Mythical and Fabulous Creatures

A Source Book and Research Guide

Edited by
Malcolm South

Greenwood Press
NEW YORK • WESTPORT, CONNECTICUT • LONDON

Library of Congress Cataloging-in-Publication Data

Mythical and fabulous creatures.

  Bibliography: p.
  Includes index.
  1. Animals, Mythical. 2. Monsters. 3. Fairies.
I. South, Malcolm, 1937–   .
GR825.M87   1987   398'.469'0321   86–14964
ISBN 0–313–24338–7 (lib. bdg. : alk. paper)

Library of Congress Catalog Card Number: 86–14964
ISBN: 0–313–24338–7

First published in 1987

Greenwood Press, Inc.
88 Post Road West, Westport, Connecticut 06881

Printed in the United States of America

The paper used in this book complies with the
Permanent Paper Standard issued by the National
Information Standards Organization (Z39.48-1984).

10 9 8 7 6 5 4 3 2 1

Mythical and Fabulous Creatures

To my Mother and Father

Contents

Part One: TWENTY FABULOUS CREATURES

Birds and Beasts

Part Two: A MISCELLANY AND TAXONOMY

Contributors

WALTRAUD BARTSCHT, *University of Dallas*

RUTH BERMAN, *Minneapolis, Minnesota*

LAURENCE A. BREINER, *Boston University*

JOHN MARSHALL CARTER, *East Carolina University*

MICHAEL CHEILIK, *Herbert H. Lehman College*

DAVID R. CHENEY, *University of Toledo*

MICHAEL J. CURLEY, *University of Puget Sound*

JONATHAN D. EVANS, *University of Georgia*

PAUL GROOTKERK, *Mississippi State University*

JAMES CRAIG HOLTE, *East Carolina University*

JUDITH J. KOLLMANN, *University of Michigan-Flint*

DAVID ADAMS LEEMING, *University of Connecticut*

DOUGLAS J. McMILLAN, *East Carolina University*

JANIS L. PALLISTER, *Bowling Green State University*

BERYL ROWLAND, *York University, Toronto, Ontario*

FRANK A. SCAFELLA, *West Virginia University*

MALCOLM SOUTH, *East Carolina University*

JUDITH D. SUTHER, *University of North Carolina at Charlotte*

Preface

This work is designed primarily as a reference and research guide that describes fabulous creatures and their appearances in history, literature, and art. The subject of imaginary beings is a large one, and I have had to establish certain focuses and emphases. Although this work discusses some creatures invented by individual artists and writers, it mainly deals with creatures that have a place in folklore, myth, or history and have a body of traditional lore connected with them. There has not been sufficient space to include some creatures, and others receive only brief or passing attention. Although gods and goddesses and angels and devils come up with some frequency in the entries, they are discussed mainly in connection with another topic. (To many persons, of course, devils and angels are in no sense "imaginary" creatures and do not rightly belong in a book on imaginary beings.)

The present volume focuses on twenty creatures that have had a major or at least a noteworthy place in the history of fabulous creatures. Each of the twenty entries in Part One discusses one of these creatures or its types as fully as space allows. In Part Two, five major groupings are used to classify most of the twenty main beings, some of their variations, and many other beings. This section concentrates on creatures that have received little or no attention in the Introduction and the previous entries. An alphabetically arranged glossary following the Introduction provides concise definitions of some of the more important fabulous creatures.

Most of the twenty creatures covered in separate entries are beings about which many readers probably know something—unicorn, dragon, phoenix, mermaid, and satyr, for example; but the basilisk and the manticora and perhaps one or two other creatures are not familiar to most readers. (Although the basilisk and the manticora have never had a central place in the history of fabulous animals, each is of sufficient significance to deserve special attention.)

Each entry on an imaginary creature describes it and the lore connected with it, discusses any different forms or types of the creature, and provides a historical survey of its manifestations. All of these entries provide a discussion of the aspects and functions of the creatures in literature, and most of them include references to visual sources in painting and the decorative arts. The entries on the vampire and the werewolf each have a section on the use of the creature in film.

The twenty entries in Part One are organized under four section headings: (1) Birds and Beasts; (2) Human-Animal Composites; (3) Creatures of Darkness; and (4) Giants and Fairies. The first section comprises seven entries, beginning with the unicorn and the dragon, two of the most important fabulous animals. There follow articles on the phoenix, the best known of mythical birds, and on another bird, the roc. The griffin and the chimera, each a composite animal, appear next; and the basilisk, which in its later history was transformed into a composite monster, concludes the section. The eighth entry, on the manticora, is the first of nine entries in the second section, Human-Animal Composites. Entries nine through thirteen are on female creatures that have been traditionally represented as destructive or seductive (mermaids, sirens, harpies, the Gorgon Medusa, and the sphinx). The final entries in the second section are on the minotaur, the satyr, and the centaur. The third section covers the vampire and the werewolf, and the fourth consists of an entry on giants and one on fairies.

As already mentioned, Part Two classifies a miscellany of creatures according to five groupings, and the discussion primarily deals with creatures that have not been discussed earlier or have been given only passing attention. Following this discussion is a list of the five categories with the twenty main creatures and many other creatures (145 in all) arranged in alphabetical order within each category.

A selected bibliography appended to each entry includes the sources cited by page references within the entry as well as other studies of the topic mentioned in the discussion. In addition, some of the bibliographies list a number of important studies not specifically cited. A large number of significant studies exist in the case of the unicorn, the dragon, the vampire, fairies, and several of the other topics; and in these cases limitations of space have dictated a high degree of selectivity in the bibliographies. The final bibliography lists more general works useful for the study of fabulous creatures.

With some modifications, the documentation style used in this book is based on that recommended by the Modern Language Association of America (see Walter S. Achtert and Joseph Gibaldi, *The MLA Style Manual*, New York: MLA, 1985). Parenthetical references within the text of an entry refer readers to the appropriate item in the appended bibliography. Most such references consist of the author's last name followed by a page reference (for example, Costello 82), or a page number alone if the author is clearly identified in the text. A volume

number usually is indicated by an Arabic numeral, with a colon separating volume
and page numbers (1:509). In general, a literary work that has divisions (books,
sections, lines, or the like) is cited by Arabic numerals, with periods separating
the divisions (for example, *Aeneid* 4.34 refers to book 4, line 34, of Virgil's
Aeneid). Occasionally, an abbreviation such as "bk." or "pt." is added for
clarity.

Acknowledgments

I wish to thank East Carolina University for giving me a semester of released time from teaching to work on this project. The Vice Chancellor for Academic Affairs at East Carolina University provided funding for some of the typing. There has been a great deal of support from William Bloodworth, Chairperson of the Department of English at East Carolina University; and the members of the departmental staff, Jane Adams, Patsy Collier, Violet Blackwelder, and Jane Schwarz, typed much of the correspondence connected with the project. Becky Latham, who typed several entries and sections, has helped me greatly. I thank Ruth Katz, the Director of Joyner Library at East Carolina University, for her generous support. Martha Lapas and other members of the reference staff of Joyner Library have answered numerous questions and helped me in countless ways. I thank Pat Guyette, our interlibrary loan librarian, for her promptness and courtesy.

Thanks to the following persons for reading sections and entries: Alex Albright, John Marshall Carter, William Cherry, Joseph Fernandez, Anne Gunn, James Holte, Jo Ann Jones, Douglas McMillan, Nancy Mayberry, John Patterson, Mary K. Thornton, and James Wilson. I owe a special debt to Joseph Fernandez and John Patterson as readers, and to James Holte and Douglas McMillan for all the help and encouragement they provided.

I am grateful to Cynthia Harris, reference book editor at Greenwood Press, for a great deal of help and much good advice. Marilyn Brownstein, my editor at Greenwood, has consistently offered valuable advice and help, and working with her has been a pleasure. I owe her a special debt for encouraging me to develop the proposal for this book.

I thank my contributors for their commitment to this project. To them I owe my greatest debt.

Laurence A. Breiner, contributor of the entry "The Basilisk," wishes to thank the American Council of Learned Societies for providing him a grant-in-aid that helped make possible some of the research for his entry.

Introduction

When the Unicorn and Alice meet in Lewis Carroll's *Through the Looking-Glass*, each has difficulty conceiving of the other as real. "I always thought they [children] were fabulous monsters!" the Unicorn says, and asks whether Alice is "alive." Moments later Alice echoes the Unicorn's words: "Do you know, I always thought Unicorns were fabulous monsters, too. I never saw one alive before!" (175). As this episode suggests, it can be difficult to determine what a fabulous being is. Both Alice and the Unicorn think that the other is the fabulous creature.

If the Unicorn from *Through the Looking-Glass* were asked to give a definition of a fabulous being, his definition might run something like this: it is something invented or made up that seems to be a living creature but does not actually exist. Although this definition has a certain merit, it may be somewhat misleading. In a sense all fantastic beings are "invented" or "made up" (that is, they do not actually exist in nature), but, in "inventing" them, people have usually drawn upon natural forms in some way such as combining the parts of two or more actual creatures or exaggerating or distorting features of real creatures. In many cases where a fabulous being may be considered a successful creation, fact and fantasy have been fused in such a way that the being takes on a life of its own and has its own reality.

In a broad sense the term "imaginary creature" can be taken to include any being that is a creation of the human imagination. If the term is used in this way, any fictional character or any being invented by an artist might be considered a fabulous being. Thus, David Copperfield would be a fabulous being as well as Dracula. In general, this work does not employ the broader sense of the term but instead defines it to mean a being that differs from an actual being because of its form and/or its powers, characteristics, and attributes; that is the term as used here applies to creatures whose forms are unlike those of any actual beings, but it includes beings (Superman, for example) that look like real beings but possess powers and characteristics that real beings do not possess.

A fantastic being can be animal, vegetable, or mineral—or a combination of two or all three of these. Indeed, it can consist of anything that the human mind is capable of conceiving. Most fabulous beings are created by making composites—that is, creatures made up of the parts of two or more other beings. Other methods of creating fabulous beings include modifying the body of a real being (such as giving a man two heads), using one part of the anatomy of an animal or a human being as a living entity (for example, a disembodied brain), investing inanimate things with life (for example, a statue), and increasing or decreasing the size of a real being to a degree that is not found in nature ("Monstrous and Imaginary Subjects" 250). In the case of some creatures (for example, the dragon), a general form exists, but variations on that form are possible. Shape-shifting is characteristic of many fabulous beings, and the form of one being may change: certain beings (like Proteus in Greek myth) can assume a sequence of forms, and others (like the werewolf) can change from a human being into an animal. A popular theme in science fiction is that of a shape-changer that can transform itself to look like any living creature that has become its victim. (The malevolent alien in John W. Campbell's story *Who Goes There?* has this power and can also read minds.) Certain fabulous beings can make themselves invisible (a power attributed to many fairies); and some beings have an amorphous or uncertain form, as in Algernon Blackwood's story *The Willows*, where terrifying forces that nearly destroy two men are never clearly seen but at one point are perceived to look somewhat like "several animals grouped together" or "a clump of willow bushes" (47).

Although no system of classifying fabulous beings is entirely satisfactory (some overlapping will always take place), a classification using their physical makeup and/or their form seems the best way to group them. Five groupings that provide a means of classifying most fabulous beings are the following: (1) human-animal combinations such as the centaur and the mermaid; (2) fabulous animals such as the unicorn and the dragon; (3) fabulous peoples and imaginary beings with a human or humanlike makeup; (4) imaginary beings with forms differing somehow from those of the beings in the previous groupings (of primary importance here are beings made up of trees, plants, or inanimate things); and (5) beings with a variety of forms. Part Two of this work discusses these groupings and places many creatures in them.

What should be present to make a fabulous being a successful creation? Above all, if it is to have a profound effect on us, it must reflect something meaningful about human experience and engage our emotions in a powerful way. Those imaginary creatures that have universal appeal (like the unicorn and the dragon) are complex beings that have rich symbolic meanings. The form of an imaginary creature is also an important consideration. The being can have the shape of a real creature and appeal to us, but there is usually a likelihood of greater appeal if the being does not look exactly like any actual creature. For instance, when the unicorn is depicted in equine form (only one of a number of forms of the creature), it is not simply a horse. The horn sets it off as a magical animal, and some element or elements from one or more other animals are often present in representations of equine unicorns. If the form of an imaginary creature is highly unusual, we may have trouble grasping the total effect; and if the impression created is too odd, the effect may wear thin after initial impact. This seems to take place with most of the creatures that Gustave Flaubert "invented" for the section of his novel *The Temptation of St. Antony* where various monsters appear before Antony. Among these monsters are "goats with asses' rumps, frogs covered with hairs like bears . . . four foetuses holding each other by the navel and spinning like tops, and winged bellies which flutter like gnats" (166–67). When a fantastic creature has a form that is unlike that of any actual being, its form should have an internal consistency and logic—that is, the parts should seem to belong together, without creating the impression of contrivance. Part of the reason for the limited appeal of the chimera may be that the three animals in its makeup (lion, goat, snake) do not seem to blend into a coherent whole; in many representations the chimera looks disjointed, as though the three animals are in an uneasy alliance. In addition, a fabulous creature should have a "character" and a distinctive personality if it is to appeal to us deeply. An imaginary creature with such a personality is the Psammead or "Sand-fairy" in E. Nesbit's books *Five Children and It* (1902) and *The Story of the Amulet* (1906). A furry creature with a tubby, spiderlike body and monkeylike hands and feet, the Psammead must grant any wish that anyone demands of it, however absurd the wish may be. To bring the wish about, it must puff itself up until it nearly bursts, a tiring and exasperating business. Although it is nearly always out of patience and makes sarcastic comments, it remains a lovable creature that "is quirky, surprising, crusty as an old misogynist, irrepressible and unforgettably strange" (Blount 103).

Fabulous creatures reflect both the dark and the bright side of human nature. They range from completely good and gentle creatures such as the ki-lin, a type of Chinese unicorn (too gentle to step on a blade of grass for fear of injuring it), to completely evil and vicious beings such as the windigo of Algonkian myth (an immensely strong monster of manlike form that feeds on human flesh [see Colombo]). The evil or terrifying creatures in world mythology seem to outnumber the good or gentle ones. Creatures such as vampires, werewolves, and man-eating giants are only a few of a multitude of nightmarish beings that appear in the mythologies of numerous cultures. Moreover, in some cases, a creature has negative associations in one culture but positive ones in another. For instance, whereas the dragon in the West is mostly sinister and evil, the dragon in the East is usually beneficent and good. In addition, some beings (like many of those in Indian mythology) are a combination of good and evil, and their nature may change from one state to another.

According to Heinz Mode (12–13), fabulous beings were not given a visual form until "a relatively late stage of cultural development," with the first clear-cut use of such creatures in art occurring in the ancient Near East about 3000 B.C. Many of the traditional types of imaginary beings that have been found in various cultures throughout the ages appeared in ancient Egypt and ancient Mesopotamia. Ancient Egyptian art contained a host of human-animal beings (especially animal-headed deities with human bodies); and the art of ancient Mesopotamia included traditional types such as the centaur, the sphinx, the griffin, the dragon, the scorpion-man, winged and human-headed bulls and lions, and human-fish composites ("Monstrous and Imaginary Subjects" 253–55). As Rudolf Wittkower has pointed out (10–14), an exchange of many types of fabulous beings took place between East and West. The ancient Greeks borrowed many imaginary creatures from the Near East; they modified and changed some of them (for example, the sphinx); they added beings of their own invention or largely of their own invention (for example, the sirens and the harpies); then they handed back or passed on the creatures in their repertory to the East, where they sometimes underwent additional changes.

By the time of the Middle Ages, there existed a large body of imaginary subjects that have continued to appear in art and literature ("Monstrous and Imaginary Subjects" 251). People during the Middle Ages saw a moral and symbolic significance in everything in the natural world, and in some cases they attached new or different meanings to certain creatures. Thus the unicorn (and most people in the Middle Ages regarded the unicorn and many other "fabulous" creatures as real and not as imaginary) became a symbol of Christ and was associated with the Annunciation and the Incarnation. In fact, fabulous and monstrous beings held such a powerful appeal during the Middle Ages that some churchmen feared that they diverted people's minds from more serious matters (Randall 3–5). In a well-known denunciation of exuberant elements in monastic art during the early part of the twelfth century, Bernard of Clairvaux deplored the use of subjects such as "centaurs . . . half-men . . . striped tigers" and fish with the heads of beasts (" 'Apologia' to William, Abbot of St.-Thierry" 19). However, denunciations like this were largely ignored, and medieval artists portrayed fantastic creatures of every imaginable shape and nature (for example, one-legged people with a foot large enough to use as an umbrella or sunscreen; people or animals composed of letters of the alphabet; plant- and tree-men; beings composed of one or several parts of the human anatomy; and gargoyles of various types).

During the European Renaissance, many people began to question the existence of certain fabulous creatures. However, writers of natural histories during the Renaissance included in their works most of the fantastic creatures that had appeared in the medieval natural histories; and Renaissance writers elaborated upon the symbolism connected with such creatures. Monstrous and fantastic creatures continued to have great appeal to artists, especially those in northern and central Europe. The Dutch artist Hieronymus Bosch (d. 1516) in particular was a master of fantasy; his work is full of strange creatures such as bird-fish, plant-monsters, tree-men, and hybrid animals and people of various kinds. As new geographical discoveries took place, the repertory of fantastic animals increased because travelers brought back stories of many new kinds of creatures in the newly discovered lands. During the Renaissance, fantastic creatures in art and literature were given an increasingly secular treatment; and from that time onward the contributions of individual artists and writers have "come to the fore, either derived from a personal vision or as adaptations of the traditional cultural heritage" ("Monstrous and Imaginary Subjects" 251).

Modern artists and writers have often reinterpreted traditional types of fantastic beings and invented new kinds of creatures. Psychoanalysis and psychology have played a significant part in the representation and the interpretation of the fantastic in modern literature and art. In many modern stories in which a monster appears, the monster is not something with an external existence but is centered in the human psyche and consciousness. Some of the most interesting fabulous creatures in twentieth-century literature appear in science fiction—creatures like androids (robots with a human form and appearance), cyborgs (human beings part machine and part human), symbiotes (two separate life forms that mutually depend on each other), and aliens of every sort.

Fabulous creatures have been the subject of numerous studies ranging from those of a popular to those of a scholarly nature. One of the most enjoyable books with a popular slant is *The Book of Imaginary Beings* by Jorge Luis Borges and Margarita Guerrero. The latest edition of this book (1970) has 120 entries, with discussion of a being usually running from one to three pages. Like *The Book of Imaginary Beings, A Dictionary of Fabulous Beasts* (1971) by Richard W. Barber and Anne Riches has an alphabetical arrangement; in general, its entries provide useful summaries of the main ideas connected with a large number of creatures from a variety of cultures. Another book with an alphabetical arrangement is Jean-Paul Clébert's *Bestiaire fabuleux* (1971), which covers both real and fantastic creatures and discusses them in terms of history, literature, and art. Peter Costello's *The Magic Zoo* (1979), which has fairly detailed discussions of about twenty fabulous creatures, explores what real creatures might be the basis of legendary beings. *I mostri e l'immaginario* (1982) by Massimo Izzi describes a broad range of imaginary beings such as sirens, the dragon, the unicorn, the vampire, and the golem, and uses typological approaches to classify various kinds of monstrous creatures. Heinz Mode's *Fabulous Beasts and Demons* (1975; originally published under the title *Fabeltiere und Dämonen*) groups hundreds of fabulous creatures according to five categories, traces these beings through different historical periods, and discusses the numerous variants of the major types of these creatures in world art. Mode's book contains excellent illustrations, with 52 color plates, 93 plates in black and white, and 260 line drawings. Richard Huber's *Treasury of Fantastic and Mythological Creatures* (1981) has no descriptive text but contains over 1,000 black-and-white illustrations of imaginary creatures from many cultures. Some other works of value include *Mythical Monsters* (1886) by Charles Gould; *Fabulous Beasts* (1951) by Peter Lum; and *Monstres, démons et merveilles à la fin du moyen âge* (1980) by Claude Kappler.

The final bibliography in this present volume lists over twenty-five secondary sources that deal solely or largely with fabulous beings. Useful bibliographies pertaining to imaginary creatures can be found also in the following: Robinson, Mode, Costello, Izzi (includes many studies published in French and Italian) and Eberhart. *Ancient Greek Art and Iconography* (1983; ed. Warren G. Moon) contains a bibliography pertaining to animals and fabulous beasts in Greek art (326–27).

Phoenix Feathers (1973; ed. Barbara Silverberg) and *Bestiary!* (1985; ed. Jack Dann and Gardner Dozois) are two of various anthologies of stories about fabulous creatures. The recent publication of a number of books on imaginary creatures indicates their current popularity. For example, Ace Books is publishing anthologies of stories about fabulous creatures (for example, *Dragons of Darkness, Dragons of Light,* and *Unicorns!*); and Time-Life Books has published *The Enchanted World,* a series designed for general readers (some of the individual volumes have titles such as *Dragons, Fairies and Elves, Magical Beasts, Giants and Ogres, Water Spirits, Night Creatures,* and *Dwarfs*).

Two areas with a special importance to the study of fabulous creatures are fantasy and science fiction. Works of fantasy contain some of the most interesting and important descriptions of fabulous creatures. A book that provides a good introduction to fantasy literature and explores critical theories concerning the nature of fantasy is Eric S. Rabkin's *The Fantastic in Literature* (1976). *Fantasy Literature: A Core Collection and Reference Guide* (1979) by Marshall B. Tymn, Kenneth J. Zahorski, and Robert H. Boyer discusses several different kinds of fantasy and provides an annotated guide to about 240 of the most important works of high fantasy (works with a setting in a secondary world). Roger C. Schlobin's *The Literature of Fantasy: A Comprehensive, Annotated Bibliography of Modern Fantasy Fiction* (1979) cites and indexes "over 800 authors, 100 editors, 721 novels, 244 collections, 100 anthologies, 3,610 short stories, and 165 author bibliographies" (preface x). Some other important works dealing with fantasy are Lin Carter's *Imaginary Worlds: The Art of Fantasy* (1973); Diana Waggoner's *The Hills of Faraway: A Guide to Fantasy* (1978); and Ann Swinfen's *In Defence of Fantasy: A Study of the Genre in English and American Literature since 1945* (1984). No thorough study of the aliens and other fabulous beings in science fiction exists. Three entries ("Aliens," "Monsters," and "Supernatural Creatures") in *The Science Fiction Encyclopedia* (1979; ed. Peter Nicholls) provide an overview of types of these beings and trace the trends in portraying them. The entry "Biologies and Environments" (90–100) in *The Visual Encyclopedia of Science Fiction* (1977; ed. Brian Ash) discusses aliens in terms of their biologies and environments and describes different "species" of aliens: tree- and plant-beings, reptilian creatures; dragons; insects; humanoid aliens; creatures composed of crystal or mineral forms; aliens having bodies of "pure energy," gas, or flames; and certain types of aliens more or less defying any categorization. The entry points out that in general the conception of aliens has evolved from an unsympathetic portrayal (aliens as bug-eyed monsters and other hostile, repugnant beings) to a more sympathetic and thoughtful depiction. In addition, *The Visual Encyclopedia of Science Fiction* discusses robots, androids, cyborgs, symbiotes, and mutants (172–203). Of course, it should be kept in mind that robots (in certain forms at least) exist in the real world and should not necessarily be characterized as "fabulous beings." Anthologies of stories about aliens include *Invaders of Earth* (1952; ed. Groff Conklin); *Encounters with Aliens* (1968; ed. George W. Earley); and *Aliens!* (1980; ed. Gardner Dozois and Jack Dann). Useful to the student interested in science fiction illustration are Anthony Frewin's *One Hundred Years of Science Fiction Illustration, 1840–1940* (1975) and Brian Aldiss' *Science Fiction Art* (1975). *Barlowe's Guide to Extraterrestrials* (1979) features excellent color drawings by Wayne Douglas Barlowe of aliens from a number of science fiction works. One of the best critical guides to science fiction is Neil Barron's *Anatomy of Wonder* (2nd ed. 1981), which evaluates about 1,900 titles.

Gods and goddesses and other mythological figures occupy a central place in the study of fabulous beings. An excellent single-volume work dealing with various mythologies is the *New Larousse Encyclopedia of Mythology* (1968; ed. Felix Guirand). The thirteen-volume *Mythology of All Races* contains much valuable information but is now dated. Although the volumes in the *Library of the World's Myths and Legends* (now being published in new revised editions) vary somewhat in quality, most of them provide reliable coverage of the specific mythology that is the subject of each volume. *A Dictionary of World Mythology* (1980) by Arthur Cotterell, which has seven geographical groupings with an alphabetical listing of figures in each group, has concise entries on a large number of mythological beings. Numerous other works deal with mythologies of the world, with a selected number of mythologies, or with one mythology. Ron Smith in *Mythologies of the World: A Guide to Sources* (1981) covers a broad range of sources and evaluates their merits.

Readers who wish to enter some of the imaginary worlds where strange beings live should look at *The Dictionary of Imaginary Places* (1980) by Alberto Manguel and Gianni Guadalupi, which has the design of a nineteenth-century gazetteer: here one can read about places like Malacovia (described in Amedeo Tosetti's *Pedali sul Mar Nero*), where dwell fierce Tartars who ride on bicycles; Selene, the city of vampires described in Paul Féval's *La Ville Vampire*; and the elfin kingdoms described in Sylvia Townsend Warner's *Kingdoms of Elfin*. *The Dictionary of Imaginary Places* furnishes a wealth of information about imaginary beings and is a joy in itself to read.

Fabulous creatures in literature often inhabit a secondary world separate from the primary or "real" world. In his essay *On Fairy-Stories*, J. R. R. Tolkien says that in a successful work of fantasy the writer creates a secondary world that induces us to believe in it while we are part of it: "He [the writer] makes a Secondary World which your mind can enter. Inside it, what he relates is 'true': it accords with the laws of that world. You therefore believe it, while you are, as it were, inside" (37). If a writer can create the sense of belief that Tolkien describes and can portray fabulous creatures with truth and power, they can take on a life of their own and seem real and "true." Tolkien's hobbits have this kind of reality. Anyone who has once read the description of hobbits in *The Hobbit* has to believe in them: "They are (or were) a little people, about half our height, and smaller than the bearded Dwarves. Hobbits have no beards. . . . They are inclined to be fat in the stomach; they dress in bright colours (chiefly green and yellow); wear no shoes, because their feet grow natural leathery soles and thick warm brown hair like the stuff on their heads (which is curly); have long clever brown fingers, good-natured faces and laugh deep laughs (especially after dinner, which they have twice a day when they can get it)" (16). Of course, hobbits largely appeal to us because they are likeable, but they also have an appeal because they have courage and perseverance.

Fabulous creatures in literature may appear in the primary world as well as in secondary worlds. Sometimes a writer's aim in placing fabulous creatures in the primary world is to satirize the inability of human beings to perceive the marvelous, as in Charles G. Finney's novel *The Circus of Dr. Lao*, in which Doctor Lao brings his circus consisting of a unicorn, a satyr, a mermaid, and some other fabulous beings to a small town in Arizona. In other cases, human beings are able to recognize fabulous beings, and the experience changes their lives in some significant way. For example, in Rob Chilson's short story "The Last of His Breed," the cowboy Ken Hastie finds in Arizona the ultimate horse for himself, the winged horse Pegasus. Both are the last of their breed; Hastie mounts the creature, tames it, and rides off into the sunset. In his short story "The Troll," which has its setting in modern Lapland, T. H. White explores questions about belief and disbelief, about the difficulty of accepting something that seems beyond reality. After a Mr. Marx awakes from a dream in which he saw blood streaming through the keyhole of a locked door of a hotel room that adjoins his room, he gets up, looks through the keyhole, and sees in the next room a blue-faced, yellow-eyed troll devour a woman "in two bites" (260). The story emphasizes the very tangible nature of Marx's experience. The killing of the woman does not occur in a dark or shadowy place but in a sunlit room, and the troll itself is "eminently solid, about eight feet high, and dressed in brightly ornamented skins" (259–60). In this story the fact that the events occur in the primary world makes them all the more chilling and terrifying. These are only a few of a variety of aims that writers have had in placing fabulous beings in the primary world.

In Maurice Sendak's well-known picture book *Where the Wild Things Are*, the wild things are types of monsters that all of us have known in one form or another. After the boy Max has been banished to his room for misbehaving, the room changes into a magical forest; he enters it and finds a boat that takes him to the land where the wild things are. The wild things—large humanoid monsters with hairy bodies, sharp claws and teeth, and big yellow eyes—are universal types of monsters. (They have many of the physical characteristics that we associate with monsters. Despite their threatening appearance, these wild things are not evil; but, portrayed in a different context, they could be trolls or other kinds of evil monsters.) Max overcomes the wild things by staring into their eyes without blinking and becomes "king of all wild things." Eventually he leaves the wild things and returns home (Lanes 85–107). Max's journey to the land of the wild things is a journey that all of us have made in one form or another. An eight-year-old boy wrote Sendak a letter asking him: "How much does it cost to get to where the wild things are? If it is not expensive, my sister and I would like to spend the summer there" (quoted in Lanes 107). The powerful wish to visit the country of the wild things is one that we all should have; and if we have imagination and a willingness to experience wonder, we can make the journey.

BIBLIOGRAPHY

Aldiss, Brian W., comp. *Science Fiction Art*. New York: Crown, 1975.

Ash, Brian, ed. *The Visual Encyclopedia of Science Fiction*. New York: Harmony Books, 1977.

Barber, Richard W., and Anne Riches. *A Dictionary of Fabulous Beasts*. London: Macmillan, 1971.

Barlowe, Wayne Douglas, and Ian Summers. *Barlowe's Guide to Extraterrestrials*. New York: Workman, 1979.

Barron, Neil, ed. *Anatomy of Wonder: A Critical Guide to Science Fiction*. 2nd ed. New York: Bowker, 1981.

Bernard of Clairvaux, St. " 'Apologia' to William, Abbot of St.-Thierry." In *Literary Sources of Art History: An Anthology of Texts from Theophilus to Goethe*. Ed. Elizabeth Gilmore Holt. Princeton: Princeton University Press, 1947. 17–19.

Blackwood, Algernon. *The Willows*. In *In the Realm of Terror*. New York: Pantheon, 1957. 3–53.

Blount, Margaret. *Animal Land: The Creatures of Children's Fiction*. New York: William Morrow, 1975.

Borges, Jorge Luis, with Margarita Guerrero. *The Book of Imaginary Beings*. Trans. Norman Thomas di Giovanni. New York: Discus-Avon, 1970.

Campbell, John W. *Who Goes There*? In *Who Goes There*? 2nd ed. Chicago: Shasta, 1951. 7–75.

Carroll, Lewis. *Through the Looking-Glass*. In *Alice in Wonderland*. Ed. Donald J. Gray. New York: Norton, 1971. 101–209.

Carter, Lin. *Imaginary Worlds: The Art of Fantasy*. New York: Ballantine, 1973.

Chilson, Rob. "The Last of His Breed." In *Bestiary!* Ed. Jack Dann and Gardner Dozois. New York: Ace, 1985. 290–304.

Clébert, Jean-Paul. *Bestiaire fabuleux*. Paris: Albin Michel, 1971.

Colombo, John Robert, ed. *Windigo: An Anthology of Fact and Fantastic Fiction*. Saskatoon, Saskatchewan: Western Producer Prairie Books, 1982.

Conklin, Groff, ed. *Invaders of Earth*. New York: Vanguard Press, 1952.

Costello, Peter. *The Magic Zoo: The Natural History of Fabulous Animals*. New York: St. Martin's, 1979.

Cotterell, Arthur. *A Dictionary of World Mythology*. New York: Putnam's, 1980.

Dann, Jack, and Gardner Dozois, eds. *Bestiary!* New York: Ace, 1985.

Dozois, Gardner, and Jack Dann, eds. *Aliens!* New York: Pocket Books, 1980.

Earley, George W., ed. *Encounters with Aliens*. Los Angeles: Sherbourne Press, 1968.

Eberhart, George M. *Monsters: A Guide to Information on Unaccounted For Creatures, Including Bigfoot, Many Water Monsters, and Other Irregular Animals*. New York: Garland, 1983.

Finney, Charles G. *The Circus of Dr. Lao*. 1935. New York: Ben Abramson, 1946.

Flaubert, Gustave. *The Temptation of St. Antony, or A Revelation of the Soul*. In Vol. 8 of *The Complete Works of Gustave Flaubert*. New York: M. W. Dunne, 1904.

Frewin, Anthony, comp. *One Hundred Years of Science Fiction Illustration, 1840–1940*. New York: Pyramid Books, 1975.

Gould, Charles. *Mythical Monsters*. London, 1886.

Guirand, Felix, ed. *New Larousse Encyclopedia of Mythology*. New ed. London: Hamlyn, 1968.

Huber, Richard. *Treasury of Fantastic and Mythological Creatures: 1,087 Renderings from Historic Sources*. New York: Dover, 1981.

Izzi, Massimo. *I mostri e l'immaginario*. Rome: Edizioni del Graal, 1982.

Kappler, Claude. *Monstres, démons et merveilles à la fin du moyen âge*. Paris: Payot, 1980.

Lanes, Selma G. *The Art of Maurice Sendak*. New York: Abrams, 1980.

Lum, Peter. *Fabulous Beasts*. New York: Pantheon, 1951.

Manguel, Alberto, and Gianni Guadalupi. *The Dictionary of Imaginary Places*. New York: Macmillan, 1980.

Mode, Heinz. *Fabulous Beasts and Demons*. London: Phaidon, 1975.

"Monstrous and Imaginary Subjects." In *Encyclopedia of World Art*. New York: McGraw-Hill, 1965. 10:250–72.

Moon, Warren G. *Ancient Greek Art and Iconography*. Madison: University of Wisconsin Press, 1983.

The Mythology of All Races. Ed. Louis Herbert Gray et al. 13 volumes. Boston: Archaeological Institute of America, Marshall Jones Company, 1916–32.

Nesbit, E. [Edith Nesbit Bland]. *Five Children and It. The Story of the Amulet*. In *Five Children and It: The Phoenix and the Carpet: The Story of the Amulet*. 1902, 1906; rpt. London: Octopus, 1979.

Nicholls, Peter, ed. *The Science Fiction Encyclopedia*. Garden City, N.Y.: Doubleday, 1979.

Rabkin, Eric S. *The Fantastic in Literature*. Princeton: Princeton University Press, 1976.

Randall, Lilian M. C. *Images in the Margins of Gothic Manuscripts*. Berkeley and Los Angeles: University of California Press, 1966.

Robinson, Margaret W. *Fictitious Beasts: A Bibliography*. London: The Library Association, 1961.

Schlobin, Roger C., comp. *The Literature of Fantasy: A Comprehensive, Annotated Bibliography of Modern Fantasy Fiction*. Garland Reference Library of the Humanities, vol. 176. New York: Garland, 1979.

Silverberg, Barbara, ed. *Phoenix Feathers: A Collection of Mythical Monsters*. New York: Dutton, 1973.

Smith, Ron. *Mythologies of the World: A Guide to Sources*. Urbana, Ill.: National Council
    of Teachers of English, 1981.

Swinfen, Ann. *In Defence of Fantasy: A Study of the Genre in English and American
    Literature since 1945*. London: Routledge and Kegan Paul, 1984.

Tolkien, J. R. R. *The Hobbit*. Rev. ed. 1966. New York: Ballantine, 1981.

———. *On Fairy-Stories*. In *Tree and Leaf*. Boston: Houghton Mifflin, 1964. 3–84.

Tymn, Marshall B., Kenneth J. Zahorski, and Robert H. Boyer. *Fantasy Literature: A
    Core Collection and Reference Guide*. New York: Bowker, 1979.

Waggoner, Diana. *The Hills of Faraway: A Guide to Fantasy*. New York. Atheneum,
    1978.

White, T. H. "The Troll." In *Bestiary!* Ed. Jack Dann and Gardner Dozois. New York:
    Ace, 1985. 258–69.

Wittkower, Rudolf. *Allegory and the Migration of Symbols*. London: Thames and Hudson,
    1977.

A Glossary of Some of the More Important Fabulous Creatures

Amphisbaena.   A serpent with two heads, one at each end of its body.

Amun.   In Egyptian mythology, a monster with a lion's body, the hindquarters of a hippopotamus, and a crocodile's head. Called the "devourer of the dead" because he eats the hearts of those who are judged unfit after their souls are weighed during the final judgment in the hall of Osiris.

Ba.   In ancient Egypt, the soul was conceived of as living on after death in the form of a ba, a bird-bodied creature with a human head.

Barnacle Goose.   A goose that was said to originate from a barnacle formed on wood soaked in the sea, or from a tree that grew beside the sea shore.

Basilisk.   According to ancient writers, a serpent that was supposed to have deadly venom and was said to be able to move with its head held upright. In later times the basilisk was transformed into a monster part serpent, part rooster (also called a cockatrice). A basilisk can kill a person by its gaze or its breath.

Brownie.   A small fairy being of the hobgoblin type who wears ragged clothes of a brown color. If he receives good treatment, he will perform many tasks. Ill treatment may cause him to leave a house, and at his departure the good luck attached to him is supposed to leave the house.

Caladrius (Charadrius).   A completely white bird that turns its head away from a sick person who will die, but looks at a sick person destined to live and draws the illness to itself.

Catoblepas.   An animal that holds its head downward, close to the ground. Anyone who looks at its eyes will die at once.

Centaur.   A being part human and part horse. Usually the head and upper body are human, and the lower body is equine, but various types of centaurs exist. Centaurs have been associated with lust and licentiousness.

Cerberus.   The three-headed dog that guards the entrance to Hades.

Chimera.   In Greek mythology, a fire-breathing monster slain by Bellerophon. In its customary form, its body is that of a lion with a goat's head emerging from the lion's back, and its tail is that of a serpent.

Cockatrice.   *See* Basilisk.

Dragon.   A general name for numerous types of a monster whose form is usually reptilian or snakelike. May or may not have wings and legs. Usually breathes fire. Guardian of treasures. The story in which a hero (for example, St. George) slays a dragon is an archetypal kind of story found in many times and places.

Dwarfs.   Small, manlike beings who live in underground kingdoms and are famous for their skill as craftsmen and smiths. They have long beards and wrinkled skin. Many dwarfs have misshapen bodies, but some dwarfs have well-proportioned bodies and a handsome appearance.

Elf.   Although the word ''elf'' is often used as a synonym for the word ''fairy,'' distinctions between elves and fairies were usually made in traditional lore. Some elves are delicate beings that live in the air and dance on the grass; others (usually of a coarser nature) live in an underground world.

Fairy.   A collective term for many different types of supernatural beings that usually possess magical powers. Many fairies have a human form, but some have animal or human-animal shapes.

Fearsome Critters.   Fabulous creatures that grew out of humorous stories and tall tales of the American frontier and backwoods. Some element of great comic exaggeration is usually present in the makeup and/or actions of fearsome critters, and they often have amusing names. Some fearsome critters are the jackalope, the sidehill dodger, the goofang, and the Funeral Mountain terrashot.

Fenrir.   In Scandinavian mythology, the fierce wolf that is bound by a chain composed of invisible things. When the end of the world takes place, Fenrir will break free and kill Odin.

Ganesha.   A potbellied Hindu god with a man's body and an elephant's head. Loves food and beautiful maidens, who are often pictured as fanning him.

Garuda.   In Hindu mythology, the mount of Vishnu. Garuda has a bird's beak and wings and a man's body, arms, and legs. Inveterate enemy of the nagas.

Ghul (plural, *ghilan*).   In Arabic lore, ghilan are monsters capable of changing their shape; they dwell in lonely places and try to lure travelers away from their companions in order to eat them. The English word ''ghoul'' refers to a monster that robs graves and feeds on corpses.

Giants.   Legendary beings of great strength and size. Often portrayed as dimwitted.

Gnomes.   Dwarflike beings who dwell beneath the earth and guard treasures. Gnomes, who are associated with the earth, are one of four types of elementals described by Paracelsus (1493–1541).

Goblins.   A collective term used to describe evil spirits. In general, goblins are thought of as misshapen beings that dwell in dark places.

Golem.   In Jewish legend, a clay figure of a man that has been brought to life.

Gorgon Medusa.   In Greek myth, one of the Gorgons, three sisters who have snakes for hair. Anyone who looked at Medusa's head would be turned into stone.

Griffin.   A fabulous animal that is usually depicted as having the body, hind legs, and tail of a lion, and the head, foreparts, and wings of an eagle. Various types of griffins appear in art and literature.

Hanuman.   The Hindu monkey-god. Ally of the god Rama.

Harpies.   In Greek mythology, evil creatures part woman and part bird. Associated with rapacity.

Hippocamp (Hippocampus).   A creature half-horse and half-fish, with a serpent's tail at the end of the body.

Hydra.   In Greek mythology, the Lernean hydra is a water-serpent or a serpentlike monster with nine heads. Slain by Hercules.

Jinn (Genies).   Good and evil spirits in Arabic lore, with transparent bodies composed of flame or vapor and with the ability to change their shapes.

Kraken.   A huge sea monster. Often mistaken by sailors for an island.

Lamassu.   Winged, human-headed lions and bulls that guarded entrances to Assyrian temples and palaces.

Lamia.   In ancient literature, a monster that drinks the blood of children and preys on young men. Although lamias have been described in a variety of ways, the term in literature sometimes refers to a serpent-woman.

Leprechaun.   The fairy shoemaker. A small, grotesque-looking man who wears a leathern apron and shoes with silver buckles. If a person can catch a leprechaun, the leprechaun will have to reveal where he keeps his buried gold. But a leprechaun is full of tricks, and getting his gold is very difficult.

Leviathan.   A huge sea-animal. More specifically, a terrible monster mentioned in the Old Testament that is the adversary of God.

Manticora.   A ferocious monster with a lion's body, human face and ears, three rows of teeth in each jaw, and poisoned spines in its tail that it can shoot like arrows.

Mermaid.   A water-dwelling being who has the body of a fair woman to the waist and is fish-tailed below. Sometimes a mermaid has legs or two tails.

Midgard Serpent.   In Scandinavian mythology, a serpent encircling the earth and holding its tail in its mouth. An example of the Uroboros, a serpent or a dragon that bites its own tail and usually appears in art in the form of a circle.

Minotaur.   Bull-man, offspring of Pasiphae and a bull. Confined in the Labyrinth on Crete and slain by Theseus.

Nagas.   In Hindu mythology, semi-divine creatures with a human form to the waist and a serpent's body below it.

Pan.   The Greek god of flocks and shepherds, usually represented as having a puck nose, shaggy hair, horns, and the feet of a goat.

Pegasus.   The winged horse in Greek mythology on which Bellerophon rides when he kills the chimera.

Phoenix.   A mythical bird that is consumed in fire, with a new bird arising from the ashes. Only one phoenix exists at one time.

Roc.   In Arabic lore, an enormous bird that is strong enough to carry off one or more elephants.

Salamander.   A mythical animal of a lizardlike shape that can survive in fire without being burned. Also a real animal—any tailed amphibian of the order Urodeles.

Satyrs.   Beings part human and part goat. Associated with wine, revelry, and lechery.

Scorpion-men.   In the art and literature of ancient Mesopotamia, beings part human and part scorpion. In some works of art, a scorpion-man is human to the waist, and the lower half of his body is that of a scorpion.

Sirens.   Women, bird-women, or mermaids who sing or sometimes play beautiful music to lure sailors to their deaths. In Greek myth, the sirens are customarily described as bird-women.

Sphinx.   In Egyptian art, the androsphinx is a lion with a human head and/or face; the criosphinx is a ram-headed lion; and the hieracosphinx is a hawk-headed lion. In Greek art the sphinx is usually represented as having the winged body of a lion and the face and breasts of a woman.

Stymphalian Birds.   In Greek mythology, birds that have brass claws and beaks and can shoot their feathers as if they were arrows. Hercules rid the lake at Stymphalus of these birds.

Tengu.   Winged Japanese spirits that are part human and part bird.

Thunderbird.   A bird in Amerindian lore, with the thunder being created by the sound of its wings.

Triton.   Son of the Greek sea-god Poseidon and the sea-goddess Amphitrite. The upper part of his body (to the waist) is human; the lower part is that of a fish.

Trolls.   In Scandinavian mythology, trolls were originally gigantic, man-eating beings who lived in mountain caverns. Sunlight turned them to stone. In later tradition, trolls were portrayed as dwarflike beings who lived in caverns or subterranean dwellings.

Unicorn. One-horned animal whose form is that of a horse, a goat, or some other creature, and whose horn has magical and curative powers. Only a virgin can capture a unicorn.

Vampire. A creature whose origin is a dead person reanimated and who sucks blood to nourish itself. A vampire is neither dead nor living but is one of the "undead."

Vegetable Lamb (Barmotez). A small lamb that grows from a fruit on a plant and remains attached to the plant by a stem.

Werewolf. A person who has been changed into a wolf or a creature with a lupine form.

Wild People. Humanoid beings having hairy bodies. Creatures of instinct and passion, they cannot control their emotions and are very lecherous.

Yale. An animal with long, movable horns that it can adjust in different directions depending on how it wishes to use them.

Zombi (Zombie). A dead person whose body has been reanimated. A zombi lacks all will of its own and mindlessly obeys its master.

Illustrations of Fabulous Creatures

1. Unicorns. From *Historiae naturalis* (Amsterdam, 1657–65) by Johannes Jonstonus. By permission of William R. Perkins Library, Duke University. From the collection of the Department of Rare Books.

2. Dragons. From *Historiae naturalis* (Amsterdam, 1657–65) by Johannes Jonstonus. By permission of William R. Perkins Library, Duke University. From the collection of the Department of Rare Books.

3. Hydras. From *Historiae naturalis* (Amsterdam, 1657–65) by Johannes Jonstonus. By permission of William R. Perkins Library, Duke University. From the Collection of the Department of Rare Books.

4. Phoenix. From *Historiae naturalis* (Amsterdam, 1657–65) by Johannes Jonstonus. By permission of William R. Perkins Library, Duke University. From the collection of the Department of Rare Books.

5. Griffin. From *Historiae naturalis* (Amsterdam, 1657–65) by Johannes Jonstonus. By permission of William R. Perkins Library, Duke University. From the collection of the Department of Rare Books.

6. Pegasus. From *Treasury of Fantastic and Mythological Creatures* (New York, 1981) by Richard Huber. By permission of Dover Publications, Inc.

7. Chimera. From *Treasury of Fantastic and Mythological Creatures* (New York, 1981) by Richard Huber. By permission of Dover Publications, Inc.

8. Cockatrice. From *Treasury of Fantastic and Mythological Creatures* (New York, 1981) by Richard Huber. By permission of Dover Publications, Inc.

9. Manticora. From *The History of Four-Footed Beasts and Serpents* . . . (London, 1658) by Edward Topsell. By permission of William R. Perkins Library, Duke University. From the collection of the Department of Rare Books.

10. Mermaid. From *Treasury of Fantastic and Mythological Creatures* (New York, 1981) by Richard Huber. By permission of Dover Publications, Inc.

11. Triton. From *Treasury of Fantastic and Mythological Creatures* (New York, 1981) by Richard Huber. By permission of Dover Publications, Inc.

12. Harpy. From *Historiae naturalis* (Amsterdam, 1657–65) by Johannes Jonstonus. By permission of William R. Perkins Library, Duke University. From the collection of the Department of Rare Books.

13. Harpy. From *Treasury of Fantastic and Mythological Creatures* (New York, 1981) by Richard Huber. By permission of Dover Publications, Inc.

14. *Sunset (Medusa)* by Eugene Berman. By permission of the North Carolina Museum of Art, Raleigh.

15. The head of Medusa. From *Treasury of Fantastic and Mythological Creatures* (New York, 1981) by Richard Huber. By permission of Dover Publications, Inc.

16. Sphinx. From *Treasury of Fantastic and Mythological Creatures* (New York, 1981) by Richard Huber. By permission of Dover Publications, Inc.

17. The Minotaur. From *Treasury of Fantastic and Mythological Creatures* (New York, 1981) by Richard Huber. By permission of Dover Publications, Inc.

18. The centaur Nessos. From *Treasury of Fantastic and Mythological Creatures* (New York, 1981) by Richard Huber. By permission of Dover Publications, Inc.

19. Centaurs holding a lion's skin. From *Historiae naturalis* (Amsterdam, 1657–65) by Johannes Jonstonus. By permission of William R. Perkins Library, Duke University. From the Collection of the Department of Rare Books.

Mythical
and
Fabulous
Creatures

TWENTY FABULOUS CREATURES

_____ **Birds and Beasts**

1

The Unicorn

Malcolm South

The unicorn legend was known in the West at least four centuries before the birth of Christ and apparently appeared in the East many centuries earlier. With the exception of the dragon, probably no imaginary beast has had a greater appeal than the unicorn. Much of his appeal comes from his mysteriousness and uniqueness: he is supposed to be a rare creature living in faraway lands and in places unfrequented by human beings; he is said to be noble and very strong; he is supposed to become meek and gentle in the presence of a virgin; and his horn is reputed to have marvelous powers. His diversity and richness as an image and symbol are also fascinating. He has a broad range of symbolic meanings, some of which involve contrasting ideas. Because his image is a varied one, it allows for new and changing interpretations and helps explain why he continues to stimulate the imagination of artists and writers. Another reason for his appeal is that he seems to be within the limits of probability. A creature such as the centaur or the griffin looks much more improbable than a unicorn does, and a case may even be made that he does not look any more improbable than certain real animals (Hathaway 11). For centuries most people accepted the unicorn as a genuine animal, and as late as the nineteenth century some educated people were still making serious claims that the unicorn might exist or actually did exist (Costello 99–102).

Numerous studies have dealt with the unicorn. The standard book on the subject is Odell Shepard's *The Lore of the Unicorn* (1930). One of the most scholarly studies of unicorns is Jürgen Einhorn's *Spiritalis Unicornis* (1976), which focuses on the animal in medieval art and literature. Robert Rüdiger Beer in *Unicorn: Myth and Reality* (originally published in West Germany in 1972 as *Einhorn: Fabelwelt und Wirklichkeit*) provides a good overall history of the unicorn and discusses the animal in literature and art. Another important book is Margaret B. Freeman's *The Unicorn Tapestries* (1976), which provides an excellent study of the set of tapestries known as *The Hunt of the Unicorn*. For information about the unicorn in the Arabian Middle Ages, readers should consult Richard Ettinghausen's book *The Unicorn* (1950). There was great interest in the unicorn between 1550 and 1700. Approximately twenty-five extended studies of the animal were published during that period (Shepard 156–83); Pierre Belon, Andrea Marini, Andrea Bacci, Ambroise Paré, Caspar Bartholinus, and Thomas Bartholinus are writers of special importance to the student of unicorn lore. In our own time the unicorn is very popular, and books and articles on the animal appear frequently. Some of these works are very superficial, and a purely commercial purpose is sometimes evident. But valuable studies such as those of Einhorn and Freeman speak well for the future of scholarship on the subject.

Most people probably envisage the unicorn as having the body of a horse. But this is only one of a number of forms that the unicorn has had through the centuries. In the West, the unicorn has often been depicted as resembling a horse or a goat (many representations combine features of these two animals by giving the unicorn a horse's body and a goatlike beard), but it has been represented in a variety of other forms as well. The East has its own traditions about the unicorn, and the animal there differs considerably from his counterpart in the West. The Chinese have several kinds of unicorns; the ki-lin, the type that has received the most attention, has been described in different ways (Gould 348–65). Japan has two types of unicorns: the kirin, which is based on the ki-lin and has resemblances to it; and the sin-you, which has lionlike features (Gould 357–59). In the Muslim world, the unicorn is known as the karkadann (this name may refer to the rhinoceros alone). The karkadann is usually a very fierce creature, and although he often has a bovine form, he may have the form of a deer, a horse, an antelope, or some other animal. Sometimes unicorned creatures in Muslim art are winged (Ettinghausen). Perhaps the strangest of all the forms of unicorned creatures is that of the three-legged ass, which is described in the sacred literature of ancient Persia. It has a white body, six eyes, nine mouths, and a golden horn that is hollow. It stands in the ocean and can use its horn to purify any uncleanliness in the water (Shepard 234–38).

Unicorns were thought to exist in the sea as well as on the land. This idea came about in part because of the existence of sea creatures such as the narwhal, but the basis for the idea was the widespread belief in earlier ages that each animal living on the land had an animal equivalent to it in the sea. Thus there were supposed to be water or sea unicorns. Sometimes the water unicorn has been depicted as having the body of a large fish or a whalelike creature, but he has been portrayed in a variety of ways.

Some of the diversity with which the unicorn can be represented is seen in two panels of *The Garden of Earthly Delights*, a triptych by Hieronymus Bosch dating from around 1500. Three unicorns appear in the left panel of the painting. One is a white unicorn that has a horse's body, cloven feet, and a straight horn with spiral twistings; next to the white unicorn is a brownish, deerlike unicorn with a curved horn having rounded knobs on it; and there is a water unicorn swimming in a pool in the right foreground, a strange-looking, composite animal with a fish's body, a horselike head, and a goatlike beard. The central panel has a water unicorn, a large fish with an extremely long horn; and at least four unicorns are among the men and animals circling a pool in the middle of the panel. The form of one of these unicorns is unclear because his body is hidden. Another unicorn is a white horse whose horn is lined at regular intervals with short, pointed barbs. A third unicorn has a deerlike body, long, erect ears, a goat's beard, and a horn of great length. The last unicorn has cloven feet, a horselike head and body, and a single horn divided into two antlered branches.

Bosch, who is one of the most inventive of all artists in the creation of fabulous creatures, shows much originality in portraying the unicorns in *The Garden of Earthly Delights*, but he does draw upon a number of traditional ideas. For instance, the white unicorn in the left panel is a traditional type of the animal: white is the predominant color of the unicorn in the West; and the equine form, cloven feet, and spiraled horn of this unicorn are all traditional elements. Bosch sometimes combines original and traditional elements in depicting unicorns. Thus the water unicorn swimming in the pool in the left panel must have come largely from Bosch's imagination, but the creature does have a horselike head, and there is the goatlike beard characteristic of many unicorns. A combination of original and traditional elements appears in two of the unicorns in the central panel. One of these—the unicorn with the body of a white horse—has the familiar equine form, but the barbs on his horn are a very unusual feature. Another unicorn— the one with the branched horn—has a horselike body and head. However, his branched horn seems to be invention on Bosch's part.

The unicorns in *The Garden of Earthly Delights* give some idea of how much the form of the unicorn can vary. Indeed, an artist (or writer) can depict almost any animal as a unicorn, for the unicorn has the form that imagination gives him. But the unicorn is firmly rooted in tradition, and although he takes a variety of forms, there are traditional ideas and patterns that give these forms underlying meanings.

The unicorn legend has many different facets. To gain a focus, we shall look at several major areas in the rest of this entry. First, we shall explore how the idea of the creature may have originated. Next there will be a historical survey of the creature. Then the following four areas will be covered: the symbolism of the unicorn; unicorn lore; unicorns in art; and unicorns in literature.

Many scholars have pointed out that the unicorn does not seem purely imaginary but is probably based on one or more actual animals. The most obvious explanation for the unicorn is that he was derived from the rhinoceros—especially from the one-horned Asian rhinoceroses (Shepard 213–19; Wendt 41–48). Although the rhinoceros with his bulky form seems to be the antithesis of the image of beauty and grace associated with the unicorn, the connection between the two creatures does not appear to be so strange if we consider the possibility that the story of the unicorn could have originated from distorted accounts of the rhinoceros. Moreover, some parallels exist between the unicorn and the rhinoceros. When attacked by hunters, the unicorn was said to be very fierce and to be hard or impossible to capture—a description that might fit a rhinoceros that is being attacked; and the unicorn's horn, like that of the rhinoceros, was reputed to have great curative and aphrodisiac powers. Some early writers merged the unicorn and rhinoceros into one animal without realizing that they were doing so. However, many writers distinguished between the two and treated them as separate animals.

The unicorn legend might have also been based on an antelope or some other animal with two horns. An antelope that has been singled out as a likely source of the legend is the oryx (Shepard 219–24). One species of the oryx, the Arabian oryx, is a large animal with white markings and long, nearly straight horns, and except for having two horns, it comes much closer to the traditional image of the unicorn than the rhinoceros. Aristotle stated that the oryx was one-horned, and it is not hard to understand why this belief came into being. When the oryx is viewed in profile, it can appear to have only one horn. In addition, an animal may sometimes be born with only one horn, or it may lose a horn while fighting.

Another animal that has contributed to the unicorn legend is the narwhal, a small whale found in arctic waters (see Vietmeyer). Extending from the upper jaw of the male narwhal is a long ivory tooth or tusk with spiral twistings. In the ancient world one or two writers speak of spirals or rings on the unicorn's horn, but usually spirals are not mentioned. Later, in the Middle Ages, unicorns were portrayed as having horns with spiral twistings, and the tusk of the narwhal was the basis for the conception of those horns. To most people in earlier times, the sight of a narwhal tusk that had been removed from the animal was proof in itself that the unicorn must exist. Even when informed that such tusks came from a marine animal, most people concluded that the tusks proved the existence of the sea unicorn and that there must be a land unicorn if a unicorn existed in the sea (Shepard 253–72).

There is one other important explanation for the unicorn: one-horned animals can be produced artificially by means of an operation. In 1933 Dr. W. Franklin Dove, a biologist at the University of Maine, performed such an operation on a male Ayrshire calf that was one day old. Describing his experiment in an article published in 1936, Dove says that the horns of ruminants are not outgrowths of the skull but are produced from horn buds or horn-producing tissues found above the frontal bones. Dove transplanted the calf's two horn buds from each corner of the skull to the middle of the forehead, bringing the buds into close contact. "The circular horn buds were trimmed flat at their point of contact so as to provide a larger fusion surface" (434–35). The horn buds fused together and became attached to the frontal bones—and in time the result was an animal with one long and straight horn. According to Dove, the adult animal exhibited a sense of the lordly power associated with the unicorn: the single horn gave the bull a sense of extraordinary power because he realized that he could use it effectively in thrusting and other ways; and on account of the consciousness of the power that he possessed and could use if he wished, he had an inner calmness and an outward meekness.

Dove says that the secret of transplanting horn buds was known in the ancient world. The Roman writer Pliny the Elder in the eleventh book of his *Natural History* refers to horn tissue transplanting (Pliny speaks of four horns being produced, but the method he mentions could produce a single horn as well as four). Dove surveys a number of reports concerning the creation of unicorned animals by artificial means (for example, a report in 1796 of unicorned oxen in Africa and a report in 1921 of unicorned sheep in Nepal), and states that the artificial production of one-horned animals may have taken place since ancient times and could help account for the unicorn.

The unicorn probably does not have a basis in any one animal. A combination of animals and concepts seems to be behind the creature. Myth has joined with fact, and fact and fantasy together have created the unicorn.

The origins of the unicorn lie in the East. India is first mentioned as the home of the unicorn, and although the use of unicorned creatures in ancient Indian art and thought is open to debate, the unicorn legend may have originated in India. Some scholars maintain that the story that the virgin can tame a unicorn grew out of an Indian legend (Beer 47). Early writers also mention Africa as the habitat of the unicorn. In addition, a long tradition concerning the unicorn exists in China.

Figures of creatures that have one horn or appear to have one horn are found in ancient Eastern art. They appear on cylinder seals from Mesopotamia, India, and some other areas of the ancient East, and they also appear on bas-reliefs found at Persepolis, Babylon, and other places. Some scholars have argued that these figures are actually of two-horned creatures that seem to have a single horn because they are shown in profile (the argument being that one horn hides the other because of the profile position). Other scholars maintain that the artists actually intended to represent one-horned creatures. Heinz Mode, for instance, states that oriental artists made the greatest possible effort "to achieve complete clarity in the representation of shapes" and that they would have shown a two-horned beast with two horns and not one (154). If the figures are of one-horned beasts (excluding the one-horned rhinoceros), then the concept of the unicorn can indeed be traced very far back, and we can conclude that the concept appeared in a number of ancient Eastern civilizations.

The first account of a one-horned animal by a writer in the West dates from about 400 B.C. and appears in a book by a Greek named Ctesias, who served as a physician at the Persian court for about seventeen years. After his return to Greece he wrote two books, one on Persia and the other on India. In the latter book he wrote:

Among the Indians . . . there are wild asses as large as horses, some being even larger. Their head is of a dark red colour, their eyes blue, and the rest of their body white. They have a horn on their forehead, a cubit in length. The filings of this horn, if given in a potion, are an antidote to poisonous drugs. This horn for about two palm-breadths upward from the base is of the purest white, where it tapers to a sharp point of a flaming crimson, and, in the middle, is black. These horns are made into drinking cups, and such as drink from them are attacked neither by convulsions nor by the sacred disease [epilepsy]. Nay, they are not even affected by poisons, if either before or after swallowing them they drink from these cups wine, water, or anything else. (McCrindle 26)

Ctesias also includes some other details about these one-horned animals: they have solid hoofs; they are very swift and strong, and no creature can overtake them; the only time that they will not flee from hunters is at the time when they lead out their young to pasture; then, because they refuse to desert their young, hunters on horseback can surround them; the animals fight by kicking and biting and butting with their heads; the hunters, unable to capture any of the animals alive, slay them with spears and arrows.

It is uncertain what animal Ctesias was attempting to describe. He never visited India himself, and he was not writing about an animal he had seen. Although he calls the animal the wild ass, the onager or wild ass was evidently not the animal he meant, for the wild ass is hornless, and Ctesias must have known what it was like because it was found in Persia and was often hunted by the Persians.

The one-horned asses are evidently based on the one-horned Indian rhinoceros and one or two other animals. Shepard believes that three animals are the basis of the description—the wild ass, some kind of antelope, and the rhinoceros (28–33). At any rate, Ctesias established the general conception of the unicorn that was to exist in the ancient world, and some features of his account (for example, the animal's white body and blue eyes and the powers of the horn) appear in many descriptions of the unicorn.

The next important description of one-horned animals is by Aristotle, who mentions two kinds: "We have seen no solid-hoofed animals with a pair of horns. But a few, e.g., the Indian ass, have a single horn and are solid-hoofed. The oryx has a single horn and cloven hooves" (*Historia Animalium* 2.1). Unlike Ctesias, Aristotle includes no colorful details. He simply states that the Indian ass is one of a few solid-hoofed animals with one horn and that the oryx, an animal with cloven feet, has one horn. The question whether unicorned animals might have cloven feet or solid hoofs must seem unimportant to modern readers, but in earlier times writers often gave the matter much attention. Aristotle added little to the unicorn legend, but he had such weight as a scientific authority that his acceptance of the existence of unicorned animals led people to believe in the unicorn.

Julius Caesar describes an unusual type of one-horned animal that was said to exist in the Hercynian forest in Germany. "There is an ox shaped like a stag, from the middle of whose forehead between the ears stands forth a single horn, taller and straighter than the horns we know. From its top branches spread out just like open hands" (*Gallic War* 6.26).

In his *Natural History* Pliny the Elder (A.D. 23–79) says that the only one-horned animal with cloven feet is the antelope. One-horned oxen, he writes, can be found in India, and also India has a fierce animal called the monoceros, "which in the rest of the body resembles a horse, but in the head a stag, in the feet an elephant, and in the tail a boar, and has a deep bellow, and a single black horn three feet long projecting from the middle of the forehead. They say that it is impossible to capture this animal alive" (8.31.76). The rhinoceros is probably behind this description, but Pliny did not realize that this was the case, and it seemed to readers that he was describing a specific animal that might be considered a unicorn—not merely a horse with a single horn. That Pliny described the monoceros as having a horselike body helped establish the concept of the equine unicorn. Like Ctesias, Pliny speaks of a fierce animal that cannot be captured alive, but the animal described by Pliny is more of a composite creature. (In most later descriptions, the unicorn is clearly a composite creature, with the body of one animal and two or three features of other animals.) Pliny and Ctesias give a different description of the horn. In Pliny it is black—not white, black, and red; and the horn in Pliny is about as twice as long as in Ctesias. Pliny says nothing about any powers attributed to the horn.

A Roman writer who had a deep impact on the unicorn legend was Claudius Aelian, who was born about A.D. 170. In his book *On the Characteristics of Animals*, three different passages pertain to unicorns. One passage—and the influence of Ctesias can be seen—states that India has one-horned horses and asses and that drinking-vessels made of their horns will protect people from poison (3.41). A second passage also owes a debt to Ctesias, for Aelian says that in India are one-horned asses with white bodies, red heads, blue eyes, and horns which are white, black, and red. The great men of that land, Aelian points out, use these horns as drinking cups; and people who drink from the horns are free from convulsions and diseases and cannot be destroyed by poison (4.52).

The third passage diverges from Ctesias and provides some new information about unicorns. According to Aelian, a one-horned animal called the *cartazon* (the Indian rhinoceros is evidently the animal being described) lives in India. This animal "is the size of a full-grown horse, has the mane of a horse, reddish hair, and is very swift of foot" (16.20). The horn grows between the eyebrows; it is black and has rings or spirals on it. Extremely sharp, it is a powerful weapon and is "invincible." The animals have very great strength. Although they are gentle towards animals of other species, they are quarrelsome among themselves; the males instinctively fight one another, and the males will fight even the females. In mating season the males become gentle toward the females and will even graze beside them, but when this time has passed and the females are with young, the males become wild once again. The animal likes solitude and prefers "lonely grazing-grounds." Nobody can recall the capture of an adult animal, but sometimes very young animals are captured, and they are taken to the king and exhibited for their strength in public festivals.

Here are ingredients that helped deepen the unicorn legend and gave the unicorn something of a distinctive character. The image is that of a very powerful and independent beast that prefers solitude and lonely places. Under certain circumstances the animal's fierceness can turn to gentleness. But there is always wildness underneath the gentleness. The female (so far the unicorn has been presented as almost exclusively male) is subordinate to the male, who becomes gentle and companionable when he wishes to mate; but once the female is pregnant, the male returns to his solitary and wild state, leaving the female to take care of the young. The animal is also associated with kings, and this is an association that will often appear in later accounts.

Some other ancient Greek and Roman authors wrote about one-horned animals, but they added nothing new to the unicorn legend. To sum up, Greek and Roman writers identified several types of unicorned animals and gave varying descriptions of their appearance. However, there did emerge a number of ideas that were to become part of the unicorn legend: unicorns are independent animals fond of solitude; they are swift and strong and cannot be captured by force; and their horns have miraculous powers.

The unicorn had great importance in ancient China, and before we trace the Western tradition any further, we need to look at the Chinese tradition in some detail. The first reference to the creature in China appears as early as 2697 B.C., and it is mentioned now and then in ancient Chinese writings. The subject of Chinese unicorns is extremely complicated, and only some of the main ideas can be given here. To begin with, it is important to emphasize that the unicorn in China has a variety of shapes and that various types of unicorned creatures can be identified. Charles Gould enumerates at least six different types: the ki-lin, the king, the kioh twan, the poh, the hiai chai, and the too jon sheu (348–65). The ki-lin, which has been given the most attention, has been represented in various ways. The body is usually that of a deer, but may be of a horse or another creature; the head may be lionlike or deerlike or resemble the head of some other animal; the tail may be like that of an ox or another animal; and the creature may or may not have scales. There may be one horn or two horns, and the horn or horns are usually said to be fleshy or to have a fleshy tip (Paludan 222–27). The ki-lin is supposed to combine both male and female attributes; it also exists in the male form (the ki) and in the female form (the lin). Whatever shape the ki-lin may have, the creature is always benevolent; it is so gentle that it will not step upon a blade of grass. It likes solitary places and likes to keep to itself. Hunters cannot catch it in snares or pitfalls. Among the 360 kinds of hairy creatures that were said to exist, the ki-lin was accorded chief place, and along with the dragon, the phoenix, and the tortoise was considered one of the four intelligent creatures. The other types of Chinese unicorns have the following appearance: the king has the shape of a large stag with the tail of an ox; the kioh twan looks like a deer with a horse's tail; the poh resembles a horse and has teeth and claws like those of a tiger; the hiai chai resembles a lion; and the too jon sheu has a lionlike head and body (Gould 352–62). The Chinese conception of the unicorn differs a great deal from the Western conception, with one of the notable differences being that the horn of Chinese unicorns has no magical or curative powers. Yet it is interesting to note that the ki-lin and the Western animal do have a few points in common. Each is a rare creature, and each likes solitary places and likes to keep to itself. Hunters cannot capture the ki-lin, and capture of the Western unicorn is not possible either unless a virgin is used. Shepard thinks that a common ancestor could lie behind the ki-lin and its Western counterpart (96).

Whereas the unicorn had a place of special importance in ancient China, the same was not true in the ancient Western world. The Greeks and Romans did not portray unicorns in their art and used them in only a very limited way in literature. Later, the unicorn took on great significance and became one of the most important animals in Christian thought. Scholars have singled out two major reasons why the unicorn gained such great importance.

The first reason is that the unicorn was included in certain translations of the Bible. This occurred because of uncertainty about the meaning of an animal that is called *re'em* in the Hebrew but is not clearly identified. In most modern translations of the Bible, *re'em* is translated as wild ox, for scholars now think that by the word *re'em* was meant the aurochs or *Bos primigenius*, a large, fierce wild ox that has been extinct for a few centuries. During approximately the third and second centuries A.D., the Old Testament was translated from Hebrew into Greek in the version known as the Septuagint; and the translators, uncertain what the word *re'em* meant, rendered it as "monoceros" (one-horned). Later, in the Vulgate (the Latin version of the Bible prepared by Saint Jerome in the fourth century A.D.), *re'em* was translated as "rhinoceros" in several cases and as "unicornis" in other cases. So it was that the unicorn came to be included in the Bible. The King James Bible has eight separate passages referring to the unicorn: Numbers 23:22, 24:8; Deuteronomy 33:17; Job 39:9–12; Psalms 22:21, 29:6, 92:10; and Isaiah 34:7. These passages speak of an untamable animal of great strength and fierceness. The inclusion of the unicorn in the Bible was sufficient proof to most Christians that he must exist, and helped give him important symbolic meanings.

The second main reason why the unicorn became more important was because of his inclusion in *Physiologus*, an allegorical bestiary that was probably written sometime between the second and fourth centuries A.D. Translated into Latin, Arabic, Syriac, and a large number of other languages, *Physiologus* had immense popularity and deeply influenced literature and art, especially during the Middle Ages (Curley ix–xliii). The earliest known use of the story of the virgin's capture of the unicorn appears in *Physiologus*. The lore found in *Physiologus* was later incorporated into the bestiaries. (For a detailed discussion of *Physiologus*, see Lauchert.)

Physiologus exists in many versions. The following summary gives a representative idea of what the typical *Physiologus* accounts say about the unicorn. He is described as a small animal that resembles a young goat and has a horn in the center of his head. He is so strong that hunters cannot capture him unless they use a stratagem. They take a virgin to a place where unicorns are supposed to be. A unicorn comes to the virgin, becomes submissive to her, and gets into her lap; then he is taken to the palace of the king. Next, after the description of the virgin-capture story, there is usually a section that gives the allegorical significance of the unicorn. He is likened to Christ, the horn symbolizing the power of Christ and the oneness of Father and Son; the virgin symbolizes the Virgin Mary, and the unicorn's getting into her lap is compared to Christ's entering the womb of the Virgin and taking on human flesh. The smallness of the unicorn is said to represent the humility of the Incarnation of Christ.

The early church fathers also compared Christ to the unicorn (Freeman 17). Saint Ambrose, for instance, asked: "Who then is this unicorn but the only begotten Son of God?" And Saint Basil stated that the might of the unicorn is invincible and therefore is a fitting symbol for the power of Christ. He also said that Christ is called a unicorn because the single horn symbolizes Christ's unity with the Father. Negative associations developed too, for the unicorn sometimes symbolized the Devil and destructive, evil forces. Thus a group of important symbols became attached to the unicorn during the early history of Christianity.

A writer who transmitted a large amount of the animal lore of the ancient world to the Middle Ages was Isidore of Seville (d. 636). In his *Etymologiae* he describes the unicorn as a fierce animal that can overcome the elephant in combat (Shepard 51–53). He includes the virgin-capture tale, saying that the unicorn falls asleep after putting his head in the virgin's lap, and that the hunters kill him. The killing of the animal was to become an important part of unicorn lore.

In the Middle Ages most people unquestionably accepted the unicorn as an actual animal. For any right-thinking Christian, the Bible attested to the unicorn's existence; *Physiologus* and the bestiaries described the creature, providing symbolic associations with Christ; and many of the encyclopedists such as Bartholomaeus Anglicus included an account of the animal in their works. In addition, some European travelers who visited the East returned with reports that they had seen unicorns themselves or that they had heard descriptions from people who had seen them. One of the most famous travelers of all, Marco Polo, saw "unicorns" in Sumatra; he declared that they were very different from what Europeans thought the unicorn to be like, for these beasts were large and ugly, fond of mud and mire. This was surely not a creature that would allow itself to be taken by a maiden, and surely no maiden would want to capture such a creature (1:372). Marco Polo was actually describing rhinoceroses, and although the animals he saw did not fit the European conception of the unicorn, he and his readers believed he had seen unicorns.

Belief in the unicorn remained strong during the Renaissance. There were more eyewitness accounts of the animal, and he was included in natural histories and books on animals. Indeed, the accounts of animals in some of these works did not differ very much from what was said in certain medieval encyclopedias, for there was the same reliance on authorities like Pliny, Aelian, and Isidore, and the same fabulous lore was repeated. Edward Topsell's *History of Four-Footed Beasts* (originally published in 1607) is a good example of a work that has this older sense of wonderment and credulity about animals. Topsell asserts that denying the unicorn's existence goes against the word of God, for the Bible proves the animal's existence. He thinks there are "divers" beasts with a single horn, but they cannot be called unicorns because there is no "virtue" in their horns. The unicorn is the only one-horned beast whose horn contains medicinal and curative powers. He characterizes the unicorn as a swift creature that lives mainly in solitary places. The virgin-capture story is one of a number of traditional beliefs that he includes in his account.

But some Renaissance writers were sceptical about the unicorn and expressed doubts about the powers attributed to the horn. In the middle of the sixteenth century, a Frenchman, Pierre Belon, and an Italian, Andrea Marini, each wrote a book that challenged traditional beliefs about the creature, and the famous French physician Ambroise Paré was sceptical about the unicorn and sought to disprove that the horn could counteract poison (Shepard 157–61, 168–72). Scepticism grew during the seventeenth and the eighteenth centuries. Some educated people in the nineteenth century still defended the unicorn as a real animal, but scientific fact was marshaled against him, and eventually it succeeded in destroying faith in him. The most telling argument against the unicorn was that made by the French naturalist Baron Cuvier, who in 1827 argued that no cloven-hoofed animal could have a single horn because such an animal has a division of the frontal bones and a horn will not grow over this division (Ley 35). Cuvier was correct in saying that a cloven-hoofed animal cannot grow a single horn naturally (the horn of the rhinoceros is not a contradiction of his argument, for its horn is made up of hair and is not attached to the bones of the skull). However, as Dr. Dove demonstrated in his experiment in 1933, a single horn can be created through tissue transplantation and will in time become fused to the frontal bones. Scientific fact undermined the unicorn legend, but Dove's experiment showed that one-horned animals are a possibility under certain circumstances.

People who are prone to reject the unicorn might be wise to remember James Thurber's fable "The Unicorn in the Garden." A man sees a unicorn in his garden, and the animal's presence uplifts his spirits. His wife will not believe in the unicorn and calls the police and a psychiatrist. However, the story has an unexpected twist: the husband is not put in the "booby hatch" but his wife is.

Much of the durability of the unicorn is because of the richness of the symbolism connected with him. He appeals to the imagination on many levels; he is mystery, beauty, power, chastity, ferocity. He is all of these things and many more. Even though he is no longer accepted as a real animal, he continues to have powerful symbolic meanings because he satisfies some deep human longing for the mysterious and the unattainable. He belongs to the world of dreams and romance, and although he may sometimes come under the power of a human being, there is always a part of him that is forever free and independent.

A major point to realize about the symbolism concerning the unicorn is that in the West he has had both negative and positive associations. He has symbolized courage, nobility, wisdom, and virtue, but he has also stood for pride, wrath, and destructive forces. He is a symbol of Christ, but he is a symbol of the Devil as well. His strength can represent the invincible power of Christ, or it can represent the destructive power of Satan. In a particular context the unicorn may symbolize either good or evil. Sometimes the context provides no clear meaning, and the animal's significance is ambiguous.

As pointed out earlier, the Chinese conception of the unicorn differs greatly from the Western conception. The ki-lin has only positive associations. It symbolizes wisdom, justice, and rectitude. It will appear only during the time of an upright ruler or before the birth or the death of a sage. In Japan the kirin, which is based on the ki-lin, is also benevolent; it has such care for living things that it will not step on a blade of grass or injure an insect; and its appearance requires a certain constellation in heaven and the birth of a man of truly great perception and understanding (Kaempfer 1:190). The sin-you, the other Japanese unicorn, can distinguish innocence from guilt; when the sage Kan You had trouble determining guilt in criminal cases involving a death, he often turned to the sin-you for help. If a person was guilty, the creature would stand still, look steadfastly at him, and then gore him with its horn (Hathaway 49).

The unicorn is often a symbol of purity and chastity. People have connected the animal with purity because of the powers attributed to the horn and because of his symbolic association with Christ and the Virgin Mary. In the virgin-capture tale, the unicorn is represented as being able to recognize purity: he will become tame if the woman is chaste; and if she is unchaste, he will know this, and will kill the woman with his horn. In art a unicorn that is depicted with a woman usually symbolizes her virtue or chastity. One of the most important uses of the unicorn as a chastity symbol was in illustrations for Petrarch's *Trionfi*, an allegorical work dealing with the Triumph of Love, Chastity, and several other themes; illustrations of chariots were made for each division of the poem, and the illustrations showing the Triumph of Chastity portray Chastity riding in a chariot drawn by two or more unicorns. As a chastity symbol, the unicorn was also an attribute of Saint Justina of Antioch and Saint Justina of Padua.

The unicorn has symbolized lust as well as chastity. The association with lust is not hard to understand. The unicorn was regarded as a very virile animal of great power and energy. He is a symbol of maleness, and his horn is an emblem of potency—a sexual symbol whose phallic significance seems natural. In the typical *Physiologus* account, the virgin does not use sexual wiles to attract the unicorn, but the story does contain ingredients that lend themselves to a sexual interpretation: only a woman can tame the unicorn; he gets into the virgin's lap and she caresses him; and he submits to her in what might seem to be the submission of one lover to another. The Arabic version of *Physiologus* departs from the typical *Physiologus* account and describes the capture in erotic terms (McCulloch 181). The woman in this version is said to be chaste, but she does not have the modesty expected of a virgin. After the unicorn has come to her, she offers him her breasts, and he begins to suck them. Then she reaches out and grasps the animal's horn. Some commentators saw the unicorn's capture as a submission to temptation. Thus Leonardo da Vinci in his *Bestiary* wrote that what attracts the unicorn to the virgin is lust: "The unicorn, through its intemperance and not knowing how to control itself, for the love it bears to fair maidens forgets its ferocity and wildness; and laying aside all fear it will go up to a seated damsel and go to sleep in her lap, and thus the hunters take it" (265). According to some accounts, the woman should carry out the capture while she was naked—or at least she should show the animal her breasts. And many writers specify that a beautiful virgin should be used.

The killing of the unicorn by hunters in the capture story also took on important symbolic meanings. His death of course can alter the interpretation of the virgin's role, for she may be seen as a decoy luring him to his death. In Christian symbolism, the hunters were often likened to Christ's enemies, with a parallel being drawn between the unicorn's death and Christ's Passion and death.

The unicorn has long been linked with nobility and kingship. Aelian mentions that young unicorns were taken to the king for public exhibition, and in *Physiologus* the captive unicorn is taken to the palace of the king. That only a king should possess the unicorn seemed right, for the animal's horn had both curative and financial value and the animal himself embodied the nobility, courage, and strength that a king should possess. European travelers reported seeing unicorns that were owned by rulers in the East. For instance, Prester John, a legendary Christian ruler of a great kingdom in Asia or Africa, was said to have tame unicorns. To Europeans, these unicorns were a sign of his wealth and power, and that he owned tame unicorns was something special, for it signified his power over nature—the submission of a fierce animal to man's will. In light of the unicorn's connection with kingship and nobility, it is understandable why the animal has an important place in heraldry (Beer 137–41). His best-known use is in the British Royal Arms, where he and the lion appear as supporters. The heraldic unicorn is white and has a horse's body, neck, and mane, a goat's beard, the tail of the heraldic lion, and a horn with spiral twistings. It is the most familiar of all images of the unicorn.

Several other symbolic meanings of the unicorn are important. He has often represented death. A miniature by Jean Colombe pictures Death riding a unicorn, and in the *Legend of Barlaam and Josaphat* the unicorn that chases and menaces the man symbolizes death. The unicorn was also associated with the infernal regions—an association found in Dürer's *Rape of Persephone*, where Pluto rides a unicorn as he carries off Persephone to the underworld. In alchemy the unicorn had a dual, hermaphroditic nature and represented mercurius, the ever-changing and transforming substance that brings unripe bodies to perfection (see Jung). The unicorn was used as a symbol of the monastic life because of his reputed love of solitude. In addition, he has represented vigor, health, and related ideas.

The lore of the unicorn comes from many times and places. The total body of beliefs about the animal is very large, and these beliefs are detailed and complex.

The virgin-capture story is the best known of all the beliefs about the unicorn. (The use of the story as a symbol of Christ's Incarnation has already been discussed.) During the latter part of the Middle Ages, the story evolved into a form called the Holy Hunt, and was used to symbolize the Annunciation. The setting of the Holy Hunt is usually in an enclosed garden; hounds that symbolize virtues chase the unicorn toward the Virgin Mary; the angel Gabriel is a huntsman and is also the divine herald announcing to Mary that she will be the mother of Jesus (Schiller 53). As already pointed out, the unicorn's capture can be interpreted in erotic and sexual terms; and the taming has often been interpreted as the submission to temptation. Yet the taming may also represent the controlling of passion or wildness by purity, or the triumph of spiritual love over profane love.

Some other ideas about the virgin-capture story need to be mentioned. Many people believed that some natural cause must be behind the capture. According to one explanation, the unicorn is attracted to the lady by a scent that only virgins are supposed to possess; and this scent—it was often described as ''sweet''—helps charm the unicorn after he has come to the lady. The virgin was said to charm the unicorn in other ways as well—by the power of her eyes or by touch (by caressing him or touching his horn).

Another story about the unicorn is that he can purify water. He appears as a water-purifier in the Greek version of *Physiologus*: animals are unable to drink from a lake because the serpent has cast poison upon its waters; they await the coming of the unicorn; when he comes he goes into the lake and purifies the water by making the sign of the cross over it with his horn; then the animals drink (Carlill 200). The text does not provide a moral, but it is obvious that the unicorn represents Christ, who offers salvation from the sin (poison) brought into the world by Satan (the serpent). Here the unicorn purifies the water by making the sign of the cross over it. In other accounts he purifies water by dipping his horn into it.

Much of the lore pertains to the powers attributed to the horn. It was used to detect poison because it was supposed to sweat in the presence of poison and because a poisoned drink was supposed to bubble up when it came into contact with the horn. Because of the belief that the horn could counteract poison, people regarded the horn as an antidote to poison. To detect poison and counteract it, they used goblets or cups made of the horn, or they used it in powdered form or in some other way. There was a traditional belief that spiders or other ''venomous'' creatures could not escape from a circle made of scrapings from a unicorn's horn.

The horn was a general cure-all. It was believed to cure epilepsy, fevers, and numerous other ailments, to prolong youth, and to stimulate sexual desire. Given all of these wonderful ''virtues,'' it is not surprising that the horn was literally worth its weight in gold. There was a thriving business in buying and selling unicorns' horns during the Renaissance. A small piece of the horn could bring a handsome price; and an entire horn (in actuality a narwhal tusk, an elephant tusk, or a horn from some other animal) could have a value that was almost priceless. By 1600 Europe had at least twelve of the horns that were very famous (Shepard 105).

The unicorn and the elephant were regarded as natural enemies. Their animosity was so great that they would begin fighting when they met, and the unicorn would kill the elephant by goring it in its stomach. The unicorn and the lion were likewise traditional enemies that fought each other. The lion defeated the unicorn by using a trick: the lion would run to a tree as the unicorn charged him, and just before being gored, the lion would jump aside; the unicorn would unintentionally stick his horn into the tree, and because he could not pull it out, the lion could kill him. Some writers have pointed out that the lion is a solar symbol and the unicorn a lunar symbol and that the joining of the animals came about because of connections between sun and moon (see Brown). At any rate, the joining seems natural. Although the lion is the "king of beasts," the unicorn is a king in his own right. Like the lion, he is strong and fierce, an animal that holds a position of primacy among beasts.

Some other lore is of interest. The unicorn was associated with the so-called wild people, savage and lustful creatures found in the art and literature of the Middle Ages and the Renaissance. Wild men and women were often depicted as riding unicorns (Bernheimer 27, 134–35). It was said that the unicorn was in the Garden of Eden and that he was among the animals that Adam named. There are works of art showing a pair of unicorns entering Noah's ark. Yet a tradition existed that the unicorn was not on the ark: he and his mate disdainfully refused to enter, or they boarded the ark, but were so unruly that Noah made them get off. Some accounts say that the unicorn drowned in the Flood, but others say that he survived by swimming until the waters went down.

Unicorns have a prominent place in art. They have been represented in book illustrations, paintings, and tapestries, and they have been portrayed on choir-stalls, church pews, chests, jewel boxes, and medals. They had a special appeal to artists during the Middle Ages and the Renaissance. The richest and most complex treatment of the unicorn in art was in the fifteenth century. After the middle of the sixteenth century, artists did not use the unicorn as often, and there was not a large use of him in art during the seventeenth, eighteenth, and nineteenth centuries. In the twentieth century, a revival of interest in the unicorn has taken place, and artists have portrayed him frequently (Hathaway 151–69). On the unicorn in art, see the following: Ettinghausen, for uses in medieval Islamic art; Freeman, for uses in the art of the Middle Ages; and Beer, for uses in the art of various ages.

Because the unicorn has a great variety of forms, artists are not bound by a fixed image of him and can represent him in different ways. We have seen that a number of traditional forms have been used. In his most familiar form—that of a white horse—the unicorn is usually depicted as a creature of surpassing beauty. Other traditional forms have their appeal too. The goatlike unicorn of *Physiologus*, for instance, can be portrayed as a charming creature with a delicate beauty. Artists have also invented new forms. Moreover, as in the case of some of Bosch's unicorns, an artist may combine traditional and invented elements. A modern artist who invents new forms and uses some traditional elements in portraying unicorns is Ernst Fuchs. He uses the equine form in some cases, but his equine unicorns have a strange appearance. Some unicorns in Fuchs's works are very unconventional (for example, a dragonlike monster in *The Transformation of Lucretia*; a creature compounded of human and animal features in *The Wedding of the Unicorn*; and a monstrous creature in *Struggle of the Changed Gods*). Fuchs has written: "The unicorn is the phallic creature and instantly becomes my synonym for overcoming death" (48). He links the unicorn with Christ, a traditional association. Yet the unicorn in his works remains a mysterious creature with meanings that defy any final explanations.

The unicorn has appeared so extensively in art that only some examples of uses can be given here. The virgin-capture story has been the most frequently used of traditional subjects. A discussion of some works involving the story will be useful in showing how the unicorn has been depicted in art. Tenderness, mystery, beauty, innocence, brutality—these are some of the themes that have appeared in representations of the story. The brutal side of the tale is seen in a miniature in a twelfth-century English bestiary. Here a blue unicorn that has an antelopelike form rests his forelegs on the lap of a seated virgin; two hunters stand behind the animal; one hunter has thrust a spear deeply into him, and the other hunter holds a heavy axe on high, poised, ready to strike a brutal blow (Freeman 44). In a German painting dating from about 1420, the story appears in the context of the Holy Hunt, one of numerous representations of this subject in art. Huntsman and divine herald, Gabriel holds a spear in his right hand and blows upon a horn held in the other hand. A goatlike unicorn rests his body on Mary's lap. "He is a most fantastic but resplendent being, fashioned entirely of shining gold, with mane and tail like darting flames" (Freeman 51). Saints behind the Virgin and the unicorn look at the pair; an angelic choir sings; and a human orchestra furnishes music. On the other hand, only virgin and unicorn appear in the painting *An Allegory of Chastity* by Giorgione (d. 1510). A seated maiden gently caresses an equine unicorn that is smaller than she is and has a delicate, exquisite beauty. A tie born of complete trust unites the two; he rests his head in her lap; she guards, protects, gives comfort. There is also trust revealed in Armand Point's *Princess and the Unicorn*, painted near the end of the nineteenth century. The princess stands beside an equine unicorn, with the fingertips of her left hand lightly touching his neck. Her purity gives her virginal mastery over the beast (Goldwater 15). It is a mastery sure and confident but tender and gentle. In each of these representations of the story, the unicorn is portrayed in a different way, and the story is given a different focus. Such variety and diversity are characteristic of much of the art involving the unicorn.

The most important works of art pertaining to the unicorn are the two sets of tapestries known as *The Lady and the Unicorn* and *The Hunt of the Unicorn*, both of which were woven in the latter part of the fifteenth century. *The Lady and the Unicorn*, at the Cluny Museum in Paris, consists of six tapestries. (For a good discussion of the series, see Verlet and Salet.) The tapestries cast a spell of enchantment. Each tapestry has a soft red background; there are flowers, trees, birds, monkeys, hares, small dogs, and other animals; on a central island in each tapestry appear the Lady in gorgeous court dress, a lion, and a white unicorn with a horse's body, a goat's beard, and a spiraled horn. The exact meaning of the series is uncertain. However, each of five of the tapestries pertains to one of the five senses, so that these tapestries seem to constitute an allegory of the senses. In light of the fact that a traditional association existed between the lion and the unicorn, their appearance in each tapestry seems natural. Each animal has a heraldic function: the lion supports a shield or banner bearing arms, and the unicorn has the same function in all the tapestries except the one pertaining to sight. *The Hunt of the Unicorn*, at The Cloisters in New York, consists of seven tapestries. They depict the hunting of the unicorn, his killing, and (in the last tapestry) his captivity, where he appears alive once more. In the first tapestry, huntsmen in bright clothes begin the hunt. The second tapestry shows the unicorn, a milk-white animal with a horse's body, dipping his horn into a stream around which hunters and other animals are gathered. In the third tapestry the unicorn leaps the stream; dogs begin the chase, and huntsmen thrust at the animal with spears, but he escapes. In the fourth tapestry the hunters and dogs have sur-rounded the unicorn; he fights for his life, goring a dog and kicking backward with his hind feet toward a hunter ready to spear him. The next tapestry, which is in fragmetary form, shows that the hunters have been unable to subdue the unicorn through force; a maiden (only one of her hands and part of one arm can be seen) has tamed the animal; a huntsman blows upon a horn to summon his fellows, and two dogs are attacking the unicorn. The sixth tapestry depicts his killing; his body, placed on the back of a horse, is taken to the lord and lady of the castle. In the final tapestry the unicorn, alive again, appears in an enclosure. Despite his captivity he seems to be free in spirit (Beer 162). Secular and religious themes are combined in *The Hunt of the Unicorn*. Margaret Freeman has made a detailed study of the series, but as she points out, the symbolism of the tapestries is so complex that "a complete understanding of all the symbolism in them may always remain elusive" (13). In *The Lady and the Unicorn* and *The Hunt of the Unicorn*, the unicorn legend reached its richest expression in art.

The unicorn has also been used extensively in literature (Cohn; Shepard; Beer; Einhorn; and Hathaway). Many literary uses of the unicorn involve only a general allusion or a passing reference. But in a large number of works unicorn lore has a significant purpose, and in some works a unicorn is used as an important or the central figure. Unicorns often appear in works of modern fantasy (see West), and they appear with some frequency in children's literature. *Unicorns!* (1982; ed. Jack Dann and Gardner Dozois) is an anthology containing sixteen stories about unicorns by modern writers.

Unicorns are usually linked with enchantment and magic. In most cases they inhabit a magical place or realm. The unicorn in Peter S. Beagle's novel *The Last Unicorn* (1968) lives in a magic forest, a place where it is always spring because she lives there; and in Lord Dunsany's *The King of Elfland's Daughter* (1924) the unicorns are inhabitants of Elfland. Unicorns often appear suddenly and unexpectedly to human beings—sometimes the passing of the animals is so swift that one may get only a glimpse of them. When they appear, they usually create a feeling of wonder and astonishment. A unicorn in *The King of Elfland's Daughter* creates such an effect: "He came, a whiteness on perfectly silent feet, four or five yards into the fields we know, and stood there still as moonlight, and listened and listened and listened" (155). Sometimes unicorns are associated with redemption and rebirth. In Alan Garner's *Elidor* (1965), four English children enter Elidor, a world existing in another dimension. Elidor is being destroyed by the forces of darkness, and it can be saved only if the unicorn Findhorn sings. Near the end of the book Findhorn enters the human world and is slain by an enemy warrior who has also come from Elidor. As he is dying the unicorn sings, and his song restores brightness to Elidor and preserves it.

In some cases unicorns are not depicted as enchanting, magical animals. There is a satirical description of unicorns in Rabelais. Pantagruel sees thirty-two unicorns in the Land of Satin, where all the birds and beasts are of tapestry work. Rabelais says that the unicorn's horn normally dangles down like the comb of a turkey cock, but that the unicorn can make the horn stand up (a reference to the erection of the penis) so that it becomes as straight as an arrow. In Lewis Carroll's *Through the Looking-Glass*, the Unicorn and the Lion fight for the crown. The Unicorn is opinionated and querulous. After he and the Lion pause for refreshments, he brags that he bested his opponent. When he sees Alice he looks at her with disgust and asks what she is. He bickers with the Lion, and at one point he complains to Alice that she has given the Lion twice as much cake as she gave him.

Writers have often drawn upon the virgin-capture story to make some point about love. The unicorn's submission can be seen as a symbol of harmonious love—fierceness transformed into gentleness by love, with the virgin and the tamed unicorn representing faithful lovers. The story was also used in the courtly love tradition: like the unicorn, the lover is bewitched by a woman, becomes her captive, and is "slain" by love. The speaker in the thirteenth-century *Bestiary of Love* of Richard de Fournival develops this comparison, saying that the huntsman Love has placed a lady in his path, that her sweet odor has captivated him as the sweet smell of the virgin captivates the unicorn and puts him to sleep, and that in his helpless state he is fated to die as the unicorn dies at the hands of the hunters (Shepard 54–55).

A simile in *The Faerie Queene* (2.5.10) is based on the story that the unicorn fights the lion and impales his horn in a tree. Shakespeare alludes to the story in *Julius Caesar* (II.i) and *Timon of Athens* (IV.iii), but he does not mention the lion-unicorn combat. In the story "The Brave Little Tailor" as related by the Brothers Grimm, capturing a unicorn is one of the deeds that the tailor must accomplish in order to win the king's daughter. Taking an axe and a halter with him, he goes into the forest. When a unicorn charges him, he springs behind a tree, and the animal impales his horn in the tree and becomes trapped. The tailor puts the halter around the unicorn's neck, cuts the horn out of the tree with the axe, and leads the animal to the king, as do the hunters in *Physiologus*.

Some other uses of the unicorn in literature are of interest. Shakespeare has a character in *The Tempest* (III.iii) say: "Now I will believe / That there are unicorns." This statement has often been taken to mean that Shakespeare was sceptical about the unicorn's existence. William Butler Yeats in his play *The Unicorn from the Stars* (1908) links the unicorn with destructive forces that bring renewal and regeneration. A poem in Rainer Maria Rilke's *Sonnets to Orpheus* (1923) was inspired by the tapestries in *The Lady and the Unicorn* series. The unicorn, Rilke writes, is the creature that "has never been," but the animal in the tapestries behaves as though it actually exists; it takes on a spiritual and idealized existence that has a greater reality than mere physical existence. In Tennessee Williams' play *The Glass Menagerie* (1945), the unicorn that Laura Wingfield has in her collection of glass animals is a symbol of her aloneness and vulnerability. When the animal's horn is broken off, Laura says that the animal will now be like the other horses and will feel more at home—a statement that seems to suggest that she will feel this way too. Yet one may get the impression that she will remain lonely and vulnerable. The white unicorn Jewel in C. S. Lewis' book *The Last Battle* (1956) fights against the forces of evil and is among those creatures that the Great Lion Aslan welcomes into paradise. Theodore Sturgeon in "The Silken-Swift" gives the unicorn-capture story an interesting and satisfying twist: a unicorn will not submit to Rita, who is a virgin but is evil; instead, he puts his head in the lap of Barbara, who is not a virgin but has a good heart. Among the many modern writers who have used the unicorn in some way are the following: Dorothy P. Lathrop, *The Colt from Moon Mountain*; Elizabeth Goudge, *The Little White Horse*; Martin Walser, *Das Einhorn*; Iris Murdoch, *The Unicorn*; Janice Elliott, *The Birthday Unicorn*; and Madeleine L'Engle, *A Swiftly Tilting Planet*. Modern poets who have referred to the unicorn include T. S. Eliot, Federico García Lorca, Dylan Thomas, and W. H. Auden. (For numerous other writers who have used the unicorn, see Einhorn.)

An important use of the unicorn legend appears in book two of T. H. White's *Once and Future King*. Four boys force a kitchenmaid named Meg to act as a decoy to attract a unicorn (257–70). Although they agree that they will try to take the animal alive, they end up killing him brutally. White uses the story to show how complex love and hate are and how the desire for recognition and glory can debase people. He also reveals how easy it is to turn beauty into ugliness.

A book that deserves special attention is Peter Beagle's novel *The Last Unicorn*. The main character of the book is a female unicorn. (She is portrayed so well that she makes up somewhat for the almost total lack of attention that the female unicorn has received in literature.) She is immortal in the sense that she cannot die from old age, but she can be killed. She lives alone in an enchanted forest, and she is happy until she hears two hunters talking about unicorns. From their conversation, she comes to fear that she may be the only unicorn left in the world, and she sets out on a quest to look for other unicorns. One day a butterfly tells her that the Red Bull has driven her people down all the roads long ago. She later learns that the Red Bull is a fearsome creature found in the kingdom of King Haggard, an old man who rules a barren land by the sea. Accompanied by the magician Schmendrick and a woman named Molly Grue, she encounters the Red Bull. He is so strong and frightening that she flees from him. Eventually, she becomes obedient to him, and as he is guiding her toward the sea, Schmendrick changes her into a girl, the Lady Amalthea. Confused by the change, the Red Bull leaves her alone and goes away. Schmendrick, Molly Grue, and the Lady Amalthea stay at Haggard's castle for a time; and Lír, the king's adopted son, falls in love with the girl. Haggard says that all the other unicorns have been imprisoned in the sea—driven there one by one by the Red Bull so that Haggard can have them for his own personal viewing. Schmendrick, Lír, Molly Grue, and the Lady Amalthea go to challenge the Red Bull in an effort to free the other unicorns, for through his power and presence they are unable to escape. The Red Bull begins pursuing the Lady Amalthea. Schmendrick restores her unicorn's form to her, but once again the Bull proves too strong for her. Then, Lír leaps into the path of the Red Bull and is killed. His death arouses her anger, and she forces the Red Bull into the sea. The other unicorns now come streaming and flowing out of the sea. Haggard's castle melts away, and the passage of the unicorns through the barren land brings back spring and begins a process of renewal. After she restores life to Lír by touching him with her horn, she leaves him and the others and sets off to return to her forest. She suspects that she may never live contentedly again, for in her human form she was mortal and now she is no longer like any other unicorn. The unicorns in *The Last Unicorn* represent the imagination and creative forces, and their freeing from the sea symbolizes the freeing of the imagination from blight, decay, and death.

At the present time the unicorn has immense popularity. Unicorn fanciers and lovers seem to be everywhere. Gift shops stock unicorn calendars, statues, napkins, paperweights, and many other items concerning the unicorn. The animal appears frequently in literature and art. In some modern representations, the unicorn has been portrayed as a weak, bland animal (Hathaway 168). Yet the symbolism connected with the unicorn is so complex and meaningful that he will surely withstand the harmful effects of commercialization and overexposure. He has an appeal that transcends any one time and place. For centuries he has satisfied some deep human need. And he will undoubtedly continue to do so for a long time to come.

BIBLIOGRAPHY

Aelian. *On the Characteristics of Animals*. Trans. A. F. Scholfield. 3 vols. Cambridge: Harvard University Press, 1958.

Aristotle. *Historia Animalium*. Trans. A. L. Peck. Cambridge: Harvard University Press, 1965. Vol. 1.

Bartholinus, Thomas. *De unicornu observationes novae*. Amsterdam, 1678.

Beagle, Peter S. *The Last Unicorn*. New York: Viking, 1968.

Beer, Robert Rüdiger. *Unicorn: Myth and Reality*. Trans. Charles M. Stern. New York: Van Nostrand Reinhold, 1977.

Belon, Pierre. *Les Observations de plusieurs singularitez et choses memorables. . . .* Paris, 1553.

Bernheimer, Richard. *Wild Men in the Middle Ages: A Study in Art, Sentiment, and Demonology*. Cambridge: Harvard University Press, 1952.

Brown, Robert. *The Unicorn: A Mythological Investigation*. London, 1881.

Caesar, C. Julius. *The Gallic War*. Trans. H. J. Edwards. 1917; rpt. Cambridge: Harvard University Press, 1952.

Carlill, James, trans. *Physiologus*. In *The Epic of the Beast*. Ed. William Rose. London: George Routledge; New York: Dutton, 1924.

Carroll, Lewis. *Through the Looking-Glass*. In *Alice in Wonderland*. Ed. Donald J. Gray. New York: Norton, 1971. 101–209.

Cohn, Carl. *Zur literarischen Geschichte des Einhorns*. Berlin, 1896.

Costello, Peter. *The Magic Zoo: The Natural History of Fabulous Animals*. New York: St. Martin's, 1979.

Curley, Michael J., trans. *Physiologus*. Austin: University of Texas Press, 1979.

Dann, Jack, and Gardner Dozois, eds. *Unicorns!* New York: Ace, 1982.

Dove, W. Franklin. "Artificial Production of the Fabulous Unicorn: A Modern Interpretation of an Ancient Myth." *Scientific Monthly* 42 (1936):431–36.

Dunsany, Lord. *The King of Elfland's Daughter*. New York: Putnam's, 1924.

Einhorn, Jürgen W. *Spiritalis Unicornis: Das Einhorn als Bedeutungsträger in Literatur und Kunst des Mittelalters*. München: Wilhelm Fink, 1976.

Ettinghausen, Richard. *The Unicorn*. Studies in Muslim Iconography 1. Smithsonian Institution: Freer Gallery of Art. Washington, 1950.

Fraenger, Wilhelm. *Hieronymus Bosch*. Trans. Helen Sebba. New York: Putnam's, 1983.

Freeman, Margaret B. *The Unicorn Tapestries*. New York: Metropolitan Museum of Art, 1976.

Fuchs, Ernst. *Ernst Fuchs*. Trans. Sophie Wilkins. New York: Harry Abrams, 1979.

Garner, Alan. *Elidor*. London, 1965; rpt. New York: Henry Z. Walck, 1967.

Goldwater, Robert. *Symbolism*. New York: Harper and Row, 1979.

Gould, Charles. *Mythical Monsters*. London, 1886.

Hathaway, Nancy. *The Unicorn*. New York, 1980; rpt. Harmondsworth and New York: Penguin, 1982.

Johnsgard, Paul, and Karin Johnsgard. *Dragons and Unicorns: A Natural History*. New York: St. Martin's, 1982.

Jung, C. G. *Psychology and Alchemy*. Vol. 12 of *The Collected Works of C. G. Jung*. Trans. R. F. C. Hull. 2nd ed. Bollingen Series 20. Princeton: Princeton University Press, 1968.

Kaempfer, Engelbert. *The History of Japan*. Trans. J. G. Scheuchzer. 3 vols. Glasgow: James MacLehose; New York: Macmillan, 1906.

Lauchert, Friedrich. *Geschichte des Physiologus*. Strassburg, 1889.

Leonardo da Vinci. *The Literary Works of Leonardo da Vinci*. Ed. Jean Paul Richter. 3rd ed. London: Phaidon, 1970. Vol. 2.

Ley, Willy. *The Lungfish and the Unicorn: An Excursion into Romantic Zoology*. New York: Modern Age Books, 1941.

McCrindle, J. W., trans. *Ancient India as Described by Ktesias the Knidian*. 1882; rpt. Delhi: Manohar Reprints, 1973.

McCulloch, Florence. *Mediaeval Latin and French Bestiaries*. Rev. ed. Chapel Hill: University of North Carolina Press, 1962.

Marini, Andrea. *Discorso de Andrea Marini, medico, contra la falsa opinione dell' alicorno*. Venice, 1566.

Mode, Heinz. *Fabulous Beasts and Demons*. London: Phaidon, 1975.

Paludan, Ann. *The Imperial Ming Tombs*. New Haven: Yale University Press, 1981.

Paré, Ambroise. *Oeuvres complètes*. Ed. J. F. Malgaigne. Paris, 1840–41; rpt. Genève: Slatkine, 1970.

Pliny the Elder. *Natural History*. Trans. H. Rackham et al. 10 vols. Cambridge: Harvard University Press, 1938–62.

Polo, Marco. *The Description of the World*. Ed. A. C. Moule and Paul Pelliot. 2 vols. 1938; rpt. London: George Routledge, 1976.

Rabelais, François. *Oeuvres complètes*. Ed. P. Jourda. 2 vols. Paris: Garnier, 1962.

Schiller, Gertrud. *Iconography of Christian Art*. Trans. Janet Seligman. Greenwich, Conn.: New York Graphic Society, 1971. Vol. 1.

Shepard, Odell. *The Lore of the Unicorn*. London, 1930; rpt. New York: Harper and Row, 1979.

Sturgeon, Theodore. "The Silken-Swift." In *Phantasmagoria: Tales of Fantasy and the Supernatural*. Ed. Jane Mobley. Garden City, N.Y.: Anchor-Doubleday, 1977. 100–20.

Tolnay, Charles de. *Hieronymus Bosch*. New York: Reynal and Company, in association with William Morrow, 1966.

Topsell, Edward. *The History of Four-Footed Beasts and Serpents and Insects*. London, 1658.

Verlet, Pierre, and Francis Salet. *The Lady and the Unicorn*. Trans. R. D. Chancellor. London: Thames and Hudson, 1961.

Vietmeyer, Noel D. "Rare Narwhals Inspired the Myth of the Unicorn." *Smithsonian* 10.11 (February 1980): 118–23.

Wendt, Herbert. *Out of Noah's Ark: The Story of Man's Discovery of the Animal Kingdom*. Trans. Michael Bullock. Boston: Houghton Mifflin, 1959.

West, Richard C. "The Sign of the Unicorn: The Unicorn Motif in Selected Works of Modern Fantasy." In *Selected Proceedings of the 1978 Science Fiction Research Association National Conference*. Ed. Thomas J. Remington. Cedar Falls, Iowa: University of Northern Iowa, 1979, 45–54.

White, T. H. *The Once and Future King*. London: Collins, 1958.

Williamson, John. *The Oak King, the Holly King, and the Unicorn: The Myths and Symbolism of the Unicorn Tapestries*. New York: Harper and Row, 1986.

2

The Dragon

Jonathan D. Evans

Of all imaginary creatures, the dragon can be said most accurately to have universal appeal. From ancient to the most recent times, in the Orient as well as in the West, in creation epics and in science fiction, dragons have served as a supreme embodiment of monstrous, superhuman power. Across the vast range of cultures that have shared belief in this fabulous creature, dragons have existed perennially as antagonists of monstrous proportions against which heroic figures struggle, the rewards for victory being of great symbolic if not practical significance: in Near Eastern cosmogonic myths, the divine king preserves the created order against primordial chaos; in classical mythology, the heroic warrior defends his lineage or earns immortality; the knight of medieval romance claims treasure or wins a kingdom or a bride; for the astral hero of science fiction, extraterrestrial worlds are won or lost in combat with a new race of dragons whose domain is only as narrow as the confines of an expanding universe. Where there have been dragons, there have always been dragon-slayers, and the story of their struggle runs as a thread through the narratives of all cultures.

The title of a book written recently for children, *Everyone Knows What a Dragon Looks Like* (Williams, 1976), suggests something of the commonplace (if not the universal) status the monster now enjoys. If this is true, it is because a number of traditions have conspired to make it so; with few exceptions, modern dragon lore offers no major departures from the medieval dragon tradition from which it borrows its most salient features. Medieval dragon lore, in turn, combines elements of earlier dragon lore drawn from scriptural exegesis, natural history, classical mythology, and Roman legend. Where the modern dragon tradition departs from its medieval and classical precursors, it either does so consciously and ironically or else is tacitly dependent upon earlier traditions for its conceptual integrity. We find this to be true especially in children's literature, where not only are many dragons not slain, but they also lack the traditional monstrous ferocity that generally provokes the combat in the first place.

As one recent scholar has pointed out, the first problem to be confronted in the historical study of dragons is that of vocabulary (Kordecki 8): a number of different words have been used for the concept of "dragon," not only the word "dragon" and its cognates in the European languages. In Latin, for example, terms like *serpens, vīpera, anguis, coluber*, and others, which were used for serpents and snakes in general, were sometimes also used specifically in texts referring to dragons—Latin *draco*. In Greek, from which the word "dragon" ultimately comes, other terms such as *ophis, sauros*, and *hydros* occur. Famous among the Germanic languages are Old English *næddre* (adder) and *wyrm* (worm), to which Old Norse *ormr* and Middle High German *wurm* (as well as Latin *vermis*) are related etymologically. Examples could be multiplied. But this problem is compounded by the fact that "dragon" and its cognates have been used in reference to serpentine animals that are not dragons in the strict sense of the word. To these two difficulties must be added a third: dragon morphology itself, the "objective" criterion upon which we might base a strict definition, has never been completely exact. The physical features associated with the dragon concept have developed over a great deal of time from the generally amorphous monstrous enemies of divine or semi-divine figures in Near and Middle Eastern mythology to the creatures of modern fantasy, where shape, size, color, appendage articulation, and offensive attributes are highly specific and meaningfully delineated.

Dragons, we must remember, are imaginary creatures, and the possibility of free variation exists here more readily than in the representation of concepts found in the natural realm. This is probably why the dragon has been so widely circulated between and within such different cultures: it is an extremely adaptable concept, drawing upon the seemingly universal fear (and sometimes respect) for snakes and serpents as well as upon the special mythic needs of particular cultures in various geographical regions and periods in history. But this is also why distinctions must be made between serpent and dragon lore, which are related yet separate phenomena.

As a provisional solution to these problems, we may make a twofold decision to regard as dragons first those that bear the name (Greek *drákon*, Latin *draco*, Old English *draca*, Old Norse *dreki*, German *Drache*, Welsh *draig*, Old Irish *drauc*, and so on) and second those that—under any denomination—exhibit the general features of dragon morphology: serpentlike creatures of exceptional size, with wings, claws, and a tail, breathing fire and/or poison, guarding treasure, living in remote areas (whether on land, or in or near water), and acting as antagonists to divine, heroic, or chivalric warriors. This decision takes in quite a lot, but it also places in an ambiguous category several kinds of creatures that by looser criteria have been regarded as dragons: the chthonic monsters of Egyptian, Semitic, Mesopotamian, and Indian mythology; the oriental dragon, which is rarely antagonistic; and the small winged serpents of classical and medieval natural history, whose antagonism is generally that of an irritant rather than of antiheroic enmity.

The dragon concept, as already indicated, developed over a long period of time. As the history of this concept is unfolded in this entry, we will see the image of the dragon come into ever sharper focus, with the gradual addition of element upon element of the concept, taking something like final shape in the Middle Ages. A major controlling factor in this process is exercised by the etymology of "dragon," which was said earlier to be based ultimately upon Greek *drákon*. Almost everyone who writes about dragons pays respects to this etymology, which locates the origin of *drákon* in the Indo-European root *derk-*, which is associated with eyesight (Pokorny 1:213). The dragon apparently is named after its sharp-sightedness, or the supposition that its eyes glitter, probably because the snake, from which the concept borrows major features, has no eyelids. This is remarkable, because almost all words for snakes and serpents are based upon Indo-European roots that seem to be connotative of snakes' means of self-propulsion: bending, twisting, writhing, creeping, turning, or weaving back and forth (Buck 193–94). We may note in passing that *t-n-n*, the probable root of a Hebrew word for dragon, is connotative of a physical feature, its great length, as opposed to the more abstract notion of eyesight. And *l-v-h*, the root for leviathan, means "turn," "twist," or "wind" (Choate 25). The dragon is exceptional insofar as its Indo-European name denotes not a physical trait but a sensory function. This function seems early to have been extended to include not merely passive visual perception but active watching, enabling the dragon to serve as a monster whose primary activity is that of watchful guardian. Coupled with the generally hostile nature of the creature—again, drawn from the probably prior fear of snakes—the dragon lends itself very early to a rudimentary narrative pattern, repeated and elaborated all over the world: the dragon guards something valuable; someone tries to take it; the dragon resists, and a battle ensues; the dragon is slain; the victor acquires the object sought. This underlying narrative structure can be seen as a logical development of the one element of the dragon concept, memorialized in its etymology and preserved in its name, that sets it apart from its serpentine heritage. The dragon is a guardian.

Because dragon lore is most fully articulated in the story of the dragon-slayer, we will pay closest attention to developments of this story in classical myth, medieval epic and romance, and modern fantasy. Before doing that, however, we must briefly consider oriental dragons; along the way we will glance peripherally at features of dragon lore that are really ancillary to dragon-slaying. But it is dragon story that unifies manifestations of the creature throughout its long history, even though certain manifestations of dragons may exhibit only isolated elements of the larger narrative pattern. As this entry moves closer to modern times, we will focus more narrowly upon antecedents and developments of dragons in English literature; our method of organization will be primarily chronological.

The scholarly literature on dragons is immense. Among the most important works, Charles Gould's *Mythical Monsters* (1886) is the first serious attempt to treat fabulous creatures in a scientific manner, with a chapter on the history of the dragon and one each on the Chinese and Japanese developments of the creature. Grafton Elliot Smith's *The Evolution of the Dragon* (1919) and C. G. Child's "The Natural History of Dragons" (1921) approach the subject, respectively, through mythology and natural history; Walter Alison Phillips' *Encyclopaedia Britannica* article on the dragon (1926), as one would expect, summarizes the major elements of the dragon tradition through mythology, natural and cultural history, etymology, and folklore. Ernest Ingersoll's *Dragons and Dragon Lore* (1928) recapitulates and extends Smith's 1919 approach. The most recent contribution surveying conceptual sources for dragons is Paul Newman's *The Hill of the Dragon* (1980).

Specialized studies on dragons include, for the oriental world, L. Newton Hayes's *The Chinese Dragon* (1922) and Marinus Willem de Visser's *The Dragon in China and Japan* (1913). John Francis Campbell's *The Celtic Dragon Myth* is concerned mostly with Irish legendary matter, and has been reprinted recently for mass market (1911; 1981). Joseph Eddy Fontenrose's massive *Python: A Study of Delphic Myth and Its Origins* (1959) is concerned primarily with ancient Greek, and is fundamental in this area, but it also treats the transmission of this and related traditions in the Middle and Far East; it also has been reprinted recently in a paperbound version (1980).

Following the appearance of an illustrated book entitled *Gnomes* (Huygen, 1977), the year 1979 saw the publication of a spate of highly glossy and profusely illustrated books on the subject of dragons, including *The Flight of Dragons* (Dickinson), *The Book of the Dragon* (Allen), *Dragon's Path* (Ruppert), *Dragons* (Hogarth), and *The Dragon: Nature of Spirit, Spirit of Nature* (Huxley). The recent publication of a book entitled *Dragons* in a Time-Life book series (always a good measurement of a subject's current, popular appeal) should dispel any remaining question of the perennial interest in the dragon (Botting, 1984).

Almost every modern scholarly attempt to deal with the dragon makes some effort to determine the ultimate origin of the dragon concept. Three general trends in this direction may be observed: the etymological approach, which we have already to some extent adopted; the naturalistic approach, which looks for dragon origins in the animal kingdom or in fossil dinosaurs; and the mythological approach, which looks mainly to chthonic creatures of a generally serpentine description in early cosmogonies. The etymological approach is only a heuristic tool, applying the philological method to questions of development but not ultimate origin. But the latter two do purport to explain where the concept originated. The first of these is probably nearer to being correct, for it suggests that the primitive fear of snakes led to an imaginative exaggeration of snakelike features to produce the idea of dragons as exceptionally large snakes. Related to this is the idea that the prehistoric discovery of fossilized dinosaurs led to the hypothetical reconstructions of huge saurians, and stories and legends to go along with them were composed. This seems to lie in part behind the wave of popular interest in dragons in the late nineteenth century, when dinosaur bones were widely exhibited in Europe and England and provoked fanciful artistic and fictional renderings of the creatures in forms evocative of earlier dragon lore (Prickett 79–84).

General mythic consciousness seems to lie behind N. Douglas' connection of the dragon's eyes with glittering springs or streams and gold (563–65). For Douglas, the dragon is "the personification of the life within the earth . . . which, being unknown and uncontrollable, is *eo ipso* hostile to man" (564). Hostility to the gods is the principal feature found by comparative mythographers in the ancient Near Eastern pantheons, where the divine hero combats a monstrous creature to preserve the world from chaos. There are such creatures in Akkadian and Sumerian, Hittite, Babylonian, and Indian cosmogonic myths; they have been discussed by a number of scholars (Choate, Kordecki, Gilbert, and Fontenrose).

Grafton Elliot Smith believed that the dragon was invented ultimately by the Egyptians, combining elements of several figures in the early divine order, and that the concept traveled eastward to India, where the idea of the dragon as a divinity of the waters was strengthened to become the major feature of the creature's habitat and function. From there, it is surmised, there were contacts between the ancient Near Eastern cultures and the Orient (Gould 216–17n), with the result that oriental dragon lore regards the dragon primarily as the benevolent protector of people, dispenser of life-giving water, and herald of fertility and good fortune in general. The Western dragon concept, on the other hand, primarily through early Greek mythology, developed the dragon's negative connotations as enemy of the sun-god, thus forever establishing the fundamental distinction between the dragons of East and West. This is a reasonable explanation, although it depends upon Smith's bias in favor of Egyptian cosmology as the fountainhead of world mythology.

As attractive as this theory may be, it is probably best to avoid the temptation to search for the original dragon and to posit the idea, as some scholars recently have done, that in the history of the dragon, "each culture responded to some similar need in their mythology to produce a dragon-like creature" (Kordecki 187) and that the dragon has been invented again and again independently throughout the world (Bernard).

Regardless of where the concept originated, the Indian nagas seem to have been carried eastward during the early spread of the Buddhist religion to the Orient. The *Rig-Veda* contains the story of the battle between Indra, the sky-god, and Vritra, a demon whose crime involved the capture of rain-clouds and retention of the waters from the earth. Vritra is conceived as a dragonlike creature. In the nagas, however, we see the idea of a race of dragonlike beings, semi-divine snakes with human faces and serpents' tails who occupy Patala, the watery region under the earth (Dowson 213). One thousand in number, they reign in great splendor and guard treasures (Savill 43). They are divided into four classes: heavenly, divine, earthly, and hidden, depending upon their function in guarding the heavenly palace, giving rainfall, draining rivers, or guarding treasures (In-gersoll 45). In Burma, the nagas combine elements of the dragon, snake, and crocodile, and give rubies to those they favor; in addition, they guard and protect several royal persons in Burmese mythology (Savill 11, 115).

The Chinese dragon, *lung*, seems to be based in part upon the four classes of nagas, where by one account the four subclasses of lung (*t'ien lung, shen lung, ti' lung*, and *fu-ts'ang lung*) perform the same respective functions as those out-lined above for the nagas (Ingersoll 46). The imperial dragon has five claws, others only four (Gould 249).

By another account, the *Ch'ien Chu'eh Lei Shu* of Ch'en Jen Hsi (cited in Williams, 1974), there are nine types of dragon in ornamental representations: *p'u lao* (bells and gongs); *ch'iu-niu* (fiddles); *pi-hsi* (stone tablets); *pa-hsia* (stone monuments); *chao-feng* (eaves of temples); *chih-wen* (beams of bridges); *suan-ni* (throne of Budda); *yai-tzu* (sword hilts); and *pi-kan* (prison gates) (Savill 176). This imaginative taxonomy has little to do with the historical significance of the dragon, for the oriental dragon is most popularly associated with royal or imperial power; the Taoist conception of dragons as benevolent was modified by contact with the Indian nagas through Buddhist influence; a number of emperors during the Hsia dynasty (ca. 2205–1766 B.C.) were associated with the great lungs; Fu Hsi, China's first emperor, was said to have a dragon's tail; his successor Shen Nung (fl. 2737 B.C.) was supposed to have been fathered by a dragon; Ta Yu was seen in the form of a dragon, whose function was the "control of waters" (Savill 176). Earlier, Huang Ti (2704–2585 B.C.) was said to have ridden to heaven on the back of a dragon or in an ivory chariot drawn by six winged dragons (Savill 173; Hayes 11).

The *yu-lung*, the "fish-dragon," exhibits the metamorphosis of the river carp into a dragon. It is said that the yu-lung leapt the great waterfall on the Yang-tse River called "the Dragon Gate," and flew to heaven. Thus, the yu-lung is symbolic of great aspiration, and is taken as a symbol for some Chinese schools, where the relationship between passing difficult examinations and leaping the cataract is seen in a metaphorical sense (Allen 40).

The oriental dragon, however, had less influence on Western developments of the dragon than ancient Greek mythology, in which manifestations of the creature set the stage for developments of classical Roman and medieval Eu-ropean dragon lore from which modern conceptions of the dragon developed. The Greeks, who gave the West their philosophy, politics, law, science, and medicine, also gave it their best monster. Though there is some variation in the ancient writers' description of dragons, we see the dragon coming into far clearer focus by comparison with the generally amorphous chthonic creatures of ancient Near Eastern cosmology. (I have cited the Loeb Classical Library editions of most of the classical texts in this entry.)

The dragon was well known to the ancient Greeks in history, natural science, and mythology; though some seem only to be proto-dragons—huge creatures, serpentine, but otherwise nondescript—in even the earliest accounts, dragons show some of the classic features later associated with them. Among these are wings and fiery breath. In a treatise on the customs and geography of India, Megasthenes (fl. 300 B.C.) wrote of small winged serpents common in that land (Kordecki 115). Likewise, in his *History* (fifth century B.C.), Herodotus says that spice-bearing trees in Arabia "are guarded by small winged snakes of varied color, many round each tree" (3.107–9).

But the source of Western dragons seems to lie in mythology, not science or history, and we notice first of all that the dragons of Greek mythology are sometimes composites of several animals and sometimes are many-headed, but they often breathe fire. Both the *Iliad* and the *Odyssey* of Homer (ca. 850 B.C.) allude to dragons, one of which breathed fire. This is the chimera, a composite monster exhibiting body parts drawn from serpents, lions, goats, and human beings, breathing blazing fire (*Iliad*, 6.180–82). In the *Odyssey*, there is a shape-shifting creature, one of whose manifestations, at least temporarily, is that of a dragon (4.457 ff.).

Almost as old are Hesiod's early accounts in the *Theogony* (ca. 750–700 B.C.) of a number of serpentine monsters who are the offspring of primordial Chaos and thus parallel to the Near Eastern dragons alluded to earlier. These are Echidna, Chimera (mentioned above), and Typhoeus—that is, Typhon, antagonist of Zeus. Echidna is also a composite creature, part nymph and partly a huge snake with a speckled hide, who dwells in the "secret parts" of the earth and eats raw flesh (295–300). This creature seems quite similar to the Old Norse Níðhoggr, discussed later in this entry, for Echidna's lair is a cave in hollow rock far from human or divine habitation; there she "keeps guard in Arima beneath the earth," a figure who "dies not nor grows old all her days" (300–305). Through a sexual union with Typhoeus, she bears the Chimera, who is described in a slightly longer account than Homer's: she breathes fire, has three heads, and is a combination of snake, goat, and dragon (319–24). This monster is later slain by Pegasus and Bellerophon.

If the Chimera is three-headed, her father Typhoeus is a hundred-headed dragon, "with dark, flickering tongues." Fire flashed from his eyes and "burned from his heads as he glared" (821–28). In a battle that causes Earth and Hades to tremble, Zeus conquers this monster and lashes him, then hurls him down "a maimed wreck, so that the huge earth groaned" (855–68).

Finally, Hesiod describes an awful snake that guards the golden apples in secret places at the ends of the earth (333–35), and in the poem *The Shield of Heracles* the shield is decorated with the image of dragons (161).

The idea that dragons guard treasures, mentioned in Hesiod, seems to have been widespread among the Greeks, and is apparently the ultimate source for this very important feature of later dragon lore, especially in the medieval period. The most famous dragon stories in ancient Greek agree on this point. For example, the Homeric Hymn to Apollo appears to be the first work to mention the dragon slain by Apollo while the god is laying the foundations for the temple at Delphi (Fontenrose 13). Although the hymn does not specifically say that the dragon (*drakaina*, "she-dragon") guards the spring in which Apollo finds her, the hymn does call her "bloated," a "fierce monster wont to do great mischief to men upon earth" (300–4); other versions of the myth discussed by Fontenrose indicate that her function is that of guardian. Apollo slays the dragon with an arrow, and her death throes rival those of the best dragons in history, complete with "great gasps for breath," "writhing" and "rolling," and even "rotting away on the spot" (356–74). The dragon's decomposition is commemorated in the name of the place where it occurred, called Pytho, which means "rotting" in Greek; hence the name "python" for a huge snake.

Apollo seems to be transitional in several respects: he was traditionally associated with the sun by the Greeks, and in fact he seems to have been seen by them as parallel to the Egyptian god Horus, whose enemy was also a dragon (Fontenrose 90, 193). Apollo's victory over the dragon was later equated with that of Zeus over Typhoeus.

Other Greek dragon tales focus on Cadmus, Perseus, and Jason. Cadmus kills a dragon sacred to Mars, and Perseus vanquishes the monstrous serpent-headed Medusa. But the latter of these three is probably the most famous of all, since it relates the story of the golden fleece and its heroic retrieval by Jason and Medea.

We first learn of Jason's adventures with the dragon in the *Fourth Pythian Ode* of Pindar (sixth century B.C.), where the golden fleece is described as lying in a thicket in the jaws of a dragon whose bulk and length are "vaster than a ship of fifty oarsmen" (4.244–46). Jason slays the dragon, and Pindar adds, uniquely, that it has "glaring eyes" (4.249).

The most famous account of this adventure is in the *Argonautica* of Apollonius Rhodius. The prior history of the fleece is too complex to trace here in detail, but its significance for Jason lies in the fact that he must somehow retrieve it in order to claim his father's kingdom. It has been placed by Aeëtes in a sacred grove in the land of Colchis, under the guardianship of a dragon, who is described as having "keen sleepless eyes." Further details are added: it is a monster rolling and writhing with "countless coils of hard dry scales." Jason receives the aid of Medea, who invokes the aid of the god Sleep; the dragon, charmed, relaxes. Medea adds a mystical soporific drug to her song, and the dragon falls asleep; its jaws relax and its coils stretch out. Jason snatches the fleece, and the two make their way back to the Argo, Jason's ship (4.123 ff.).

Other writers tell the story, adding their own twists to it. In Euripides (*Medea* 480–82), Diodorus Siculus (4.48 ff.), and Apollodorus (1.9.23), the dragon's sleepless watchfulness is emphasized, along with its monstrous coils. In some versions, Medea is credited not only with charming the dragon but actually with slaying it (*Medea* 480–82).

Jason's contact with dragons is not confined to the one guarding the fleece. In the *Argonautica*, Apollonius also describes an adventure at Colchis in which Jason is given the teeth of a dragon that he must sow by taming the fire-breathing bulls of Ares. Dragons' teeth are mentioned later in medieval sources to dramatize the fact that they might eat their opponents; but in the Jason legend, dragons' teeth, planted in the ground, can sprout forth as armed warriors. Jason invokes the aid of Hecate, who surfaces from the underworld surrounded by dragons. Jason tames the bulls, yokes them to a plow, and sows the teeth, whereupon they spring from the ground as mighty warriors. Jason slays them immediately (*Argonautica* 3.1176–1407). This adventure is also told in Apollodorus at some length.

The teeth Jason sows are those of a dragon slain earlier by Cadmus, and are identified by Apollonius as the teeth of the Aonian dragon found by Cadmus in Thebes, the guardian of the spring of Ares (3.1176 ff.). Thus, Cadmus' dragon is connected in some way with that of Apollo. Once Cadmus' dragon is slain, its teeth are torn from the dragon's body by a goddess, who gives them as gifts— half to Aeëtes and half to Cadmus himself. Cadmus, too, sows the teeth, and again they spring up immediately in human form. In Apollodorus, a fuller account is given. Cadmus, wishing to sacrifice a cow to Athena, sends his company to draw water from the Spring of Ares. But a dragon, presumed to be the offspring of Ares, is found guarding the spring; it destroys those sent on the errand. Indignant, Cadmus kills the dragon; advised by Athena, he removes its teeth and later sows them. The men who sprout from them are called the "Sparti," meaning "the sown" (3.4.1). In recompense for the dragon's death, Cadmus must serve Ares in punishment for an "eternal year"; that is eight years to you and me, says Apollodorus. Cadmus's dragon-slaying is also alluded to in Euripides' *Phoenissae*, where Ares wishes to avenge the dragon's death, and Menoeceus, of the lineage of the Sparti, must sacrifice his life (931–35; 940–42).

Other dragon allusions in Apollodorus include a "chariot of winged dragons" made by Triptolemus (1.5.2) and a similar one "drawn by winged dragons" used by Medea to escape from Corinth to Thebes after the murder of her children (1.9.28). But by far the most important is the dragon of the Hesperides, elsewhere named Ladon (Hesiod, *Theog.* 333–35), who guards the golden apples presented to Zeus when he wedded Hera. According to Apollodorus, Ladon, offspring of Typhoeus and Echidna, is an "immortal dragon" with a hundred heads who speaks "with many and divers sorts of voices" (2.5.11). Heracles must slay Ladon in order to claim the apples, one of the tasks in his quest for immortality. Diodorus expresses some scepticism about both the golden apples and the dragon guarding them, speculating that the apples were really sheep with a golden-hued wool and that the "dragon" was really a shepherd/guardian named "Dracon." Nonetheless, he repeats the story that "Heracles slew the guardian of the apples and . . . duly brought them to Eurystheus" and received the gift of immortality promised by Apollo (4.26).

It has been remarked that the Romans had no myths, but only borrowed their mythology from the Greeks. This is not entirely true, but it is fair to say that what dragon lore they had was passed on to them primarily by the Greeks. In his *Description of Greece*, the Greek geographer Pausanias (A.D. 120–180) refers to the Theban spring guarded by the dragon as well as to the sown dragon's teeth (9.10.5; 9.10.1). One of the most interesting documents in the Roman interpretation of Greek mythology is found in the *Saturnalia* of Macrobius. Harking back to the identity of Apollo as sun-god and forward to the solar mythographers of the nineteenth century, Macrobius repeats Antipater's and Euripides' theories that the dragon-slayer myth derives from the sun's drying of water vapor, which sometimes resembles a coiling serpent, and that the sun itself is a serpent symbol, with equinoctial fluctuations equivalent to the serpent's slaying and death. He also mentions the cult of Aesculapius, the healing power of the caduceus deriving from its connection with Mercury, also felt to be a solar deity (1.19, 20).

But the principal writer on the connection of Greek and Roman mythology is Ovid (43 B.C.–A.D. 17). In the *Metamorphoses*, he preserves for the Romans many of the important stories that furnish the classical and medieval periods with knowledge of Greek dragon lore. In his collection of mythological stories, he gives versions of Heracles', Cadmus', and Jason's dragon-slayings.

In Ovid's version of the Jason story, the dragon is "distinguished by a crest, a three-forked tongue, and golden fangs" and again guards the tree on which the fleece is hung. Here, the tree itself is also golden. But Jason charms the dragon not with song but with the "Lethean juices of a certain herb," and recites a triple incantation. As a result, says Ovid, "eyes which had never known sleep before" close in slumber, and Jason steals the fleece (7.149–57).

Ovid's account of Heracles' famous eleventh labor (9.190) amounts to little more than a passing allusion, though the essential information of the dragon's "sleepless eyes" is retained; but the retelling of the Cadmus legend is highly dramatic. The habitat and appearance of the dragon are very specifically detailed: the creature has "a wondrous golden crest," three tongues, three rows of teeth, and rolling knots of scaly coils; its body is swollen with venom, and fire flashes from its eyes (3.28–44). Cadmus attacks first with a javelin and then with a spear thrust in its throat. Its death-throes are particularly hideous. Elsewhere, Ovid describes the huge dragon that Atlas places to guard the tree with golden fruit (4.637–48).

In the *Aeneid*, Virgil alludes to dragons guarding the golden apples of the Hesperides (4.484) and to a pair of dragons who rise up out of the sea and kill the priest Laocoön and his two sons (2.203–25). Although the latter seem to represent a throwback to earlier concepts of the dragon as a kind of sea-monster, the description of them evokes elements of dragons already mentioned here in Greek and Roman tradition: they possess "endless coils," "blood-red crests," and "blazing eyes suffused with blood-red fire."

In his *Fabulae*, Hyginus—a Latin writer about whom nothing much is known—attempted to rewrite Greek myths apparently for use as a school text sometime in the second century A.D. The compilation is apparently full of absurdities, probably because the writer knew little Greek (Cary 443), but fable 178 does repeat the common motif of dragons' teeth being sown.

Fables of dragons appear also in Aelian's *De natura animalium* and in the fables of Phaedrus. The former, written in Attic Greek by a Roman rhetorician, includes the unusual story of a powerful but benevolent dragon who rescues a young man from brigands and kills his attackers (6.63). Similarly, in another story, the Emathian prince Pindus, who is befriended by a dragon in the wilderness, is jealously attacked by his brothers. Because the dragon can see and hear better than any other creature, says Aelian, it perceives this treachery and comes to his aid, surrounding the brothers and killing them with its coils. Pindus dies, but the dragon remains to guard the body until his people come to give him proper burial (10.48).

In the benevolent dragons of the two previous stories, we see a peculiar departure from the normal Western tradition of maleficent dragons. However, this anomaly may be explained by Aelian's overall purpose in the *De natura*: to support the idea of universal reason by finding examples of rational behavior in the animal kingdom. We should also note the unusual usage of the dragon's guarding function here in the positive sense of protection—a usage later connoted in the Vikings' decoration of their ships with dragons on the prow and, in Roman and Celtic armament, on shields and banners.

In the fables of Phaedrus, the story is told of a fox digging its hole. It penetrates the underground lair of a dragon guarding its treasure. The fox asks what benefit it gains from its vigilance in the subterranean shadows, whereupon the dragon answers that this is its fate, assigned by Jupiter. Phaedrus concludes by criticizing misers, who get no enjoyment from their wealth (4.21). This moralistic approach to the dragon's hoard-guarding function is used as well in Martial's *Epigrams*, where a wealthy citizen is criticized for brooding over his treasure "like the great dragon that poets sing of as guardian over the Scythian grove" (12.53.4), and in Cicero's *Philippics*, in which one of Marc Antony's party is likened to a dragon in embracing his estates without surrendering them to the government (13.12).

Other Roman allusions to dragons include Lucan's statement that dragons beset Cato on his voyage to Libya (*Pharsalia*; see Kordecki 52) and Propertius' claim that "Lanuvium of old is protected by an aged dragon" down in a cave, requiring a yearly food sacrifice. The poet's interest in purity of love is probably behind the additional detail that the dragon will accept the offering from only a chaste maiden; otherwise, it kills the maiden and remains unappeased. A girl who does not return from her descent into the cave thus publicizes irrevocably her bad reputation (*Elegy* 4.8; Gould 165).

Greek mythology, rendered by Roman mythographers and fabulists, attests to the great interest the dragon held during the classical period as a creature of narratives. This interest in dragon stories in turn was transmitted to the Middle Ages as part of the legacy of its classical heritage. But another body of classical learning contributed to the medieval interest in dragons; this tradition draws upon at least three fairly distinct literary genres in classical writing: encyclopedias, travel literature, and bestiaries (Kordecki 46). It is unclear just how important this body of writing was for the codification of dragon lore; but brief mention should be made of them. We have already observed the winged serpents in Herodotus and Megasthenes, whose early travel literature (with that of Ctesias; see Kordecki 46 ff.) contributed one leg of the tripod later developed in the medieval bestiaries. But the encyclopedists Pliny, Solinus, and Aelian comprise the Latin tradition that inspired Isidore of Seville, whose *Etymologiae* was "one of the most important reference books of the Middle Ages" (Harrington 75).

In sections devoted to medical cures, Pliny distinguishes between asps, basilisks, vipers, snakes, salamanders, and dragons (*Natural History* 29.18–23), giving the particular dangers associated with each one as well as any pharmaceutical properties of their various parts, if any. The dragon, he says, "has no venom," and its bodily parts, in various concoctions, are effective charms and remedies: its head buried under a threshold brings good luck to a home; an ointment made of its eyes wards off nocturnal phantasms; its teeth and vertebrae help make potentates gracious to suppliants; and so on. Elsewhere in the work, he retells the story of the Arcadian youth's rescue by his pet dragon (8.11), but Pliny's dragon is clearly not the great monster of mythology and legend, not least because of its apparently small size. Pliny here seems to think of *draco* merely as a species of serpent.

Elsewhere, Pliny alludes to Megasthenes' account of exceptionally large snakes in India, and refers to the "well-known case" of a 120-foot-long dragon killed by Regulus during the Punic wars, whose skin and jaws were exhibited in Rome for years afterward (8.14). In the text, these are called *serpentes*. But equally large are the *dracones* that "easily encircle the elephants in their coils and fetter them with a twisted knot" (8.11). Both combatants, says Pliny, fall down together and die, the elephant strangled and the dragon crushed. Whether this contest occurs on land or in water (8.11; 8.12), Pliny speculates on the cause of such a duel, and concludes that nature arranges it "to provide herself with a show" (8.12.34).

Pliny's description of the dragon/elephant battle was repeated many times, by Lucan (*Pharsalia* 9.726–32), Aelian (6.21 ff.), Philostratus (*Images* 2.17) and Solinus in the *Collectanea rerum memorabilium* (trans. Mary Ann Sullivan, 1969), which borrows wholesale from Pliny, as does Isidore's *Etymologiae* (12.4, "*De serpentibus*"). In Pliny, the eagle is also brought down by a similar ploy of dragons (10.5).

The nonnarrative texts presenting the dragon as a natural, if sometimes exotic, creature were combined with the exegetical tradition in the *Physiologus*, the most influential book in the Middle Ages other than the Bible (Courthope 2:198, cited in South 9), to produce the medieval bestiaries. *Physiologus* is "a compilation of pseudo-science in which the fantastic descriptions of real and imaginary animals, birds, and even stones were used to illustrate points of Christian dogma and morals" (McCulloch 15). The list of chapters—that is, of animals, plants, and the like—was by no means fixed, and the earliest texts of *Physiologus* do not include separate chapters on dragons (though sometimes they are mentioned in connection with the elephant and the panther). With the addition of material drawn from the encyclopedic tradition epitomized in Isidore, *Physiologus* begins to be transformed into the classic bestiary, with a chapter on the dragon in book 2 of *De bestiis et aliis rebus*, attributed (wrongly) to Hugh of St. Victor (McCulloch 30–31).

Versions in which *draco* or its grammatical equivalents are found in chapter titles include Pseudo-Hugh of St. Victor, *De bestiis* (2.24; 3.83); *Dicta Chrysostomi* (Hofer Bestiary 30); Philippe de Thaün, *Bestiaire* (3); and Guillaume le Clerc, *Bestiaire* (24). Typical of these is the chapter in a twelfth-century Latin bestiary edited by M. R. James in 1928 and translated by T. H. White (1954), where

DRACO the Dragon is the biggest of all serpents, in fact of all things on earth. The Greeks call it "draconta" and hence it has been turned into Latin under the name "draco."

When this dragon has come out of its cave, it is often carried into the sky, and the air near it becomes ardent. It has a crest, a small mouth and a narrow gullet through which it draws breath or puts out its tongue. (White 165–66)

The mystical significance of the dragon, the text goes on to say, is found in the Devil, who "translates himself into an angel of light and misleads the foolish with false hopes of glory and worldly bliss" (White 167). The dragon's crest, a regular feature of dragon physiognomy derived from ancient Greek dragon lore, is explained by the idea that the Devil is the king of pride; anyone ensnared by "the tools of crime" dies, and "no doubt goes to Hell," the chapter concludes grimly.

The dragon in Christianity represents spiritual evil, incarnate in the figure of Satan. Actually, the symbolic system into which the dragon fits is much more complicated than that, as Lesley Kordecki has recently shown (1980): the dragon in scriptural exegesis has at least ten identifiable symbolic values as Kordecki calculates them, many of which involve either the means or the results of satanic seduction: heresy, pride, wickedness, corruption, and so on (Kordecki 170). Among these is the dragon of Psalm 91, which Hugh of St. Victor describes as a beast "with fiery breath" that "kills whatever it touches; . . . this is *luxuria*, which greatly rules the unproductive" and lazy. The dragon in Psalm 148:7 is interpreted by Augustine as an encouragement to praise a God who is so great as to be the creator of even so monstrous a creature as the dragon (Kordecki 161).

But the foregoing are mere commentaries upon the one text that, probably more than any other, insured that the dragon would have a place in the medieval world: the Bible. If the Eastern dragon owes much of its development to the transmission of the Hindu mythology through Buddhist evangelism, then in the West it has been the Christian church and its central documents that have performed the parallel function of providing the resources as well as the belief-system necessary for interpreting dragon lore in its spiritual dimension.

The Bible may be said to begin and end with the dragon, for in the next to last chapters of the Apocalypse we read that St. John saw an angel coming down from heaven, holding in his hand the key of the bottomless pit and a great chain. And he seized the dragon, that ancient serpent, who is the Devil and Satan, and bound him for a thousand years, and threw him into the pit, and shut it and sealed it over him, that he should deceive the nations no more. (20:1–3)

This dragon is a *draco*, whose designation as such owes a debt to the decision of the translators of the Septuagint (third century B.C.) to render Hebrew *tanniym*, in the Old Testament, as δράκων (Kordecki 169), thus making a connection between ancient Semitic demon and dragon lore and classical Greek mythology. This is the same dragon, the same Satan, who, eight chapters earlier, is introduced as "a great red dragon, with seven heads and ten horns, and seven diadems upon his heads" (12:3), whose tail cast one-third of the stars from heaven and who waits to devour a child soon to be born of "a woman clothed with the sun, with the moon under her feet." In a passage that seems to suggest the original fall from grace of Satan and his angels, the text goes on to describe the battle between the Archangel Michael and the dragon, which ends when "the great dragon was thrown down; that ancient serpent who is called the Devil and Satan, the deceiver of the whole world—he was thrown down to the earth" (12:7–9). Cast down to earth at the beginning of sacred history and cast down into the abyss at the end of time, Satan assumes serpent form in Genesis 3, appears in the Garden of Eden, and tempts the woman to disobedience.

But there are a number of dragons besides those in Genesis and the Apocalypse just mentioned. The dragon of the Apocalypse undoubtedly owes something of its description to Greek legend, but the Old Testament dragons are clearly part of a Near Eastern tradition of cosmogonic myths and associated at some level with folklore of "a high god's slaying of the primordial dragon in his effort to bring order and life into being" (Choate 7). This motif, found in Egyptian, Babylonian, and Hittite texts, some of which we have already mentioned, lies behind certain words used for dragons in Hebrew and other Semitic languages, connecting Old Testament dragons with Tiamat, Apophis, and Illuyankas, and with dragons of Jewish folklore (Choate 10–18, 19 ff.).

The linguistic problem regarding the biblical dragons is treated by N. K. Kiessling (1948), who shows that the original Hebrew text contains three words for various kinds of sea- or land-monsters, all of them hostile to God or the people of God: *tanniyn, rachab*, and *leviyathan*. Of the passages using these terms, probably the best example is Job 40 and 41, where the monster is said to have impenetrable hide, gleaming eyes, fiery breath, and smoking nostrils. But these three terms were translated variously into Greek by the writers of the Septuagint, and later into Latin by St. Jerome, and while in many cases the original sense of dragon—an evil monstrous creature living either on land or in the sea, antagonist of God and Israel—was preserved, the misunderstanding of *rachab* and the mistranslation of a fourth term (*tan*, "jackal") extended the original Hebrew dragon concept in two new directions. First, the LXX writers translated *rachab* differently six out of seven times, in three instances rendering it in Greek words meaning pride, vanity, or idleness. Without a doubt, this is the origin of the long tradition, culminating in the medieval bestiaries, in which the dragon is an allegorical symbol for the sin of pride, personified capitally in Satan.

Tan, which scholars now recognize means "jackal," was confused with *tan-niyn*, especially when declined with the masculine plural ending *-im*; since *tan* was often used by the prophets in association with the desolation that results when a people strays from God (Kiessling 173), the LXX rendering of this word as *drákon* and St. Jerome's translation of it as *draco* meant that the dragons in the Old Testament took on yet another meaning: desolation, wilderness, and wasteland. Kiessling thinks that this error lies behind the repeated designation of the "desert wastelands of foreign enemies" as the habitation of dragons in medieval literature.

It is indeed the wastelands of the world from which dragons come to oppress the characters of history and legend in Anglo-Saxon culture. Dragons are found widely in Old English literature. The Vespasian Psalter translates the Vulgate *draco* in Psalms 73, 90, 103, and 148 in variants of Old English *draca* (Sweet 291, 320, 336, 399), and the Vespasian Hymn 7 (Sweet 412) speaks of the *hatheortnis draecena* (dragons' wrath). In the poem *Be Domes Dæge* (Of the Day of Judgement), the pains of Hell are described as bales of flame and gnawing *wyrmas* (worms, that is, dragons; Lumby 164 ff., 170 ff.), an image drawn no doubt from Mark 9:43–48 and used repeatedly in Old English homiletic tradition (see, for example, Morris 47 ff., 251 ff.) and saints' lives (for example, St. Margaret: Cockayne 39–49). Dragons are found inscribed on shields and amulets from the Anglo-Saxon period (Meaney 170). Though the *Liber monstrorum* contains a long section on serpentlike monsters, it nowhere uses the term *draco* or describes creatures that seem much like dragons either in form or function. Yet other monster literature from the period—the apocryphal *Letter of Alexander to Aristotle* and the *Wonders of the East* (Cockayne 1–38)—contains references to dragons in exotic geographical locations.

In addition, the dragon appears in Anglo-Saxon culture as a portent of calamity and, aphoristically, as a symbol of human greed. The Anglo-Saxon Chronicle says that in A.D. 793 "terrible portents appeared. . . . These were exceptional flashes of lightning, and fiery dragons were seen flying in the air, and soon followed a great famine" (Garmonsway 54, 56). The Old English maxim *draca sceal on hlæwe / frod frætwum wlanc* (the dragon shall [be] on the barrow, proud, arrogant in treasures) (Dobbie 56) bespeaks the association of dragons with wealth in a condemnation of hoarding similar to the Roman legends seen earlier.

But the epitome of Old English dragon lore is to be found in *Beowulf*, where the most elaborate dragon-slaying episode in all of medieval literature is narrated. Consisting of some 800 lines of the poem, the episode and its aftermath are told in glorious detail, from the first appearance of the dragon in line 2210 to its burial at sea fifty lines from the poem's end. In the 900 lines that intervene, the dragon's rampages are described in the most colorful terms, and from there we learn a number of things about dragon lore in Anglo-Saxon England. Among these is the fact that the *Beowulf* dragon is preeminently a guardian of treasure. This is the effective cause of the great dragon-slaying episode, for it is not until a thief breaks into the dragon's hoard that the monster begins to wreak destruction across the land, drawing Beowulf to challenge and eventually slay the marauder. The dragon is described in great detail. It is of a "hideous" color, otherwise unspecified (3041); is fifty feet long (3043); flies (3043–44) but also slithers (for example, 2287–88; 2293–94); has reptilian physiognomy (2561) but smooth skin (2273); is poisonous (2523) but also breathes fire (2270–74 et passim); and is sentient (2220, 2298, 2305). Its den is a stone barrow, its entrance a stone arch beneath a cliff near the sea (2543), where in earlier times a cursed treasure was buried (2230 ff.). The dragon is very old, for it has guarded the treasure for 300 years since its discovery of the empty barrow (2279).

The structure of Beowulf's battle with the dragon is complex, with numerous attacks and counterattacks on both sides. The dragon is nearly indestructible: Beowulf's sword fails to penetrate the dragon's hide (2577) and later it shatters against its head (2680). When he does slay the dragon, it is with the help of his loyal retainer Wiglaf, who delivers the decisive blow "a little lower" than the head, using the tradition that dragons, while generally impervious to weaponry, have a soft spot below the belly, under the wing, or elsewhere. The dragon dies, and the hero survives only long enough to examine the hoard his victory has won. Afterwards, Wiglaf and the other warriors look at the monster "Stretched out lifeless upon the sand" (3039), scorched in its own dying flames. In a digression on the Old Norse hero Sigemund, another dragon also guards a hoard in a barrow of "ancient rock" (874), and after its death, melts away—again, presumably from its own heat.

The allusion to Sigemund brings us to the vast wilderness of dragons found in Old Norse literature. There are at least three dozen dragons in Old Norse (see Evans, 1984), but the most important one of these is Fáfnir, the dragon alluded to above (though in *Beowulf* the episode is attributed to Sigemund, the father of Siegfried, to whom the main body of Norse tradition assigns the battle and victory). The earliest form of this legend is found in the *Poetic Edda*, a collection of very old mythic materials preserved in an early thirteenth-century manuscript, and it is retold in Snorri Sturluson's *Prose Edda*, among other sources. There, Fáfnir is a dragon who has become monstrous in form as a result of his greedy ownership of cursed treasure. This is an important element, rarely found elsewhere in the world's dragon lore, but frequently attested in Germanic legend: some dragons begin life as men but are later transformed into dragons as the outworking of greed. Sigurd slays him to gain the gold; before he dies, Fáfnir engages Sigurd in a long discussion consisting of riddles, mythological lore, and prophecies of Sigurd's own death resulting from the treasure's curse. By contrast, the Old Norse dragon's nature as a guardian is turned to positive value in the Viking ship-building tradition, where carved dragons' heads were frequently mounted on the prow of their ships, presumably invoking protection.

Most critics of the *Beowulf* episode allude to some of the more interesting Old Norse analogues, parallels, or sources of the episode, but few take the trouble to do a comprehensive search; one recent attempt to do this (Evans, 1984) is hampered by the fact that its motif source is incomplete. There is not space to go further into this interesting tradition, except to mention the dragon Níðhoggr, which, according to the conception of the early mythology in the *Poetic Edda*, lies at the bottom of the world-tree Yggdrasil gnawing its roots. It also is depicted as surrounding the earth—evoking the boundary function in holding back the outer chaos and protecting the world of men. This dragon is slain by Thor, son of Odin, though the god dies in the struggle.

Turning now to the medieval period, we may recognize in three genres the main lines of development in which the classical, exegetical, and biblical traditions coalesced to present a remarkably unified body of dragon lore: saints' lives, bestiaries, and chivalric romances. Of course these genres had a great influence upon one another, sometimes to a remarkable degree; yet the thematic concerns of each indicate separate trajectories for the dragon tradition. We have already looked at the bestiaries and their origins in the classical natural histories and *Physiologus*, and turn now to saints' lives and medieval romance.

The most popular dragon-slayer narratives in the Middle Ages are those of the St. George legend. The origins of the dragon episode in this legend are obscure, but the particulars of it are not. As Northrop Frye has summarized the pattern, which he regards as "the central form of quest-romance,"

a land ruled by a helpless old king is laid waste by a sea-monster, to whom one young person after another is offered to be devoured, until the lot falls on the king's daughter: at that point the hero arrives, kills the dragon, marries the daughter, and succeeds to the kingdom. (Frye 189)

However, there are many versions of the St. George legend, owing partly to a period when elements of St. George's story were fused with those of the legend of Sir Beves of Hamtoun (Gilbert 41), and later versions include a verse life of St. George by Alexander Barclay, Johannes Mirk's *Festival*, and the Scottish *Legends of the Saints*. Serious work on the development of the legend of St. George must take into account the scholarship of Bernard Myers (1933) and J. E. Matzke (1902; 1903; 1904). George was an extremely popular saint during the Middle Ages; his appeal may be seen in a number of ecclesiastical buildings dedicated to him, from the fifth century onward (Matzke, 1903: 147–49).

The earliest Greek and Latin lives of the saint say nothing about the dragon, but focus instead upon the agonizing martyrdom of St. George; not until the late twelfth or early thirteenth centuries did a dragon find its way into the story, in an episode in a French metrical *vita* by Simund de Freine, in which, late in the narrative, George is thrown into a den filled with wild beasts including dragons (Matzke, 1903: 123). But very little is made of the event. A century later, another French metrical version now kept in a library in Cheltenham included an illuminated frontispiece depicting the saint slaying a dragon. No dragon is found in the text itself, but the illumination undoubtedly attests to the influence of the *Legenda aurea*, already nearly 200 years old at that time (Matzke, 1903: 115).

The earliest full-scale version of the dragon episode as an integral element of the story occurs in a twelfth-century manuscript, and it is essentially the same story as that found in the *Legenda aurea* (Matzke, 1904: 452). The main events of this version of the story are as follows: George finds a maiden by a lakeside who tells him of a dragon that has devoured cattle and children as sacrificial tribute. Now it is the maiden's turn to share this fate. St. George at once "overcomes the dragon, binds him with the maiden's girdle and leads him captive to the city. There is much joy, and all the inhabitants accept the Christian faith" (Matzke, 1903: 452). George then goes on to another heathen city, where the traditional tortures leading to his martyrdom begin.

The *Legenda aurea* of Jacob Voragine offers several versions of the dragon's demise: first, even as St. George and the king's daughter are conversing, the dragon rises up out of the lake. George draws his sword and delivers it "a hurt that threw him to the ground." The saint does not slay the beast, but tells the maiden to throw her girdle round its neck, whereupon the dragon "followed her like a little dog on a leash" (Ryan 234). Only after 20,000 men and "a multitude of women and children" believe in Christ and are baptized" does St. George say he will slay the dragon. This done, he draws his sword and kills it; its body is carried out of the city "upon a car drawn by four yoke of oxen" (Ryan 234). "Other authors, however," the text says, "tell this story in a different way. They say at the very moment when the dragon drew nigh to devour the maiden, Saint George, making the sign of the cross, set upon him and slew him with one blow" (Ryan 235).

From this short scene, a great dragon episode grew primarily by fusion with that of *Sir Beves of Hamtoun*. We will look at the *Sir Beves* dragon later, and here will say only that as a result of this fusion, which "was accomplished during the XIII or XIV centuries" (Matzke, 1904: 473), the dragon became firmly established as the most memorable feature of the legend.

The version of the story in *The Seven Champions of Christendom*, printed in 1680, is extremely detailed and dramatic, second only to the adaptation found at the end of the first book of Edmund Spenser's *Faerie Queene*. The dragon is described here as being fifty feet from shoulder to tail, with scales "bright as Silver, but far more hard than Brass," and a belly the color of gold (3.2).

Issuing from its den, the dragon attacks the saint fiercely, nearly felling St. George on the first attack. St. George recovers himself and drives in with his spear, which "shivered in a thousand pieces." At this moment, the dragon lashes out with its poisonous tail and the saint takes refuge under an orange tree, miraculously virtuous against venomous worms.

Recovering thereby, St. George strikes the dragon in the belly with his sword Ascalon. A stream of venom springs from the wound, shattering the knight's armor and rendering him half-unconscious. Remembering the orange tree,

George seeks refuge under it; after a moment's supplication heavenward, he resumes the battle. The dragon's death scene is quite dramatic: St. George strikes the dragon under the wing, "where it was tender without scale," whereupon Ascalon, his sword, goes in up to the hilt and "through both the Dragon's Heart, Liver, Bone and Blood, where out issued such abundance of purple gore" that the grass is thoroughly soaked. The dragon loses so much blood that finally he "yielded his vital Spirits to the force of the conquering Champion." St. George beheads the dragon after first "yielding due honour to Almyghty God for the Victory" (3.2).

Of a different order is the great dragon fight between the Redcrosse Knight and "his foe, a Dragon horrible and stearne," announced as the goal of the prospective saint's quest in the opening lines of book 1 of *The Faerie Queene* (1.1.3), which falls between the *Legenda aurea* version and that of the *Seven Champions* quoted above. It has been noted that Spenser's great episode is based primarily upon the iconographic rather than the narrative tradition (Kellogg 11; Williams, 1948).

St. George is by no means the only medieval figure who slays a dragon. A large number of dragon-slayers populate the pages of medieval literature and legend. Among the Christian saints whose careers boast dragon fights may be listed Philip, Matthew, Silvester, and Martha (Gilbert 33–40). Others include Saints Flovent, Cado, Maudet, Paul, Keyne, Michael, Samson, Clement, and Romain (Gould 198–99), as well as Saints Leonard, Carantoc of Somerset, and Petroc of Cornwall in British hagiography (Simpson, 1980: 48–49). A number of Celtic saints are mentioned in Campbell (1911); most dragons who threaten the saints present a ferocious appearance, but are easily defeated in an apparent allegory of the Christian's defeat of sin through grace. Thus, for example, St. Donatus slays his dragon by spitting in its mouth (Gilbert 37), and the Old Norse saint Guthmund defeats a dragon with a prayer and a sprinkling of holy water (Evans, 1984: 307–8).

Dragon-slaying knights in chivalric romances also abound. Among the most prominent is Sir Beves, whose dragon-slayings contributed to the details and format of those in the early St. George legends, as we have noted. Others in Middle English include the knights Sir Torrent, Degaré, Lancelot, Eglamour, and the Knight of Curtesy. The adventures of these heroes differ in many particulars, but they fit a common narrative pattern, that of the quest romance, of which the "central form," according to Frye, "is the dragon-slaying theme" (Frye 189).

The events in the dragon-slaying scene in *Sir Beves of Hamtoun*, as indicated earlier, run much the same as those in the St. George episode. In one version, the dragon is described quite simply: "His skales bryhter were than glasse / And muche harder than any brasse / Bytwene his shulders and his tayle / Was XL fote, withouten fayle." But in another version, the dragon has long ears, eight tusks (the smallest seventeen inches around), a beard, and a mane; it is twenty-four feet from its shoulders to its tail, which is sixteen feet long; its body is bright as the sun and its wings like glass, its sides as "hard ase eni bras" (2661–78). The dragon lives in a cliff about a mile from the sea; significantly, one version indicates that the dragon was originally a man—one of two fierce kings who, dying in sin, became "dragouns vile" (Kölbing 123). Beves is wounded and poisoned and twice falls into a well once bathed in by a virgin, and so by its virtue he recovers. Though his lance is shattered—as is St. George's—Beves draws a sword, hits the dragon in a traditional soft spot "vnder the wynge, / . . . / There was he tender wythout skale," with his good sword named Morglay. It goes in to the hilt, penetrating "Thoroughe hert, lyuer, bone and blode," and the dragon falls dead. As in the St. George legend, the hero strikes off the dragon's head and mounts it on the hilt of his shattered lance. Beves enters the town of Coleyne to the sound of joyous pealing bells.

The dragon slain by Degaré is described as a "dragon grim" full of venom and filth, with large teeth and a wide throat, wings, a long tail, and feet like a dragon; smoke comes out of its nose "ase fer out of a chimenai" (345–52). After a series of attacks and counterattacks, Degaré batters the dragon with his cudgel. In its death throes, the dragon's tail strikes Degaré, knocking him upside down. But the knight rights himself and breaks all the dragon's bones, so that it "lai ded, stille as a ston" (382).

Guy of Warwick kills two dragons—one in order to rescue a lion harried by a dragon, the other to rid a foreign country of a national menace. The descriptions of the dragons are dramatic; they are full of fire, with blazing eyes, huge bodies, and grinning jaws; one is said to be sixty feet long; slaying them is no easy task. Guy's sword breaks, he is unhorsed, his sword glances off the dragon's hard skin; the monster rends his hauberk, strikes him with its tail, and breaks two of his ribs before Guy discovers that, unlike the rest of its body, the dragon's tail is not impervious to steel. He cuts if off. Guy locates another traditional vulnerable spot—behind the wings—and the dragon falls down and dies amid cries and groans. Guy decapitates it and the head is carried to the king at York and hung up as a trophy (6959–66).

Dragons are slain in various versions of Arthurian knights' adventures, including those by Sir Tristrem, Sir Lancelot, Yvain, and Gawain. For Gawain and Lancelot, the episode is of minor importance. Lancelot's adventure occurs in book 11 of Malory's *Morte Darthur*, where the knight is asked by townspeople under Pelles, king of the Foreign Country, to deliver them from a dragon who inhabits a tomb. Lancelot lifts the lid of the tomb, and "there came oute an orryble and fyendely dragon spyttynge wylde fyre oute of hys mowthe" (Vinaver 3:793). Though the ensuing fight is called "longe," the narration expends only one sentence: "Than Sir Launcelotte drew his swerde and faught wyth that dragon longe, and at the laste wyth grete payne Sir Launcelot slew that dragon."

In *Sir Gawain and the Green Knight*, Sir Gawain's adventure with dragons consumes even less story-telling than this. On his journey through Wales, the knight passes through a wilderness, where he must fight a number of foes: "Sum whyle wyth wormes he werres, and with wolues als,'' the poem says (line 720), going on to list the other monstrous impediments to speedy passage.

Yvain, the title character of a French romance by Chrétien de Troyes, slays a dragon in a scene that is "structurally the central episode" in the story (Comfort 371). This is the scene in which Yvain earns his epithet "the knight of the lion," for here he discovers a dragon holding a lion by the tail and "burning its hind-quarters with flames of fire" (Comfort 223). Yvain, urged by pity for the captive lion, cleaves the dragon in two and cuts it to bits. The lion follows him ever afterward as a loyal companion. The source of this story is the Welsh romance *Owein*, where the same events occur in slightly shorter form; an Old Icelandic translation of the story (*Ívens saga*) is very close to the French original.

For Sir Tristrem as for Yvain, the dragon-slaying is fundamental to the plot of the story in which he appears. The dragon-slaying is in all the major versions of the story except Malory's, and the encounter with the dragon (and its consequences) enables Tristrem to woo Isolt on behalf of the Cornish King Mark. After having slain the dragon, Tristrem cuts out the monster's tongue and keeps it as a trophy. This has been connected with a folktale pattern of which one scholar has collected 109 examples, 76 of which include the motif of the removal of the tongue (see Eisner 125 ff., 134).

In the Lancelot episode described earlier, the dragon issues from a tomb, whose cover is inscribed with a message predicting both the dragon-slaying and the slayer's fathering of a great hero—Sir Galahad. Here, just as in the Anglo-Saxon Chronicle, the dragon is taken as a portent; this same function is found several places in the Arthurian canon with reference to the coming of King Arthur, where the discovery of fighting dragons beneath the castle of Vortigern prompts Merlin to utter oracular statements. This is found in Wace (Mason 18–19), Geoffrey of Monmouth (7.3), and Layamon (lines 231 ff.; Brock 8 ff.). Elsewhere in Geoffrey, a celestial dragon portends Uther's rise to kingship. Uther has two dragons made of gold, earning him the epithet "Pendragon," Welsh for "dragon-head," since Merlin had prophesied that he should be king by means of the dragon (Geoffrey 8.17; Evans, 1958: 171–72). Also, in many versions of Arthurian material, Arthur himself has dreams of dragons fighting each other, interpreted similarly as prophetic portents (Geoffrey 10.2; Brock 760–830).

Early printed romances in which dragons appear include those concerning Tom a Lincoln and Chinon of England. But during the Renaissance, the most important vehicle of dragon lore was the popular St. George legend, described earlier in this entry. There are allusions to dragons in Shakespeare and in Ben Jonson's *The Alchemist* (2.1.26–28), where the character Face, who tends the alchemist's fire, is described as a dragon who "watches over the place from which the treasure will come" (South 147)—indicating that the monster's most interesting function has not yet been forgotten. The natural histories have not forgotten the dragon either, nor have the encyclopedias: writers such as Alexander

Neckham, Ulisse Aldrovandus, and Edward Topsell all pay attention to dragons (for an account, see Gould 201–10). But the most dramatically impressive Renaissance dragon is without doubt the one slain by the Redcrosse Knight in *The Faerie Queene*. The battle scene is anticipated within the first 30 lines of the first book, where the Gentle Knight, "pricking on the plaine," yearns in his heart "to prove his puissance in battell brave" against "his foe, a Dragon horrible and stearne" (1.1.3); the scene itself, which takes up all but 35 of canto 11's 495 lines, is divided into three days of combat. The dragon, which the Redcrosse Knight and his lady Una hear before they see, is described as massive: it lies stretched on the side of "a great hill, himself like a great hill" (33); elsewhere, airborne, its shadow is wide as that of a "mountaine" (68); when dead, it lies "like an heaped mountaine" (486). So huge is it, in fact, that in its ascent aloft, it draws near to the knight "halfe flying, and halfe footing in his hast" (65), running along the ground in an image that cannot help but call to the modern mind the image of a large cargo-carrying aircraft. But the Spenserian image is that of an airborne sea-vessel with large sails. This dragon's flight is lumbering and ponderous, and the air is barely able to keep it aloft (154–61). The battle is long and complicated, filled with flames and sparks, with the traditional failure of the first weapon-blows, the penetration of a spear under the wing; the dragon counterattacks with wings and the stings in its tail. Redcrosse retaliates by cutting off first its tail, then one of its claws, and the dragon, enraged, exhales such heat that the warrior falls backward under an apple tree (not orange, as in the St. George legends), from which flows a stream of healing balm which—together with Una's prayers—enables the knight to recover in time for the third day's fighting. He rises, arms, and drives his weapon into the gaping jaws of the dragon; the blade's withdrawal is followed by a gush of dragon's blood. The dragon's downfall is so precipitous as to evoke from the poet the fourfold repetition of the phrase "so downe he fell"; he collapses like a rocky cliff collapsing into the sea, and he is "so huge and horrible a mass" that "the knight himselfe even trembled at his fall" (487–88). Even the dragon's dead body inspires such fear that, in canto 12, the townsfolk nearby will not touch or come near it (78–81), fearing that from its womb might spring dragonets; some think they see the flicker of fire yet in its eyes (88–90). Redcrosse, now identified as St. George, is rewarded with "princely gifts of yvorie and gold" (105), and is married to Una near the end of the twelfth canto.

Spenser's dragon represents the apex of medieval dragon lore; with its death, the dragon itself passes from English literature—or at least goes dormant. On the Continent, dragons remained active only as subspecies of serpents in encyclopedias and works of natural history (Gould). Apart from literary allusions referred to earlier, the Renaissance comes to a close, drawing a curtain on dragon lore that was not to be lifted for almost 300 years. Whether this is because of a growing scepticism in the wake of the Enlightenment, or because of the burden of theological symbolism that had been loaded on the dragon throughout the Middle Ages and Renaissance, or because after the St. George legend there was simply nothing to add to the tradition that had not already been said, the dragon now passes out of literature and into the secondary realm of literary allusion— which is to say, that of metaphor, simile, poetic decoration. At least one scholar thinks that the dragon-slayer was overused in the Middle Ages (Hume 20); its overuse may have turned exaggeration into melodrama—perhaps anticipating the comical tone later exploited by writers of children's literature (Stein, 1968). Thus one can find a fair number of allusions to dragons in the poetic and dramatic works of Milton, Shakespeare, Jonson, Dryden, Pope, the Romantic poets, Tennyson, and Browning; most of them refer to specific dragons in earlier literature (especially classical mythology), but none develops the dragon as an actual element of plot or theme in any of their works.

An interesting commentary on the collapse of literary dragon lore during this period can be elucidated from the entry for "Dragon" in Samuel Johnson's great *Dictionary* (1755), which falls almost exactly in the middle of the 300-year period of dormancy for the dragon. Johnson defines the dragon thus: "A Kind of winged serpent, perhaps imaginary, much celebrated in the romances of the Middle Ages." Whether the word "perhaps" in this definition is an instance of Johnson's lexicographic fun or, instead, evidence of a lingering belief in the dragon as a subspecies of reptiles, the definition seals the dragon off as a relic of medieval lore.

When the dragon does reemerge as an element of narrative plot, at the end of the nineteenth century, it is as a creature of folktales, the unsophisticated stories of low, not high, culture. This does not mean that the dragon was entirely forgotten in the literary world during this period. The late Romantic revival of interest in the Middle Ages explains most dragon allusions in the later nineteenth century: Tennyson used Arthurian material in allusions to Celtic dragons in the *Idylls of the King* (1859); William Morris translated Old Norse legends, which no doubt inspired his adaptation of Sigurd's victory over Fáfnir in *Sigurd the Volsung* (1876). But the interest in mythology and folklore that developed as a result of the growth of philology in the latter half of the 1800s brought into print a number of stories collected from a variety of hitherto untapped sources, and dragons occur in many of the tales.

A thorough study of dragons in British folktales has been made by Jacqueline Simpson in an article-length analysis of fifty dragon tales (1978) and a book entitled *British Dragons* (1980). Numerous uses of the dragon in folk literature are listed in Stith Thompson's *Motif-Index* (1955–58); Thompson analyzes the dragon tale in *The Folktale* (1977: 22–52), of which there are supposed to be about 1,100 examples extant, the classic version being "Die Zwei Brüder" (The Two Brothers) in the Grimms' collection. An illustrative sampling of folktales and legends concerning the dragon is found in Katharine Briggs's *Dictionary of British Folktales in the English Language* (1970), where some two dozen texts gathered from many sources are reproduced. No more mention can be made here of them, except for the observation that in these tales, the dragons conform to the classic medieval type; the courageous men who go against them in battle employ the traditional weapons—sword, lance, spear—as well as untraditional ones such as live coals of peat, large stones, or camels filled with water, emphasizing the ingenuity (to a sometimes comic degree) of the human combatants. In a number of instances, local legends attach the story of the dragon's destruction to some geographical feature; indeed, several scholars have studied the use of "dragon" or "worm" and their cognates in English place-names as evidence of popular belief in the idea that dragons guard treasure-mounds—typically, hills and barrows of local geography (Davidson, 1950; Whitman, 1907).

The dragons of twentieth-century children's literature grow out of dragon folktales and fairy tales of the late nineteenth century, and the prototype is probably Kenneth Grahame's *The Reluctant Dragon* (1898). E. Nesbit's *Book of Dragons* (1900) is one of the first collections of dragon stories for children; there are dragons in the variously colored fairy-tale books edited by Andrew Lang. But in Grahame's story, dragon lore takes a new direction, reversing the narrative pattern outlined at the beginning of this entry. With few exceptions, dragons from earliest mythology on have been hostile, most of them being combatants against heroes of various sorts; most dragons end up dead. But the title character of *The Reluctant Dragon* is peaceful and gentle; though it is physically a member of its class—with scales, claw, tail, fire, and so on—it is by conviction a noncombatant. This dragon speaks, and it says of itself that, by contrast with its more ferocious colleagues, "I liked to get my meals regular and then to prop my back against a bit of rock and snooze a bit, and wake up and think of things going on and how they kept going on just the same" (Grahame, 1983: 8). This dragon, in a word, is civilized—just the opposite of chaos, disorder, or enmity. It likes to tell stories, compose poetry, reminisce about "old, old times when dragons were quite plentiful and the world was a livelier place than it is now" (10). Nevertheless, St. George is called in to deal with it, and the mock battle that results is carefully choreographed to give the appearance of genuine struggle, with a decisive spear-blow designed to look mortal and at the same time not *tickle* the dragon. The story ends with St. George, the dragon, and the local townsfolk all together at a banquet at which the dragon "[said] the right thing to everybody, and proved to be the life and soul of the evening" (40). Grahame's dragon is the first in a long lineage of peaceful dragons in children's stories, where the dragons are generally affable, cute, misunderstood, but always nonthreatening creatures more like overgrown puppies.

The interest in dragons among writers of children's literature is nothing short of explosive. Indexes of twentieth-century children's literature (Eastman, 1926, 1937, 1952; Ireland, 1973, 1979) list literally hundreds of stories, books, songs, and poems about dragons. These may be grouped under three headings: (1) translations, retellings, or adaptations of classical and medieval dragon stories, (2) dragon tales from more recent world folklore, and (3) new tales unconnected with prior literary or ethnic tradition, the dominant theme of which is the reluctant, tame, or otherwise nonthreatening dragon of the Kenneth Grahame variety. Examples of the first are found in the numerous retellings of the St.

George legend, one of the most recent being Margaret Hodges' *Saint George and the Dragon* (1984), which is based on the episode in the *Faerie Queene*; examples taken at random from the third category include Irwin Shapiro's *Jonathan and the Dragon* (1962), in which the townspeople of Kell try unsuccessfully to drive out a dragon, until young Jonathan succeeds merely by whispering in its ear, "Please, Mr. Dragon, won't you go away?" and Jack Kent's *There's No Such Thing as a Dragon* (1975), in which Billy Bixbee's mother refuses to acknowledge the presence of a small dragon in the house. She continually repeats the sentence that makes the book's title, and only admits its existence after it has grown so large that it carries the house away on its back. Once she does so, it returns the house to its foundations and shrinks back to "kitten size." Mrs. Bixbee says, "I don't mind dragons this size," and Billy replies, "I think it just wanted to be noticed!" This is of course a long way from the cosmological dragons, for whom being noticed is not a matter of great difficulty.

More prominent are the dragons of J. R. R. Tolkien and C. S. Lewis, whose imaginative fictions cross the boundary between children's literature and adult fantasy. These authors' dragons and their antecedents are discussed by Ruth Berman (1984); we can only allude to C. S. Lewis's dragons in *The Voyage of the 'Dawn Treader'* and his poem "The Dragon Speaks" (1935). But Tolkien's Smaug (*The Hobbit*, 1937), Chrysophylax (*Farmer Giles of Ham*, 1949), Ancalagon and Glaurung (*The Silmarillion*, 1977), and Scatha the Worm (*The Lord of the Rings*, 1954–55) are better known. In them, Tolkien's knowledge of medieval dragon lore is put to full narrative effect. Smaug, the gold-stealing enemy of the dwarves in *The Hobbit*, is described in a semi-humorous style befitting its juvenile audience, but he is fully ferocious: his fascination with riddles and susceptibility to flattery contain hints of the comical (234, 238–39), but his fiery rampages and dramatic death rival the most colorful in medieval literature, recalling the *Beowulf* episode and the *Poetic* and *Prose Eddas* with which it has many features in common. Smaug is sharp-sighted, but his hearing and sense of smell are also highly developed (230–31; *Unfinished Tales* 323). Smaug can speak, like Fáfnir in the *Eddas*, and his voice is enchanting (237, 241). Bilbo falls in danger of "coming under the dragon-spell" and telling Smaug all the truth of his plot to reclaim the dragon's treasure (236). Smaug also has the traditional weak spot in his armor, on his underside in the hollow of his left breast, which in his pride he reveals accidentally to Bilbo. This spot later proves his undoing, for Bard the Bowman's last arrow pierces this spot, penetrating completely and disappearing into the wound. Smaug crashes "down from on high in ruin" and sinks into Lake Esgaroth. True to Old English and Old Norse tradition, Smaug's treasure is cursed, and its possession ends in tragedy for the dwarves and men who claim it greedily.

In *The Silmarillion*, Tolkien develops dragon origins within his own mythic framework: the *Urulóki*, Quenya for "fiery dragons," were created by Morgoth for use in his wars against the Valar, Elves, and Men. Of these, Glaurung is the first, coming forth "young and scarce half-grown" in the 260th year of the

Sun. Since he is "not yet come to his full armoury" then (116), he cannot endure the arrows of his opponents; but later in the cycle of wars he comes forth fully armed and withers his foes (192). Later, a new strain of dragons, the flying dragons, is introduced; of these, Ancalagon the Black is the greatest (*LOTR* 1:70; *Silmarillion* 252).

The most fully conceived dragon-slaying in Tolkien's mythology is that of the battle between Glaurung the golden dragon of Angband and Turin Turambar the hero in both *The Silmarillion* (213–23) and *Unfinished Tales* (117–45). And in the appendix to *The Lord of the Rings*, we find mention of Scatha the Worm, slain by Fram of the kingdom of Rohan (*LOTR* 3:346), from whose hoard an ancient horn is taken and given later to Merry Brandybuck (3:256).

Probably riding partly on the coat-tails of Lewis' and Tolkien's fiction, modern fantasy is filled with dragons, principally in the novels of Anne McCaffrey (1969 et seq.) and Ursula K. Le Guin (1968; 1972), and in Gordon Dickson's *The Dragon and the George* (1976), which turns the St. George legend inside out. Orson Scott Card has edited two volumes of short fantasy stories about dragons (1980; 1981). In McCaffrey's novels, dragons are telepathically controlled by their riders, who are psychically mated to them in the youth of both monster and human master. In Hazard Adams's *The Truth about Dragons* (1977), the dragon's hoarding propensities are turned to archival usage: this dragon preserves countless artifacts of human culture for posterity.

The dragon has been a popular motif in art as well as in literature almost as long as dragons have existed in human imagination; in fact, one interesting avenue of research is the investigation of interdependencies between dragons as they are described in literary (and other) texts and as they are depicted in artistic material. Two essential books providing a general introduction to this subject are Francis Huxley's *The Dragon* (1979) and Judy Allen and Jeanne Griffiths' *The Book of the Dragon* (1979), both of which are filled with photographs of dragon motifs drawn from all epochs and cultures. In this genre, Peter Dickinson's *The Flight of Dragons* (1979) adds beautiful modern illustrations to some of the most important dragon myths and legends in world history.

Dragons have been both described and depicted in literature and in art. Indeed, one of the earliest accounts of the dragon, from Hesiod's poem *The Shield of Heracles*, does both at the same time: in it, the ancient Greek hero's shield features artistic depictions of colorful dragons (160). Dragons have been popular as ornamental decorations in both East and West; the artistic representations of them in Buddhist temples and Scandinavian churches, particularly on the eaves of these buildings, suggests a conceptual connection between the dragon as guardian in the West and as benevolent tutelary image in oriental religion. A further similarity between the famous dragon-ships popular in both China and Japan and the Norse usage of dragons as the prow of Viking sea-vessels probably evokes the same conceptual similarity (Allen 50–51). Scandinavian art in particular abounds with stylized representations of intricately coiled serpentine forms, a feature that may be found in objects ranging from cloisonné jewelry to sword-hilts.

The dragon-slaying associated with St. George was an immensely popular artistic motif in the Middle Ages; interrelations between the legend and its representations in art have been studied in detail by Bernard Myers (1933). Heraldic and cartographic illustrations have used dragon images to great effect in representing the regal ferocity of royal houses and the dangers lying in uncharted territories (Allen 108–9, 78–85).

Modern popular culture shows a remarkable love of dragons: video-game parlors now feature dragon-slayer computer games; in 1981, Paramount Pictures/ Walt Disney Productions released a film entitled *Dragonslayer* (Barwood, 1981); dragons have appeared in cinematic versions of *Conan the Barbarian* and Arthurian legends. But popular culture dragon lore is most evident in role-playing fantasy games. ''Dungeons and Dragons,'' which is the most important, and which has gone through three versions since its invention in the early 1970s, has the most fully developed dragon lore of all. According to the *Dungeon-Master's Guide* (Gygax, 1979), dragons are ''immense creatures whose main occupation is sleeping, dreaming . . . and entertaining emissaries of the warring factions of the area'' (77). Dragons are ''above such things as the collection of gold,'' and they ''have no hoards to tempt the unwary'' (ibid.). This is not true of a sleeping dragon, for ''while it dreams, its baser nature, the suppressed desires for blood and gold, comes out'' (ibid.); thus, the ''dream dragon'' is the monster to be feared. Dream dragons sit alone on ''a heap of money and gems,'' and they possess four legs and two wings, and have ''a fiery or poisonous breath'' (ibid.). As delineated in the *Advanced Dungeons and Dragons Monster Manual* (Gygax, 1978), the breath-weapons that dragons possess come in several varieties: cold, acid, gas, electricity, and fire, all of which are powerful to various statistical degrees and may be neutralized by combinations of the same sort of weaponry (1978: 30). Dragons are of two orders: Chaotic and Lawful; within each order, dragons may be aligned with either evil or good forces. Dragons are of two physiognomic types: metallic or chromatic; in the former one finds brass, bronze, copper, gold, platinum, and silver dragons; in the latter, dragons may be colored black, blue, green, red, or white (1979: 201; 1978: 31–34). Dragons pass through eight growth stages, ranging from ''very young'' (1–5 years) to ''ancient'' (401 years or more) and gain offensive/defensive strength as they pass through these stages (1978: 29). There are two offensive strategies to be used against dragons: attack to kill or to subdue (ibid., 30). The strength of the attack is determined by roll of dice, the dragon's defensive power also being determined in this way; the ratio between the two determines the outcome of the encounter. Most dragons can be subdued, showing the ''innate cowardice of dragonkind'' (1978: 31); they are also egotistical, and thus susceptible to flattery; they are greedy and avaricious and ''subject to manipulation by very clever persons or the prospect of actual treasure'' (ibid.). Most can speak ''one or more human languages in addition to the language of their species'' (ibid., 30); all have excellent sight, smell, and hearing, and though they "see equally well in daylight or darkness," they are "able to detect *hidden* or *invisible creatures*," depending upon their age-level (determined also by throws of the dice) (ibid., 29). Two dragons are individuals of their kind: the five-headed Chromatic Dragon named "Tiamat," ruler of plane one of the Nine Hells and progenitor of "all of evil dragonkind" (ibid., 32); and the Platinum Dragon named "Bahamut," the "King of good dragons," whose palace is behind the east wind and who "roams the earth in the guise of human or nearly any other form he chooses" (ibid., 33). Bahamut "can travel astrally or ethereally" (ibid.).

The role-playing games in which these dragons appear have been exceedingly popular, their success guaranteed by an apparent subsegment of the science fiction/fantasy readership that has emerged since the late 1950s. This *subcultus* is served by an entrepreneurial legion of game manufacturers and distributors, whose products include not only individual games but also whole game-systems. Ancillary products including models, sculptures, and maps are produced by another set of manufacturers; a commercial franchise, The Compleat Strategist, Inc., billing itself as a "fantasy and adventure game headquarters," had (as of 1985) retail outlets in seven states. Their apparent clientele meet frequently for conventions—seventeen separate advertised meetings being listed for the month of March/April 1985 alone—and are kept informed of new games and game developments through *Polyhedron*, the bimonthly newsletter of an international Role Playing Game Association Network, and through *Dragon* magazine, published monthly by TSR, Inc., the manufacturer of the *Dungeons and Dragons* series.

What does this fanatical popularity of science fiction, fantasy, and dragon lore mean apart from the success of its commercial promoters? If we accept Casey Fredericks' recent surmises (1982: 174–82), this is a "return to myth" of the kind observed and in large part anticipated by Northrop Frye in 1959:

Even popular literature appears to be slowly shifting its center of gravity from murder stories to science fiction—or at any rate a rapid growth of science fiction is certainly a fact about contemporary popular literature. . . . It is thus a mode of romance with a strong inherent tendency to myth. (Frye 48–49)

This shift, noticeable in other areas of recent cultural activity besides popular literature, reveals a need demonstrable over the long course of human history but perceived anew only recently: the need for a universe larger than its physical limits, more desirable than the tedium of modern life, more meaningful than the mere details of biography and history. This is the need for myth, realized most fully in religion but partly satisfied by mythmaking in fiction and fantasy. As the world shrinks to ever smaller proportions, the monsters that once inhabited uncharted realms are either driven inward—emerging as the repressed urges of our psychological selves—or reinvented on a larger scale; it is a fair guess that mankind's oldest and greatest monster—the dragon—will continue to play its terrible part in our imaginations.

BIBLIOGRAPHY

Adams, Hazard. *The Truth about Dragons*. New York: Holt, Rinehart, and Winston, 1977.

Allen, Judy, and Jeanne Griffiths. *The Book of the Dragon*. London: Orbis, 1979.

Barwood, Hal, and Matthew Robbins. *Dragonslayer*. Screenplay. Paramount Pictures/ Walt Disney Productions, 1981.

Berman, Ruth. "Dragons for Tolkien and Lewis."*Mythlore* 39 (1984): 53–58.

Bernard, Mary. "A Dragon Hunt." *American Scholar* 33 (1964): 422–27.

Botting, Douglas. *Dragons*. Time-Life Books. Boston: Little, Brown, 1984.

Briggs, Katharine. *A Dictionary of British Folktales in the English Language*. 4 vols. Bloomington: Indiana University Press, 1970.

Brock, Edmund, ed. *Morte Arthure*. Early English Text Society, o.s. 8. London: Oxford University Press, 1871.

Buck, Carl Darling. *A Dictionary of Selected Synonyms in the Principal Indo-European Languages*. Chicago: University of Chicago Press, 1949.

Campbell, John Francis. *The Celtic Dragon Myth*. Edinburgh: John Grant, 1911. Rpt. North Hollywood, Calif.: Newcastle, 1981.

Card, Orson Scott, ed. *Dragons of Darkness*. New York: Ace, 1980.

———, ed. *Dragons of Light*. New York: Ace, 1981.

Carlson, Signe M. "The Giant and the Dragon of the Folk Epic." Ph.D. diss. University of Southern California, 1966.

Cary, M., et al. *The Oxford Classical Dictionary*. Oxford: Clarendon, 1949.

Child, C. G. "The Natural History of Dragons." *University of Pennsylvania University Lectures* 7 (1921): 103–24.

Choate, Bonniejean McGuire. "A Study of Word Parallelism Significant to the Dragon Motif in the Old Testament." Master's thesis. University of Southern California, 1953.

Cockayne, O., ed. *Narratiunculae Anglice Conscriptae*. London, 1881.

Comfort, W. W., trans. Chrétien de Troyes. *Arthurian Romances*. London: Dent, 1975.

Courthope, W. J. *A History of English Poetry*. 6 vols. London: Macmillan, 1935.

Davidson, H. R. Ellis. "The Hill of the Dragon." *Folklore* 61 (1950): 169–85.

Dickinson, Peter. *The Flight of Dragons*. New York: Harper and Row, 1979.

Dickson, Gordon. *The Dragon and the George*. New York: Ballantine, 1976.

Dobbie, Elliott van Kirk, ed. *The Anglo-Saxon Minor Poems*. New York: Columbia University Press, 1942.

Douglas, N. "Dragons." *English Review* 16 (1914): 562–68.

Dowson, John. *A Classical Dictionary of Hindu Mythology and Religion, Geography, History, and Literature*. 8th ed. London: Routledge and Kegan Paul, 1953.

Eastman, Mary Huse, ed. *Index to Fairy Tales, Myths and Legends*. 2nd ed., rev. and enl. Boston: F. W. Faxon, 1926. Supplement, 1937; 2nd Supplement, 1952.

Eisner, Sigmund. *The Tristan Legend*. Evanston, Ill.: Northwestern University Press, 1969.

Evans, Jonathan D. "A Semiotic of the Old English Dragon." Ph.D. diss. Indiana
    University, 1984.
Evans, Sebastian, trans. *Geoffrey of Monmouth, History of the Kings of Britain*. New
    York: Dutton, 1904. Rpt. 1958.
Fontenrose, Joseph Eddy. *Python: A Study of Delphic Myth and Its Origins*. Berkeley
    and Los Angeles: University of California Press, 1959. Rpt. 1980.
Fredericks, Casey. *The Future of Eternity*. Bloomington: Indiana University Press, 1982.
French, W. H., and C. B. Halle, eds. *Sir Degaré. Middle English Metrical Romances*.
    2 vols. New York: Russell and Russell, 1930. 1:287–320.
Frye, Northrop. *Anatomy of Criticism*. Princeton: Princeton University Press, 1957.
Garmonsway, G. N., trans. *The Anglo-Saxon Chronicle*. New York: Dutton, 1972.
Gilbert, Dorothy Lloyd. "The Medieval Dragon: A Study Based on English Literature
    Exclusive of Romance up to 1400." Master's thesis. Columbia University, 1929.
Gould, Charles. *Mythical Monsters*. London, 1886.
Grahame, Kenneth. *The Reluctant Dragon*. 1898. Rpt. New York: Holt, Rinehart, and
    Winston, 1983.
Gygax, Gary. *Advanced Dungeons and Dragons Monster Manual*. Lake Geneva, Wis.:
    TSR Games, 1978.
———. *Dungeon-Master's Guide*. Lake Geneva, Wis.: TSR Games, 1979.
Harrington, K. P. *Mediaeval Latin*. Chicago: University of Chicago Press, 1962.
Hartland, Edwin S. *The Legend of Perseus: A Study of Tradition in Story, Custom and
    Belief*. 3 vols. London, 1894–96; rpt. New York: AMS Press, 1973.
Hayes, L. Newton. *The Chinese Dragon*. Shanghai: Commercial Press, 1922.
Hodges, Margaret. *Saint George and the Dragon*. Boston: Little, Brown, 1984.
Hogarth, Peter, and Val Clery. *Dragons*. New York: Viking, 1979.
Hume, Kathryn. "From Saga to Romance: The Use of Monsters in Old Norse Literature."
    Studies in Philology 77 (1980): 1–25.
Huxley, Francis. *The Dragon: Nature of Spirit, Spirit of Nature*. New York: Collier,
    1979.
Huygen, Wil. *Gnomes*. New York: Harry Abrams, 1977.
Ingersoll, Ernest. *Dragons and Dragon Lore*. New York: Payson and Clarke, 1928.
Ireland, Norma Olin. *Index to Fairy Tales, 1949–1972, Including Folklore, Legends and
    Myths in Collections*. Westwood, Mass.: F. W. Faxon, 1973.
———. *Index to Fairy Tales, 1973–1977, Including Folklore, Legends and Myths in
    Collections*. Fourth Supplement. Boston: F. W. Faxon, 1979.
Johnson, Richard. *The Seven Champions of Christendom*. n.p., 1670.
Kellogg, Robert, and Oliver Steel, eds. *Edmund Spenser: The Faerie Queene*. India-
    napolis: Odyssey, 1965.
Kent, Jack. *There's No Such Thing as a Dragon*. New York: Golden Press, 1975.
Kiessling, N. K. "Antecedents of the Medieval Dragon in Sacred History." *Journal of
    Biblical Literature* 89 (1970): 167–77.
Kölbing, Eugen, ed. *Beves of Hamtoun*. EETS, e.s. 46, 48, 65. London, 1855–94.
Kordecki, Lesley Catherine. "Traditions and Developments of the Medieval English
    Dragon." Ph.D. diss. University of Toronto, 1980.
Le Guin, Ursula K. *The Farthest Shore*. New York: Atheneum, 1972.
———. *A Wizard of Earthsea*. Berkeley: Parnassus, 1968.
Lewis, C. S. "The Dragon Speaks." *Lysistrata* 2 (May 1935): 16. Rpt. *Rehabilitations*
    (1939): 122.

————. *The Voyage of the Dawn Treader*. New York: Macmillan, 1952.

Lumby, J. Rawson. *Be Domes Dæge*. EETS, o.s. 65. London, 1876. Rpt. 1974.

McCaffrey, Anne. *Dragonflight*. London: Rapp and Whiting; New York: Walker, 1969.

McCulloch, Florence. *Medieval Latin and French Bestiaries*. Rev. ed. Chapel Hill: University of North Carolina Press, 1962.

Mason, Eugene, tr. *Wace: Roman de Brut*. New York: Dutton, 1962.

Matzke, J. E. "Contributions to the History of the Legend of St. George." *PMLA* 17 (1902): 464–535; 18 (1903): 99–171; 19 (1904): 449–78.

Meaney, Audrey L. *Anglo-Saxon Amulets and Curing Stones*. Oxford: British Archaeological Reports. British Series 96, 1981.

Morris, Richard, ed. *Old English Homilies and Homiletic Treatises*. EETS, o.s. 29, 34. London, 1868.

Myers, Bernard. "St. George and the Dragon." Ph.D. diss. New York University, 1933.

Nesbit, E. *The Book of Dragons*. New York: Harpers, 1900.

Newman, Paul. *The Hill of the Dragon*. Totowa, N.J.: Rowman and Littlefield, 1980.

Phillips, Walter Alison. "Dragon." *Encyclopaedia Britannica*. 13th ed. 1926.

Pokorny, Julius. *Indogermanisches Etymologisches Wörterbuch*. 2 vols. Bern and München: Francke, 1959.

Prickett, Stephen. *Victorian Fantasy*. Bloomington: Indiana University Press, 1979.

Ruppert, Donna. *Dragon's Path*. San Rafael, Calif.: Dawne-Leigh, 1979.

Ryan, Granger, and Helmut Ripperger, trans. and eds. *The Golden Legend of Jacobus de Voragine*. 2 vols. New York: Arno, 1941. Rpt. 1969.

Savill, Sheila. *The Orient. Pear's Encyclopedia of Myths and Legends*. London: Pilham, 1977.

Shapiro, Irwin. *Jonathan and the Dragon*. New York: Golden Press, 1962.

Simpson, Jacqueline. *British Dragons*. London: B. T. Batsford, 1980.

————. "Fifty British Dragon Tales: An Analysis." *Folklore* 89 (1978): 79–93.

Smith, Grafton Elliot. *The Evolution of the Dragon*. Manchester: The University Press; London and New York: Longmans, Green and Company, 1919.

South, Malcolm Hudson. "Animal Imagery in Ben Jonson's Plays." Ph.D. diss. University of Georgia, 1968.

Stein, Ruth M. "The Changing Styles in Dragons—From Fáfnir to Smaug." *Elementary English* 45 (1968): 179–83.

Sullivan, Mary Ann, trans. "Collectanea Rerum Memorabilium of Gaius Julius Solinus." Master's thesis. University of Georgia, 1969.

Sweet, Henry, ed. *The Oldest English Texts*. EETS, o.s. 83. London, 1885. Rpt. 1966.

Thompson, Stith. *The Folktale*. Berkeley and Los Angeles: University of California Press, 1977.

————. *Motif-Index of Folk-Literature*. Rev. and enl. ed. 6 vols. Bloomington: Indiana University Press, 1955–58.

Tolkien, J. R. R. *Farmer Giles of Ham*. London: Allen and Unwin, 1949; Boston: Houghton Mifflin, 1950.

————. *The Hobbit*. London: Allen and Unwin, 1937; Boston: Houghton Mifflin, 1938.

————. *The Lord of the Rings*. 3 vols. London: Allen and Unwin, 1954–55; Boston: Houghton Mifflin, 1955–56.

————. *The Silmarillion*. London: Allen and Unwin, 1977; Boston: Houghton Mifflin, 1977.

————. *Unfinished Tales*. Boston: Houghton Mifflin, 1980.

Vinaver, Eugène, ed. *The Works of Sir Thomas Malory*. 3 vols. Oxford: Clarendon, 1947; rpt. 1948; 2nd ed., 1967.

Visser, Marinus Willem de. *The Dragon in China and Japan*. Amsterdam: J. Muller, 1913.

White, T. H., ed. and trans. *The Bestiary: A Book of Beasts, Being a Translation from a Latin Bestiary of the Twelfth Century*. New York: Putnam's, 1954.

Whitman, C. H. "The Old English Animal Names." *Anglia* 30 (1907): 380–93.

Williams, C. A. S. *Outlines of Chinese Symbolism and Art Motives*. Tokyo: Charles E. Tuttle, 1941; 3rd ed., rev., 1974.

Williams, Ethel Carleton. "Mural Paintings of St. George in England." *Journal of the British Archaeological Association* 11 (1948): 19–36.

Williams, Jay. *Everyone Knows What a Dragon Looks Like*. New York: Four Winds, 1976.

Zupitza, J. *The Romance of Guy of Warwick*. EETS, e.s. 25–26. London, 1875; 1876. Rpt. 1 vol., 1966.

3

The Phoenix

Douglas J. McMillan

The phoenix (phenix), the best known of all fabulous birds, is a large eaglelike or heronlike sacred bird with gold and red feathers that is said to be self-reincarnated, often from its own ashes. There is just one phoenix at a time, and it usually lives for 500 years. Indeed, some say that it lives 540, 1,000, 1,461, or even 12,994 years (Vries 364). The phoenix in the Western world is usually considered a bird of Egypt with probable Arabian ties. From Egypt, knowledge of the phoenix spread to Greece, to Rome, to Christian Europe, and to the rest of the modern world. This fabulous bird usually is considered to be a symbol for the sun as well as for life after death.

This phoenix of the Western world is sometimes identified with oriental birds such as the anka ('anḵā', 'anqā', anqua) of Arabia, the roc (the rukh) of Arabia, the simurgh (sīmorgh) of Persia, or the garuda (garida) of India (Pellat 509). Indeed all of these fabulous birds may be related to one another and to a common solar myth and/or to some real bird such as the eagle, heron, albatross, condor, or the like.

The Western phoenix is also probably related to the Chinese phoenix, the fêng-huang, which originated in the sun, and which is a mysterious and beautiful bird with plumage blending the five colors and with a sweet call which is a harmony of the five notes (Ferguson, *Chinese Mythology* 98–99). The Western phoenix may also be related to the Japanese hō-ō, a phoenixlike bird which came to earth to do good deeds for people (Mercatante 206). Some also say that the firebird of Russian legend (best known outside the USSR through Stravinsky's ballet *The Firebird*) is a blend of the Western and the oriental phoenix (Mercatante 206). However, because the firebird talks, it might be safer to compare it to the falconlike karshipta of Persian mythology, which also is said to know how to speak (Ingersoll 206). "But phenix, rukh, anka, simurgh, garuda, feng-huang and others . . . such as Yel, the mythical raven of our Northwest, and those of Malaya . . . are all, apparently, members of the brood hatched ages ago in that same sunrise nest and still flying amid rosy clouds of prehistoric fable'' (Ingersoll 202).

The phoenix, although unique, has had many names over the years. It has been called ''the bird of the sun,'' ''of incense,'' ''of fire,'' ''of second birth,'' ''of the Ganges,'' ''of Assyria,'' ''of Arabia,'' ''the long-lived bird,'' and ''the Egyptian bird'' (Lum 237).

The account of the phoenix has continued to be very popular from Herodotus in the fifth century B.C. (and known at least from the eighth century B.C. through references by Hesiod) to the present time. Currently, in addition to countless literary and artistic examples of the myth, there are, to mention just a few modern reappearances of the fabulous bird, insurance companies, cities, and journals of learned societies called Phoenix; we refer to Atlanta, Georgia, and other cities rebuilt after drastic burning as phoenix cities, and bombed-out cathedrals like Coventry are said to have been rebuilt from their own ashes (Mercatante 207). The appearance of the phoenix from Hesiod and Herodotus to the present is one of the most widespread, best known, and vibrant of all myths. No other fabulous bird has so captured the imagination and the aspirations of the peoples of the world as has the sacred phoenix of Heliopolis, the mystical and mythical bird of the city of the sun.

Suggested explanations for the origin of the phoenix include the possibility that it is an astrological symbol for the sun setting and rising and/or a religious symbol of eternal life with the soul (and sometimes the body) rising to ''heaven'' after death. The phoenix may have originated as a misunderstanding of the appearance and the nature of the eagle, condor, albatross, heron, or some other actual bird. And it is also possible that the phoenix was an early human aspiration for immortality: if a bird can be reborn, perhaps a person could too.

Another possible explanation for the origin of the phoenix is to be found in the known ''anting'' behavior or posture of some species of birds. Some birds control parasites on their feathers by allowing ants to run over their bodies or by allowing smoke to rise through their feathers (Burton 15). Maurice Burton observed a tame rook's ''anting'' behavior using flames and smoke: ''He flapped his wings, snatched at the burning embers with his beak and appeared to be trying to put them under his wing'' (9). Another possible scientific explanation for the origin of the phoenix seems to me to be found in the molting process. A bird observed going through a complete feather molt appears to be becoming new again, perhaps even young again. The ''anting'' posture using smoke and fire plus the molting process of feather renewal may provide scientific clues to the possible origin of the phoenix seemingly rising anew (or with new feathers) out of its own ashes (or out of smoke or incense).

All of these possible origins are hypotheses, of course. Any one of them or any combination of them may be the truth. (A very thorough exploration of the surviving written and pictorial evidence for speculation on origins may be found in Broek [393–422: ch. 11, "The Development of the Myth of the Phoenix: Some Conclusions"].) Or the truth may be found in a hypothesis that we have yet to formulate. Whatever its origin, the phoenix has captured the imagination of the peoples of the world in ways that no other fabulous bird has.

Let us now turn to a historical survey of the appearance and use of the phoenix in different cultures.

The phoenix is first known to be mentioned by the ancient Greek poet Hesiod in the eighth century B.C. when he implies that the phoenix is already very well known and that it lives for a very long time (Broek 394). However, the most detailed and the most influential early (pre-Christian) account is that of the Greek historian Herodotus in the fifth century B.C. (Herodotus' account is now thought to be based at least partially on the *Periegesis* of Hecataeus of Miletus.) "This report, by virtue of its great age and relative abundance of detail, has been taken as the point of departure for all the discussions of the development of the phoenix myth" (Broek 395). In the second book of his *History*, Herodotus says that the phoenix is sacred to the Egyptians, although he has not seen one himself except in pictures. According to accounts given to him by the people of Heliopolis, the new phoenix comes there only once in 500 years at the death of the old phoenix. The pictures Herodotus has seen suggest to him that the phoenix looks like, and is the size of, an eagle with red and golden feathers. The story of the phoenix, which Herodotus finds hard to believe, is as follows: it comes to Egypt from Arabia with the parent bird's body completely plastered over in a ball of myrrh. It buries the ball with the body enclosed at the temple of the sun at Heliopolis (Herodotus 2.73). At least from the fifth century B.C. on, the phoenix has been famous beyond Egypt, eventually famous the world around.

The Greek comic poet Antiphanes, in the fourth century B.C., also associates phoenixes with Heliopolis in Egypt (Broek 395). The Hellenistic Jew Ezekiel the Dramatist, in the second century B.C., says that the phoenix has a beautiful song and is the king of birds (Broek 395). And Diogenes Laertius reports that Aenesidemus (first century B.C.) referred to the phoenix as an instance of an animal that reproduces itself asexually, giving us the first known reference to the unusual genesis of the phoenix (Broek 395–96).

The first complete account of the genesis of the phoenix, however, is given by the Roman senator Manilius as reported by Pliny the Elder (A.D. 23–79) in the tenth book of his *Natural History*. In this account, the phoenix lives in Arabia for 540 years and then dies on a sweet-smelling nest. A small worm which becomes the new phoenix develops from the bones and marrow of the dead phoenix (Pliny 10.2; Broek 396).

The fragmentary nature of these early references suggests that the authors could assume that the audience already knew the myths of the phoenix, and therefore they could mention relevant details only (Broek 396). Indeed, all the variations of the phoenix myth have several permanent elements: (1) the bird lives a long time, (2) it appears immediately before or after its death, (3) through death it lives again, (4) it is a bird of the sun (Broek 10).

At the time of Christ's youth we find the most interesting and influential Latin account of the phoenix in the *Metamorphoses* of Ovid (43 B.C.–A.D. 17). Just as Herodotus' version is the key Greek version, so Ovid's is the key Latin version, a major source for later writers in the Western tradition (McMillan 242–43). In the final book of the *Metamorphoses*, Ovid presents the phoenix as immortal but living through 500-year cycles. At the end of each cycle it builds a nest high in a palm tree covered with cassia, spikenard, myrrh, and cinnamon. There it dies; however, a little phoenix rises through the fragrance of the spices from the body of the old phoenix and lives the next 500-year cycle. When the new phoenix is strong enough it takes its nest, which is also its father's tomb, to the temple in the city of the sun, Heliopolis (5.393–407).

"In the first century A.D. the phoenix is mentioned twenty-one times by ten authors. From the preceding eight centuries we have only nine mentions of the bird, eight of them known only from quotations from later authors" (Broek 393–94). The total number of classical and early Christian references is given as 128, with all the passages identified in Fitzpatrick. Once we move beyond early Christian times the references to the phoenix become innumerable.

Closely related to the classical and the Christian phoenix (some would say identical to this Western phoenix) is the Egyptian benu or purple heron (*Ardea purpurea*), which is what Pliny's description of the phoenix would suggest to an ornithologist. The Egyptian word "benu" means both purple heron and palm tree. (Note in Ovid's account the appearance of the phoenix in a palm tree.) From the *Book of the Dead* we learn that the benu was one of several Egyptian symbols for the worship of the sun-god at Heliopolis (Carrington 87–88).

Probably related to the Western phoenix because they are also solar birds are the Chinese phoenix, the fêng-huang, and the Japanese phoenix, the hō-ō. In Chinese culture, according to the *Li Ki* (Book of Rites), there are four spiritual animals: the unicorn, the phoenix, the tortoise, and the dragon. The Chinese phoenix is mysterious but beautiful with its feathers a blend of the five colors and its song a harmony of the five notes. It originated in the sun, and it represents nature. It is said to have appeared several times bringing prosperity. Calamity occurs at its departure (Ferguson, *Chinese Mythology* 98–99). The Japanese phoenix is very much like the Chinese. In Japan, the phoenix has been an emblem used by the royal family, but particularly by the empress (Lum 243). The Japanese phoenix is said to be the sun descending to earth as a messenger of goodness (Ingersoll 208).

Probably also related, although less closely, are some other oriental solar birds like the garuda of India, the simurgh of Persia, the anka (which is said to live 1,700 years), and the roc, both of Arabia—all sun-birds that sometimes are said to feed mainly on elephants.

In the Western tradition after Ovid, we find many phoenix accounts besides that of the Roman writer Pliny the Elder (already mentioned). The Roman Tacitus notes in his *Annals* (6.28, for the year A.D. 34) the 500-year cycle but adds that some say the interval between appearances is 1,461 years. He also notes that the old phoenix sheds a genital substance in its nest from which the new phoenix arises. St. Clement of Rome (ca. A.D. 90–99), third successor to St. Peter as bishop of Rome, was one of Tacitus' contemporaries and is the first known (and because of his position the best-known and most widely influential) Christian to use the phoenix as an illustration for Christian teaching. In chapters 25 and 26 of "The Letter of St. Clement of Rome to the Corinthians" we find the already well-established account of the phoenix in Arabia, one of a kind, living 500 years, and the nest of spice made as death nears. But after death, according to St. Clement, a worm is born as the flesh decays. The worm develops wings, and when strength allows, the new phoenix flies with the nest and the bones of the old phoenix to Heliopolis in Egypt. Then St. Clement asks if we still think it marvelous that the creator will bring about the resurrection of those who served him and had faith in him after this demonstration of his promise of everlasting life by means of this bird (St. Clement 30–31). The fact that St. Clement really seems to believe the story of the phoenix has given some later commentators on the phoenix much trouble.

Other church fathers use the phoenix much as St. Clement does. Notable is Tertullian (b. ca. 150–60), who in chapter 13 of his *De resurrectione carnis* elaborates on the myth and uses it to prove the doctrine of the resurrection of the body. The Greek *Physiologus* (probably composed as early as ca. A.D. 200), its Latin translation (known before 431), and the bestiaries (expansions of the *Physiologus*) give us the core religious accounts known throughout the Christian Middle Ages and well into modern times. The *Physiologus* and the bestiaries are natural histories with Christian allegorical interpretations. All versions are in agreement that the phoenix represents Christ, who died and who came back to life. (This tradition may be approached through Curley 13–14 and White 125–28).

Other interesting early Christian accounts of the phoenix are those of Lactantius, Rufinus, St. Gregory of Tours, the Old English *Phoenix*, and "The Phoenix Homily." Those readers interested may find the relevant portions of these accounts reprinted in my earlier article on the phoenix (McMillan 250–56). This Hellenized, Romanized, and Christianized Egyptian phoenix is the fabulous bird known in the West from these early authors and artists through countless other authors and visual artists up to the present day.

The key to the oral lore of the phoenix is Thompson's *Motif-Index* and its supplements, particularly Cross's *Motif-Index of Early Irish Literature*. Three motifs refer specifically to the phoenix: B32. *Phoenix*; B32.1. *Phoenix renews youth*; and B32.1.1. *Phoenix renews youth when 1,000 years old*. References to oral lore collected about the phoenix listed under one or more of these motifs indicate that there is an oral tradition (folklore) concerning the phoenix in Egyptian, Chinese, Irish, and Jewish lore, among others. Indeed, as is the case with many folk motifs, it is likely that there has been a much wider oral circulation of phoenix lore than has been committed to print. The phoenix has not only been popular with elite (literate) levels of cultures but also, as the many entries in the *Motif-Index* prove, with so-called less sophisticated levels.

The symbolism attached to the phoenix is multiple and inspiring. Some of humanity's highest aspirations and most intimate desires are and have been represented by the phoenix. Essentially, the phoenix is a symbol of the sun. Secondarily, but no less important, it is a symbol of life after death. In Christian cultures the phoenix also becomes a symbol of the Son, the second person of the Trinity, of his resurrection, and of the resurrection (soul and body) of the faithful.

The basic association of the phoenix as a symbol for the sun seems to be a constant interpretation as far back as we can trace the phoenix. But, according to E. A. Wallis Budge, the Greek and Roman (and therefore later) accounts of the phoenix are all the result of misunderstandings of the Egyptian myth of the benu (Bennu) bird "which declared that the renewed morning sun rose in the form of a Bennu, and of the belief which declared that this bird was the soul of Rā and also the living symbol of Osiris, and that it came forth from the very heart of the god" (96–97). The renewal too, on Budge's evidence, is universal: "From many passages we learn that the Bennu, the Soul of Rā, which appeared each morning under the form of the rising sun, was supposed to shine upon the world from the top of the famous Persea tree wherein he renewed himself" (97).

R. T. Rundle Clark is even more emphatic in pointing out the shift in symbolism from the divine symbol it was in ancient Egypt to the supernatural but somewhat less sacred symbol it became through Herodotus and his followers: "This great symbol, the most persuasive in the Egyptian repertoire, was misunderstood by Herodotus who . . . brought it down to the level of a fairy-tale" (248). Clark holds that the phoenix was known to the Egyptians as the benu bird and that it was "one of the primeval forms of the High God." The benu is the first light and life; it is the patron of time. "But the heron form is not to be taken too literally; it is a way of expressing one of the basic activities of God." Indeed, concludes Clark, "the phoenix is the principle of life" (246, 249).

Outside Egypt, without losing its essential connections to the sun and to renewal, the phoenix became more of a thing in itself in addition to being a symbol. Later, after the many Greek and Roman accounts of the phoenix, the bird took on the symbolic meaning of political perfection: "Depicted on a pyre, and encircled by a halo of glory, this solar Bird became, amongst the Romans, the emblem of the imperial apotheosis" (Goblet d'Alviella 95). And, in the Christian era, the phoenix appeared again and again as a symbol for the immortal soul, for eternal bliss, for the resurrection of the body, and for love. But the main Christian symbolic use of the phoenix is as a symbol for the resurrected Christ. St. Clement mentioned the phoenix in the first century, as noted already, and the phoenix appeared often on funeral stones and sarcophagi, and in churches, religious paintings, religious embroidery, and religious stonework.

The phoenix as a solar symbol is often seen as the eastern and the western sun, as the morning and the evening sun, and by extension as the sun of spring and the sun of autumn (Gubernatis 1:200–1). In addition to being a solar symbol, the phoenix also is a symbol, among other things, for resurrection, immortality, eternal youth, chastity, temperance, a paragon or unique person, self-sufficiency, self-immolation, a storm, justice, royal succession, Christ's suffering and resurrection, hope, perseverance, and the complete alchemical transmutation (Vries 364). The phoenix is a unique symbol with the power in one word to evoke all or any of these meanings. Because of its uniqueness and its power, however, it could easily be misunderstood. One clearly needs to know the context within which this symbol appears before attempting to understand and to interpret it.

The uses of the phoenix in art are overwhelming in number and variety. Two very useful assemblages of reproductions of visual sources are to be found in Broek (following ch. 11) and in Poesch (between 208 and 229). Broek presents forty black-and-white plates depicting the phoenix from a mural painting in the Tomb of Irenifer, Dêr el Medineh (1345–1200 B.C.) to a ceiling painting in a burgomaster's residence in Arnhem (seventeenth century A.D.). In between are phoenixes on coins, seals, sculptures, and so on. In addition, Broek gives twenty-five descriptions of dubious phoenixes in art. Poesch presents twenty-one black-and-white figures; and one figure, a fragment of a mosaic from Old St. Peter's, Rome, late twelfth century, is in vivid color. In this mosaic in color depicting a phoenix, the gold and red wing feathers are set off with mainly white, but also with some blue, body feathers. The head is presented against a gold and white circular nimbus. A larger series of circles encloses the whole bird, which here looks much more like an eagle than a heron. The total impression is one of wonder, awe, and admiration for this bird which is a bird but which also is the sun, immortality, and deity. Poesch's black-and-white figures show the phoenix on Roman imperial coins, other mosaics, a manuscript illumination from a twelfth-century bestiary, a fifteenth-century engraving, a seventeenth-century painting, seventeenth-century armorial bearings of the Worshipful Company of Blacksmiths of London, an eighteenth-century letterhead of the Phoenix Assurance Co., and an American eighteenth-century mirror with a phoenix at the top center of the frame. All these are among other very interesting representations of the Western phoenix. The Chinese phoenix (pheasantlike, with long flowing tail) is represented in figures 18–20. Poesch concludes her very informative illustrated essay on visual portrayals of the phoenix by saying, ''I have seen the phoenix emblem used as the symbol of an employment agency; a chance for a new beginning is certainly implied. The emblem renews itself with each new interpretation'' (232).

The phoenix, as already noted, is depicted in many Christian buildings. Perhaps most notable are those in the cathedrals of Tours, Le Mans, Magdeburg, and Basel (Armstrong 81).

Although the phoenix was very popular in medieval art, it is rare in paintings of the Italian Renaissance (Ferguson, *Signs and Symbols* 24). Yet the phoenix was a popular emblem in Renaissance emblem books. At least in heraldry, the Renaissance continued the visual and symbolic use of the phoenix: Joan of Arc's device had a painted phoenix in flames; Vittoria Colonna (wife of the Marquis of Pescara) used the phoenix on her medal; Mary Queen of Scots used the impress of her mother, a phoenix in flames; Jane Seymour's badge was a phoenix in flames on a castle; Queen Elizabeth I used a phoenix on her medals and tokens (Vinycomb 174–75).

Rembrandt did an etching in 1658 called *The Phoenix, or the Statue Toppled*. An eaglelike phoenix is at center top with outstretched wings. This etching "may allude to Rembrandt's own bankruptcy or that of Joost van den Vondel of 1657. Vondel was frequently referred to as *Fenicks van uns Landt* [Phoenix of our country]. . . . The suggestion has also been made that some connection exists with the emblem of the Jewish community of Amsterdam which also featured a Phoenix" (Strauss and Meulen 408, etching 409; etching also Poesch 221).

There seems to be no limit and no end to the visual representations of the phoenix. Some are inspiring (the religious); some are decorative (the mirror frame, for example); some are practical (the letterhead, for instance); all are instantly recognized and all are moving and meaningful. The phoenix, we see, rises again and again all around us.

The use of the phoenix in literature is widespread. Indeed, T. H. White, who translated and edited a Latin twelfth-century bestiary, remarked as follows in 1954: "Everybody has heard of the Phoenix, and half the poets who have written have mentioned it" (128n).

Aside from historical and religious accounts, the most important and influential classical literary account of the phoenix is to be found in the *Metamorphoses* of Ovid, as already mentioned. Ovid's work is an anthology of the myths of Greece and Rome using the central notion of transformation or change or metamorphosis as its theme. The phoenix really does belong in such a poem.

The most influential medieval literary account of the phoenix is found, as has been noted, in the Greek and Latin versions of the *Physiologus* and in its derivative the bestiaries (twelfth and thirteenth centuries). These allegorical natural histories correlate the death and rebirth of the phoenix with the saying of Christ: "Therefore doth the Father love me: because I lay down my life, that I may take it again. / No man taketh it away from me: but I lay it down of myself, and I have power to lay it down: and I have power to take it up again. This commandment have I received of My Father" (John 10:17–18). In the *Physiologus*, the phoenix signals the priest of Heliopolis to prepare the altar with brushwood. The phoenix ignites the fire and burns itself up. The next day the priest finds a worm; the second day the priest finds a little bird; the third day he finds an "eagle" which flies off. The phoenix, of course, represents Christ (Curley 13–14). In the bestiaries, the phoenix makes a coffin of spices, enters, and dies. A worm emerges from the body liquid, and the worm becomes a phoenix. This teaches the faithful to believe in the resurrection (White 126–27).

Ovid, the *Physiologus*, and the bestiaries were widely read and vastly influential throughout the Middle Ages and beyond.

Other noteworthy medieval literary references to the phoenix are to be found in the Old English ninth-century poem *The Phoenix* (a retelling of the myth based on the account of Lactantius plus a Christian allegorical interpretation concerning life after death); the twelfth-century English "The Phoenix Homily" (an account of St. John's visit to paradise, wherein is a phoenix which every 1,000 years is burned to dust and then rises from the dead on the third day); the early twelfth-century German *Parzival* of Wolfram von Eschenbach (an account of the Holy Grail in which the Grail—a stone here—keeps a person and the phoenix young and rejuvenated); the French thirteenth-century *Romance of the Rose* of Guillaume de Lorris and Jean de Meun (with a comparison of the rarity of both the phoenix and a virtuous maid [Dunn 175] and with a full history of the ever-living phoenix as an example of Nature's creation of new creatures [Dunn 341]—this work was also very influential); the Italian early fourteenth-century *Inferno* of Dante (a reference in canto 24 to the 500-year cycle of restoration of the phoenix); the English fourteenth-century *Book of the Duchess* of Chaucer (an allusion to the unique phoenix of Arabia); the fourteenth-century English anonymous *Pearl* (a reference to Mary, Christ's Mother, as the phoenix of Arabia); three fourteenth-century Italian sonnets of Petrarch (a reference to the purple and gold feathers of the phoenix, a reference to its golden plumes, a reference to its unique nature, all comparing the phoenix story to Petrarch's love for Laura); and the fifteenth-century English translation by William Caxton of the *Image du monde* (a highly detailed description of the phoenix's plumage and its burning and rejuvenation) (McMillan 254–60).

Another major, influential, encyclopedia-type medieval account of the phoenix is to be found in Bartholomaeus Anglicus' *De proprietatibus rerum* (ca. 1230) and its English translation by John Trevisa, *On the Properties of Things* (1398/99). The section on the phoenix informs us that the phoenix (fenyx) is a bird and that there is only one of the type in the world. It is bred among the Arabs, has no mate, and lives 300 or 500 years. After that time it makes a nest of sweet-smelling dry sticks that is set on fire by the sun in the summer when the western wind blows. The phoenix enters the burning nest, and in three days a little worm is produced from the ashes and little by little the worm turns into a bird (1:625; Trevisa's translation).

The phoenix was also very popular in Renaissance literature. A few representative examples of its literary uses in that major period are discussed here; there are, of course, many others.

Rabelais (d. 1553), one of the most widely read of French Renaissance authors, refers to the phoenix in chapter 30 of book 5 of *Gargantua and Pantagruel*; in the visit to Satinland, among other fabulous birds, beasts, and trees were seen fourteen phoenixes in spite of earlier authors' statements to the contrary about only one existing at a time (Rabelais 676).

The Phoenix Nest, an Elizabethan poetical miscellany, 1593, with the phoenix in its title and with five separate poetical appearances of the phoenix, attests to the popularity of the image, used here primarily as an Elizabethan conceit (Rollins x, 9, 10, 15, 58, 69, 106).

Shakespeare was fond of the phoenix, too, and used its story in "The Phoenix and the Turtle," where the phoenix seems to represent immortality and truth and the turtledove seems to represent true love and beauty. Both seem to burn to death because of "married chastity." In addition, we can note the following six appearances of, and allusions to, the phoenix in Shakespeare's plays: "In Arabia / There is one tree, the phoenix' throne, one phoenix / At this hour reigning there" (*The Tempest* III.iii.22–24); "And that she could not love me, / Were man as rare as phoenix" (*As You Like It* IV.iii.17–18); "A phoenix, captain, and an enemy, / A Guide, a goddess" (*All's Well That Ends Well* I.i.162–63); "from their ashes shall be rear'd / A Phoenix that shall make all France affear'd" (*Henry VI, Part I* IV.vii.92–93); "But as when / The bird of wonder dies, the maiden phoenix, / Her ashes new create another heir, / As great in admiration as herself" (*The Life of King Henry the Eighth* V.v.39–42); and "Lord Timon will be left a naked gull, / Which flashes now a phoenix" (*Timon of Athens* II.i.31–32).

The literary uses of the phoenix after Shakespeare are astronomical in number. There is an excellent survey of them in English in the important essay by Montgomery, from which I select these outstanding examples.

Several references to the phoenix appear in Milton's poetry (Montgomery 271–74). Milton alludes to the phoenix in "Epitaphium Damonis" (an elegy for his friend Charles Diodati, in which the phoenix is called divine and unique and is said to have parti-colored wings); in *Paradise Lost*, book 5 (in which God sends the archangel Raphael to Adam before the fall—to all the birds Raphael in his downward flight seems to be a phoenix); and at the end of *Samson Agonistes* Milton has the chorus report to Samson's father that Samson died like a dragon, an eagle, and a phoenix:

> So virtue giv'n for lost,
> Deprest, and overthrown, as seem'd
> Like that self-begott'n bird
> In the Arabian woods embost,
> That no second knows nor third,
> And lay erewhile a Holocaust,
> From out her ashy womb now teem'd,
> Revives, reflourishes, then vigorous most
> When most unactive deem'd,
> And though her body die, her fame survives,
> A secular bird ages of lives.
> (lines 1697–1707; qtd. in Montgomery 274)

Sir Thomas Browne devotes a chapter of his *Pseudodoxia Epidemica or Enquiries into . . . Vulgar and Common Errors*, 1646, to the phoenix. Chapter 12 of book 3 is called "Of the Phoenix." Sir Thomas reviews the findings of all authorities of the phoenix—classical, biblical, church fathers, and so on. His conclusion is that we cannot say that there ever was a real phoenix because no one ever saw one. He also doubts many of the attributes the phoenix is said to have, particularly its uniqueness, its long life (1,000 or more years), and its method of reproduction (nonsexual, worm, and so on) (Browne 437–45). This is a very scientific, nonsymbolic view. However, it appears in the work of one of the early masters of English literary prose and is therefore not only very interesting in itself for its grand summary of phoenix lore from Herodotus to Browne, but also as an appropriate vehicle for our literary study of uses of the phoenix.

The phoenix appears also in the poetry of Henry Vaughan (Montgomery 269–71) and of Richard Crashaw (Montgomery 274–77), where it is used mainly in religious ways. For an example of an early secular, sexual use of the phoenix, we should turn to John Donne's "The Canonization." Here we have a man and woman in love who give a new meaning to the phoenix story:

> Call us what you will, wee are made such by love;
>   Call her one, mee another flye,
> We'are Tapers too, and at our owne cost die,
>   And wee in us finde the'Eagle and the Dove.
>   The Phoenix ridle hath more wit
>   By us, we two being one, are it.
> So to one neutrall thing both sexes fit,
>   Wee dye and rise the same, and prove
>   Mysterious by this love.
>   (lines 19–27; qtd. in Montgomery 277)

A similarly secular, sexual use of the phoenix is found in Donne's "An Epithalamion, or Mariage Song . . . ," a marriage poem in which the speaker says to the celebrant at the wedding:

> Till now, Thou warmd'st with multiplying loves
>   Two larkes, two sparrowes, or two Doves,
>   All that is nothing unto this,
> For thou this day couplest two Phoenixes;
> . . . .
> And by this act of these two phenixes,
>   Nature againe restored is,
>   For since these two are two no more,
> Ther's but one phenix still, as was before.
>   (lines 15–18, 99–102; qtd. in Montgomery 277–78)

Among seventeenth-century poets using the phoenix we may note in passing Ben Jonson, William Drummond, Giles Fletcher, Thomas Carew, James Shirley,

Thomas Stanley, Richard Crashaw, Robert Herrick, John Wilmot, Earl of Rochester, and John Dryden, among others (Montgomery 278–87).

We then run into a lull in the use of the phoenix in English literature. The major writers of the eighteenth century rarely used the phoenix for literary imagery (Montgomery 287).

In the nineteenth century there is something of a revival of interest in the use of the phoenix image among great writers. We find Keats in "On Sitting Down to Read *King Lear* Once Again" saying "Give me new Phoenix wings to fly at my desire," and in *Otho the Great* (V.v.130–34) he has Prince Ludolph say "Carve it on my tomb, that, when I rest beneath / Men shall confess, this Prince was gull'd and cheated, / But from the ashes of disgrace he rose / More than a fiery Phoenix, and did burn / His ignominy up in purging fires!" Tennyson refers in *The Ring* to "a fiery phoenix rising from the smoke," and Browning in book 3 of *The Ring and the Book* has Abate Paolo refer to the myth in these words: "The rare bird, sprinkle salt on phoenix' tail, / And so secure the nest a sparrow-hawk." (For these quotations, I am indebted to Montgomery 299–301.)

Several twentieth-century poets have satirical and/or humorous poems devoted to the phoenix. Howard Nemerov's "The Phoenix" recalls the unique bird rejuvenating itself in Heliopolis, committing incest, murder, and suicide to survive. Siegfried Sassoon's "Phoenix" is even more satirical and concludes that the bird of fame is a "Pseudomorphous Hieroglyphic." And Ogden Nash notes that it lays one egg out of which it pops itself (Montgomery 306–7).

William Butler Yeats refers to the place where the last phoenix died in "The Lover Asks Forgiveness because of His Many Moods" and he uses the phoenix as a symbol for Maude Gonne in "The People" and in "His Phoenix" (Montgomery 307–10).

Other noteworthy twentieth-century literary uses of the phoenix include Hart Crane's "Voyages," C. Day Lewis's "Do Not Expect Again a Phoenix," Louis Untermeyer's "Appeal to the Phoenix," Christopher Fry's *A Phoenix Too Frequent*, Nathanael West's *The Dream Life of Balso Snell*, Eudora Welty's *A Worn Path*, and Tennessee Williams' *Camino Real* and *I Rise in Flame, Cried the Phoenix* (Montgomery 310–21). Particularly noteworthy among twentieth-century literary users of the phoenix is D. H. Lawrence. He chose the phoenix as his personal emblem for the theme of death and rebirth. His presentation of the phoenix can best be read in *The Crown* (1915), *The Rainbow* (1915), *Aaron's Rod* (1922), *Kangaroo* (1923), and in the final poem, "Phoenix," in the posthumous volume *Last Poems* (1930). "Having committed himself to life, Lawrence came finally to incorporate, as both literary metaphor and psychological task, the fact of his own death. . . . The phoenix, always an emblem for creative living, in Lawrence's last poem defines the nature of the coming change, the quality of immortality" (Cowan 198).

Although this discussion of the literary uses of the phoenix since the Middle Ages has focused mainly on English literature, I do not mean to suggest at all that the phoenix was ignored by writers using other languages. Indeed, I selected the emphasis on English by way of primary example. One could also trace the uses of the phoenix in any of the other modern literatures and use that as further exemplification. I mention just a few more examples of uses of the phoenix in the literature, folk and otherwise, of the twentieth century.

Allowing for the possibility that the talking Russian firebird is a phoenix, we note that its long feathers are yellow and red like fire, that its eyes flash like diamonds, and that its wings are like flames. The firebird is captured by Koschtchei and rescued by Prince Ivan. The version used by Igor Stravinsky for his ballet *Firebird* can be read in summary in Appleby and Fowler, and some Russian folk versions can be read in Guterman's translation of Afanas'ev, where one will find "The Maiden Tsar," "The Firebird and Princess Vasilisa," and "Prince Ivan, The Firebird, and the Gray Wolf."

A very interesting and entertaining book for children by Edith Nesbit appeared in 1904 called *The Phoenix and the Carpet*. In this story a phoenix is delivered still in its egg all wrapped up in a magic carpet. (The carpet had just been purchased for the room of four children.) The children make a fire in the fireplace using sweet scented woods and gum to heat their room, and the phoenix hatches from its egg after 2,000 years in that egg (and magic blanket). The children recognize the phoenix from a picture in their encyclopedia. The phoenix is pleased that it is still remembered after all these years but disagrees with the statement in the encyclopedia about its reincarnation via a worm. It explains that it tired of appearing every 500 years and had made a 2,000 year arrangement with the magic carpet. The 2,000 years are up and here is the phoenix again. The magic carpet takes the children and the phoenix where they want to go. Finally, the phoenix lays an egg to be placed in the carpet for another 2,000 years, burns itself, and the carpet flies off (Nesbit 179–394).

And still the phoenix continues to rise. I will mention just two more twentieth-century reappearances of the phoenix in literature: a fantasy novel by Avram Davidson appeared in 1969 with the title *The Phoenix and the Mirror*, and a romantic historical novel set in Atlanta, the phoenix city, by Frances Patton Statham appeared in 1982 with the title *Phoenix Rising*. The phoenix is immortal.

The single most useful and detailed study of the phoenix is that by Broek (early history, art, and bibliography). There are also many valuable shorter studies; among them, I would particularly recommend the following: Costello (natural history and bibliography), Ingersoll (legend and lore), Lum (lore), McDonald (early history), Montgomery (modern English literature), Poesch (art), Rowland (symbolism and bibliography), and Rusch (classical antiquity and bibliography). These studies are valuable in themselves and they contain extremely valuable bibliographical references.

The phoenix has been, is, and will be the best known fabulous bird in the world. It is truly immortal. It has survived from Hesiod and Herodotus to our own day in history, myth, lore, art, and literature. It has commercial connections, especially with insurance companies, and it is intimately connected with many cities, particularly the sun cities of Phoenix in Arizona, Venice in Italy, and Heliopolis in Egypt. Long live the unique phoenix!

BIBLIOGRAPHY

Appleby, William, and Frederick Fowler. *The Sleeping Beauty and The Firebird: Stories from the Ballet.* The Young Reader's Guides to Music. New York: Henry Z. Walck, 1965.

Armstrong, Edward A. *The Life and Lore of the Bird: In Nature, Art, Myth, and Literature.* A Chanticleer Press Edition. New York: Crown, 1975.

Broek, R. Van den. *The Myth of the Phoenix According to Classical and Early Christian Traditions.* Trans. Mrs. I. Seeger. Études Préliminaires aux Religions Orientales dans L'Empire Romain, 24. Diss. Utrecht 1969. Leiden: Brill, 1972.

Browne, Sir Thomas. *Pseudodoxia Epidemica.* In *Sir Thomas Browne's Works.* Ed. Simon Wilkin. London, 1835; rpt. New York: AMS, 1968. Vol. 2.

Budge, E. A. Wallis. *The Gods of the Egyptians or Studies in Egyptian Mythology.* 1904; rpt. New York: Dover, 1969. Vol. 2.

Burton, Maurice. *Phoenix Re-born.* London: Hutchinson, 1959.

Carrington, Richard. *Mermaids and Mastodons: A Book of Natural and Unnatural History.* New York: Rinehart, 1957.

Chevalier, Jean, and Alain Gheerbrant. "Phénix." In *Dictionnaire des symboles.* 2nd ed. Paris: Seghers, 1974. Vol. 3.

Clark, R. T. Rundle. *Myth and Symbol in Ancient Egypt.* 1960; rpt. London: Thames and Hudson, 1978.

Clébert, Jean-Paul. "Phénix." In *Bestiaire fabuleux.* Paris: Albin Michel, 1971. 298–302.

Clement, St. "The Letter of St. Clement of Rome to the Corinthians." Trans. Francis X. Glimm. In *The Apostolic Fathers.* Ed. Ludwig Schopp. New York: Cima, 1947.

Costello, Peter. *The Magic Zoo: The Natural History of Fabulous Animals.* New York: St. Martin's, 1979.

Cowan, James C. "Lawrence's Phoenix: An Introduction." *The D. H. Lawrence Review* 5 (Fall 1972): 187–99.

Cross, Tom Peete. *Motif-Index of Early Irish Literature.* n.d.; rpt. New York: Kraus, 1969.

Curley, Michael J., trans. *Physiologus.* Austin: University of Texas Press, 1979.

Dunn, Charles W., ed. *The Romance of the Rose.* By Guillaume de Lorris and Jean de Meun. Trans. Harry W. Robbins. New York: Dutton, 1962.

Ferguson, George. *Signs and Symbols in Christian Art.* 2nd ed. New York: Oxford University Press, 1955.

Ferguson, John C. *Chinese Mythology.* In *The Mythology of All Races.* Ed. Canon John Arnott MacCulloch. Boston: Archaeological Institute, 1932. Vol. 8.

Fitzpatrick, Mary Cletus. *Lactanti De Ave Phoenice.* Philadelphia: University of Pennsylvania Press, 1933.

Goblet d'Alviella, Eugène Félicien. *The Migration of Symbols.* London, 1894; rpt. New York: University Books, 1956.

Gubernatis, Angelo de. *Zoological Mythology or The Legends of Animals*. 2 vols. London, 1872; rpt. Detroit: Singing Tree Press, 1968.

Guterman, Norbert, trans. *Russian Fairy Tales*. Ed. A. Afanas'ev. London: George Routledge, n.d.

Herodotus. *The Histories*. Trans. George Rawlinson. 2 vols. 1858; rpt. Everyman's Library. London: Dent, 1964.

The Holy Bible: Translated From the Latin Vulgate. 1899; rpt. Rockford, Ill.: Tan Books, 1971.

Ingersoll, Ernest. *Birds in Legend, Fable and Folklore*. 1923; rpt. Detroit: Singing Tree Press, 1968.

Lum, Peter. *Fabulous Beasts*. London: Thames and Hudson, n.d.

McDonald, Sister Mary Francis. "Phoenix Redivivus." *The Phoenix* 14 (Winter 1960): 187–206.

McMillan, Douglas J. "The Phoenix in the Western World from Herodotus to Shakespeare." *The D. H. Lawrence Review* 5 (Fall 1972): 238–67.

Mercatante, Anthony S. *Zoo of the Gods: Animals in Myth, Legend and Fable*. New York: Harper and Row, 1974.

Montgomery, Lyna Lee. "The Phoenix: Its Use as a Literary Device in English from the Seventeenth Century to the Twentieth Century." *The D. H. Lawrence Review* 5 (Fall 1972): 268–323.

Nesbit, E. [Edith Nesbit Bland]. *The Phoenix and the Carpet*. In *Five Children and It: The Phoenix and the Carpet: The Story of the Amulet*. 1904; rpt. London: Octopus, 1979.

Ovid. *Metamorphoses*. Trans. Frank Justus Miller. 2 vols. 1916; rpt. Cambridge: Harvard University Press, 1929.

Pellat, Charles. " 'Anḳā'." *The Encyclopaedia of Islam*. New ed. Leiden: Brill, 1961. 1:509.

Pliny the Elder. *The Natural History*. Trans. John Bostock and H. T. Riley. London, 1855. Vol. 2.

Poesch, Jessie. "The Phoenix Portrayed." *The D. H. Lawrence Review* 5 (Fall 1972): 200–37.

Rabelais, François. *The Histories of Gargantua and Pantagruel*. Trans. J. M. Cohen. 1955; rpt. New York: Penguin, 1979.

Robin, P. Ansell. *Animal Lore in English Literature*. London: John Murray, 1932.

Rollins, Hyder Edward, ed. *The Phoenix Nest* (1593). Cambridge: Harvard University Press, 1931.

Rowland, Beryl. *Birds with Human Souls: A Guide to Bird Symbolism*. Knoxville: University of Tennessee Press, 1978.

Rusch, Adolf. "Der Wundervogel." *Paulys Real-Encyclopädie der classischen Altertumswissenschaft*. Neue Bearbeitung. Stuttgart: Metzlersche, 1941, 20: pt. 1, cols. 414–23.

Strauss, Walter L., and Marjon van der Meulen. *The Rembrandt Documents*. New York: Abaris, 1979.

Thompson, Stith. *Motif-Index of Folk-Literature*. Rev. and enl. ed. 6 vols. Bloomington: Indiana University Press, 1955–58.

Trevisa, John, trans. *On the Properties of Things: John Trevisa's Translation of Bartholomaeus Anglicus*, De Proprietatibus Rerum. Ed. M. C. Seymour et al. 2 vols. Oxford: Clarendon, 1975.

Vinycomb, John. *Fictitious and Symbolic Creatures in Art, with Special Reference to Their Use in British Heraldry*. London, 1906; rpt. Detroit: Gale, 1969.

Vries, Ad de. *Dictionary of Symbols and Imagery*. Amsterdam: North-Holland, 1974.

White, T. H., ed. and trans. *The Bestiary: A Book of Beasts, Being a Translation from a Latin Bestiary of the Twelfth Century*. London: Jonathan Cape, 1954.

4

The Roc

Douglas J. McMillan

The roc (rukh) is a huge fabulous bird which can fly carrying an elephant and is best known in the Western world through its appearances in both the *Arabian Nights* and the *Travels of Marco Polo*. It seems, also, however, to be related to solar myths of the eagle, to the anka ('anḳā', 'anqā', anqua) of Arabia, to the simurgh (sīmorgh) of Persia, to the garuda (garida) of India, to the phoenix of Egypt, to the albatross and heron (and to other large real birds), to huge birds of European and Native American folktales, and just possibly even to Big Bird of *Sesame Street*. The roc is a huge white bird, and it looks something like an eagle, vulture, condor, or albatross; yet it is much, much larger than even these large birds. The wings of the roc are said to spread over sixteen paces (yards?) and the feathers are said to be over eight paces long. Indeed, the roc is so large that it not only can lift a full-grown person high into the air, but it can (so it is said) easily lift three full-grown elephants high into the air. Actually, carrying persons or elephants through the air, over seas, on to mountains seems to be one of the major tasks of the roc. The egg of the roc is said to be over fifty paces in circumference.

We learn first of the fabulous roc from Arabia and China. Then we learn of roclike birds in European and Native American folktales. Finally, we learn of the roc of Arabia in modern children's stories and in contemporary science fiction. Many persons believe that the roc of literature and lore is based on a real bird such as an eagle. This may be true, of course. But also possibly true is the hypothesis that the roc represents a mythical creation of human aspiration to be like the sun, to leave the earth, to escape the ordinary, to get to "heaven." In addition, it is also possible that the roc represents a human wish to be helped by a bird (a real bird and/or an agent of deity). I doubt that we will ever know what ingredients actually went into the "original" creation of the roc; whatever they were, we are most grateful for the "existence" of the roc, for it is truly one of the most wonderful birds in the world. The name "roc" or "rukh," according to Burton, is Persian and means among other things a "cheek," a "rook" (hero) in chess, and a "rhinoceros" (4:2093).

Let us now attempt to look more deeply into some of the major possible explanations for the origin of the roc. One possibility is that the roc is a variation on the anka, a phoenixlike fabulous bird of Arabia. The anka was believed by the Arabs to have been created by God originally as a perfect bird but one that later became a plague. The anka merged with the Persian simurgh and possibly with the Indian garuda. Some Arabic authors describe the anka but acknowledge that it is extinct. Other Arabic authors say that the Fatimids had heronlike ankas in their zoos (Pellat 509). Although the anka is phoenixlike (it lived 1,700 years and then burned itself), it is particularly distinguished by its huge size and by its ability to carry off an elephant (Ingersoll 198–99). Perhaps this specialty of the anka gave rise to the belief in the separate, non-phoenixlike bird, the eaglelike bird called the roc (Carrington 92).

It is also possible that the roc is one manifestation of an ornithological solar myth including the eagle, the anka, the simurgh, the garuda, and the phoenix: they "are all, apparently, members of the brood hatched ages ago in that same sunrise nest and still flying amid rosy clouds of prehistoric fable" (Ingersoll 202).

Another possibility is that the roc was created to explain showers of meteorites, for some stories of the roc portray the bird as carrying huge stones and dropping them, particularly on ships. The assumption is that premodern people would explain the meteorites by creating vengeful giant bird-gods (rocs) which sometimes drop stones out of the sky (Carrington 93).

Yet another theory holds that the roc and the now extinct Aepyornis bird (*Aepyornis maximus*—great giant bird, nicknamed "elephant-bird") of Madagascar are identical. Unfortunately for that theory, the Aepyornis was a huge running bird, not a huge flying bird (Heuvelmans 501–3). However, Arab explorers may have seen Aepyornis (and perhaps the dodo and other large birds) on their travels and may have created the tale of the roc or recreated the tale of the anka based on what they had actually seen by way of fifteen-foot-tall birds with proportionately large eggs (Wendt 141). David Attenborough visited Madagascar some years ago and found pieces of an Aepyornis egg. He reconstructed an egg from the pieces (which he estimated to be anywhere from two or three centuries to several thousand years old). "The complete egg was of astonishing size. In length it was almost exactly a foot. Its girth was 27 inches; its longest circumference, measuring over the two ends, 32 inches" (Attenborough 42).

Yet another possibility is that the roc developed via oral tradition from mythology into folklore before being recorded in literature. According to Anthony S. Mercatante, "Arabic folklore, based in part on Persian mythology, developed the Roc" (206). There may also be some Asian source (possibly the Chinese phoenix [fêng-huang], the Japanese hō-ō [a phoenixlike bird], or the Indian garuda) for the roc of Arabia, but what the source of that source may be must remain as tantalizing and as wondrous as the roc itself.

Turning now to a brief historical survey of the appearances and manifestations of the roc in different cultures, we find the earliest literary mention of this fabulous bird in the *Arabian Nights*, suggesting that this giant bird of legend has been famous for at least a thousand years (Carrington 89). Indeed, the story without the name of the roc appears in the *Jatakas*, the great compendium of tales of India, dating from the fourth century B.C. at the latest (Armstrong, *Folklore* 128). This takes the story, if not the bird, back almost 2,400 years. Also, Herodotus (ca. 484 B.C.–ca. 424 B.C.) was told by priests of Egypt about giant birds which were so huge they could carry off a person (Heuvelmans 500). From the East, crusaders brought the story of the roc back to Europe in the Middle Ages (Clébert 333), and Marco Polo described the roc in detail in the thirteenth century (Attenborough 32).

Admiral Etienne de Flacourt, governor of Madagascar and director of the French East India Company, published in 1658 *Histoire de la Grande Isle de Madagascar*, the first book about the island, in which he described a giant bird, the *vouron patra*, which lived in southern Madagascar. He called the bird a species of ostrich (Attenborough 33). In 1851, on the evidence of eggs and bones, the earlier "existence of a giant bird in Madagascar was at last officially admitted"; and in 1866, the "huge bones in a perfect state of preservation" were revealed to be those of Aepyornis (Heuvelmans 502). Many attempts were made to prove that the Aepyornis and the roc were identical, "but . . . unlike the legendary roc, it [Aepyornis] could no more fly than the ostrich, cassowary, emu and other running birds" (Heuvelmans 503). For a slightly different historical view of the study of Aepyornis and its possible relevance to the legend of the roc see Wendt (141–45), and for the exciting contemporary eyewitness exploration of traces of the giant birds see Attenborough (31–43). In modern times the roc or a roclike bird has appeared in European and Native American folktales and in children's stories and science fiction writing.

The symbolism suggested by the roc seems limited in comparison to that of some other fabulous birds and beasts, yet there are several interesting possibilities. The roc may symbolize divine reward or punishment, the human desire to escape the here and now, the human desire to fly (particularly noteworthy in the days before the Wright brothers), and perhaps the human desire to follow the sun or to be with the sun or even to be the sun rising and setting. The symbolism is very broad and quite overpowering in its imaginative appeal, yet it is very human and understandable—it bridges the unknown and the known.

The wide occurrence of the roc in the lore of the world can best be attested through reference to Thompson, *Motif-Index of Folk-Literature*, in which one finds numerous references to the appearance of folk motifs concerning the roc in world oral tradition. Three motifs in volume one refer specifically to the roc: B31.1. *Roc*. A giant bird which carries off men in its claws; B31.1.1. *Roc's egg*; B31.1.2. *Roc drops rock on ship*. Beyond these specific references one finds the following related motifs: B30.1. *Mythical white albatross*; B30.2. *Mythical cock*; B31.1.0.1. *The bird Ziz*, Hebrew counterpart of roc; B31.2. *The Bird Gam*; B31.3. *Giant ravens*; B31.3.1. *Giant swimming raven*; B31.4. *Giant bat*; B31.5. *Simorg*: giant bird; B31.6. *Other giant birds*; and B31.6.1. *Giant blackbird*. One interested in the folklore of the roc should turn to these motif numbers in Thompson and also in Cross, *Motif-Index of Early Irish Literature*, where specific references to appearances of these motifs are to be found. The roc is indeed a major motif in world folk literature and in world oral culture. Wittkower notes, for example, that the Chukchee, a tribe from Siberia, tell roclike tales about a giant Noga-bird which eats reindeer, elks, persons, and whales. The same legends are also known in Alaska (Wittkower, *Allegory* 24).

The uses of the roc in art give us our visual sources for the appearance of this fabulous creature and for selected episodes in its activities. Attenborough provides a drawing, showing the roc much bigger than the elephant it has in its talons, entitled *The rukh: from* Americae pars quarta *by Theodor de Bry, 1594* (35); and in relation to his own adventures in Madagascar in search of traces of the big bird, Attenborough provides the drawing *A reconstruction of Aepyornis* (41) and two photographs, "a pile of egg fragments over a foot high" and "the completed Aepyornis Egg" (between 32 and 33). The 1594 drawing seems to be as close to a "typical" view of the roc as one is likely to get, and the Aepyornis illustrations are fascinating whatever their relationships to the roc and its legends may be.

Perhaps the most interesting combination of illustrations and discussions of the roc, however, is to be found in Wittkower's study " 'Roc': An Eastern Prodigy in a Dutch Engraving." The engraving is by the Italianized Dutch painter Johannes Stradanus (1523–1605) and is called *Magellan's Discovery of the Straits*. In the upper left corner there is a roc with an elephant in its talons. The roc is at least twice the size of the elephant, has eaglelike wings each double the length of the elephant's body, and has an enormous beak. The engraving must have been issued shortly before 1590 (206). Wittkower's illustration (95) is from a seventeenth-century edition. Wittkower provides another illustration (93) showing that Stradanus' representation of the roc was changed from an account of exploration and history to an ornithological bird of fable classification in Ulisse Aldrovandi's *Ornithologia* (1599). Here again the roc with an elephant in its talons is shown.

A modern illustration of the underside of a flying roc with four children tied to its legs can be seen in *Magic by the Lake* (Eager 139). (An illustration of the simurgh showing it bigger than a person and with an impressive tail more than twice the length of its body from a Persian manuscript of the *Shāhnāmah*, dated 1587–88, now in the Metropolitan Museum of Art, is reproduced as plate 37 in Gray, opposite p. 290. An illustration of an ebony carving of the eaglelike garuda can be seen as plate 16 in Gray, opposite p. 140.) Also, an awe-inspiring huge grey eaglelike roc in flight with a tent and person on its back can be seen in color (along with a relatively miniature basilisk, phoenix, unicorn, Scythian lamb, and dragon) among fabulous creatures from a children's picture book by F. J. Bertuch, reproduced in Mode (19). It is important to note too that illustrations of the roc appear in some editions of the *Arabian Nights*.

It is, however, in literature (written and oral) that we find our best sources of information on the roc. The literary base for stories of the roc is the *Arabian Nights*, also called *The Book of the Thousand Nights and a Night* (although older in oral tradition, the work was first collected and compiled between 988 and 1011). In this entry references to this work are to the translation and scholarly edition by Richard F. Burton.

On the 404th Arabian night we hear Abd al-Rahman's story of the roc. A man from West Africa was lost on an island. When he finally returned home he brought the quill of a wing-feather of an unhatched roc; the wing of the chick is said to be a thousand fathoms long (Burton 3:1691).

On the 405th Arabian night we hear that Abd al-Rahman on a voyage in the China seas went ashore on an island with a huge, gleaming white dome, a hundred cubits long. He and his companions discovered that the dome was a roc's egg, and they broke it open and removed one of the wing-feathers from the chick. They left the island with the chick, but the parent roc followed them and dropped a stone bigger than the ship. Luckily it missed the ship, and the crew was safe. Then members of the crew cooked the chick and ate it and magically their youth was restored or retained (Burton 3:1692).

On the 543rd Arabian night we hear the tale of Sinbad's second voyage. Sinbad had been left on an island where he eventually saw a huge white dome fifty paces in circumference. Suddenly the sun was blotted out by the appearance of an enormous bird in the sky (Burton 4:2025–26). This story continues on the 544th Arabian night when Sinbad remembers a story he had heard about the immense bird called the roc which feeds its young with elephants. Looking again at the dome, Sinbad determined that it was a roc's egg. Then the parent roc settled on its egg, and Sinbad tied himself to the sleeping roc's legs in an attempt to escape from the island. In the morning, the roc flew away and finally landed on a high hill where Sinbad escaped. The roc picked up a huge serpent and flew off (Burton 4:2026–27).

On the 556th Arabian night we hear the tale of the fifth voyage of Sinbad. One day Sinbad and others came to an island on which they saw an immense white dome. The merchants went ashore to examine the dome while Sinbad remained on the ship. The merchants discovered that it was a roc's egg, broke it open, killed the chick, and removed large portions of meat. Sinbad tried to stop this activity in order to prevent retribution from the parent roc, but to no avail. Finally two rocs flew over the ship, circling. Sinbad tried to sail away. The rocs returned with very large boulders. The she-roc had the bigger boulder, which struck the poop of the ship, breaking the rudder. All aboard were thrown into the sea, but Sinbad found a plank and made his way to an island (Burton 4:2056–58).

The *Arabian Nights* is not, of course, the only Arabic work in which the story of the roc is told. The roc also appears in some Arabic scientific works. For example, it is to be found in Al Kazwini's geography and in Ibn Al Wardi's natural history, both of the thirteenth century (Costello 85).

The second core literary source for information on the roc is found in Marco Polo's *Travels* (ca. 1298–99). Within book 3 (Japan and Archipelago, Southern India, and the Coasts and Islands of the Indian Sea), chapter 33 is titled "Of the Great Island of Madagascar." Marco Polo notes that the people of the island say that at a certain time of year the roc makes an appearance from the south. It is said to resemble an eagle, although it is so much larger that it can carry elephants into the air in order to kill them by dropping them. Those who have seen the bird say that the spread wings measure sixteen paces and the feathers measure eight paces. Marco Polo thought such birds might be griffins but emphasized that they did not resemble the traditional griffin, which is a combination of lion and eagle. (See the entry on the griffin.) He questioned those who had seen these birds, and they insisted they were totally birdlike, eaglelike. Later when the great khan heard about the roc, he sent messengers to Madagascar (who pretended to seek the release of one of the khan's servants) to investigate the roc. They returned to the khan with a roc feather that measured ninety spans and that gave the khan great pleasure to own (313–14).

Although the roc has not appeared in Western literature as frequently as the gorgons, the sphinx, the griffin, and some other fabulous creatures, its appeal has been continuous in the West, particularly (it seems) after the first European translations of the *Arabian Nights*. The main entry for "roc" in *The Oxford English Dictionary* corroborates this with representative references to written appearances of the roc for the years 1579, 1598, 1621, 1631, 1635, 1691, 1774, 1802, 1839–52, 1841, 1855, and 1865. Not listed in the *OED* but of particular additional interest is the reference which Michael Drayton (1563--1631) makes to the roc in his poem "Noah's Flood": among the beasts and birds brought to the ark by the angels, Drayton chooses to name particularly the largest, the roc, and the smallest, the wren, in lines 447–52:

> All feathered things yet ever knowne to men,
> From the huge Rucke, unto the little Wren;
> From Forrests, Fields, from Rivers, and from Pons,
> All that have webs, or cloven-footed ones;
> To the Grand Arke, together friendly came,
> Whose severall species were too long to name.
>
> (Drayton 338)

From the world of folk literature we should note first a Native American mythological analogue to the roc story from the Jicarilla Apache tribe. In "The Attack on the Giant Elk" (Thompson, ed.) we hear about a giant "eagle" which devoured people. A hero killed the parent eagles and struck the eaglets on their heads, preventing their full growth. All of this is said to have happened, of course, in "the early days." The giant male eagle's wing bones were as large as a man's arm (101–3). There are many other Native American tales of this sort, particularly in the Southwest, on the plains, and on the plateaus (318–19, n. 151). Also from the world of folk literature we should note two folk analogues to the roc story from the Brothers Grimm collection. In "Snow-White and Rose-Red" the two girls see a huge bird soaring in the air. Finally the "eagle" seized a dwarf, but the children prevented it from carrying the dwarf off (531). In "Foundling Bird" we hear of a gamekeeper who found a child up in a tall tree. A bird of prey had carried the child in its beak from the ground up into the tall tree. The gamekeeper, therefore, named the child Foundling Bird (185–86). And a very contemporary analogue to the roc story may just possibly be seen Monday through Friday in the form of Big Bird on the television show *Sesame Street*.

Although certainly not called a roc, the albatross in Samuel Taylor Coleridge's *The Rime of the Ancient Mariner* suggests something of the sea connection and mystery of the roc. So too does Herman Melville's apotheosis of the albatross (*Moby-Dick*, ch. 42, n. 2) suggest something of the roc of Arabia. The connections of Coleridge and Melville to the albatross are brilliantly discussed by Lowes (202–7, 484–85, 516–17). It would not take much imagination to make many more cautious literary connections to the roc.

There is a wonderful example in contemporary children's literature of a modern use of the roc based on the *Arabian Nights*. Chapter 7 ("The Treasure") in Edward Eager's *Magic by the Lake* begins with four children wishing they could find buried treasure. They are carried by magic to an island which they mistake for Treasure Island. Katharine recognizes the island, however, from a picture in one of her books at home. Mark identifies that book as the *Arabian Nights* and the island as one on which Sinbad had found a roc's egg. The children then see an enormous round white object. They hope a roc is near that would appear and fly them away from the island. The roc then does appear as an immense cloud darkening the sun. When the roc descends and goes to sleep, Mark ties himself to one claw using the belt from his blue jeans, Jane and Katharine use their hair ribbons, and Martha uses Jane's long white socks. Finally the roc awakes; it makes a loud cry, and rises from the egg with the children attached to its claws. They fly over a sea, a vast continent with a field and forest, a city, and then another forest. The roc hovers low over a clearing in the forest for just an instant, and the children free themselves and jump to the soft earth. The roc wings away (143–49). The rest of the adventures in this story involve not the roc, but Ali Baba's cave and the genie.

A fitting final modern appearance of the roc can be noted in the science fiction account of a zoo in the future with animals from the past by Larry Niven called "Bird in the Hand." In this story we have the traditional picture and account of the roc including the elephant connection (173). Here is the roc of the past, in our present, yet in a future zoo. Surely this is not the "final" appearance of the roc in literature.

The major studies of the roc include Armstrong's two books (lore, literature, art, nature) and the books by Attenborough (Madagascar), Burton (*Arabian Nights*), Costello (natural history and bibliography), Ingersoll (lore), and Wittkower (art and symbolism).

The huge roc has fascinated audiences from Arabia to Persia to Europe and to America from at least a thousand years ago. And the roc seems to be a lasting and continuing theme in contemporary scholarship and in contemporary creative writing.

BIBLIOGRAPHY

Armstrong, Edward A. *The Folklore of Birds: An Enquiry into the Origin and Distribution of Some Magico-Religious Traditions*. The New Naturalist: A Survey of British Natural History. London: Collins, 1958.

————. *The Life and Lore of the Bird: In Nature, Art, Myth, and Literature*. A Chanticleer Press Edition. New York: Crown, 1975.

Attenborough, David. "The Giant Birds." In *Bridge to the Past: Animals and People of Madagascar*. (In Great Britain published under the title: *Zoo Quest to Madagascar*). New York: Harper and Row, 1961. 31–43.

Borges, Jorge Luis, with Margarita Guerrero. "The Rukh." In *The Book of Imaginary Beings*. Trans. Thomas di Giovanni. New York: Discus-Avon, 1970. 192–93.

Burton, Richard F., trans. *The Book of the Thousand Nights and a Night: A Plain and Literal Translation of the Arabian Nights Entertainments*. 6 vols. in 3. 1934; rpt. New York: Heritage, 1962. Vols. 3–4.

Carrington, Richard. *Mermaids and Mastodons: A Book of Natural and Unnatural History*. New York: Rinehart, 1957.

Clébert, Jean-Paul. "Rokh." In *Bestiaire fabuleux*. Paris: Albin Michel, 1971. 333.

Costello, Peter. *The Magic Zoo: The Natural History of Fabulous Animals*. New York: St. Martin's, 1979.

Cross, Tom Peete. *Motif-Index of Early Irish Literature*. n.d.; rpt. New York: Kraus, 1969.

Drayton, Michael. *The Works of Michael Drayton*. Ed. J. William Hebel. Oxford: Basil Blackwell, 1961. Vol. 3.

Eager, Edward. *Magic by the Lake*. New York: Harcourt, 1957.

Gray, Herbert, ed. *The Mythology of All Races*. Boston: Archaeological Institute, 1932. Vol. 6.

Grimm, Jacob and Wilhelm. "Snow-White and Rose-Red," no. 161, and "Foundling Bird," no. 51. In *The Grimms' German Folk Tales* (1857). Trans. Francis P. Magoun, Jr., and Alexander H. Krappe. Carbondale: Southern Illinois University Press, 1960. 526–32, 185–87.

Heuvelmans, Bernard. *On the Track of Unknown Animals*. Trans. Richard Garnett. New York: Hill and Wang, 1959.

Ingersoll, Ernest. *Birds in Legend, Fable and Folklore*. 1923; rpt. Detroit: Singing Tree Press, 1968.

Lowes, John Livingston. *The Road to Xanadu: A Study in the Ways of the Imagination*. 1927; rpt. Boston: Houghton Mifflin, 1964.

Mercatante, Anthony S. *Zoo of the Gods: Animals in Myth, Legend and Fable*. New York: Harper and Row, 1974.

Mode, Heinz. *Fabulous Beasts and Demons*. London: Phaidon, 1975.

Niven, Larry. "Bird in the Hand" (1970). Rpt. in *Phoenix Feathers: A Collection of Mythical Monsters*. Ed. Barbara Silverberg. New York: Dutton, 1973. 151–76.

Pellat, Charles. " 'Anḳā'." *The Encyclopaedia of Islam*. New ed. Leiden: Brill, 1961. 1:509.

Polo, Marco. *The Travels of Marco Polo [The Venetian]: Revised from Marsden's Translation*. Ed. Manuel Komroff. New York: Liveright, 1930.

Thompson, Stith. *Motif-Index of Folk-Literature*. Rev. and enl. ed. 6 vols. Bloomington: Indiana University Press, 1955–58.

———, ed. "The Attack on the Giant Elk." In *Tales of the North American Indians*. 1929; rpt. Bloomington: Indiana University Press, 1966. 101–4, 318–19.

Wendt, Herbert. *Out of Noah's Ark: The Story of Man's Discovery of the Animal Kingdom*. Trans. Michael Bullock. Boston: Houghton Mifflin, 1959.

Wittkower, Rudolf. " 'Roc': An Eastern Prodigy in a Dutch Engraving." In *Allegory and the Migration of Symbols*. Boulder, Colo.: Westview, 1977. 93–96, 206–7.

5

The Griffin

_____ **Waltraud Bartscht**

"This is called a GRIFFIN because it is a winged quadruped. This kind of wild animal is born in Hyperborean parts, or in mountains. All its bodily members are like a lion's, but its wings and mask are like an eagle's. It is vehemently hostile to horses. But it will also tear to pieces any human beings which it happens to come across" (White 22–24). These words from a medieval bestiary describe one of the most enigmatic creatures in the kingdom of fabulous animals. An ambiguous being, the griffin combines the qualities of bird and beast, heaven and earth, good and evil. It can be aggressor or victim, marauder or guardian.

The concept of the griffin, also called gryphon, originated somewhere in the Middle East at least five thousand years ago. Long before written words could refer to it, its likeness was depicted in stone, ivory, silk, felt, bronze, silver, and gold; it could be found on vases, palace walls, mosaic floors, and in tombs. By means of trade routes, conquering armies, and migrating tribes, the griffin image traveled from the highlands of Iran eastward to the Himalayas and into China, westward as far as the coast of Ireland. During the Middle Ages, griffins appeared frequently on coats of arms, in manuscripts, and on cathedral walls. Most people took the griffin's physical existence for granted. But in the intellectual revolution of the sixteenth century, doubts began to rise about all the fabulous creatures that were said to populate remote parts of the ancient world. By the end of the seventeenth century, it had become an accepted fact that there were no such beasts as griffins in nature. This does not mean that they had ceased to capture the human imagination; to this very day, griffins are still very much with us.

Whenever daily life threatens to become too rational and science attempts to explain away all the mysteries of the universe, the human spirit resorts to fantasy as if to counteract the intellectual desiccation. New myths are created and old ones revitalized. This may be one reason for the current interest in fabulous beasts such as the unicorn, the dragon, and the griffin.

Since the late 1950s, a fairly large number of studies on the griffin have been published, some of them book-length. One of the most appealing works is Joe Nigg's *Book of Gryphons* (1982). The author has lovingly traced the history of the composite beast, which he calls ''the most majestic of all mythical creatures,'' from its advent in the Near East to the present time. Although the book does not go into great detail, it quotes a large number of literary sources and is magnificently illustrated with griffin images, from Assyrian temple walls to contemporary logotypes. An Italian study, *Il grifone* (1965) by Anna M. Bisi, offers an extensive history of griffin iconography in the ancient Eastern Mediterranean. Bisi's very informative text is augmented with excellent line drawings and photographs. A German dissertation by Ingeborg Flagge, later published under the title *Untersuchungen zur Bedeutung des Greifen* (1975), complements Bisi's work by including Roman and Etruscan griffin effigies and by exploring their mythological and ritual significance.

While the griffin is the exclusive subject of these books, it is just one of many creatures which Peter Costello examines in *The Magic Zoo: The Natural History of Fabulous Animals* (1979). Emphasizing historical accounts, Costello tries to ascertain which real animals could have been the models for imaginary beasts.

Two more works deserve to be mentioned. *Fabulous Beasts and Demons* by Heinz Mode (1975), with a profusion of beautiful pictures, classifies types of monsters from many cultures and offers some speculations about their origin. Rudolf Wittkower's *Allegory and the Migration of Symbols* (1977), also richly illustrated, stresses the relationship between Western and Eastern cultures in the interpretation of their iconography.

The griffin's form and nature vary from culture to culture, revealing the outlook and values of different societies (Nigg 19). Most frequently, it is shown with a lion's hindquarters; but it can also have the legs of a panther or of a dog, or even the tail of a dragon or a serpent. When its beak is shown open, it may display a tongue and teeth; on its handsome head it can wear a peacock's crest or ram's horns, a royal crown, or merely a decorative knob, as in most Greek representations. Although the griffin is counted among the birds, it is often shown with ears to indicate its keen sense of hearing; Scythian griffins have antelope horns as a symbol for swiftness. The neck of the griffin can be adorned with a row of spikes (as in Etruscan art) or with a lion's or a horses's mane; sometimes a beardlike tuft of feathers appears under its beak.

An unusual type of griffin can be found in English heraldry. It has no wings, but sharp spikes in groups of three sprouting from its body. One of these so-called ''male'' griffins supports the coat of arms of Anne Boleyn, the ill-fated wife of Henry VIII (Dennys, *Heraldry* 121–22). Another heraldic animal, the opinicus, is also a variant form of the griffin. Only its head and wings resemble an eagle, while its body and legs are those of a lion; its tail, which is short and thin and has a little tuft on the end, has some resemblance to a camel's tail

(Dennys, *Heraldic Imagination* 177, 180). Although griffins are the deadly enemies of horses, there is one hybrid offspring of the two, the hippogryph, which has the head, wings, and front legs of a griffin and the back and hind legs of a horse. "Unknown to antiquity, this monster was a creation of the poets of the late middle ages" (Hall 154). As one of several variants of the flying horse, the hippogryph has a connection with the winged Pegasus of Greece, the eight-legged Sleipnir belonging to the Norse god Odin, and the silver horse that was given to Mohammed by the Angel Gabriel (Nigg 32, 34).

One scholar, H. Prinz, has tried to classify the various permutations into the categories of bird-griffin, snake-griffin, and lion-griffin. But Heinz Mode argues that the snake-griffin and the lion-griffin are nothing but variants of the dragon, since both are usually shown with reptilelike scales covering their bodies. Only the bird-griffin, which has a bird's head and a lion's body, should deserve the name "griffin," whether it is shown with or without wings (Mode 128–29). Perhaps such a rigorous classification is impossible. For one thing, some dragons on Chinese artifacts strongly resemble griffins; also, as Karl Bartsch points out, medieval texts do not always make a clear distinction between griffins and dragons; sometimes the terms are interchangeable (see Karl Bartsch's introduction to *Herzog Ernst* cliv). As a composite figure, the griffin is related to the sphinx, the chimera, the harpies, and similar monsters which originated about the same time and in the same region of Western Asia.

The griffin's temper is thought to match its fierce countenance. The creature is belligerent, rapacious, and vigilant. When entrusted with guardianship, it is protective and, occasionally, even gentle; as an avenger, it is relentless in the pursuit of evildoers. These traits may account for the fact that the griffin image has been used as an emblem since classical antiquity. Joe Nigg explains the griffin's appeal: "Possessing the strength of heroes and the splendor of gods, the Gryphon is a natural choice as a heraldic animal. A regal beast, the Gryphon has always been associated with the rulers of earth and sky, from Pharaoh and the Cretan kings to Alexander the Great, and even God" (84). After having appeared on royal seals and coins in ancient times, the griffin image was chosen by Christian noblemen to be emblazoned on their arms—the knights may have been impressed by Arabian traditions during the Crusades. One of the earliest heraldic griffins is found on the shield of Richard de Revers, Earl of Exeter, in 1167 (Nigg 82). The use of griffins and griffin heads flourished especially between the fifteenth and the seventeenth centuries. A work compiled in the early part of the seventeenth century lists eighty-six griffins and three demi-griffins "in English arms alone" (see Dennys, *Heraldic Imagination* 176–77). Even today, griffins are in favor as emblems for business firms, from insurance companies to publishing houses.

The griffin's prevalence in heraldry is probably the reason for many family names derived from it, such as Grifford, Griffen, Griffith, and the regular Griffin, filling a large number of columns in some English or American telephone books. The German form *Greif* is just as widespread in the central European countries.

Sometimes is it latinized as *Gryphius*, the form preferred by a famous German Baroque poet. In Germany, Austria, and Switzerland there is also an abundance of place names related to the griffin, such as Greifswald, Greifenberg, Greifenhagen, Greifensee, and many more.

The name "gryphon" or "griffin" is borrowed from the Greek word *grups*, a griffin (Latin *gryphus*). There is a possibility that *grups* is related to the Greek word *grupos*, which means "hooked" and "curved." The Brothers Grimm presumed that the Greek word *grups*, together with the concept, was borrowed from oriental languages, for example the Assyrian *k'rub*, "winged fabulous being," or Hebrew *kerub*, "winged angel" (*Deutsches Wörterbuch*, cols. 5–6). There may be a connection to the German word *greifen*, "to seize," and the English *grip*, but I have not been able to verify it. The German language still has the term *Greifvögel* for all birds of prey such as eagles, hawks, falcons, or vultures. There is a good reason to believe that such birds were prototypes of the mythical griffin and that its leonine attributes are a later embellishment.

Fabulous birds have been part of ancient mythologies for thousands of years. It seems that primitive tribes all over the world venerated the sun or the sky in the effigy of a large bird, but, as Heinz Mode states, only more advanced civilizations were capable of combining several divine attributes and of representing them by means of compound images (12). One of those is the heavenly bird Garuda from India, part eagle, part man, and a symbol of speed and strength; he is the son of heaven and king of all the birds. According to certain Vedic texts, Garuda is even older than Vishnu, the anthropomorphic god of Hindu mythology with whom he is usually associated (*Indische Märchen* 5, 344–66). Garuda's primeval struggle against the nagas, or snakes, may be the basis for a legendary feat ascribed to many fabulous birds. Perhaps derived from a physical analogy, the Hindu word for "snake" is the same as that for "elephant" (*Indische Märchen* 88). Used as a pun in ancient Indian tales, this could be the origin of stories about gigantic birds that can carry elephants into the air.

Folklore from Persia and Turkey also contains an ancient bird of divine origin, the senmurv or simurgh. Sometimes the simurgh is shown with a human face, perhaps because of the Muslim belief in its power of speech and reasoning. According to popular tradition, the simurgh lives for two thousand years. It is so large that its wingspread darkens the sunlight, and it is strong enough to carry a camel or an elephant (*Märchen aus Turkestan und Tibet* 296). It shares this trait with Garuda, with the legendary roc (a gigantic bird often mentioned in Arabian fairy tales), and with the gryphon bird (described by Marco Polo and apparently the same creature as the roc). Traces of these legends can even be found in the Jewish tradition, where rabbinical writings refer to the ziz, a huge creature similar to the other fabulous birds (Costello 82). It is peculiar that griffins seem to be confined to the continents of Asia, Africa, and Europe; indigenous American cultures know of winged snakes and many other monsters, but not of griffins.

Some scholars believe that the mythical griffin might have its origin in vague collective memories of an early flying reptile like the pterodactyl or a prehistoric bird like the archaeopteryx. Others point out that the tusks of an extinct Siberian animal had once been thought to be griffin claws. But Costello is not satisfied with these explanations. In his opinion there is only one bird that comes close to the descriptions ancient observers gave of the griffin, the Lammergeier or bearded vulture, *Gypaetus barbatus aureus* (80). At home in the mountains of Southern Europe, Central Asia, and parts of Africa, the areas where the "griffins" were first reported to live, "this largest old-world bird of prey . . . has a tuft of long bristly hairs on the chin, and stiff bristles hide the nostrils. It is blackish-grey above, otherwise pale tawny; the white cap is bordered black" ("Lammergeier," *Encyclopaedia Britannica*). The body of the bird measures between forty and forty-six inches, and its wingspread is close to ten feet. There are tales of the Lammergeier carrying away lambs (hence the name) or young children, but zoologists say there is no basis for the allegation. At any rate, it is a fierce and impressive creature and, according to Costello, "a worthy original of the griffin of legend" (80). Whether one accepts or rejects his theory, it is easy to understand why prehistoric men may have conceived of large birds of prey as visible messengers of a divine or demonic power.

The first written reference to griffins was made by the Greek writer Aristeas of Proconnesus, who lived during the seventh century B.C. (For an excellent study of Aristeas, see Bolton). Aristeas had traveled deep into Central Asia in search of the Hyperboreans and their sanctuary of Apollo, worshiped in that region as a ruler of both light and darkness. In his travels, Aristeas encountered a tribe called the Issedonians, who told him about a mountain range, home of cold storms, to the north of their country. The Greek traveler thought those were the Caucasus Mountains, although modern scholars assume they were the Urals or even the Altai. Rivers of that area were said to bear gold, and a race of one-eyed men, called Arimaspoi, habitually stole this gold from swift and ferocious monsters who guarded it. The Issedonian name for these monsters is not known, but Aristeas called them "griffins," using a term which his Greek audience would understand. The image of the griffin as a composite creature was already established in Greek art of that time; later writers adopted Aristeas' name for the gold-guarding monsters without question. The Arimaspoi, or Arimaspians, as they are usually called in English, might have been Eurasian nomads or a tribe of gold miners wearing bright lamps on their foreheads. They were reputed to conduct their raids on horseback—hence the traditional hostility of the griffins against horses (Costello 73–76).

Herodotus, living about two hundred years after Aristeas, repeated the story of the griffins (*History* 3.116). Ctesias of Knidos, a Greek physician slightly younger than Herodotus, wrote a geographical treatise on India that was accepted as a factual account for many centuries. Among many other marvels, Ctesias gave this detailed description of the griffin: "a race of four-footed birds, almost as large as wolves, having legs and claws like those of a lion and covered all over the body with black feathers, except only on the breast, where they are red'' (qtd. in Costello 76). The plumage corresponds somewhat to that of the Lammergeier; but the image of a four-footed bird may well have originated in the art work which Ctesias could see at the royal court in Persepolis, where he lived for many years. It was also Ctesias who claimed that the griffin could "only be conquered by the lion and the elephant" (Vries 229). The Roman writer Claudius Aelian, writing a few centuries after Ctesias, claims in his book *On the Characteristics of Animals* that griffins have white wings and variegated necks "with feathers of a dark blue" (4.27).

Later writers relied mostly on Aristeas and Herodotus as authoritative witnesses for their own reports, especially Pliny the Elder in his *Natural History*, completed in A.D. 77. According to Pliny, the griffin is "a kind of wild beast with wings . . . that digs gold out of mines, which the creatures guard and the Arimaspi try to take from them, both with remarkable covetousness" (7.2.10). With each recounting the story became more elaborate. In the ancient world, Scythia was considered the most abundant source of gold, and griffins were frequently portrayed on Scythian artifacts. So it is understandable that people thought griffins were hunting for treasure in the Caucasus Mountains, making their nests of gold and laying agate eggs in them (Nigg 50–52).

Well into the Christian Middle Ages, most people accepted the veracity of the ancient reports, although not even Aristeas had claimed that he ever laid eyes on a griffin. The bird was represented in countless bestiaries, together with other animals, fabulous or real. Creatures catalogued in these books were divided into "good" and "wicked," symbolizing human virtues and vices. As Margaret Blount remarks, "it did not particularly matter if certain animals existed at all— the important thing was what they *meant*" (96). The griffin was usually counted among the wicked, but some authors conceded its good qualities. For example, according to Beryl Rowland, "the griffin was made the emblem of *scientia* or knowledge" because it knew where gold could be found. She also adds that "the alleged habit of building its nest of gold was sometimes construed as generosity" (71). This interpretation disregards the griffin's jealous guardianship of the gold; but then the griffin's role has always been ambivalent.

Marco Polo, who traveled as far as China during the thirteenth century, was one of the first writers to attempt a modicum of realism. After hearing of some gigantic birds that were known to the inhabitants of Madagascar, he decided that they must be "gryphons." He took great pains to point out that they were not "a blend of bird and lion; but . . . in build they are just like eagles but of the most colossal size" (274). Traditional griffins were familiar to him not only from stories but also from images on the walls of Saint Mark's Cathedral in Venice and from illustrated manuscripts (for example, bestiaries or devotional books); decorated initials showed all kinds of fabulous animals; and St. Mark's emblem, the winged lion, often resembled a griffin. As Wittkower notes, Marco Polo "compares his actual experience with, and often rejects, the traditional image; but sometimes the traditional image colours or even submerges his true impressions'' (86). This happens especially when Marco Polo has not personally seen what he describes. His report on the gryphon bird is evidently based on Islamic stories. He says that in Madagascar this bird is called the "rukh"—a term for the roc bird (see the entry on the roc). According to Polo, these birds are so strong "that one of them can pounce on an elephant and carry it up to a great height in the air. Then it lets go, so that the elephant drops to earth and is smashed to pulp, whereupon the gryphon bird perches on the carcase and feeds at its ease" (274). In general, however, Marco Polo's chronicles were so realistic that they disappointed his readers' expectations and therefore met with incredulity.

Much more appealing was *Mandeville's Travels*, also first published in the fourteenth century. Mandeville (the identity of the author is uncertain) wrote about a journey to Africa and Asia—which may have never occurred—replete with tales of marvels and fabulous races, both human and animal. Numerous illuminated manuscripts attest to the popularity of the work; and, after the invention of printing, it appeared in many editions illustrated with woodcuts. Naturally, Mandeville mentions griffins, and they are at least as formidable as their ancestors: "But one griffon hath the body more great and is more strong than eight lions . . . and more great and stronger than a hundred eagles. For one griffon there will bear flying to his nest a great horse . . . or two oxen yoked together as they go at the plough" (207–8). He adds that the talons of these creatures are as long as the horns of oxen and are big enough to be used as drinking cups.

Such stories supported medieval notions which not only took fabulous beasts for real but attributed healing power to their body parts. Like the horn of the unicorn, the claw of a griffin was supposed to possess magical faculties (Shepard 130–31). Made into a drinking cup, a claw was said to change color when it came into contact with poison. To acquire such a claw was not easy, of course. Only a holy man who had cured a griffin of an illness could receive one as a reward for his kindness. Many such alleged griffin claws were known during the Middle Ages—in actuality they were animal horns, often elaborately combined with gold and precious stones. A griffin's feather, passed before the patient's eyes, allegedly could heal blindness. An early German medical manual even prescribed putting a live griffin on a woman's breast as a means of curing infertility (Nigg 69, 71–72, 74).

Gradually, however, science began to question traditional lore. In the sixteenth century, Konrad Gesner published his *Historia animalium*, in which he attempted to document actual animals. In 1646, Sir Thomas Browne argued against the existence of many mythical beasts in his *Pseudodoxia Epidemica*. He asserted that the griffin was not an authentic animal but only a symbolic one. Although Andrew Ross tried six years later to refute Browne's statements with elaborate arguments and copious quotations from classical writers, it was in vain. After 1662, when the English Royal Society had been founded to promote scientific inquiry, empirical knowledge began to replace the venerable traditions, and soon the griffin was banished to the world of art and poetry, its original habitat (Nigg 87–94).

Visual representations of the griffin are actually much older than any written texts. Their meaning is not always clear, but their outward form, their relationship to other images, and the circumstances of their placement can serve as clues for interpretation.

The very earliest picture of a griffin has been found near Susa, a city in the ancient kingdom of Elam, now Iran. It was carved on a seal dating from about 3000 B.C.; a griffin seal from Byblos, hundreds of miles west of Susa, is not much younger (Mode 127; Nigg 39). Composite animal figures originated at this time among the highly developed civilizations of Mesopotamia and were transmitted to neighboring countries. Towards the end of the third millennium B.C. they appeared in northern Babylonia, influencing a succession of cultures in that region. Obviously, the demon images of Assyria and Syria, such as bird-men and winged lions, are close relatives of the griffin.

In Egypt, griffins occurred rather early, probably due to Sumerian and Elamitic influences. Ingeborg Flagge's study offers some interesting details on the subject. In predynastic times, about 3000 B.C., griffin images were carved on small personal articles where they may have had some magic or ritual connotations. Six hundred years later, in the Fifth Dynasty, the king himself was portrayed in the form of a griffin who crushes his enemies underfoot. This representation seems to express the immense strength of the ruler and his readiness for battle. It proclaims the king's valiant deeds during his lifetime and makes him the awe-inspiring guardian of his own tomb (12–13). The sun, as it rises anew every morning from the dark of night, was closely connected with Egyptian ideas of life's victory over death. According to some theories, the griffin may have denoted a union between the falcon-headed sun god and the feline goddess of night and the sky. In this form it would aid the pharaoh's soul in its ascent to heaven (13–14). In one Egyptian papyrus the griffin is acclaimed as the most powerful creature, "with the beak of a falcon, the eyes of a man, the body of a lion, the ears of a fish, the tail of a snake." Since it has attributes from every part of the animal kingdom, the griffin is the most powerful being, the shepherd and avenger of everything on earth (14–15). A variant of the Egyptian griffin is associated with Seth, the enemy of the sun god Horus. In this aspect the griffin represents the terrors of death, which is the inescapable fate of all living things. During the New Kingdom (after 1500 B.C.) Seth was gradually identified with the griffin image and thereby assimilated the positive aspects of Horus (20). So the Egyptian griffin became a mediator between light and darkness, good and evil.

The culture of Egypt apparently influenced Minoan art, which, in turn, affected other civilizations (Bisi 37). On the island of Crete, large painted griffins without wings adorned the walls of the throne room in the royal palace at Knossos (Evans 4:910–14). Griffins were also found painted on coffins and placed in special sacred association with the great Minoan goddess. In Flagge's interpretation, the demonic creature intensifies the power of the deity whom it serves as a companion or a guardian. The Cretan griffin does not have the warlike spirit of its Egyptian counterpart, but it is shown in pursuit of other animals and occasionally as a victim of the hunt. The griffin seems to be part of a negative power which has been defeated and tamed by the goddess; in this aspect it serves the souls of the dead as a guide into the other world (22, 24–25).

By 1500 B.C., griffins could be found on seals and ivory plaques, atop monumental columns, and as delicately wrought gold and silver ornaments all over Western Asia. At the palace of Tell Halaf, a griffin of black basalt with white limestone eyes escorted the Great Goddess of the Hittites who ruled the darkness of the heavens and the shadowy realm of the underworld. This figure "has been interpreted as both a bird of the sun and a symbol of the night sky" (Nigg 45–46). The griffin's composite nature, being both bird and beast, seems to invite such dualistic interpretations.

Although the griffin is fierce and strong, some of the ancient pictures show it as victim, defeated in the struggle against other animals or a human warrior. The latter scene may be a parallel to the mythical slaying of dragons or to Oedipus' victory over the sphinx. In Assyrian art, the bird-griffin often represents the "angel of death," which is vanquished by a deity with griffin head and human body (Flagge 46, 123). On Etruscan graves, fight scenes between animals involving griffins, lions, or cattle apparently symbolize the cruelty and terror of death. In contrast to this view, Greek sepulchral art shows griffins fighting with Arimaspians; but here the griffins represent the rising sun and the Arimaspians are forces of darkness. As symbols of Apollo, the griffins must be victorious (Flagge 124).

By the ninth century B.C., Assyrian art had adopted the griffin image and raised it to extraordinary prominence. It could be seen on monumental wall reliefs and, again, on seals and coins. Splendid examples of Assyrian gold jewelry adorned with griffins have been found at Ziwiyeh in northwestern Iran, part of a hoard that had been buried for more than two thousand years—it was accidentally discovered by a shepherd boy in 1946. In Anatolia and the Persian province of Luristan, home of a prehistoric tribe of horsemen whose name is not known, griffin figures were cast in bronze and used as ornaments for horses' bits (von Soden 83). They were probably meant to impart the griffin's legendary swiftness to the steeds.

The griffin image was established in Greek art by 1400 B.C. and became popular for many centuries. In Greece and in related pagan cultures, griffins were associated predominantly with Apollo, Dionysos, and Nemesis. The gold which the griffins were said to guard was identified with the rising sun; therefore, Apollo was shown riding on a griffin or using griffins to draw his chariot (Flagge 73–75, 125). In spring, when the sun returns from the land of the Hyperboreans and the light increases, plants begin to sprout again. The griffin's role as a guardian of the rising sun may have led to its connection with Dionysos, who was originally a god of vegetation (Flagge 83–85). When Greek influence was extended to Alexandria, the griffin became most intimately attached to the goddess Nemesis. Like Nemesis, the griffin was known as swift, ferocious, and a punisher of evildoers. It was often shown as her companion; a griffin with a wheel under its paw could even replace an image of the goddess (Flagge 106–21).

Over the centuries, the griffin was conveyed to every area under Greek influence; it followed Alexander the Great as far as India; it was adopted by the Etruscans and the Romans; and it was especially well received by the Scythians and Sarmatians. Some scholars assume that Greek traders introduced the griffin to these nomadic tribes north of the Black Sea by selling them silverware that was embossed with its image. It is true that whole colonies of Greek artisans worked for the Scythians and that a Graeco-Scythian style developed during the fourth century B.C. But Georges Charrière points out that there is probably as strong an influence from Iran, if any, as from Greece (184–85). The art of ancient Persia shows an abundance of griffin portrayals, from the time of Cyrus, 550 B.C., to the end of the Sassanian empire in A.D. 641, when it left its mark on the developing art of Islam. The area that is now Iran was famous for its elaborate metal pieces and for its rich fabrics, which were exported as far as Byzantium and Western Europe (Gardner 92). Many griffins found their way abroad on silver dishes and the splendid patterns of silk brocades.

Strange aggregates of animal and human forms had long been typical of the indigenous art of the steppes in Central Asia and could have served as ideograms in a culture without writing. Scythian and Sarmatian artists took the most prominent parts of an animal, such as wings, horns, or claws, and combined them into new images to express characteristics they admired (Charrière 134–40). The griffin is frequently shown as aggressor, attacking an ibex, a horse, or men. In all probability, Scythians identified with the strength, mobility, and ferocity of a beast that combined the attributes of two predators. Nomads preferred scenes with wild animals, unlike the settled peoples, who portrayed domesticated cattle or sheep.

Some of the images in this art of the steppes are quite lifelike, but more often they typify the so-called "animal style" which combines an observation of nature with completely abstract, geometric decoration and intricately interweaving forms. Charrière suggests that "the delirium of colors and forms" characteristic of Scythian art may have sprung from hallucinations induced by substances such as hashish, which was used as a tranquilizer during funeral rites (87–95). Other nomadic tribes were known for intoxicating drinks, an important element in their religious ceremonies, so Charrière's theory is not without foundation. But the "animal style" was sustained over such a long period of time and spread over such vast geographical areas that it must have more profound origins than mere hallucinatory experiences.

Wittkower points out that the steppes of the northern Asiatic land-mass, separated from urban civilizations by large mountain ranges, brought about a fairly uniform nomad culture reaching from China to Central Europe. Those semi-barbaric tribes played a significant role in the history of the ancient world, partly by periodic invasions, partly by trade relations. The nomads served, indirectly, as a connecting link between their southern and western neighbors. In Wittkower's words, "The interpenetration of nomad and high-culture art continued without interruption for over two thousand years" (14). It is therefore difficult to determine whether the fabulous birds of India and Persia are precursors of the Scythian griffins or whether they are their descendants.

The influence of nomad or "barbaric" art was especially strong after the fall of the Roman Empire, during the time of the Great Migrations between the fourth and the seventh centuries A.D. It continued after the wandering ethnic groups had accepted Christianity, settled in new homelands, and established the new social system of feudalism. Now the "animal style" merged with the vestiges of classical art and gradually evolved into the style known as Romanesque (Gardner 217–18, 226–27). The griffin had accompanied the migrating tribes on belt buckles, scabbards, and other portable objects. Now it made its transition from pagan to Christian iconography. With heathen gods being demoted to the rank of demons, the griffin became an emblem of Satan, the archenemy of men, who is constantly on the prowl in search of sinners. But griffin images were also placed on the outside walls of churches to ward off evil spirits, resuming their ancient function of guardians and protectors. Again, the symbolic meaning of the griffin was ambiguous. "This fabulous creature . . . is used with two different and opposite meanings: on the one hand to represent the Saviour; on the other, because it is a combination of the preying of an eagle and the fierceness of the lion, to symbolize those who oppress and persecute the Christians" (Ferguson 7). The lion-bird as a symbol of the Incarnation of Christ signified "the two-fold nature of our Lord, also His omnipotence and omniscience" (Webber 370). The griffin was also considered a symbol of the pope, who at that time was both priest and worldly ruler (Borges 84).

Romanesque churches and monasteries from Italy to Ireland were richly ornamented with griffins and other composite monsters. These gradually disappeared, possibly under the influence of St. Bernard of Clairvaux (1090–1153), who called for a new spirituality within the Church. Griffins still kept a stronghold in heraldry, where they could be seen *segreant* (aggressively erect with outspread wings) painted on shields and woven into tapestries, but their power was waning. With the revival of Graeco-Roman art during the Renaissance and early Baroque, there was some renewed interest in griffins, but it was only a faint reflection of their former glory. Although artists such as Dürer and Altdorfer drew some magnificent specimens and goldsmiths formed ornate cups and other objects in their image, griffins served as mere allegorical devices, no longer endowed with numinous powers. This is also true for their last rebirth in the early nineteenth century, when Napoleon Bonaparte enriched the neoclassical style of the time with motifs from Pompeii and Egypt to glorify his empire ("Empire Style," *Encyclopaedia Britannica*). There may be an abundance of griffins and sphinxes on Empire furniture, but they are only decorations, not avengers or guardians. To this day, artists use the griffin occasionally, but mostly for trademark designs or illustrations of fantastic fiction.

Literature has always been a hospitable abode for the griffin, beginning with ancient Greece. Aeschylus, for example, was apparently inspired by Aristeas' reports to choose the Caucasus Mountains as the setting for his drama *Prometheus Bound*. In one scene the protagonist speaks about the dangers of that country, including "the sharp-beaked griffins" (qtd. in Costello 75). Poetry and history frequently intermingled, as in *The Romance of Alexander*, a work written about A.D. 400 and based on the exploits of the mighty conqueror. It became eminently popular and was retold in many versions well into the Middle Ages. One episode shows the strength and cunning of the king who can subjugate even griffins. When he has reached the end of the known world, Alexander wants to conquer the sky. To this end, he has a chariotlike chair built and four griffins tied to it with iron chains. Meat is placed above their heads; and when the griffins try to reach it, they lift the chariot up toward the heavens. Alexander soars to a great height; but before he can reach the heavens, God forces the griffins back to earth.

In this as in later stories, it is not quite clear whether the griffins are composite creatures or just gigantic birds of prey, since they are often described in similar terms to the roc bird or the simurgh. Much of griffin lore has indeed been borrowed from oriental sources; there were ample opportunities for contact between Christian Europe and the world of Islam, from the Moorish occupation of Spain to the Crusades and the Turkish Wars.

Numerous romances from the early Middle Ages tell of fierce griffins, strong enough to carry full-grown men. In the German story of *Herzog Ernst*, written around 1180, the shipwrecked hero and his companions observe griffins carrying away corpses as food for their young. The knights cover themselves with the skins of slaughtered "sea-cattle" (perhaps manatees?) and are carried across the ocean to the griffins' nest. When they arrive there, the men cut the skins open and escape. After many hardships they find a way home. Karl Bartsch, editor of the old chapbook, has found many similar episodes in other medieval tales (clii–clx).

More aggressive are the fabulous birds in the German epic *Kudrun*, which originated around 1230. Young prince Hagen has been abducted by a huge griffin and taken to its nest as food for the young griffins. Hagen escapes and lives for many years in a cave with three princesses whom the monstrous birds had also carried off. When Hagen has grown tall and strong, he finds the armor of a drowned knight and is able to kill all the griffins in a terrifying struggle. Eventually he and the princesses are rescued by a passing ship.

The simurgh, too, is known to take children to its nest, but not as food. The tenth-century epic *Shah Nameh* by Firdausi tells of a young prince who is abandoned in the wilderness by his father because of an evil omen. Nursed by the simurgh with its own young until he has grown to manhood, the prince returns to his kingdom after the father has repented. As a farewell gift, the bird presents the young man with a magical feather, which he may burn whenever he needs help.

Italian poetry assigns a more symbolic role to the griffin. Its most sublime apotheosis can be found in the *Divine Comedy* when Dante describes the triumphal chariot of the church, drawn by the sacred griffin who represents the Lord Jesus Christ. His divine nature is symbolized by the golden feathered head, neck, and wings, while the animal limbs of red and white color symbolize Christ's human nature. After restoring the tree of knowledge, which had withered since the fall of Adam and Eve, the griffin returns to heaven (*Purgatorio*, cantos 29–32). Another emblematic bird is the hippogryph, described by Lodovico Ariosto in his epic *Orlando Furioso*. As mentioned before, it is the unlikely offspring of a griffin and a horse. A large, powerful creature that can move through the air more swiftly than lightning, the hippogryph has been tamed by the magician Atlas, who rides upon it. The knights Ruggiero and Astolfo also use it as a mount, and finally Astolfo sets it free (canto 44). A line in Virgil's *Eclogues* gave Ariosto the inspiration for the hippogryph: "Now griffins will be mated with horses." According to Nigg, Ariosto combined the two to symbolize love (32).

In folktales, the griffin can be both frightening and benevolent. In a German version of "Beauty and the Beast," it transports an enchanted prince and his bride across the Red Sea. When they have reached the middle of the sea, the bride must drop a magical walnut into the water, and the walnut immediately grows into a large tree. The griffin can sit on it and rest for a while; otherwise it would get too tired and cast its burden into the waves ("Das singende springende Löweneckerchen," Grimm, *Märchen* 261–65). In another fairy tale, an evil king sends young Hans to the griffin's house to bring back a magical feather before he may marry the princess. On the way, the youth encounters three groups of people with different problems. When he arrives at his destination, the man-eating griffin is not home, but the griffin's wife takes pity on Hans and hides him under the bed. At night she asks the griffin for solutions to all the problems, and the wise bird tells her the answers. She also manages to procure a beautiful tail feather for Hans, who has overheard everything and returns to the princess happy and wealthy ("Der Vogel Greif," Grimm, *Märchen* 449–53).

After the sixteenth century, griffins were used more as figures of speech than as fear-inspiring monsters. More than two thousand years after Herodotus, European poets still showed their classical erudition by alluding to griffins and their traditional enemies. Milton, in book 2 of *Paradise Lost*, describes Satan traversing the abyss between Hell and the newly created earth with these words:

> As when a Gryfon through the Wilderness
> With winged course o'er Hill or moory Dale,
> Pursues the Arimaspian, who by stealth
> Had from his wakeful custody purloined

> The guarded Gold.
>
> (lines 943–47)

Goethe, in the second part of his drama *Faust*, is not as serious. The hero and his companion Mephisto encounter a group of griffins and Arimaspians during the "Klassische Walpurgisnacht," a Grecian witches' sabbath near the Peneios river. The griffins are properly forbidding, speaking in gruff and snarling voices throughout the brief scene, but Mephisto answers them in puns, and the mood is ironic rather than terrifying.

Goethe's *Faust* was completed in 1831. From then on literature was not much concerned with griffins; only occasionally were they allowed to make an appearance in children's books. Alice, in Lewis Carroll's *Alice in Wonderland*, meets an impatient and testy griffin that takes her to the Mock Turtle. In an illustration by Carroll, it is an absurd-looking scaled creature that barely resembles a griffin (it even lacks wings). Tenniel's well-known illustration showing the griffin "lying fast asleep" does it more justice. In Frank Stockton's children's tale *The Griffin and the Minor Canon* (first published in the 1870s), the griffin is the central character, a haughty and domineering creature. It visits a small French town, where it admires its likeness on the cathedral and befriends a young cleric, the minor canon. The townspeople are petty and selfish. They do not like the griffin, who tries to improve their ways by using force. The tale has an unhappy ending, because the griffin must leave town. It loses the only friend it ever had, and it dies after it refuses to eat. Margaret Blount suspects that the griffin is disliked by the people because of "that strange harshness that seems to be the property of mythical birds." She notes that "bird omens and oracles are more familiar than bird friends," and that maybe "we love birds less than we think," no matter how ancient, powerful, experienced, educated, and erudite they may be (100).

The creature described in Vachel Lindsay's poem "Yet Gentle Will the Griffin Be" is tame by comparison. Grandfather tells the children that the moon is a griffin's egg, but when the bird hatches, there is nothing to fear:

> Yet gentle will the griffin be,
> Most decorous and fat,
> And walk up to the Milky Way
> And lap it like a cat.

While the image has a certain charm, it is not really befitting for a griffin to be "gentle," "decorous," and "fat." Such a griffin appears to be rather senile or degenerate. In a fairly new children's book, *Sir Toby Jingle's Beastly Journey* by Wallace Tripp, the griffin looks formidable, to be sure. But it is easily duped and captured by an old, experienced knight, together with a number of other wild creatures in an enchanted forest.

Modern authors of fantastic novels for grownups have come to the rescue.

Piers Anthony, for example, has designated a whole province of legendary Xanth as a griffin refuge. There they can fight among themselves and menace traveling ogres or centaurs to their heart's content (*Ogre, Ogre*). It is even possible that a knight is magically transformed into a griffin and must undergo many tribulations before he can regain his human form (Anthony, *The Source of Magic*). In *The Fellowship of the Talisman* by Clifford Simak, an old griffin serves a young sorceress as companion and mount. But when her uncle, the archwizard, dies and his magic castle crumbles to dust, the griffin disappears without a trace.

Griffins have been a part of Western civilization since its beginnings. They have been represented in art and poetry, as servants of gods and of demons. They are still exerting their power, no matter how much we may try to demystify them. Their meaning still can be interpreted in many ways. But if we contemplate their proud images intently enough, we come to the realization that they hold up a mirror to humankind—showing us our own dual nature, composed of spirit and matter, good and evil.

BIBLIOGRAPHY

Aelian. *On the Characteristics of Animals*. Trans. A. F. Scholfield. 3 vols. Cambridge: Harvard University Press, 1958.

Anthony, Piers. *The Source of Magic*. New York: Ballantine, 1979.

———. *Ogre, Ogre*. New York: Ballantine, 1982.

Ariosto, Lodovico. *Orlando Furioso*. Trans. Allan Gilbert. 2 vols. New York: S. F. Vanni, 1954.

Bisi, A. M. *Il grifone: storia di un motivo iconografico nell'antico oriente mediterraneo*. Roma: Università di Roma, Centro di Studi Semitici. Studi Semitici 13, 1965.

Blount, Margaret. *Animal Land: The Creatures of Children's Fiction*. New York: William Morrow, 1975.

Bolton, J. D. P. *Aristeas of Proconnesus*. Oxford: Clarendon, 1962.

Borges, Jorge Luis, with Margarita Guerrero. *The Book of Imaginary Beings*. Trans. Norman Thomas di Giovanni. New York: Discus-Avon, 1970.

Carroll, Lewis (see Dodgson).

Cary, George. *The Medieval Alexander*. Cambridge: Cambridge University Press, 1956.

Charrière, Georges. *Scythian Art: Crafts of the Early Eurasian Nomads*. New York: Alpine Fine Arts Collection, 1979.

Costello, Peter. *The Magic Zoo: The Natural History of Fabulous Animals*. New York: St. Martin's, 1979.

Dante. *The Divine Comedy*. Trans. Laurence Binyon. New York: Viking, 1957.

Dennys, Rodney. *The Heraldic Imagination*. New York: Clarkson N. Potter, 1975.

———. *Heraldry and the Heralds*. London: Jonathan Cape, 1982.

Dodgson, Charles Lutwidge (Lewis Carroll). *Alice in Wonderland, Through the Looking-Glass and Other Comic Pieces*. Introd. Ernest Rhys. London: Dent; New York: Dutton, 1929.

Duden Etymologie. Ed. Paul Grebe. In *Der Grosse Duden*. Vol. 7. Mannheim: Bibliographisches Institut, 1963.

"Empire Style." *Encyclopaedia Britannica*. 1970 ed.

Evans, Sir Arthur. *The Palace of Minos*. 4 vols. London: Macmillan, 1921–35.

Ferguson, George. *Signs and Symbols in Christian Art*. New York: Oxford University Press, 1959.

Firdausi. *The Shah Nameh*. Trans. James Atkinson. London: Frederick Warne, 1886.

Flagge, Ingeborg. *Untersuchungen zur Bedeutung des Greifen*. Sankt Augustin: Hans Richarz, 1975.

Gardner, Helen. *Art through the Ages*. 4th ed. New York: Harcourt, Brace and Company, 1959.

Goethe, Johann Wolfgang von. *Faust*. In *Werke*. Ed. Erich Trunz. 11th ed. Vol. 3. München: Beck, 1981.

Grimm, Jacob, and Wilhelm Grimm. *Kinder- und Hausmärchen*. Stuttgart and Leipzig: Deutsche Verlagsanstalt, n.d.

————. *Deutsches Wörterbuch*. Vol. 9. München: Deutscher Taschenbuchverlag, 1984.

Hall, James. *Dictionary of Subjects and Symbols in Art*. New York: Harper and Row, 1974.

Herodotus. *The History of Herodotus*. Trans. George Rawlinson. 4 vols. New York: Appleton, 1859–60.

Herzog Ernst. Ed. Karl Bartsch. Hildesheim: Georg Olms, 1969.

Indische Märchen. Ed. Johannes Hertel. Jena: Eugen Diederichs, 1921.

Jantzen, Ulf. *Griechische Greifenkessel*. Berlin: Gebr. Mann, 1955.

Kudrun. Ed. Karl Bartsch. 5th ed. Wiesbaden: F. A. Brockhaus, 1965.

"Lammergeier." *Encyclopaedia Britannica*. 1970 ed.

Lindsay, Vachel. *Collected Poems*. Rev. ed. New York: Macmillan, 1925.

Mandeville, John. *Mandeville's Travels*. Ed. M. C. Seymour. London: Oxford University Press, 1968.

Märchen aus Turkestan und Tibet. Ed. Gustav Jungbauer. Jena: Eugen Diederichs, 1923.

Milton, John. *Complete Poems and Major Prose*. Ed. Merritt Y. Hughes. New York: Odyssey Press, 1957.

Mode, Heinz. *Fabulous Beasts and Demons*. London: Phaidon, 1975.

Nigg, Joe. *The Book of Gryphons*. Cambridge, Mass.: Apple-Wood Books, 1982.

Pliny the Elder. *Natural History*. Trans. H. Rackham et al. 10 vols. Cambridge: Harvard University Press, 1938–62.

Polo, Marco. *The Travels of Marco Polo*. Trans. R. E. Latham. Baltimore: Penguin, 1958.

Prinz, H. "Der Greif in den orientalischen Kulturkreisen." *Paulys Real-Encyclopädie der classischen Altertumswissenschaft*. Neue Bearbeitung. Stuttgart: A. Druckenmüller, 1912, 7: pt. 2, cols. 1904–18.

Rowland, Beryl. *Birds with Human Souls: A Guide to Bird Symbolism*. Knoxville: University of Tennessee Press, 1978.

Shepard, Odell. *The Lore of the Unicorn*. London, 1930; rpt. New York: Harper and Row, 1979.

Simak, Clifford D. *The Fellowship of the Talisman*. New York: Ballantine, 1978.

Soden, Wolfram von. "Der Nahe Osten im Altertum." In *Hochkulturen des mittleren und östlichen Asiens*. Vol. 2 of *Propyläen-Weltgeschichte*. Berlin, Frankfurt, and Wien: Propyläen Verlag, 1962.

Stockton, Frank. *The Griffin and the Minor Canon*. New York: Holt, Rinehart and Winston, 1963.

Tripp, Wallace. *Sir Toby Jingle's Beastly Journey*. New York: Coward, McCann and
    Geoghegan, 1976.
Vries, Ad de. *Dictionary of Symbols and Imagery*. Amsterdam: North-Holland, 1974.
Webber, F. R. *Church Symbolism*. 2nd ed. rev. Cleveland: J. H. Jansen, 1938.
White, T. H., ed. and trans. *The Bestiary: A Book of Beasts, Being a Translation from
    a Latin Bestiary of the Twelfth Century*. New York: Putnam's, 1954.
Wittkower, Rudolf. *Allegory and the Migration of Symbols*. Boulder, Colo.: Westview,
    1977.

6

The Chimera

David Adams Leeming

In Greek mythology the chimera (kī-mêr-́a < Latin *chimera* < Greek *khimaira*, "she-goat") is the she-monster killed by the hero Bellerophon. The earliest descriptions of the chimera in literature are found in Homer and Hesiod. According to Homer, she is a fire-breathing monster that is "in the fore part a lion, in the hinder a serpent, and in the midst a goat" (*Iliad* 6.181–82). Hesiod also says that the chimera is a fire-breathing monster, and he describes her as "a creature fearful, great, swift-footed and strong, who had three heads, one of a grim-eyed lion, another of a goat, and another of a snake, a fierce dragon" (*Theogony* 319 ff.). In Greek art the chimera was mainly depicted as a creature with a lion's body, with a goat's head emerging from the lion's body, and with a snake for a tail. However, as we shall see, the creature has had a variety of forms.

Over the years the word "chimera" has come to be associated with any grotesque monster made up of various animals. A typical variation is that of an eighteenth-century blazonry expert named Coats, who refers to "an imaginary creature invented by the poets, and represented by them as having the face of a beautiful maiden, the two forelegs and the main of a lyon, the body like a goat, the hinder-legs like a griffin, and the tayl like a serpent or dragon turned in a ring" (qtd. in Hulme 84).

In modern English, of course, a chimera is any foolish idea. To quote the *Oxford English Dictionary*, a chimera is "a mere wild fancy; an unfounded conception." Thus the adjective "chimerical," meaning imaginary or unreal.

Not a great deal has been written about the chimera by scholars. Four studies that provide useful information about the creature are: "Bellerophon" by L. Malten; "The Origin of the Chimaera" by Anne Roes; "Bellerophon, Herakles and Chimaera" by T. J. Dunbabin; and "Bellerophon and the Chimaera in

Archaic Greek Art'' by Marilyn Low Schmitt. Discussion of the chimera is included in S. Hiller's *Bellerophon* and Nikolas Yalouris' *Pegasus*. There is an essay on the monster in Jean-Paul Clébert's bestiary, and a brief discussion can be found in John Ashton's *Curious Creatures in Zoology*, Anthony Mercatante's *Zoo of the Gods*, and Jorge Luis Borges' *The Book of Imaginary Beings*. In general, the chimera has somehow avoided the kind of attention that is paid to such monsters as the Gorgon Medusa or the sphinx. She remains "chimerical" to scholars.

According to our primary sources, Homer and Hesiod, the chimera was of divine origin. Homer speaks of the creature as "of divine stock" (*Iliad* 6.180), and Hesiod says that her mother was Echidna, herself a terrible monster—half a girl "with glancing eyes and fair cheeks: and half a large and frightening snake" (*Theogony* 298 ff.). The father of the chimera was said to be the monster Typhon, the youngest son of Gaea and Tartarus. Typhon was taller than any mountain. He had great wings, eyes of fire, hands made of dragons, and a lower body of vipers. Later he was to fight Zeus himself. The chimera had appropriately grotesque brothers: Cerberus, the dog-headed creature who conducted souls to the underworld, and Orthus, the two-headed dog who guarded the cattle of Geryon. There are numerous variants to the "tree" of this remarkable family. Some of the ancients held, for instance, that Orthus was the chimera's father or that the terrible many-headed Hydra was her mother. Whatever her specific parentage, our heroine is of that archaic, chthonic, and chaotic class of monsters and giants who would eventually struggle with the Olympians for control of the universe. (Although the chimera is usually identified as female in literature, the creature is often depicted as male in art. For the most part, this entry will treat the chimera as a female monster.)

The chimera's home was in Lycia in Asia Minor. Some have tried to "explain" her existence by associating her with a volcanic mountain there called Chimaera or Yanar. Servius, the Virgil commentator, pointed out that flames issued from the mouth of the mountain, that lions lived near its top, that goats grazed in its upper meadows, and that serpents infested its base. More farfetched explanations have been proposed. Plutarch believed the chimera legend was the result of a pirate whose ship was decorated with images of a snake, a lion, and a goat (see Borges 62). A later commentator, the Count Goblet d'Alviella, finds the origin of the chimera in an artist's misinterpretation of a lion devouring a goat (24).

Whatever the explanation of the chimera's nature, it seems evident that she has ancient origins. L. Malten (see Nilsson 53) finds oriental sources, and certain bronze figurines of the Han dynasty in China would seem to suggest an Asian version of the monster. Anne Roes, who also finds oriental sources for the chimera, thinks that the creature originated in art from a type of winged quadruped that has a head appearing on the top of its wings. Martin Nilsson argues for a preclassical, Mycenaean version, using as evidence a representation of the creature in a glass plaque found in a beehive tomb at Dendra, near old Mideia (53–54). This plaque shows a hero fighting a lion from whose back emerges a goat's head. There is a still earlier depiction of the chimera as a calendar symbol in ancient Caria in Asia Minor, and there is a chimera represented on a Hittite ruin in Carehemish. Something like a chimera appears on stamp seals of the ancient Harappa culture in India.

According to Roes, Greek art had three different ways of combining the lion and the goat in representations of the chimera. The customary way was to depict a goat's head emerging from a lion's back (1156). The second way placed the goat's head on the top of wings; this method of representation was extremely rare in Greek art but was well known in Persian art (1157). The third combination showed the entire forequarters of a goat growing out of the lion's back (1157).

Although the chimera has not been depicted in art as frequently as creatures such as the Gorgon Medusa and the sphinx, there are numerous depictions of the creature from different periods. The chimera may be shown alone, or the creature may be represented in conjunction with Bellerophon and Pegasus, the winged horse on which that hero rode when he slew the monster.

The Bellerophon-chimera legend was one of the earliest legends depicted in Greek art (Dunbabin 1164; Schmitt 341). A pictorial tradition concerning the legend developed in Corinthian art and reached a point of high development about the middle of the seventh century B.C. (Schmitt 341–43). Two of the earliest representations of the combat between Bellerophon and the chimera are found on two Protocorinthian vases that have been dated a little before 650 B.C. (Dunbabin 1164; Yalouris, figs. 6 and 7). In one representation (on a kotyle in Aegina), Bellerophon astride his winged steed charges the chimera "with cries of triumph (notice his half-opened mouth) and gestures of self-assurance" (Yalouris, note to fig. 7); in the other representation (on an aryballos in Boston), the hero rides on Pegasus and is about to throw his spear at the monster. Marilyn Low Schmitt says that both of these works reveal "a strongly established conception of the legend" (342). Sometime before 630 B.C. the Corinthian Bellerophon-chimera tradition underwent a decline, and a period of about thirty years passed before there was a revival of interest in the chimera. This revival saw the production of some outstanding works dealing with the story, especially those by the Corinthian Chimaera Painter, who had great "technical mastery" and displayed "delicacy of detail" and "boldness of composition" (Schmitt 345). Attic artists also produced some outstanding examples of the legend. In the Attic tradition the chimera usually has a leonine form, and the head of the lion and that of the goat are turned to the rear (Schmitt 343–44). According to Schmitt, interest in the legend declined in Greek vase-painting after the Archaic period (346). It should be pointed out, however, that some noteworthy uses of the story in later Greek painting can be found. For example, on an Attic red-figure epinetron (ca. 430 B.C.), which shows Bellerophon about to plunge his spear into a lion-bodied chimera with a goat's forequarters emerging from the lion's back, the artist focuses on a new relationship involving Bellerophon, Pegasus, and the chimera. "Their eyes meet and for the first time their gazes express the deep inner link among adversaries in a fatal encounter" (Yalouris, note to fig. 31).

The most famous depiction of the chimera in art is the fifth-century B.C. bronze figure found in Arezzo, Italy. Here the chimera is a lionlike beast whose tail is a serpent and out of whose back emerges a goat's head.

In postclassical times the chimera has remained a subject of interest. The creature appeared in the Middle Ages, for example, on coats of arms, in mosaics, and in Bible decorations. The combat between Bellerophon and the chimera continued to receive attention during the Renaissance and later. For instance, Francesco di Giorgio on a fifteenth-century bronze plaquette depicts the killing of the chimera, and Peter Paul Rubens (1577–1640) in a painted sketch portrays Bellerophon slaying a leonine chimera (Yalouris, fig. 115). The word "chimera" in reference to a painting may not refer to the mythological animal but to something strange or mysterious or puzzling. For the French painter Gustave Moreau (1826–98), the word as it is used in reference to his unfinished painting *Chimeras* signifies a strange dream. The painting does contain several monsters, but no chimera seems to be among them. Although the exact meaning of the work remains ambiguous, it depicts "a sort of pandemonium where all passions, perverse desires and monstrous, fantastic dreams weigh heavily on woman, conceived as being possessed by mystery and fascinated by evil" (Paladilhe 67). Moreau said of the work that it dealt with a "chimerical dream, the terrible dream of destruction, pain and death" (qtd. in Paladilhe 67).

The chimera appears with fair frequency in the literature of various periods. Besides Homer and Hesiod, some of the other classical authors who refer to the creature are Euripides (*Ion* 201 ff.), Ovid (*Metamorphoses* 9.647–48), and Virgil (*Aeneid* 6.288). In the *Aeneid* the chimera is among the frightening forms that Aeneas sees in the underworld. Milton in *Paradise Lost* also connects the creature with Hell when he speaks of "Gorgons and Hydras, and Chimeras dire" (2.628). As Merritt Hughes points out (p. 247, note to line 628), Milton treats these monsters as "vague monsters" rather than as specific mythological creatures. In doing so, Milton followed an established tradition in English literature. For example, John Lyly says that "chymeraes" are "monsters" of the "imagination" (3:402). Thomas Nashe speaks, in the same manner, of a "*Chimera* of imagination" (3:217). It is worth noting, however, that Nashe also refers to the specific mythological monster in her form as a volcano in Lycia (2:181). The reference is essentially metaphorical, "the fires of *Chimera*," being compared to "some mens furie." Another such metaphorical volcano reference is found in Robert Greene's *Venus Tragedie* (5:76), where the quenching of the "Hill *Chymera*" is used as a model for the use of reason as opposed to brute force. In Gustave Flaubert's *The Temptation of St. Anthony* (1874), the Chimera (a symbol of fantasy) is a green-eyed monster that barks and spirts fire through its nostrils. It talks with the Sphinx (a symbol of reality), and "their grotesque and futile efforts at intercourse" seem to suggest "the essential cleavage between the orders of experience" (Brombert 204). In Charles G. Finney's *The Circus of Dr. Lao* (1935), a chimera is one of the strange creatures that Doctor Lao has on exhibit. A combination of lion, lizard, and eagle, the monster has an eagle's wings and a dragon's tail. The attributes of lion, lizard, and eagle are "so perfectly blended together" that it is impossible to tell where one creature leaves off and another begins (79). Doctor Lao says that the chimera cannot expel "waste matter through the bowels" but must burn it up within: "Yes, a chimera is its own incinerator plant. Very unusual beast" (77). John Barth's novel *Chimera* (1972) is a brilliant adaptation of the chimera myth to modern concerns. In his novel, Barth uses the old myth as a basis for an elaborate metaphor for the art of fiction itself. Myths are, of course, inventions, and each of the three sections of *Chimera* is a fiction about the process of fictional invention. *Chimera* becomes a reflection of the ultimately chimerical nature of a world which can only explore reality by way of its own inventions, its own illusions about itself.

A summary of the story of Bellerophon will be helpful in providing a clearer understanding of the myth of the chimera. The account that follows is a composite one drawn from Homer, Hesiod, Pindar, Apollodorus, Pausanias, Plutarch, and Ovid. (For a listing of the classical sources concerning Bellerophon, see Graves, *Greek Myths* 1:254).

The son of King Glaucus of Corinth took the name Bellerophon after killing a man called Bellerus and his own brother. Some say that Bellerophon was really the son of Poseidon; true heroes usually had divine origins, and Bellerophon had all the physical attributes of the true hero. Whatever his parentage, trouble came naturally to his human family. Glaucus' father was the famous stone-rolling Sisyphus, who had once revealed a secret of Zeus. Glaucus himself displeased the gods by feeding human flesh to his horses to make them more ardent at war. The gods punished him by causing him to be eaten by the horses after he was thrown from his chariot.

After killing his brother, Bellerophon fled to Tiryns, where King Proetus agreed to give him asylum and to purify him. But the king's wife, Anteia, fell in love with the young hero and, when her advances were refused, took revenge by accusing him before the court of trying to seduce her. Furious, but unwilling to risk the anger of the Furies by killing a guest, Proetus sent Bellerophon to Anteia's father, King Iobates of Lycia, with a sealed letter accusing the hero of attempted adultery and requesting that he be executed. After entertaining Bellerophon for nine days, Iobates asked for news of his daughter and his son-in-law and was presented with the still-sealed letter. Its contents horrified the king, who had grown genuinely fond of his guest. He could not bring himself to fulfill Proetus' commission, but he challenged Bellerophon with a task that he believed would result in his death anyway. A supposedly invincible monster with "lion's head, goat's body, and serpent's tail"—a monster we will no doubt recognize—was wasting Lycia with her flame-throwing breath. Iobates found the chimera particularly irritating because she had become a favorite of his mortal enemy, the king of Caria. Bellerophon's task was to kill the chimera.

Bellerophon wisely consulted the seer Polyeidus before attempting the assigned task. Polyeidus advised him to capture the winged horse Pegasus and to use him as a steed in the battle with the monster. It was Pegasus who, with his hoof, had made the famous Hippocrene fountain that was sacred to the Muses on Mount Helicon. Pegasus, like so many others in this story, was of "monstrous" lineage. He was born of the blood of the Medusa's head after it was severed by the hero Perseus. (For Pegasus, see Yalouris.)

Bellerophon found Pegasus in Corinth and with Athena's help (or that of the horse-god Poseidon) caught him in a golden bridle. He then flew to Lycia on the horse's back and was able to shoot the chimera with arrows from a safe distance above her. Finally, he threw a spear with a lead point into her gaping mouth and watched as the fiery breath melted the lead, which in turn burnt out the monster's insides and caused her death.

Iobates was to assign Bellerophon other herculean tasks, but eventually he learned the truth about the affair with Anteia and rewarded his guest by marrying him to his daughter Philonoe and making him heir to this throne. Unfortunately, Bellerophon's pride grew with his good fortune. He made the mistake of trying to ride Pegasus to Mount Olympus and was punished for his arrogance by being flung to the earth, where he was left to wander lame and blind until his pitiful death some years later. So ends the only mythological tale in which the chimera plays a significant role.

What, then, are we to make of this "chimerical" monster? It is important to note first that the chimera is female and that she is a composite figure—that is to say, she is an aberration of earthly forms, a monster. In this she is decidedly not alone. Other she-monsters of Greek mythology include the sphinx, the Gorgon Medusa, and the Hydra. There are counterparts in other cultures: Vritra in India, Tiamat in Babylon. The female monsters, as Sir James Frazer in *The Golden Bough* and Robert Graves in *The White Goddess* have suggested, might well be representations of the destructive side of the Great Goddess of the ancient matriarchal fertility cults. Graves sees the chimera specifically as a symbol for the Great Goddess's tripartite year—the lion for the spring, the goat for summer, the snake for winter (*Greek Myths* 1:130, 254).

In the matriarchal religions, a predominant practice was that of the periodical sacrifice of the Sacred King to the Sacred Queen, the human representative of the Great Goddess. So it is that the she-monster is a devastator and an eater of raw flesh. But the matriarchal cultures were to be challenged by patriarchal ones, such as, for example, the Hellenes, who invaded Greece in the second millennium B.C. In Greek mythology these Hellenes might be said to be represented by the shining male heroes who destroy the multiformed she-monsters. Perseus kills the Gorgon Medusa, Hercules kills the Hydra, and Bellerophon kills the chimera. Graves (*Greek Myths* 2:17) and Jane Harrison (ch. 5) suggest that the horrible forms and deeds of the she-monsters are warnings against those who would profane the mysteries of the Great Goddess. Yet the killing of these monsters marks the new Hellenic culture's defeat of the old cult. Thus Bellerophon's defeat of the chimera is a specific metaphor for the Hellenic suppression of the ancient tripartite calendar in favor of the new two-part Greek one. This suppression coincides with the Achaean religious changes that left Zeus dominant over the goddess Hera. Still more specifically, says Graves (*Greek Myths* 1:255), the defeat of the chimera on the mountain in Lycia can be seen as a reflection of the Hellenic invaders' actual seizure of the matriarchal shrines of the Triple Muse or "Mountain Goddess" on Mount Helicon and Corinth.

Finally, in a modern psychological context, it would seem to be safe to suggest that the many-faceted chimera is a representation of the dark side of the unconscious that must be brought to the light of consciousness by the probing ego, itself represented by the male hero figure. As lion, goat, and snake, the chimera is a metaphor for the combination of destruction and fertility, the death and rebirth process that is so basic to physical existence and to psychic growth. Ideally, of course, the monster demons of the depths must be recognized as necessary to the whole psyche and must be assimilated by the ego. If they are merely suppressed or killed the ego will almost certainly pay later by itself becoming in some sense monstrous. Bellerophon kills the she-monster but later emerges as a perversion of male reason and spirituality as he foolishly attempts to fly to Mount Olympus and is flung back lame and blind to the maternal earth.

The chimera is indeed a monster to be feared. She must, of course, be confronted if we are to pass on to a new stage on the "hero journey." But we must beware too of the arrogance that might lead us to think that the force that takes form in her can ever be killed.

BIBLIOGRAPHY

Apollodorus. *The Library*. Trans. Sir James George Frazer. 2 vols. 1921; rpt. Cambridge: Harvard University Press, 1961.

Ashton, John. *Curious Creatures in Zoology*. New York: Cassell, n.d.

Avery, Catherine B., ed. *The New Century Classical Handbook*. New York: Appleton, 1962.

Barth, John. *Chimera*. New York: Random House, 1972.

Borges, Jorge Luis, with Margarita Guerrero. *The Book of Imaginary Beings*. Trans. Norman Thomas di Giovanni. New York, Discus-Avon, 1970.

Bridaham, Lester B. *Gargoyles, Chimeres, and the Grotesque in French Gothic Sculpture*. 2nd ed. New York: Da Capo Press, 1969.

Brombert, Victor. *The Novels of Flaubert: A Study of Themes and Techniques*. Princeton: Princeton University Press, 1966.

Campbell, Joseph. *The Masks of God: Primitive Mythology*. New York: Viking, 1969.

Clébert, Jean-Paul. *Bestiaire fabuleux*. Paris: Albin Michel, 1971.

Dennys, Rodney. *The Heraldic Imagination*. London: Barrie and Jenkins, 1975.

Dunbabin, T. J. "Bellerophon, Herakles and Chimaera." In *Studies Presented to David Moore Robinson*. Ed. G. E. Mylonas and D. Raymond. Vol. 2. St. Louis: Washington University, 1953. 1164–84.

Encyclopedia of World Art. 16 vols. New York: McGraw-Hill, 1957–83.

Finney, Charles G. *The Circus of Dr. Lao*. 1935. New York: Ben Abramson, 1946.

Frazer, Sir James George. *The New Golden Bough*. Ed. Theodor H. Gaster. New York: Mentor, 1964.

Goblet d'Alviella, Eugène. *The Migration of Symbols*. London, 1894; rpt. New York: Burt Franklin, 1972.

Goldsmith, Elisabeth. *Ancient Pagan Symbols*. New York: Putnam's, 1929.

Graves, Robert. *The Greek Myths*. 2 vols. Baltimore: Penguin, 1955.

————. *The White Goddess: A Historical Grammar of Poetic Myth*. Amended and enl. ed. New York: Farrar, Straus and Giroux, 1966.

Greene, Robert. *The Life and Complete Works in Prose and Verse of Robert Greene*. Ed. Alexander Grosart. 15 vols. London, 1881–86; rpt. New York: Russell and Russell, 1964.

Grimal, Pierre, ed. *Larousse World Mythology*. Trans. Patricia Beardsworth. London: Hamlyn, 1965.

Harrison, Jane Ellen. *Prolegomena to the Study of Greek Religion*. 3rd ed. New York: Meridian, 1955.

Hesiod, the Homeric Hymns and Homerica. Trans. Hugh G. Evelyn-White. Cambridge: Harvard University Press, 1936.

Hiller, S. *Bellerophon: Ein griechischer Mythos in der römischen Kunst*. Munich: Fink, 1970.

Homer. *The Iliad*. Trans. A. T. Murray. 2 vols. 1924; rpt. Cambridge: Harvard University Press, 1946.

Huber, Richard. *Treasury of Fantastic and Mythological Creatures: 1,087 Renderings from Historic Sources*. New York: Dover, 1981.

Hulme, F. Edward. *Myth-land*. London, 1886.

Klingender, Francis. *Animals in Art and Thought to the End of the Middle Ages*. Ed. Evelyn Antal and John Harthan. London: Routledge and Kegan Paul, 1971.

Lyly, John. *The Complete Works of John Lyly*. Ed. R. Warwick Bond. 3 vols. Oxford: Clarendon, 1902.

Malten, L. "Bellerophon." *Jahrbuch des Deutschen Archäologischen Instituts* 40 (1925): 121–60.

Mercatante, Anthony S. *Zoo of the Gods: Animals in Myth, Legend and Fable*. New York: Harper and Row, 1974.

Milton, John. *Complete Poems and Major Prose*. Ed. Merritt Y. Hughes. New York: Odyssey Press, 1957.

Mode, Heinz. *Fabulous Beasts and Demons*. London: Phaidon, 1975.

Nashe, Thomas. *The Works of Thomas Nashe*. Ed. Ronald B. McKerrow. 5 vols. London: Sidgwick and Jackson, 1910.

Nilsson, Martin P. *The Mycenaean Origin of Greek Mythology*. 1932. New York: Norton, 1963.

Ovid. *Metamorphoses*. Trans. Frank Justus Miller. 2 vols. Cambridge: Harvard University Press, 1916.

Paladilhe, Jean, and José Pierre. *Gustave Moreau*. Trans. Bettina Wadia. New York: Praeger, 1972.

Pausanias. *Description of Greece*. Trans. W. H. S. Jones. 5 vols. Cambridge: Harvard University Press, 1918–35.

Pindar. *The Odes of Pindar: Including the Principal Fragments*. Trans. John Sandys. 1915; rpt. Cambridge: Harvard University Press, 1968.

Plutarch. *Concerning the Virtues of Women*. In *Plutarch's Morals*. Ed. William W. Goodwin. Vol. 1. Boston, 1878.

Roes, Anne. "The Origin of the Chimaera." In *Studies Presented to David Moore*

Robinson. Ed. G. E. Mylonas and D. Raymond. Vol. 2. St. Louis: Washington University, 1953. 1155–63.

Schmitt, Marilyn Low. "Bellerophon and the Chimaera in Archaic Greek Art." *American Journal of Archaeology* 70 (1966): 341–47.

Vinycomb, John. *Fictitious and Symbolic Creatures in Art, with Special Reference to Their Use in British Heraldry*. London: Chapman and Hall, 1906.

Warner, Rex. *Men and Gods*. New York. Farrar, Straus and Giroux, 1959.

Yalouris, Nikolas. *Pegasus: The Art of the Legend*. Trans. Helen Zigada. N.p.: Mobil Oil Corporation, 1975.

7

The Basilisk

Laurence A. Breiner

In antiquity the basilisk was a small snake of the Libyan desert, probably the Egyptian cobra, notable for a white marking on its head, for its venom, and for its ability to move with its head held upright. It seems correct to identify it with the upright snake that appears on the foreheads of Egyptian pharaohs and gods. Horapollo's *Hieroglyphics* was written too late by more than a millennium to claim any authority, but it offers our only glimpse, however distorted, of what the Egyptians themselves thought about this indigenous creature: "When they wish to symbolize Eternity, . . . they draw a serpent with its tail concealed by the rest of its body. This the Egyptians call *Ouraion*, but the Greeks a *Basilisk*. . . . Should it blow upon any other animal, even without biting it, its victim dies. Wherefore, since it seems to have power over life and death, they put it on the heads of the gods" (57).

Our word "basilisk" comes from the Greek *basiliskos*, meaning "little king" (*basileus* plus diminutive). The term is taken over into Latin as *basiliscus*, and used alongside a native translation, *regulus* (*rex* plus diminutive). The creature is also occasionally called, or confused with, the *sibilus* and the *armene*. All European vernaculars including English adopted cognates of the Greek term; since the late Middle Ages the word "cockatrice" and its cognates have been mistakenly but chronically treated as synonyms for "basilisk."

Like its name, our knowledge of the basilisk comes originally through the Greeks, for whom it was one of the marvels of the strange desert on the other side of the Mediterranean. But no extended account in Greek survives from the classical period. We rely instead on Pliny's encyclopedic *Natural History* (A.D. 77), a Latin compilation based on an impressive array of ancient sources—book 8, for example, in which the chief entry on the basilisk appears, lists over sixty sources in Greek and Latin, many of them no longer extant. Here is Pliny's description:

The basilisk serpent also has the same power [whoever sees its eyes dies at once]. It is a native of Cyrenaica, not more than 12 inches long, and adorned with a bright white marking on the head like a sort of diadem. It routs all snakes with its hiss, and does not move its body forward in manifold coils like the other snakes but advancing with its middle raised high. It kills bushes not only by its touch but also by its breath, scorches up grass and bursts rocks. Its effect on other animals is disastrous: it is believed that once one was killed with a spear by a man on horseback and the infection rising through the spear killed not only the rider but also the horse. Yet to a creature so marvellous as this—indeed kings have often wished to see a specimen when safely dead—the venom of weasels is fatal: so fixed is the decree of nature that nothing shall be without its match. . . . The basilisk, which puts to flight even the very serpents, killing them sometimes by its smell, is said to be fatal to a man if it only looks at him. Its blood the Magi praise to the skies, telling how it thickens as does pitch, and resembles pitch in color, but becomes brighter red than cinnabar when diluted. (8.33 and 29.19)

This, if anything, is the "real" basilisk. Its primary feature is its kingliness, as its name indicates. This may be associated with the peculiar marking of its head, or may reflect the regal upright posture (the aspect that seems to have been most compelling for the ancient Egyptians). The combination of extreme virulence and small size also commands respect, as does the power to destroy literally everything in sight. But the Greeks reserved the word *basileus* for foreign rulers, and *basiliskos* in other contexts can imply "petty tyrant." So it is not surprising that the creature's potential as an image of royal power is usually overshadowed by its negative aspects, above all the ineluctability of its poison.

The basilisk hardly appears at all in classical literature. Apart from two passages in the Greek translation of the Old Testament (Psalm 90:13 and Isaiah 59:5), the only Greek instance known to me is in Heliodorus' late romance, the *Aethiopica*, where the reality of such phenomena as love at first sight and the evil eye is argued from the fact that the basilisk "by its mere breath and glance will shrivel and cripple whatever comes its way" (3.8). In Latin the basilisk plays a similar brief role in the fourth-century *History* of Ammianus, when someone is described as "like the basilisk, . . . harmful even from a distance" (28.1.41). But it has only a single substantial role in Latin literature, during the great battle between Cato's army and the desert serpents in book 9 of Lucan's *Pharsalia* (ca. A.D. 65). Here the basilisk drives off all other serpents and reigns alone in the empty sand; when a soldier encounters it in battle he avoids the fate of Pliny's horseman only by cutting off his own hand as the poison reaches it (9.724–26, 825–33).

In each of these literary instances, the basilisk is equated with its virulence; there is no regard for its posture, its "crown," or any other feature. Evidently the basilisk did not fire the imaginations of classical writers, though the nature of the references to it indicates that at least some of its properties were common knowledge. Pliny's report about the properties of its blood, attributed to the mysterious Magi, points to an early, protoscientific interest in the uses of the creature; it was also sometimes said that basilisk skins were hung in temples because they repel snakes and spiders, or that silver rubbed with the creature's ashes took on all the appearances of gold. Such lore persists and accumulates in the medieval bestiaries and the alchemical tracts of the Renaissance. The antagonism between the basilisk and the weasel is attested at least as early as the third century B.C., in a work attributed mistakenly to Democritus (Diels 127), and the impulse behind the idea is similarly practical: if you are travelling in Libya, bring a weasel. But as Pliny's remark about "the decree of nature" makes plain, the faith in such inherent antipathies is fundamental to a certain understanding of nature according to which every creature exists in a mesh of relations or correspondences. As the conception of the basilisk becomes increasingly complex through the ages, so too does the system of its affinities and antipathies. Thus, for example, its fatal breath and venom are overcome by the venom and stench of the weasel; its hiss is fatal, but it can be killed by the sound of a rooster (Aelian 3.31); and its fatal glance can be turned against it with a mirror.

With the end of the Roman Empire, Europe lost regular contact with Africa; in succeeding centuries the continent and its contents became more and more fabulous. Medieval Europe came to imagine the basilisk not as a marvel but as a full-fledged monster. And remarkably, as it became more monstrous it became less exotic. It was no longer thought of as something over in Africa, but as a peril you might stumble upon, with fatal consequences, just outside your door— one story insists that even England was once full of basilisks (Topsell 681). Knowledge of the Plinian original was faithfully transmitted by the more reliable writers through the Middle Ages and even into the seventeenth century, just before the creature disappears under the weight of its accumulated attributes. But the transformation of the basilisk into a fabulous monster begins with the story of its birth, and the seed of that story is to be found in the third century B.C., in the Septuagint's translation of Isaiah 59:5—"They break the eggs of asps and weave the spider's web; he who would eat their eggs, having crushed the wind egg [ourion] finds in it a basilisk." The obscurity of this passage is reflected in the great diversity of subsequent translations. The Vulgate intensifies the statement: "He who would eat of their eggs will die, and the one that is broken produces a basilisk [regulum]," while the King James Bible turns it inside out: "They hatch cockatrice' eggs, and weave the spider's web; he that eateth of their eggs dieth, and that which is crushed breaketh out into a viper." But the passage clearly says that the birth of the basilisk is anomalous, not part of a normal reproductive cycle but a genetic sport, a monster. This is at the heart of the medieval development of the basilisk. The context in Isaiah also encouraged an association of the creature with evil, and this underlies its treatment in Christian commentary as a type of the Devil, a wickedly fascinating serpent that, like Milton's Satan before the Fall, still carries himself upright. Thus while the mention of the basilisk in Holy Scripture established its existence with the highest possible authority, the view of the creature as diabolic invited increasingly grotesque visualization, and the lack of any descriptive detail in the biblical passages licensed radical transformation of its appearance so long as the name was preserved.

The idea that the egg in this story is a bird's seems to derive from statements about the ibis. Ammianus in his *History* mentions the basilisk immediately after recounting that the ibis controls the population of serpents in Egypt by carrying their eggs to its nestlings for food, and that ibises are reported to lay their eggs through their beaks (22.15.25–27). This invites possible confusion about whether the egg seen in an ibis' beak was its own or a serpent's. Thomas Browne reports an Egyptian opinion that the bird's diet of serpents sometimes caused it to produce serpentine eggs (178). In either case we find Ammianus' contemporary Cassianus, who knew Egypt very well, asserting categorically that "there can be no doubt that basilisks are born from the eggs of birds which in Egypt are called ibises" (Migne 210–11).

Though the idea of an antipathy between cock and basilisk, similar to that between weasel and basilisk, is attested as early as the second century A.D., there seems to be no further evidence to show when or why this story of the serpent's birth was transferred to the ordinary rooster, though it is probably linked to the familiar antipathy of demons and ghosts to cockcrow, and may be part of the general shift of the basilisk into a domestic European monster. The earliest surviving version of the story of the monstrous birth is in Alexander Neckam's *De naturis rerum* (A.D. 1180); interestingly enough it appears not in the chapter about the basilisk, which simply paraphrases Pliny, but in the chapter on the barnyard cock (1.175). This story enters the mainstream of the tradition shortly afterwards, when included in Pierre de Beauvais' enlarged bestiary (A.D. 1218); according to Pierre, an egg begins to form in the body of an aged cock. He lays it secretly in a dung heap, where it is hatched by a toad. The animal produced from the egg has the upper body of a rooster and the lower body of a snake (McCulloch 62–69, 199). Pierre is also the first surviving witness for the notion that the basilisk can be overcome with a mirror—we have the details of a hunt for a basilisk using this method in the year 1202 (Ley 42–45). The idea is probably of ancient origin; it is sometimes traced to Aristotle (Lum 41), and, since it recalls the myth of Medusa, who is defeated by her own reflection in the shield of Perseus, it may be related to Lucan's poetic conceit that the basilisk is one of the serpents generated from her blood (9.696 ff.).

The medieval image of the basilisk as a chimerical monster, part serpent, part cock, derives from this story of its birth. The precise moment of invention is untraceable, but at least from the twelfth century the classical snake remains at the heart of all verbal accounts, while the medieval monster continues to be developed and enriched in visual representations. A convenient milestone of this persistent incongruity is the twelfth-century bestiary manuscript translated by T. H. White; here the description of a Plinian basilisk is illustrated by what looks like a rooster with a long serpentine tail ((White 168). From this point on the two creatures continue to meet on the page, but each has its own relatively independent tradition.

At about the same time the word "cockatrice" comes into play. The history of this term is a long comedy of errors that can only be summarized here (Breiner; Robin 85–91 and Appendix). At first it was simply the name for the crocodile (*cocodrillus*). Through an accumulation of sound shifts, scribal errors, and mis-information, it served as the name for several different things, among them the ichneumon, trochilus, and hydra; it even seems to function as a kind of all-purpose word for a monster. Finally it comes to rest as the name for the basilisk born of a cock's egg. The first surviving instances of the word with this meaning appear in France at the end of the twelfth century (in a few cases it seems to have been used to name the peculiar egg involved in the story). "Cockatrice" comes into English as a translation of *basiliscus* at the end of the fourteenth century through two influential books: Trevisa's English version of Bartholo-maeus Anglicus' encyclopedia *De proprietatibus rerum*, in which Neckam's story of the birth is retold, and Wyclif's Bible, in which instances of both *basiliscus* and *regulus* are translated from the Vulgate. The most rigorous writers properly tried to reserve "cockatrice" as a name for the chimerical monster, as distinct from the Plinian snake, but since the two were rarely distinguished in ordinary medieval practice, "cockatrice" became interchangeable with "basilisk."

By the High Middle Ages the lore of the basilisk was complete; one of the most learned and comprehensive accounts of the creature from any period is that of Albertus Magnus' *De animalibus*, which incidentally rejects both the story of birth from a cock's egg and the idea of a basilisk with wings (666–67). The same account mentions that in alchemical writings the elixir or Philosopher's Stone is called "the basilisk"; in England the term "cockatrice" was also used in this sense (Ripley 127).

The climax of the basilisk's story comes with the Renaissance, which brings to bear on it a new passion for scholarship, new scientific instincts for orderly theory and empirical research, and considerable new technology. When the new science came to investigate the lore of the basilisk, most of it had to be discarded. What may be the last documented appearance of a basilisk occurred in Warsaw in 1587 (Lum 42–43); in the same year Conrad Gesner's sceptical account of the creature was published as part of his *Historia animalium*. Relying heavily on Gesner, Edward Topsell in his *History of Serpents* allowed that there might be a cockatrice born from a cock's egg (to deny this meant an apparent contra-diction of scriptural authority), but insisted that this was not the real basilisk, and that in any case the idea of a composite winged monster was impossible (678). Aldrovandi in 1640 and Browne in 1646 essentially agreed: "Nor is this Cockatrice only unlike the Basilisk, but of no real shape in Nature; and rather an Hierogyphical fansie" (Browne 175).

Paradoxically, after the reality of the cockatrice was denied, the original

African basilisk was forgotten, but the cockatrice flourished as a creature of pure fantasy. One reason for this surprising outcome was that Renaissance technology made possible a tremendous proliferation of images of the creature at its most chimerical. The oddest sort of representation was the contrivance of "actual" basilisks, little mummified monsters put together out of pieces of marine rays and other fish, often with painted glass eyes. Gesner, Aldrovandi, and Browne all warn their readers against these impostures—or at least against spending too much for them. Several of these so-called "jenny hanivers" can still be seen in the museums of Venice and Verona (Forti 229 f.), and many of the drawings of basilisks published in the sixteenth and seventeenth centuries are patently based on these contrivances; this is true, for example, of some of Aldrovandi's illustrations (Gudger 512–19).

It was printing, however, that made the basilisk available to the largest public it ever enjoyed. During the Middle Ages the monster had been depicted in a limited number of illuminated manuscripts and, more accessibly, as an ornamental detail in church architecture. In this form it can be seen adorning capitals, medallions, and misericords particularly in England and France. Toward the end of the Middle Ages the physical appearance of the cockatrice achieved its sharpest definition in the arcane system of heraldry: here it has the head and legs of a cock, a snakelike tail, and a body like a bird's, but covered with scales like a snake (whether the wings were feathered or scaled seems not to have been legislated). Its two legs set it apart from the four-legged dragons and griffins, while the two-legged wyvern differed in having a serpent's head and the feet of an eagle (Gough 122). But the application of such rigor to a group of chimerical monsters was too misguided to prevail. What appealed to artists, and even to illustrators, was the imaginative license that such creatures allow. What the cockatrice contributed to the arts was not so much its form as the freedom of conception behind its form—the freedom that produces the grotesque.

During the Renaissance, basilisks and near-basilisks are common in the decorative arts and rare in paintings. The reason may be that, in a sense, the basilisk has form but no content. It is very successful as an element of grotesque decoration, because it has a striking appearance with which an artist can play very freely. Whatever distortion might be necessary to fit it into the available space, its monstrosity survives intact. In painting, however, which is more or less anecdotal, there can be few reasons to include a basilisk as such, because it can bring little more than its monstrosity to the composition. There is, for example, something like a basilisk among Giotto's frescoes in the Scrovegni Chapel in Padua. But it is playing the role of the biblical brazen serpent (Numbers 21:9), and in the immediate context the creature on its pillar is a prototype of Christ on the cross; neither of these functions is appropriate to the basilisk. In effect, Giotto was painting not the basilisk in particular, but a generalized desert serpent.

Carpaccio's painting usually called *St. Tryphonius Subduing the Basilisk* is a more complex case. What attributes of a basilisk are engaged in this picture or in the anecdote it represents? The legend is about the saint's exorcism of a demon, so the creature is in the picture to suggest what a demon looks like. If it is a basilisk, no attribute except its monstrosity comes into play. It is a form, not a content. For that matter, the demon does not even look like a proper basilisk: it has four legs, a lion's body, and a head like a mule. Carpaccio may not have thought of a basilisk except insofar as he was thinking of a composite monster; the title is of course not the artist's. Yet the fact that the picture is known by this title has the peculiar result that, for art history, the creature depicted here is a basilisk in spite of its appearance, and moreover is a factor in all subsequent conceptions of what a basilisk looks like.

In literature for similar reasons the basilisk tends to adorn a tale and rarely plays a central role. We have seen already that it hardly appears in classical literature. Christianity then rediscovered the basilisk in the Old Testament context as an emblem of sin and of the Devil. This interest is apparent in moralizing bestiaries and biblical commentaries, where the moral implications of the creature's attributes are explored; it certainly found expression too in sermons and other unrecorded forms. Then, with the emergence of secular literature at the end of the Middle Ages, new possibilities opened up. The basilisk appears frequently in French literature, less often in Italian and Spanish. But it will be most instructive to trace his progress through the shifting fortunes of English literature.

Our creature appears in Chaucer's *Parson's Tale* under the name "basilicoc," but the basilisk is most popular with English writers during certain periods. He figures prominently in literature (especially drama) around the year 1600; that is, just at the time of sceptical revaluation of his legend. He then all but disappears, except for a resurgence of interest among the Romantic poets, and another among twentieth-century writers of fantasy. Among the Renaissance poets Donne mentions the cockatrice only once, in a comic elegy ("The Perfume"); Herbert uniquely draws on its alchemical implications for "Sinnes Round." Milton never used the words "cockatrice" or "basilisk," but it is difficult not to sense Pliny's regal serpent behind Milton's conception of Satan in prelapsarian Eden. Both words were heard most often from the stage, in part because "cockatrice" had become a slang term for a prostitute. When the creature itself was being invoked, the reason was almost always its "death-darting eye." This is, for example, the sole content of seven of the twelve instances of the terms in Shakespeare's plays. But the dramatist's most thoughtful uses of the basilisk all occur in the histories, which are linked in small measure by images of venomous animals and poisons overcome (note for example the language of *Richard II* III.ii, *2 Henry VI* III.ii, and *Richard III* I.iii). Perhaps the most complex instance is appropriately in *Richard III*, the play most overtly concerned with a venomous reptile. Richard has just proposed to Lady Anne over the fresh corpse of Henry VI, and these lines follow:

> *R.:* Why dost thou spit at me?
> *A.:* Would it were mortal poison, for thy sake!

> R.: Never came poison from so sweet a place.
> A.: Never hung poison on a fouler toad.
>   Out of my sight! thou dost infect my eyes.
> R.: Thine eyes, sweet lady, have infected mine.
> A.: Would they were basilisks, to strike thee dead!
> R.: I would they were, that I might die at once;
>   For now they kill me with a living death.
>
> (I.ii.144–52)

Here Anne's own action leads to imagery that presents her as a snake, spitting poison at a toad which it has hypnotized with its stare. When she tries to take control of the drift of the imagery (line 150) she is a snake wishing to be a basilisk—to be more poisonous, but perhaps also more regal, the wife of a king. And the new image only plays into Richard's hands: he is precisely the toad seeking to hatch this basilisk's eggs.

When the basilisk reappears among the Romantic poets, it comes directly from their interest in the Elizabethan dramatists. Coleridge uses "cockatrice" only twice, in his play *Zapolya*, an overt imitation of *The Winter's Tale*, and Keats uses it only in his play *Otho the Great*. Shelley is more interesting. Three times he envisions an infant sharing a meal with a basilisk ("Daemon of the World" 2.91; *Queen Mab* 8.86; *Revolt of Islam* 5.50.3), an image that derives from the apocalyptic vision of peace in Isaiah 11:8. It is in effect a redemption of the basilisk from his fallen, demonic role in Christianity and a restoration of his original Egyptian nobility; a version of the Romantic glorification of demonic heroes like Prometheus and Milton's Satan. The same spirit is behind his only other use of the word, when in the "Ode to Naples" he urges the city, "Be thou like the imperial basilisk / Killing thy foe with unapparent wounds."

In all of these instances, the basilisk finds a place in the realm of imagery, not in the narrative; its function (as in the plastic arts) is ornamental. The same is usually true in modern fantasy, thanks to the freedom with which alien creatures can now be invented. Even the most monstrous basilisk seems rather quaint, a relic from a primitive period in the history of the imagination, but some writers, like Piers Anthony or Roger Zelazny, still find uses for the traditional monsters. At the opening of Anthony's *A Spell for Chameleon*, a chameleon takes on the form of a basilisk, foreshadowing the temporary transformation of the hero into a cockatrice and the female lead (named Chameleon) into a basilisk (185–91). In the same author's *Ogre, Ogre*, a more significant adventure is ornamented by a brief encounter with a basilisk, here a small lizard with a pungent smell. Its corrosive body will eventually eat through a metal gauntlet, but its killing glance is met with the mirror defense; the mirror is shattered, the basilisk stunned (21).

Only very recently has an author introduced the basilisk, apparently for the first time since Lucan, as a character fully involved in an action. Walter Wangerin's fantasy *The Book of the Dun Cow* recounts a battle for the fate of the world in which a rooster is the hero and the villains are the subterranean Wyrm, his creature Cockatrice, and Cockatrice's countless basilisk-children. Wangerin is scrupulous about detail. His basilisks are Plinian snakes that move with heads erect; they are born of Cockatrice and his hens. Cockatrice himself is the medieval monster, born of a cock's egg hatched by a toad. But none of these creatures has the characteristic deadly glance, for good reason: it is awkward to introduce into a narrative an element that immediately destroys all other features of the landscape. The basilisk typically rules over a desert because its presence creates a desert. Wangerin's compromise here is successful for his purposes, but even so his Cockatrice remains an unmotivated blank, the basilisks mere engines of evil. The basilisk, alas, has great looks but no personality, and this helps to explain its oddly marginal role in literature.

The basilisk is not otherwise very familiar today. For one thing, such chimerical creatures are difficult to associate clearly with a symbolic valence. Many fabulous beings are highly suggestive. The unicorn, for example, presents a fine visual image, but it is also a regal ennobling of the domesticated horse, and an Apollonian version of the centaur, its phallic power absolutely patent in icon as in anecdote, but somehow purified. The mermaid offers a complex of fertile ideas by bringing together land and sea, the human and the far from human; by contrast the melding of a chicken and a snake does not invite much thought. The basilisk has little resonance; it is merely monstrous, not in any way emblematical. What might have been the creature's niche has been taken over by the dragon, which is also lordly, dangerous, and a little ludicrous, but enjoys a longer history and richer lore. Sadly, most of us, coming across a representation of a basilisk, would mistake it for a dragon. Yet there is a kind of poetic justice in the decline of the basilisk. In its heyday, its sight could kill. But as pictures of the monster proliferated, there were those who wondered how it could be spied upon so readily; perhaps there was some truth to the lingering opinion that if you saw it first, you were safe (Albertus 666). For whatever reason, after centuries of stealing glimpses, we can stare at a basilisk on a wellhead or a facade and, far from catching our death, not even see him.

BIBLIOGRAPHY

Aelian, Claudius. *On the Characteristics of Animals*. Trans. A. F. Scholfield. 3 vols. Cambridge: Harvard University Press, 1958.

Albertus Magnus. *De animalibus*. In *Opera omnia*. Lyons, 1651. Vol. 6, lib. 25.

Aldrovandi, Ulisse. *Serpentum, et draconum historiae*. Bologna, 1640.

Ammianus Marcellinus. *Ammianus Marcellinus*. Trans. John Rolfe. 3 vols. Cambridge: Harvard University Press, 1950.

Anthony, Piers. *A Spell for Chameleon*. New York: Ballantine, 1977.

———. *Ogre, Ogre*. New York: Ballantine, 1982.

Borges, Jorge Luis, with Margarita Guerrero. *The Book of Imaginary Beings*. Trans. Norman Thomas di Giovanni. New York: Discus-Avon, 1970.

Breiner, Laurence A. "The Career of the Cockatrice." *Isis* 70.251 (1979): 30–47.

Browne, Thomas. *The Works of Sir Thomas Browne*. Ed. Geoffrey Keynes. Chicago: University of Chicago Press, 1964. Vol. 2.

Costello, Peter. *The Magic Zoo: The Natural History of Fabulous Animals*. New York: St. Martin's, 1979.

Diels, H. *Die Fragmente der Vorsokratiker*. Berlin: Weidemann, 1922. Vol. 2.

Forti, Achille. "Il basilisco esistente al Museo Civico di storia naturale a Venezia." *Atti del R. Istituto Veneto* 88 (1929): 225–38.

Gesner, Conrad. *Historia animalium*. Zurich, 1587. Vol. 5.

Gough, Henry, and James Parker, eds. *A Glossary of Terms Used in Heraldry*. Oxford, 1894.

Gudger, E. W. "Jenny Hanivers, Dragons and Basilisks in the Old Natural History Books and in Modern Times." *Scientific Monthly* 38 (1934): 511–23.

Heliodorus. *Ethiopian Story*. Trans. Walter Lamb. London: J. M. Dent, 1961.

Horapollo. *The Hieroglyphics of Horapollo*. Trans. George Boas. New York: Pantheon, 1950.

Ley, Willy. *Exotic Zoology*. New York: Capricorn, 1966.

Lucan. *The Civil War [Pharsalia]*. Trans. J. D. Duff. Cambridge: Harvard University Press, 1928.

Lum, Peter. *Fabulous Beasts*. New York: Pantheon, 1951.

McCulloch, Florence. *Medieval Latin and French Bestiaries*. Chapel Hill: University of North Carolina Press, 1960.

Migne, J.-P. *Patrologia Latina*. Paris, 1865. Vol. 50.

Neckam, Alexander. *De naturis rerum*. Ed. and trans. Thomas Wright. Rolls Series no. 34. London, 1863.

Phillips, Henry. *Basilisks and Cockatrices*. Philadelphia, 1882.

Pliny the Elder. *Natural History*. Trans. H. Rackham et al. 10 vols. Cambridge: Harvard University Press, 1938–62.

Ripley, George. *The Compound of Alchemy* (1471). In *Theatrum chemicum britannicum*. Ed. Elias Ashmole. London, 1652; rpt. New York: Johnson Reprint, 1967.

Robin, P. Ansell. *Animal Lore in English Literature*. London: John Murray, 1932.

Topsell, Edward. *The History of Four-Footed Beasts and Serpents and Insects*. London, 1658.

Wangerin, Walter, Jr. *The Book of the Dun Cow*. New York: Harper and Row, 1978.

White, T. H., ed. and trans. *The Bestiary: A Book of Beasts, Being a Translation from a Latin Bestiary of the Twelfth Century*. New York: Putnam's, 1954.

_____ Human-Animal Composites

8

The Manticora

David R. Cheney

The manticora is perhaps the most fearsome and ferocious monster ever imagined. It has a red lion's body; a human face, ears, and blue eyes; and a voice like the mingling of panpipes and trumpet. But the distinctive and terrible features are three rows of teeth in each jaw, a fatal sting like a scorpion's in the end of the tail, and poisoned spines along the tail which may be shot like arrows in any direction. It is exceedingly swift, with leaps so powerful that the loftiest objects and largest spaces cannot hold it. Finally, it is a man-eater.

The manticora has over three dozen different names deriving ultimately from the Old Persian *martikhoras*, meaning "man-eater," or *mantichoras*, a corrupt reading in Aristotle. Indeed, most of the changes have been rung on "manti," "manty," "mard," "marti," and "merdi" of the first part of the name and "chora," "chore," "chors," "cor," "cora," "core," "cors," "khor," and "khora" of the second part. In addition, it has been called mantiserra, manticero, and man-tiger.

In spite of A. H. L. Heeren's suggestion that the source of the manticora is to be found in a mythological system of Bactro-Indian origin that blended real animals together in a variety of monstrous combinations (Wilson 40), the actual origin seems to have been the account by Ctesias, a Greek physician at the Persian court in the fifth century B.C. and credulous purveyor of many Persian tales of natural history. As evidence, the earliest description of the manticora yet discovered is by Ctesias, and it contains all the basic characteristics of the beast—lion's body, man's face, triple row of teeth, tail with a sting and darts, and red color (McCrindle 11). Furthermore, all the accounts of the manticora by ancient Greeks and Romans apparently were derived directly or indirectly from Ctesias. For instance, among others, Aristotle in the fourth century B.C.

(*Historia animalium* 2.1) and Pliny the Elder in the first century A.D. (*Natural History* 8.30.75) attributed their accounts of the manticora to Ctesias.

Of the ancients, Aelian, in the second century A.D., gave the fullest account of the manticora. He did not add anything new to Ctesias' description, but he did elaborate on several points. For example, he said that "the tip of the tail gives a fatal sting to anyone who encounters it," that the darts in its tail are "a foot long and the thickness of a bulrush," and that it defeats all animals but the lion. While it is true that Aelian, like Aristotle, Pliny, and Pausanias (9.21.4), questioned Ctesias' veracity, he immediately added, "At any rate after hearing of the peculiarities of this animal, one must pay heed to the historian of Cnidos" (4.21).

Also in the second century A.D., Philostratus of Lemnos mentioned the "martichora" as one of the marvels Apollonius asked Iarchas about before his departure from the hill of the sages (3.45), and in the third century A.D. Solinus repeated essentially what Pliny had said (52.37).

The manticora does not seem to have appeared in the *Physiologus*, but it did appear as early as the second-family bestiaries in, for example, the so-called Pseudo-Hugo of Saint Victor, where it occurs as number 21 (3.8; McCulloch 37). It also appeared in later bestiaries such as MS. Harleian 3244 in the British Library. From the bestiaries it passed into natural histories and also into medieval church decoration and thence into folklore (Costello 104).

In the thirteenth century Bartholomaeus Anglicus included a description of the manticora, calling it "baricos," in book 18 of his treatise on scientific and humane knowledge *De proprietatibus rerum* (Steele 139), and in the fifteenth century the manticora appeared in William Caxton's *Mirrour of the World*, which was translated from a French version of an early Latin original. The account included two notable variations: the three rows of teeth became "thre huge grete teeth in his throte" and the voice like panpipes and trumpets became "the voys of a serpente in suche wyse that by his swete songe he draweth to hym the peple and deuoureth them" (e viii). This may be the only time the manticora was confused with sirens.

In the Renaissance some descriptive natural histories treated the manticora. For example, Conrad Gesner in the sixteenth century included a lengthy history and description in his *Historia animalium* (1:631), and in the early seventeenth century Edward Topsell drew heavily on Gesner for his *History of Four-Footed Beasts* (1:343–45).

Manticoras seem not to have been mentioned in any serious studies in the eighteenth century and in only one in the late nineteenth century, F. Edward Hulme's *Myth-land*, but they have appeared in many twentieth-century books about fabulous beasts, such as Daniel Cohen's *Modern Look at Monsters*, Peter Costello's *Magic Zoo*, Ernst and Johanna Lehner's *A Fantastic Bestiary*, Heinz Mode's *Fabulous Beasts and Demons*, P. Ansell Robin's *Animal Lore in English Literature*, and T. H. White's *Book of Beasts*, a translation of a bestiary with copious notes.

Throughout the history of the beast, the basic description, as far as written accounts are concerned, has been adhered to closely with only an occasional variation. For example, Pliny says its eyes are gray instead of blue (8.30.75), Bartholomaeus Anglicus says the beast is "like to the bear in body and in hair" (Steele 139), and the rare heraldic figure has curved or spiral horns and sometimes dragon's wings and feet (*Oxford English Dictionary*; Franklyn and Tanner 215). But none of these variations seems to have been accepted by many other writers, and since all references seem to have sprung from the single source, Ctesias, there have never been what could be called different forms of manticoras.

Although the manticora has been equated with the fabulous Indian beast called the makara, and has been said to be an uncanny creature like the werewolf, or an Eastern hieroglyphic or god (T. H. White 52), or a composite of lion, man, scorpion, and porcupine (Wilson 42–43), the likely original is the Indian tiger. In any case, as early as the second century A.D., Pausanias, in recording Ctesias' description of the manticora, said, "I am inclined to think [it] is the tiger." He accounted for the three rows of teeth, the scorpion's sting, the darts, and the man's face by saying that these are false details that "the Indians pass on from one to another owing to their excessive dread of the beast" (9.21.4), and P. Ansell Robin agrees that the embellishments are merely those of "panic-stricken witnesses after headlong flight" (81). However, others give a more detailed explanation for the fabulous elements. For example, Valentine Ball suggests that "the idea of the three rows of teeth probably had its origin in the three lobes of the carnivorous molar," and that "at the extremity of the tail of the tiger . . . there is a little horny dermal structure like a claw or nail, which, I doubt not, the natives regard as analogous to the sting of the scorpion." He adds that the spines may be derived from the whiskers of the tiger, which "are by many natives regarded as capable of causing injury" (311). Wilson suggests that the human face may have been a Persian embellishment or have been derived from some "grotesque specimen of Indian sculpture," or from Hindu stories about cannibals, since the manticora is a man-eater (41–42).

In the Middle Ages the manticora was the emblem of the prophet Jeremiah because the manticora lives in the depths of the earth and Jeremiah was thrown into a dung pit (Réau 1:124). It had no symbolic meaning until it passed into folklore. Then, according to D. Philippo Picinello in his *Mundus Symbolicus*, it became the symbol of tyranny, disparagement, and envy (Henkel and Schöne 2161), and finally the embodiment of evil (Costello 104). As late as the 1930s it was still considered by peasants in Spain to be a beast of ill omen (Costello 110).

There have been sporadic references to the manticora in literature ever since the Middle Ages. Usually it is presented as a dangerous, cruel, or vicious beast. The earliest literary reference seems to be that in the thirteenth-century romance *Kyng Alisaunder*. At Caspias, says the romance in the lengthy section on Alexander's travels in the East, he lost thirty thousand men to wild beasts, such as adders, lions, bears, dragons, unicorns, and manticeros (1:383; lines 7078–99).

A later allusion to the manticora is found in John Skelton's early sixteenth-century poem "Phyllyp Sparowe" in which a young girl, in her bitterness toward a cat that had killed her pet bird, prays that

> The mantycors of the montaynes
> Myght fede them on thy braynes!
> (79; lines 294–95)

In George Wilkins' seventeenth-century play *The Miseries of Inforst Marriage*, usurers are compared to manticoras by Scarborrow's butler, who tells Scarborrow that all the people outside his door are "mantichoras, monstrous beastes, enemies to mankinde, that ha double rowes of teeth in their mouthes. They are Vsurers, they come yawning for money" (I2v).

Leigh Hunt, in his *Autobiography*, written in the mid–nineteenth century, tells at some length how he was terrorized in childhood by an older brother telling him tales of the manticora and then grinning and roaring like one (33–34).

Among the monsters that tempt St. Anthony in Gustave Flaubert's nineteenth-century novel *The Temptation of Saint Anthony* is a martichoras that is the traditional huge red lion with human face, three rows of teeth, and spines in its tail that it can throw in all directions. But it also spits plague and devours armies (227).

Later in the nineteenth century Charles Kingsley, in the novel *Water Babies*, used the manticora in a humorous way. Because Professor Ptthmllnsprts refused to believe in water babies, even after he had seen them, the old fairy, for revenge, made him believe in worse things such as firedrakes, manticoras, basilisks, and the like, which so "terrified" and "flabbergasted" the professor that he was out of his wits for three months (179).

In the twentieth century the manticora seems to have become gentler. At any rate, in Menotti's madrigal fable *The Unicorn, the Gorgon, and the Manticore*, the manticora really loves mankind. It is only out of its loneliness and shyness and feeling unloved that it bites sometimes the hand it really meant to kiss. Dorothy Spicer has contributed further to its domestication by writing a tale for children called "The Manticore of North Cerney." Her manticora, a man to the waist and the rest a lion, is a gentle, freedom-loving, joyful, sensitive creature (116–17).

Additional contemporary interest is suggested by the recent publication of two novels which include symbolic uses of the manticora. Robertson Davies' novel *The Manticore*, published in 1972, has a lawyer protagonist who dreams of himself as a manticora, and his psychoanalyst suggests that it is a good picture of him in court—the rational "head of a man, brave and dangerous as a lion, capable of wounding with barbs" (179). Piers Anthony's fantasy novel, *A Spell for Chameleon*, published in 1977, contains, once more, a ferocious manticora as a substantial character, guardian of the good wizard's privacy. Anthony describes his manticora, except for the wings, very much as Ctesias originally described it:

It was a manticora—a creature the size of a horse, with the head of a man, the body of a lion, wings of a dragon, and tail of a scorpion. One of the most ferocious magical monsters known. . . . Its mouth was strange, with three rows of teeth, one inside another—but its voice was stranger. It was something like a flute, and something like a trumpet. (126–27)

Thus, though the manticora has appeared infrequently in literature, it has appeared in every century, with the possible exception of the eighteenth, since the Middle Ages.

Visual presentations of the manticora have the same low frequency as literary appearances. Most of them are illustrations, and because, unlike writers, artists sometimes allowed their imaginations freer rein, some of them are rather fantastic. The earliest surviving pictures of the manticora are illustrations for the bestiaries. The most well known of these is probably the one that pictures a manticora as graceful as a gazelle and with a Phrygian cap on its head (Bodleian 764). Two other interesting illustrations are the one with the head of a woman (Cambridge, Gonville and Caius College 384, f. 175v) and the one having an odd tail that looks like a clarinet with a small spear sticking out of its bell (British Library, Harleian 3244, f. 43v; McCulloch 142–43). The only one that shows the three rows of teeth distinctly is the Westminster Bestiary (Druce 47). Probably the most complex illustration is a pen drawing from a seventeenth-century bestiary manuscript. It has the shape and mane of a lion, the scales and wings of a dragon, the head of a man with perhaps three rows of teeth, the horns of a cow, the tail of a scorpion with an arrowhead tip, seemingly three goat's dugs on the chest, and the toes of an eagle or dragon (Lehner and Lehner 69).

Apparently the bestiary pictures influenced decoration in ecclesiastical architecture, where some of the creatures appear as examples of exotic animals of the world. For instance, the twelfth-century Abbey of Souvigny has an octagonal column with various monsters, including the manticora, on four sides of it (Mâle 324); the Cathedral of Aosta has a representation of the manticora in a mosaic (Weerth 17); the Cathedral of Cahors has a fresco in which the manticora is an emblem of the prophet Jeremiah; and the capital from the ancient church Saint-Sauveur de Nevers, now in the Archeological Museum of the Porte du Croux, Nevers, has a representation of the manticora (Réau 1:124).

The manticora also appeared in other forms of art. For example, a drawing of the manticora appears on the thirteenth-century Hereford World Map (Costello 108). From the early fifteenth century there is an engraving of two fighting manticoras by a middle-Rhenish master (Lehner and Lehner 72), and in the fifteenth-century "Will of Eburton" at Somerset House there is a reference to a standing silver cup with a manticora imprinted in its bottom (*OED*).

The most elaborate illustration of the manticora is found in Topsell's *History of Four-Footed Beasts*, originally published in 1607 (1:344). The picture is of a lion with a very long tail, the tip of which is covered by spines pointing in all directions, and a man's head with moustache, beard, meticulously combed hair, mild eyes, and a mouth stretched from ear to ear and filled with three rows of pointed teeth both upper and lower.

The most recent illustration of the manticora probably is the one for Anthony's *A Spell for Chameleon*. The front cover of the paperback shows a lion with a long, jointed scorpion's tail and a man's face surrounded by a full mane, so that the head looks much like that of Bert Lahr as the lion in the *Wizard of Oz* movie.

The manticora has had a long—twenty-five century—history, and, considering the widespread knowledge of it throughout Western culture, has remained singularly true to its original description. Though at present there seems to be new interest in the manticora in fiction and books on fabulous beasts, it is unlikely that it will ever attain to the familiarity or popularity of such creatures as the unicorn or dragon. However, in spite of recent attempts to domesticate it, the manticora still remains, among fabulous beasts, a prime symbol of ferocity.

BIBLIOGRAPHY

Aelian. *On the Characteristics of Animals*. Trans. A. F. Scholfield. 3 vols. Cambridge: Harvard University Press, 1958.

Anthony, Piers. *A Spell for Chameleon*. New York: Ballantine, 1977.

Aristotle. *Historia Animalium*. Trans. A. L. Peck. Cambridge: Harvard University Press, 1965. Vol. 1.

Ball, Valentine. "On the Identification of the Animals and Plants of India Which Were Known to Early Greek Authors." *Proceedings of the Royal Irish Academy* 2 (1884): 302–45.

Caxton, William. *The Mirrour of the World*. London, 1480.

Cohen, Daniel. *A Modern Look at Monsters*. New York: Dodd, 1970.

Costello, Peter. *The Magic Zoo: The Natural History of Fabulous Animals*. New York: St. Martin's, 1979.

Davies, Robertson. *The Manticore*. New York: Viking, 1972.

Druce, George C. "The Mediaeval Bestiaries, and Their Influence on Ecclesiastical Decorative Art." *British Archaeological Association Journal* 25–26 (1919–20): 41–82.

Flaubert, Gustave. *The Temptation of Saint Anthony*. Trans. Kitty Mrosovsky. Ithaca, N.Y.: Cornell University Press, 1981.

Franklyn, Julian, and John Tanner. *An Encyclopaedic Dictionary of Heraldry*. Oxford: Pergamon, 1970.

Gesner, Conrad. *Historia animalium*. 5 vols. Zurich, 1551–87.

Henkel, Arthur, and Albrecht Schöne. *Emblemata: Handbuch zur Sinnbildkunst des XVI. und XVII. Jahrhunderts*. Stuttgart: Metzlersche Verlagsbuchhandlung, 1967.

Hulme, F. Edward. *Myth-land*. London, 1886.

Hunt, Leigh. *The Autobiography of Leigh Hunt*. Ed. J. E. Morpurgo. London: Cresset Press, 1949.

Kingsley, Charles. *The Water Babies: A Fairy Tale for a Land-Baby*. New York: A. L. Burt, n.d.

Kyng Alisaunder. Ed. G. V. Smithers. 2 vols. The Early English Text Society. London: Oxford University Press, 1952–57.

Lehner, Ernst, and Johanna Lehner. *A Fantastic Bestiary: Beasts and Monsters in Myth and Folklore*. New York: Tudor Publishing Company, 1969.

McCrindle, J. W., trans. *Ancient India as Described by Ktesias the Knidian*. 1882; rpt. Delhi: Manohar Reprints, 1973.

McCulloch, Florence. *Mediaeval Latin and French Bestiaries*. Rev. ed. Chapel Hill: University of North Carolina Press, 1962.

Mâle, Emile. *Religious Art in France: The Twelfth Century*. Princeton, N.J.: Princeton University Press, 1978.

Menotti, Gian Carlo. *The Unicorn, the Gorgon, and the Manticore, or the Three Sundays of a Poet*. New York: G. Ricordi and Company, 1957.

Mode, Heinz. *Fabulous Beasts and Demons*. London: Phaidon, 1975.

Pausanias. *Description of Greece*. Trans. W. H. S. Jones. 5 vols. Cambridge: Harvard University Press, 1926–54.

Philostratus. *The Life of Apollonius of Tyana*. Trans. F. C. Conybeare. 2 vols. 1912; rpt. Cambridge: Harvard University Press, 1958–60.

Picinello, D. Philippo. *Mundus Symbolicus in Emblematum Universitate*. 2 vols. Coloniae Agrippinae, 1681.

Pliny the Elder. *Natural History*. Trans. H. Rackham et al. 10 vols. Cambridge: Harvard University Press, 1938–62.

Réau, Louis. *Iconographie de l'art chrétien*. 3 vols. Paris: Presses Universitaires de France, 1955–59.

Robin, P. Ansell. *Animal Lore in English Literature*. London: John Murray, 1932.

Skelton, John. *The Complete English Poems*. Ed. John Scattergood. New Haven: Yale University Press, 1983.

Solinus. *The Excellent and Pleasant Works of Julius Solinus Polyhistor*. Trans. Arthur Golding. London, 1587.

Spicer, Dorothy. *13 Monsters*. New York: Coward-McCann, 1964.

Steele, Robert. *Mediaeval Lore from Bartholomew Anglicus*. Preface by William Morris. London: De La More Press, 1905.

Topsell, Edward. *The History of Four-Footed Beasts and Serpents and Insects*. London, 1658.

Weerth, Ernst Aus'm. *Der Mosaikboden in St. Gereon zu Cöln*. Bonn, 1873.

White, Beatrice. "Medieval Animal Lore." *Anglia* 72 (1954): 21–30.

White, T. H., ed. and trans. *The Bestiary: A Book of Beasts, Being a Translation from a Latin Bestiary of the Twelfth Century*. New York: Putnam's, 1954.

Wilkins, George. *The Miseries of Inforst Marriage*. 1607; rpt. New York: AMS Press, 1970.

Wilson, Horace Hayman. *Notes on the Indica of Ctesias*. Oxford, 1836.

9

Mermaids

Ruth Berman

The mermaid is a water-dwelling being, usually a fair woman down to the waist, and fish-tailed below. She may, however, have legs or two tails; the tail may be fishlike, dolphinlike, or snaky. She is usually musical, singing beautifully, or sometimes harping. Although mermaids appear much more often, there are also mermen, sometimes correspondingly fair, sometimes rough and stormy in appearance. Mermaids like to sun themselves on sands or rocks, letting their hair dry and arranging it with the aid of comb and mirror. They mostly live in the sea, as the name implies (Old English *mere*, sea), but are also to be found in lakes, rivers, wells, and other watery places.

With the specific identifying details of long hair, comb and mirror, beauty, fishtail, and sirenlike music, the mermaid is a late-developing legend, taking shape chiefly in the Middle Ages in the countries of northern Europe. The earliest citations for both mermaiden and mermaid in the *Oxford English Dictionary* are from Chaucer: in *The Romaunt of the Rose*, 1366, "But it was wondir lyke to be / Song of meremaydens of the see"; and in *The Nun's Priest's Tale*, 1386, "Chauntecleer so free / Soong murier than the Mermayde in the see."

The major studies of mermaids are: *Sea Enchantress* by Gwen Benwell and Arthur Waugh, a full-length study; *Havfruens Saga* by Georg Koës Brøndsted, on Scandinavian mermaids and their origins; *Mermaids* by Beatrice Phillpotts, an art-book; *Der Wassermensch* by Klaus J. Heinisch, a study of humans metamorphosed to sea-people, in the line of the classical Glaucus and Scylla, or the Italian Cola Pesce (Nick Fish), as symbols of alienation; and "The Natural History of Mermaids" by Richard Carrington in his *Mermaids and Mastodons*, on the natural phenomena which have contributed to the development of the legend. *A Book of Mermaids* by Ruth Manning-Sanders is a collection of legends retold for young people.

Every culture has legends of gods or spirits of the water, often fair women, sometimes fish-tailed and musical, who incarnate the beauty of the sight and sounds of water. As water-beings, mermaids and their kin tend to be capricious and powerful; they may either enrich or endanger a land-dweller.

The oldest known sea-god is the Babylonian Ea (or Oannes, in the form derived from Greek texts), who rose out of the Erythrean Sea and taught the arts and sciences to men. An eighth-century B.C. wall-scene, now in the Louvre, shows Oannes as a merman, human to the waist and fish-tailed below; a photo of it is reproduced in Benwell and Waugh (pl. 2b). A Semitic mermaid moon-goddess, called Atargatis among the Syrians and Derceto among the Philistines, was widely worshiped.

Benwell and Waugh discuss among other examples of the ubiquitous water-gods in the ancient world various gods of India, especially the Apsaras, celestial lute-playing water-nymphs (not fish-tailed); the Chinese and Japanese sea-drag-ons and the dragon-wives; and the Greek and Roman Poseidon/Neptune, along with his son Triton, the sea-nymphs, daughters of Nereus (the nereids), and their counterparts of Ocean (the oceanides) and fresh water (naiads). Triton is usually portrayed with a fishtail; the other classical water-spirits were usually human in shape.

Examples of mermaidlike water-spirits in other lands are also discussed by Benwell and Waugh. In the British islands, there are the Cornish merrymaid, the Irish merrow (Irish *muir*, sea; *oigh*, maid), and the Shetland sea-trow, who puts on the shape of a tailed creature to travel in the water and, like the selchies, the seal-folk, of the same waters, is able to remove the animal-skin to walk on land. In Scandinavia, there are the neck, a merman of both salt and fresh water, and the havfrue and havmand (mermaid and merman). In German lands are the meerfrau, the fresh-water nix (male) and nixe (female), and the Lorelei of the Rhine. There are sirens in France, Italy, Portugal, and Spain. The French Mé-lusine, ancestress of the house of Lusignan, was a snake-woman in most forms of the legend, but sometimes a mermaid; in German heraldry, a Melusine is a double-tailed mermaid. In Russia are the daughters of the water-king, who live beneath the sea; the rusalka, a water-nymph which drowns swimmers; and the vodyany, a tricky male spirit who follows sailors and fishers. In Africa are folktales of a fish-wife and of river-witches. A two-tailed sea-god led the Shawano Amerindians to their home, and various Amerindian groups have stories of fish maidens.

Although "siren" became the standard term for a mermaid throughout most of Southern Europe, the original sirens of Greek mythology (see the entry on sirens) were not mermaids, but bird-women.

The worship of the ancient deities of river and sea gradually faded, but belief in mermaids—in some kind of intelligent and powerful humanoid water-creature to be placated for safety's sake—remained. Stories which would seem originally to have been told of humans sacrificed to water-goddesses could be retold as stories of drowned humans transformed to water-spirits. For example, Habren (or Sabrina), the illegitimate daughter of King Locrine in Geoffrey of Monmouth's *History of the Kings of Britain*, was drowned in the river Severn by her father's wife, and the river took its name from her. Milton drew on this legend in his masque *Comus* for his portrait of "Sabrina fair" as Goddess of the River, invoked in the names of classical water-gods from Oceanus to the Sirens, to protect virgins like herself.

A similar transformation, with grimmer results, occurred at the death of a servant, Peg o' Nell, who broke her neck drawing water from a well on a winter's icy day, and who haunts the river Ribble and claims a death by drowning every seven years; Katharine Briggs, in *An Encyclopedia of Fairies*, points out that such figures also serve as cautionary bogies to frighten children away from potentially dangerous playgrounds. In addition to Peg o' Nell, some of her examples are Peg Powler of the river Tees, Jenny Greenteeth of Lancashire, the Grundylow of Yorkshire, and the Scottish water-wraiths such as haunted the river Conan and the Linn of Lynturk. The Lorelei of the Rhine, in Germany, best known in Heinrich Heine's poem, "Die Lorelei," is a similarly dangerous river-spirit; the beautiful song with which she draws travelers to death on the rocks around her suggests the influence of the classical siren.

On the more beneficent side, there are stories of mermaids who warn of storms, or other future events (sometimes voluntarily, sometimes under compulsion—a mermaid may be compelled to answer by the seizure of her cap or belt), grant wishes or bestow supernatural powers, bring up drowned treasure or show its location, or teach wisdom (as in the Welsh tale of the lady of the lake, Llyn y Fan Fach, who married a mortal and later left him, but, according to the story of the three physicians of Mydfai, visited her sons to teach them the arts of medicine). More ambiguous in their results are the stories of mermaids who take mortal men into their favor. A youth adopted by a mermaid as a ward usually has a strong and faithful protector, but marriage with mermaids is usually conditional, and the conditions are usually broken, ending the marriage. Men who are drawn under the sea to live with the mermaids in their underwater realms (such as blind Maurice Connor, king of the bagpipers in Munster, who followed a sea-lady and is still to be heard playing under the water) may be thought of either as living in bliss—or drowned.

As the Christian church became dominant in Europe, its leaders tried to suppress belief in all pagan deities. Minor supernatural figures such as mermaids, however, lacking the powers of major gods, presented less of a threat, and were not attacked as vigorously. Moreover, there were two factors which made the Church accept belief in mermaids: their value as moral emblems of one type of sin, and the quantity of evidence in contemporary and classical authors showing proof of their existence.

Emblematically, the mermaid with her comb and mirror was a figure of vanity and of that female beauty which lures males to destruction. This misogynistic view served to encourage depictions of mermaids, thus increasing the fascination with the figure it was intended to deplore.

Like many other imaginary creatures, the mermaid-siren and its emblematic significance were made widely known in the bestiaries of *Physiologus* and its successors. As T. H. White pointed out in the appendix to his translation of a twelfth-century bestiary, the bestiaries were intended to be compilations of (real) zoological information, and included emblematic significance as an appropriate scientific datum, given their belief that Creation was orderly and therefore full of obvious parallels between the domains of land and sea, heaven and earth, or morality and nature (243–47).

The early bestiaries included sirens (bird-women), not mermaids, in the entries. As sirens and mermaids became merged in popular conception, however, so did they in the bestiaries. In White's bestiary, the text carefully described sirens as half-human, half-avian, but the picture showed a human (holding a fish in one hand) with wings at the waist and with both bird-legs and a large fishtail below (134–35). An early thirteenth-century bestiary, Guillaume le Clerc's *Le Bestiaire divin*, said the siren's lower half was shaped like a fish or like a bird (224). In the mid–thirteenth century, Bartholomaeus Anglicus, in the book on animals in his *De proprietatibus rerum* (On the Properties of Things), although remarking that some men said sirens were fishes like women, while others said they were part maiden and part bird, gave it as the opinion of *Physiologus* that a siren was a maid above the navel and a fish below (2:1248; Trevisa's translation).

On the scientific side, in addition to the accounts of the siren repeated by *Physiologus* and its followers, there were Pliny's descriptions, apparently based on eyewitness accounts, of various sea-folk in the section on aquatic monsters in his *Natural History* (9.4; first century A.D.). Pliny's tritons and nereids were probably seals and sea-cows; he mentions the bristly, scaly appearance of a nereid.

Besides such older authorities, there were contemporary mermaid sightings. Benwell and Waugh list examples dating from the twelfth century (a monster like a woman to the waist and a fish below, with a horrible face, wide-mouthed and double-chinned, seen near Greenland, according to an Icelandic work, the *Speculum Regale*) to the end of the nineteenth century—as well as a few more in the twentieth century. For example, the Elizabethan historian, Raphael Holinshed, in his *Chronicles* (1587), reported that in the reign of John or Henry II (his sources disagreed), some fishers of Oreford in Suffolk caught a man-shaped fish, who would not or could not speak, and ate fish either raw or cooked. He escaped after two months and fled back to the sea (Benwell and Waugh 74, 76). In 1403, after a storm in West Friesland, a mermaid was found stranded in the mud. John Swan, in his *Speculum Mundi* (1635), reported that she was taken and allowed herself to be clothed and fed ordinary food, but often tried to escape back to the sea; she learned to spin and to kneel to the crucifix, but was unable to speak. According to some informants, she lived for fifteen years after her capture (Benwell and Waugh 81). Samuel Purchas, in *Purchas His Pilgrimes* (1625), quoted from Henry Hudson's log a report of a mermaid, seen on June

15, 1608, during his second attempt to find a northern passage to the East Indies. Two of his company, Thomas Hilles and Robert Raynor, said they had seen a mermaid: "From the Navill upward, her backe and breasts were like a womans . . . her skin was very white; and long haire hanging down behinde, of colour blacke; in her going downe they saw her tayle, which was like the tayle of a Porposse, and speckled like a Macrell" (qtd. in Benwell and Waugh 95). In 1809, William Munro, a schoolmaster of Thurso, in Caithness, wrote an account, which was published in *The Times* on September 8. About twelve years earlier, while walking on the shore, he had seen what he first took to be a naked woman sitting on a rock and combing her light brown hair. The face was plump, with ruddy cheeks and blue eyes. Had not the rock on which the creature was sitting been dangerous for swimmers, Munro would have assumed it was human. After a few minutes it dropped into the sea and swam away. Others had seen it there (Benwell and Waugh 111–13).

The weight of such examples is still enough to cause some commentators to argue for the possibility that mermaids (that is to say, some kind of large sea-going mammal, much more human in appearance than those known) could exist, even though no naturalist has succeeded in catching one or finding the body of one. Benwell and Waugh (275–77) and Peter Costello (56) take this position. Others, such as Richard Carrington (in "The Natural History of Mermaids" in *Mermaids and Mastodons*), argue that even views apparently as close as those of Hudson's men or Munro were sightings of known sea-mammals, distorted by distance, unfamiliarity, and the desire to believe.

The animals most likely to be mistaken for mermaids, according to Carrington, have been the tropical manatee and dugong, some of the smaller whales, and seals and walruses. None of these looks much like a traditional mermaid from close up, but their postures and cries are often very humanlike. Legged merfolk taken in captivity (such as the merman of Oreford or the mermaid of West Friesland) sound likely to have been mute humans (perhaps retarded or psychotic) with a gift for swimming.

Deliberate hoax has occasionally played a part in drawing attention to mermaids, although not on a large scale, except during the nineteenth century. By then, scientific and geographical investigation had made it increasingly difficult to accept wonder-tales as literally true, and yet the need for wonder continued. The development of fantasy as a genre of literature—using the impossible as a basis of art for its emotional and symbolic truths—during the nineteenth century was one solution. Hoaxes were another.

Mermaid corpses were manufactured out of monkey tops and fishtails, skillfully stitched together. P. T. Barnum had a "Feejee mermaid" on display. A reproduction of one of Barnum's ads (Phillpotts 55) shows a mermaid sexy enough in general outline to attract customers and ugly enough in face to prevent cries of fraud when they got inside and saw a monkey-faced, "hideous-looking" mermaid (Barnum 238).

Until the age of global explorations, however, the weight of available evidence made the existence of mermaids plausible, and their symbolic value as images of temptation made them theologically acceptable. There was thus no bar to the use of mermaids in the various arts, and gradually mermaids came to be used in many art forms.

In literature, the mermaid, as opposed to such older kindred spirits as nereids or naiads, was rare at first. The various folk-narratives of mermaids did not become a major source for literary treatment until the nineteenth century. (The age of the folk-narratives is uncertain, as they were generally not recorded until modern times; they may be medieval in origin, or may be more recent, but they are certainly older than the late eighteenth century, when scholars began studying them seriously.) In the popular ballad tradition, merfolk were often central characters, particularly in Denmark; indeed, the Danish ballad "Agnete og Havmanden" (Agnes and the Merman) inspired what is perhaps the best known of all mer-poems, Matthew Arnold's sequel, "The Forsaken Merman." Among the mermaids of British balladry, those of "Clerk Colville" (Child, no. 42), and "The Mermaid" (Child, no. 289) are major characters. In the poetry of Chaucer, however, the mermaid was merely a scholarly metaphor from *Physiologus* for beautiful, if dangerous, song.

In the Elizabethan period, the mermaid was still primarily a metaphor in literature, but was beginning to be used as a character. In Shakespeare's *Comedy of Errors* (III.ii), Antipholus of Syracuse cries to Luciana:

> O, train me not, sweet mermaid, with thy note,
> To drown me in thy sister's flood of tears:
> Sing, siren, for thyself and I will dote.

Sceptical John Donne, doubting the possibility of constancy in woman, asked in his "Song" for discoveries less unlikely than such constancy:

> Goe, and catche a falling starre,
> . . . .
> Teach me to heare Mermaids singing,
> Or to keep off envies stinging.

In contrast to these metaphors, the mermaid of Oberon's vision in Shakespeare's *A Midsummer Night's Dream* (II.i) is literal, although not present in the action:

> Once I sat upon a promontory,
> And heard a mermaid on a dolphin's back
> Uttering such dulcet and harmonious breath
> That the rude sea grew civil at her song
> And certain stars shot madly from their spheres,
> To hear the sea-maid's music.

(The passage was probably suggested by some actual pageant staged for Queen Elizabeth, with mermaids in the cast, such as those put on by the Earl of Leicester in 1575 at Kenilworth, or by the Earl of Hertford in 1591 at Elvetham.) Five mermaids, symbolizing the temptations to intemperance of the five senses, played a minor role in tempting Guyon, the Knight of Temperance, in Spenser's *Faerie Queene* (bk. 2, canto 12).

The interest in the sea that grew with the voyages of exploration stimulated Elizabethan interest in mermaids. Mermaids were an apt symbol for a nation winning riches from sea-voyages. It is not surprising, therefore, that mermaids were included in many coats of arms granted during the Elizabethan period (for example, as supports in the arms of the borough of Boston, Lincolnshire, and of the Fishmongers' Company of the City of London), and that the favorite gathering-place of writers in London was called the Mermaid Tavern. Keats, only half-joking, asked in his "Lines on the Mermaid Tavern" (1818/1820) what Elysium could poets know "Choicer than the Mermaid Tavern?"

In the seventeenth century, Milton's *Comus*, as mentioned before, portrayed Sabrina as a river-goddess. In the eighteenth century, most writers turned away from all forms of the wondrous, considering fairy tales childish and unbelievable.

The Romantic movement, at the turn of the eighteenth century and in the nineteenth century, looked again to wonder, holding childhood as a symbol of freedom and imagination, and discovering that wonders might be literally un-believable yet emotionally true. The mermaid quickly became a dominant figure in nineteenth-century fantasy, both in fiction and in poetry, and was generally used to express a sense of divisions in human nature, in particular, a division between the "animal," sexual nature symbolized by the tail, and the reasoning intellect, which longs for an immortal soul and for release from the demands of the body. This division could be made the more striking in the mermaid, because love between humans and merfolk made them subject in the action of a story to the sexual delights and the corresponding sexual fears which the mermaid's form symbolized.

In 1811 appeared Baron de la Motte Fouqué's *Undine*. This name for water-spirits had been coined by the sixteenth-century alchemist Paracelsus, who had invented a systematic mythology to combine beings of folklore with the ancient Greek division of the world into the four elements of earth, air, fire, and water. The undine (from Latin *unda*, water) was the spirit of water, corresponding to the Greek water-nymphs. This story (turned into an opera, *Undine*, by E. T. A. Hoffmann, and a play, *Ondine*, by Jean Giraudoux) tells of the marriage of the river-spirit Undine and a mortal; he is untrue to her, and she returns to the water. Fouqué added the motif of the longing for an immortal soul: Undine would have won a soul and a feeling heart if her lover had been true.

This motif had appeared before in connection with merfolk, most notably in the Swedish folktale (recorded in Thomas Keightley's *The Fairy Mythology*) of the neck who wept and flung away his harp when told that he could not be saved. (Matthew Arnold wrote a poem on this story, "The Neckan.") Fouqué was the first to combine the longing for a soul with the mermaid's wedding. Hans Christian Andersen's "Little Mermaid" wins a soul, although not the prince himself, through the strength of her devotion. In Arnold's "The Forsaken Merman" Margaret's fear for her soul makes her untrue to her merman, and in Oscar Wilde's "The Fisherman and His Soul" the Fisherman tries to be rid of his soul to be able to marry the mermaid.

A related motif was the mermaid as guardian or avenger of women. In James Hogg's "Mary Burnet," the Mermaid of the Loch takes on Mary's shape to bring vengeance to her seducer. In Sir Walter Scott's *The Bride of Lammermoor*, the legendary lover's betrayal at the Mermaid's Well is acted anew by Edgar and Lucy; in *The Monastery*, the White Lady, the spirit of the Fountain of Avenel, watches after the fortunes of the family. In Alexander Pushkin's "Rusalka," the Rusalka who punishes the seducer is the spirit of the victim, who drowned herself.

Heine in "Die Lorelei" and Tennyson in "The Sea-Fairies," "The Merman," and "The Mermaid" concentrated on the observer enchanted rather than on the psychology of the water-spirit. In Heine's poem, the beauty of the Lorelei and her song are the chief peril. For Tennyson, although the sea-fairies are lovely, the chief danger to the mariners who hear them, and to the singer who wants to imagine himself as merman and mermaid, is the desire to be free of human cares in a world of vegetative and animal beauty. (It is interesting to note that Tennyson's mermaid has "silver feet"; his sea-fairies, who are not described below the waist, are evidently the Homeric sirens singing to the mariners of Odysseus. Mermaid and siren are fused so deftly as to show no division.)

Charles Kingsley in *The Water Babies* invented a new sort of water-people, and turned them to a theme of maturation instead of passion. The water-world of Tom and the other babies is ruled by motherly spirits whose care of their charges is one element of the moral beneficence Kingsley saw in all nature. Louisa May Alcott, although all her best work was in the realistic mode, wrote some fairy tales, including two of water-folk, beneficent elementals in "Ripple, or the Water Sprite," and heartless, thoughtless spirits in "The Mermaids."

The humorist Thomas Hood used mermaids for comically improbable psychic divisions. In "A Sea-Totaller," too much abstinence turns Bob Bunce into a merman; in "The Repeal of the Union," the merman who wants his Saxon tail amputated so that he can be purely human symbolizes Irish independence. (In a serious poem, a version of the legend of "Hero and Leander," he made a sea-nymph's unfulfillable love for the drowning Leander the central incident.)

In the twentieth century, the mermaid became a less important figure than in the nineteenth century, but remained popular. Mermaids might appear as one among many wonders, like the mermaids of J. M. Barrie's *Peter Pan*, or the mermaid that Doctor Lao dreams of setting free (without doing it) in Charles G. Finney's *The Circus of Dr. Lao*, or the "Water Midden" briefly met and loved by Nod, the youngest Royal Monkey, in Walter de la Mare's *The Three*

Mulla-Mulgars; but they were slightly less likely to figure as central characters in major works.

Themes changed also. The mermaid bride was no longer taken seriously, probably because sexuality had come to seem less threatening as sexual mores became freer. T. S. Eliot's J. Alfred Prufrock had heard the mermaids singing each to each, but did not expect that they would sing to him. H. G. Wells, in *The Sea Lady*, treated the theme of the mermaid bride satirically, using the mermaid's innocent inability to understand human restrictions.

Later comic portraits of mermaid brides, although including much clever social satire, as in Lord Dunsany's "Mrs. Jorkens," have sometimes resulted in amusing, but repetitious farces, as in Guy Pearce Jones and Constance Bridges Jones's novel *Peabody's Mermaid* and its film adaptation, or Peter Blackmore's play *Miranda*, and the sequel, *Mad about Men*. More successful are the stories in which the comedy turns on an unusual characterization of the irresistibly beautiful mermaid. In Theodore Sturgeon's "A Touch of Strange," the merfolk are conventionally heartless for an unconventional reason: their sexual organs are in the fish half, and sex in fishes is not the intimate process it is in mammals. In L. Sprague de Camp's "Nothing in the Rules," the thwarted romance is a minor element in the story; the comedy rises from the legalistic complexities of entering a mermaid in a women's swimming meet. Fritz Leiber's Gray Mouser encountered "The Mer-She," a creature conventionally beautiful in her human guise, but actually a hungry sharklike sea demon; the two Sea-Queens in his "When the Sea-King's Away" act like conventional mermaids interested in mortal lovers, but the story hints that they and the Sea-Witch with them may be a water-aspect of the Greek Triple Goddess, playing with mortals.

The nineteenth-century theme of mermaids as elemental spirits of a beneficent nature has been continued by some twentieth-century writers. Examples are L. Frank Baum's *The Sea Fairies* or E. Nesbit's *Wet Magic*. In both, the mermaids are semi-deities ruling the waters. In the inset story of Mensje told by a "Liar" in Jan de Hartog's *The Lost Sea*, Mensje becomes a mermaid so that she may save the life of her sailor-lover, and, unable to return to human form, she becomes the guardian spirit of all sailors from her home.

The theme which has been perhaps most popular among twentieth-century mermaid stories is that of tolerance, with the mermaid representing whatever is alien and different. One consequence of this theme is an interest in using a wide variety of merfolk. In the title story of Barbara Leonie Picard's *The Mermaid and the Simpleton*, the mermaid and the dreamer rescue each other from the arrogance of the worldly-wise. In Joyce Gard's *The Mermaid's Daughter*, the mermaid is the goddess Derceto; the Daughter is a British priestess of the goddess in the time of the Roman Empire, trying to preserve freedom of worship and her own freedom against patriarchal, exclusive Mithraism. Smaragthi, reputed to be a mermaid's daughter in Stratis Myrivilis' *The Mermaid Madonna*, tries unsuccessfully to be treated as the human she is instead of as an object of desire.

In Poul Anderson's *The Merman's Children*, a sequel to the Danish legend of Agnete and the merman, the merfolk are legged, human in appearance but for their bluish or greenish hair. In Avram Davidson's "The Case of the Mother-in-Law of Pearl," a deformed human with fused legs hiding in the river is perceived by others as a doom-portending lurley, like the Lorelei of the Rhine. In Jane Yolen's *The Mermaid's Three Wisdoms*, based on such mutes as the mermaid of West Friesland, the merfolk speak by sign language, and the encounter between hearing-impaired Jess and Melusine reconciles Jess to herself and to the use of sign language. Yolen has written many short stories and poems about merfolk, most of them in her collection *Neptune Rising*, and a few others in her *Tales of Wonder*, including figures as diverse as Neptune, Proteus, an animate monkey-fish fake, and selchies, as well as mermen and mermaids. In Randall Jarrell's *The Animal Family*, the theme of the mermaid bride is transformed into a celebration of difference as part of family love—a family of hunter, mermaid, and their adopted bear, lynx, and boy. A similar theme in reverse appears in the title novella of Thomas Burnett Swann's *The Dolphin and the Deep*, in which the adoptive family of male human, female dolphin, and triton-boy are united (the dolphin and triton metamorphosed to humans) in the end through their faithful love.

Mermaids have figured notably in the other arts as well, if not as prominently as in literature. In film, the comedy of the man in love with the mermaid has been the chief subject, including, besides the film versions of Blackmore's plays and *Peabody's Mermaid*, such movies as *The Mermaids of Tiburon* (1962), *Beach Blanket Bingo* (1965), *Sirène* (1968, Belgian), and *Splash* (1984). Serious treatments of the theme include various adaptations of "The Little Mermaid," as well as *Night Tide* (1963), a love story of a man and a woman who works as a mermaid in an amusement park. Walt Lee's *Reference Guide to Fantastic Films* lists several films about mermaids, the earliest being *La Sirène* (1904), by film pioneer Méliès.

In music, mermaids have often been the subject of tone portraits, although few such works are well known. The most familiar are Haydn's pianoforte canzonet *Mermaid's Song*; Dvořák's symphonic poem *The Water Goblin* and opera *Rusalka*; Mendelssohn's unfinished opera *Lorelei* and overture *Die schöne Melusine*; and Rimsky-Korsakov's opera *Sadko* (the youth in Russian folklore who loved one of the daughters of the water-king). A mermaid plays a small role in Handel's opera *Rinaldo*, and the Rhinemaidens are instrumental in the opening and close of Wagner's opera cycle *The Ring of the Nibelungs*.

In art, portrayals of the mermaid as such have followed the literary mermaid, and many of the best known examples are illustrations of literature, such as Arthur Rackham's sea-maid in *A Midsummer Night's Dream*, or Edvard Eriksen's statue of the Little Mermaid in Copenhagen harbor. Georg Koës Brøndsted believes that the visual forms go back much further than the literature; he considers the two-tailed mermaid a direct descendant of a version of the oriental goddess of fertility and the single-tailed mermaid of the Greek female triton.

In devotional art, a curious paradox of the theological acceptance of the mermaid as a symbol of evil was that mermaids became popular as an ornament in churches. Benwell and Waugh devote a chapter (127–39) to documenting this popularity. The devotional mermaid, however, did not produce works of out-standing artistry, except perhaps in the fictional *Mermaid Madonna* painted on the chapel wall in Stratis Myrivilis' novel.

Tritons became popular in Baroque art as an element in sea-scenes from classical mythology, as in Raphael's *Triumph of Galatea*. Mermaids as such were rare until the nineteenth century. Phillpotts' *Mermaids* has reproductions of assorted ancient sea-deities, and their Baroque counterparts; mermaids from medieval churches and books of learning; a woodcut from the Nuremberg Bible (1483) of Noah's ark floating between two mermaids; and an engraving of the Entry of the Sirens (1581), depicted as double-tailed mermaids, as staged in a ballet. Her earliest example of a mermaid in painting, however, is Daniel Ma-clise's *The Origin of the Harp* (1842), illustrating Thomas Moore's poem, on the metamorphosis into a harp of a siren weeping for her lost lover.

Phillpotts comments that unlike the Greek sea-gods of Renaissance Classicism, the mermaid of late nineteenth-century art fascinated artists "in a more personal, frequently mystical sense. . . . As subconscious *femme fatale*, the mermaid was the perfect symbol of the attractions of doomed passion" (68). Examples re-produced include works of Arnold Böcklin, Edvard Munch, Gustav Klimt, and Edward Burne-Jones. In twentieth-century art, as in literature, comic treatment of this passion became popular; examples include works of René Magritte and Paul Delvaux.

Benwell and Waugh devote a chapter (213–33) to mermaids in art-for-use, "Heraldry, Sign, Map, Coinage and Philately." The heraldic mermaid is also discussed in Rodney Dennys' art book, *The Heraldic Imagination* (121–24).

Water is the element of both death and rebirth. The sea-changes of the fair, rough, storm-bringing, storm-averting, dangerous, helpful merfolk of legend have been mirrored by the sexual, spiritual, alien, natural merfolk of literature and art. They lend themselves in both to a wide variety of meanings and of moods, and the future may bring yet more changes, equally rich and strange.

BIBLIOGRAPHY

Alcott, Louisa May. *Lulu's Library.* 2 vols. Boston, 1887.

Andersen, Hans Christian. "The Little Mermaid." In *The Complete Fairy Tales*. Trans. Erik Christian Haugaard. Garden City, N.Y.: Doubleday, 1974. 57–76.

Anderson, Poul. *The Merman's Children.* New York: Berkley-Putnam, 1979.

Arnold, Matthew. *Poems.* Ed. Kenneth Allott. London: Longmans, Green, 1965.

Barnum, Phineas Taylor. *The Life of P. T. Barnum, Written by Himself.* New York, 1885.

Barrie, J. M. *Peter Pan, or The Boy Who Would Not Grow Up.* 1904. London: Hodder and Stoughton, 1928. [The play.]

———. *Peter and Wendy.* London: Hodder and Stoughton, 1911. [The novel.]

Baum, L. Frank. *The Sea Fairies*. Chicago: Reilly and Britton, 1911.

Benwell, Gwen, and Arthur Waugh. *Sea Enchantress: The Tale of the Mermaid and her Kin*. London: Hutchinson, 1961.

Blackmore, Peter. *Miranda, a Comedy in Three Acts*. London: Deane; Boston: Baker, 1948.

———. *Mad about Men, a New Comedy about Miranda*. London: Deane; Boston: Baker, 1956.

Briggs, Katharine. *An Encyclopedia of Fairies: Hobgoblins, Brownies, Bogies, and Other Supernatural Creatures*. New York: Pantheon, 1976.

Brøndsted, Georg Koës. *Havfruens Saga: En literaer-kunsthistorisk orientering*. Copenhagen: G. E. C. Gads Forlag, 1965.

Calvino, Italo, ed. "Nick Fish." In *Italian Folktales*. Trans. George Martin. New York: Harcourt Brace Jovanovich, 1980. 521–23.

Carrington, Richard. "The Natural History of Mermaids." In *Mermaids and Mastodons: A Book of Natural and Unnatural History*. London: Chatto and Windus, 1957. 3–19.

Child, Francis James, ed. *The English and Scottish Popular Ballads*. 5 vols. 1882–98; rpt. New York: Dover, 1965.

Costello, Peter. *The Magic Zoo: The Natural History of Fabulous Animals*. New York: St. Martin's, 1979.

Dann, Jack, and Gardner Dozois, eds. *Mermaids!* New York: Ace, 1986.

Davidson, Avram. "The Case of the Mother-in-Law of Pearl." In *The Enquiries of Doctor Eszterhazy*. New York: Warner, 1975. 153–78.

de Camp, L. Sprague. "Nothing in the Rules." In *The Best of L. Sprague de Camp*. Garden City, N.Y.: Doubleday, 1978. 95–123.

de la Mare, Walter. *The Three Mulla-Mulgars*. New York: Knopf, 1919.

Dennys, Rodney. *The Heraldic Imagination*. London: Barrie and Jenkins, 1975.

Dunsany, Lord. "Mrs. Jorkens." In *The Travel Tales of Mr. Joseph Jorkens*. London and New York: Putnam's, 1931. 242–71.

Finney, Charles G. *The Circus of Dr. Lao*. New York: Viking, 1935.

Fouqué, Baron Friedrich de la Motte. *Undine*. Berlin, 1811.

Gard, Joyce. *The Mermaid's Daughter*. London: Gollancz, 1969.

Geoffrey of Monmouth. *History of the Kings of Britain*. Trans. Sebastian Evans. Rev. Charles W. Dunn. New York: Dutton, 1958.

Guillaume le Clerc. *Le Bestiaire divin*. Ed. C. Hippeau. Genève: Slatkine Reprints, 1970.

Hartog, Jan de. *The Lost Sea*. New York: Harper, 1951.

Heine, Heinrich. *Buch der Lieder*. Berlin, 1827.

Heinisch, Klaus J. *Der Wassermensch*. Stuttgart: Klett-Cotta, 1981.

Hogg, James. *Tales and Sketches by the Ettrick Shepherd*. 6 vols. Glasgow, Edinburgh, and London, 1837.

Hood, Thomas. *Works*. Ed. by his son and daughter [T. Hood, Jr., and F. F. Broderip]. 10 vols. London, 1869–73.

Jarrell, Randall. *The Animal Family*. New York: Random House, 1965.

Jones, Guy Pearce, and Constance Bridges. *Peabody's Mermaid*. New York: Random House, 1945.

Keightley, Thomas. *The Fairy Mythology*. London, 1850.

Kingsley, Charles. *The Water Babies: A Fairy Tale for a Land-Baby*. London, 1863.

Lee, Walt. *Reference Guide to Fantastic Films*. 3 vols. Los Angeles: Chelsea-Lee Books, 1972–74.

Leiber, Fritz. "When the Sea-King's Away." In *Swords in the Mist*. New York: Ace, 1968. 70–95.

———. "Under the Thumbs of the Gods." In *Swords and Ice Magic*. New York: Ace, 1977. 33–52.

———. "The Mer-She." In *The Year's Best Fantasy Stories: Six*. Ed. Lin Carter. New York: DAW, 1980. 85–113.

Manning-Sanders, Ruth. *A Book of Mermaids*. New York: Dutton, 1968.

Moore, Thomas. *Poetical Works*. 10 vols. London, 1840–41.

Myrivilis, Stratis. *The Mermaid Madonna*. Trans. Abbot Rick. New York: Thomas Y. Crowell, 1959.

Nesbit, E. [Edith Nesbit Bland.] *Wet Magic*. London: T. Werner Laurie, 1913.

Phillpotts, Beatrice. *Mermaids*. London: Russell Ash; New York: Ballantine, 1980.

Picard, Barbara Leonie. *The Mermaid and the Simpleton*. London: Oxford University Press, 1949.

Pliny the Elder. *Natural History*. Trans. H. Rackham et al. 10 vols. Cambridge: Harvard University Press, 1938–62.

Pushkin, Alexander. "The Rusalka." In *The Bronze Horseman: Selected Poems of Alexander Pushkin*. Trans. D. M. Thomas. New York: Viking, 1982. 216–38.

Scott, Sir Walter. *The Bride of Lammermoor*. Edinburgh, 1819.

———. *The Monastery*. Edinburgh, 1820.

Sturgeon, Theodore. "A Touch of Strange." In *A Touch of Strange*. Garden City, N.Y.: Doubleday, 1958. 160–73.

Swann, Thomas Burnett. *The Dolphin and the Deep*. New York: Ace, 1968.

Tennyson, Alfred. *Poems and Plays*. Ed. T. Herbert Warren. Rev. Frederic Page. London: Oxford University Press, 1965.

Trevisa, John, trans. *On the Properties of Things: John Trevisa's Translation of Bartholomaeus Anglicus*, De Proprietatibus Rerum. Ed. M. C. Seymour et al. 2 vols. Oxford: Clarendon, 1975.

Wells, H. G. *The Sea Lady: A Tissue of Moonshine*. Leipzig: Bernhard Tauchnitz, 1902.

White, T. H., ed. and trans. *The Bestiary: A Book of Beasts, Being a Translation from a Latin Bestiary of the Twelfth Century*. New York: Putnam's, 1954.

Wilde, Oscar. "The Fisherman and His Soul." In *A House of Pomegranates*. London, 1891. 63–128.

Yolen, Jane. *The Mermaid's Three Wisdoms*. Cleveland: Collins and World, 1978.

———. *Neptune Rising: Songs and Tales of the Undersea Folk*. New York: Putnam's, 1982.

———. *Tales of Wonder*. New York: Schocken Books, 1983.

10

Sirens

Ruth Berman

Sirens are women, bird-women, or mermaids, who sing or sometimes play alluringly beautiful music, drawing sailors off course to their deaths.

Studies of sirens include a survey, *A sereia*, by Fernando de Castro Pires de Lima, and a psychoanalytic discussion, *La Candeur d'un monstre*, by Silla Consoli. A chapter of John Pollard's *Seers, Shrines and Sirens* (137–45) discusses the development of the classical siren. Most of a chapter ("In Classical Times," pp. 35–50) in *Sea Enchantress* by Gwen Benwell and Arthur Waugh discusses the classical siren and the change from avian to mermaidlike sirens. Although outdated (1858) in its research, *Les Sirènes* by Georges Kastner is the most comprehensive consideration of musical supernatural beings, and includes a wide variety of engravings. *Siren Land* by Norman Douglas is a description of the islands around Capri traditionally associated with the sirens and the influence of the legends in their history.

Sirens come from Greek mythology, chiefly from the legends of Jason and Odysseus (Ulysses, in Latin). Jason and the Argonauts, in the *Argonautica* of Apollonius of Rhodes (third century B.C.), passed the sirens, who are the daughters of the river Achelous and the muse Terpsichore, and who are in shape part bird and part maiden; their siren song would have drawn the Argonauts to their deaths had not Orpheus drowned it out playing his lyre (4.893–921). In Homer's *Odyssey* (ca. 850 B.C.), Odysseus had his men plug their ears and tie him to the mast so that he could hear the sirens and live (bk. 12). Homer did not describe the sirens as having any nonhuman characteristics; his use of the dual number implied that there were two of them.

Although Apollonius wrote later than Homer, the story of Jason is older than Homer's *Odyssey*. The tradition of sirens as women-headed birds is more authentic than the tradition of fair women implied by Homer's absence of description. Classical writers who described the sirens always gave avian characteristics. In the *Library* of Apollodorus (ca. first or second century A.D.), they are birds from the thighs down, named Pisinoe, Aglaope, and Thelxiepia, daughters of Achelous and the muse Melpomene, one a lyre-player, one a singer, and one a flutist (*Epitome* 7.18–19; vol. 2, pp. 290–91). Sir James George Frazer's notes to the passage summarize other classical writers' data. Descriptions of avian sirens occur in Aelian (*De natura animalium* 17.23), Ovid (*Metamorphoses* 5.552–62), Hyginus (*Fabulae* 125, 141), Eustathius (*On Homer's Odyssey* 12.47), and Pausanias (*Description of Greece* 9.34.3). Different versions give their number as two, three, or four; their father as Achelous or Phorcys, a sea-god; their mother as Melpomene, Terpsichore, or Sterope; their names as Teles, Raidne, Molpe, and Thelxiope, or Parthenope, Leucosia, and Ligia, or Thelxione, Molpe, and Aglaophonus, or Aglaopheme and Thelxiepia. Apollodorus and Hyginus said that the sirens died after Odysseus went by, fulfilling a prophecy that they would die when a ship passed them safely. Others said rather that they drowned themselves in vexation at Odysseus' escape.

A third myth is known from a brief mention in Pausanias' *Description of Greece* (9.34.3; vol. 4, pp. 322–23): in Coroneia was a statue of Hera with sirens in her hand, "for the story goes that the daughters of Achelous were persuaded by Hera to compete with the Muses in singing. The Muses won, plucked out the Sirens' feathers . . . and made crowns for themselves out of them." Spenser told this myth in terms of mermaids symbolizing sensual temptation (*Faerie Queene*, bk. 2, canto 12), originally "faire Ladies," punished with fishtails for their "bold surquedry" in challenging the Muses.

Paintings and sculptures of the sirens surviving from classical and preclassical art also show them as bird-bodied, and, indeed, difficult to distinguish from harpies (see the entry on harpies), except by labels or Odysseus' presence. As Benwell and Waugh point out (45–47), sirens frequently decorated classical tombs, and may have represented the dead soul, or spirits which convey the soul to Hades. Denys Page, in his *Folktales in Homer's Odyssey* suggests that Homer may have created his implicitly human sirens by combining the idea of soul-conveying sirens with legends of evil female demons who use beauty to lure men to their deaths (83). Joseph Campbell, in *The Hero with a Thousand Faces*, suggests that sirens and kindred figures represent the male fear of incestuous *libido*, projected onto the figure of a sensual female tempter (79).

John Pollard points out that the surviving art shows that sirens originally had a wider range of associations and meanings than has survived in literature (137–42). In addition to the many sirens on tombs and depicted with Odysseus, sirens are shown with Theseus, Artemis, Hera, Athene, and Dionysus; although most sirens are female, some, especially among the earliest, are bearded. In addition to mourning death or causing it, they may have represented otherworldly musical joys, or animal powers.

Almost the only classical writer to present sirens favorably was Plato. In the myth of Er, which closes the dialogue of the *Republic*, Socrates imagines the

Music of the Spheres as the singing of eight sirens, one on each of the circles of the planets and one on the circle of the fixed stars.

It is not known precisely when or how sirens became identified with mermaids and left their perches on rocky islands to go down into the waves, losing their wings. The increasing closeness of the identification can be traced in the development of the bestiaries (see the entry on mermaids). In the Romance languages (and some others), "siren," in its various cognate forms, became simply the word for "mermaid," although some uses might show more or less influence of the classical siren.

In the Italian folktale of "The Siren Wife," the sirens who rescue and adopt the drowned wife like to sing to sailors (a trait found among some mermaids, as well as in classical sirens); Italo Calvino, in his retelling of the story, increased the classical effect by inventing the words of their song, making the lyrics an invitation to the sailors to jump overboard (456); the fish-tailed siren in Giuseppe Tomasi di Lampedusa's "Lighea" (in the English translation titled "The Professor and the Mermaid") has one of the classical siren-names; Eléonore, however, "la petite sirène" in Jean de Brunhoff's *Les Vacances de Zéphir*, is fish-tailed, benevolent, and nonseductive, with no hint of musical interests.

In *The Book of Imaginary Beings* by Jorge Luis Borges, with Margarita Guerrero, the entry on sirens (206–8) notes that the difference between a "mermaid" and a "siren" is in having a tail or not, but this difference sometimes disappears in practice. The mermaid in Tennyson's "The Mermaid" has "silver feet"; the siren tempting Pen away from Laura's domestic love in Thackeray's title-page illustration to his *Pendennis* is tailed.

Legged or tailed, sirens have not been as widely used as mermaids. The influence of Odysseus and Jason restricted sirens to acting primarily as expressions of male fear of female sexuality, without the variety of other moods and themes found in mermaid literature. Nevertheless, sirens have appeared in a number of works of literature and other arts.

In three famous works with sirens, the sirens are only one in a vast array of unusual beings. Dante, in the *Purgatory* of his *Divine Comedy*, portrayed himself as dreaming (canto 19) that he saw a siren, an ugly woman, who, as she sings of her temptation of Ulysses, seems to become beautiful. Goethe, who is one of the few postclassical writers to represent sirens as bird-bodied, included sirens among the crowd of monsters and lesser deities from Greek mythology in the Classical Walpurgis Night of *Faust, The Second Part* (balancing the medieval Walpurgis Night of Faust's own era in the first part). These sirens are also unusual in apparently representing healthy sensuality; although the Sphinx accuses them (Goethe 87–88) of luring men to love in order to tear their victims with their claws, by the end of the act the sirens lead all the characters in a paean to Eros, the creator and ruler of all Nature (Goethe 132). In James Joyce's *Ulysses*, the odyssey of Leopold Bloom in contemporary Dublin, the sirens are two barmaids, serving gold beer; the siren-song is represented by the songs sung in the bar.

Sirens also appear briefly in versions of the story of Jason, as in William Morris' poem *The Life and Death of Jason*, or Robert Graves' novel *Hercules, My Shipmate*. In Graves' version, the sirens are humans, priestesses of the Mother Goddess, in accordance with his belief (discussed in his book on the Mother Goddess, *The White Goddess*, pp. 417–18) that the sirens were originally a symbolic representation of priestesses in charge of sacrificing the old king and the original siren-song a hymn as part of the rite. He composed such a hymn, "The Sirens' Welcome to Cronus" (*The White Goddess* 418–19). In his poem "Ulysses," however, he portrayed the sirens as projections of one aspect of Ulysses' fear of and desire for any woman.

Short poems on sirens in their conventional role as supernatural seductresses include Samuel Daniel's "Vlisses and the Syrens," Pierre de Béranger's "La Sirène," Tennyson's "The Sea-Fairies," and D. G. Rossetti's "A Sea-Spell." (Rossetti planned a larger work, a verse-tragedy, "The Doom of the Sirens," but wrote only its outline.) Of these, only Tennyson's, which never uses the word "siren," is well known. Matthew Arnold used sirens as seductresses in "The New Sirens," but in an unusual way. His "new sirens," seen by the speaker in a dream as the old Homeric ones, are spirits of romantic enthusiasm, overvaluing emotion at the expense of thought. Margaret Atwood used bird-bodied sirens as figures of temptation rebelling against their own nature in "The Sirens"; their alluring song is a plea to be rescued from the doom of life as temptresses.

Many writers have used "sirens" not literally, as supernatural figures, but metaphorically, to describe anyone alluring. This metaphor has become a cliché. Some interesting examples of the metaphorical siren, however, are Ligeia, who has a siren's name and whose beauty haunts the narrator from beyond the grave in Edgar Allan Poe's story "Ligeia"; the sirens of Titan, constructs of the alien Tralfamadorians in Kurt Vonnegut's novel *The Sirens of Titan*; and the hungry man whose praise of dinner draws all his colleagues from their work in Anton Chekhov's story "The Siren."

A few writers have used themes other than seduction. Thomas Moore depicted a faithful, Undine-like siren deserted by a faithless human lover in a poem, "The Origin of the Harp." In E. M. Forster's "The Story of the Siren," the siren is a goddess whose emergence into the world is resisted from fear of change (even if it might be change for good). In Laurence Binyon's "The Sirens (an Ode)," the sirens are a symbol of the longing to explore and conquer, including, finally, self-exploration and self-mastery.

In works needing a great many fantasy-beings, sirens may be part of the landscape. Two recent examples are Piers Anthony's *The Source of Magic* and Elizabeth Scarborough's *Song of Sorcery* (and a sequel, *Bronwyn's Bane*), light comedies including tailed sirens.

Sirens have been rare in film and drama. Walt Lee's *Reference Guide to Fantastic Films* lists only ten films with sirens in the title, and half are in languages which do not distinguish between sirens and mermaids (for example,

La Sirène, 1904, by Georges Méliès). An interesting metaphorical use of a "siren" is *The Siren's Song*, a 1911 silent starring Theda Bara as a singer whose father curses her and who loses her voice from the curse. The various film adaptations of the stories of Jason and Odysseus have mostly omitted sirens.

In music, sirens are rarer than mermaids, rusalkas, or the Lorelei. Debussy's nocturne *Sirènes* is the best known siren-composition. Some other well-known composers who have written of sirens are Daniel Auber (an opera, *La Sirène*), Reinhold Glière (a symphony, *Les Sirènes*), and Deems Taylor (a symphonic poem, *The Siren Song*). Georges Kastner included in his book *Les Sirènes* a symphonic drama, *Le Rêve d'Oswald, ou, Les Sirènes*.

In paintings, artists sometimes attach the label "siren" to leggier, more overtly dangerous sea-women. In John William Waterhouse's *The Siren*, the woman is legged, with scales from the calves down, and she stares at a drowning man; in his *A Mermaid*, the woman has a full fishtail and sits alone. Both are reproduced in Beatrice Phillpotts' *Mermaids* (23, 29). Daniel Maclise's painting for Thomas Moore's "The Origin of the Harp" shows a legged siren mourning her lost love; the same figure, however, in his engraved illustration is tailed (Phillpotts 2, 74).

Artists whose native tongues do not distinguish between "mermaid" and "siren" are likely to draw sirens as tailed figures, not overtly dangerous, as in Paul Delvaux's *Siren in Full Moonlight* (Phillpotts 8). A rare example of a siren with classically avian characteristics is Armand Point's *The Siren*, shown as a winged woman (Phillpotts 33).

Sirens will probably continue to be rare. Mermaids have taken over most of their functions as characters in fantasy, leaving their predecessors a role primarily metaphorical. In addition to the metaphor of the "siren" who is any pretty face or voice, the sirens gave their names to the much less musical sirens which warn of attack or emergency and to the order of the Sirenia, the manatees, dugongs, and sea-cows, which from a distance have sometimes been mistaken for mermaids. Suetonius (in his *Lives of the Twelve Caesars*) thought Tiberius foolish in the intensity of his interest in mythology, which led him to stump scholars by asking such questions as what the sirens sang and what name Achilles took in disguise. Sir Thomas Browne retorted in his *Hydriotaphia, or Urne-Buriall*: "What Song the *Syrens* sang, or what name *Achilles* assumed when he hid himself among women, though puzzling Questions are not beyond all conjecture" (165).

BIBLIOGRAPHY

Anthony, Piers. *The Source of Magic*. New York: Ballantine, 1979.
Apollodorus. *The Library*. Trans. Sir James George Frazer. 2 vols. Cambridge: Harvard University Press; London: Heinemann, 1921.
Apollonius Rhodius. *The Argonautica*. Trans. R. C. Seaton. London: Heinemann; New York: Macmillan, 1912.
Arnold, Matthew. *Poems*. Ed. Kenneth Allott. London: Longmans, Green, 1965.

Atwood, Margaret. *Selected Poems*. New York: Simon and Schuster, 1976.

Benwell, Gwen, and Arthur Waugh. *Sea Enchantress: The Tale of the Mermaid and her Kin*. London: Hutchinson, 1961.

Béranger, Pierre Jean de. *Dernières Chansons . . . 1834 à 1851*. Paris, 1857.

Binyon, Laurence. *Collected Poems: Lyrical Poems*. Vol. 1. London: Macmillan, 1931.

Borges, Jorge Luis, with Margarita Guerrero. *The Book of Imaginary Beings*. Trans. Norman Thomas di Giovanni. New York: Discus-Avon, 1970.

Browne, Sir Thomas. *Hydriotaphia, or Urne-Buriall*. In *The Works of Sir Thomas Browne*. 4 vols. Ed. Geoffrey Keynes. London: Faber and Faber, 1964. Vol. 1, 129–71. (Originally published 1658.)

Brunhoff, Jean de. *Les Vacances de Zéphir*. Paris: Hachette, 1936. (Available in English as *Babar and Zephir*. Trans. Merle S. Haas. New York: Random House, 1937.)

Calvino, Italo, ed. *Italian Folktales*. Trans. George Martin. New York: Harcourt Brace Jovanovich, 1980.

Campbell, Joseph. *The Hero with a Thousand Faces*. 2nd ed. Bollingen Series 17. Princeton: Princeton University Press, 1968.

Castro Pires de Lima, Fernando de. *A sereia na historia e na lenda*. Porto: Porto Editora, 1952.

Chekhov, Anton. *The Portable Chekov*. Trans. Avrahm Yarmolinsky. New York: Viking, 1947.

Consoli, Silla. *La Candeur d'un monstre: Essai psychoanalytique sur le mythe de la sirène*. Paris: Editions du Centurion, 1980.

Daniel, Samuel. *Poems and a Defence of Ryme*. Ed. Arthur Colby Sprague. Cambridge: Harvard University Press, 1930.

Dante. *The Divine Comedy, II: Purgatory*. Trans. and ed. Dorothy L. Sayers. Harmondsworth: Penguin, 1955.

Douglas, Norman. *Siren Land*. London: J. M. Dent, 1911.

Forster, E. M. *The Collected Tales*. New York: Knopf, 1966.

Goethe, Johann Wolfgang von. *Faust, The Second Part of the Tragedy*. Trans. Bayard Taylor. Boston, 1879.

Graves, Robert. *Hercules, My Shipmate*. New York: Creative Age Press, 1945.

———. *Poems, 1930–1933*. London: Arthur Barker, 1933.

———. *The White Goddess: A Historical Grammar of Poetic Myth*. Amended and enl. ed. New York: Farrar, Straus and Giroux, 1966.

Homer. *The Odyssey*. Trans. T. E. Shaw (T. E. Lawrence). New York: Oxford University Press, 1932.

Joyce, James. *Ulysses*. New York: Random House, 1934.

Kastner, Georges. *Les Sirènes, essai sur les principaux mythes . . . et suivi de Le Rêve d'Oswald, ou, Les Sirènes, grande symphonie dramatique et instrumentale*. Paris, 1858.

Lee, Walt. *Reference Guide to Fantastic Films*. 3 vols. Los Angeles: Chelsea-Lee Books, 1972–74.

Moore, Thomas. *Poetical Works*. 10 vols. London: 1840–41.

Morris, William. *The Life and Death of Jason. A Poem*. 9th ed., rev. London, 1889.

Page, Denys. *Folktales in Homer's Odyssey*. Cambridge: Harvard University Press, 1973.

Pausanias. *Description of Greece*. Trans. W. H. S. Jones. 5 vols. London: Heinemann; Cambridge: Harvard University Press, 1918–35.

Phillpotts, Beatrice. *Mermaids*. London: Russell Ash; New York: Ballantine, 1980.

Pollard, John. *Seers, Shrines and Sirens: The Greek Religious Revolution in the Sixth Century B.C.* London: Allen and Unwin, 1965.

Rossetti, Dante Gabriel. *The Collected Works.* Ed. William M. Rossetti. 2 vols. London, 1887–1901.

Scarborough, Elizabeth. *Bronwyn's Bane.* New York: Bantam, 1983.

———. *Song of Sorcery.* New York: Bantam, 1982.

Tomasi di Lampedusa, Giuseppi. *Two Stories and a Memory.* Trans. Archibald Colquhoun. London: Wm. Collins Sons; New York: Pantheon, 1962. (*Racconti.* Milan: Feltrinelli Editore, 1961.)

Vonnegut, Kurt. *The Sirens of Titan.* New York: Dell, 1959.

11

Ḥarpies

Beryl Rowland

In contemporary song, the Harpy is a convivial, musical creature, subscribing to the modern preference for entertainment that is vigorous and noisy:

> I took my Harp to a Harpy.
> Together we harped and sang.
> No one can harp like a Harpy,
> Not with a whimp but a bang.

There is no hint here of those predatory creatures, usually three in number, who swooped down from the clouds, snatched up all the food they could find, either in their talons or in their long arms, and then proceeded to vomit or excrete it over anyone who happened to be dining below them. Today, even when the word "harpy" is used pejoratively, the exact nature of her antisocial behaviour appears to have been forgotten.

Nor were the Harpies originally famed for their disgusting table manners. Etymologically the name derives from the Greek verb *harpazein*, to snatch. In ancient myth they were associated with storm winds, and they were wind-spirits that carried off anyone whom the gods wished to cause to disappear. Homer in the *Iliad* mentions only one of them by name, Podarge, the mother of the horses of Achilles by Zephyrus, the generative wind (16.150); Hesiod in his *Theogony* names two, "fair-tressed" Aello and Ocypete, who "accompany the wind-blasts and birds, with swift wings, for they are wont to fly high above the earth" (267). Represented as vulturelike creatures with women's heads and breasts, more commonly they were known as Celaeno, Nicotheon, and Thyella.

Aeschylus seems to have been one of the earliest writers to find them ugly and misshapen (*Eumenides* 50). But the fullest account of their repulsive behaviour and appearance occurs in the epics of the Argonauts. In their quest for the golden fleece, the Argonauts meet Phineus, who has been punished by the gods with blindness and premature old age for abusing the gift of prophecy. Phineus is starving because of the Harpies.

The Harpies always watch my food. Never, alas! can I escape them; they immediately all swoop down like the black cloud of a whirling tornado. Already, by the sound of her wings, I know Celaeno from afar. They ravage and sweep away my feast, and pollute and upset the cups. There is a violent stench, and a most wretched battle arises because the monsters are as famished as I am. (Valerius Flaccus, *Arg.* 4.450–56; my translation)

In return for the benefit of Phineus' prophetic powers to aid them in their quest, Argonauts Zetes and Calais fight the Harpies and drive them off to the Strophades in the Aegean, where they promise never to torment Phineus again. There they are waiting when Aeneas, fleeing from burning Troy, disembarks and prepares a feast for his hungry companions. Virgil's hero graphically describes the incident later to Queen Dido:

No monster is more terrible than the Harpies, no plague, no wrath of the gods more dire, surging upwards from the Stygian waters. They are birds with the faces of young girls. Disgusting filth comes from their stomachs; their hands have claws and they are always pale from hunger. . . . Suddenly, with a fearful swoop from the mountains they are upon us, and with a loud clang they flap their wings, plunder the feast, making every dish filthy with their dirty hands; with the foul stench comes a hideous scream. (*Aeneid* 3.214–28; my translation)

The Harpies are finally driven off, and one of them, Celaeno, perching on a rock, curses Aeneas from a distance. He will not build his promised city in Italy, she says, before he has been forced through hunger to gnaw and consume his own tables.

Gluttony was, of course, the quality with which the Harpies were proverbially associated even in Horace's day (*Sat.* 2.2.40). Much earlier, however, the Harpies were interpreted allegorically. To the Greek philosopher Heraclitus, the Harpies who robbed Phineus of his food were high-priced prostitutes devouring the patrimony of young men. This idea was repeated by Eustathius and others throughout the centuries. In Eustathius' time, when allegory became the common vehicle for all pious expression, and mythological exegesis reached astonishing proportions, the Third Vatican Mythographer united the Furies and the Harpies and declared that misers were supposed to be tormented by them (5.5). In the fifteenth century Giovanni Bellini gave the Harpies similar values. In a series of panels illustrating the Seven Deadly Sins, he depicted a Harpy as Avarice, mounting her on two golden balls. The balls were due to the confusion of Harpies with the Hesperides, the four daughters of Atlas, who ate the apples they were supposed to guard—a confusion that also reinforced the Harpies' reputation for avarice. In the sixteenth century, the Italian mythographer, Natale Conti, declared that the bodies of Harpies exactly expressed the souls of misers (7.6).

While harpies were, in general, a subject well suited to didacticism, medieval moralists and Renaissance emblem writers made particular use of a tradition that emphasized a sense of guilt. According to the *Tretyse of Love*:

The Harpy has the semblance of a man's visage, and her nature is to slay the first man she finds, and then she goes to some water where she beholds herself and sees that she has slain her own likeness, and then she makes a full great sorrow alway that ever she saw any man. This signifieth the soul that slew Christ by her sin, whose semblance is in her, for to his semblance she was created. And when she remembers how Jesus was dead for our sins, then ought she to make great sorrow and lamentation. (113)

Vincent of Beauvais repeated the same story in his encyclopedic work (*Spec. Nat.* xvi–xciv), and on the rare occasions that the harpy is included in the bestiaries, it appears as the repentant murderer. In one bestiary (Cahier and Martin 2:xx) a winged, man-headed monster with leonine paws stands over a serene-looking corpse, and according to Pierre of Beauvais in his bestiary compiled before 1218, this homicidal harpy resembles a horse and a man, with a lion's body, a serpent's wings, and a horse's tail (McCulloch 64, 202). In one version of the story, the harpy's remorse is such that she commits suicide. A reflection of the sequel may be contained in Dante's curious introduction of the Harpies into the seventh circle of Hell. In a characteristically elaborate and violent figure, he depicts the Harpies as feeding upon the leaves of thorny trees in which are encased all the souls of those who have committed suicide. Only when bleeding from wounds inflicted by these creatures that defile everything they touch can the sinners sob out their mournful stories (*Inf.* 13.10–15).

Although not widely used, the harpy as murderess appeared alongside the bulimiac of classical tradition in those Renaissance collections of illustrated moralized verses known as emblem books. Under the caption *Homicidia sui ipsius Ultor* (Murder is its own avenger), Laurentius Haechtanus and Jacobus de Zetter tell of the harpy who sinks her teeth into the entrails of a man. But her rejoicing does not last long, for when she sees in the water a likeness of herself as she would appear in death, grief (''dolor'') snatches her into the watery depths below, and she perishes. The verse ends with a general exhortation to the evildoer to repent his crime. Although only one harpy is mentioned, the engraving shows three, and the well-known emblem writer, Reusner, refers to the harpies as ''Tria Animi Monstra,'' the three monsters of the mind (Henkel and Schöne 1635–36). An English contemporary of these writers, Henry Peacham, transfers the harpies in his emblem to the Royal Courts and employs a striking engraving of a female-headed bird with well-developed breasts and shoulder-length hair. Princes are like Phineus, and in their blindness they are preyed upon by three kinds of harpies—the liar, the courtier who is easily bribed, and the parasite (115).

By this time the predominant values attributed to the Harpies were well established. Indeed, the great ornithologist Konrad von Gesner (1516–65), while noting that scholars interpreted harpies as winged demons, swift winds, or ravenous dogs, expressed scepticism (II.ii.544–66). The indefatigable encyclopedist Aldrovandi, who summed up the classical and medieval history of harpies, produced the rubric *Rapacitas, Ingluvies, Foeditas* (rapacity, voraciousness, filthiness). Described as having bodies of vultures, bears' ears, feathered arms, human feet, huge claws, and white female breasts, they were variously conceived of as ill-omened goddesses, demons, and allegories of the winds. They were also called *canes Jovis* (Jove's dogs) because they were the Furies, ministers of the vengeance of Zeus. Noting that they could not retain food and that as a result everything they touched was contaminated from horrible emissions pouring from their bowels, he observed that they had a medical condition which doctors called in man "the dog-like appetite" (611–18).

Aldrovandi's discussions anticipate less didactic references to the Harpies. Prospero in Shakespeare's *Tempest*, III.iii.83–84, recommends Ariel for assuming the guise of a harpy to make a banquet vanish before it is tasted, and Benedick in *Much Ado About Nothing*, II.i.260, declares that as far as Beatrice is concerned, he would rather go to the ends of the earth "than hold three words' conference with this Harpy." In *Pericles*, IV.iii.46–48, Shakespeare emphasized the paradox inherent in the harpy's appearance: "Thou art like the Harpy," says Cleon to his wicked wife, "which, to betray, dost, with thine angel's face, / Seize with thine eagle's talents [talons]." Such are the features given by the late Elizabethan authority on heraldry, John Guillim. He places harpies in his class of "exorbitant animals" and gives two armorial bearings. In the one, a woman's face looks out from the body, wings, and talons of a plump vulture; in the other, the harpy has a woman's face and body but bird's wings and talons. Guillim remarks of the first:

He beareth Azure, an Harpey with her wings disclosed, her Haire flotant, Or, Armed of the same. This Coat standeth in Huntington Church. Of this kind of bird (or rather Monster) Virgil writeth in this manner;

> "Of Monsters all, most Monstrous this; no greater wrath
> God sends 'mongst men; it comes from dephth of pitchy Hell;
> And Virgins face, but wombe-like gulfe unsatiat hath,
> Her hands are griping clawes, her colour pale and fell."
>
> (183)

The second, states Guillim, forms the arms of the city of Nuremberg, and he cites Upton that the Harpies "should be given to such persons as have committed manslaughter, to the end that by the often view of their Ensigns they might be moved to bewail the foulness of their offence" (183). Contemporaneous with Guillim's book on heraldry is a monument erected in the south transept of the collegiate church of St. Saviour, Southwark, in South London. Apparently the Harpies' association with horses had not been forgotten, for the inscription, flanked with a pair of boldly carved harpies, is to John Bingham, saddler to Elizabeth I and James I. Such representations seem to have been exceptional, however, and Upton's pejorative view appears to have discouraged its application in heraldry. By the late nineteenth century, according to William Norman, its heraldic use was largely limited to common charges, and it even became a subject for humour: "this creature," stated R. H. Edgar, "is half a woman and half a bird, the upper part thus resembling one of the fair and the lower part one of the fowl" (85). In the accompanying illustration a young woman with the body of a bird smokes a cigarette and holds a glass of wine in her dexter claw.

The association with avarice lasted until this century, and one of the definitions given by the *Oxford English Dictionary* s.v. "Harpy" (2) is "a rapacious, plundering or grasping person; one who preys on others." Samuel Butler no doubt had this significance in mind in *The Way of All Flesh* when Ernest is discovered to be in debt to the school shopkeeper and to the landlord of the Swan and Bottle, and his father asks indignantly: "What boys, then, owed money to these Harpies?" (178). The same meaning is reflected in the Reverend E. Cobham Brewer's definition in 1900: "He is a regular Harpy, signifying 'one who wants to appropriate everything; one who sponges on another without mercy.' " More commonly, however, the word is used to suggest shrewishness rather than avarice and is applied exclusively to women. An expressive use, in this sense, was made earlier by Thackeray: "Was it my mother-in-law, the grasping, odious, abandoned, brazen Harpy?" asks Lady Maria, when she learns that someone has revealed her age (139). More recently Dylan Thomas in "Lament" shows some indication of the Harpies' origins and of their more ambivalent features. When the reformed rake finally settles down to marriage, he states:

> For, oh, my soul found a Sunday wife
> In the coal black sky and she bore angels!
> Harpies around me out of her womb!
>
> (207)

The child-harpies reflect the virtues of their mother and the vices of their father.

Psychologically, these creatures are not difficult to explain. As I have observed elsewhere, the wings and avian body symbolize feminine, nurturing characteristics; the talons represent an infantile projection of destructive impulses which converts the maternal figure into a cruel predator (76). For this reason nearly all the great mother-goddesses had birdlike features. Horapollo described the Egyptian mother-goddess as a vulture (23–27). She possessed traits sometimes ascribed to the Harpies—she was made pregnant by the wind, and she had the gift of prophecy. She was also death-bringing and corpse-devouring. In the case of the Harpies, Greek and Roman writers simply chose to emphasize their negative role as destroyers of life and the object of masculine fear and hatred. Yet references to the Harpies' flowing hair and virginal faces as well as subsequent illustrations of firm, seductive breasts or soft avian curves suggestive of fecundity point to their dual role. The so-called Harpy monument brought to the British Museum from the ruins of Xanthos, the ancient capital of Lycia in Asia Minor, shows a flying Harpy holding a child in a suckling position in her arms while she clings to the child's lower limbs with her talons. Centuries earlier, features of the Harpy were represented in the winged mother-goddess of the Isin-Larsa period in Mesopotamia (Neumann 145). In a Sumerian terra-cotta relief (ca. 2000 B.C.), Lilith, the goddess of death, has wings and talons (Neumann, pl. 126).

Such examples raise the possibility that the harpy figure may have been more widely disseminated and more ancient than her appearance in classical literature suggests. Human-headed birds have been found in the ancient art of India, Iran, Persia, Turkistan, and elsewhere. Harpies, together with sphinxes, were a popular motif in medieval Islamic art—in tapestries, embroidery, manuscripts, wall-paintings, architecture, pottery, figurines, and even on everyday utensils. The identity of the stylized figures on the lustre bowls of the Fatimid is unmistakable. Despite their elaborate female headdresses and dark hair tidily draped over their ears, they have the characteristic wings and vulture's body and talons (Baer, pls. 6, 7). Baer found no evidence of "an immediate or direct connection between the creatures of classical antiquity and the human-headed bird in the Muslim world" (47). Nevertheless, their traditional features, and in addition, the dour, even malign, expressions on their faces, seem to unite them with their infernal sisters of the pagan and Christian underworld. They, too, are the "hellish Harpies, prophets of sad destiny."

BIBLIOGRAPHY

Aldrovandi, Ulisse. *Ornithologia, hoc est de avibus historia libri XII*. Bologna, 1599.

Baer, Eva. *Sphinxes and Harpies in Medieval Islamic Art*. Jerusalem: The Israel Oriental Society, 1965.

Bellini, Giovanni. See Sir Guy de Tervarent. *Attributs et symboles dans l'art profane, 1450–1600*. Genève. Droz, 1958. Cols. 206, 207, 313.

Butler, Samuel. *The Way of All Flesh*. 1903. Rpt. London: Jonathan Cape, 1970.

Cahier, Charles, and Arthur Martin. *Mélanges d'archéologie*. 4 vols. Paris, 1847–56.

Conti, Natale. *Mythologiae sive Explicationis fabularum libri decem*. 1551. Padua, 1637.

Edgar, R. H. *Ye Comic History of Heraldry*. 2nd ed. London, 1878.

Gesner, Konrad von. *Historiae animalium liber III qui est de avium natura*. Frankfurt, 1585.

Guillim, John. *A Display of Heraldry*. London, 1610.

Henkel, Arthur, and Albrecht Schöne. *Emblemata: Handbuch zur Sinnbildkunst des XVI. und XVII. Jahrhunderts*. Stuttgart: Metzlersche Verlagsbuchhandlung, 1967.

Heraclitus. *De Incredibilibus*. Rome, 1641.

Hesiod. *The Works of Hesiod, Callimachus, and Theognis*. Trans. J. Banks. London, 1889.

Horapollo. *The Hieroglyphics of Horapollo Nilous*. Ed. Alexander Turner Cory. London, 1840.

Neumann, Erich. *The Great Mother*. 1955. Trans. Ralph Manheim. 2nd ed. Princeton: Princeton University Press, 1972.

Norman, William. " 'Harpie' or 'Harpy.' " *Notes and Queries*. 11, 8th ser. (1897): 216.

Peacham, Henry. *Minerva Britanna*. London, 1612.

Pierre de Beauvais. See Florence McCulloch. *Mediaeval Latin and French Bestiaries*. Rev. ed. Chapel Hill: University of North Carolina Press, 1962.

Rowland, Beryl. *Birds with Human Souls: A Guide to Bird Symbolism*. Knoxville: University of Tennessee Press, 1978.

Thackeray, William Makepeace. *The Virginians*. London, 1858.

Third Vatican Mythographer [Albericus?]. *Scriptores rerum mythicarum Latini libri III*. Ed. Georg Heinrich Bode. Celle, 1834.

Thomas, Dylan. *The Poems of Dylan Thomas*. Ed. Daniel Jones. New York: New Directions, 1971.

The Tretyse of Love. Ed. John H. Fisher. Early English Text Society, o.s. 223. 1945; rpt. London: Oxford University Press, 1970.

Valerius Flaccus. *Argonautica*. Trans. J. H. Mozley. 1934; rpt. Cambridge: Harvard University Press, 1958.

Vincent de Beauvais. *Speculum naturale*. Douai, 1624.

12

The Gorgon Medusa

Judith D. Suther

The earliest known use of the name Gorgon incorporates it into the word *Gorgoneion*, a talismanic mask or emblem which the Greeks, long before Homer, placed on their clothing, household items, weapons, tools, jewelry, money, and buildings. Referring to the legend of the Gorgoneion as it had developed before the classical Greek and Roman uses familiar to Western Europeans, ethnographers fuse "the Gorgon" and "the Medusa" into one type. The history of the monstrous siblings and their one mortal sister is thus intertwined very early, and the two names are virtually synonymous in popular usage.

Elworthy sums up the fusing of the general (the Gorgon) and the particular (Medusa) in the phrase "the central idea embodied in the Medusa" (165). In naming Medusa, the archetypal Gorgon, one implies the whole ambiguous tradition that invests the Gorgon with the power of beauty and hideousness inextricably combined in the face and specifically in the eyes to exercise fascination on a victim. Depending on circumstances, his own and his culture's, the victim may be enraptured, spellbound, immobilized, rendered senseless, castrated, petrified, or destroyed. In like manner, he may capture Medusa's power and turn it on victims whom he wishes to enrapture, spellbind, and so forth.

From numerous sources, often contradictory, the Gorgon Medusa emerges in classical Greek literature and iconography as a female monster with the power of arresting all who gaze on her. "Arresting" is a deliberately neutral term designating the imprecision inherent in the earliest accounts of her attributes. By the time she enters the record of history through artifacts and literature, she has been concentrated into a severed head surrounded by snakes. The head is further intensified by the attribution of destructive energy to the eyes. This distilling of the Gorgon's power antedates the earliest mention of her in extant Western literature (Homer, ca. 850 B.C., *Iliad* 5.741; 8.348; 11.36–37).

Although its origins are multiple and obscure, the story of the Gorgon Medusa can be constructed from textual and other anthropological evidence dating at least to the eighth century B.C., beginning with the Homeric passages and the everyday talismans just mentioned. By Homer's time the Gorgon has become so much a symbol that he introduces her only as a detail, calling up but never retelling the full biography which listeners are presumed to know. As the centerpiece of Athena's shield, or aegis, Medusa's potent head is a portent of Zeus calculated to stun the enemy. How she acquired this power is not even alluded to. Analogous signs of her totemic function, however, are already evident in the images affixed to numerous artifacts familiar to Homer's contemporaries. The image is embedded in kilns used to bake pottery, stamped on coins and on the bottom of drinking glasses, placed over doorways, attached to the base of lamps suspended overhead, and hung in prominent positions near Athenian hearths. Hollowed-out versions containing drops of the Gorgon's blood are used as amulets to protect the bearer against harm. The story behind these minatory uses of the Gorgon figure, while known before Homer, emerges in varying degrees of coherence throughout the classical period of Greek literature and art into Graeco-Roman times.

After Homer the first significant pieces in the jigsaw of the legend are added by Hesiod (ca. late 8th century B.C.) in the *Theogony* and the *Shield*. In these works two of the Gorgon's five sisters are named (Stheno and Euryale), their status established as monsters inhabiting the edge of the world, and Medusa's death at the hand of Perseus recorded. This is a wealth of information compared to the almost decorative allusions in Homer. With Aeschylus (525–456 B.C.) further details are added. In the *Prometheus* the hero refers to both triads of Medusa's unholy sisters—the Graeae, or Gray Ones, and the Gorgons, who are winged, dragon-tressed, and deadly if looked upon (798–800). In two other plays Aeschylus develops the Gorgon reference, using it as a literary image to point up the loathsomeness of guilt and the pitilessness of conscience (*Choephori* 1048–1051; *Eumenides* 49–53).

It is Pindar (ca. 522–443 B.C.), however, who provides the first real complexities in the story, in the *Twelfth Pythian Ode*. After relating the origin of flute-playing—Athena derived the art from the dirge sung by Medusa's sisters the day Perseus killed her—Pindar speaks of "the head of the fair-cheeked Medusa." In this line is the first hint of Medusa's beauty, which will become the hallmark of the Romantics' use of the Medusa figure twenty-four centuries later. Pindar is also the first to attribute to the Medusa head the power of inflicting death by petrifaction. Ambiguity again enters into his account of this power: the severed head that Perseus bears aloft as a trophy of his conquest is not only "dragon-maned" (snaky) but also "changeful" (the face is expressive, blushing, capable of attracting).

An important dimension to the story comes from Euripides, in the *Ion* (989–1015). Here, in a drawn-out conversation indicating the focal speaker's unwillingness to divulge her terrible secret, Creusa describes two small hollow amulets which she has inherited from her grandfather Erichthonius, who was given them by Athena. Each amulet contains a drop of the Gorgon's blood. One drop is benign, possessed of healing properties; the other drop is malignant, a poison from the snakes' venom. Again the complexity seen in Pindar emerges.

By far the best known, fullest, and most influential account of the Medusa story in Greek or Roman literature comes in books 4 and 5 of the *Metamorphoses* of Ovid (43 B.C.–A.D. 17). The focus of the story is now on Perseus, Medusa's youthful slayer, whom Ovid portrays as dashing, brave, and ruthless. In order to set the hero up as unsurpassed in these qualities, Ovid spins out the tale of Medusa's lineage and her fearsome powers, so that Perseus can triumph over an extraordinary adversary. As the Ovidian tale unfolds, Medusa's story takes on the shape in which it will be transmitted to artists and writers in succeeding centuries.

Under Ovid's pen the Medusa story is transformed into legend. Daughter of Phorcys, the son of sea and earth, and Ceto, Medusa belongs to a second set of three sisters, the Gorgons. (Ovid numbers the first set, the Gray Ones, at two. They were born old and share a single eye and a single tooth which they pass between themselves.) Although all three Gorgons are endowed with snake hair and generally noisome countenance, only Medusa embodies the power to fascinate, in both the negative and positive aspects of the term, and only she is mortal. Using his wits to deal her the death blow, Perseus avoids direct contact with her eyes by mirroring her in his polished shield as she sleeps, striking off her head. From the blood that spurts from the death wound, "as though it were a mother," spring Pegasus and Chrysaor, Medusa's twin sons, engendered, it must be supposed, by the sword of Perseus.

Safely stowed in the kibisis or pouch which Athena has provided for the purpose, Medusa's severed head is neutralized until Perseus takes it out. He does this three times on his return trip to Ethiopia, where he will claim Andromeda as his bride. Once he takes the head out and carries it streaming across the desert, causing snakes in great numbers to rise up where the blood falls. A second time he takes the head out and brandishes it at Atlas, who has scorned the young warrior's boasting and refused him hospitality. For his boorishness Atlas is turned into a mountain. A third time Perseus removes the head from safekeeping, this time as he is resting beside his prize, Andromeda. He sets the head down "among sweet ferns and seaweed," where the "magic fluid" of Medusa's powers performs one of the most astonishing of its legendary feats: it petrifies the ferns and seaweeds, turning them into coral. The transformation as told by Ovid is quite beautiful. There is no question of horror, nor does Perseus give a thought to his new bride's safety when he lays the Gorgon's head at her side.

To round out the tale of his heroic adventures, Perseus recounts Medusa's lineage and the curse put on her by a jealous, perhaps a prudish, Athena. Once, confides Perseus, Medusa was beautiful, her hair her greatest glory. But her fortune changed when Poseidon raped her in Athena's temple. Shocked by the desecration of her holy place—or envious of Medusa's beauty—Athena raised her shield to protect her eyes. She turned the beauty's hair to snakes, banished her to the end of the earth, and forever after bore the Gorgon's head on her shield as an armorial device to stun the enemy.

In Ovid, then, are concentrated the lavish detail and ambiguity of feeling that mark the Gorgon's history as regenerative—that is, repeatedly fascinating to artists and writers of widely varied sensibilities. After Ovid the only classical continuator of the Medusa story to offer more than reiteration or exclamatory reference is Apollodorus (ca. first or second century A.D.), in the *Library* (2.4.1– 3). His account of the legend is a cultural historian's record, objective in so far as that is possible, and complete with variants. Inheritors of the material do not take cues from Apollodorus, though they may consult him as one consults a reference work. They take cues from Pindar and Ovid and even from the abbreviated images of Homer, the tragedians, Greek and Roman prose writers like Xenophon (ca. 430–355 B.C., *Symposium* 4:24–25), and Lucian (ca. A.D. 120– 80, "The Hall"), and from medalists and craftsmen. Apollodorus is to the legend of Medusa as a careful journalist is to the subject of a retrospective: he is the commentator who gathers sources, reporting them all for future historiographers.

To what extent Medusa's powers should be linked with the universal belief in the evil eye remains an open question. As one of the premier researchers puts it, "the story of the Medusa is but an incident in the early belief in the evil eye" (Elworthy 166). Another researcher traces a long tradition of people alleged to be turned to stone by a malevolent glance in Europe, India, Australia, China, Africa, South America, North America (primarily among Indians and Eskimos), and the Slavic and Scandinavian countries (Hartland, chs. 9–10). Linking the worldwide superstition of the evil eye to contemporary Western culture, Hartland recounts the tale of a Brazilian bird whose eye was believed to possess the power to petrify. A hunter was able to capture one of these birds and decapitate it without having the eye turned on him. He then used the bird head as a weapon, training the eye on his enemies. Hartland concludes: "The awful weapon of the mythical Brazilian bird was Medusa's power, the same as is today the terror of the Italian peasant, and is not yet regarded with indifference even in lands, like our own, which boast of being in the van of civilisation" (146). There is also abundant evidence, Hartland points out, "that the form assumed [in numerous cultures] by the Quest of the Gorgon's Head . . . is not confined . . . to tales of the Perseus cycle" (95).

The origin of the ancient and widespread custom of emblazoning strange devices on warriors' shields to catch and thereby disengage the eye of the enemy is also unknown. The relation of the practice, however, has long been established with anti–evil-eye precautions like the placing of protective eyes on the prows of ships, around the necks of domestic animals, on infants' shawls, and on all the paraphernalia of public and private life. While the Gorgon's eye is neither the source nor the fruition of evil-eye practices, it figures prominently in the tradition and gives its name to the particular type of prophylactic known as the Gorgoneion.

Works of pictorial artists, from the Orientalizing (ca. 725–650 B.C.) through the Archaic (ca. 650–480 B.C.), Classical (fifth–late fourth century B.C.) and Hellenistic periods (ca. 300–180 B.C.), provide a rich record of the Gorgon's currency. Unlike the craftsmen who fashioned the ubiquitous Gorgoneions, artists responded to the nuances of the legend, portraying Medusa in the varied and paradoxical guises seen in literature. One of the best preserved examples of a Medusa icon is the marble mask now owned by the state art museum of Monaco. Dating to ca. 400–350 B.C., the mask is particularly interesting as a contrast to the Gorgoneion-like relief pieces of the Archaic period which push the Gorgonian, negative aspect of the figure to a caricatural extreme. The Monaco Medusa, on the other hand, shows the serene countenance which Italian art historians call the *tipo bello*. An almost round, smooth female face with strong, very human features casts its eyes slightly downward. Two snakes are knotted under her chin. This is the Medusa that Goethe so admired and that he saw in the Rondanini Palace in Rome. In ''the noble semi-transparency of the yellow stone,'' Goethe writes home, ''the attempt to portray a lofty and beautiful countenance in the numbing agony of death has been indescribably successful'' (*Letters from Italy* 253). Because it is associated with the palace where Goethe saw it, the mask is still referred to as the Rondanini Medusa.

The fullest surviving visual evidence of the Medusa figure is in vase-painting, on red-figured and black-figured kylikes and amphorae. In the earliest examples the artists' preoccupation with Medusa's monstrous side is obvious. Archaic initiation scenes, depicting a grotesque female warrior beheaded by Perseus, are popular in pre-Classical painting. Later, as more complex conceptions of the Gorgon's meaning develop, interest in the act of beheading wanes and the element of pathos enters into the artists' representations. Medusa herself becomes the victim, beautiful and heart-rending in death. ''Once the monster had become attractive and appealing, she engaged the sympathy of her audience and the latter could no longer take pleasure in her killing'' (Phinney 452–53). Phinney concludes, in a quotation from a fellow art historian, that ''the artistic possibilities of her character had been exhausted'' (453). The exhaustion, it will later be seen, was temporary.

The Gorgon Medusa that comes into Western art and literature by way of the Greeks and Romans is, at any rate, an amply explored figure. The degree to which she is known to any one postclassical reinterpreter varies greatly with availability of sources and, as competence in Greek declines, with the linguistic tools the interpreter can wield. Access to the pictorial record is also gradually reduced as what Western commentators are pleased to call ''civilization'' disperses and its artifacts are scattered during the Hellenistic and later Roman expansion periods. Eventually, by the time of the transfer of the Roman capital to Constantinople in the fourth century A.D., there is no center of Western civilization and its artifacts, so that the transmission of any one set of them becomes random and difficult to trace. This is the case with the legend of the Gorgon. She persists as a member of the medieval pantheon of monsters, and her minor contribution to the lore of the evil eye is undeniable. As a central figure in a work of visual art or literature, however, she does not reemerge until the Renaissance.

One of the most haunting uses of the image before modern times is in canto 9 of Dante's *Inferno* (lines 49–63). It seems to combine the covalent qualities of horror and beauty in a way peculiarly suited to Dante's Christian imagination. As a horrible figure made enticing through sexual overtones, Medusa serves Dante as the negative pole of his contradictory urges, to which the virtuous Matelda is juxtaposed at the opposite pole (Freccero 37). Since Dante's characteristic treatment of erotic themes is ambivalent, the Medusa figure in the *Inferno* is one of the key icons in the postclassical canon. She stands as the ultimate temptation to a pilgrim of radically divided longings. His passage beyond her gaze to redemption is effected only because he is prevented from looking at her; Virgil, his guide, covers the pilgrim's eyes.

By positing links with a long passage on the Medusa in Jean de Meung's portion of the *Romance of the Rose* (late thirteenth century) and Dante's own brilliant juvenilia, the *Rime petrose* or *Stony Rhymes*, Freccero further develops the damnation/redemption pattern epitomized by Dante's Medusa. In the *Romance of the Rose* sequence, the lover is faced with an extended description of Medusa and her potency just as he approaches the castle where he comes upon a sculpted image of overwhelming erotic beauty. He is in effect presented with a long moral oxymoron. Although the passage, occurring at line 20,811 of the *Romance*, is rejected by some commentators as an interpolation, Freccero points out that it occurs in several thirteenth-century manuscripts and provides "an extraordinary parallel to the action in Canto nine of the *Inferno*" (39). The fact that in his youth Dante did a poetic paraphrase of the *Romance* reinforces the aptness of Freccero's thesis; the paraphrase, unfortunately, has not survived.

The link between the Medusa of the *Inferno* and Dante's own *Stony Rhymes*, on the other hand, is beyond question. The hard, unyielding lady to whom the verses are addressed turns the poet into stone—that is, into a despairing suitor stopped dead on his quest for redemption through love. Dante's Christian allegory of petrifaction and sexual vulnerability as a source of spiritual paralysis, in the *Stony Rhymes* as well as the *Inferno*, represents one of the great incarnations of the Medusa figure.

Odd as this may seem, Dante's Medusa emerges as a bland, sexless head in Blake's illustration of canto 9 (Klonsky 44). The head peers benignly over the entry to the city of Dis, while a vaguely sketched Dante, his eyes covered by Virgil, cowers in the lower left corner of the drawing. Like many of Blake's scenes from the *Inferno*, this one seems almost to ignore Dante's text in favor of a pastel dream world where monsters become lap dogs and even the flames of Hell are friendly.

The numerous literary uses of the figure from the late Middle Ages through the seventeenth century concentrate almost exclusively on Medusa's negative aspect. Writers frequently pair her with Athena, so that the two become short-cut renderings of evil and good, vice and virtue, lust and chastity. Once again displayed on Athena's shield, the Gorgon now becomes a convention for rage, disorder, madness, or death. Among characteristic uses are those in Petrarch, Du Bellay, Spenser, and Milton. Petrarch, in the *Canzoniere*, effects one of his more cogent conceits when he equates his love for Laura, his own Pygmalion-esque creation, with the sin of idolatry. She then becomes Medusa the petrifier: "Medusa and my sin have made me a stone" (poem 366, line 111). Later, in the "Trionfo della castità," Petrarch anticipates the use to which the image will be put in the Renaissance love lyric: Laura-Athena, the epitome of virtue-chastity, holds a shield in the center of which a prophylactic Gorgon head glowers (lines 189–90). Du Bellay develops the image more fully by making it the focus of one of his poems of praise addressed to Margaret of Valois. In an antithetical structure, he rejects the paradigm of Margaret-Athena versus the Gorgon, preferring "simple poetry" freed from the conventions of a "moldy fable" (sonnet 188 in *Les Regrets*). The irony of Du Bellay's denial is that his entire "simple poem" owes its life to the "moldy fable" of Medusa. Spenser too exploits the image, this time in a marriage song, by contrasting the bride's physical and spiritual beauty with the physical and spiritual ugliness of Medusa (*Epithalamion*, st. 11, lines 1–6). In the *Faerie Queene* he echoes the same convention when Britomart, champion of chastity, bears a "Gorgonian shield" (3.9.22.8). In *Comus* (lines 447–52), Milton's description of the Gorgon face on the shield and its function is explicit and chilling, reminiscent of the Homeric epithet "the blank-eyed face of the Gorgon with her stare of horror" (*Iliad* 11.36–37). The Renaissance references to the Gorgon which place her on Athena's shield function only in inverse relation to the proud goddess figure, but this fact scarcely reduces the potency of the image, especially in the hands of consummate poet-mythographers like Petrarch, Du Bellay, Spenser, and Milton.

The Gorgon may function only through her complement in the iconographic tradition just described, but she is accorded spectacular vengeance in Cellini's free-standing bronze statue of Perseus (1553). Were it not for Medusa's head which he holds aloft in his left hand and her headless body at his feet, he might be any well-favored young man. Her head, although proportionately smaller than his, identifies the hero and signals the magnitude of his feat. Yet it is the viewers' knowledge of the legend, not the head itself, that triggers admiration for Perseus, because the head is in no way threatening. In fact, it is a double of Perseus' own. The finely modeled eyebrows, the sensual lips, the straight-bridged nose, and the downcast eyes of the trophy and the hero mirror each other. Even the hair is similar. Medusa's hair is not made of snakes. Rather, a cohort of small snakes the size of the curls of her hair has settled itself into a flowing composition with the curls. Perseus' own curls continue the design. Seen from behind, the two heads are almost interchangeable, as Perseus' curls mimic Medusa's snakes. The only discordant element in Cellini's masterpiece is the somber, mature male face that forms the rear portion of Perseus' helmet. The face has tusks and is clearly a Janus mask offsetting the beauty of the young hero and his Doppelgänger trophy. Siebers identifies the mask as the god of death who "stares to the rear, counting the victims left in the wake of the hero's swift and relentless advance" (12).

Cellini's statue and Ovid's account of the Perseus-Medusa story are cast in the same mold of revelatory brilliance. With them the ambiguities of the Gorgon figure reach an apogee. After Cellini, visual artists especially work in the shadow of a rare genius of transformation. Caravaggio's somewhat silly Medusa (1600–1601) is a case in point. Mounted on a wooden shield as part of the parade equipment of an equestrian statue, the painting represents what is obviously a boy model trying to look fierce. Instead, he seems concerned that the snakes in his headpiece are going to bite his nose. Equally unconvincing, although not silly, is an illustration of the constellation Perseus in a sky atlas published by Jan Hevelius in 1687. In the illustration, Perseus, in rear view, swings a full-face, placid Medusa head through the skies after him. The head, trailing two or three anodyne snakes, is as big as Perseus' considerable torso.

Edward Topsell offers a number of fantastic word portraits of the Gorgon in his *History of Four-Footed Beasts*, originally published in 1607. The section in question is for the most part a translation from volume one of Conrad Gesner's *Historiae animalium* (1551). Topsell-Gesner portray the Gorgon as an animal with dragon scales, swine teeth, a poisonous mane, wings, human hands, and lethal breath. This animal, they explain, is native to Africa and is actually bred in Libya. Barely disguising their scorn for "poets' fictions" which make of the Gorgon a human female, they say he is nonhuman and male, between a calf and a bull in size.

A male Gorgon is not unknown in the tradition, although the bestial composite described by Topsell and Gesner is unique, with only slight indebtedness to the *Natural History* of Pliny the Elder (A.D. 23–79). Male Gorgoneions were fairly common even before Homer, and he is the first to make a literary reference to the male aspect of the Gorgon. "The stark eyes of a Gorgon, or murderous Ares" (*Iliad* 8.348–49) refers to the raging Hector. Shakespeare has Cleopatra make a similar allusion in her anger at Antony's marriage to Octavia. "Though he be painted one way like a Gorgon, / The other way's a Mars" (II.v.116–17), she says, meaning, from her perspective, that Antony is alternately bestial and heroic but certainly not female. In the *Hercules Furens* Euripides characterizes the demented hero's gaze as that of a "wild Gorgon eye" (990). Fontenrose also records the existence of Ketos, a male counterpart to Medusa, in Mediterranean creation myths (ch. 11). None of these references to the Gorgon in its male aspect, however, seems related to Topsell-Gesner's strange portrait of the male beast. Both the sex and the species they posit represent aberrations from the mainstream of the Medusa's history.

Beginning with the antirationalist sensibilities that develop with pre-Romantics like Rousseau and the early Goethe, that mainstream is very clear. The advent of Romanticism in the late eighteenth century marks the most concentrated attention accorded Medusa since classical times. The place she occupies in the

Romantic imagination can be called obsessive, because the Romantics saw her not only as herself, the single Gorgon named Medusa, but as the embodiment of the dark lady, the contaminated and irresistible beauty whose real name was Death. Writers' and artists' fascination with her radical ambiguity elevates her to the status of Muse. She occupies this position under various pseudonyms until well into the Decadent period at the end of the nineteenth century. Mario Praz says that the symbiosis between the artist and Medusa epitomizes "the whole of Romanticism. This glassy-eyed, severed female head, this horrible, fascinating Medusa, was to be the object of the dark loves of the Romantics and the Decadents throughout the whole of the century" (26–27). Praz is referring in particular to Faust's vision of a mysterious young girl on the night of the witches' sabbath, but he might be characterizing the ideal of Poe, Baudelaire, Coleridge, Keats, Shelley, Rossetti, Swinburne, Pater, or D'Annunzio, among many others.

The extent to which the contaminated beauty permeates Romantic literature can best be seen in two exemplars of the type, not precisely Medusa figures but first cousins traveling under other guises: Geraldine in Coleridge's "Christabel" (1797–1800), and Lamia in Keats's long poem of the same name (1819). Geraldine, the mysterious serpent-woman who is compellingly beautiful and hideously powerful, destroys both her innocent counterpart Christabel and Christabel's aged father Leoline. The young girl, powerless in the face of the stranger's spell, is slowly transformed into a snake herself, hissing when words fail. The old baron is rendered senseless by the memories the intruder evokes, so that he repudiates his own child and follows Geraldine into the nether world. While Geraldine is not, strictly speaking, a Medusa figure, she is, like her, a "lovely demon" of the Gorgon family, in the Romantics' lexicon. Keats's Lamia is certainly of the same family. She herself is destroyed in a reversal of the evil-eye spell—Apollonius, the friend of her lover Lycius, shoots his "sophist's eye" through her "like a sharp spear" (lines 299–300). But by then Lycius has died through his union with her. In Coleridge's and Keats's heroines, there is a risk of broadening the Gorgon family beyond manageable bounds. There is no doubt, however, that the head of the family, so to speak, fits the esthetic that requires mystery, perversity, and transforming power as components of beauty.

The most explicit manifesto of this esthetic is Shelley's "On the Medusa of Leonardo da Vinci in the Florentine Gallery" (1819). The poem which so fired Shelley's admirers is technically a fragment—the concluding stanza was not published until 1961 (Rogers). The original five pentametric octaves, however, evoke through the Medusa figure the quintessentially Romantic "tempestuous loveliness of terror" (line 33). Shelley's inspiration for the poem was a painting of the Medusa in the Uffizi gallery. He and his contemporaries accepted the gallery's inaccurate attribution of the painting to Leonardo. That it was actually done by an unidentified seventeenth-century Flemish artist does not alter the importance of the painting for Shelley and for those who read and were captivated by his poem.

The painting, as transmogrified by Shelley, shows the Medusa head "surrounded by a mist in which can be faintly seen a variety of bats, mice, and other more ambiguous and sinister creatures. . . . Out of the half-open mouth issues a whitish cloud of breath, the 'thrilling vapour' referred to by Shelley'' (McGann 7–8). McGann's excellent interpretation of the poem hinges on the meaning of the ''thrilling vapour,'' the creative energy that emerges from destruction and death regenerated. ''Shelley's Medusa seeks to terrorize whatever in the observer is still committed to evil and to invigorate in him everything that strives for life'' (McGann 10).

Following the lead of Keats and Shelley and Coleridge, other writers of like inclination respond to the spirit of the Florentine Medusa as a catalyst for their own syntheses of the death and life forces. One of the most notorious syntheses occurs in the erotic poetry and sensually charged critical writings of Swinburne. In ''Notes on the Designs of the Old Masters at Florence'' (ca. 1866) and in much of his poetry, Swinburne celebrates ''masochistic and sadistic love, and his Medusan allusions exhibit the masochistic side of the nineteenth-century obsession with the ambivalent female'' (Patterson 118). The popularly perceived danger to public morals inherent in this ambivalent figure is well illustrated by Rossetti's loss of a commission for a Perseus-Medusa painting in 1868. The would-be patron, a wealthy brewer, cancelled the commission on grounds that Rossetti's preliminary sketches revealed the severed head as an indecent object. Rossetti's subsequent defense of his design reveals the core of ''the nineteenth-century obsession'': he declares his intention of treating the head ''as a pure ideal,'' avoiding ''the least degree of . . . repugnant reality'' (Rossetti 281). Pater too extols the idealizing qualities of the figure, in his essay in *The Renaissance* (1873) entitled ''Leonardo da Vinci.'' He sees in the equipoise of beauty and horror the seed of the creative energy that will lead Leonardo to the perfection of the *Gioconda* or the *Mona Lisa*. D'Annunzio, in the poem ''Gorgon'' (1885), expresses the identical sentiment. At the other end of the scale, perhaps the most insipid use of the Medusa figure in the Keats-Shelley-Coleridge lineage is that of William Morris, in ''The Doom of King Acrisius'' from *The Earthly Paradise* (1871). There, Medusa, pathetic and Victorian, ''resembles the heroine of a sentimental best seller'' (Patterson 115). Poseidon has seduced her and then abandoned her, so that the whole of her fate, to Morris, is to be a victim of lust, an indecent urge whose expression taints its victim.

If these encounters with the Medusa figure add up to any one conclusion, it is that the image in all its guises represents vitality. The last guise it takes, by the turn of the century, is the highly stylized surface representation of Symbolist painting. The prototype of the genre, for the Medusa figure, is *The Blood of the Medusa*, painted around 1895 by the Belgian Fernand Khnopff. There is no blood at all in this elegant portrait of a refined and inscrutable woman seen in a close-up of the face looking straight forward. The pupils in the transparent eyes are placed strangely high in the cornea, and the head is cropped just above the eyebrows. A miniature hissing snake with visible fangs peeps coyly out of the high neck of the woman's dress. Two other small snakes seem to lick affectionately at her temples. According to Emile Verhaeren, Khnopff's women have a "glacial attraction and medusa-like perversity" (qtd. in Goldwater 208–9). These qualities can be seen in the Medusa figure in *The Blood of the Medusa* as well as in some of the other women depicted by Symbolists.

Perhaps the fullest assimilation of the Gorgonian duality, in visual art, comes with Beardsley, whose illustrations for Wilde's *Salomé* (1894) evoke a "suggestion of evil . . . conveyed without representation" (Goldwater 65). In *The Dancer's Reward* Salomé grasps a strand of the hair of the severed head offered her on a platter. The head is Medusa's, not John the Baptist's. The remaining strands of its hair drip over the sides of the platter, "animized strands that menace" (65), while the faces of the two women, dancer/artist and Muse/Gorgon, gaze on each other in amazement. This image of the twin female faces is new in the Medusa tradition, and points toward the final transformation of the figure in the twentieth century.

The single most subtle transformation of the image since Pindar's fair-cheeked beauty is the insistent denial by contemporary writers and artists of the Gorgonian aspect of the Medusa. Both male and female interpreters embrace this unmonstrous Medusa. The essay of Hélène Cixous, "The Laugh of the Medusa" (1976), provides a good model for the most recent turns the image has taken. Portrayed as deadly by patriarchal culture, Medusa, for Cixous, is not deadly at all. She is a bogy invented by moral cowards or interpreters whose self-knowledge remains at the infantile stage. She laughs at the nightmarish feats of destruction attributed to her. She especially laughs at the feat of castration attributed to her by Freud ("Medusa's Head," 1922). Among other observations it offers, Cixous' analysis recognizes a potentially comic strain in the tradition. Such a dimension is central to twentieth-century versions of the image. These modern Medusas are not necessarily funny—although some of them are—but they are very human. They live among us, they wear jeans (in Barthelme's story "A Shower of Gold" in *Come Back, Dr. Caligari*, 1964), they frequent beauty shops (in Welty's story "Petrified Man" in *The Collected Stories of Eudora Welty*, 1980), they reverse the ancient formula of creator/created to act out their own stories (in Barth, *Chimera*, 1972).

One of the first twentieth-century instances of the new Medusa story is *Perseus and the Head of Medusa* (various versions, 1898–1902), a marble statue by Rodin's pupil Camille Claudel. Like Cixous offering a revisionist view of Medusa's meaning, Claudel had broken with the master before she designed and executed her statue. In it the Medusa head, neither horrible nor beautiful, forms a block with the left arm of Perseus and is raised beside and above his head. His smooth, youthful face is uninteresting beside the image of bewildered suffering he holds up. Medusa's chin line is no longer firm; lines sag in her cheeks. Rather than the image of pathos which the contrast between young Perseus and middle-aged Medusa might suggest, Claudel's piece shows a dignified woman misused and tragically bound to the victorious arm of her rather stupid tormenter.

In its blurring of the horror-beauty syndrome, Claudel's turn-of-the-century piece typifies expressions of the Medusa image down to the present time. Except in rare instances—in José Emilio Pacheco's short story "The Blood of Medusa" (1958), for example—the Gorgonian aspect gives way to a more subtly assimilated expression of sorrow or blocked creative energies or thwarted aspiration. Daryl Hine's poem "Tableau vivant" from *Minutes* (1969) and Louise Bogan's pair of poems "The Sleeping Fury" and "Medusa" from *The Blue Estuaries* (1968) crystallize the *aggiornamento* of the image. In the thirteen compact lines of "Tableau vivant," a stylized, predictable Perseus is suspended in time above "the slumbering Medusa / Like a buzzing fly or a mosquito / On beaten, golden wings." Unlike the Medusas of earlier ages, this one bears fruit within her own dreaming, where she creates "the mate that she will never meet / Who will look into her eyes and live." As McGann points out, the mate is the new artist (24). For Bogan the Medusa figure is equally unthreatening. "The Sleeping Fury" opens with this unpretentious address to Medusa: "You are here now, / Who were so loud and feared, in a symbol before me, / Alone and asleep, and I at last look long upon you." Nine brief stanzas later, the voice of the poem expresses the catharsis that follows the long looking: "And now I may look upon you, / Having once met your eyes. You lie in sleep and forget me. / Alone and strong in my peace, I look upon you in yours." It is hard to read the "I" as other than Bogan, a woman who has made peace with one of her culture's most ambiguous female icons. That reading is not prerequisite, however, to a recognition of "The Sleeping Fury" and its earlier, simpler counterpart, "Medusa," as a bold reinvention of the old myth. The same boldness marks Hine's distinctly modern Medusa.

Among twentieth-century artists, Eugene Berman has probably made the most extensive use of the Medusa figure. She is the explicit subject of a series of watercolors, pastels, oils, and lithographs he completed in 1968 and 1969. In the characteristic back or top-of-the-head, hunched view he adopted for the great *Sunset (Medusa)* oil painting from 1945 [see illustration 14], she is the sometimes named, sometimes implicit, subject of a whole range of oils from the 1940s, including, among others, *View in Prospect of a Perfect Sunset* (1941), *Medusa's Corner* (1943), and *Perpetuum Immobile* (1945). Berman's lifelong preoccupation with mythological figures informs *Sunset (Medusa)* with a profusion of ambiguous images from the Gorgonian and the redemptive aspects of the tradition. The former emerge in the foreboding, derelict atmosphere of the painting; the latter, in the strange beauty of the young woman's hair and her evident mourning.

Sylvia Plath's two explicit Medusa poems span the register of possibility in the image (both from *Collected Poems*, 1981). In "Medusa" (1962) the voice of the poem violently rejects the "unnerving head—God-ball." Ending eight five-line stanzas of abuse, the last line stands alone: "There is nothing between us." This is a poem of particularly concentrated intensity in which the poet's voice cedes not a decibel to the hated antagonist invoked. In "Perseus: The Triumph of Wit Over Suffering" (1958), Plath uses the Medusa head to mock the victory of Perseus over his adversary. After centuries of sufferers have battled the Gorgon, this upstart bounds across the stage with "a fun-house mirror" that keeps her head "In safe perspective." Her decapitated head becomes "the beheaded head of a sullen doll." Plath manages to suggest not that Medusa is a rag doll but that Perseus is a fool.

The artistic variety in these modern Medusas marks a distinctive revitalizing of the figure. Just as the petrifying power once ascribed to her drops away, so poets shift from the immobility of stone to water and other fluid imagery. In "The Muse as Medusa" from *Collected Poems, 1930–1973* (1974), May Sarton develops the I-poet-acolyte figure as a fish which looks Medusa "straight in the cold eye, cold" (line 2), "Prepared to be hooked, gutted, caught" (line 6). Instead, the fish is left free to explore "Through the great deep and on the rising tide, / Flashing wild streams" where it "did not come to grief, / But swims still in a fluid mystery" (lines 10–11, 15–16). In the story "The Letting Down of the Hair" (*Atlantic*, March 1972), Anne Sexton's Medusa protagonist constantly washes her long yellow hair, which is like sea grass. "The parts that are washed sit in coils on the floor and wait patiently. . . . As it dries it is owned by the wind; as it dries it moves swiftly like a thousand minnows" (41–42). These are images of growth, movement, change, certainly not of the arrest or petrifaction recorded in the origins of the myth. These are images that corroborate Jung's reflections in *Aion* (1959) on the Medusa-jellyfish-*stella maris* (star of the sea) configuration, the "fiery centre in us from which creative or destructive influences come" (137). For Jung, destruction leads to reconstruction in a continual process of making and becoming. The process occurs repeatedly in twentieth-century versions of the Medusa story, as outworn assumptions are cast off and new ones take their place.

Even if no new synthesis is offered, the material itself is invariably explored from angles not taken before. This is the case in Iris Murdoch's novel *A Severed Head* (1961), in which a sculptor keeps a number of heads in varying states of incompletion. When questioned as to why modern sculptors do not do realistic heads anymore, he answers, "I don't know. We don't believe in human nature in the old Greek way any more. There is nothing between schematized symbols and caricature. What I want here is some sort of impossible liberation. Never mind. I shall go on playing with it and interrogating it and perhaps it will tell me something" (49). A moment later he makes a throwaway remark, musing that his heads may be "an obsession. Freud on Medusa. The head can represent the female genitals, feared not desired" (50). While this worldly banter does not say much about heads in general or Medusa's in particular, it is vintage Murdoch and affords a quirky vignette of Medusa's adaptability. In this case the real Medusa figure is not to be found among the sculpted heads, but in the androgynous person of Honor Klein, who disdains (read enraptures, spellbinds, renders senseless, castrates, petrifies) men.

Another ambitious recent use of the Medusa legend is in Emilio Carballido's five-act play *Medusa* (1958). For Carballido the legend is the stuff of an existentialist political allegory, a call to social revolution. The hero Perseus, conditioned to regard Medusa as a monster whom he must kill, realizes, at the moment of truth, that she is no more monstrous than he is. He struggles to translate his realization into personal choices and thus to reverse the patterns of action laid out for him. He only succeeds, however, in alienating himself from the social order he seeks to change. Medusa as recast by Carballido becomes an emblem of disillusionment. It is important to note that Medusa herself does nothing disillusioning. She mediates the young man's passage from stereotyped notions of good and evil to an acceptance of the inevitable intermingling of the two. This is a role that the contemporary Medusa will often play.

In *Perseid*, the central section of the triptych novel *Chimera* (1972), John Barth's Medusa combines the qualities of antagonist-destroyer and muse-nurturer. Perseus, at the midpoint in his life, appears stymied by disorder and impotence. Long ago he conquered their outward sign, the Gorgon Medusa, as she then seemed to him, but now they have returned. Rejecting battle as an appropriate metaphor for the search to regain his own creative powers, sexual and artistic, Perseus must learn to love Medusa. In a marvelous Barthian series of metamorphoses he does this and is reborn through love. As Perseus puts it to Medusa at the end of *Perseid*:

Now listen and believe me, if there's any truth in words: it wasn't you who discovered your beauty to me, but I who finally unveiled it to myself. And what I saw, exactly, when I opened my eyes, were two things in instantaneous succession, reflected in yours: the first was a reasonably healthy, no-longer-heroic mortal with more than half his life behind him, less potent and less proud than he was at twenty but still vigorous after all, don't interrupt me, and grown too wise to wish his time turned back. The second, one second after, was the stars in your own eyes, reflected from mine and rereflected to infinity—stars of a quite miraculous, yes blinding love, which transfigured everything in view. Perhaps you find the image trite; I beg you not to say so. (Barth 132–33)

Although Barth's re-enactment of the combat myth is deliciously ironic, it also strikes at the heart of Medusa's meaning. She is both adversary and partner to all who seek self-knowledge and the power to create—to create life and to create art. If heroism must figure in the early stages of the apprentice's quest, so be it; that strain in the tradition is rich. It is understanding, however, that finally brings the hero to maturity and the Gorgon to its full strength as a universal symbol. Fear changes to love and the regenerative cycle is complete.

Fear, translated into the evil-eye component of Medusa's ancestry, seems rooted in primitive belief, whether temporally (in archaic societies) or psychologically (in individual experience). The positive elements associated with her redemptive qualities, however, do not enter the written or visual record before the Greek classical period. What Pindar began continues to the present day, making for the persistent ambiguity that attaches two names to the figure: the Gorgon, which evokes dread, and Medusa, which may evoke anything from helpless fascination to creative powers regained.

The two faces of Medusa are now a critical paradigm for the Dionysian/ Apollonian register. The paradigm signifies not only chaos and order within an individual, but extends to analyses of self and society, freedom and determinism, and, of course, life and art. Siebers, in *The Mirror of Medusa*, proposes a "logic of superstition" that links archaic and modern societies' myth-based practices "as a universal human activity" (Preface). For anyone inclined to relegate Medusa to a graveyard of classical allusions, Siebers has news. To read it is to look into the mirror.

BIBLIOGRAPHY

Barth, John. *Chimera*. New York: Random House, 1972.

Bogan, Louise. "Medusa" and "The Sleeping Fury." In *Blue Estuaries: Poems 1923–1968*. New York: Ecco Press, 1968. 4, 78–79.

Callois, Roger. *Méduse et Cie*. Paris: Gallimard, 1960.

Carballido, Emilio. *Medusa*. Ed. J. Gaucher–Schultz and Alfredo Morales. Englewood Cliffs, N.J.: Prentice-Hall, 1972.

Cather, Willa. *Youth and the Bright Medusa*. New York: Knopf, 1920.

Cixous, Hélène. "The Laugh of the Medusa." Trans. Keith and Paula Cohen. *Signs* 1.4 (1976): 875–93.

Claudel, Camille. *Perseus and the Head of Medusa*. In catalog of Claudel exhibit at the Rodin Museum. Paris, 1984.

Cornille, Jean-Louis. "L'Oeil, la gorgone." *Littérature* 25 (1977): 83–99.

Davey, Frank. "Atwood's Gorgon Touch." *Studies in Canadian Literature* 2 (1977): 146–53.

Davidson, Cathy N., and E. M. Broner, eds. "Mother as Medusa." In *The Lost Tradition: Mothers and Daughters in Literature*. New York: Frederick Ungar, 1980. 190–252.

Elworthy, Frederick. *The Evil Eye*. London, 1895; rpt. New York: The Julian Press, 1958.

Fontenrose, Joseph. *Python: A Study of Delphic Myth and Its Origins*. Berkeley and Los Angeles: University of California Press, 1959.

Freccero, John. "Dante's Medusa: Allegory and Autobiography." In *By Things Seen: Reference and Recognition in Medieval Thought*. Ed. David L. Jeffrey. Ottawa: University of Ottawa Press, 1979. 33–46.

Goethe, Johann Wolfgang von. *Letters from Italy*. In *The Works of J. W. von Goethe*. Trans. A. J. W. Morrison, Anna Swanwick, and Sir Walter Scott. Ed. Nathan Haskell Dole. Boston: Wyman-Fogg, 1902. 253.

Goldwater, Robert. *Symbolism*. New York: Harper and Row, 1979.

"Gorgo." *Paulys Real-Encyclopädie der classichen Altertumswissenschaft*. Neue Bearbeitung. Stuttgart: A. Druckenmüller, 1912, 7: pt. 2, cols. 1630–55.

"Gorgona." *Enciclopedia Italiana di Scienze, Lettere ed Arti*. 1933 ed.

Hartland, Edwin S. *The Legend of Perseus: A Study of Tradition in Story, Custom and Belief*. 3 vols. London, 1894–96; rpt. New York: AMS Press, 1973.

Helterman, Jeffrey. "Gorgons in Mississippi: Eudora Welty's 'Petrified Man.' " *Notes on Mississippi Writers* 7 (1974): 12–20.

Hine, Daryl. "Tableau vivant." In *Minutes*. New York: Atheneum, 1969. 45.

Holzapfel, Tamara. "A Mexican Medusa" [on Carballido]. *Modern Drama* 12 (1969): 231–37.

Howe, Thalia P. "An Interpretation of the Perseus-Gorgon Myth in Greek Literature and Monuments through the Classical Period." *Dissertation Abstracts* 12.5 (1952): 613. Abstract of Ph.D. diss. Columbia University.

Jung, C. G. *Aion: Researches into the Phenomenology of the Self.* Vol. 9, pt. 2 of *The Collected Works of C. G. Jung.* Trans. R. F. C. Hull. 2nd ed. Bollingen Series 20. Princeton: Princeton University Press, 1968.

Klonsky, Milton, ed. *Blake's Dante: The Complete Illustrations to the Divine Comedy.* New York: Harmony Books, 1980. Plate 20, "Hell, Canto 9."

Lettvin, Jerome Y. "The Gorgon's Eye." In *Astronomy of the Ancients.* Ed. Kenneth Brecher and Michael Feirtag. Cambridge, Mass., and London: MIT Press, 1979. 133–51.

McGann, Jerome J. "The Beauty of the Medusa: A Study in Romantic Literary Iconology." *Studies in Romanticism* 11 (1972): 3–25.

Maloney, Clarence, ed. *The Evil Eye.* New York: Columbia University Press, 1976.

Mode, Heinz. *Fabulous Beasts and Demons.* London: Phaidon, 1975.

Murdoch, Iris. *A Severed Head.* London: Chatto and Windus, 1961.

Patterson, Kent. "A Terrible Beauty: Medusa in Three Victorian Poets." *Tennessee Studies in Literature* 17 (1972): 111–120.

Phinney, Edward, Jr. "Perseus' Battle with the Gorgons." *Transactions and Proceedings of the American Philological Association* 102 (1971): 445–63.

Plath, Sylvia. "Medusa" and "Perseus: The Triumph of Wit Over Suffering." In *The Collected Poems.* Ed. Ted Hughes. New York: Harper and Row, 1981. 82–84, 224–26.

Praz, Mario. *The Romantic Agony.* New York: Meridian Books, 1960.

Rogers, Neville. "Shelley and the Visual Arts." *Keats-Shelley Memorial Bulletin* 12 (1961): 9–17.

Rossetti, Dante Gabriel. *Rossetti Papers, 1862–1870.* Ed. William M. Rossetti. London: Sands, 1902. 281–82.

Sarton, May. "The Muse as Medusa." In *Collected Poems, 1930–1973.* New York: Norton, 1974. 332.

Sexton, Anne. "The Letting Down of the Hair." *Atlantic,* March 1972, 40–43.

Siebers, Tobin. *The Mirror of Medusa.* Berkeley and Los Angeles: University of California Press, 1983.

Topsell, Edward. *The History of Four-Footed Beasts and Serpents and Insects.* London, 1658.

Wagoner, David. "Medusa's Lover." In *First Light.* Boston: Little, Brown, 1983. 41–42.

13

The Sphinx

Frank A. Scafella

"Sphinx" is a Greek name deriving from *sphiggein*, "to draw tight or to bind together." So the Greek sphinx, a winged monster with a lion's body and the head and breasts of a woman, is understood as a strangler. (See Graves 417.) But if the name "sphinx" is Greek, the monster thus named seems to have originated in Egypt. Heinz Mode identifies the Great Sphinx of Giza, a wingless monster with a lion's body and the head of a man, as the oldest representation of its kind. If this is so, the idea of the sphinx passed from Egypt into Assyria and ancient Greece, and thence to the rest of the Western world.

In ancient Assyrian and Greek civilizations the sphinx was represented in architecture, on vases, shields, sarcophagi, gems, and intaglios, on columns and sculpture, in ivory, terra-cotta, and bone, on gold plates, glass plates, and even on the helmet of Athena in the Parthenon at Athens. If we accept Mode's thesis that the sphinx originates in Egypt, it would have been during this first long period of transition and adaptation (from approximately the twenty-sixth to the fourth centuries B.C.) that the sphinx lost its direct association with divine kingship, acquired its female character, and was associated with other beasts and monsters from the ram and the bull, the falcon and the eagle, to harpies and sirens.

The sphinx had a variety of forms in the ancient world. In ancient Egypt, the sphinx was male and wingless and was often recumbent. Three major types of the creature can be found in Egyptian art: the androsphinx, a lion with a human head and/or face; the criosphinx, a ram-headed lion; and the hieracosphinx, a hawk-headed lion. In ancient Mesopotamia, the sphinx appeared in both male and female forms and could be winged or wingless. Female sphinxes are often found in the art of Phoenicia and Syria. In ancient Greece, the customary type of the sphinx had a woman's head and breasts, the wings of an eagle, and the body and feet of a lion ("Sphinx," *Encyclopaedia Britannica*). The Greek sphinx was not usually depicted as recumbent. (For a detailed study of the sphinx in the ancient world and other times, see Demisch, *Die Sphinx*.)

In spite of the diversity of artistic use and the transforming effects of cultural adaptation, the sphinx of ancient art remains quite stable in form. One need only glance through the numerous representations of the sphinx gathered from all parts of the ancient world by A. Dessenne to see the extent to which this is so. Mode suggests that the Great Sphinx of Giza is responsible for this stability of form: "As it has exercised an enormous influence right down to our time, it must be considered the most permanent and significant among all the monsters. In this instance it is not so much the type, but a particular ancient monument, that has been of decisive importance" (76). It follows that ancient man's conception of the sphinx would have been gained primarily through the plastic arts.

But there was a literary tradition that developed along with the pictorial. In the *Enuma elish*, a Sumero-Akkadian creation myth dating from the beginning of the second milennium before our era, we find what may be the earliest literary representation of the sphinx. In this myth, Tiamat, the primordial mother (who represents the vastness of the marine waters), and Apsu, the primordial father (who represents the fresh waters), produced a host of younger gods whose daily revelry disturbed the primeval peace of the old couple. To gain repose, Apsu devised a plan whereby to destroy the younger gods. But learning of his plan, the revellers turned the tables on Apsu and killed him before he could carry out his plan. Then Tiamat, inflamed with rage over the death of Apsu, declared war on the younger gods, her children, and gave birth to a horde of monsters to avenge her—viper, dragon, sphinx, great lion, mad dog, scorpion-man.

> When Tiamat had thus lent import to her handiwork,
> She prepared for battle against the gods, her offspring.
> To avenge Apsu, Tiamat wrought evil.
> (Tablet 2, lines 1–3; translation by E. A. Speiser,
> in Pritchard, p. 63)

This account of the origin of gods and monsters suggests a very different genealogy for the sphinx than is implied in Mode's thesis that the sphinx originates in Egypt. For if the Great Sphinx of Giza was symbolic of divine kingship, the sphinx of the *Enuma elish* (an offspring of rage and the desire for revenge) is an embodiment of evil. It may well be, as Mode observes, that "the literary tradition lags far behind the visual repertory" in the representation of monsters. When monsters of classical antiquity appear in literary works (such as the *Enuma elish*) "there is seldom a detailed description" of them, Mode says, "since they are either assumed to be known, or it is left to the reader to imagine them for himself" (13, 14). But in view of the fact that the *Enuma elish* is roughly contemporary with the Great Sphinx of Giza, Mode's thesis merits some examination.

Mode has given us one of the fullest and most provocative accounts of the origin and use of monsters in the art of the ancient world, but he is surprisingly conservative (one might even say reactionary) in his account of modern man's use of the sphinx. In modern Western art the "genuine" sphinx is rare, Mode says, and almost always it is mistakenly female.

Only more recently has European art again taken up the sphinx without *falsifying* it, deriving it directly from Egypt. In the nineteenth century it was *misused* for all kinds of symbolic fantasies. Many genre painters and late romantics attempted to portray the eternal feminine, enigmatic, erotically dangerous, by a more or less deliberate *distortion* of the *original work*. Thus for example Franz von Stuck painted not only the sphinx in its animal-human shape but also, as a parallel, a female nude lying on its stomach with the upper part of the body raised up. Other artists—Kubin for instance—stressed the ghostly sense of a "laughing sphinx." (78; italics added)

By "genuine" Mode means the "original work" of the Great Sphinx of Giza. It is this monument that von Stuck and others have distorted and falsified with erotic and comic notions derived from sources other than the monument itself. By implication, the literary tradition is partly to blame because it did not give us "detailed descriptions" of the sphinx when it figured in the epic musings of the poets. It is further implied that distortion and falsification began as far back as the Greeks when they depicted the sphinx not as masculine and kingly but as feminine and erotic, a strangler of man. Apparently all that is necessary for ridding modern art of its tendency to falsify the sphinx is for the artist to derive his image directly from the Great Sphinx of Egypt. Francis Bacon, a twentieth-century British painter, seems to have done this in a painting entitled *Sphinx I* (1953).

The viewer's perspective in Bacon's painting is from above a massive skylight in the roof of a large apartment building. Resting on the skylight, supported by heavy dark beams which hold the glass, is a likeness of the Great Sphinx. Except for the head, shoulder, and left front leg and paw, the figure is not drawn in great detail; in fact, the body itself is transparent to the window frames and to the large, lighted room beneath the skylight. The eyes of the viewer are held only momentarily by the figure of the sphinx itself before they are drawn to a very dark shadow on the far wall of the room below the skylight—a shadow of the slouching shoulders and head of a man holding a pistol in his hand. Apparently the man is stalking someone or something. Then the viewer realizes with a start that the shadow is not cast by a man at all, but by the head and upper torso of the Great Sphinx itself (Russell 93). It is discernibly the figure of the Great Sphinx that we see, yet it casts a shadow foreboding skulduggery, perhaps even murder. How do we explain this? Why is it that this contemporary painter, when he takes up the image of the "genuine" sphinx, finds it casting a shadow not of royalty and divinity but of evil? Is the shadow of evil merely the legacy of a falsifying literary tradition?

Or consider the image of the Great Sphinx as it appears in a prose sketch and a sonnet by W. H. Auden. These pieces were written in 1938 after Auden stopped in Egypt on a trip East to cover the Sino-Japanese War (Fuller 199–20). Of the Great Sphinx, Auden writes:

There it lies, in the utter stillness of its mortal injuries; the flat cruel face of a scarred and blinded baboon, face of a circus monstrosity, no longer a statue but a living, changing creature of stone. A camera, if cameras had been invented, could have shown how that face has changed through the centuries, growing old and blind and terrible in the blaze of the sun, under the lash of the wind and the desert sand. Once, no doubt, it was beautiful. Long ago, it could see. Now it lies there mutilated and sightless, its paws clumsily bandaged with bricks, its mane like an old actor's wig, asking no riddle, turning its back upon America—injured baboon with a lion's cruel mouth, in the middle of invaded Egypt. (qtd. in Fuller 199–20)

There is interpretation here, to be sure. But interpretation is not the result of the failure of the writer to describe in detail the monument that is being contemplated; the writer stands directly before the monument itself. To him its very form and presence speak of mortal injury, of cruelty and blindness and beauty lost to the "lash" of wind and sand and time. It is the physical presence of the Great Sphinx itself that presses Auden to ask in his sonnet, "The Sphinx," whether it issued "Healthy" from the hand of its carver. For he knows that even the earliest "conquerors" of Egypt saw, as he sees, "the face of a sick ape, a bandaged paw," a presence that does not like youth or love or learning. Apparently, then, even when he takes up the image of the Great Sphinx of Giza, the contemporary artist is put in mind by that monument of cruelty, intrigue, bestiality, murder, disease—in a word, evil. This is the "rough beast"—a creature with a lion's body and a man's head—that William Butler Yeats sees slouching (like the shadow of Bacon's man with the pistol in his hand) "towards Bethlehem to be born" ("The Second Coming," 1920).

So the question is, whence the association of the sphinx with disease? If originally the sphinx was a symbol of divine kingship, where and when did it begin to be associated with evil? The *Enuma elish* leads us to believe that the sphinx was an evil monster before it came to represent divine kingship in the Great Sphinx of Giza. In any case it seems fair to say that the sphinx of the literary tradition, once it was established, all but determined Western man's understanding even of the Great Sphinx. This is not to say that disease of mind or heart is the only or original reality associated with the sphinx in Western thought. Associations of the sphinx with kingship and wisdom carry over from the ancient world into the Renaissance and beyond. Pico della Mirandola, for example, expressing an idea that he may have taken directly from Plutarch (first century A.D.), says that the Egyptians sculpted sphinxes in all of their temples "to indicate that divine knowledge, if committed to writing at all, must be covered with enigmatic veils and poetic dissimulation" (qtd. in Wind 24). Pico undoubtedly knew that in ancient Egypt the sphinx was used as a hieroglyph of *neb*—that is, master or lord ("Sphinx," *Encyclopaedia Britannica*). He also knew that the sphinx was an emblem of the achievement of wisdom; Pharaoh seated on a lion throne is an image of self-mastery (Norman 75). Frances Yates shows that Marsilio Ficino and Giulio Camillo also knew of the sphinx as a guard against profanation of the temple and as a discloser of divine mysteries in Egypt (150–51). Moreover, the use of the sphinx as a guardian of mysteries carries over into Renaissance humanism, as Jean Seznec shows, since the science of emblems was placed under the patronage of the sphinx (102). And Marie-Louise von Franz tells us that the sphinx in Egypt was a symbol of resurrection (35). All of this, no doubt, is what Mode refers to as the "genuine" tradition, and it appears that he has a point.

Nevertheless, there is the *Enuma elish*. And there is Hesiod, who, in implicit agreement with this creation myth, calls the sphinx the daughter of Orthos and Echidna (*Theogony* 326). Apollodorus regards the sphinx as a daughter of Typhon and Echidna, and says that the Muses taught her a riddle (*Library* 3.5.8). Against this background Graves observes that in Greece the sphinx was very early associated with disease and death, and that as a daughter of Typhon her breath is to be understood as the unhealthy sirocco (417). This interpretation comes directly into modern Western thought by way of Apollodorus' *Library* and Seneca's *Oedipus*. It comes forward toward our own time through "Fulgentius, Neckam, Boccaccio, and the whole tribe of authors who had made mythology safe for the world" (Bush 31). Following these mythographers, Andrea Alciati (1492–1550) presents the sphinx as the embodiment of the nature of ignorance; Edmund Spenser (1552?–1599) regards her as an appropriate embodiment of the Inquisition; Ben Jonson (1611) sees her as one who binds men's minds, as "Ignorance, who is alwaies the enemie of Love, and Beauty, and lyes still in wait to entrap them" (*Love Freed from Ignorance and Folly*); and Sir Francis Bacon presents her, in *The Wisdom of the Ancients* (1609), as the symbol of Science (or knowledge). By the beginning of the seventeenth century, then, it seems safe to say (with Charles Lemmi) that when it comes to Bacon, "the symbolism of the sphinx has long been conventional. Whatever is enigmatic and disquieting has at one time or another, we may feel sure of it, been compared with the famous woman-headed monster" (141).

Whence the association of the sphinx with evil? The ancient Greeks, if not first to associate the sphinx explicitly with disease of mind (ignorance, forgetfulness, thought-crippling fear) and death, were almost certainly first to elaborate this association in detail. The Oedipus legend, an early (perhaps *the* early) example of such detailed elaboration, is well known. Bulfinch summarizes Oedipus' encounter with the sphinx as follows:

The city of Thebes was afflicted with a monster which infested the highroad. It was called the Sphinx. It had the body of a lion and the upper part of a woman. It lay crouched on the top of a rock, and arrested all travellers who came that way, proposing to them a riddle, with the condition that those who could solve it should pass safe, but those who failed should be killed. Not one had yet succeeded in solving it, and all had been slain. Oedipus was not daunted by these alarming accounts, but boldly advanced to the trial. The Sphinx asked him, "What animal is that which in the morning goes on four feet, at noon on two, and in the evening upon three?" Oedipus replied, "Man, who in childhood creeps on hands and knees, in manhood walks erect, and in old age with the aid of a staff." The Sphinx was so mortified at the solving of her riddle that she cast herself down from the rock and perished. (125)

Sophocles' *Oedipus Rex* draws on this legend. In the play, twenty years have passed since Oedipus vanquished the sphinx and became king of Thebes. It has been twenty years, too, since he unwittingly murdered his father and married his mother in fulfillment of the prophecy of an oracle. Yet Oedipus has sought to discover the murderer, and when he asks Creon why the murder of Laius has never been investigated, Creon answers: "The riddling Sphinx compelled us to let slide / The dim past and attend to instant needs" (130–31). In other words, the sphinx is the cause of *lēthē* (concealment, oblivion) in the minds of the Thebans; she is the enemy of *alētheia*, truth (literally "unconcealing" or "unforgetting") (see Mueller 107). At least from the time of Sophocles, then, the sphinx and disease of mind were synonymous in the mind of Western man. From Sophocles onward, originality in pictorial, literary, philosophical, theological, and psychological treatments of the sphinx consists principally in searching out the origins of, explaining the nature of, offering solutions to, or simply dramatizing the conflict between man and the "monstrous" distortions of thought, word and deed visited on him by the forces which the sphinx symbolizes. Sir Francis Bacon synthesizes the tradition of the diseased or evil sphinx in his "Sphinx; or, Science."

By "Science" Bacon means knowledge in general. But as Lemmi points out, Bacon "deals rather with the discomforts of ignorance than with the conscious power of knowledge." For him, knowledge is a kingdom yet unconquered, a riddle to be solved, and knowledge in its unformed state may become tormenting and cruel to the man who takes up its challenge of precise formulation. So the symbol of the sphinx "came spontaneously to Bacon's mind" out of his familiarity with Natalis Comes and Andrea Alciati, says Lemmi. In Comes, the sphinx symbolizes the "lacerating anxieties which beset men" who seek knowledge, and "the life-and-death importance of facing them with a clear mind"; in Alciati, "the multiform Sphinx is declared to symbolize different kinds of ignorance, . . . and Oedipus, in contrast with the ignorant and hasty, who are devoured, the prudent judge of human nature" (Lemmi 142–43). With this in mind, Bacon locates the origin of the sphinx in the allegorical imagination of the ancients, and he interprets the sphinx allegorically as follows:

Science, being the wonder of the ignorant and unskilful, may be not absurdly called a monster. In figure and aspect it is represented as many-shaped, in allusion to the immense variety of matter with which it deals. It is said to have the face and voice of a woman, in respect of its beauty and facility of utterance. Wings are added because the sciences and the discoveries of science spread and fly abroad in an instant; the communication of knowledge being like that of one candle with another, which lights up at once. Claws, sharp and hooked, are ascribed to it with great elegance, because the axioms and arguments of science penetrate and hold fast the mind, so that it has no means of evasion or escape; . . . and unless they be solved and disposed of, they strangely torment and worry the mind, pulling it first this way and then that, and fairly tearing it to pieces. (Bacon 160–61)

The sphinx of Bacon's vision is thoroughly Greek; it is quite clear too that in Bacon's mind man's actions with respect to knowledge are to be modeled on those of Oedipus with respect to the sphinx.

Michael Maier, a contemporary of Bacon, states quite explicitly the philosophical implications of Bacon's allegory of knowledge. Maier counsels every man of intellect to remember that truth is gained only by way of many errors, and that falling into errors is always painful. "It is this that the ancient philosophers wished to stamp on our minds when they told us of the sphinx." He regards the sphinx as a symbol of "the difficulty and vexatiousness of the art" of philosophy—not only "to the Thebans" but "to the Egyptians before them" and to all men. The sphinx proposes enigmas, standing as she does "at the entrance to the works of the philosophers," and

he who passes by and goes his way receives no hurt from the monster; but he who, trusting in his boldness and his intelligence, attempts to solve the enigma,—he, I say, if he fails, prepares his own destruction: that is, the laceration of his heart and the loss of his substance. . . . Such are the doctrines of philosophy, as he who is versed in them can readily understand. (qtd. in Lemmi 143–44)

Friedrich Hegel's remark, some two centuries after Bacon and Maier, might be taken as a footnote to their interpretation of the sphinx: "The human head that bursts from the animal body represents Mind as it begins to raise itself above Nature . . . without, however, being able to liberate itself wholly from its fetters" (qtd. in Moore 68). And a poem by Ralph Waldo Emerson, "The Sphinx" (1841), affords us a summary account of the philosophical understanding of man's encounter with the sphinx.

Emerson's poem is faithful to the main elements of the Oedipus legend: the sphinx arrests the traveler, poses a riddle, the traveler answers it correctly, and the sphinx is vanquished. Yet Emerson does more than represent the Oedipus story. His sphinx, drowsy with age, all but deaf, her wings furled, sits brooding on the world. She understands the fate and meaning of nature, but through the long ages she has found no seer to answer the question she poses on the fate and nature of man. The riddle itself, as one might expect, has to do directly with the relations of Man and Nature. All nature is enchanted by one music, she knows, and one deity stirs nature to life. But man is an enigma:

> . . . man crouches and blushes
> Absconds and conceals;

He creepeth and peepeth,
  He palters and steals;
Infirm, melancholy,
  Jealous glancing around,
An oaf, an accomplice,
  He poisons the ground.

So the question, posed through the sphinx by "the great mother," Earth, is: "Who has drugged my boy's cup? / Who, with sadness and madness, / Has turned my child's head?"

Then the traveler-poet readily discerns the "meaning sublime" of the riddle, for the poet sees perfectly because he sees not with his eyes only, but with his soul. And what he sees is that in Nature Love works, "Heart-heaving alway." Not surprisingly, this answer discloses the sphinx herself as an element of the poet's own spirit, "yoke-fellow: / Of thine eye I am eyebeam," she says. The sphinx is the poet's intellect calling for reunion with his seeing soul. Her vanquishment is her reunion with the soul, where she takes her rightful place as an element of his Reason and counsels the poet thus: "Ask on, thou clothed eternity; / Time is the false reply." And immediately,

Uprose the merry Sphinx,
  And crouched no more in stone;
She melted into purple cloud,
  She silvered in the moon;
She spired into a yellow flame;
  She flowered in blossoms red;
She flowed into the foaming wave;
  She stood Monadnoc's head.

Thorough a thousand voices
  Spoke the universal dame:
"Who telleth one of my meanings
  Is master of all I am."

In the last words of the sphinx we hear the voice of Reason, whose "thousand voices" are the firmament itself.

Thus Emerson's sphinx is Reason dis-eased in estrangement from the soul. Her dwelling is the poet's disordered mind. This subjectivization of the sphinx is not surprising, given Emerson's understanding of Man in his relations with Nature. But what is surprising is the extent to which other poets and novelists in the nineteenth and twentieth centuries have treated the sphinx solely as a reality within the mind of man. In Edgar Allan Poe's narrative, "The Sphinx," the monster has no objective existence at all, but is strictly a projection of the diseased imagination of a man whose "dread" of dying of cholera has taken "entire possession of my soul." In chapter 70 of Melville's *Moby-Dick*, entitled "The Sphynx," there is no physical object that has the likeness of the monster, but only a whale's head that, severed from the body and hanging there at the side of the *Pequod*, "seemed" to Ahab "the Sphynx's in the desert." In Oscar Wilde's "The Sphinx" (1894) the poet's fancy makes him conscious of a "curious cat" which lies crouching in the corner of his room "on the Chinese mat with eyes of / satin rimmed with gold"—in other words, a thoroughly personal and private "sphinx" whose malevolence and oppressive presence turn out to be "foul dreams of sensual life" which dominate the poet's thought. And in H. G. Wells's *The Time Machine* (1895) the blind and diseased White Sphinx (which I have treated at length elsewhere) is an objectification of the diseased mind of a cannibalistic remnant of the human race.

Perhaps Sir Francis Bacon sowed the wind and it is we who reap the whirlwind. For it is Sigmund Freud in *The Interpretation of Dreams* (1900) who carries to its ultimate the extreme subjectivization of the sphinx that I have sketched above. Stating that the fate of Oedipus in Sophocles' *Oedipus Rex* "moves us only because it might have been ours," Freud believes that "the legend of Oedipus sprang from some primaeval dream-material which had as its content the distressing disturbance of a child's relation to his parents owing to the first stirrings of sexuality" (262–64). This is to say that the Oedipus fable is a fantasy response to the dream of having sexual relations with one's mother. And with this explanation of the root of Oedipus' problem the sphinx ceases to exist and figures not at all in Freud's discussion of the Oedipus complex. It was left to his disciples to recall the sphinx (somewhat) from the oblivion of man's unconscious into which Freud cast her.

For Mark Kanzer, the sphinx is an embodiment of "the mysteries of intercourse and birth" which Oedipus solves. For George Devereux, Oedipus' victory over the sphinx "represents both a heterosexual and a homosexual victory and gesture of triumph" (Ruitenbeek 172). And so it goes in essay after essay right down to Bruno Bettelheim's *Freud and Man's Soul* (1983), in which one finds one more very typical, unimaginative reading of the Oedipus legend. "Because we are told that the Sphinx posed all sorts of riddles, we must assume that the one she asked Oedipus was designed specifically for him," says Bettelheim.

Certainly Oedipus, owing to the lasting effects of his early trauma, must have been more concerned with the problems posed by walking than most people are, and more likely to think of walking and what it means at various ages; as an infant, crawling on all fours, he must have been more keenly aware than an ordinary child of his inability to walk on two feet. What the story of the Sphinx seems to emphasize is that the answer to the riddle of life is not just man, but each person himself. (26–27)

Here the sphinx has become a most considerate and helpful monster indeed, always with the best interests of her client in mind. Knowing Oedipus' deep longing to walk normally, and knowing that this longing stems from the sexual trauma of his infancy, the sphinx, like any analyst worth his salt, not only asks Oedipus a leading question but elicits the right answer from him. One finds himself wishing that the Freudians had not seen fit to drag the sphinx back into their picture.

Given the erotic nature and the therapeutic aims of the Freudian concern with the Oedipus legend, a far more constructive way of recovering the sphinx from the depths of "each person himself" would be to contemplate two nineteenth-century paintings whose subject is "Oedipus and the Sphinx"—one by J.-A.-D. Ingres (1808) and the other by Gustave Moreau (1864). In Ingres' painting, attention falls directly on Oedipus in the center of the picture. Nude, standing sideways, he has placed his left foot on a boulder (knee-high) and is leaning forward, his left elbow resting on his knee, and looking into the face of the sphinx, who stands before him on a pile of boulders at the mouth of her cave. Oedipus' entire figure is a study in relaxation. Light falls full on his face and on his abundant, dark, and curly hair. But the same light bathes the full and abundant breasts of the sphinx; the rest of her figure (head, wings, front legs) is in the shadow of the wall of rock that rises out of the top of the picture behind her.

She and Oedipus seem to have paused in the course of their conversation to contemplate one another. Their relaxed dispositions permit the viewer's eye to wander—down from those full breasts (eye-level to Oedipus, although he looks directly into the sphinx's eyes) to the pile of boulders on which she stands, to a rib-cage of a man (picked clean) at the base of the boulder on which Oedipus rests his foot. To the left of the rib-cage, stark against the blackness of the mouth of the cave, appears the bottom of a man's foot, the rest of his body concealed by the inner darkness of the cave. But off to the right and beyond Oedipus on the mountain pass, at a distance sufficient to render him a figure knee-high to Oedipus, stands a man in a state of alarm: his arms are thrown out as his upper body swings to flee, his face full on the sphinx, his garment thrown out from his shoulder by the force of his whirling. And beyond him, through a narrow passage between the rock walls of the soaring mountain peaks, one has a glimpse of Thebes—a dome dimly visible, the slanting roof of a columned building.

José Pierre says that in concept and plastic expression, Moreau's *Oedipus and the Sphinx* derives from the painting of Ingres that I have just described. Yet there is a world of difference between the two works. The sphinx occupies the center of Moreau's work, and an impressive figure she is. Her body is that of a very large cat which has just leaped onto Oedipus as onto the trunk of a tree and clings there—her back arched, the tendons and muscles in her legs taut, her claws sunk deep in. Her eagle's wings are fully unfurled, each filament of each feather sharply defined. She has the head of a fair maiden, her long hair braided and coiled, on her head a pearl-studded crown, her skin milky and fair, her features delicate, her soft and exposed breast touching the chest of Oedipus, and her large soft eyes looking deep into his, for his body is the trunk to which she clings. Here, says Pierre, is the *femme fatale*—Alfred de Musset's "exhausting and lethal, but nonetheless beautiful" maiden; here are Keats's "La Belle Dame sans Merci,'' Heine's "Lorelei,'' Mérimée's *Carmen.* So "not the least of Moreau's achievements [was] to have introduced this fascinating, evil presence into Romantic painting where its absence had been remarkable'' (98). The terrible beauty of this sphinx is perfectly paradoxical, utterly mysterious, and not to be rationalized as a projection of the human psyche or dismissed as an illusion. The sphinx in Ingres and Moreau is a being in her own right, an original mystery of the world at large, in whose presence we find ourselves once more reaching (imaginatively and intellectually) toward the timeless and the immortal rather than, as with the Freudians, toward a scientific language "to express the instinctual roots of cravings for and projections of omnipotence'' (Feder 56). By way of Ingres and Moreau we find ourselves taking something of the Jungian view of the sphinx as the terrible and devouring mother, Tiamat. Thus we come full circle to face once more (in something of the manner of ancient man before the monuments of his day) the visual presence of one of those beings who make myth.

In the poem "The Double Vision of Michael Robartes'' (1919) by William Butler Yeats, the speaker sees in "the mind's eye'' (line 25) a Buddha and a Sphinx, with a girl dancing between them. In commenting upon this poem, Yeats identified the Buddha with "the outward-looking mind, love and its lure'' and the Sphinx "with introspective knowledge of the mind's self-begotten unity, an intellectual excitement'' (qtd. in Feder 77). The girl, whom the speaker associates with Helen of Troy, is an image of beauty: she is found in his dreams, and although her image is elusive, she affects him in such a powerful way that he feels "undone.'' The Sphinx, the Buddha, and the girl "are symbols of a knowledge of past and present, of beauty, and love in all its sadness and potential destruction contained in the unconscious'' (Feder 78). Although the form of this Sphinx is of the Greek type (a female creature), she is not a predatory creature such as the sphinx in the Oedipus myth, but is a self-contained being identified with intellect and knowledge. She gazes on all things "In triumph of intellect'' (line 31). Yeats has used here some of the traditional associations (with intellect and knowledge); but his Sphinx, as is often the case in portrayals of the creature, has such complexity that her symbolic meaning defies any precise categorization.

The symbolism associated with the sphinx has varied throughout human history. The creature has represented both creative and destructive powers. Above all, it is a symbol of the mysterious and the inexpressible, and as such it remains and will remain a symbol that appeals to us deeply.

The sphinx has been the subject of numerous books and articles. Among books that deal with the sphinx are: *Le Sphinx: Etude iconographique* (1957) by A. Dessenne; *Die Sphinx: Geschichte ihrer Darstellung von den Anfängen bis zur Gegenwart* (1977) by H. Demisch; and *The Riddle of the Sphinx: The Calendric Symbolism in Myth and Icon* (1979) by C. F. Herberger. Demisch's *Die Sphinx* provides the best and most thorough study of the sphinx in art, history, and literature. The book traces uses of the creature from the ancient world to the present time and contains excellent illustrations from different periods.

BIBLIOGRAPHY

Bacon, Francis. *The Works of Francis Bacon.* Ed. James Spedding, Robert Ellis, and Douglas Heath. 15 vols. Boston: Brown and Taggard, 1860–64. Vol. 13.

Bettelheim, Bruno. *Freud and Man's Soul.* New York: Knopf, 1983.

Borges, Jorge Luis, with Margarita Guerrero. *The Book of Imaginary Beings.* Trans. Norman Thomas di Giovanni. New York: Discus-Avon, 1970.

Bulfinch, Thomas. *The Age of Fable: Or the Beauties of Mythology.* New York: Heritage Press, 1942.

Bush, Douglas. *Mythology and the Renaissance Tradition in English Poetry.* Minneapolis: University of Minnesota Press, 1932.

Charrière, Georges. *Scythian Art: Crafts of the Early Eurasian Nomads.* New York: Alpine Fine Arts Collection, 1979.

Cox, George W. *An Introduction to the Science of Comparative Mythology and Folklore.* London: Kegan Paul, 1883; rpt. Detroit: Singing Tree Press, 1968.

Delcourt, Marie. *Oedipe ou la légende du conquérant.* Liége, 1944.

Demisch, H. *Die Sphinx: Geschichte ihrer Darstellung von den Anfängen bis zur Gegenwart.* Stuttgart: Urachhaus, 1977.

Dessenne, A. *Le Sphinx: Etude iconographique. Des Origines à la fin du second millénaire.* Paris: E. de Boccard, 1957.

Devereux, George. "Why Oedipus Killed Laius: A Note on the Complementary Oedipus Complex in Greek Drama." *International Journal of Psychoanalysis* 34.2 (1953): 1–10.

Eliot, Alexander. *Myths.* New York: McGraw-Hill, 1976.

Encyclopedia of World Art. 16 vols. New York: McGraw-Hill, 1957–83.

Feder, Lillian. *Ancient Myth in Modern Poetry.* Princeton: Princeton University Press, 1971.

Freud, Sigmund. *The Interpretation of Dreams* (First Part). Vol. 4 of *The Standard Edition of the Complete Psychological Works of Sigmund Freud.* Trans. James Strachey. London: Hogarth Press, 1958.

Fuller, John. *A Reader's Guide to W. H. Auden.* New York: Farrar, Straus and Giroux, 1970.

Gide, André. *Two Legends: Oedipus and Theseus.* Trans. John Russell. New York: Knopf, 1950.

Graves, Robert. *The White Goddess: A Historical Grammar of Poetic Myth.* Amended and enl. ed. New York: Farrar, Straus, and Giroux, 1966.

Herberger, C. F. *The Riddle of the Sphinx: The Calendric Symbolism in Myth and Icon.* New York: Vantage Press, 1979.

Jung, C. G. *Symbols of Transformation.* Vol. 5 of *The Collected Works of C. G. Jung.* Trans. R. F. C. Hull. Bollingen Series 20. New York: Pantheon, 1956.

Leibovitch, J. *La Sphinge.* Cairo, 1947.

Lemmi, Charles. *The Classic Deities in Bacon: A Study in Mythological Symbolism.* Baltimore: Johns Hopkins University Press, 1933.

Lévi-Strauss, Claude. *Structural Anthropology.* Trans. Claire Jacobson and Brooke Grundfest Schoepf. New York: Anchor, 1967.

Mode, Heinz. *Fabulous Beasts and Demons.* London: Phaidon, 1975.

Moore, Albert C. *Iconography of Religions: An Introduction.* Philadelphia: Fortress Press, 1977.

Mueller, Martin. *Children of Oedipus and Other Essays on the Imitation of Greek Tragedy, 1550–1800*. Buffalo: University of Toronto Press, 1980.

Neumann, Erich. *The Origins and History of Consciousness*. Trans. R. F. C. Hull. Bollingen Series 42. Princeton: Princeton University Press, 1970.

Norman, Dorothy. *The Hero: Myth, Image, Symbol*. New York: The World Publishing Co., 1969.

Paladilhe, Jean, and José Pierre. *Gustave Moreau*. Trans. Bettina Wadia. New York: Praeger, 1972.

Pritchard, James B., ed. *Ancient Near Eastern Texts Relating to the Old Testament*. 2nd ed. Princeton: Princeton University Press, 1955.

Réau, Louis. *Iconographie de l'art chrétien*. 3 vols. Paris: Presses Universitaires de France, 1955–59.

Rhyne, N. A. "The Aegean Animal Style: A Study of the Lion, Griffin, and Sphinx." Diss. University of North Carolina at Chapel Hill, 1970.

Ricoeur, Paul. *The Symbolism of Evil*. Trans. Emerson Buchanan. New York: Harper and Row, 1967.

Rowland, Beryl. *Animals with Human Faces: A Guide to Animal Symbolism*. Knoxville: University of Tennessee Press, 1973.

Ruitenbeek, Hendrik M., ed. *Psychoanalysis and Literature*. New York: Dutton, 1964.

Russell, John. *Francis Bacon*. New York: Oxford University Press, 1971.

Scafella, Frank A. "The White Sphinx and *The Time Machine*." *Science-Fiction Studies* 8.25 (1981): 255–65.

Seznec, Jean. *The Survival of the Pagan Gods: The Mythological Tradition and Its Place in Renaissance Humanism and Art*. Trans. Barbara Sessions. Bollingen Series 38. New York: Pantheon, 1953.

Sophocles. *Oedipus the King*. In *Sophocles*. Trans. F. Storr. Cambridge: Harvard University Press, 1912, Vol. 1.

"Sphinx." *Encyclopaedia Britannica*. 11th ed.

Starnes, DeWitt, and Ernest Talbert. *Classical Myth and Legend in Renaissance Dictionaries*. Westport, Conn.: Greenwood Press, 1973.

Thompson, Stith. *The Folktale*. Berkeley and Los Angeles: University of California Press, 1977.

von Franz, Marie-Louise. *Interpretation of Fairy Tales*. Dallas, Tex.: Spring Publications, 1978.

Wind, Edgar. *Pagan Mysteries in the Renaissance*. New Haven: Yale University Press, 1958.

Yates, Frances. *The Art of Memory*. Chicago: University of Chicago Press, 1966.

14

The Minotaur

Michael J. Curley

The Minotaur (The Bull of Minos) was a hybrid creature, part man and part bull, whose legend was associated with the family of Minos, king of Crete, and with the exploits of the Athenian hero Theseus. While representations of the Minotaur date back to the Archaic period of Greek art, the first continuous accounts of the creature's history are found in Apollodorus and Plutarch.

The story as told by Apollodorus in the *Library* is as follows: Asterius, a prince of the Cretans, married Europa and brought up the children she had by Zeus, namely, Sarpedon, Rhadamanthys, and Minos. As the children grew up they fell into discord over the love of the boy Miletus, son of Apollo by Aria. In the war that ensued, Minos succeeded in driving his brothers into exile, and then claimed sovereignty over all of Crete. In order to silence local opponents, Minos alleged that he was favored by the gods, and as proof of this, prayed to Poseidon to send a bull from the depths of the sea, promising to sacrifice it when it appeared. Poseidon did send a fine bull, but Minos sent it off to the herds and sacrificed another in its place. Angry at this breach of promise, Poseidon turned the bull wild and contrived that Minos' wife Pasiphae should conceive passion for it. In order to satisfy her passion, Pasiphae sought the help of Daedalus, an Athenian who had been sent into exile for murder. He carved and hollowed out a wooden cow and covered it with the hide of one recently slain; he then set Pasiphae inside this effigy and placed it in a field where the bull grazed. Having coupled with the bull, Pasiphae became pregnant and gave birth to Asterius, who was called the Minotaur. This creature had the head of a bull and the body of a man. In accord with the oracles, Minos had him confined in the Labyrinth, a structure built by Daedalus of such intricacy as to defy all attempts to escape by those placed within it.

Later, another of Minos' offspring, Androgeus, traveled to the Panathenian games, where he defeated all the other competitors. He was sent by King Aegeus to vanquish the Bull of Marathon, which was roaming the plains of Marathon destroying men and livestock. Androgeus found this bull, which had been brought to Marathon from Crete by Hercules as one of his twelve labors, but was killed by it. Apollodorus records another version of the story in which Androgeus was murdered by the jealous competitors whom he had overcome in the recent games at Athens. Hearing this, Minos attacked Athens with his fleet and captured Megara. Unable to take Athens itself, Minos prayed to Zeus that he might be avenged on the Athenians. When a terrible plague struck the city, the citizens consulted the oracle, which advised that they submit to whatever demands Minos should make. He ordered them to send seven youths and seven maidens every year as fodder for the Minotaur. Theseus, the son of Aegeus, was chosen or volunteered to be among the third tribute to the Minotaur. When he arrived in Crete, however, Ariadne, the daughter of Minos, fell in love with him and offered to save him if he agreed to take her back to Athens as his wife. This he swore to do, and she persuaded Daedalus to devise a method by which Theseus might escape from the Labyrinth. Upon Daedalus' advice, Ariadne gave Theseus the clue, a ball of thread which he fastened to the lintel of the Labyrinth and then unravelled continuously as he proceeded deeper and deeper into the maze. At the heart of the Labyrinth, he found the Minotaur asleep and beat him to death with his fists. Then, retracing his way, he led the other hostages along with Ariadne to the sea, where they set sail for Athens (Apollodorus 3.1; 3.15.7–9).

Not all ancient sources concur with Apollodorus' version of the story. Diodorus Siculus (4.61) and Plutarch (*Theseus* 15.1) claim the hostages were given to the Minotaur every nine years for as long as he should live. Plutarch (*Theseus* 17.3) adds on the authority of Hellanicus that Minos himself traveled to Athens to select the youths to be sacrificed, and that while some versions of the story maintain that the Minotaur destroyed the hostages, others claim that they simply wandered about at their own will and, being unable to find their way out, died there. Not all Greek sources, moreover, agree on the death of the Minotaur. Plutarch says that the hostages who went to Crete carried no warlike weapon (*Theseus* 17.3); yet representations of this popular scene in black- and red-figure Greek pottery generally depict Theseus grasping the Minotaur by the horns, the ear, the hair, or the arm and dispatching him with a sword or a club. On what appears to be one of the earliest representations of the death of the Minotaur, a seventh-century gold ornament from Corinth (Ward, ill. 27), Theseus is shown grasping the Minotaur's ear and piercing his breast with a sword. The Minotaur's death is similarly portrayed on a fragment of a late seventh-century shield relief (Ward, ill. 25). Pausanias (3.18.11) mentions a Spartan throne in Amyclae made by Bathycles of Magnesia on which the Minotaur was shown bound and being led along alive by Theseus, but he claims not to know why the story was represented this way.

An unusual variation on the scene of the slaying of the Minotaur is found on a relief-decorated amphora in Basel (ca. 670–660 B.C.), where Theseus and Ariadne are both shown throwing stones at the Minotaur, who is depicted, not as the bull-headed man of the later classical tradition, but rather as a creature with a bull's body and a horned human head. On the frieze just above this, the Athenian children are shown helping in the task of stoning the monster (Schefold, pl. 25a). The Etruscans seem to have been particularly interested in the Minotaur, who appears in their art from the archaic through the postclassical period. There are some two dozen examples of the theme of the battle between Theseus and the Minotaur in Etruscan art. Characteristic of the manner in which they received most Greek legends and myths, however, the Etruscans sometimes represented the Minotaur in rather unusual ways. The figure who grasps a bow in his left hand and triumphantly sits over the prostrate form of the Minotaur on the Civita Castellana mirror, for example, is not Theseus but Hercules (Hercle). And in another Etruscan work, a black-figure vase in the Louvre, it is Hercules again, clad in his lionskin, who strikes the Minotaur with a club (Brommer, fig. 10, and pp. 4 and 9). In describing the figures emblazoned on Theseus' shield, the Roman poet Statius (ca. 45–96 A.D.) mentions the Athenian hero's "twisting the shaggy neck of the struggling bull, and binding him fast with sinewy arms and grip of either hand" (*Thebaid* 12.668–71).

The ancients seemed to have entertained a similar range of views concerning the Minotaur's physical appearance. Among the Greeks, Apollodorus' opinion was that he had the face of a bull (ταύρου πρόσωπον) and the body of a man (3.1.4). This was also the view of Diodorus (4.77), who states that the creature was "of double form, the upper part of the body as far as the shoulders being those of a bull, and the remaining parts those of a man." A black-figure amphora from Vulci, however, shows the Minotaur with a tail and skin speckled like the pelt of a leopard (Ward, ill. 41). Similar depictions can be found on a red-figure vase by Epiktetos (Ward, ill. 15) and on a band-cup by Archikles and Glaukytes (Ward, ill. 30), all sixth-century artists. Pausanias, who refers to the Minotaur as "the so-called Bull of Minos," is not certain whether he was "a man or a beast of the nature he is said to have been in the accepted story" (1.24.1). Roman authors appear to have had a somewhat more vague impression of the Minotaur's form. Catullus (64.101) simply calls him a "savage monster" (*saevum monstrum*), while Virgil (*Aeneid* 6.25) speaks of him as "a hybrid offspring, a two-shaped progeny" (*mixtumque genus prolesque biformis*). Ovid speaks of the Minotaur as a "two-shaped monster" in the *Metamorphoses* (8.156), and in the *Heroides* (10.102) claims him to be "in part man, in part bull." This vagueness among Roman authors in regard to the Minotaur's appearance may have suggested to medieval authors and artists the idea that the Minotaur was a creature half-man and half-bull.

The legend of the Minotaur, being part of the heroic saga of Theseus, has come down to us with a strong Athenian coloration. Not infrequently in Greek vase-paintings Theseus is depicted as being directed or encouraged by Athena as he plunges his sword into the Minotaur or drags his limp body through the gates of the Labyrinth (Ward, ills. 30 and 42). Noting the abuse that Minos always suffered at the hands of Attic dramatists, Plutarch commented that it was "a grievous thing for a man to be at enmity with a city which has a language and a literature" (*Theseus* 16.2). Accordingly, he records a number of euhemerized versions of the legend of Theseus' slaying of the Minotaur, one of which, on the authority of Philochorus, derived from the citizens of Crete themselves. They maintain, Plutarch says (*Theseus* 16.1–2; 19.2), that the Minotaur was actually one of Minos' generals who was called Taurus. As the prize for his victory in the first funeral games that Minos established in memory of his son Androgeus, Taurus was given the young Athenian hostages who up to this point had been detained in the impregnable Cretan dungeon known as the Labyrinth. Being a man of violent disposition, Taurus treated the youths with extreme cruelty. On the third occasion of the funeral games, however, Theseus put himself forward as a competitor and soundly defeated all other contestants including Taurus. As a result of Theseus' athletic prowess, Ariadne fell in love with him. Minos, too, was delighted with the Athenian's victory, for he despised the powerful Taurus for his violent character and suspected him of having an affair with Queen Pasiphae. As a reward Minos returned the Athenian youths to Theseus and remitted all future Athenian tribute to Crete.

While the Minotaur himself was seldom if ever the principal subject of Greek or Roman literature, he must have been alluded to in Euripides' lost play, *The Cretans* (see Page, *Literary Papyri* 75–76), in which Pasiphae makes a spirited defense of herself as having been driven mad by Poseidon to lust after the Cretan bull. Among the Romans, Catullus compared the Minotaur's death at the hands of Theseus to the uprooting of a giant oak or pine tree by a vehement storm (64.76 f.). Virgil and Ovid both interpreted the Minotaur as the monstrous consequence of Pasiphae's passion (Virgil, *Aeneid* 6.26: *Veneris monumenta nefandae; Eclogue* 6.45 f.; Ovid, *Metamorphoses* 8.152 f.; *Heroides* 10.99–111). On a less lofty plane, the scene of Pasiphae begetting the Minotaur featured among the obscene vignettes enacted by Greek dancers in the public spectacles sponsored by Nero (Suetonius, *Nero* 12.2) and Domitian (Martial, *On the Spectacles* 5). Theseus slaying the Minotaur was represented on a wall painting in the Villa Imperiale at Pompeii, while two fragmentary Roman busts of the monster indicate that he was also thought an attractive subject for Roman sculpture.

But it is in their labyrinth-patterned mosaic floors that the Romans treated the Minotaur most suggestively. Among the numerous examples of intricate labyrinth mosaics which have survived from disparate corners of the Roman world, those at Pompeii, Cremona, Brindisi, Nea Paphos, Aix-en-Provence, Susa (Tunisia), Cormerod (Switzerland), and Salzburg all represent the Minotaur as the central figure of the design. The mosaic pavement in the Casa del Labirinto at Pompeii depicts Theseus and the Minotaur locked in deadly combat while a group of frightened girls looks on. In the central chamber of the Salzburg labyrinth mosaic (Ward, ill. 192), Theseus is shown in a flowing cape grasping the Minotaur by the right horn and preparing to strike him with an upraised club. Symmetrically arranged around the circumference of the round mosaic labyrinth at Cormerod are eight birds, perhaps as an allusion to Daedalus' and Icarus' use of mechanical wings to escape from the Cretan Labyrinth where Minos had imprisoned them.

The labyrinth-patterned mosaic at Susa comes from a family necropolis (Matthews, fig. 37; Bord, fig. 117) and represents the Minotaur vanquished in the central chamber; in the border, Theseus and the Athenian youths are depicted sailing away from (towards?) the Labyrinth's gate, over which the motto *Hic inclusus vitam perdit* (Whoever is enclosed herein loses his life) is inscribed. While mosaics portraying the Minotaur's death in the Labyrinth may have had no special allegorical significance for the owners of Roman villas, their presence as decorations in burial chambers and on sarcophagi (McCann 25–29) suggests that they expressed the patron's desire for some form of transcendence of death. The potential for such an interpretation, of course, was implicit in the Minotaur's legend from its origins. Greek coins dating from the classical period onwards represented the labyrinth in the unicursal pattern which became standard in Roman mosaics. While the head of a bull was the usual image on the opposite face of such coins, female figures usually thought to be Demeter or Persephone not infrequently came to replace the bull, suggesting a view of the labyrinth as a symbol of the underworld, and the Minotaur as the personification of death.

The tools of euhemerism and allegory, already applied to the legend of the Minotaur in the ancient world, allowed the Middle Ages and the Renaissance to preserve and elaborate upon the story without fear of reproach on the score of impiety. The Minotaur continued to be a popular subject in church labyrinths, in manuscript illuminations, in the numerous medieval chrestomathies of classical myths, in the encyclopedias, in commentaries on the ancient authors, and in the works of the medieval poets themselves. The Minotaur's dwelling place in particular provided the Middle Ages with a very rich and suggestive image of the temptations of the world. The four hexameters which accompany the labyrinth design in the church of San Savino at Piacenza (tenth century?) proclaim that the labyrinth symbolizes the world, broad at its entrance, narrow at its exit, in which man, once he is ensnared by the joys of the world, can find his way out only with great difficulty. Guido da Pisa goes even further in his commentary on Dante's *Inferno* (before 1333). The Minotaur, says Guido, was the offspring of Pasiphae and Taurus, a notary in the court of King Minos. In his legend, however, he represents allegorically the Devil, while his labyrinth (from *labor* "I slip, fall" and *intus* "within") stands for the world of error. The Minotaur accordingly devours the Athenian youths when they fall within his dwelling as the Devil consumes our spirit when we slip into the errors of the world. Just as Theseus was assisted by Ariadne, so Christ was guided by the Holy Spirit in his encounter with death and in leading the lost souls up to the light of eternal life. On the scriptural plane, Theseus' conquest of the Minotaur and liberation of the youths stands for Christ's harrowing of Hell and freeing of the holy fathers (*Expositiones et Glose* 222–23).

Boccaccio extracted a similar spiritual lesson from the legend of the Minotaur. In his *Genealogy of the Gods* (4.10), Boccaccio claims that by this story we learn that from the union of the soul (Pasiphae, daughter of the Sun) with earthly pleasure (the Bull) comes the Minotaur, the vice of bestiality. Visually, the Middle Ages often conceived of the Minotaur as a creature with a bull's body and human torso, arms, and head, that is, in the shape of a centaur. The origin of this confusion may be found in the vague descriptions of the Minotaur in some of the Latin poets such as Ovid, who refers to him in the *Heroides* (10.102) as *parte virum . . . parte bovem*, or Virgil, who describes him in *Aeneid* 6, as *mixtumque genus prolesque biformis*. Isidore of Seville includes the Minotaur among the centaurs, onocentaurs, and hippocentaurs (*Etymologiae* 11.3.35). And it is in the centaur shape that he is depicted in the tenth-century wall labyrinth in San Michele Maggiore at Pavia (Matthews, fig. 44, where the analogous biblical story of David slaying Goliath is also represented) and in the majority of illustrations to Dante's *Inferno* (Brieger, Meiss, and Singleton 2:150–64). More difficult to account for is the statement in King Alfred's translation of Orosius that the Minotaur was half-man and half-lion.

Perhaps the most famous literary representation of the Minotaur in the Middle Ages occurs in Dante's *Inferno* 12, where the monster is found as the guardian of the violent of the seventh circle. As Dante and Virgil begin their descent into this circle, they come upon the Minotaur stretched out before them. Dante refrains from naming him initially, calling him instead *l'infamia di Creti, bestia* and *ira bestial*. Catching sight of the two pilgrims as they make their way, the Minotaur becomes enraged and bites himself. Thereupon Virgil taunts him by reminding him of his death in Crete at the hands of Theseus and Ariadne. Stung by the poet's words, the Minotaur leaps about in blind fury, thus allowing the two pilgrims to proceed along their way unimpeded. As with all the denizens of Dante's Hell, the Minotaur is shown to be the victim of his own passion. Virgil's taunt is epecially effective since it forces upon the Minotaur's consciousness the scene of his death, the moment at which his eternal fate was unalterably fixed.

According to one peculiar late-medieval variation on the legend of the Minotaur, found in Chaucer's *Legend of Good Women*, Gower's *Confessio Amantis*, and elsewhere, Theseus carried with him, in addition to Ariadne's thread, a ball of wax and pitch which he hurled into the Minotaur's mouth in order to slake his hunger and seal his gnashing teeth. This action was interpreted allegorically by Guido da Pisa to represent the sacrifice of flesh and blood on the cross in order to liberate mankind from the snares of the Devil.

During the sixteenth and seventeenth centuries, the story of the Minotaur continued to be of interest to artists and scholars, if somewhat less to literary men. Allegorizations of the medieval sort continued to be popular, as in George Sandys' 1632 translation of Ovid with commentary on the philosophical sense of Ovid's fables. Sandys interpreted the labyrinth as the condition of man on earth, the Minotaur as sensual delights, and Ariadne as sincere affection. Alexander Ross's *Mystogagus Poeticus* (1647) kept alive the analogy of Theseus slaying the Minotaur with Christ's harrowing of Hell. Numerous engravings of the Minotaur and the labyrinth can be found in sixteenth- and seventeenth-century editions of Ovid's *Metamorphoses*, and in the ever-popular handbooks of emblems and heraldry. In the edifying and often idiosyncratic personal maxims that accompany the labyrinth *cum* Minotaur devices of the sixteenth and seventeenth centuries, one can discern an extension of the ingenious moralizing proclivities of the Middle Ages. Gonzalo Perez, secretary to Emperor Charles V at Naples, for example, adopted the Minotaur in the labyrinth as his personal device. Its accompanying motto *In silentio et spe* (In silence and hope) was taken over from Isaiah 30:15 "In silence and hope shall be your strength."

While reserving a special place for myths and fables as part of the allegorical or emblematic quality of poetry, the eighteenth century often sought to explain myths such as that of the Minotaur as a kind of distorted recollection of history. The article on the Minotaur in Diderot's *Encyclopedia* (ed. 1765), for example, falls back confidently on the euhemerized interpretation of the monster's origin in Pasiphae's adulterous liaison with Minos' functionary Taurus. Theseus slaying the Minotaur reflects the historical counteraction of the Athenians against Minos' unreasonable demands for tribute following his son Androgeus' death. "There you have," the *Encyclopedia* states, "the basis of the fable of Pasiphae who shut herself up in a bronze cow in order to have intercourse with a bull; and beyond that, the birth of this monster who has become so famous under the name of Minotaur."

In the plastic arts, Canova's marble statue *Theseus Triumphant* (1781–82) used the Athenian hero's victory over the Minotaur to celebrate the power of reason and beauty over bestiality. Apparently inspired by the Pompeian wall fresco on the same theme, Canova chose to represent Theseus in a contemplative moment just after his victory over the Minotaur. He sits on the outstretched body of the bull-headed creature, supporting himself with his right hand, which rests on the Minotaur's left knee, while in his left hand he holds a club. Theseus' lightly muscled form and calm, reflective expression contrast sharply with the bulky shape and slightly opened mouth of his defeated bovine opponent.

While Canova's *Theseus Triumphant* used the Minotaur to depict the moment following the defeat of irrationality and brutality, Antoine-Louis Barye's small (eighteen-inch) bronze statue (1846) shows the Minotaur still locked in dynamic conflict with Theseus. Barye, who is perhaps more widely known for his representations of fighting animals, shows the Minotaur in his final desperate attempt to throw Theseus off balance; his left leg hooks around Theseus' firmly planted right leg, while his left hand clutches the hero's right shoulder. Theseus stands with both legs set stolidly apart, and with his left hand forces the Minotaur's head downward into a posture of submission and vulnerability. His upraised right hand points a short sword directly at the undefended brow of his bull-headed adversary. The calm and confident expression on Theseus' face combined with the bent, sinewy form of the stocky Minotaur leaves no doubt that the struggle is about to end in a victory of beauty and grace over brutality. The same self-confident Theseus finds his way into Thomas Erat Harrison's illustration of the death of the Minotaur (Bord, pl. 59).

In Gustave Moreau's painting *The Athenians Sacrificed to the Minotaur in the Labyrinth on Crete* (1855; Kaplan, pls. 4 and 5), however, Theseus does not appear at all. Moreau's initial sketch for the work featured the Minotaur grappling with one of his victims while trampling on the broken bodies of others. He rejected this scheme in his final version, concentrating instead on the less violent but perhaps no less terrifying moment when the Athenian youths become aware of the approach of the Minotaur. In the left of the painting, whose composition bears a striking similarity to that of an ancient frieze, maidens clutch one another in a posture of grief, while at the center several young men stand intently listening and looking to their left. Another youth crouches on his knee, hand outstretched in the direction of an adjacent corridor of the Labyrinth, down which the Minotaur approaches. He is centaur-shaped, with a bull's body and head, but with a human torso and arms.

In some ways, Moreau's painting anticipated the direction that would be taken by artists and writers concerned with the Minotaur in the twentieth century. Since his first appearance iconographically and literarily, the Minotaur had served as a foil to the heroic Theseus or as an emblem of the mystery of the labyrinth. By excluding Theseus from his canvas, Moreau implicitly rejected the redemptive content of the legend which had been an essential part of its message from the classical age down to the Romantic period. As the fledgling disciplines of archaeology and comparative mythology began to cast new light on the historical background of the legend, the combined impact of Darwin and Freud enabled moderns to explore in the figure of the Minotaur the humanity of the man in the beast as well as the brutality of the beast in the man.

The change can be seen in *The Minotaur*, a painting by the Englishman George Frederic Watts (1817–1904). Watts's moral indignation was aroused by a description of prostitution which he read in the *Pall Mall Gazette*, and he resolved to register his outrage by setting forth on his canvas the destruction of innocence by brutality. He pictures the Minotaur gazing into the distance from the walls of a citadel, seemingly oblivious to the crushed body of a dove which he grasps in his left hand. While Watts's allegorical intention may have been clear, his Minotaur is scarcely the monster the painter wished him to be. Rather, he is a sad and pathetic creature in whose expression human intelligence and self-aware-ness struggle dimly against mute torpidity.

With the advent of the new methodologies of comparative anthropology and classical archaeology in the nineteenth century, the legend of the Minotaur came under fresh scrutiny. In his *Golden Bough*, Frazer categorized the story of Minos, Pasiphae, and the Minotaur as a variant of the theme of the killing of the divine king, examples of which could be found in nearly all cultures. Struck by the Cretan king's need to renew his kingship through contact with divinity every eight years, and the octennial conjunction of the sun and moon "in the same heavenly bridal chamber where they first met" (4:74), Frazer concluded that the story of the genesis of the Minotaur was a reflection of "a mythical marriage of the sun and moon, which was acted as a solemn rite by the king and queen of Cnossus, wearing the masks of a bull and a cow respectively" (4:71). Through the enactment of this ritual, the king renewed divine sanction for his rule for a period of another eight years. The Athenian youths who were fodder for the Minotaur were sacrificial victims, according to Frazer, who were perhaps roasted alive every eight years in a bronze image of a bull in order to renew the power of the king and the sun whom the king personified.

Frazer's *Golden Bough* established a certain vogue among later students of the legend of the Minotaur. They continued to interpret the monster as a figure in a universal human drama in which man attempts to control the powers of the gods and nature by a mimetic ritual. Jane Harrison concluded that behind the legend of Pasiphae conceiving the Minotaur by union with the bull from the sea, "it can scarcely be doubted that there lurks some sacred mystical ceremony of ritual wedlock (ιερòς γάμος) with a primitive bull-headed divinity" (*Prolegomena* 482). More closely following Frazer's solar theory, A. B. Cook noted that the labyrinth was often depicted on coins and on vases as a meander or a swastika, and suggested that this was simply "a stylised representation of the revolving sun" (*Zeus* 478). Cook drew on the archaeological discoveries of Sir Arthur Evans at Knossos to formulate the theory that the palace's orchestra was intended for the performance of a mimetic dance (479) in which the participants were guided by labyrinthine lines drawn on the pavement in a solar pattern. The Minotaur, according to Cook, was probably nothing else than the crown prince of Knossos in ritual attire, including a bull-mask which proclaimed his solar character (491), while his dance itself was a bit of mimetic ritual serving to promote the year's vegetation. The Minotaur's name, Asterius, was one further indication that his legend originated in some astral ceremony.

As the importance of Minoan civilization in the eastern Mediterranean became clearer, the legend of the Minotaur was interpreted as a reflection of Minoan dominance of the sea. W. F. Jackson Knight (*Cumaean Gates* 138) traced the story of the Minotaur back to the Athenian youths who brought Attic tribute to Crete (and possibly were themselves part of that tribute). They reported on a culture which they only dimly understood, telling of an intricate palace, rituals of bull-masked priests, and maze and thread dances, perhaps sometimes performed at the entrance to caves. The Minotaur was, in Knight's view, a purely Attic creation derived from Cretan "bull-masked priests, from the bull King Minos, or from the Minotaur of the pictures" (140).

The theory that the legend of the Minotaur could be accounted for by Cretan sacred ritual, however, was undercut by Martin Nilsson (*The Minoan-Mycenaean Religion* 373–76), who insisted that while it was natural to attempt to explain the story of the Minotaur by reference to a bull-cult, "there is no evidence for a bull-cult among the Minoans" (373). Bullfighting was not sacral in Crete, but simply a very popular secular activity. Nilsson claimed that depictions of hybrid beasts, part man, part animal, sufficiently accounted for the origin of the Minotaur legend. Others have seen in the depictions of bull-leaping on Cretan frescos a reflection of just such an ancient secular activity that pitted young acrobats against a bull in the central courtyard of the regal palace. The gruesome fate which befell these contenders, combined with the later sacrifice of the bull with the double-headed axe (the *labrys*), suggests again a historical core based in Minoan ceremony for the legend of the Minotaur.

Surely the most complex and innovative treatment of the Minotaur in modern times occurred in the series of engravings and sketches which Picasso executed on the subject between 1933 and 1937. The Minotaur had already been discussed by the Surrealists as an emblem of the conflicting forces of the conscious and the subconscious when Picasso was commissioned to provide the cover for the first issue of Albert Skira's avant-garde magazine *Minotaure*. The cover of each subsequent volume of the publication until its demise in 1939 featured the subject of the Minotaur interpreted by a different artist. Dali, Magritte, Max Ernst, and Diego Rivera were numbered among the contributing artists in addition to Picasso. Having thus been initially stimulated by the subject, Picasso went on to reinvent the Minotaur in a wide range of unprecedented and imaginative settings. In keeping with tradition are his scenes representing the Minotaur as the dark and brutal force in man, especially as it expresses itself in the violence of rape. At the other end of the spectrum are the convivial scenes in which the Minotaur carouses playfully in the studio with a sculptor and his naked models. In between are a number of complex symbolic representations. *The Minotaur Asleep* (1932) depicts the monster resting peacefully behind a flower-decorated gossamer curtain while a young girl looks on. The situation is reversed in *Minotaur and Sleeping Girl* (1933), in which the beast crouches over a slumbering girl, gazing with jaw agape into her face with a pitiable and melancholy expression. The delicate features of the maiden contrast sharply with the massive hirsute head of the Minotaur, as if to emphasize the incongruity of his awakened passion and her peaceful slumber.

In his representations of the death of the Minotaur, Picasso fused together the ancient Spanish ceremony of the *corrida* with the bull ritual of Minoan Crete. In one composition reminiscent of the Minotaur mosaic in the Pompeian Casa del Labirinto (*The Minotaur in the Bull-ring*, 1933), a naked classical youth is seen plunging his sword between the shoulder blades of the crumpled Minotaur as a curious but detached audience looks on. In another (*The Death of the Minotaur*, 1933), the sinking monster, now alone in the ring, raises his head and eyes to the sky while one member of the impassive crowd reaches out to touch the hump of his back. In two other etchings completed in 1936, Picasso emphasizes the pathos of the Minotaur's death. In the first of these, a naked classical girl with her hands raised before her looks through the transparent sail of the bark on which she is sailing to witness the scene of the Minotaur's death in the ring. In another, a fierce bird-headed man carries along the limp body of the Minotaur dressed in a harlequin costume; to the left, a bearded figure dressed in a horse's hide prepares to hurl a stone at the bird-man. In the enigmatic

Minotauromachy (1935), the Minotaur prepares to stab a disemboweled horse over whose back a half-naked female figure is draped. Before them stands a little girl with a candle raised on high. The monster holds his hand out to block her light while a bearded man flees in fear up a ladder. Meanwhile, two girls with a dove gaze down on the scene from a window above. And in a sequence of compositions intended presumably to represent the redemption of the Mino-taur, Picasso pictures the now blind beast being led along docilely, like Oedipus at Colonus, by a young girl carrying flowers or a dove.

In these and in his other Minotaur sketches and engravings, Picasso was not merely translating a classical figure into a contemporary idiom, but inventing a kind of drama with the Minotaur as the tragic hero. He was unique among artists in grasping the rich suggestiveness of the Minotaur as a symbol of the human condition. As a complex amalgamation of conflicting forces, violence, passion, amiability, melancholy, docility, the Minotaur became for Picasso a figure ca-pable of arousing our deepest feelings of pity and fear. In his recreation of the Minotaur we understand how destructive fury is counterbalanced by suffering, rejection by reconciliation, monstrosity by humanity, and death by boundless vitality.

Among other treatments of the Minotaur in the modern period are Michael Aryton's bronze statue of the Minotaur in his brick and stone labyrinth at Dry Brook, Arkville, New York (also in London's Postman's Park), Kazantzakis' play *Theseus*, Gide's novel of the same title (1946), Mary Renault's novel *The King Must Die* (1958), and Jorge Luis Borges' short story/monologue "The House of Asterion" in *El Aleph* (1949; also in *Labyrinths*). Each of these, with the possible exception of Renault's novel, demonstrates the tendency of the modern writer and artist to seek in the hybrid creature itself a rich expression of the complexity of twentieth-century consciousness.

BIBLIOGRAPHY

Apollodorus. *The Library*. Trans. Sir James George Frazer. 2 vols. 1921; rpt. Cambridge: Harvard University Press, 1961.

Boccaccio, Giovanni. *Genealogie deorum gentilium libri*. Ed. Vincenzo Romano. 2 vols. Bari: Gius. Laterza e Figli, 1951.

Boer, W. den."Theseus, The Growth of a Myth in History." *Greece and Rome* 16 (1969): 1–13.

Bord, Janet. *Mazes and Labyrinths of the World*. New York: Dutton, 1976.

Borges, Jorge Luis. *Labyrinths: Selected Stories and Other Writings*. Ed. Donald Yates and James E. Irby. New York: New Directions, 1962.

————, with Margarita Guerrero. *The Book of Imaginary Beings*. Trans. Norman Thomas di Giovanni. New York: Discus-Avon, 1970.

Brieger, Peter, Millard Meiss, and Charles Singleton. *Illuminated Manuscripts of the Divine Comedy*. 2 vols. Bollingen Series 81. Princeton: Princeton University Press, 1969.

Brommer, Frank. "Theseus und Minotauros in der etruskischen Kunst." *Mitteilungen des Deutschen Archaeologischen Instituts, Roemische Abteilung* 88 (1981): 1–12.

Catullus. *Catullus, Tibullus and Pervigilium Veneris*. Trans. F. W. Cornish, J. P. Postgate, and J. W. Mackail. 1913; rpt. Cambridge: Harvard University Press, 1962.

Chaucer, Geoffrey. *The Works of Geoffrey Chaucer*. Ed. F. N. Robinson. 2nd ed. Boston: Houghton Mifflin, 1957.

Cook, A. B. *Zeus, A Study in Ancient Religion*. Vol. 1. Cambridge: Cambridge University Press, 1914.

Dante Alighieri. *The Divine Comedy*. Trans. with a commentary by Charles Singleton. 6 vols. Princeton: Princeton University Press, 1970–75.

Diodorus of Sicily. *Library of History*. Trans. C. H. Oldfather et al. 12 vols. Cambridge: Harvard University Press, 1933–67.

Frazer, Sir James George. *The Golden Bough: A Study in Magic and Religion*. 3rd ed. 12 vols. London: Macmillan, 1911–15.

Green, André. "Thésée et Oedipe, une interprétation psychanalytique de la Théséide." In *Il mito greco, Atti del convegno internazionale* (Urbino 7–12 maggio 1973). Ed. Bruno Gentili and Giuseppe Paione. Rome: Edizioni dell'Ateneo e Bizzari, 1973. 137–89.

Guido da Pisa. *Guido da Pisa's Expositiones et Glose super Comediam Dantis or Commentary on Dante's Inferno*. Ed. Vincenzo Cioffari. Albany: State University of New York Press, 1974.

Harrison, Jane Ellen. *Prolegomena to the Study of Greek Religion*. Cambridge: Cambridge University Press, 1903.

Hyginus. *The Myths of Hyginus*. Trans. Mary Grant. University of Kansas Publications, Humanistic Studies 34. Lawrence: University of Kansas, 1960.

Isidore of Seville. *Etymologiarvm sive originvm libri xx*. Ed. W. M. Lindsay. 2 vols. 1911; rpt. Oxford: Clarendon, 1971.

Kaplan, Julius. *The Art of Gustave Moreau: Theory, Style and Content*. Ann Arbor: UMI Research Press, 1982.

Knight, W. F. Jackson. *Cumaean Gates: A Reference of the Sixth Aeneid to the Initiation Pattern*. Oxford: Blackwell, 1936.

McCann, Anna Marguerite. *Roman Sarcophagi in the Metropolitan Museum of Art*. New York: The Museum, 1978.

Martial. *Epigrams*. Trans. Walter C. A. Ker. 2 vols. 1919; rpt. Cambridge: Harvard University Press, 1961.

Matthews, William Henry. *Mazes and Labyrinths: A General Account of Their History and Developments*. London and New York: Longmans, Green, 1922.

"Minotauros." *Paulys Real-Encyclopädie der classischen Altertumswissenschaft*. Neue Bearbeitung. Stuttgart. A. Druckenmüller, 1932, 15: pt. 2, cols. 1927–34.

Nilsson, Martin P. *The Minoan-Mycenaean Religion and Its Survival in Greek Religion*. 2nd ed. Lund: C. W. K. Gleerup, 1968.

Orosius. *Seven Books of History against the Pagans, The Apology of Paulus Orosius*. Trans. Irving Woodworth Raymond. New York: Columbia University Press, 1936.

Ovid. *Heroides and Amores*. Trans. Grant Showerman. 1914; rpt. Cambridge: Harvard University Press, 1963.

———. *Metamorphoses*. Trans. Frank Justus Miller. 2 vols. 1916; rpt. Cambridge: Harvard University Press, 1929.

Page, D. L., trans. *Literary Papyri: Poetry*. Vol. 3 of *Select Papyri*. Ed. Arthur Surridge

Hunt and C. C. Edgar. 1941; rev. and rpt. Cambridge: Harvard University Press, 1942.

Pausanias. *Description of Greece*. Trans. W. H. S. Jones. 5 vols. 1918–35; rpt. Cambridge: Harvard University Press, 1964.

Plutarch. *Plutarch's Lives*. Trans. Bernadotte Perrin. 11 vols. 1914–26; rpt. Cambridge: Harvard University Press, 1959.

Sandys, George. *Ovid's Metamorphoses, Englished, Mythologized, and Represented in Figures*. Ed. Kark K. Hulley and Stanley T. Vandersall. Lincoln: University of Nebraska Press, 1970.

Schefold, K. *Myth and Legend in Early Greek Art*. Trans. Audrey Hicks. London: Thames and Hudson, 1966.

Seznec, Jean. *The Survival of the Pagan Gods: The Mythological Tradition and Its Place in Renaissance Humanism and Art*. Trans. Barbara Sessions. Bollingen Series 38. New York: Pantheon, 1953.

Statius. *Thebaid*. Trans. J. H. Mozley. 2 vols. 1928; rpt. Cambridge: Harvard University Press, 1961.

Suetonius. *Lives of the Caesars*. Trans. J. C. Rolfe. 2 vols. 1913; rpt. Cambridge: Harvard University Press, 1960.

Virgil. *Eclogues, Georgics, Aeneid*. Trans. H. Rushton Fairclough. 2 vols. 1918; rpt. Cambridge: Harvard University Press, 1960.

Ward, Anne, W. R. Connor et al. *The Quest for Theseus*. New York: Praeger, 1970.

15

The Satyr

Paul Grootkerk

Satyrs, woodland creatures who are part man and part goat, have been described in Western literature since the eighth century B.C. Representing the luxuriant forces of nature, the satyr became associated with the Greek cult of Dionysus, god of wine and revelry, later called Bacchus by the Romans. Referred to by various names by the Greeks and Romans, the satyr became a symbol of mischief, buffoonery, cowardliness, drunkenness, phallicism, fertility, lasciviousness, lechery, and irrationality. Though not originally conceived of as a demon, the satyr was transformed by Christianity, which regarded satyric associations as being satanic, into the Devil. This contrasting of symbolic associations has made the satyr one of the most popular images for both artists and writers throughout history, so that even in the twentieth century the satyr is interpreted as the personification both of innocence and of evil.

Numerous contemporary scholarly studies have dealt with the various forms, aspects, and interpretations of the satyr. Especially significant is Frank Brommer's *Satyroi* (1937), which traces the development of goat-beings (satyrs, fauns, silvans, ''sileni,'' Pan) as manifested in their representation in Greek vase-paintings of the sixth and fifth centuries B.C. Antique erotic depictions of these goat-beings are examined in Catherine Johns' *Sex or Symbol: Erotic Images of Greece and Rome* (1982). Margarete Bieber in *The History of the Greek and Roman Theater* (1939; 1961) discusses the evolution of the classical satyr play. Lynn Frier Kaufmann's *The Noble Savage: Satyrs and Satyr Families in Renaissance Art* (1984) traces conceptions of satyrs from the ancient world through the Renaissance and focuses on their portrayal in the art of Northern Europe and Italy during the Renaissance. Several major works explore the history of Pan from antiquity to the present. Among these is *Pan the Goat-God* by Patricia Merivale (1969), a survey of the literary and artistic heritage of Pan throughout Western history. Reinhard Herbig's book *Pan der griechische Bocksgott: Versuch einer Monographie* (1949) is an anthropological, archaeological, and art historical study of Pan. A critical examination of the relationship between the satyr and satire in Elizabethan literature and theatre is studied in Alvin Kernan's *The Cankered Muse* (1959). The coalescence of the satyr/devil image is chronicled in Robert Hughes's book *Heaven and Hell in Western Art* (1968). The Christian conception of the satyr is also explored in *Wild Men in the Middle Ages* by Richard Bernheimer (1952), a scholarly investigation of the medieval counterpart of the satyr, the wild man.

As mentioned previously, the satyr is but one of numerous creatures (satyrs, fauns, silvans, "sileni," Pan) that can be classified as "goat-beings." Even though most artists and writers intertwined the iconography of these various mythological beings into one general form, it is necessary to define each group's physical characteristics as originally conceived by the Greeks and Romans.

In Greek mythology satyrs were first envisioned as Dionysian male spirits of the forests and mountains having "puck noses, bristling hair, goat-like ears, short tails," and human feet (Seyffert 559). By the time of the Romans there had also developed female satyrs. Closely related to the satyr was Pan, also a member of the retinue of Dionysus. The name "Pan" is derived from the early Greek *Paon*, literally meaning "feeder," referring to Pan's pastoral functions (Grant and Hazel 312). Like satyrs, Pan was a male god of hills and woods, imagined as having a puck nose, beard, shaggy hair, two horns, and goat's feet. In late Greek history Pan was converted into the pans or "panisci," young forest imps who were both male and female (Seyffert 453).

Every region of ancient Greece had its own version of Pan with accompanying mythological descriptions. The Pan of Thessaly was called Aristaeus, god of flocks and agriculture. The Pan of Asia Minor was Priapus, god of procreation, meaning "phallus," referring to his enormous penis (Aldington and Ames 183–84). Statues known as "herms," named after Hermes, father of Pan, were often placed in Greek (and Roman) gardens. Herms were quadrangular pillars with a god's torso represented at the top of the pillar; herms of Priapus usually show the god with an erection.

One of the sons of Pan was Silenus, supposed teacher of Dionysus, who prompted the latter to invent wine. Considered to be the oldest of the satyrs, Silenus was usually portrayed as a fat, drunken old man with a potbelly, a bald head, and a puck nose, his entire body covered with hair (Seyffert 586–87). The followers of Silenus were called "sileni," male and female personifications of springs and rivers. The "sileni" derive from the horse, not from the he-goat; however, the most famous of the "sileni," Marsyas, is generally portrayed as a satyr (Aldington and Ames 182–83). Like the "sileni," satyrs were at "first represented as uncouth men, each with a horse's tail" (*New Britannica* 10:471). Later the distinction between "sileni" and satyrs became more distinct, the latter deriving from a goat, the former from a horse.

The Romans identified Pan with the rustic male fertility god Faunus, whose attributes are almost identical to those of Pan. The name "Faunus" is derived from the Latin *fari*, meaning "the speaker," since the god could reveal the future through dreams. This association is seen in the contemporary concept of fairies. The followers of Faunus were the fauns or "fauni," mischievous male and female creatures who caused nightmares (Seyffert 235).

Related to the Roman god Faunus was Silvanus, an Italian male god of woods and gardens. Since his physical appearance is so close to that of Pan, Silvanus is often identified with the former. The male and female followers of Silvanus were called silvans or "silvani" (Seyffert 587).

Distinguishing these multiple rustic goat-gods is very difficult. Jorge Luis Borges considers them all one, saying satyrs is the Greek name for these creatures, while fauns, pans, and silvans are the equivalent in Rome. He describes them as being goats in the lower parts of their bodies, while their torsos, arms, and heads are human. "Satyrs were thickly covered with hair and had short horns, pointed ears, active eyes, and hooked noses" (198). Naturally, this description is a blending of multiple goat-beings. For the remainder of this entry the term "satyr" will be used accordingly, except in those cases where a distinction must be made between the various goatlike gods.

The Greek poet Hesiod (eighth century B.C.) says that the satyrs, nymphs, and Curetes were born of the five daughters of Hecaterus and that the satyrs are worthless and unfit for work (fragment 6 in *Hesiod*, p. 277; see also Strabo, *Geography* 10.3.19). Hesiod may be suggesting that satyrs are worthless because they are given to pleasure, but this meaning is uncertain. Hesiod may also be suggesting that satyrs are worthless since they are supposed to be of a cowardly nature (Seyffert 559), except at those times when the Dionysiac frenzy is upon them.

Though satyrs are not specifically described by Hesiod, Pan is vividly portrayed in the Homeric Hymn to Pan, an anonymous hymn of uncertain date, but probably post-Homeric according to Merivale (1). The opening verses of this hymn (in a translation by George Chapman) are:

> Sing, Muse, this chiefe of Hermes' love-got Joies,
> Goate-footed, Two-horn'd, amorous of noise,
> That through the faire-Greenes, al adorn'd with Trees,
> Together goes with Nymphs, whose nimble knees
> Can every Dance foot, that affect to scale
> The most inaccessible Tops of all
> Uprightest rocks, and ever use to call
> On Pan, the bright-hayr'd God of Pastorall—
>
> (1–8; qtd. in Merivale 231)

The visible image of the satyr was established in Greece about 500 B.C. with the development of the satyr play, an outgrowth of the worship of Dionysus, who according to the fifth-century B.C. Greek playwright Aeschylus in *The Edonians* was tutored as a child by Silenus, father of the satyrs. Part of the worship of Dionysus consisted of songs of rejoicing known as dithyrambs, accompanied by a choral dance. In his *Poetics* Aristotle claims that Greek tragedy developed from "the leaders of the dithyramb" (Bieber 6).

The dithyramb was originally performed by men disguised as satyrs, wearing equine ears and tails, a subject found on countless Greek vases. The satyr play was the final adaptation of the dithyramb. After the performance in Greek theatre of three tragedies, there was customarily a satyr play where choruses of satyrs and "sileni" would act in a wanton and sometimes obscene manner to break up the solemnity of the three preceding plays as well as to indicate the connection between Dionysus and the drama (Seyffert 559).

Satyr plays were usually set under an open sky in a lonely forest with actors wearing an ugly mask and the skin of a goat, panther, or deer over their naked bodies (Seyffert 559). Sometimes loin cloths with tails and an artificial leather phallus of considerable size were also worn, with the total costume conveying the quality of a coarse, ugly, rustic creature (Bieber 1–17).

Part of the satyr play consisted of a wild dance, the "sikinnis," where actors often played the double flute, sometimes known as the panpipe or "syrinx." In the *Dialogue of the Gods* by the second-century A.D. Greek writer Lucian, the author narrates the story of how Pan pursued the chaste nymph Syrinx, who, to save herself, became a reed by the river Ladon. Pan, unable to distinguish Syrinx from the other reeds, cut several reeds at random and made them into the traditional panpipe, a very common attribute of satyrs. The story of Pan and Syrinx is also contained in the *Metamorphoses* by the Roman poet Ovid (43 B.C.–A.D. 17), who elaborates that not only did Syrinx elude Pan, but she also evaded satyrs and other gods of the woods and fields (1.659–712). This variation of the story is noteworthy since the interrelationship of the multiple classical goat-beings is emphasized.

In the previously discussed satyr plays the actor always had human legs; however, as noted, Pan is described as being "goat-footed" in the Homeric Hymn to Pan. The coalescence of the satyr and Pan images is clearly presented by the first-century B.C. Roman poet Horace in his poem "Bacchus' Might," which describes satyrs as being "goat-footed" (*Odes* 2.19).

One of the most significant tales about satyrs developed as a result of the fourth-century B.C. military conquests of Alexander the Great. According to this fable, Dionysus and his retinue of Pan, Silenus, satyrs, and maenads (female worshipers of Dionysus) conquered India, introducing wine to this culture (Seyffert 191). The association of satyrs with India was exploited by later authors, who recorded that satyrs were not fictional but rather actual creatures who resided in India. The earliest of these reports were by two Greek writers, Ctesias and Megasthenes. Ctesias of Cnidos was a physician at the Persian court during the late fifth century B.C.; Megasthenes went to India as ambassador of Seleucus I to the court of King Chandragupta in 303 B.C. According to these two authors, satyrs were found on the central Indian plateau (Hughes 216).

The Roman encyclopedist Pliny the Elder (ca. A.D. 23–79) based his own accounts of satyrs on the writings of Ctesias and Megasthenes. Pliny's *Natural*

History notes that satyrs got their name from the Greek *sathe*, the "membrum virile," since they are "always prone to lust" (White 36 n. 1). Pliny further states that satyrs are found not only in India but also in Ethiopia, an idea reiterated by the third-century A.D. Roman writer Solinus in his *Polyhistor* (Wittkower 68). This belief in actual satyrs continued into the late Middle Ages, as noted in the 1493 edition of Schedel's *Nuremberg Chronicle*, an illustrated anthology of the fabulous creatures of India (including satyrs), with many of the races having their origin in Pliny (Hughes 225).

The concept of satyrs being actual animals living in India is but one example of the survival of the satyr during the Middle Ages. The acceptance of the satyr as a real animal during the Middle Ages was due to the inclusion of satyrs in the Bible. In the Vulgate, the Latin version of the Bible prepared by Saint Jerome, Jerome had used the term "pilosi" as the translation for a word in Isaiah concerning the demons that would inhabit Babylon and Edom after their destruction. Jerome interpreted the term to mean satyrs or incubi (Bernheimer 96–97). According to Isaiah 13:21, from the King James Bible, Babylon will be home to creatures of evil after its destruction: "But wild beasts of the desert shall lie there; and their houses shall be full of doleful creatures; and owls shall dwell there, and satyrs shall dance there." Likewise, in Isaiah 34:14, wild beasts will make the gutted city of Edom their home, and "the satyr shall cry to his fellow."

Many authors, including Dante, have based their images of Hell on Isaiah's metaphors, especially noting his bestiary of "unclean animals," some of which are also listed in the *Golden Legend*, a French thirteenth-century collection of the legends of the saints by Jacobus de Voragine. In his account of Saint Paul the Hermit, Voragine relates how Saint Anthony attempted to find Saint Paul in the wilderness, encountering on his journey many diabolical animals including a satyr, a "creature which the pagans mistake for wood-gods" (89). The inclusion of the satyr by Isaiah and Voragine in their descriptions of demonic creatures is especially noteworthy since the satyr was to become transformed during the Middle Ages into the epitome of evil, the Devil.

Though satyrs were originally pictured by the Greeks and Romans as rowdy and mischievous, they were not considered evil; however, their transformation into the satanic was partially enhanced by the medieval interpretation of the classical story of the satyr Marsyas (Hyginus, *Fabula* 165). After Marsyas learned to play the flute, he challenged Apollo to a musical contest. Having lost the contest, Marsyas was mercilessly skinned alive. This myth represented to various Christian theologians the destruction of darkness and evil by Apollo, the personification of light and clarity (Hughes 237).

Another element that abetted the transformation of the satyr into the Devil was the former's association with Pan and Dionysus. Both Pan and Dionysus were often portrayed as horned gods with insatiable appetites for sex. Pan is also a goat-footed, hairy creature, having large ears and nostrils, a wide mouth, and slanting eyes, attributes which are satanic in quality; he could instill "panic" into people, just as the English word suggests, by making horrible noises creating hysteria. Pan, son of Hermes, leader of the dead to the underworld, and Dionysus, the "giver of the underworld," meaning by extension that he was able to give man life after death, were accordingly viewed by medieval theologians as symbols of darkness (Hughes 237–40).

As late as the seventh century A.D., groups of women in England still imitated the mythological maenads worshiping Bacchus (that is, Dionysus) by dressing in skins and dancing and singing at night, sometimes around a goat. This image recalls a sixth-century A.D. Coptic ivory now in Aachen, Germany, showing a dancing maenad and Pan. In this sculpture Pan and the Devil are one: cloven hooves, goat's legs, beast's ears, saturine face, and goatee; only the panpipes identify the figure as Pan. In the seventh century A.D., Theodore, archbishop of Canterbury, in the *Book of Penitences* condemned these ancient fertility practices as being "devilish" (Hughes 241).

Even though Theodore may have denounced the Dionysian revelries, they were to continue for more than another thousand years, transformed into the witches' sabbat, a satanic event at which male and female followers of the Devil worshiped Satan, often portrayed in the form of a goat, with orgies recalling the worship of Dionysus (Robbins 414–24). During the Middle Ages witches were believed to be real, resulting in countless monographs on witchcraft, the most famous being the *Malleus Maleficarum* by James Sprenger and Heinrich Kramer, first published in Germany in 1486. Two references to satyrs and fauns are included in this book. The first is a lengthy interpretation of classical and Christian descriptions of satyrs, calling them "incubi," that is, devils who have intercourse with women: "Blessed Isidore, in the last chapter of his 8th book, says: Satyrs are they who are called Pans in Greek and Incubi in Latin. And they are called Incubi from their practices of overlaying, that is debauching. . . . But the devil which the common people call an Incubus, the Romans called a fig Faun" (24). The second reference in the *Malleus Maleficarum* describes the nature and home of these demonic creatures, saying that fauns, also called trolls, are "buffoons and jokers" that "abound in Norway" (106). One could accordingly conclude that for medieval man the Devil and the satyr were factual, interchangeable creatures of evil. This concept is clearly supported in a line from the *Carmina Burana*, a thirteenth-century collection of Latin songs sung by itinerant religious men in Germany. Song number fifty-four in the original manuscript from the monastery of Benedictbeuern in Upper Bavaria includes the passage, "I exorcize you . . . Fauns . . . Nymphs . . . Satyrs . . . all species of demons" (qtd. in Merivale 246 n. 65).

The image of the Devil as satyr was enriched by another medieval source: the wild man. The wild man was a distinct human species who supposedly lived in the woods and was covered with a thick mat of hair. During the Middle Ages, hair was considered to be a sign of sexuality (Sprenger and Kramer 166), an idea already found in Aristotle's *Generation of Animals*, which states that "men that are hairy are more prone to sexual intercourse" (4.5). The relationship of the satyr and the wild man can be traced to the satyr play, where actors wore goat skins over their naked bodies. As previously noted, Silenus was sometimes portrayed with his entire body covered with hair. In the third century A.D. the Greek rhetorician and writer Philostratus reported in his *Vita Apollonii* that he had seen a man who was considered to be the son of a satyr because there was a dense covering of hair like an animal's fleece on his back and part of his chest (Bernheimer 100). St. Jerome in his commentary on Isaiah speculates on his use of the term "pilosi," saying: "When in the following it is said that 'the hairy ones will dance here' we must understand this to mean either incubi or satyrs or a certain kind of wild men whom some call 'fatui ficarii' and regard as of the nature of demons" (qtd. in Bernheimer 97). As Jerome infers, the Devil as satyr was closely related to the concept of the wild man.

Another major variation that satyrs underwent during the Middle Ages was their association with monkeys and apes. This relationship is apparent in modern terminology, with the orangutan being *Simia satyrus* (White 36 n. 1). The identification of the satyr with the monkey is first found in book 7 of Pliny's *Natural History*, where in one case satyrs are described as swift animals that walk on all fours and can stand upright like human beings. Such an association extended into the Middle Ages, when countless bestiaries from the twelfth to the fifteenth centuries classified and illustrated satyrs and monkeys together (Wittkower 68–69).

Various medieval authors wrote about the association of the satyr and the ape. Bartholomaeus Anglicus in *De proprietatibus rerum* (written about 1230) notes that not only do satyrs come in the form of apes, but some are also cyclopes, some are headless and noseless, and some have an eye in their shoulders. These mutants all seem to be variations of Pliny's original list of Indian freaks, yet now all were classified as satyrs. These creatures are illustrated in the fifteenth-century *Livre des merveilles*, which deals with the travel accounts of Marco Polo and certain other writers.

Satyr-apes and satyrs are distinguished, yet grouped together, by Edward Topsell in *The History of Foure-Footed Beasts* (originally published in 1607) since they have rough hair and lust after women. This reference to hair recalls the account of Petrus Martyr, who in *De orbe novo* (Basel, 1511) identified the satyr-apes with the wild men of the woods, living in the manner of troglodytes in underground caves and hovels (Clair 84–85). Caspar Bauhin, a Swiss anatomist, concluded in *De Hermaphroditorum monstrorumque partuum natura* (Oppenheim, 1614) that two classes of satyrs exist, actual and fictitious ones. He believed that actual satyrs are either human beings or a species of ape and that fictitious ones are either demonical or poetical (Wittkower 68).

By the time of the Renaissance the demonic medieval image of the satyr began fading. The original, more arcadian, classical form of the satyr returned. This is seen in John Fletcher's play *The Faithful Shepherdess* (circa 1608–9), a pastoral drama whose action is directed by Pan through his agent, the satyr. In the lines, "Pan, the father of our sheep . . . Thou that keepst us chaste and free" (1.2), a complete reversal of the medieval satyr symbol is evident (Merivale 18).

Likewise, in 1620, Ben Jonson in *Pan's Anniversarie* compares King James I to Pan as the protector of shepherds. Both authors conveniently avoid any references to the goat-god's shaggy animal elements (Merivale 19).

This romanticized vision of the satyr is best expressed in chapter 36 of Edward Gibbon's *Decline and Fall of the Roman Empire* (London, 1776–88). When discussing the ancient Feast of Lupercalia, Gibbon notes: "The rustic deities who presided over the toils and pleasures of the pastoral life, Pan, Faunus and their train of satyrs, were such as the fancy of shepherds might create, sportive, petulant and lascivious, whose power was limited and whose malice was inoffensive" (qtd. in Merivale 40).

The multiple meanings of the satyr, that is, demonic versus pastoral, were questioned by Friedrich Nietzsche in part four of the introduction to his 1872 book *The Birth of Tragedy*. Nietzsche asked, "What does the union of goat and god mean in the satyr; what life force or impulse caused the Greeks to think of the Dionysian revelers and the fictitious satyrs?" For Nietzsche satyrs had become a philosophical metaphor for Greek civilization: satyrs can be beautiful, idyllic, sexual, primitive, and evil.

As diverse as the interpretations of the satyr have been throughout history, equally varied are the representations of the satyr in art and literature. There are such extensive and assorted representations of satyrs and other goat-beings in art that only a cursory review can be given in this entry. Among the earliest representations of satyrs are those on Greek vase-paintings, around 500 B.C., which are usually portrayals of lost satyr plays. For example, Aeschylus wrote the lost satyr play *Prometheus and Satyrs*, first performed in 472 B.C., a play represented on numerous vases of that date depicting dancing satyrs lighting their torches from Prometheus' narthex, a giant fennel stalk that Prometheus used to steal fire from the gods (Beazley 619). On many of these vase-paintings Greek artists distinguished between satyr players, with their loin cloths incorporating a phallus and tail, and a "real" satyr. However, in both cases satyrs are represented with pointed ears, long hair and beards, tails, and smooth hairless human bodies with huge erect phalluses. Many of these satyr images are graphically erotic, showing that satyrs will resort to any form of sexual gratification, including masturbation, oral sex, anal sex, or vaginal sex, with each other, maenads, or animals. These images were meant to be enjoyed as pure bawdy humor, since sexual comedy was a part of the satyr play (Johns 88–90).

Whereas Greek vase-painters often showed satyrs as purely sexual creatures, the famous early fourth-century B.C. Greek sculptor Praxiteles depicted in marble a satyr (Rome, Capitoline Museum) as an idealized human being with no references to the traditional animal quality of the satyr except for his pointed ears and an animal skin thrown over his shoulders. Likewise, the late fourth-century B.C. marble *Barberini Satyr* (Munich, Glyptothek) shows a peacefully sleeping satyr with pointed ears partially covered by an animal skin. Some historians have suggested that the *Barberini Satyr* may represent the story of King Midas, who intoxicated a satyr to capture him so that he might prophesy for him (Elderkin 28–31).

Pan was generally represented in Greek and Roman art as much more ani-mallike. This is clearly seen in an early Roman marble sculpture of Pan teaching Olympus to play the syrinx (Naples, National Museum), with Pan having a coarse, satanic face, long hair and beard, horns, and the lower body of a goat. Often Pan is represented in overtly sexual situations, as noted in a first-century B.C. marble statue of Pan copulating with a she-goat (Naples, National Museum). In a second-century A.D. Roman marble sarcophagus (Naples, National Mu-seum), male and female pans are shown in Dionysian revelry, with one young female pan impaling herself on the phallus of a Pan-headed herm. By the second century A.D. Pan and satyrs had been assimilated into one general image, as seen in the marble portrayal of a young satyr playing the flute (Rome, Villa Albani), with the satyr now having acquired the lower body of a goat.

With the coming of the Middle Ages, the satyr was to be transformed in Christian art into the Devil. This image is so common that only a few examples need to be mentioned. In a thirteenth-century Spanish altarpiece (Barcelona, Museum of Catalan Art), St. Michael is portrayed bargaining with the Devil in the weighing of souls. The Devil is a satyr with a goatlike head, ears, and horns, yet somewhat altered, as shown by its clawed feet and hairless, emaciated body. A similar figure is seen in a portrayal of the Devil's temptation of St. Anthony in a fifteenth-century illuminated manuscript (Florence, Laurentian Library). In an engraving from Pierre Boaistuau's *Histoires prodigieuses* (Paris, 1597) de-picting the Devil tempting St. Jerome, the Devil is a full satyr with a hideous face, large nose, hairy body, and the legs and cloven feet of a goat. The identical figure is seen in Frans Hogenberg's 1559 etching *Al Hoy*, where the Devil in the form of a satyr is shown three times cultivating seeds of evil.

In numerous late medieval prints the Devil/satyr is often portrayed with various musical instruments. The most common of these instruments is the bagpipe, a traditional medieval symbol of satanism as shown by its German name, "bock," or he-goat (Hughes 232). Among these prints are a woodcut illustration from Olaus Magnus' *Historia de gentibus septentrionalibus* (Rome, 1555) delineating a bagpipe-playing satyr/devil and a lute-playing satyr/devil dancing around a "magic circle," a protective circle drawn on the ground by witches when in-voking demons. The lute was sometimes associated with secular versus sacred music and accordingly considered evil (Harrison 21). Other sixteenth-century prints of the satyr with a bagpipe include Hans Sebald Beham's woodcuts *Satyress Playing the Bagpipe* and *Satyr Family in a Vine Pattern* depicting four satyrs playing bagpipes.

Another instrument associated with satyrs/devils in late medieval prints was the cornetto. This is vividly seen in a woodcut illustration from Ludovicus Caelius Rhodiginus Ricchierus' *Lectionum antiquarum* (Basel, 1517). This satyr and cornetto image is repeated in Hans Sebald Beham's woodcut *Satyr Blowing Horn* and Albrecht Dürer's engraving *The Satyr Family*. The cornetto would appear to be a variation of the classical panpipes.

In both Dürer's *The Satyr Family* and Beham's *Satyr Family in A Vine Pattern*, images of hairy satyrs are seen in a forest setting. The satyr family theme is repeated in Cornelis Metsys' 1550 engraving where two baby satyrs are portrayed suckling the breasts of their satyr mother. These depictions closely parallel a fifteenth-century miniature by Jean Bourdichon (Paris, Ecole des Beaux-Arts) showing a wild man, woman, and baby outside their cave. This series of representations recalls the medieval belief in wild men as well as their relationship to the satyr and Devil.

During the Renaissance, with the rediscovery of the classical world, pagan themes were revived, with countless ancient books and plays being translatad into the vernacular. Accordingly, satyrs became but one of many classical themes depicted by Renaissance artists throughout Europe. (For a useful study of satyrs in Renaissance art, see Kaufmann.)

In Italy around 1485 Botticelli painted *Mars and Venus*, representing Mars asleep in a forest with Venus watching. Generally regarded as an allegory of love and strength, the painting also shows four mischievous satyr children as rustic symbols. Piero di Cosimo painted three major works containing satyrs: *The Discovery of Honey* (ca. 1498; Massachusetts, Worcester Art Museum) depicts a band of somewhat domesticated satyrs collecting honey to make mead; *Cephalus and Procris* (ca. 1515; London, National Gallery) illustrates the ancient story of the satyr Cephalus who unwillingly killed his beloved, the nymph Procris (Hyginus, *Fabula* 189); *Hunting Scene* (ca. 1490; New York, Metropolitan Museum of Art) depicts a universal warfare raging between humans, animals, centaurs and satyrs in a wild forest. No other Renaissance artist better captured the rusticity of the satyr than di Cosimo.

About 1516 the High Renaissance artist Raphael began painting the frescos *The Marriage of Cupid and Psyche* and *The Marriage Feast of Cupid and Psyche* in the Villa Farnesina in Rome. Completed by his assistant Giulio Romano, the marriage feast represents numerous pagan gods, including satyrs, attending the festivities. These two frescos are especially significant since they inspired a generation of European artists who represented pagan wedding and feast scenes primarily as an excuse to portray the pantheon of ancient deities, including satyrs. These works are well illustrated and interpreted in Henry Bardon's study *Le Festin des Dieux*. One visibly aroused satyr in *The Marriage Feast of Cupid and Psyche* is shown leering at two nymphs who are decorating the wedding table. This vignette is commonly attributed to Raphael's assistant Giulio Romano, who was a painter of the last phase of the Italian Renaissance, known as Mannerism, which, among other qualities, was known for its eroticism. Representative of this erogenous element was a series of sixteenth-century engravings by Romano known as the *Sedici Modi*, which explicitly depict male satyrs having sexual intercourse with female satyrs or women.

Numerous Italian Mannerist artists went to France during the reign of Francis

I, who beginning in 1528 was patron to a school of artists at the royal Château of Fontainebleau. At Fontainebleau these Italian artists, as well as French artists, produced numerous erotic prints of satyrs, some extremely violent in context. Among these Fontainebleau prints is Antonio Fantuzzi's engraving *A Satyr Assaulting a Woman Defended by Three Cupids* (ca. 1542–45), showing a demonic satyr attempting to rape a woman, with his enormous erection visible behind her thighs, while three cupids futilely try to restrain the satyr. A somewhat less graphic representation of the same subject is seen in Master L. D.'s etching *A Woman Being Carried to a Libidinous Satyr* (dated 1547), showing a rather violently struggling woman being carried by two other women to a visibly aroused satyr. A third variation of this subject is Master L. D.'s etching of *A Woman Assaulted by a Satyr* (ca. 1545), depicting a young woman being carried off by a satyr while other women run away in fear. One of the most unusual etchings printed at Fontainebleau was Master L. D.'s *Satyr Being Carried to a Woman* (1547), a companion sheet to his *Woman Being Carried to a Libidinous Satyr*. This print may be seen as reverse rape, that is, the rape of the satyr by the female. The artist shows a struggling satyr being borne to a woman with open legs, ready to receive him.

Between 1545 and 1563 there took place the Council of Trent, the nineteenth Ecumenical Council, which was convened to define Catholic doctrine and to bring about reforms in the Church. The Council condemned the use of erotic images in art—a condemnation that had a restraining effect on the erotic portrayal of satyrs. In the seventeenth and eighteenth centuries an idyllic representation of satyrs returned, as seen in countless paintings by seventeenth-century French artist Nicolas Poussin, whose *oeuvre* is well documented in Anthony Blunt's monograph. Poussin distinguishes between satyrs and fauns by showing satyrs with goat legs and fauns with human legs.

In the nineteenth century numerous variations of the satyr image were produced. Especially noteworthy among these images was the development in England of "fairy painting," a uniquely nationalistic phenomenon largely based upon William Shakespeare's *A Midsummer Night's Dream* and *The Tempest*. Among the most important characters in the former is Puck, described by Shakespeare as a "Robin Goodfellow" (II.i. 34). Thomas Nashe in his 1594 *Terrors of the Night* wrote of "Robbin-good-fellowes . . . which idolatrous former daies and the fantasticall world of Greece ycleaped *Fawnes, Satyrs*" (qtd. in Merivale 246 n. 65). In a seventeenth-century English blackletter ballad woodcut illustration "The Mad Merry Pranks of Robin Goodfellow," a priapic satyr/devil is shown dancing at a witches' sabbat. However, by the nineteenth century the demonic representations of Robin Goodfellow, that is, Shakespeare's Puck, had become idyllic, rustic, fairy-tale satyrs, as shown in the illustrations in Beatrice Phillpotts' *Book of Fairies*.

The late nineteenth-century illustrator Aubrey Beardsley created various drawings containing satyrs for books, plays, magazines, and catalogues. Many of these illustrations are to be noted for their humor, as evident in a drawing of a satyr hairdresser cutting a woman's hair. Others are more traditional, showing satyr herms or Pan playing his syrinx for a group of dancing wood-nymphs. Some of Beardsley's satyr illustrations were designed by the artist for a romantic novel *Under the Hill*, left incomplete at his death in 1898. This short novel is the story of Venus and Tannhäuser, with chapter 5 depicting a ballet in a "remote Arcadian valley" stage setting, when "suddenly, to the music of pipe and horn, a troop of satyrs stepped out from the recesses of the woods" (43–44).

The most significant twentieth-century artist to represent satyrs was Pablo Picasso. Beginning in 1944 just after the liberation of Paris, Picasso produced at least three paintings containing satyrs: *Bacchanal* (Picasso estate), dated 1944, is a variation of Poussin's 1635 *Triumph of Pan; Joie de vivre* (Antibes, Musée Grimaldi), dated 1946, is a joyful, childlike mural of satyrs and centaurs reveling in nature; *Faun Piping* (Antibes, Château Picasso), also dated 1946, is similar in imagery. Undoubtedly these portrayals of satyrs are a rapturous celebration of life after the nightmare of the Second World War.

As varied as the artistic interpretations of satyrs have been over the centuries, equally diverse are the literary portrayals of satyrs. This literary tradition begins in classical Greece, as evident in the numerous references to Greek literature throughout this entry. Among the most significant of these Greek works is the only surviving satyr play, *The Cyclops*, by Euripides. The action takes place in front of a cave where the satyr Silenus is being held prisoner by the Cyclops Polyphemus, who has also captured Odysseus and his men. Odysseus and his men free themselves by blinding Polyphemus, who, however, keeps Silenus as his lover. The entire satyr comedy becomes a satire about the meaning of justice (Grene and Lattimore 230).

Euripides' play is illustrated in James Barry's 1803 *Self-Portrait* (Dublin, National Gallery of Ireland), depicting the artist displaying a painting of the giant Cyclops surrounded by tiny satyrs, that is, the satyr chorus. Though this work was painted while Barry was sixty-two years of age, he "represents himself in imagination as a young artist again, now identified with a legendary Greek painter, Timanthes, described by Pliny" (Rosenblum and Janson 63).

Another significant classical work is *The Satyricon* by the Roman satirist Petronius (d. A.D. 66). The meaning of "satyr" as used in Petronius' title is "satire," with perhaps the latter derived from the former. Some scholars believe, however, "satire" is derived from the Latin *satura* (a dish of different ingredients), with the term being modified in literature to mean a form that loosely connects a variety of topics (Introduction, *The Satyricon of Petronius Arbiter* xxv).

During the Middle Ages the satyr became the Devil not only in art but also in literature. This demonic interpretation was associated with sexuality and the witches' sabbat, as indicated by the previously discussed *Malleus Maleficarum*. This medieval theme of satyr-satanism continued in literature into the seventeenth century. An outstanding example of this is John Milton's *Paradise Regained*

(1671), as seen in Satan's charge against Belial that satyrs and all woodland gods are but demonic disguises for perpetrating sexual crimes:

> Too long, then layst thy scapes on names adored,
> Apollo, Neptune, Jupiter, or Pan.
> Satyr, or Faun, or Silvan.
>
> (2.189–91)

The *Hymne des daimons* (1555) by poet Pierre de Ronsard describes the gathering of similarly disguised woodland demons at what would appear to be a witches' sabbat. Ronsard says that they are often transformed into fauns, satyrs, and pans with hairy bodies, and that they dance all night (Merivale 29–30). Poet Henry More wrote several poems relating to the witches' sabbat. *The Argument of Psychozoia or, the Life of the Soul* (ca. 1650) describes the harsh sounds of woodland demons: "the woods with black bedight / Answer rough Pan, his pipe and eke his skill, / And all the Satyr-routs rude whoops and shouting shrill" (qtd. in Merivale 31). In *Praeexistency of the Soul* (ca. 1647) More also yearned for a day when no longer the "filthy lust" and "sinful dust" of the witches' sabbat will exist, a metaphor for human purification: "Pans pipe shall then be mute, and Satyrs heel / Shall cease to dance ybrent in scorching fire" (qtd. in Merivale 31).

During the Elizabethan era the satyr became a frequent literary symbol for several major writers. William Shakespeare, for example, had Hamlet compare his father to his uncle as "So excellent a king, that was to this / Hyperion to a satyr, so loving to my mother" (I.ii. 139–40). However, no other Elizabethan author alluded to satyrs as much as Edmund Spenser in *The Faerie Queene*. One of the characters in Spenser's epic poem is Sir Satyrane, the son of a satyr and a woman whom the satyr had raped after finding her in the forest. Sir Satyrane is the medieval wild man living in the woods, and he has learned from his father how to dominate through force the animals there (1.6.22 ff.). Sir Satyrane and the satyrs discovered the virgin Una in a forest, the victim of an attempted rape. After the satyrs had taken her home, Una taught them the "true sacred lore," and was worshiped by them until her eventual departure. Richard D. Jordan has interpreted this canto as representing an anti-Semitic tradition, with the horned satyr symbolizing the medieval belief of the "horned Jew" (125–26). The satyrs' worship of Una represents idolatry, interpreted by Christians as the "mindless performance of ritual" by the Jews (Jordan 130). Also, Dionysus was believed to be the god of the Jews, an argument found in the *Histories* of the Roman historian Tacitus (ca. 55–117 A.D.). Tacitus also claimed that Jews are given to lust, like Spenser's satyrs (5.5). Another segment of Spenser's poem relates the tale of Hellenore, who spent a night of debauchery with a satyr, probably an allusion to Christian versus pagan love:

> ... his lovely wife [Hellenore] emongst them lay
> Embraced of a Satyre rough and nude,

> Who all the night did minde his joyous play.
>
> (3.10.48)

A curious Elizabethan etymological development was the spelling of "satire" as "satyr." The significance of this relationship is that the Elizabethans to a degree associated satyrs and satire in the manner of the Greeks, with the author assuming the "guise" of the satyr instead of the "role" of the satyr (as in the original satyr plays) to deliver a satire (Kernan 54–58). Accordingly, at the beginning of George Wither's satire "Vices Executioner: or the Satyrs Self-description of Himself," the author introduces himself as a satyr:

> Though in shape I seeme a Man
> Yet a Satyr wilde I am:
>   Bred in Woods and Desert places,
>   Where men seldom shew their faces;
> Rough and hayrie like a Goate,
> Clothed with Dame Natures coate.
>
> (1–6; qtd. in Kernan 57)

Wither's satire is contained in an anthology *The Workes of Master George Wither* (London, 1620), where the satire is illustrated with a picture of a fierce, shaggy satyr. The Elizabethans depicted satyrs "as half-man and half-goat with a long tail" (Kernan 62); such a representation can be found on the title pages of numerous Elizabethan satires, and was used as late as 1726 by William Hogarth in his frontispiece for *Hudibras*.

Numerous major authors referred to satyrs during the nineteenth century. John Keats wrote several poems where Pan was a major subject, including "The Hymn to Pan" (in *Endymion*, 1818). The first three stanzas of this poem list the functions of Pan: "forester, hunter, shepherd, leader of fauns and satyrs, would-be lover of nymphs" (Merivale 53–59). Percy Bysshe Shelley's romantic poem *The Witch of Atlas* (1820) lists in stanza 8 the various classical woodland goat deities:

> And old Silenus, shaking a green stick
>   Of lilies, and the wood-gods in a crew
> Came . . .
> And Dryope and Faunus followed quick,
>   Teasing the God to sing them something new.
>
> (qtd. in Merivale 62)

Thomas Peacock in his 1817 satiric poem *Melincourt* compares his main character Sir Oran, a "natural and original man . . . caught . . . in the woods of Angola," to "the very same beings whom the ancients worshipped as divinities under the names of Fauns and Satyrs, Silenus and Pan" (qtd. in Merivale 68). In Victor Hugo's 1859 poem *Le Satyre*, the satyr is pictured as a symbol of evil, representing the outdated forces of false pagan mythology which have been replaced by the "Christian supernatural" (Merivale 105).

Amusing nineteenth-century allusions to satyrs are the references by certain authors to each other as "goat-beings." In 1842 Ralph Waldo Emerson adverted to Henry David Thoreau as "young Pan under another name." Likewise, when Walt Whitman met Thoreau, Bronson Alcott in a diary entry described Whitman as "Walt the satyr, the Bacchus, the very god Pan" (Merivale 130).

Numerous Victorian authors wrote poems about Pan. Among these authors were Robert Browning, "Pan and Luna" (1880); Robert Louis Stevenson, "Pan's Pipes" (1878); and Oscar Wilde, "Santa Deca" (1881). Algernon Charles Swinburne wrote three major poems about Pan: "Pan and Thalassius," "A Nympholept," and "The Palace of Pan" (1887–93).

The most significant twentieth-century author to write about satyrs and Pan was D. H. Lawrence. Throughout his career Lawrence made repeated references in his poems and novels to Pan and satyrs. For Lawrence, Pan and satyrs were conflicting symbols of evil and goodness, Christianity and paganism. This is noted in *The Plumed Serpent* (1926), where Pan's face is pictured as being that "at once of a god and a devil" (qtd. in Merivale 206). Lawrence's conflicting symbolism is also revealed in his review of *Georgian Poetry: 1911–1912*: "I worship Christ, I worship Jehovah, I worship Pan, I worship Aphrodite. But I do not worship hands nailed and running with blood upon a cross, nor licentiousness, nor lust. I want them all, all the gods. They are all God" (307; qtd. in Merivale 196). The universalism of Lawrence's concept of God is seen in Dorothy Brett's painting *Crucifixion Scene* (ca. 1920), portraying Lawrence both as Christ upon the cross and as Pan offering grapes to him.

Satyrs and their variations continue to be popular images today. Both "Pan" and "satyr" have been incorporated into our vocabulary. The word "panic" describes a state of sudden overpowering fear such as that the god Pan was supposed to induce. "Satyriasis" is a condition of uncontrollable sexual desire in males. Various major porcelain companies, including Mettlach and Royal Copenhagen, have produced decorative satyr/Pan figurines. Pan has been included in a Walt Disney comic book, where Pan and Pluto meet in a forest and Pluto dances to Pan's music (Dell Giant, 33, 1960). "Pan" was even the trade name of a prophylactic manufactured during the 1920s, picturing a harmless classicized satyr playing a pipe. In a somewhat more traditional manner, one also has to mention the faun costume worn by Vaslav Nijinsky for the 1912 Russian Ballet performance of *Afternoon of a Faun*. Like the Pan prophylactic trademark, Nijinsky's satyr/faun costume denotes romantic harmlessness.

A rather opposite interpretation of the concept of the "harmless" satyr has been offered by Dr. Andrew K. Bernath, M.D. Dr. Bernath believes that in our contemporary society there has evolved a new satyr, the satyr of "Hollywood and Rome's Cine Citta." This satyr dresses and grooms in immaculate taste, sleeps by day and prowls by night, copulating with several beautiful women, consuming large quantities of alcohol and cigarettes, and alienting himself from society with his suicidal sexual tendencies, never knowing love or generosity (405–12). One could say that Dr. Bernath's modern satyr is but a summation of satyrs in general: the personification of lechery, fertility, phallicism, carnality, and demonism.

BIBLIOGRAPHY

Aldington, Richard, and Delano Ames, trans. *Larousse Encyclopedia of Mythology*. New York: Prometheus Press, 1960.

Aristotle. *Generation of Animals*. Trans. A. L. Peck. Rev. ed. Cambridge: Harvard University Press, 1953.

Bardon, Henry. *Le Festin des Dieux*. Paris: Presses Universitaires de France, 1960.

Beardsley, Aubrey. *The Story of Venus and Tannhäuser or "Under the Hill."* Ed. Robert Oresko. New York: St. Martin's, 1974.

Beazley, J. D. "Prometheus Fire-Lighter." *American Journal of Archaeology* 43 (1939): 618–39.

Bernath, Andrew K. "The World of a Satyr, A Case History." *Journal of Existential Psychiatry* 3, no. 12 (Spring 1963): 405–12.

Bernheimer, Richard. *Wild Men in the Middle Ages: A Study in Art, Sentiment, and Demonology*. Cambridge: Harvard University Press, 1952.

Bieber, Margarete. *The History of the Greek and Roman Theater*. 2nd ed., rev. and enl. Princeton: Princeton University Press, 1961.

Blunt, Anthony. *Nicolas Poussin*. 2 vols. New York: Bollingen Foundation, 1967.

Borges, Jorge Luis, with Margarita Guerrero. *The Book of Imaginary Beings*. Trans. Norman Thomas di Giovanni. New York: Discus-Avon, 1970.

Brommer, Frank. *Satyroi*. Würzburg: Konrad Triltsch Verlag, 1937.

Campbell, F. Leota. "The God Pan in Greek and Latin Literature." M.A. thesis. University of Southern California, 1918.

Clair, Colin. *Unnatural History: An Illustrated Bestiary*. London: Abelard-Schuman, 1967.

Curious Woodcuts of Fanciful and Real Beasts. New York: Dover, 1971.

Elderkin, George W. "The Barberini Satyr." *Art in America* 27, no. 1 (January 1939): 28–31.

Grant, Michael, and John Hazel. *Gods and Mortals in Classical Mythology*. Springfield, Mass.: G. and C. Merriam Co., 1973.

Grene, David, and Richmond Lattimore, eds. *Euripides*. Chicago: University of Chicago Press, 1959.

Harrison, Frank, and Joan Rimmer. *European Musical Instruments*. New York: Norton, 1964.

Herbig, Reinhard. *Pan der griechische Bocksgott: Versuch einer Monographie*. Frankfurt am Main: V. Klostermann, 1949.

Hesiod, the Homeric Hymns and Homerica. Trans. Hugh G. Evelyn-White. Cambridge: Harvard University Press, 1936.

Hilton, Timothy. *Piccaso*. New York: Oxford University Press, 1975.

Hughes, Robert. *Heaven and Hell in Western Art*. New York: Stein and Day, 1968.

Irwin, W. R. "The Survival of Pan." *PMLA* 76 (June 1961): 159–67.

Johns, Catherine. *Sex or Symbol: Erotic Images of Greece and Rome*. Austin: University of Texas Press, 1982.

Jordan, Richard Douglas. "Una Among The Satyrs: *The Faerie Queene*, 1.6." *Modern Language Quarterly* 38 (1977): 123–31.

Kaufmann, Lynn Frier. *The Noble Savage: Satyrs and Satyr Families in Renaissance Art*. Ann Arbor: UMI Research Press, 1984.

Kernan, Alvin. *The Cankered Muse*. New Haven: Yale University Press, 1959.

Lawrence, D. H. Review of *Georgian Poetry: 1911–1913*. In *Phoenix: The Posthumous Papers of D. H. Lawrence*. Ed. Edward McDonald. London: William Heinemann, 1936.

Melville, Robert. *Erotic Art of the West*. New York: Putnam's, 1973.

Merivale, Patricia. *Pan the Goat-God: His Myth in Modern Times*. Cambridge: Harvard University Press, 1969.

Mode, Heinz. *Fabulous Beasts and Demons*. London: Phaidon, 1975.

New Encyclopaedia Britannica. 15th ed. Chicago: University of Chicago, 1985.

Ovid. *Metamorphoses*. Trans. Frank Justus Miller. 2 vols. 1916; rpt. Cambridge: Harvard University Press, 1929.

Petronius Arbiter. *The Satyricon of Petronius Arbiter*. Trans. W. C. Firebaugh. New York: Boni and Liveright, 1922.

Philadelpheus, Alexander. *Der Pan in der antiken Kunst*. Athens, 1899.

Phillpotts, Beatrice. *The Book of Fairies*. New York: Ballantine, 1979.

Robbins, Rossell Hope. *The Encyclopedia of Witchcraft and Demonology*. New York: Crown, 1959.

Rosenblum, Robert, and H. W. Janson. *19th-Century Art*. New York: Abrams, 1984.

Seyffert, Oskar. *Dictionary of Classical Antiquities, Mythology, Religion, Literature, and Art*. 1891. Cleveland: World Publishing Co., 1956.

Sprenger, James, and Heinrich Kramer. *Malleus Maleficarum*. Cologne, 1486. Trans. Montague Summers. London: John Rodker, 1928.

Symons, Arthur. *The Collected Drawings of Aubrey Beardsley*. New York: Bounty Books, 1967.

Voragine, Jacobus de. *The Golden Legend*. Trans. Granger Ryan and Helmut Ripperger. New York: Arno Press, 1969.

White, T. H., ed. and trans. *The Bestiary: A Book of Beasts, Being a Translation from a Latin Bestiary of the Twelfth Century*. New York: Putnam's, 1954.

Winternitz, Emanuel. *Musical Instruments and Their Symbolism in Western Art*. New York: Norton, 1967.

Wittkower, Rudolf. *Allegory and the Migration of Symbols*. London: Thames and Hudson, 1977.

Zerner, Henri. *The School of Fontainebleau: Etchings and Engravings*. New York: Abrams, 1969.

16

The Centaur

Judith J. Kollmann

Fundamentally the centaur is a creature whose torso (including head and ears) is human and whose lower body is equine, possessing four equine legs. However, a number of variations exist, of which the most significant in antiquity was a type having a human body terminating in human legs and feet; the equine barrel and hindlegs extended behind the waist or buttocks. Still another form was the winged centaur. In both these cases the centaur is a combination of man with horse, and, strictly speaking, this is the true form, regardless of lesser details such as wings or types of legs. During the Middle Ages the onocentaur, part man and part donkey (most readily distinguished by its tufted ass's tail), became widespread due to *Physiologus*. As, however, *Equus asinus* is a member of the equine family, and as manuscript illuminations usually show the onocentaur performing traditional centaur functions, it, too, can be considered a member of the true centaur family. But there are other forms that have also been called centaurs. These include bucentaurs and leontocentaurs (Mode 90), which have the bodies of bulls and lions respectively. In Indian art there exist combinations of ''a snake's body and fish-tail with a human thorax, human arms and horse (or bull) legs'' (Mode 92). Perhaps the term ''centauroid,'' first used (as far as I am aware) by Poul Anderson to describe his creatures in *Fire Time* (1974), would be a more accurate word for man-beast composites that deviate markedly from the equine form but manifest characteristic centaur behavior.

The centaur apparently originated in Babylonia during the late second millennium B.C., and the consensus of scholarly opinion is that the Kassites (a barbaric group that moved into the Fertile Crescent ca. 1750 B.C. from Iran or further east) might have been responsible for creating the centaur, while the Hittites might have disseminated it to its place of greatest religious, literary, and artistic development: Greek culture. The Kassites, who once contended with

Egypt and Assyria for supremacy in the Near East, customarily set up boundary stones, not only to mark but also to protect the perimeters of their lands; consequently, the stones were incised with figures of gods or guardian spirits as well as protective curses. Among many different beings there are those that are half-man and half-horse. On one stone, the centaur is double-faced (a man's facing front, and a dragon's facing to the rear) as well as double-tailed (a horse's and a scorpion's). He is winged, and bends a bow while galloping. Beneath him is a scorpion (Baur 2). On another example the centaur is "wingless, has only one head and one tail. He is walking to the l. [sic] and is about to shoot an arrow" (Baur 2). Of course, because the Kassites depicted the centaur on their stones does not necessarily mean they invented it; however, as the Kassite empire ended ca. 1150 B.C., we can at least be certain that the beast was in existence by the mid–twelfth century, giving us a *terminus ad quem* for its invention.

The *terminus a quo* must be not only the introduction of the horse but also its distribution. The *Cambridge Ancient History* notes that the earliest "positive record [of the horse] is in a Babylonian tablet of about 2100 B.C., where it is described as the 'ass from the east,' or 'from the mountains' " (107). It took, however, centuries before the horse became common in the Near East, and there is every possibility that the people who distributed the horse were, in fact, the Kassites. As barbarian nomads, they might have ridden their horses, and, to the Near-Eastern cultures that were accustomed to chariots and asses, such a sight might have been sensational enough to have caused the same kind of confusion that the Indians were said to have experienced when faced by the mounted conquistadores, and believed that horse and man were one animal. This is possible, of course, but, given the penchant among Mediterranean peoples for creating hybrid man-beast forms, I suspect that once the horse was well known the invention of a semi-equine being would have been an almost foregone conclusion.

Thus, the creature that became known as the centaur originated in the Near East at some time between 1750 and 1150 B.C., and functioned as a guardian spirit. It is depicted as a hunter, and uses the bow as its principal weapon. It probably came into existence some centuries before 1150, as not only Kassite but also Mycenaean civilization ended in the mid–twelfth century, and, if Thomas Webster is correct, the centaur had been imported to Mycenaean Greece by means of the Hittites, with whom the Mycenaeans had maintained excellent trade relations. Webster believes that "the battle between Theseus and Peirithoos and the Centaurs is a very early story. It has been recognized on a Geometric [725–700 B.C.] neck-amphora in Copenhagen" (175), which means not only that the centaur had been imported by the eighth century but that specifically Greek mythology involving Mycenaean heroes had had time to develop around it.

Upon arriving in Greek culture, the centaur appears to have undergone significant modifications in its symbolic or mythic purpose as well as in its appearance. A sharp distinction was made between the centaur Cheiron (and, to a lesser degree, the centaur Pholos) and the rest of the centaurs: Cheiron was perceived as wise, benevolent to mankind, and universally beloved. He, or his type, is also present on the Copenhagen vase: "on the front of the neck a Centaur holding a branch in each hand approaches a man wearing a *petasos* and also holding a branch in each hand. He is a traveller and they are not fighting. The branches are not weapons but the kind of branches carried by dancers or suppliants. The meeting is peaceful, and we should not think of a battle but perhaps of Peleus and Cheiron" (Webster 175). If Richmond Lattimore's date for Homer is correct (the late eighth or early seventh centuries B.C.; *Iliad* 28–29), the Copenhagen vase is approximately contemporary to the *Iliad* and the *Odyssey*, and the literature discusses what the art depicts. In the *Iliad*, Cheiron is a celebrated healer and a friend to man (4.218–19), the teacher of heroes (11.831), the maker of sophisticated weapons (16.143–44; 19.389–91), and, in summation, "the most righteous of the Centaurs" (11.831).

But the centaur population as a whole was associated with drunkenness and physical, especially sexual, violence. Perhaps this dichotomy between wisdom and violence was already implicit in the figures portrayed on Kassite boundary stones: on the one hand, the human face of the centaurs might have represented benevolence and guardianship; on the other, the dragon heads and scorpion tails might have suggested eroticism or the tendency to uncontrollable violence. In any case the Greeks seem to have made the dichotomy explicit early in the evolution of the Greek centaur. The Copenhagen vase depicts both types of centaur; so does Homer. Allusions to the Battle of the Lapiths and Centaurs are made in the *Iliad* (1.261 ff.; 2.740 ff.), while a more complete version of the story is told in the *Odyssey* (21.295–304): the centaur Eurytion, invited to the wedding of Peirithoos, became drunk with wine and created a disturbance (presumably he attempted to rape the bride, which is the traditional story, but this is not specified in the *Odyssey*). His ears and nose were cut off, he was thrown out, and he subsequently roused the centaurs to avenge his shame. After a lapse of several months there was a formal battle that the centaurs lost. The story is one of the most enduring and popular of centaur myths because it is one of the most significant, demonstrating what the centaur normally represented to the Greek: that element of human behavior which blazes up suddenly due to some stimulus. It is irrational, and violent to the point of threatening the human social fabric. The Greeks, a horse-loving and horse-breeding people, were familiar with the erotic reaction of a stallion presented with a mare in estrus, and this equine behavior may well be the reason why the semi-equine centaur became so apt a symbol for sudden irrational violence, particularly sexual violence. It took several centuries for this symbolism to evolve completely, but by Homer's time the average centaur is a potentially uncontrollable creature, although the violence does not manifest itself specifically as sexual violence in Homer's work. Rather,

It was wine . . . that drove the Centaur, famous Eurytion, distracted in the palace of great-hearted Peirithoos he visited the Lapiths. His brain went wild with drinking, and in his fury he did much harm in the house of Peirithoos. . . . Since his time there has been a feud between men and Centaurs, and he was the first who found his own evil in heavy drinking. (21.295–98; 303–04)

The centaur was a popular subject for vase-painting, and its appearance had changed since its arrival in Greece. The variety possessing four equine legs was retained as far as its basic shape was concerned, but underwent profound changes in details; in addition, a new variety was developed, a type having a complete human body which terminated in human legs and feet. Both are represented on vases from the Late Geometric Period, when centaurs first appear in art (ca. 725 B.C.), and both are to be found, sometimes on the same vase, through the Attic Period (ca. 750–480 B.C.). At first the types appear to have no significant distinction, but eventually they became polarized so that form followed function: Cheiron and Pholos were the two most civilized centaurs, Cheiron more so than Pholos. Both (Cheiron invariably, Pholos at times) are depicted with complete human bodies. If the centaur is Cheiron, he is always human-legged, usually fully clothed, and may or may not have equine ears. If Pholos, he is usually nude, equine-eared, and with equine forelegs. However, he can be equine-legged, yet draped; and, when human-legged, may sometimes be nude (Baur 137).

The centaur with four equine legs is, in general, more like beast and less like man. While he has a human head, he almost always has equine ears, is coarse-featured, and, in the Archaic Period, is always bearded. He is usually nude, and may have both human and equine genitals. There may, of course, be variations due to local customs in depicting centaurs; for example, in continental Greece they are typically shaggy-haired, while in Ionia and Etruria they are short-haired (Baur 137). These centaurs do not, as a rule, carry sophisticated weapons such as bows, but appear to prefer pine trunks, branches, or boulders. A favorite scene is the death of the hero Kaineus during the battle of the Lapiths and the Centaurs; the centaurs killed him by burying him beneath pine trunks and rocks.

A notable use of both types of centaurs occurs on the François vase, which dates from 560 B.C. and was painted by Klitias. It depicts the human-legged Cheiron, wearing a chiton and "[l]eading the procession of gods to honor the newly wedded pair, Peleus and Thetis . . . who grasps the r. [sic] hand of his old friend in hearty greeting" (Baur 100). In another band, the vase shows seven scenes from the battle of the Lapiths with equine-legged Centaurs (Baur 100 and Minto). Thus the vase juxtaposes the opposing roles of the centaurs: on the one hand is Cheiron, who upholds the human social structure by blessing a marriage; on the other are the centaurs who threaten to destroy society by their feral impulses.

These two types do not exhaust the centaurs of Greece, but they do constitute the major forms. In addition, a few winged centaurs are noteworthy, indicating that this type has not been entirely lost. There are also a number of sixth-century terra-cotta figures from Cyprus that might be more accurately termed centauroids, as they are combinations of man and bull rather than man and horse. Unlike the Minotaur, which is bull-headed and human-bodied, these possess human heads and bodies often terminating in human legs. Their heads have bulls' horns, their barrels are indeterminately equine or bovine, but the legs appear to end in cloven hoofs. They frequently have both human and animal sexual organs and are occasionally double-faced as well as double-torsoed. In these cases one body is male; the other, female. They seem to be fertility figures or spirits worshipping a bull-god. Statues of the bull-god have also been found at the sites (see Karageorghis).

Not the least among the numerous puzzles and unanswered questions clustering about the early development of this creature is the name ''centaur'' itself. Although Homer is the first poet to name the beast, calling it the κένταυρος, we know neither what, precisely, he thought they were, nor what the word itself means. Homer might have meant the half-equine creature; on the other hand, he may have been thinking simply of a tribe of rather wild human beings. Neither Homer nor Hesiod alludes to any specifically equine characteristic when discussing centaurs, unless calling them the ''beast men'' or ''hairy beast men'' (φῆρες [*Il.* 1.268; 2.743]), can be so construed. Although the half-equine creatures are found portrayed on pottery by 725 B.C., that does not mean the semiferine form was so widely disseminated by that time that it would have been familiar to everyone. Robert Graves claims that the centaurs Homer knew were a tribe of Pelasgians, ''the most warlike'' of whom ''were the Centaurs of Magnesia, whose clan totems included the wryneck and mountain lion. They also worshiped the horse. . . . The Centaurs under their sacred king Cheiron welcomed Achaean aid against their enemies the Lapiths, of Northern Thessaly'' (*Goddess*, rev.ed., 62).

The etymology of ''centaur''is also under debate. In the first edition of *The White Goddess* (1948, 45–46), and in *The Greek Myths* (sec. 7.7), Graves conjectured that the word derived from ''the Latin word *centuria*, or band of one hundred.'' In the amended edition of *The White Goddess* (1966, 63) he speculated that centaur derived from the Greek ''*centron*, a goat.'' Vinycomb (143) suggests that the term ''is most probably derived from the words κεντέω (to hunt, or to pursue) and ταῦρος (a bull)''; Jobes suggests that ''the origin of the name is uncertain; probably derived from kenteo, Greek for goad or spear'' (303). Less innocuously, Jeffrey Henderson has noted that ''κέντρον, any point or goad, was common for phallus'' (122), that ''ταῦρος . . . is the phallus'' (127) and also the cunt (133). It ''can also indicate the hindquarters. . . . This usage is reflected in . . . comic terms for aggressive (as opposed to pathic) homosexuals'' (202–3).

Pindar is the first poet to describe centaurs explicitly as semi-equine and to assign them myths of origin. In *Pythian 2* (475? B.C.) Pindar recounts how the race of centaurs began. The Lapith, Ixion, aspired to the love of Hera, and Zeus, in revenge, sent him a cloud that appeared to be the goddess. He made love to her, siring a son:

Without the blessing of the Graces did that mother bear him a monstrous offspring, there was never such a mother, never such a son—an offspring unhonoured either among men or amid the ordinances of the gods. And she reared him up, and called him by the name of Centaurus, who consorted with the Magnesian mares by the spurs of Pêlion, and thence there came into being a host wondrous to look upon, resembling both their parents, the dam's side down, the upper side the sire's. (lines 44–48)

Centaurus, the result of presumptuous and unlawful appetite, is himself the inheritor of perverted sexual appetite, and the final result is a race of beings that manifest impulsive, violent behavior and unlawful desires.

On the other hand, in *Pythian 3* (474? B.C.) Pindar informs us that Cheiron's parentage is completely different:

I would pray that Cheiron, son of Philyra, who is dead and gone, were now alive again,— he who once ruled far and wide as the offspring of Cronus, who was the son of Heaven. Would that that rugged monster with spirit kindly unto men, were reigning still in Pêlion's glens, even such as when, in olden days, he reared Asclêpius. (lines 1–11)

Pindar seems to have been nostalgically fond of Cheiron, to whom is also attributed an exalted and, for an immortal, natural conception which is directly opposed to the doubly depraved engendering of the centaurs as a race. Moreover, in other odes Pindar relates that Cheiron was married to Chariclo, had "pure daughters," and was obviously the only domestic centaur.

By the Attic Period virtually every myth concerned with centaurs was represented on vase-paintings or other artifacts; besides the battle with the Lapiths, the stories dealing with Herakles (particularly the Nessos story and Herakles' reception by Pholos in his cave) were common. Also found are the wooing and marriage of Peleus and Thetis, and the bringing of the infant heroes (especially Achilles and Herakles) to Cheiron for tutoring. In addition there is a small host of lesser, and at times unidentifiable, incidents. The "Nessos story was the most popular, though in the later [red-figure] period it is extremely rare" (Baur 136).

While in red-figure vase-painting (after 500 B.C.: attains peak between 500 and 480) the Nessos tale might have been on the wane, it found eloquent expression in drama when Sophocles composed *The Women of Trachis* in the mid– fifth century. To be sure, Nessos, long dead by the time the play opens, does not himself appear on stage. Nevertheless, he is central to both plot and theme: Herakles had been bringing home his bride, Deianeira, when, at the river Evenus (where Nessos earned a living by carrying people across the ford) the centaur attempted to rape her. According to Deianeira, she rode on the centaur's shoulders, but in the center of the stream "he grossly handled me" (line 565). Herakles rescued her by shooting the centaur through the lungs, and Nessos, as he was dying, instructed her to save his blood as a charm to bring Herakles back to her if he should ever love another woman more than herself. During the course of events, Deianeira finds use for the blood, which she had preserved by dipping a tunic into the poisoned liquid. When worn by Herakles, the garment clings to him and burns him so painfully that he is forced to make a funeral pyre and immolate himself. On one level, as duBois states, "the tragedy traces the consequences of Nessos' violation of Deianeira. The centaur, in laying his hands on her, broke into the human exchange of women and caused disaster to the house of Herakles. His intervention leads to the death of both the violated woman and her husband" (98). However, the play moves on deeper levels as well; as Dorothea Wender has argued, this is a play about sex, but not one in which "sex is . . . fructifying or fun or funny, but sinister and tragic" (4). The sexuality is polarized between Herakles, "the archetypal rapist-philanderer hero" who is a failure as husband and father because he fears women, and Deianeira, who "is precisely the sort of motherly, 'clinging' woman he fears most" (4). She is "clingy" because she is afraid of being hurt physically, sexually, or emotionally by men. This is a mutually destructive situation. The several monsters—the "river who took the form of . . . a bull (the masculine beast *par excellence*)" (Wender 4–5), the recurrent serpents, and, of course, Nessos—symbolize what Herakles is, and what Deianeira fears. When the elements they represent manifest themselves externally, in the shape of monsters, they can be destroyed by Herakles; but they also represent that which is within and not eradicable, and which destroys both protagonists.

The violent, sexually-charged, feral centaur was very much alive in late Archaic and Classical Greece, and, in the centauromachia of the Lapiths and Centaurs, found its place in the monumental sculpture of the pediments and metopes in the new temples. However, the story had changed since Homer's allusions to it in the *Iliad* and *Odyssey*. In all the early versions the battle took place outdoors after a lapse of some months. Nestor speaks in the *Iliad* (1.262 ff.) of coming to the aid of the Lapiths, which suggests that the Lapiths had time to summon help and that their allies were able to marshal their forces. Moreover, Peirithoos' son, who was not conceived prior to the wedding night, was born on the day of the battle, so the time lapse had minimally to be nine months. Thus it was a formally arranged battle held in a suitable place outdoors: vase-paintings usually indicate uneven ground; Kaineus is buried alive; no women are ever present; and the Lapiths wear armor and fight with weapons. This is the version represented on the François vase (ca. 570–560 B.C.). "But in the Early Classical period the scene changes. . . . In sculpture the new version appears for the first time in the west pediment of the temple of Zeus at Olympia" (Barron 26). Now the battle takes place at the wedding; characteristics of the banqueting hall include level terrain, the presence of women and boys (both of whom are sexually menaced by the centaurs), the absence of all weapons with the exception of Theseus' ax, and evidence of haste in the swirling garments. Page duBois calls the centaurs "anticulture personified" (29) to the Greeks of the fifth and fourth centuries B.C.; their chief purpose was as the symbol of bestiality, a destructive force:

They are not simply nature spirits, or river creatures, but also hybrid monsters whose existence in myth permitted speculation about boundaries and kinds. The centaurs formed an asymmetrical, overly masculine, violently bestial alternative to the norm of what was seen by the Greeks as human culture. They were hyper-masculine; the violence and sexuality of horses was super-added to human virility in their bodies. (31)

In the monumental sculpture of Classical Greece, the centaur represents everything that is to be excluded from the Polis. Other examples of the centauromachy of the Lapiths and Centaurs include the metopes of the Parthenon at Athens, and the metopes of the temple of Apollo Epikouris at Bassae. Later, a frieze was also sculpted for the tomb of Mausolus (ca. 350 B.C.).

In the following centuries centaurs appear to have, on the whole, become the "peaceful followers of Dionysius and Eros" (Avery 267). Artistically, perhaps because of the influence of monumental sculpture, the Roman centaur became the typical human-torsoed creature with four equine legs.

The most significant Roman contribution to the history of the centaur is, of course, Ovid's *Metamorphoses* (completed 7 A.D.). Ovid makes numerous allusions to centaurs in his work as a whole, but treats the battle with the Lapiths extensively (12.210–535). Nestor tells the story of Peirithoos' marriage and describes a battle that can only be a burlesque of battle scenes in the *Iliad*. There is a whole army of centaurs, including Pholos and Nessos, and some of them must be Ovid's invention. Two, Cyllarus and Hylonome, are particularly interesting. Cyllarus was young, a handsome blond in his human part and a fabulous horse in his equine part. He was loved by Hylonome, and

there was no other centaur-maid more comely in all the forest depths. She, by her coaxing ways, by loving and confessing love, alone possessed Cyllarus; and by her toilet, too, so far as such a thing was possible to such a form; for now she smoothed her long locks with a comb, now twined rosemary, now violets or roses in her hair, and sometimes wore white lilies. (12. 405–11)

When Cyllarus was killed, Hylonome "threw himself upon the spear which had pierced Cyllarus and fell in a dying embrace upon her lover" (12.426–28). With the presence of handsome males, of feminine females, monogamous romance, and sentimental suicide, we are far indeed from the feral centaurs of Archaic and Classical Greece.

One more development, dating from perhaps the fifth century B.C., should be noted: this is the formation of the signs of the zodiac. The year "410 is the date of the earliest surviving personal horoscope" (Gleadow 162); this horoscope is Babylonian, and there is not much doubt that Sagittarius was derived from Kassite boundary stones. Over the centuries Sagittarius appears to have been transposed to the skies along with other guardian figures from the stones, such as the scorpion-man, which became Scorpio, and Ea, the "antelope of the subterranean ocean" (Gleadow 166), which became Capricorn. There are, of course, two constellations having centaur associations: Sagittarius the Archer in the Northern Hemisphere, and Centaurus, "the southern Centaur" (Lum 186). As Sagittarius, the centaur was known in Islamic art.

The centaur was not forgotten in Western Europe during the Middle Ages. Its position in the zodiac would have kept it from extinction, but, perhaps because of its connection with sexual licentiousness and because of the *Physiologus*, which characterized the only type of centaur of which it was aware (the ono-centaur or ass-centaur) as a symbol of the Devil (Curley 24), the centaur flour-ished mainly in the marginalia of European art and literature, where it served decorative (and occasionally allegorical) purposes. It is, of course, to be found in bestiaries as well as in books of hours (as Sagittarius), and in heraldry (King Stephen I of England, for example [Vinycomb 142]). The creature usually has four equine legs; if it has only two equine legs then it stands awkwardly upright upon them, having no human legs (to my knowledge) during the Middle Ages (or, for that matter, at any time since Classical Greece). Sometimes the medieval centaur has a nude torso, but it is usually clothed with a tunic or jacket, and carries a bow.

The Bayeux Tapestry (ca. 1073–83 [MacLagan 27]) contains two borders, each approximately three inches wide and running the length of the tapestry (about 231 feet [MacLagan 16]); these borders are "made up of repeating or-nament, in slanting lines, and more or less fantastic birds and beasts, single or in pairs" (MacLagan 15). Among these animals cavort five centaurs: there are two winged but armless beasts below the scene of Harold on his way to visit Duke William. Two long-haired and clothed centaurs with outstretched arms are to be found in the upper border above "William's Messengers on their Way," while still another clothed beast is beneath "Harold Rescues Two Soldiers." This specimen is a centauroid, possessing leonine paws; it is clothed, and part of an unidentified little scene. Leontocentaurs appear to have enjoyed a slight vogue during the Middle Ages. Another is found on a stone boss in the Muniment room at Westminster Abbey (Stone, pl. 93), while a female was carved on the West Portal of San Michele in Lucca (thirteenth century [Mode 89]).

The most significant literary use of the centaur during medieval times occurs in the *Commedia* when Dante meets Cheiron, Nessos, and Pholos in the seventh circle of Hell (12.55–138), the Circle of Violence, where the centaurs gallop around the circle to shoot any soul who attempts to lift itself out of the boiling river of blood (Phlegethon). Dante's use of the centaurs is extraordinary in its complete understanding of the beast. In a passage of less than a hundred lines, Dante captured everything of significance about the appearance, nature, legends, and functions of the creature. When Cheiron first sees Dante and Virgil, he takes an arrow from the quiver at his waist. With its notched end, he brushes "back his beard along his jaws" (Singleton, in Brieger 1:13) in order to speak. Thus

Dante has reminded us twice that in these creatures two natures join: the quiver hangs at the waist, where the man is attached to the horse, and his beard, reminiscent of Homer's description of centaurs as the "shaggy-haired people," is so thick, so animallike, that it has to be pushed away to permit speech. However, when Cheiron does speak, it is to observe "how the feet of the one behind move what they touch" (Sayers 12.81); in short, he has seen that Dante is alive. Cheiron has not lost his scientific perception or his intellect. When Virgil introduces the beasts to Dante he touches upon their violent traits as well as Cheiron's intellect and the centaurs' legendary roles. Finally, since Nessos in life carried people across fords, he does so now, taking Dante and Virgil across Phlegethon. With seeming effortlessness, Dante has presented us with a complete portrait of the two types of classical centaur and has demonstrated their suitability as "guardians and ministers of eternal justice" (Brieger 1:16) in the Circle of the Violent.

The only thing Dante did not do, beyond calling them *fiere isnelle* (Grandgent 12.76), "swift creatures," was to describe them specifically as semi-equine. As an educated Italian, Dante had no doubt not only read Ovid but had also seen a few Roman bronzes of centaurs. He may have assumed that all his readers would be familiar with the beast, but, in fact, occasionally illuminators of the *Commedia* did become confused. For one thing, a few illustrators of the Minotaur (also found in canto 12 of *Hell*) made it look like a centaur (see Brieger 1:95–96 for a discussion of minotaur-centaurs). For another, the illuminator of MS. Egerton 943 evidently knew that centaurs were supposed to be half-man and half-horse, but had never seen an example. So at one point this artist created a centaur whose human head and neck were stuck directly on the equine breast; there were, of course, no human torso and arms. Then, when the artist had to portray Cheiron, Pholos, and Nessos as archers, he was totally at a loss, and depicted the three centaurs as simply naked human beings (Brieger 2:151).

Among the oddities spawned in centaur lore during the Middle Ages is a comment in Mandeville's *Travels*, informing its readers that, in the land of Bacharia "be many hippotaynes that dwell sometime in the water and sometime on the land. And they be half man and half horse. . . . And they eat men when they may take them" (Pollard 177). Chaucer, incidentally, was aware of the centaur, probably from Ovid and also from Statius' *Thebaid* (2.563–64), and, of course, from Sagittarius, but beyond references made in passing was uninterested in the creature. Caxton translated Le Fevre's *The Recuile of the Histories of Troie*, in which the centaur appears on the battlefield as a Trojan ally. He is described as having "herye lyke an horse & had his eyen red as a cole and shotte ryght wel wyth a bowe, this beast made ye Grekes sore aferde, and slewe manye of hem wt his bowe" (bk. 3, f. 17v).

Caxton's translation was used by Shakespeare for *Troilus and Cressida*. Jeanne Addison Roberts notes that "Menelaus, at a moment of Greek rout, echoes the idea, 'The dreadful Sagittary / Appalls our numbers' " (2). As Roberts observes, "If Shakespeare's audience would truly have favored the Trojans in this war, the Sagittary is a political savior; but the fact that . . . he fights for the Trojans suggests, I think, the Greek origin of the tale—centaurs and Amazons embody fears of threats to the sovereignty of the Greek state and to the definition of Greek man'' (7).

There are several passing allusions to centaurs in Shakespeare, but perhaps the most significant, beyond the one from *Troilus and Cressida*, is Lear's assessment of Goneril and Regan: ''Down from the waist they are Centaurs, / Though women all above'' (IV.vi.124–25). Of this statement Roberts notes that ''Lear's image-sequence is doubly disturbing because it evokes not only the collapsing of human and bestial but also the reversal of male and female roles. In the course of his speech the woman has moved from the position of horse to that of rider, although the final metaphor is blurred—in fact down from the waist most centaurs are horses'' (10). Both allusions suggest that to Shakespeare the centaur meant something fairly similar to what it had represented in Classical Greece: namely, a threat to established social order. The centaur remains a creature of two worlds, yet belonging to neither, and continues to serve as a means of exploring boundaries between the human and the bestial.

In the nineteenth century the centaur, never forgotten, suddenly aroused greater literary interest. Goethe made Cheiron a figure of central importance to the Classical Walpurgis Night of *Faust, Part 2*, while Maurice de Guérin wrote the prose poem, *Le Centaure*. Goethe's Cheiron makes a brief appearance, but in both works while the centaurs are present they are the focus of interest, and no longer brief allusions. In *Faust*, literature returns to the myth of Cheiron; he is the wise centaur who instructs Faust and carries him on a physical and spiritual journey to Helen. Thus Cheiron has returned to his age-old roles of teacher and blesser-of-wedlock. To these functions, Goethe added the sexual symbolism of the centaur; however, Cheiron is not the representative of violent sexuality but what Goethe conceived to be the epitome of masculinity: movement, kinesis. ''Cheiron is half man and perfectly in motion'' (Borchardt 249).

Guérin's *Le Centaure* is a monologue. The centaur, Macareus, speaks; he is the last of his race, and recounts his life to a human being, Melampus. The work is unique; told from the perspective of the centaur, it attempts to understand what the life, perceptions, and sensations of such a being might be like. There is no suggestion that Macareus ever felt himself to be other than well adapted to his pastoral world and totally in harmony with nature.

In art the centaur had become popular during the Italian Renaissance, and its popularity has continued into the twentieth century: Pisanello, Botticelli, Michelangelo, Giovanni da Bologna, Baldung-Grien, Rubens, Böcklin, Menzel, Rodin, and Picasso (Mode 90), among others, have worked with centaurs. Böcklin, a Swiss painter active through much of the nineteenth century, is noteworthy. Fascinated by mythological subjects in general, he painted various feral beings. Among his works are several studies of centaurs, and while his *Battle of the Centaurs* is the most renowned, perhaps the most amusing is a study of a centaur conferring with a smith over the state of his right forehoof.

The twentieth century has been a rich one for centaurs in literature. In my opinion the finest use of the figure in mimetic literature is that of John Updike's Cheiron in *The Centaur*. This novel, which is structurally as twi-formed as the creature itself (see Vickery for a discussion of Updike's narrative art), deals profoundly with the myth of Cheiron the teacher and self-sacrificer, superimposing the centaur, his mountain environment, and his beautiful, brilliant students (all of whom became heroes or benefactors to mankind) directly upon a middle-aged teacher in Pennsylvania and his puberty-stricken, anti-intellectual American teenagers. The idyllic world of pastoral Greece is thus juxtaposed to an ugly modern city in the middle of a poverty-stricken rural district. Still another work of realistic fiction that might be considered to explore a centaurlike concept is Shaffer's *Equus*, with its use of human figures to represent horses and the identification the boy makes between himself and the animals when he rides them.

It is, of course, in science fiction and fantasy that centaurs abound. Sometimes, as in C. S. Lewis' *Chronicles of Narnia*, they exist mainly for background color, but often they form an integral part of the narrative. The centaurs in these works represent all aspects of the ancient myths, and writers frequently create their own hybrids. Philip José Farmer, for instance, has "half-horses" (his term) in his "World of Tiers" series (see especially *A Private Cosmos*). These creatures are a combination of horse and Plains Indian, and, having inherited not only the appearance of the Indians but also their culture, gallop about wearing war paint and trying to sate their bloodlust. Poul Anderson, on the other hand, went back to Babylonian myth for *Fire Time*, which deals with a planet called Ishtar and has, as its native sentient species, leontocentaurs that are clearly derived from Assyrian art (Parrot, figs. 199, 224).

Most contemporary centaurs, however, are taken from Greek myth and have the traditional form with human torso, arms, and head and a horse's body with four equine legs. These creatures are usually rich combinations in personality, often blending knowledge with turbulence (or at least the potential for turbulence). Examples include John Varley's gaudy, multi-sexed centaurs in *Titan*, *Wizard and Demon*, James Kahn's *World Enough, and Time* and *Time's Dark Laughter*, Thomas Burnett Swann's *Cry Silver Bells, Day of the Minotaur, The Forest of Forever*, and *The Weirwoods*, and, of course, Piers Anthony's Xanth series—particularly *Castle Roogna, A Spell for Chameleon*, and *Centaur Aisle*. Anthony's novels also demonstrate that centaurs can be treated with affectionate humor; a notable example is Arnolde the Archivist of *Centaur Aisle*, who is a myopic, pedantic Appaloosa centaur, appalled to discover he possesses magical powers. Still another centaur on the lighter side is Cairon, the black-man, zebra-striped-horse centaur in Michael Ende's *The Neverending Story*. The centaur is in no danger of extinction today.

For those who might be interested in further research, the finest and most recent work on the creature is Page duBois' *Centaurs and Amazons*. In addition, the beast attracted great attention from art historians and classicists during the late nineteenth and early twentieth centuries. Although dated, many of these works are still helpful; I am particularly grateful to Paul V. C. Baur's *Centaurs in Ancient Art*. Thomas B. L. Webster's *From Mycenae to Homer* deals only in passing with centaurs, but is most helpful in bridging that mysterious and important gap between Mycenaean and Archaic Greece when the Greeks incorporated the centaur and its symbolism into their lifeblood. John P. Barron's "New Light on Old Walls: The Murals of the Theseion" contains a superb discussion of the Battle between the Lapiths and the Centaurs.

BIBLIOGRAPHY

Anderson, Poul. *Fire Time*. New York: Ballantine, 1974.

Andree, Rolf. *Arnold Böcklin: Die Gemälde*. Zurich: Schweizerisches Institut für Kunstwissenschaft, 1977.

Anthony, Piers. *Castle Roogna*, New York: Ballantine, 1979.

———. *Centaur Aisle*. New York: Ballantine, 1981.

———. *The Source of Magic*. New York: Ballantine, 1979.

———. *A Spell for Chameleon*. New York: Ballantine, 1977.

Ashmole, Bernard. *Architect and Sculptor in Classical Greece: The Wrightsman Lectures*. New York: New York University Press, 1972.

Avery, Catherine B., ed. *The New Century Classical Handbook*. New York: Appleton, 1962.

Barron, John P. "New Light on Old Walls: The Murals of the Theseion," *Journal of Hellenic Studies* 92 (1972): 20–45.

Baur, Paul V. C. *Centaurs in Ancient Art: The Archaic Period*. Berlin: Karl Curtius, 1912.

Borchardt, Frank L. "Goethe, Schiller, Sphinx, Centaur and Sex." *Monatshefte für Deutschen Unterricht, Deutsche Sprache und Literatur*. 64 (1972): 247–55.

Brieger, Peter, Millard Meiss, and Charles Singleton. *Illuminated Manuscripts of the Divine Comedy*. 2 vols. Bollingen Series 81. Princeton: Princeton University Press, 1969.

The Cambridge Ancient History. Ed. J. B. Bury, S. A. Cook, and F. E. Adcock. 2nd ed. London: Cambridge University Press, 1924. Vol. 1.

Colvin, Sidney. "On Representations of Centaurs in Greek Vase-Painting." *Journal of Hellenic Studies* 1 (1881): 107–67.

Curley, Michael J., trans. *Physiologus*. Austin: University of Texas Press, 1979.

Dante Alighieri. *La divina commedia*. Ed. C. H. Grandgent. Rev. Charles Singleton. Cambridge: Harvard University Press, 1972.

———. *The Divine Comedy: Hell*. Trans. and ed. Dorothy L. Sayers. Harmondsworth: Penguin, 1949.

Detienne, Marcel. *The Gardens of Adonis*. Trans. J. Lloyd. Atlantic Highlands, N.J.: Humanities Press, 1977.

duBois, Page. *Centaurs and Amazons*. Ann Arbor: University of Michigan Press, 1982.

Dumézil, Georges. *Le Problème des centaures: Etude de mythologie comparée indo-européene*. Paris: Librairie Orientaliste Paul Geuthner, 1929.

Ende, Michael. *The Neverending Story*. Trans. Ralph Manheim. New York: Doubleday, 1983.

Farmer, Philip José. *A Private Cosmos*. 1968; rpt. New York: Ace, 1981.

Gleadow, Rupert. *The Origin of the Zodiac*. New York: Castle, 1968.

Goethe, Johann Wolfgang von. *Faust*. Trans. George M. Priest. 1941; rpt. New York: Knopf, 1950.

Graves, Robert. *The Greek Myths*. 1955; rpt. Baltimore: Penguin, 1957. Vol. 1.

————. *The White Goddess: A Historical Grammar of Poetic Myth*. New York: Creative Age Press, 1948.

————. *The White Goddess: A Historical Grammar of Poetic Myth*. Amended and enl. ed. New York: Farrar, Straus and Giroux, 1966.

Guérin, Maurice de. *From Centaur to Cross*. Trans. H. Bedford-Jones. New York: Covici-Friede, 1929.

Hammond, N. G. L., and H. H. Scullard, eds. *The Oxford Classical Dictionary*. 2nd ed. Oxford: Clarendon Press, 1970.

Henderson, Jeffrey. *The Maculate Muse: Obscene Language in Attic Comedy*. New Haven: Yale University Press, 1975.

Hesiod. *Hesiod: The Works and Days, Theogony, The Shield of Herakles*. Trans. Richmond Lattimore. 1959; rpt. Ann Arbor: University of Michigan Press, 1977.

Hinks, Roger. *Myth and Allegory in Ancient Art*. London: The Warburg Institute, 1939.

Homer. *The Iliad of Homer*. Trans. Richmond Lattimore. Chicago: University of Chicago Press, 1951.

————. *The Odyssey of Homer*. Trans. Richmond Lattimore. 1965; rpt. New York: Harper and Row, 1967.

Jobes, Gertrude. *Dictionary of Mythology, Folklore and Symbols*. Pt. 1. New York: Scarecrow Press, 1962.

Kahn, James. *Time's Dark Laughter*. New York: Ballantine, 1982.

————. *World Enough, and Time*. New York: Ballantine, 1980.

Karageorghis, V. "Notes on Some Centaurs from Cyprus." In *Charisterīon eis A.K. Orlandon*. Bibliothēkēt en Athēnais Archaiologikēs Hetaireias. Tome 54, 1–4. Athens, 1965–68. 2:160–69.

Le Fevre, Raoul. *The Recuile of the Histories of Troie*. Trans. William Caxton, London, 1553.

Lum, Peter. *The Stars in Our Heaven: Myths and Fables*. New York: Pantheon, 1948.

MacLagan, Eric. *The Bayeux Tapestry*. 1943; rpt. Harmondsworth: Penguin, 1949.

Mandeville, John. *Travels of Sir John Mandeville*. Ed. A. W. Pollard. London: Macmillan, 1923.

Michaelis, A. T. F. "Kentaurenkopf von einer Parthenonmetope." *Deutsches Archäologisches Institut. Jahrbuch* 11 (1896):300–304.

Minto, Antonio. "La centauromachia del vaso François." In *Anthemon: scritti di archeologia e di antichità classiche in onore di Carlo Anti*. Firenze: G. C. Sansoni, 1955, 21–40.

Mode, Heinz. *Fabulous Beasts and Demons*. London: Phaidon, 1975.

Oelschig, P. *De Centauromachiae in Arte Graeca Figuris*. Halle, 1911.

Ovid. *Metamorphoses*. Trans. Frank Justus Miller. Vol. 2. 1916; rpt. Cambridge: Harvard University Press, 1976.

Parrot, André. *The Arts of Assyria*. Trans. Stuart Gilbert and James Emmons. New York: Golden Press, 1961.

Pausanias. *Description of Greece*. Trans. W. H. S. Jones. 5 vols. Cambridge: Harvard University Press, 1918–35.

Peck, Harry Thurston, ed. *Harper's Dictionary of Classical Literature and Antiquities*. New York: Cooper Square, 1965.

Pindar. *The Odes of Pindar: Including the Principal Fragments*. Trans. John Sandys. 1915; rpt. Cambridge: Harvard University Press, 1968.

Pollitt, J. J. *Art and Experience in Classical Greece*. Cambridge: Cambridge University Press, 1972.

Robert, Carl. *Kentaurenkampf und Tragoedienscene: Zwei Marmorbilder aus Herculaneum*. Halle, 1898.

Roberts, Jeanne Addison. "The Dreadful Sagittary and Other Shakespearean Nightmares." Paper presented at Shakespeare Association of America Annual Meeting, Cambridge, Mass., April 20, 1984.

Rowland, Beryl. *Animals with Human Faces: A Guide to Animal Symbolism*. Knoxville: University of Tennessee Press, 1973.

Schiffler, Birgitt. *Die Typologie des Kentauren in der antiken Kunst: vom 10. bis zum Ende d. 4. Jhs. v. Chr.* Frankfurt: Lang, 1976.

Seznec, Jean. *The Survival of the Pagan Gods: The Mythological Tradition and Its Place in Renaissance Humanism and Art*. Trans. Barbara Sessions. Bollingen Series 38. New York: Pantheon, 1953.

Sophocles. *Electra and Other Plays*. Trans. E. F. Watling. 1953; rpt. Harmondsworth: Penguin, 1954.

Stone, Lawrence. *Sculpture in Britain: The Middle Ages*. Baltimore: Penguin, 1955.

Swann, Thomas Burnett. *Cry Silver Bells*. New York: Daw, 1977.

———. *Day of the Minotaur*. New York: Ace, 1966.

———. *The Forest of Forever*. New York: Ace, 1971.

———. *The Weirwoods*. New York: Ace, 1967.

Tarbell, F. B. "*Centauromachy* and *Amazonomachy* in Greek Art: The Reasons for their Popularity." *American Journal of Archeology* 24, 2nd ser. (1920): 226–31.

Updike, John. *The Centaur*. New York: Knopf, 1972.

Varley, John. *Demon*. New York: Berkley, 1984.

———. *Titan*. New York: Berkley, 1980.

———. *Wizard*. New York: Berkley, 1981.

Vickery, John B. "The Centaur: Myth, History and Narrative." *Modern Fiction Studies* 20 (1974): 29–43.

Vinycomb, John. *Fictitious and Symbolic Creatures in Art, with Special Reference to Their Use in British Heraldry*. London: Chapman and Hall, 1906.

Webster, Thomas B. L. *From Mycenae to Homer*. London: Metheun, 1958.

Wender, Dorothea. "The Will of the Beast: Sexual Imagery in the *Trachiniae*." *Ramus* 3 (1974): 1–17.

_____ Creatures of Darkness

17

The Vampire

James Craig Holte

The dark images abound. Caped Bela Lugosi pointing out the beautiful sounds of the children of the night. The outline of a bat against a full moon. Mirrors refusing to return a reflection. Windows hung with garlic and coffin lids closing at dawn. Erotic vampire paintings by Boleslas Biegas and Edvard Munch. The castle, graveyard, blood.

The undead are undergoing a renaissance. In various shapes, vampires can be found in comic books, on Broadway, on television serials, and in the movies, in drugstore paperback racks, and in works of literary scholarship, and even on the front of cereal boxes. They have become a standard feature on music videos, and they occasionally grace the front pages of newspaper tabloids. The vampire, a figure as ancient as recorded history and one of the central mythic figures in English literature since the eighteenth century, has been adopted by contemporary popular culture and transformed from mythic symbol to popular entertainment. Vampires are everywhere.

The *Oxford English Dictionary* defines the vampire as "a preternatural being of a malignant nature (in the original and usual form of the belief, a reanimated corpse), supposed to seek nourishment, or do harm, by sucking the blood of sleeping persons; a man or woman abnormally endowed with similar habits." Because of the popularity and influence of Bram Stoker's novel *Dracula* and the Lugosi film of 1931, the most popular image of the vampire is that of Dracula, a Transylvanian count with dark hair and formal dress who lusts after the blood of beautiful young women and can transform himself into a bat, a wolf, or a wisp of smoke. The image of the vampire is far older than Stoker, however, and far more complex.

While related to, and often confused with, the werewolf, the vampire is a separate creature. Its origin is a dead person reanimated; it is not controlled by the moon, and it needs blood for nourishment. The vampire is not possessed by a demon, although some writers state that this is the case; rather the spirit of the dead person inhabits its own body. Neither ghost nor animal, neither dead nor alive, the vampire is a thing unto itself, undead.

The vampire is ancient. Devendra Varma, in his introduction to *Varney the Vampire or the Feast of Blood*, traces the vampire into the Himalayan Mountains, where over three thousand years ago the earliest vampire lived in a variety of forms including the bloodthirsty mother goddess, Kali, and the Tibetan lord of death, Yama. From this homeland, according to Varma, vampires and vampire legends moved westward into Eastern Europe, Greece, Arabia, and Africa. Whatever the origins, vampire myths and legends existed long before Christianity in such diverse places as Egypt, India, China, and Greece. In addition, vampire myths have been unearthed in Malaysia, South and Central America, and Southern Africa.

Specific references to vampirism abound in the records of Babylonia and Assyria. R. Campbell Thompson, in *The Devils and Evil Spirits of Babylonia*, discusses the belief in the Ekimmu, the soul of a dead person that could not rest and wandered about the earth tormenting the living until a priest could exorcise it (1:xxiii–xxv). In addition, Assyrian, Babylonian, and ancient Hebrew legends refer to Lilitu, Lilith, Lamia, Lamme, or Lamashto, a night-roaming female monster who sought the blood of young children. According to the Talmud, Lilith was Adam's original wife. She argued with him over his authority and left him, but her children were destroyed on account of her disobedience. After the creation of Eve, Lilith—undead, immortal, and vengeful—attempted to kill all of Eve's children. A similar legend appears in Greek mythology. Lamia bears Zeus' children, but jealous Hera kills them. Seeking revenge, Lamia wanders the earth attempting to kill as many children as possible.

Violence and sexuality, the two most consistent elements in vampire lore, are present in these early stories. Sexuality begets jealousy and violence. The vampire in legend, literature, and art provides a figure which unites the lust for blood and the lust for sex. It is always depicted as a creature with great hungers.

Modern vampire scholarship recognizes this combination as one of the main reasons for the attractiveness of the vampire as a figure for storytellers. Such works as James Twitchell's *The Living Dead*, Montague Summers' *The Vampire: His Kith and Kin* and *The Vampire in Europe*, Dudley Wright's *The Book of Vampires*, Raymond McNally's *A Clutch of Vampires*, and Anthony Masters' *The Natural History of the Vampire* guide readers to an understanding of the vampire and its popularity. In doing so, they suggest four general areas of study: the vampire in classical myth and literature, non-European vampires, the influence of Christianity on vampire legends, and the modern vampire.

Classical literature provides a rich field for vampire hunters. Blood sacrifices to appease the dead are mentioned frequently in Greek literature, and Wright and Summers see them as references to vampirism. Euripides, Sophocles, Homer, Pausanias, Strabo, Aelian, and Suidas refer to the lust of the dead for blood, and the Greeks believed in the strigae, dangerous birds which flew by night seeking infants to devour and blood to drink. More specifically, Summers and McNally direct readers to two explicit vampire tales.

The first is the story of Philinnion from Phlegon's "Concerning Wonderous Things" in *Fragmenta Historicorum Graecorum* (see Summers, *Vampire in Europe* 35–37). This second-century tale, which influenced Goethe's "The Bride of Corinth," describes how Machates, a handsome young man, was visited at night by a beautiful young woman while staying at the house of Demostratus in Corinth. Appearing only at night and leaving before dawn, the woman turns out to be Philinnion, Demostratus' daughter, who has been dead for six months. Compelled to remain after sunrise, Philinnion falls lifeless. Her grave is searched, found to be empty, and Hyllus, a local seer, orders her to be burned outside the city walls. Machates kills himself in grief.

The second vampire story can be found in Philostratus' third-century *Life of Apollonius of Tyana* (4.25). Apollonius was a first-century Pythagorean philosopher and ascetic reputed to have magical powers. Menippus, a handsome young man and student of philosophy, is in love with a mysterious young woman. Apollonius discovers that the woman is a vampire who wishes to have pleasure with Menippus before she devours him. The philosopher eventually makes the vampire depart.

The vampires mentioned above have some of the characteristics of their modern kin—night walking, a taste for blood, and sexual motivation. Vampirism in other cultures can be quite different. In *The Vampire in Legend, Fact and Art* Basil Copper notes that Indian belief accepts female vampires who haunt crossroads and drink the blood of elephants. In Japan, the medieval folk tale of the Vampire Cat of Nabeshima depicts a large cat which attacks people and sucks blood from their necks. In Malaysia, the vampires known as Langsuirs are predominantly female, and in addition to attacking people they have a fondness for fish. Numerous vampire stories exist in Chinese mythology (see Willoughby-Meade). One Chinese belief was that a demon would take over a dead body, preserve it from corruption, and prey upon the living. Another Chinese superstition was that each man has two souls. If the moon or the sun should shine on an unburied body, the evil soul would gain strength and would come searching for human blood. Unlike the Western vampire, which infects its victim with vampiristic tendencies, the Chinese vampire apparently does not.

Even within the Western tradition there is little uniformity of belief concerning vampires. The word "vampire" itself has a confusing history. It first appeared in English in 1734 in *The Travels of Three English Gentlemen*. The word derives from the Magyar *vampir*, a word loosely translated as "undead" and which occurs in similar form in Russian, Polish, Bulgarian, Serbian, and Czech. The Greek word for vampire is *vrykolakas*, which means "drumlike" and describes the rough skin of the vampire. *Nosferatu* or "living corpse" is another Eastern European term for vampire. In Latin *strix*, which means "screech owl," is often used to denote a vampire, and in Portuguese the word *bruxsa*, signifying "a bird-woman who sucks the blood of children'' (Robbins 522), is used. Vampires are sometimes called revenants, or the dead who return, but that term refers to a larger category of beings which includes ghosts.

While vampire beliefs are varied, certain elements of the vampire myth are consistent. The most important are the inability to experience death, the importance of blood, and the sexual connection between vampire and victim. In addition, vampires usually are pallid in appearance before drinking blood, they take little or no food, and they have a foul odor.

In placing the vampire within a cultural framework, scholars like Twitchell and Summers observe that blood seems forever imbued in man's consciousness with mythic importance. In both classical myth and early Christianity the blood-is-life motif is continually repeated as an objective statement and psychological fact. In ancient times blood sacrifice appears to be almost universal, often employed as a means to acquire strength or power, and the sacrament of the Eucharist is based on the transfer of power through the sharing of blood. A vampire cheats death by taking blood, the life force, from the living.

The importance of the erotic elements of the vampire myth cannot be overstated. With the rare exceptions of vampires who prey on children and animals, vampires combine sexual and blood hungers. Male vampires lust after young women, and female vampires thirst for virile young men. The penetration of the victim with phallic teeth is obviously sexual, as is the ecstasy produced by the actual blood-taking.

Aside from these core elements, there is no consistency in vampire lore. Romanian, Russian, Greek, and other traditions list multitudes of ways to become a vampire (Summers, *Vampire: Kith and Kin* 77–170). In Greek folklore, suicides, excommunicates, people who die in mortal sin, people born between Christmas and Epiphany, people who eat the flesh of a sheep killed by a wolf, and people with blue eyes or red hair may become vampires. In Eastern Europe an unbaptized child will become a vampire, as will a man who sought wealth too zealously, the seventh child of the same sex born into a single family, a child whose mother did not eat salt during pregnancy, and a man who was cursed by his parents. In Russian legends a corpse can be turned into a vampire if a human shadow falls upon it, a bird flies over it, or a cat or young boy jumps over it. The most common way a vampire is created, however, is by the attack of another vampire.

Similarly diverse are the accepted methods of defeating a vampire (Summers, *Vampire: Kith and Kin* 202–10). The most universally accepted ways to destroy a vampire are to drive a stake through its heart, chop off its head, and burn the body. Some authorities maintain that each of these actions alone is sufficient, while others hold that all three must be performed. Some traditions stipulate a particular kind of wood must be used for the stake, often hawthorn or maple, both thought to be the wood of the cross; and most traditions state that the stake must be driven and the head cut with a single stroke. The only universal antidote for vampires is garlic, although there is no explanation provided other than the "virtu" of the plant itself. Greek belief suggests that vampires cannot cross running water, while European legends hold that a suspected vampire should be buried at a crossroads so that when it rises from the grave it will become confused and remain transfixed at the spot.

Shape-shifting has also been associated with vampires. Generally, vampires are thought to be able to take the shapes of animals often associated with witchcraft and other evils; the most common forms are the dog, the wolf, the cat, and the bat. In addition, vampires, according to some legends, can change into smoke, mist, and fog. Particularly in Eastern Europe, it is believed that vampires escape from their graves in this manner.

Christian belief played an important part in the development of vampire lore. According to Montague Summers, who describes the Christian position in detail in *The Vampire: His Kith and Kin*, Christianity accepts the existence of vampires and sees the power of the Devil working in their creation. Since vampires become the servants of Satan, the Church has power over them. Thus vampires flee from and can be destroyed by the crucifix, relics of the saints, the sign of the cross, holy water, and above all, a consecrated host. A book that influenced the Christian attitude toward vampires is the *Malleus Maleficarum* (Witch Hammer), written by two Dominican priests, Jakob Sprenger and Prior Heinrich Kramer, and published in 1486. Written as a question-and-answer catechism, the *Malleus Maleficarum* defined and described a variety of evil beings and prescribed the proper way to deal with them. Although the book does not specifically discuss vampires, it does describe incubi and succubi, demons that take human form and prey upon human beings, and it includes one story that has some features of vampirism (part I, question 15). Accepted as authoritative by both Catholics and Protestants, the book helped create a climate of superstitious fear.

Even with the official sanction of the Church, belief in vampires required some external corroboration. It was not difficult to find. Following the report of a vampire, people set out to exhume suspects during the light of day. Evidence of nocturnal activity was often found—ripped burial shrouds, fresh blood, twisted positions. The vampire hunters would then decapitate, stake, and burn the body. Modern medical research has provided other explanations for these phenomena. Premature burial was common, as living victims of anemia, comas, shock, and various kinds of fits were often entombed. Localities visited by tuberculosis or the plague were thought to be attacked by hordes of vampires, and the daytime visits to the graveyards in search of vampires often turned up what seemed to be evidence. The Spanish conquest of the Americas provided even more apparent confirmation. The discovery of extensive blood sacrifices to demons (Inca and Aztec deities) and the vampire bat (*Desmodus rotundus*) confirmed European belief in its own legends.

Belief in the vampire varied throughout Europe, lasting longer in Eastern Europe than Western Europe. Indeed, belief in vampires remained very much alive in parts of Eastern Europe until recent times, and the belief is undoubtedly alive in certain regions even today. The vampire legends have had a particular vigor in the Balkans, especially in Transylvania and Romania, and these and the surrounding areas have become known as "vampire country."

From these superstitions, discoveries, folklores, and legends, creative artists wove new stories. The vampire became a popular literary figure in the nineteenth century, and even more popular in the twentieth. Another influence remains to be explained, however. Records exist of instances of people actually delighting in the taking of human blood. These are, in a sense, real vampires, and their activities fascinated people. The most famous is, of course, Dracula.

The name of Dracula has become synonymous with vampires since Bram Stoker published his novel in 1897. Dracula, however, was not a figment of Stoker's imagination. The work of Raymond McNally and Radu Florescu, *In Search of Dracula: A True History of Dracula and Vampire Legends* and *Dracula: A Biography of Vlad the Impaler*, provides an extensive account of the actual figure behind Stoker's character.

Dracula, born in 1430 or 1431, was the son of Vlad, a Wallachian prince rewarded by King Sigismund of Hungary for his valor in battle against the Turks with induction into the Order of the Dragon. Since the Latin word for dragon is *draco* Vlad became known as Vlad Dracul, or Vlad the Dragon. But *draco* has a second meaning, "devil," and since Vlad was known as a cruel prince, his people relished the pun. Dracula is the diminutive of *draco*, and Vlad's son became Dracula, son of the dragon or son of the Devil. The name fits. He is also known as Vlad Tepes, or Vlad the Impaler, since impaling people on long stakes was his favorite method of both torture and execution. Some scholars estimate that he impaled over one hundred thousand people in his lifetime.

Vlad Dracula ruled Wallachia, the southern half of modern Romania, three different times in his life: in 1448, from 1456 to 1462, and for two months in 1476. Accurate information about much of Dracula's life is difficult to find. The exact location of his infamous castle, for example, is a matter of dispute. In 1453 Constantinople fell to the Ottoman Empire, and Turkish forces pushed northward through the Balkans into Europe. Wallachia, and the neighboring province of Transylvania, became the bloodly frontier between Islam and Christianity. Vlad Dracula, who had been a hostage of the Turks in his youth, led his army in a guerrilla war against the Turks with astounding success. His favorite tactic was to attack at night, causing confusion and terror, and then retreat, carrying away prisoners to be impaled. Faced with such fanatic fighting, the Turkish forces withdrew. Dracula turned his attention to ruling his territory, again impaling large numbers of victims to insure law and order. In one memorable incident, Dracula attacked the Transylvanian city of Sibiu, killing over ten thousand of the inhabitants. Eventually King Matthias of Hungary intervened at the request of some of Dracula's subjects and forced him from his throne. Dracula was a prisoner of Matthias for twelve years. He has released in 1476, and died, under mysterious circumstances, shortly thereafter.

Accounts of Dracula's bloody activities spread quickly. With the aid of the newly invented printing press, the Dracula legend, complete with embellishments, appeared first in Germany and then throughout Europe. Because of the extent of his tortures, it is no wonder that his name became linked with the vampires of legend. McNally and Florescu provide the most complete information about Vlad Dracula, and additional commentary is available in the work of Twitchell and Donald Glut.

A second "living vampire" was Elizabeth Bathory, a Hungarian countess born in 1560 and brought to trial in 1611 for the torture and murder of somewhere between 150 and 650 young women. After hearing rumors of the disappearance of young women, Hungarian authorities raided the Bathory castle on either December 19 or 20, 1610, and discovered the body of one dead girl before the door of the manorhouse and two other victims inside. During two trials, evidence was given that the countess and accomplices had killed a large number of young women after torturing them. Her acts gave her erotic pleasure (her captives were usually stripped naked). She also took pleasure in bleeding her victims. Some were stuck with needles, and most were cut and slashed. It has often been said the countess drank blood and that she bathed in her victims' blood to keep herself young, but Raymond McNally in *Dracula Was a Woman* points out that there was no evidence given during the trials that she drank blood or bathed in it (82). After the trials, four of the accomplices were executed, but because of her aristocratic connections, Bathory was imprisoned for life in her own castle.

Another historical figure often included in studies of vampires is Gilles de Laval, Baron de Rais. He was a contemporary of Dracula, a Marshal of France who fought alongside Joan of Arc against the English, and a cultured and pious man in public life. In 1440, however, he was brought to trial for the murder of 140 young children. In addition, he was charged with sodomy. Contemporary records indicate that de Rais would habitually kidnap young boys whom he found attractive, rape them, and slash or bite their necks. Like Elizabeth Bathory, he found pleasure in bloodletting. He may have drunk his victims' blood, but there is uncertainty about this. At his trial he confessed to the charges and begged forgiveness of the parents of his victims. He was executed shortly after the trial.

If Bathory and de Rais actually did drink their victims' blood, they may have suffered from haematomania, the medical term for a literal lusting for blood. More significant is their combination of erotic and violent behavior, which is at the heart of the vampire legend. Both showed erotic behavior connected with bloodletting. De Rais raped his victims, and Bathory may have done this in one or more cases, although this is uncertain. Both became sources for later vampire stories. Bathory's life was portrayed in the film *Countess Dracula* (1970), and de Rais inspired Joris-Karl Huysmans' *Là-Bas* (1891).

Tales of actual humans who lusted for blood did not end with the Middle Ages or the Renaissance, nor does the evidence for blood-drinking consist solely of hearsay and questionable documents. Three famous twentieth-century cases attest to the timeless attraction of blood.

Between 1918 and 1924, Fritz Haarmann killed between twenty-seven and fifty young men between the ages of twelve and eighteen by biting them in the neck and drinking their blood (Summers, *Vampire: Kith and Kin* 188–93). Afterwards he cut up the bodies, made sausages out of the meat, and ate them. What he could not devour he sold to the public in his Hanover butcher shop. In 1924 Haarmann was arrested and subsequently confessed. In 1925 he was executed by decapitation, ironically one of the traditional methods of destroying a vampire.

John George Haigh also drank human blood, and his activities also conform to the habits of the vampire of legend. Haigh was arrested in England in 1949 for murder; and although charged with only one crime, he admitted killing and drinking the blood of nine people. He drank the blood, he confessed, after visions which left him with an intense thirst for blood. He admitted that after each incident he felt powerful and peaceful, and his thirst was gone (see Dunboyne).

Kuno Hofmann, a deaf German laborer, also drank human blood to satisfy powerful urges. Between 1971 and 1972 Hofmann broke into cemeteries around Nuremberg and on at least thirty-five occasions drank the blood of the newly buried. Although the practice of the living feeding on the blood of the newly dead is almost vampirism in reverse, Hofmann is usually considered the most recent "real vampire."

Haarmann, Haigh, and Hofmann provide links between the reality of horror and the horror of the imagination. It is not such a great leap from the bloody actions of the criminally insane to the exploits of characters of legends and literature.

Although the vampire was kept alive by folklore, demonologies, and occasional human horrors, it did not become a widespread figure until the eighteenth century, when it began to appear in drama, poetry, and prose. Except for references in classical Greek and Roman literature, a number of fifteenth-century German pamphlets about Dracula, and a few references in English ballads ("Margaret's Ghost" and "Sweet William's Ghost"), the vampire was absent from Western literature. The familiar figure of the modern vampire appeared with the rise of Romanticism.

The first literary vampires were German. Twitchell notes that "in the early eighteenth century as a result of the 'vampire epidemics' in the Balkans, the vampire had become a serious subject of study on the Continent. Treatise after treatise was written, not necessarily affirming the vampire's existence (that was already generally accepted), but rather explaining the vampire as a personification of demonic energies on earth"(33). German poets followed where the scholars led. In 1748 Ossenfelder wrote "The Vampire," in 1773 Burger wrote "Lenore," and in 1797 Goethe created "The Bride of Cornith." All three poems were popular and were often translated. Interest in vampires spread throughout Europe. French and Italian vampire poems, stories, and operas appeared in the eighteenth and nineteenth centuries, including such well-known works as Prosper Mérimée's *La Guzla* and Baudelaire's vampire poems. "Lenore," the story of a dead crusader returning to gather up his bride, inspired such early English

Romantic poets as Robert Southey and John Stagg to write vampire poems. Others followed.

Twitchell notes that the English Romantics were more interested in the vampire as metaphor or symbol than as a character. The image of the vampire appears in two forms: the male vampire as sexual predator and the female vampire as sexual seductress. In both types, evil, sexuality, and violence are combined. In such works as Keats's "Lamia," Coleridge's "Christabel," and Poe's "Ligeia," the female character with features of a vampire is a grand seductress—passionate, unfeeling, and eternal, an object of adolescent desire. The male character of the vampire, which appears in such works as Byron's *Manfred* and *The Giaour*, and Shelley's *The Cenci*, is an extension of the Byronic hero—isolated, moody, powerful, and threatening. Whether male or female, the vampire in English Romantic poetry is usually used imaginatively rather than literally; the vampire is the representation of the sexual and psychological uneasiness within the individual. While given the traditional characteristics—bloody, sexually attractive, and demonic—the Romantic vampire itself is not of primary concern to the poets. It is to the novelists.

In April of 1819 the first vampire story in English prose appeared in Colburn's *New Monthly Magazine*. Written by John Polidori, Lord Byron's physician and travelling companion, *The Vampyre* was a tremendous immediate success. It generated numerous French and German vampire dramas and began a tradition of vampire fiction which continues to this day. Polidori took a creature of legend and turned it into a cultural symbol. *The Vampyre* is a full-blown Gothic novella, complete with "local color, melodrama, suspense," and horror (Twitchell 107). More importantly, *The Vampyre* established the conventions of the modern vampire story and made the vampire a popular literary figure.

Polidori's vampire, Lord Ruthven, seems familiar to modern readers weaned on Stoker's *Dracula* and Hollywood vampire films. Ruthven is an adult sexual predator who can mingle undiscovered with humanity while he kills young women. Polidori includes elements which later writers and directors have made essential—retelling vampire legends from Eastern Europe, young innocents caught in the vampire's power, glittering social evenings, the discovery and hunt of evil, and, perhaps most important, the combination of sexuality and violence. Ruthven is an actual vampire, a bloodthirsty monster who is the embodiment of the destructive power of sexuality masked by wealth, intelligence, and culture. Like later vampire stories, Polidori's tale is as much a culturally significant morality play as an entertaining horror story.

The first full vampire novel written in English, and one of the most popular of all vampire novels, was *Varney the Vampire or the Feast of Blood*, first published in 1847 and reprinted in 1853 in installments. *Varney* has been attributed to Thomas Peckett Prest and/or James Malcolm Rymer (the latter is now favored by some scholars as the major author), but there is a good probability that the novel was produced by several writers working in collaboration. Such collaboration may help explain the novel's lack of consistency (Twitchell 123). *Varney* is important for more than its popularity; it continued the motifs established by Polidori and influenced many later vampire writers with such elements as "the initiation of the heroine through sex, the vampire's middle-European background, the quasi–medical-scientific explanations, the midnight vigils, the mob scene . . . and the hunt and the chase" (Twitchell 124). Unlike *The Vampyre*, *Varney* never attempts to be a psychological study; it is a horror story pure and simple.

The prototype of the female vampire appeared in Joseph Sheridan Le Fanu's 1871 novella, *Carmilla*, a tale which inspired Bram Stoker to write *Dracula*. Le Fanu deliberately adapted Coleridge's "Christabel" into a prose narrative, recognizing and emphasizing the elements of perversion in his source. Twitchell notes that *Carmilla*, like "Christabel," is "a story of a lesbian entanglement, a story of the sterile love of homosexuality expressed through the analogy of vampirism" (129).

Carmilla is a story of seduction and addiction. Laura, the narrator, writes of an experience more than ten years prior to the tale's opening. After an accident involving a stagecoach, a young woman who has been injured in the accident is left by the woman's "mother" at the castle of Laura's father. During her recuperation, the woman, Carmilla, draws Laura to her, first attracting her with erotic dreams and then transforming herself into a cat and biting her on the breast. Laura begins to succumb; but it is discovered that Carmilla is a vampire, actually the Countess Karnstein, who has been ravaging the neighborhood for about 150 years. A doctor, a general, and a local clergyman join forces and hunt her down, discovering her coffin and destroying her. The story ends with Laura saying that often in a reverie she has fancied hearing Carmilla's footsteps at her door. The reader is left to imagine if Carmilla has returned or not.

Later versions of the female vampire story, especially film versions, play down the homosexual elements of Le Fanu's story but remain faithful to much of the rest. While domination remains the province of the male vampire, erotic seduction belongs to the female.

Bram Stoker published *Dracula* in 1897, and it has been in print and popular ever since. To most people, Dracula is *the* vampire. *Dracula* and Mary Shelley's *Frankenstein* remain the two outstanding works of horror within the Gothic tradition, yet neither is a true Gothic novel. *Frankenstein* is an essay on the moral and philosophical dilemmas of modern science, and *Dracula* is a study of psychological terror. Unlike most Gothic novels, *Dracula* is neither action-packed nor full of physical violence. Yet *Dracula* succeeds where some other horror novels fail because it is about the nature of terror. Dracula is more than a mere monster; he is evil incarnate.

The story of *Dracula* is familiar to most readers. The Transylvanian count wishes to move from his castle to England and invites Jonathan Harker to make the arrangements. While at Castle Dracula, Harker is seduced/attacked by female vampires. Dracula moves, enters English society, and begins to prey on Lucy

Westenra, a close friend of Mina Murray, who is Harker's fiancée. The vampire-hunter Van Helsing attempts to save Lucy but is unable to do so. Dracula next preys on Mina, and although he contaminates her, she is saved. He is finally destroyed after he has returned to his homeland. First-time readers of Stoker's novel are often put off by its structure, that of the epistolary novel, and its shifting focus. Yet the book remains popular because it has power.

Dracula is effective because Stoker did not dilute the psychological content of the vampire legend. As Twitchell brilliantly observes: "Dracula is terrifically alluring; he has everything we want: he has money and power without responsibilities; he parties all night with the best people, yet he doesn't need friends; he can be violent and aggressive without guilt or punishment; he has life without death; but most attractive of all, he has sex without confusion (i.e., genitalia, pregnancy . . . love). It's all take, no give" (134). The story of *Dracula* is a psychological story and a story of revenge: the group destruction of a father figure who controls all the available women. The Freudian interpretation, first offered by English anthropologist Maurice Richardson, goes a long way in explaining the popularity of *Dracula* in particular and vampire stories in general.

Dracula spawned a horde of horrors. It has generated literally hundreds of plays, films, novels, and stories. Since *Dracula*, it is impossible to think of the vampire without imagining the Transylvanian count, but some modern writers have used the figure of the vampire in other ways.

Most twentieth-century vampire literature draws directly upon Stoker. Many works of fiction are straight adaptations of *Dracula* written for specific audiences. *Monsters* is a children's book containing a condensed version of *Dracula*. Such works as *The Adult Version of Dracula, Monster Sex Stories*, "Lust of the Vampire," *County Dracula's Canadian Affair*, and *The Orgy at Madam Dracula's* involve the Count in explicit erotic adventures. French, German, and Italian publishers have issued series with similar themes. In 1973 Pinnacle Books inaugurated "The Dracula Horror Series" with *Dracula Returns*. It was followed by such forgettable pulps as *The Hand of Dracula!, Dracula's Brothers, Dracula's Gold*, and *The Drums of Dracula* (Glut 307–18). While this vampire literature is derivative and without serious merit, some first-rate vampire fiction has been written.

Richard Matheson's novel, *I Am Legend*, combines vampirism with science fiction in an effective story about the last man on earth, who is forced to barricade himself at home during the night against a screaming crowd of vampires made up of his ex-friends and neighbors. His short story "Drink My Red Blood" is more widely known. Often anthologized, "Drink My Red Blood" is a haunting story of a boy named Jules who desires to become a vampire. He discovers the movie *Dracula* and Stoker's novel, steals a vampire bat from the zoo, and finally cuts his own neck and forces the bat to drink the blood. As he is dying, Jules sees looming over him a tall, dark man whose eyes shine "like rubies." The man calls him "my son." In both works Matheson draws upon vampire literature and lore, but he uses the material in original and striking ways.

Raymond Rudorff's *The Dracula Archives* is an impressive novel written as a series of first-person accounts. Rudorff consciously imitates Stoker's style as he provides a story of the origins of Dracula and links him directly with Elizabeth Bathory. *The Dracula Archives* is a historical novel which expands on Stoker's work and is successful in its own right.

Jeff Rice's *The Night Stalker*, originally titled *The Kolchak Tapes*, is the story of vampire Janos Skorzeny running loose in contemporary Las Vegas. Unlike Rudorff, who set his story within the mainstream of vampire fiction, Rice combines two genres—horror and detective fiction. The hero of the novel, a newspaperman named Kolchak, tries to convince an unbelieving world of the actual existence of a vampire and in the end manages to confront the vampire and drive a stake through its heart. *The Night Stalker* was shown on television in 1972 and was the highest-rated film made for television to that date.

The Dracula Archives is the only serious work of vampire fiction which is a deliberate imitation of Stoker. Some other writers besides Matheson and Rice have also adapted the vampire to new situations and settings. Theodore Sturgeon's *Some of Your Blood*, John Rechy's *The Vampires*, Fred Saberhagen's *The Dracula Tape*, Desmond Stewart's *The Vampire of Mons*, Colin Wilson's *The Space Vampires*, and Chelsea Quinn Yarbro's *Hôtel Transylvania* are all serious novels which use the lore of vampires effectively. The range to which vampire material is currently being used by serious writers of fiction can be seen in Stephen King's *'Salem's Lot* and Anne Rice's *Interview with the Vampire*.

In *Danse Macabre*, Stephen King confesses that "when I conceived of the vampire novel which became *'Salem's Lot*, I decided I wanted to try to use the book partially as a form of literary homage. . . . So my novel bears an intentional similarity to Bram Stoker's *Dracula*" (37–38). King constructed his novel by creating twentieth-century scenes which run parallel to Stoker's nineteenth-century ones, and the result is a haunting combination of the traditional and the new.

Familiar to readers of *Dracula* are King's use of the staking of a loved one, the effect of a consecrated host, the burning of a hand at the church door, the initiation by drinking the vampire's blood, and the band of fearless vampire-killers. King's achievement rests not on his use of these incidents, but rather in his ability to transfer the vampire story from the European past to the American present. He also makes the vampire story democratic; vampirism is not the curse of the aristocracy; rather, it spreads like a contagion throughout an entire New England community. King creates a horde of vampires and lets them loose as a group. As a result, the erotic elements of the vampire legend are downplayed while the violent ones are emphasized.

If *'Salem's Lot* can be considered a study in the sociology of vampirism, Anne Rice's *Interview with the Vampire* is an examination into the psychology of vampirism. Written in the form of a tape-recorded autobiography of a two-hundred-year-old vampire, Rice's novel chronicles the initiation, education, and ultimate disillusionment of a New Orleans vampire who has searched the earth to find out what he really is. *Interview with the Vampire* is unique in that it focuses on the motivations, feelings, and thoughts of a vampire, not on the terror it spreads. Rice's vampire comes closer to being human, and thus understandable, than any fictive vampire since Polidori's.

Although contemporary writers continue to experiment with a variety of settings in which to place their vampires, few have achieved the success of King and Rice. Three recent vampire novels illustrate the kinds of nontraditional stories vampires find themselves in.

F. Paul Wilson's *The Keep*, the source for the film by the same name, combines vampire material with Star Wars theology—a force with good and evil emanations—and Nazis. In *The Keep* the vampire's traditional Transylvanian castle is a prison for a supervampire whoses evil transcends mere nightwalking and bloodletting. During the Second World War German troops occupy the castle and begin to release the evil buried within. The world is saved from contamination by a mysterious agent of light and goodness who forces the father of vampires back into his prison.

Dean R. Koontz's *The Vision* combines parapsychology and vampirism in a psychic detective tale set in modern California. The protagonist is a woman who can "see" violent murders before they occur, and the vampire is the seer's brother, a character reminiscent of Matheson's young Jules. Koontz presents parapsychology as real, but leaves the question of vampirism open. Ultimately, *The Vision* is more concerned with prophecy than it is with vampires.

Scott Baker's *Dhampire* is a curious combination of vampire lore, eroticism, oriental philosophy, and anti-Christianity. The title comes from a Russian word for the son of a vampire, and the story involves a direct descendant of Elizabeth Bathory who must fight all the members of his family, all actual or potential vampires, to rid the world of the curse of the living dead.

Short stories and novels are not the only forms of prose employed by the creators of vampire stories. Two other sources exist and deserve at least a brief mention: the pulps and the comics.

Donald Glut's *The Dracula Book* is an excellent source for the discovery of vampire stories in magazines and comic books. Among the pulp magazines listed as containing vampire material are *Horror Stories, Unknown Worlds, Imagination, Famous Monsters, Monster Worlds*, and *The Magazine of Fantasy and Science Fiction*. Vampires appear in comics with equal frequency. Prior to the institution of the Comics Code Authority in the mid-fifties, vampires were staple characters in *Eerie*. Dell published a Dracula series in the sixties, and D.C., Gold Key, and the Marvel Comics group joined the field in the late sixties and early seventies. Many of the vampire stories which appear in the comics come directly from Stoker's *Dracula*, but the Marvel adventures show a good deal of imagination and skill in linking vampires with other characters.

The vampire has fared better than other famous creatures of horror in print. Unlike mummies, werewolves, and zombies, vampires have been served by a number of serious writers. Surprisingly, pictorial artists have not adopted the vampire with equal enthusiasm. Although not a major subject of a large number of artists, the vampire can be found in the works of such painters and illustrators as Francisco de Goya, Edvard Munch, Max Klinger, Boleslas Biegas, and Edward Gorey. The turn-of-the-century work of Munch and Biegas is most widely known. Both artists emphasize erotic female vampires attacking helpless victims. In addition, numerous book illustrations of vampires can be found in nineteenth-century texts. The vampire has flourished at the hands of one kind of visual artist, the filmmaker. The vampire is more popular on screen than it ever was in legend or literature.

The film vampire has generated a small industry. Since the turn of the century, over five hundred vampire films have been produced, and dozens of books and articles have appeared examining the vampire on the screen. The most comprehensive study is Michael Murphy's *The Celluloid Vampires*, although useful information can be found in Ivan Butler's *Horror in the Cinema*, Carlos Claren's *An Illustrated History of the Horror Film*, Lotte Eisner's *The Haunted Screen*, Denis Gifford's *Movie Monsters*, Donald Glut's *The Dracula Book*, Walt Lee's *Reference Guide to Fantastic Films*, David Pirie's *The Vampire Cinema*, and Donald Reed's *The Vampire on the Screen*. From the first days of the movies, the vampire has haunted the theater. It has soared to the heights of art with the work of Bela Lugosi and Christopher Lee and fallen to the depths of parody at the hands of Abbott and Costello. With its unique ability to communicate vivid imagery within a fast-paced narrative, film has made the vampire come alive for millions of viewers.

George Méliès, a French magician and showman, was one of the first film producers to see the entertainment potential of the newly invented genre. He also created the first vampire film, an 1897 three-minute story of a bat transforming into a devil, called *Le Manoir du diable*. Few of the earliest films exist today; many titles do remain, and they suggest that French, Russian, German, British, and American directors were making vampire films.

In 1922 the vampire came to the screen full-blown in Friederich Murnau's masterful *Nosferatu, eine Symphonie des Grauens*. *Nosferatu*, an adaptation of Stoker's novel, follows *Dracula*'s characters and sequences closely. Unfortunately, the filmmakers never sought permission to use the Stoker material, and in 1925 a German court ruled that the film be taken out of circulation and all copies destroyed. Fortunately, a number of prints survived.

Nosferatu is noteworthy for more than being the first full-length treatment of the vampire in film. Murnau was an exceptionally talented Expressionist director, and he adapted Stoker's narrative with skill and creativity. In *Nosferatu* Murnau transforms the character of the vampire. Arthur Lennig says of Nosferatu: ''A kind of abstract thing of evil, he has no nobility, nor does he inhabit the dark world of majestic satanic villains. Instead, he is a lower kind of evil, an obscene and loathsome creature that dwells amid decay and slime and crawling rats'' (qtd. in Murphy 6). Unlike the vampires created by Lugosi and Lee, Murnau's vampire is at most a personification of evil; he has not yet risen to the status of hero.

The earliest vampire films seem to have been cursed. The other major vampire film of the twenties, *London after Midnight*, has been lost. Nothing remains of this 1927 Lon Chaney, Sr. production except some still photographs and the recollections of viewers. Apparently *London after Midnight* was a combination vampire/detective film with Chaney playing both roles. Available information indicates that the film borrowed much from Stoker and pitted a man of science and occult learning against the vampire, or a man pretending to be a vampire, in London. *London after Midnight* was directed by Tod Browning for MGM, and in 1931 Browning was hired by Universal Pictures to direct *Dracula*. He was considering Chaney for the role of the vampire, but Chaney died. He settled for Bela Lugosi (Murphy 10–15).

Most filmgoers recognize Lugosi as Dracula. Although he appeared in numerous other roles, Lugosi made a career of playing vampires. His selection was obvious. Lugosi was touring the United States in a successful stage production of Stoker's novel, and his Hungarian accent seemed perfect for the new technology of the sound screen. The film, justly famous, is a photographic representation of the stage play, which itself was Stoker simplified. Although far less graphic than later vampire films, Lugosi's *Dracula* is still effective in its evocation of horror and the link between vampirism and sexuality. In a sense, the image of the vampire in *Dracula* is the opposite of the image presented in *Nosferatu*; the former depicts the vampire as a type of noble sufferer, while the latter shows it to be something utterly inhuman. Most subsequent vampire films fall somewhere in between.

Carl Theodor Dreyer's 1932 French film *Vampyr*, which was based loosely on Le Fanu's *Carmilla*, brought the female vampire to the screen. The vampire is a wrinkled old woman who is preying on a young woman. "The plot has the main character, David Gray, moving in an eerie dreamlike environment of bizarre supernatural experiences as he tracks down the vampire" (Riccardo 66). Although viewers who were expecting a sequel to *Dracula* were disappointed by the film, *Vampyr* is an evocative movie which was in advance of its time.

In 1936 Universal Studios released its sequel to *Dracula*, *Dracula's Daughter*. "This film picked up where *Dracula* left off, and brazenly assumed that everyone had seen *Dracula*" (Murphy 34). Van Helsing is in possession of the bodies of Dracula and Renfield, but because he is unable to convince the police of the existence of vampires, he is accused of murder and imprisoned. A mysterious woman in black, Dracula's daughter, appears and steals her father's body. She burns it in an isolated forest and exorcises the evil. The rest of the film recounts her attempts to seek release from vampirism between episodes of seduction of both a handsome young man and his fiancée.

The serious vampire films of the thirties employed the conventions of the vampire fiction of the nineteenth century: the male vampires combined eroticism and domination, while the female vampires were seductive and terrible. During the next decade, vampire films would move away from serious themes and become either cheap thrillers or parodies.

The 1943 film, *The Return of the Vampire*, starring Bela Lugosi, inaugurated the trend of multiple-monster movies which became popular in this period. Lugosi is again a noble vampire, but here he is assisted by a wolfman named Andreas. In addition, the second half of the film is set in London during the Nazi blitz. This combination of mixing monsters and changing the setting continued in *Son of Dracula*, starring Lon Chaney, Jr. In this film the setting is the Southeastern United States, and the vampire is involved with a swamp witch.

Universal Pictures continued this popular formula in *House of Frankenstein* (1944) and *House of Dracula* (1945). In both films John Carradine played Dracula, and in both the vampire must confront the Frankenstein monster and a wolfman. The character of the vampire gets lost in the mash of monsters, and while the films are fun to watch, they are hard to take seriously. The trend toward group horrors reached its height, or depth, in 1948 with *Abbott and Costello Meet Frankenstein*, in which the two comics confront Dracula, the Frankenstein monster, the Wolfman, and the Invisible Man.

In 1945 RKO Pictures released *Isle of the Dead*, the one original vampire film of the forties. Starring Boris Karloff as a Greek general trapped on a Mediterranean island by the plague, the film draws on Greek folklore rather than Stoker for its dramatization of the superstitious belief in the living dead.

Several new trends emerged in the vampire films of the fifties. First, vampire films spread from Hollywood around the world. British filmmakers released humorous vampire films, Italian producers made sexy vampire movies, and in the Far East the Shaw brothers made a popular series of Pontianak (Malaysian for "vampire") films. In the United States scientific vampire films and teenage-vampire films were popular in the first part of the decade. In 1957, however, the vampire returned as a serious character in United Artist's *The Return of Dracula*. In this film Czechoslovakian actor Francis Lederer plays the traditional vampire in a low-budget, black-and-white film set in contemporary America. Without the theatrics of the Lugosi films or the absurdities of some of the later American movies, *The Return of Dracula* is a serious, straightforward horror film. More dramatic and influential, however, was the 1958 British film *The Horror of Dracula*, also known as *Dracula*, which starred Christopher Lee.

For many modern movie viewers, Christopher Lee has replaced Bela Lugosi as the most prominent portrayer of vampires. Lee, who had not seen the Lugosi films, drew upon Stoker for his inspiration, and his Dracula is a terrifying combination of arrogant aristocrat and menacing monster. In *The Horror of Dracula*, which is a faithful adaptation of Stoker's novel, Lee emphasized the sexuality inherent in the narrative. His Dracula is a creature who literally lusts after the blood of beautiful young women. Unlike the earlier films, in which much of the action took place offscreen, *The Horror of Dracula* and such other Christopher Lee vampire films as *Dracula, Prince of Darkness* (1965), *Dracula*

Has Risen from the Grave (1968), and *Taste the Blood of Dracula* (1970) are full of visual violence, gore, and eroticism. With Lee, the film vampire became a visual as well as imaginative horror (Murphy 76, 78; Glut 158–59).

The popularity of vampire films increased in the sixties. Italian vampire films featuring beautiful young victims remained available, and the Mexican film industry created a huge success with "Nostradamus" pictures, inexpensive thrillers somehow combining the character of Nostradamus, vampirism, and scientific paraphernalia. In the United States, a surprising number of pornographic vampire films were released. The major vampire films, however, continued to be the Hammer films with Christopher Lee, and Roman Polanski's 1967 *Dance of the Vampires*, also known as *The Fearless Vampire Killers*.

Polanski's film is a delightful satire which employs nearly all of the conventions and mannerisms made popular by Lugosi and Lee. It even includes a Jewish vampire who, when confronted with a crucifix, laughs and responds "Oivay . . . have *you* got the wrong vampayah!" (qtd. in Murphy 117). *Dance of the Vampires* is an entertaining film rich in both vampire lore and laughter.

There has been no letup in the production of vampire films since 1970, and while many follow old formulas, a number provide examples of new treatments of the vampire. Perhaps the most unusual contemporary vampire film is German director Hans Geissendorfer's *Jonathan, Vampire Sterben Nicht* (1970). Geissendorfer's film is "an intellectual commentary on Nazism and fascism, set in the black and white world of the vampire" (Murphy 140). It is a morality play that has been called by critics an intellectual's vampire film. Geissendorfer uses the domination, terror, and violence inherent in the vampire story as a metaphor for Hitler's control of Germany in an explicit manner, even employing an actor with a striking resemblance to Hitler as his vampire. The film, though successful in Europe, did not fare well in the United States.

Less intellectual, but far more popular, are two American films, *Count Yorga, Vampire* (1970) and its sequel, *The Return of Count Yorga* (1971). Count Yorga, played by Robert Quarry, is an aristocratic and sarcastic vampire, modeled somewhat after Lee's Dracula, who wanders the wilderness of modern California. Quarry is successful in making the vampire's lust seem real in a setting far removed from nineteenth-century Transylvania, and audiences responded to the idea of sex and violence in modern America.

Another popular contemporary vampire film is *Blacula* (1972), featuring William Marshall. *Blacula* is significant for several reasons. First, it was the first film to use a black actor in the leading role. Second, the main characters are all portrayed by black actors and actresses. More importantly, the movie is more than a cheap horror production aimed at a black audience. Marshall portrays his vampire as a sympathetic character (Glut 230). The black vampire is a creature doomed to immortality because he is opposed to the slave trade; he is as much victim as victimizer. By the end of the film Blacula has developed as a character to the point where he willingly destroys himself, a transformation seldom seen in vampire films (Murphy 166–73).

Film history repeated itself in 1979 when Universal Pictures adapted the stage play *Dracula* to the screen for a second time. Frank Langella played the Count both on Broadway and in the film, and his performances were exceptional. Langella's film Dracula is a recreation of his stage character, and the film has the feel of a play—dialogue and acting take the place of special effects, and Langella manages to make his vampire sympathetic, menacing, and erotic. While less animalistic than Lee's Dracula, Langella's is a convincing creation.

Two recent vampire films have been less successful in creating nontraditional vampires. George Hamilton's *Love at First Bite* is a mere parody, while David Bowie's *The Hunger* fails either to engross or to horrify viewers.

Werner Herzog's *Nosferatu* (1979), a remake of Murnau's 1922 masterpiece, shows vampire films coming full circle. It is an elaborate and well-made film which treats the vampire as a plaguelike horror. Filmed in black and white to recreate the mood of the original, *Nosferatu* is a truly terrifying film which avoids all attempts at humanizing the vampire.

The figure of the vampire has become a staple of the small screen as well as the large one, and with the same mixed success. John Carradine recreated his film role for television in 1957, Jack Palance played Dracula in 1973 for CBS television, and Louis Jordan recently provided an excellent Dracula for viewers of PBS.

While Rod Serling's *Night Gallery* aired several vampire stories between 1971 and 1973, the most famous television vampires appeared in two very different popular serials, *The Munsters* and *Dark Shadows*. In *The Munsters* Dracula is defanged. Al Lewis played Count Dracula as a kindly grandfather with a vampire daughter married to a Frankenstein monster named Herman. *The Munsters*, a children's version of *Ozzie and Harriet* in Halloween costumes, was popular, spawning a film, three novels, several records, and an animated cartoon (Glut 293–300).

In order to boost its ratings, *Dark Shadows*, an afternoon soap opera about a Gothic New England family, introduced the character of Barnabas Collins, a vampire played by Shakespearean actor Jonathan Frid. The ploy worked, and although the series went off the air in 1971, it generated a movie and a series of novels.

Vampires continue to appear on television, perhaps nowhere else with more frequency than on MTV, the cable rock network. Numerous videos contain the figures of vampires, but the most famous is Michael Jackson's video "Thriller," which features images of the undead rising from their graves to seek out the blood of the living. The reference to vampires in music is not new. In 1957 John Zacherle recorded the popular "Dinner With Drac," and Bobby "Boris" Pickett had a series of hits in the early sixties entitled "Monster Mash," "Bella's Bash," and "The Transylvanian Twist."

Contemporary popular culture has embraced vampires. They can be found selling breakfast foods, nasal spray, and socks on television. Vampire games, kits, dart boards, puzzles, stamps, and greeting cards are available almost everywhere. While the vampire remains a figure for serious artists, it is also a friendly character for children.

The popularity of the vampire in the second half of the twentieth century can be partly explained by the pervasiveness of mass communications, which can spread any image around the world in minutes. But why has the vampire in particular become so popular? The answers lie in the nature of the creature. In nearly all of its manifestations, the vampire has served as a metaphor for the dark side of human emotions and behavior. In mid-Eastern legends, European folktales, and the fiction of the nineteenth century and the films of the twentieth, vampires have been depicted as creatures with voracious appetites. They literally hunger for sex, violence, and power. The vampire, more so than other monsters of the imagination, appears to spring out of the human subsconscious. It is a creature of boundless selfishness, a creature of childish wish fulfillment that demands everything. Civilization demands cooperation and self-denial, and as Western culture grows more civilized, we are forced to deny ourselves much that would gratify. The vampire represents the denied gratification of a civilized society. It wants—and gets—sex, blood, and eternal life. Who could ask for more?

BIBLIOGRAPHY

Abbott and Costello Meet Frankenstein. Universal International, 1948.

Arnold, Theador Ferdinand Kajetan. *Der Vampir*. Schneeburg, 1801.

Baker, Scott. *Dhampire*. New York: Pocket Books, 1982.

Billy the Kid vs. Dracula. Embassy, 1965.

Blacula. Powers Productions, 1972.

The Brides of Dracula. Hammer Films, 1960.

Burton, Sir Richard. *Vikram and the Vampire or Tales of Hindu Devilry*. London, 1870.

Butler, Ivan. *Horror in the Cinema*. New York: A. S. Barnes, 1970.

Calmet, Dom Augustin. *Traité sur les apparitions des esprits, et sur les vampires, ou les revenants de Hongrie, de Moravie....* 2 vols. Paris, 1751.

Clarens, Carlos. *An Illustrated History of the Horror Film*. New York: Capricorn Books, 1967.

Collin de Plancy, J. A. S. *Dictionnaire infernal*. Paris, 1818.

———. *Histoire des vampires*. Paris, 1820.

Copper, Basil. *The Vampire in Legend, Fact and Art*. London, 1973; rpt. Secaucus, N.J.: The Citadel Press, 1974.

Count Yorga, Vampire. Erica Productions, 1970.

Dance of the Vampires. Cadre, 1967.

Douglas, Drake. *Horror!* New York: Macmillan, 1966.

Dracula. Universal Pictures, 1931.

Dracula. Hammer Films, 1958.

Dracula. Universal International, 1979.

Dracula Has Risen from the Grave. Hammer Films, 1968.

Dracula, Prince of Darkness. Hammer Films, 1965.

Dumas, Alexandre (père). *Le Vampire*. Paris, 1865.

Dunboyne, Lord, ed. *The Trial of John George Haigh*. London: William Hodge, 1953.

Eisner, Lotte H. *The Haunted Screen: Expressionism in the German Cinema and the Influence of Max Reinhardt*. Berkeley and Los Angeles: University of California Press, 1969.

Epaulard, Alexis. *Vampyrisme, nécrophilie, nécrosadisme, nécrophagie*. Lyon, 1901.

Farson, Daniel. *Vampires, Zombies, and Monster Men*. London, 1975; rpt. Garden City, N.Y.: Doubleday, 1976.

Florescu, Radu, and Raymond McNally. *Dracula: A Biography of Vlad the Impaler, 1431–1476*. London: Robert Hale, 1974.

Gerard, Emily de Laszowska. *The Land Beyond the Forest: Facts, Figures, and Fancies from Transylvania*. London, 1888.

Gifford, Denis. *Movie Monsters*. London: Dutton Press, 1969.

Glut, Donald. *The Dracula Book*. Metuchen, N.J.: Scarecrow Press, 1975.

Haining, Peter, ed. *The Midnight People*. New York: Popular Library, 1968.

Hock, Stefan. *Die Vampyrsagen und ihre Verwertung in der Deutschen Literatur*. Berlin, 1900.

House of Dark Shadows. MGM, 1970.

House of Dracula. Universal Pictures, 1945.

House of Frankenstein. Universal Pictures, 1944.

Huysmans, Joris-Karl. *Là-Bas*. Paris, 1891.

I Was a Teenage Vampire. Donald Glut, 1959.

Isle of the Dead. RKO Pictures, 1945.

Jonathan, Vampire Sterben Nicht. Beta Films/Iduna Films, 1970.

King, Stephen. *Danse Macabre*. New York: Everest House, 1981.

———. *'Salem's Lot*. Garden City, N.Y.: Doubleday, 1975.

Koontz, Dean R. *The Vision*. New York: Putnam's, 1977.

Lawson, John Cuthbert. *Modern Greek Folklore and Ancient Greek Religion*. London: Cambridge University Press, 1910.

Le Fanu, Joseph Sheridan. *Carmilla*. 1871. In *In A Glass Darkly*. 3 vols. London, 1872. Vol. 3. 52–270.

The Legend of the Seven Golden Vampires. Hammer Films/Shaw Bros., 1974.

London after Midnight. MGM, 1927.

La Maldicion de Nostradamus. Produciones Bosas Priego S.A., 1960.

McHargue, Georgess. *Meet the Vampire*. New York: Dell, 1979.

McNally, Raymond. *A Clutch of Vampires*. Greenwich, Conn.: New York Graphic Society, 1974.

———. *Dracula Was a Woman: In Search of the Blood Countess of Transylvania*. New York: McGraw-Hill, 1983.

McNally, Raymond, and Radu Florescu. *In Search of Dracula: A True History of Dracula and Vampire Legends*. Greenwich, Conn.: New York Graphic Society, 1972.

Mark of the Vampire. MGM, 1935.

Masters, Anthony. *The Natural History of the Vampire*. New York: Putnam's, 1972.

Matheson, Richard. "Drink My Red Blood." In *A Clutch of Vampires*. Ed. Raymond McNally. Greenwich, Conn.: New York Graphic Society, 1974. 223–34.

———. *I Am Legend*. New York: Fawcett, 1954.

Munster, Go Home! Universal Pictures, 1966.

Murphy, Michael. *The Celluloid Vampires: A History and Filmography, 1897–1979*. Ann Arbor: Pierian Press, 1979.

The Night Stalker. ABC Television, 1972.

Nosferatu. 20th Century Fox, 1979.

Nosferatu, eine Symphonie des Grauens. Prana Films, 1922.

Paban, Madame Gabrielle de. *Histoire des fantômes et des démons*. Paris, 1819.

Philostratus. *The Life of Apollonius of Tyana*. Trans. F. C. Conybeare. 2 vols. 1912; rpt. Cambridge: Harvard University Press, 1958–60.

Pirie, David. *The Vampire Cinema*. New York: Crown Publishers, 1977.

Plan Nine From Outer Space. Distribution Corporation of America, 1956.

Polidori, John William. *The Vampyre*. London, 1819.

Pontianak. Keris, 1957.

Rechy, John. *The Vampires*. New York: Grove Press, 1973.

Reed, Donald. *The Vampire on the Screen*. Inglewood, Calif.: Wagon and Star Publishers, 1965.

The Return of Count Yorga. American International, 1971.

The Return of Dracula. United Artists, 1957.

Return of the Vampire. Columbia Pictures, 1943.

Riccardo, Martin V. *Vampires Unearthed: The Complete Multi-Media Vampire and Dracula Bibliography*. New York: Garland, 1983.

Rice, Anne. *Interview with the Vampire*. New York: Knopf, 1976.

Rice, Jeff. *The Night Stalker*. New York: Pocket Books, 1973.

Robbins, Rossell Hope. *The Encyclopedia of Witchcraft and Demonology*. New York: Crown Publishers, 1959.

Rudorff, Raymond. *The Dracula Archives*. New York: Arbor House, 1971.

Saberhagen, Fred. *The Dracula Tape*. New York: Warner Paperbacks, 1975.

The Scars of Dracula. Hammer Films, 1970.

Silver, Alain, and James Ursini. *The Vampire Film*. Cranbury, N.J.: A. S. Barnes, 1975.

Son of Dracula. Universal Pictures, 1943.

Sprenger, James, and Heinrich Kramer. *Malleus Malifecarum*. Cologne, 1486. Trans. Montague Summers. London: John Rodker, 1928.

Stewart, Desmond. *The Vampire of Mons*. New York: Harper and Row, 1976.

Stoker, Bram. *Dracula*. London, 1897.

Sturgeon, Theodore. *Some of Your Blood*. New York: Harper and Row, 1961.

Summers, Montague. *The Vampire: His Kith and Kin*. London, 1928; rpt. New Hyde Park, N.Y.: University Books, 1960.

———. *The Vampire in Europe*. London, 1929; rpt. New Hyde Park, N.Y.: University Books, 1961.

Taste the Blood of Dracula. Hammer Films, 1970.

Thompson, R. Campbell, trans. *The Devils and Evil Spirits of Babylonia*. 2 vols. London: Luzac, 1903–4.

Turolzi, Laszlo. *Erzebet Bathory*. Budapest, 1744.

Twitchell, James B. *The Living Dead: A Study of the Vampire in Romantic Literature*. Durham, N.C.: Duke University Press, 1981.

Vampyr. Tobes Klangfilm, 1932.

Varney the Vampire or the Feast of Blood. Presumed authorship by James Malcolm Rymer and/or Thomas Peckett Prest. London, 1847. Rpt. New York: Arno Press, 1970. Introduction by Devendra Varma. 3 vols.

Villeneuve, Roland. *Loups-garous et vampires*. Paris and Genève: La Palatine, 1963.

Willoughby-Meade, G. *Chinese Ghouls and Goblins*. London: Constable, 1928.

Wilson, Colin. *The Space Vampires*. New York: Random House, 1976.

Wilson, F. Paul. *The Keep*. New York: Berkley Books, 1981.

Wright, Dudley. *Vampires and Vampirism*. 1914; rpt. as *The Book of Vampires*. New York: Causeway Books, 1973.

Yarbro, Chelsea Quinn. *Hôtel Transylvania: A Novel of Forbidden Love*. New York: New American Library, 1979.

18

The Werewolf

Michael Cheilik

Unlike the vampire, which is neither alive nor dead, the werewolf is very much a living creature. According to traditional belief, the werewolf is a person who has been changed into a wolf or a creature with a lupine form. In some cases people transform themselves into werewolves, but in other cases someone else brings about the transformation. Often this is accomplished by some specific agency such as an ointment, belt or garment. A werewolf is usually larger and more powerful than an ordinary wolf, and he possesses a craving for human flesh.

The werewolf has great popular appeal today. There are werewolf masks, costumes, T-shirts, and many other commercial items connected with the creature. The werewolf is a popular figure in comic books, and he often appears in literature and films.

Indeed, the werewolf has been a feature of movies since 1913, but has recently increased in popularity because of most realistic lupine makeup and special effects. So close is the tie between werewolves and films that many people think that this monster is a creation of cinema. In reality, the werewolf and other human-animal combinations are basic archetypes of the psyche. A clinical psychological condition known as lycanthropy has always existed and continues to exist in modern times. In more archaic periods, what is now a pathological state was the norm for certain elements of society. For example, warrior clans among early Indo-European peoples identified themselves with the wolf, and indeed, in certain situations, acted like wolves. Many details of this can be traced to Greece, Rome, and the Germanic and Slavic areas, as well as to other cultures with an Indo-European derivation. Official lupine and/or lycanthropic cults such as these were ultimately transposed to folklore when these archaic societies changed and became more complex. Even before the advent of Christianity, which eliminated or demonized pagan beliefs, or transformed them into folklore, some archaic Roman myths had become folktales and ultimately minor literary genres. Werewolf stories and beliefs have been common enough in Western Europe, especially in Brittany, but they have retained even more vitality in Eastern Europe, which converted to Christianity at a later date. It is from both these areas that we get a large number of our ideas about werewolves. Still, because of its archetypical nature, the man-wolf is found in non–Indo-European cultures as well: where there are wolves there are werewolves.

I will attempt to trace and describe the werewolf figure from early hunting societies through the Greek and Roman world, the Middle Ages, and modern times. It will be shown that the werewolf lore of such non-Western cultures as the American Indian and the Chinese confirms certain archetypes. Then there will be an attempt to construct a composite model of a werewolf's life cycle. Finally, I will focus on the use of the werewolf in literature and in films.

Anthropomorphism is a characteristic attitude of human beings. If we look at early or archaic cultures, we can see that animals with human characteristics are frequently represented in art. Indeed, as early as the Upper Paleolithic period, groups of men who formed hunting clans identified with animals (totems), and considered themselves to have been descended from them. Transformations from man to at least partial beast can be seen in Cro-Magnon wall-paintings where certain man-beasts appear to be dancing. Thus, the "Sorcerer" from the Trois Frères cave shows a deerman (Ucko 204, fig. 89). Such man-animal combinations continued into early agricultural and pastoral societies.

According to Stig Wikander, Bruce Lincoln, and others, the Indo-European warrior clans were descended from such hunting bands. Further, a reconstruction of the structure of early Indo-European society has shown that these warriors identified with wolves (Przyluski 128–45). Lincoln has demonstrated this from Sanskrit, Avestan, and Greek texts, as well as from Baltic, Slavic, and Germanic sources. "At that time [the proto–Indo-European period] and for millennia thereafter, the ability to magically or ritually transform oneself into a ravening predator, possibly by the donning of a wolf's skin or a wolf's helmet, was valued as the highest accomplishment of the warrior's art, at once terrifying and glorious" (Lincoln 126).

It has been disputed whether or not the Greek cults of Zeus Lykaios (Greek *lykos*, wolf) and of the hero Lykaon are of Indo-European origin. In any case lycanthropy played a major role in their rituals. A condensation of the Lykaon myth is as follows: On a visit by Zeus and other gods, Lykaon served them the remains of a sacrificed boy instead of the customary meal offered to such guests. In retribution, Zeus changed Lykaon into a wolf (Ovid, *Metamorphoses* 1.177–343). Walter Burkert sees a connection between the Lykaon myth and the Arcadian festival, the Lykaia, where an initiate became a "wolf" for nine years after he had performed a human sacrifice. The ritual took place on Mount Lykaion at the altar of Zeus Lykaios in Arcadia. Lykaon ultimately became the totem clan founder of Arcadia, its first king (Burkert 84–93). Less in the realm of ritual and more literary in nature is Homer's description of Dolon, the Trojan spy in the *Iliad*: "Immediately Dolon threw on his shoulders the bent bow, and put on top of it the skin of a grey wolf" (10.333–34; my translation). A more fully detailed description of Dolon is given by Euripides in his *Rhesos*: "On my back I will attach a wolf-skin; on my head I will put the open jaws of the beast; to my hands I will apply the front paws and to my legs the rear paws" (208–11; my translation). Thus transformed, Dolon believes that he will be unrecognizable to his enemies the Greeks. Unfortunately for Dolon, Odysseus and Diomedes see through his trick, and the latter decapitates him. Louis Gernet considers the Dolon tale to be related to the wolf cult of Lykaon and Zeus Lykaios (192–94). In both cases the man-wolf becomes an outcast or *pharmakos*, a victim. In the ritual he suffers a symbolic death; in the Homeric tale, a real one. Gernet, Burkert, and others think that all of this goes back to "mask" rituals which admitted new warriors into wolf clans after a ritual death.

Herodotus did not believe the report that each of the Nueri, a nomad people of Northern Europe, changed into a wolf for a few days each year (4.105). But most ancient Greeks were apparently not sceptical about the possibility of such transformations, and the survival of werewolf lore to this day in Greece seems to indicate its vitality in the ancient period. An example of such vitality is probably seen in the transposed werewolf warrior Lykourgos (wolf-work), who came to be considered the Spartan lawgiver. He might originally have been a totem clan founder like Lykaon. Another of the wolf-gods is Apollo Lykeios. In the *Iliad* this god is referred to as being "born of the she-wolf" (4.101; my translation). Occasionally, the wolf form was taken on by the god (Summers 143).

Another Indo-European people, the Romans, had equally close ties to wolves. The wolf who suckled Romulus and Remus, the legendary founders of Rome, is one such totem. An actual survival of a wolf clan transposed to the realm of religion was the wolf priests or *luperci* who celebrated the Lupercalia festival on 15 February (Eisler 254–58). Still, the werewolf as a literary figure does not appear in the works of Roman writers until the first century B.C. and then in a mythical context. It is only in the Silver Age (mid–first century A.D. and later) that Latin literature deals with the supernatural to any great degree. Characteristic of these works is a love for the archaic, recondite, and bizarre. Thus, among its other adventures it is not surprising that the now fragmentary novel written by Petronius during the reign of Nero, the *Satyricon*, contains a werewolf story as well as a witch's tale. The former is probably the most celebrated lycanthropic tale from classical antiquity, and is related by the freedman Niceros at a lavish dinner given by the parvenu Trimalchio. He assures the guests that everything he is about to tell is true. The following is a condensed version of the story:

When I was still a slave I became very friendly with Melissa. After her husband died, I wanted to visit her at her farm [not too far from the city]. As luck would have it, my master was out of town on business and I took the opportunity to go see her. I had no difficulty in persuading a young man who was visiting to accompany me. He was a soldier and strong as Orcus [an underworld deity]. We departed during the last watch of night when the moon was still shining as brightly as at midday. We arrived at that part of the road lined with tombs, and my companion turned aside to do his business among the monuments. I sat down singing nervously. Then when I looked around to see what the soldier was doing, Heavens! My heart jumped into my mouth. He had taken off all his clothes and had put them at the side of the road. After he had urinated around them in a circle, he immediately changed into a wolf. Howling, he fled. When I tried to gather up his clothes, they had changed to stone. Half dead with fear, I finally made it to Melissa's house holding a drawn sword. She told me that just before, a wolf had broken in and had struck down the sheep. Before it got away, one of the farmhands had stabbed it in the neck with a spear. I hastened home. When I passed the graves, I could not find the soldier's clothes. Instead, there was a pool of blood. Finally, I reached the house where I found the soldier bleeding profusely from a deep gash in his neck; he was being cared for by a doctor. Then I knew he was a *versipellis* [literally, "turnskin"], a werewolf. (*Satyricon*, chs. 61–62; my translation).

This werewolf story has been interpreted in a variety of ways. According to Mauriz Schuster, it is fairly significant that the werewolf is a soldier in human form. This indicates his great strength ("strong as Orcus") in his human form and is typical of most lycanthropes (155–56). Although the soldier takes off his clothes, missing in this story are the more typical triggers of metamorphosis: the wolf garment, belt, or salve. Schuster thinks that Petronius' version reflects the prototypical werewolf tale, while Konrad Müller (33–35) believes that in the archetypal lycanthropic saga a wolf shirt must have been involved. Montague Summers (155) disagrees with Schuster that urinating in a circle is parody, stating that in Indian and Italian folklore, urinating ritually in a circle is supposed to immobilize all objects it surrounds. This would protect the soldier's means of returning to human form.

These analyses of Niceros' tale answer many questions raised by the story, but some basic ones remain unanswered. It seems to me that the fact that Niceros' companion is a soldier is of major significance. It appears to indicate that this is a transposed myth which originally concerned the Indo-European wolf-warriors. As has been seen, these lycanthropes acted like vicious wolves in certain situations. It is probable that these men stripped off their ordinary clothing before donning wolfskins that effected their transformation. In returning to society in human form they probably reversed the process. This fits in with the evidence of Niceros' tale. The only thing missing for transformation is the wolf garment, but the implication of the full moon is enough. Another trace of Indo-European ideology might be the lance wound inflicted on the wolf. Scholars have shown that each caste in Indo-European society had its own method of executing its criminals. Relevant here is that warriors who failed to return to a human frame of mind, if caught, were killed by spear point (Gerstein 131–56). Thus, in attempting to kill the wolf, the servant of Melissa attempts the proper execution of an Indo-European warrior gone mad, most importantly in his destruction of societal property, the sheep.

As in the case of other peoples of Indo-European origin, the Baltic and Slavic tribes retained werewolf traditions. Indeed, so entrenched did they become in the folk psyches of the region that some of this lore still survives in remote villages of the Balkans. Richard A. Ridley and others have suggested that the Indo-European warrior bands with werewolf tendencies worshiped a wolf deity. Ridley believes that there was "a specifically Baltic tradition of the Männerbund [warrior band] in service of the wolf god, men who commit acts of carnage in the near-hallucinatory state resulting from the ritual imbibing of a sacred intoxicant, and who think that they and their fellows are, indeed, ravening wolves" (330).

Another characteristic of the wolf deity or at any rate his Balto-Slavic manifestation, Velinas/Velnias/Volos or Veles, is an association with the guarding of flocks. As has just been seen from the analysis of the Petronius story, the wolf guardian (the soldier) has his ambivalences and can turn on his charges. Ridley sees the Eastern European St. George as a lightly Christianized wolf-god. "Both saint and god(s) reflect—on the folkloristic and mythological levels respectively—the Baltic/Slavic version of the Indo-European Männerbund" (330). A story retold by Ridley is sufficient to affirm the lupine and death-dealing aspects of St. George. St. George and his wolf companion Lisun are herding sheep and are observed by a poor man. After feeding loaves of bread to the sheep, George gives an extra loaf to the poor man. The loaf proves to be inexhaustible. The poor man's rich brother, wanting a similar magic loaf, goes back to the same place. This time George lacks enough bread and consequently feeds the rich brother as food to one of the wolves (Ridley 329). The wolf as destroyer of flocks and the Devil in lupine form (to be discussed subsequently) are basically similar.

The Germanic tribes also preserved warrior-wolf traditions. The god most closely associated with these werewolf fighters was Odin in the Scandinavian regions or Wotan on the Continent. So ferocious were these wolfmen that they required no arms, supposedly chewed their shields, and slaughtered man and beast that crossed their paths (Przyluski 133). They in short became berserk, or literally "enveloped in bear skin." Apparently, the ferocity of bear and wolf transformations had become synonymous. Even closer to werewolf lore of later periods is the story of Ûlfr (Wolf) described in the *Saga of Egil*, which was committed to writing in Iceland before 1000 A.D. but reflects traditions of several hundred years earlier. Ûlfr was an aged berserk who spent his days resting. When evening came, however, he was said to become a wolf. On his last nocturnal foray, he and his companions were transformed into wolves and slaughtered people who crossed their paths. Then Ûlfr died (Przyluski 134).

Here, as in other Indo-European traditions, the instability of these wolf bands created an ambivalent attitude toward them. Thus the *warg* (wolf) is a warrior who remains mad and an outlaw who is a danger to society (Gerstein 131–56).

But to return for a moment to the positive aspect of wolves in the Germanic tradition: when heroic ancestors died, they were transformed into wolves. By taking on a wolf name such as Wolfhard, Wolfbrand, Wolfgang, one assumed the strength and power of these forefathers. Indeed, the use of such a magical appellation provides for an incarnation of the wolf spirit in the body of the descendent (Kienle 38).

Not only was the death of warriors connected with lupine transformation, but the death of the universe was described in the sagas as wolf-time. In addition to other apocalyptic events, the cosmic wolf Fenrir will be released. His gaping mouth will reach from earth to sky. He will even eat up Odin, but Fenrir will also meet his doom (Davidson 37–38).

Christianity officially frowned on pagan beliefs and deities, but where these were too deeply rooted, they were often transformed into accceptable rituals and saints. This has been seen in the Balto-Slavic region. Where pagan cults were deemed incompatible with Christianity, they were proscribed. Still, they survived as folklore, fairy tales or, in a more vital para- and anti-Christian way, as part of the cult of the Devil. The latter was facilitated by the medieval Church's assertion that paganism was not so much baseless superstitution as the work of Satan.

Consequently, everywhere in Europe the positive aspect of the pre-Christian wolf cults was eliminated, leaving only the negative elements. St. Boniface of Mainz had a typical early medieval attitude toward lycanthropy. Unlike such early church fathers as Augustine and Jerome, who denied the possibility of human-to-animal metamorphosis, Boniface did not reject this concept. He, however, renounced all kinds of horrid diabolical things such as putting ''one's trust in the power of sorcerers'' and believing ''that the devil is able of his own might to transform men into wolves'' (Summers 6). Yet many writers believed that Satan was capable of effecting such transformations. If a person uses diabolical means to bring about transformation, he must first make a pact with the Devil. He receives in turn an unguent which will enable him to become a wolf (Villeneuve 10).

Satan himself was believed to be able to appear in a variety of animal forms including that of wolf. In an allegorical interpretation typical of the medieval period, the wolf as destroyer of flocks corresponds with the Devil's lupine form: if people are the sheep of God, then their devourer is the enemy of God. Since Christ is the Lamb of God, his enemy is, consequently, the wolf-Devil (Villeneuve 36). According to Harry A. Senn, the belief that the Devil was responsible for transforming people into werewolves gained widespread acceptance in the later fifteenth century, and this acceptance came about because of papal bulls passed at that time against sorcery and heresy (73).

During the Renaissance, Reformation, and beyond, lycanthropy was seen as diabolical possession. This in some cases might be exorcised, with the victim remaining alive, if it had been established that he was unwillingly possessed by demonic forces. More frequently, since transformation into a wolf had long been linked to Devil worship, lycanthropy was considered to have been voluntary. Thus, as in the case of witches, the werewolf had to be killed. This had to be done properly, according to set formulas, because if not, a lycanthrope could become a vampire.

A more rational attitude toward werewolves can also be seen. In medical works of the Persian philosopher Avicenna (980–1037) and the Spanish-Arabian thinker Averroës (1126–98), which were translated into Latin and diffused in Western Europe during the High Middle Ages, lycanthropy was considered a mental disease, not diabolical possession. By the sixteenth century, a German professor of medicine, Herman Neuwalldt, reflected this rational approach: "Whoever pretends that the Devil can change the nature of a creature of God misses the point; he has lost his mind; he ignores the principles of true philosophy" (qtd. in Villeneuve 88; my translation). As will be seen shortly, however, a substantial number of critics in the sixteenth and seventeenth centuries still continued to believe that lycanthropy was the work of the Devil.

As the Enlightenment progressed, more and more of the educated began to doubt the existence of werewolves. With the rise and continued growth of an urban middle class, diabolical lycanthropy as a reality receded in Western Europe to remote rural villages. There it joined other pagan survivals as folklore. As has been pointed out, much of Eastern Europe was different: Christianity came later here than in the West and the Enlightenment was long delayed. Consequently, in that region the werewolf continued to live a relatively full life (Senn 1–37).

In the Romantic period, however, the demonic and irrational made themselves felt again. Thus, with the rise of the Gothic novel and horror story, folkloric themes and peasant superstitions were drawn upon in profusion. In addition to Devil worship and witchcraft, such supernatural genres as the werewolf were mined for sensational themes.

Contemporary psychiatry attempts to analyze and treat neuroses and psychoses. Until fairly recently, however, theology and para-religious activities such as exorcism played such a role. It will be seen that lycanthropy is now considered to be a psychosis. Although far from common in the modern industrial world, sensational cases of lycanthropy can occasionally be found in screaming tabloid headlines. In more remote areas of less-developed countries, the psychosis of people changing into animals, acting like these beasts, even devouring human flesh—if not an everyday phenomenon—is relatively more frequent. In all such cases of the multiple personality variety, the individual returns to a relatively normal state before being set off again by an external stimulus.

This syndrome was the case from the Middle Ages until the modern period. Students of history are well acquainted with mass psychoses—the twentieth century has been replete with those based on ideologies of various sorts. A medieval example was that of the Crusades, above all the Children's Crusade.

But together with such seemingly irrational movements as Nazism, the Crusades had an economic and/or religious program as their base. Spontaneous, unplanned psychoses and resulting hysteria are not typical of the contemporary world.

During the medieval and early modern periods, however, there were waves of phenomena of this kind. A fourteenth-century example of such hysteria, although it is ostensibly based on one of the more extreme aspects of Christianity, the mortification of the flesh, can be seen in the behavior of the flagellants. Bands of them passed from town to town whipping themselves into ecstasy. There were outbreaks of witchcraft, and people lived in fear of attacks by were-cats, were-dogs, werewolves, and other were-animals. As late as the sixteenth century a wave of werewolfism made itself felt. In France, particularly between the 1570s and 1610, the fear of werewolves seems to have reached epidemic proportions (Villeneuve 70). Essays and treatises were written to try to explain the phenomenon, the most influential of which was a 1580 treatise on lycanthropy by Jean Bodin. This work (to be discussed subsequently) attempts to understand lycanthropy and allied phenomena rationally but within the limitations of the period. It must be remembered that no matter how seemingly secular France was becoming during the Renaissance, this was also a period of religious turmoils and wars. Consequently, Bodin and many of his contemporaries interpreted werewolfism in theological terms.

The Devil was thought to play a major part in werewolfism. As has been seen, many pre-Christian beliefs which had not been absorbed were proscribed as the work of Satan. This resulted in a parallel mirror-image religion, with its own rituals, which was proscribed by the Church. The question of evil, as opposed to good, is basically archetypal to religious thought, but dualistic representation is ambivalent in early Christianity. Polarization of God and Devil is of Persian Zoroastrian derivation and is not characteristic of the early Judaic tradition. During the sixth century B.C. and later, Judaism was influenced by Iranian dualism, but not in its central doctrines. Consequently, when Christianity arose from Judaism at the beginning of the current era, the strong dualism of Zoroastrianism was not sharply delineated. Only during the period of the Roman Empire and beyond did such dualistic cults as Mithraism and Manichaeism greatly influence Christianity. This presented an extraordinary problem. If God is omnipotent in the Hebraic sense, how can he tolerate the more flagrant works of the Devil which go against his basic precepts? Consequently, lycanthropy presented a major theological issue.

If we are all made by God in his image, God therefore has total control over our external forms. This line of reasoning implies that the Devil cannot really change a person to lupine form. As a result, if a person seems to become a wolf, it is only an illusion imposed by Satan, a cloud. The body within the cloud is unchanged. On the other hand, many theologians, more in the spirit of dualism, gave the Devil his due, and stated that he does cause external changes of human beings. Jean Bodin belongs to this latter school.

Before discussing the scholarly-theological arguments of the sixteenth and seventeenth centuries concerning lycanthropy, it would probably be instructive to discuss actual examples of this phenomenon which caused these works to be written in the first place. The most notorious of sixteenth-century "werewolves" was Gilles Garnier (Villeneuve 75–76; Summers 225–28). Garnier and other lycanthropes were active in the mountains of the future French province of Franche-Comté, filling the night (and day) with terror. A German studying at Dôle has left an account of the contemporary situation: "Rumor had it that the surrounding villages were infested by wolves the size of the average donkey. They devoured people, above all women" (qtd. in Villeneuve 75; my translation). As an academic, he had doubts about the gigantic man-wolves.

A less sceptical account is by Daniel d'Ange, who said that Gilles Garnier in a state of total indigence met a sort of spirit in the forest. The latter gave him the power, in the form of an unguent, to change into a variety of beasts, including a wolf (Summers 225–26; Villenueve 75). Whether or not his contemporaries considered Gilles Garnier a werewolf, his victims were real enough. They were stripped of their clothing, raped, and killed; and parts of their bodies, particularly the genital area, were eaten (Villeneuve 76). Garnier was ultimately caught and tried in Dôle in 1574. The transcript of his trial makes sensational reading. Catalogues of murdered young men and women and the circumstances of their deaths are described in detail. One of the least gory examples is the following: "*Item* by the said defendant, eight days after All Saints Day appearing in the form of a wolf, having taken another girl to the same place, near the meadow of La Ruppe . . . a bit before noon of the said day he strangled her and killed her with five wounds. He attempted to eat her but was so prevented by three people" (qtd. in Villeneuve 77–78; my translation).

Transcripts of quite a few such trials exist. Many "werewolves" may have been falsely accused during this hysterical period, and many who engaged in lycanthropy were never caught. Those who were tried were quickly burned at the stake like witches and sorcerers.

It seems that lycanthropy, in addition to appearing as an individual psychosis, was even more bizarre in such group manifestations as para-religious forest clans. For example, one youth, Jean Grenier (in 1603), was brought to the forest by an acquaintance of his. There he met the Lord of the Forest. "The Lord was a tall dark man, dressed all in black, riding a black charger. He saluted the two lads. . . . On a second meeting he [Jean Grenier] had given himself as his bond-slave" (Summers 233). After being marked on their thighs, the two boys received wolfskins, which after being put on seemed to change them into wolves. In that state they scoured the countryside accompanied by the Lord in a shape the size of a leopard (Summers 233). Necessary to transformation was an unguent which was applied before donning the wolfskin. Both salve and skin were held by the Lord, who gave them to Grenier whenever he wanted to be transformed. Another of the characteristics of the initiate into this strange clan was that the left thumbnail was not to be cut, but left to grow clawlike. After committing infanticide and cannibalism, Grenier was caught and tried. Strangely enough, considering the hysteria of the period, Grenier was granted clemency due to his youth and callowness (Summers 233–34). He was imprisoned in a monastery, where several years later a visitor claimed that Grenier continued to have sunken, burning eyes, sharp teeth, and clawlike hands. Grenier claimed that he had been visited at the monastery by the Lord of the Forest, but that he had repelled him with a crucifix (Summers 234). Perhaps this forest clan was a survival of the Indo-European wolfmen.

Lycanthropy diminished in virulence in France, but as late as 1925 there was a werewolf case. This time it was at Uttenheim, an Alsatian village not far from Strasbourg.

These are some of the kinds of phenomena that prompted Jean Bodin to write his treatise on lycanthropy. As can be seen from the transcript of Gilles Garnier's trial, both defendant and accusers actually believed that shape-shifting was involved. Bodin follows this point of view and uses corroborating evidence of St. Thomas Aquinas, who stated that all angels whether bad or good have the power by their very nature to change the shapes of our bodies (Summers 73). Further, Bodin uses the alchemical argument that, if man can change rose bushes to cherry trees, or apples to cabbages, then Satan can change one form of the body into another, a great power given to him by God (Summers 73). As in alchemy, however, special evocations (in this case black magic) are necessary for transformation.

An entirely different point of view is espoused by other theologians and observers. The *Canon Episcopi*, one in a series of ecclesiastical decrees collected in *De ecclesiasticis disciplinis*, had an enormous influence. Supposedly from the tenth century or earlier, the *Canon* rejects the idea of actual transformation (Regino 354–56; Summers 84) and says that whatever change seems to be effected is mere illusion. Following this line of reasoning is the *Malleus Maleficarum*, first printed in 1486 (Sprenger and Kramer 122–24). Moreover, in *De spirituum apparitionibus* (1594), Peter Thyraeus argues that transformation only seems to be real. According to Summers, Thyraeus favors the following explanation: "By the power and agency of the fiend both the man himself and all who espy him are fully persuaded and convinced that he is metamorphosed into the shape of some animal . . . whereas actually he is not so transformed" (92). Thyraeus inclines toward diabolical possession of both observer and "werewolf," although he does not reject the idea that the diabolical illusion of an animal superimposed on human form is possible.

Countless publications in the early modern period, then, tried to discover the nature of lycanthropy, but it was not until the nineteenth century that psychoanalysis was utilized in explaining the phenomenon. In his book *Man into Wolf* (1951), Robert Eisler uses the analytic methods of Jung to explain the phenomenon of lycanthropy. According to Eisler, although the werewolf exists among the archetypes of our collective unconscious, its outward manifestation must be considered a clinical psychosis. Consequently, on the one hand lycanthropy is caused by internal means, not by a more archaic agent such as the Devil, via salves, clothing, and the like. On the other hand, the fact that werewolfism is part of our collective unconscious makes it seem like an agent outside the conscious ego. As a result, the differences between lupine possession (as in the more Christian past) and the reification of an unconscious archetype all seem various modes of expressing the same thing.

Eisler delves into history to try to explain the lycanthropic phenomenon. In essence, he states, this took place in the transition our ancestors went through from being vegetarian apes to becoming carnivorous ones. "We are all descended from males of the carnivorous lycanthropic variety, a mutation evolved under the pressure of hunger caused by the climatic change at the end of the pluvial period, which induced indiscriminate, even cannibalistic predatory aggression, culminating in the rape and sometimes even in the devouring of the females of the original peaceful fruit-eating *bon sauvage* remaining in the primeval virgin forests" (Eisler 42). In this bloodletting and cannibalism, there is always an accompanying feeling of guilt which required expiatory rites. Consequently, the aggressor had to be purified. In many cases, as part of the induction into a hunting group, the initiate was branded as an outlaw. As has been seen from ancient Greek evidence, Lykaon was forced to live as a wolf in isolation for nine years, but subsequently became the founding totem-king of Arcadia. In addition, the Germanic military werewolf figure the *warg* became an outlaw in Frankish Salic law.

Dream analysis has revealed similarities to archaic rituals and myths. In one example a patient dreams he has been in a herd (society) from which he withdraws. On leaving he puts on a " 'strange hat': This is, of course, the disguising headgear . . . of the werewolf about to take to the woods and to become an outlaw" (Eisler 45). This pattern is repeated endlessly in the actual reports of lycanthropy, such as the one of Gilles Garnier. Eisler and others believe that this werewolfism includes not only such obvious lupine "transformations," but also such psychotic behavior as rape, murder, dismemberment, and subsequent cannibalism. This syndrome, although not obviously lupine, does appear in the modern world. A psychosexual explanation complements this: "Sexual pathologists put down this particular idea of a man changing himself into an animal for cannibalistic purposes to the desire to devour both the loved and hated objects, and see in the werewolf's lust the symbolism of repressed aggression" (Hannum 76). In the same category belongs Sigmund Freud's famous case history of the "Wolf-Man."

Burkert agrees with Eisler in the following: "In hunting societies accessible to ethnological study, hunters are said to have expressed clear feelings of guilt with regard to the slaughtered animal" (Burkert 16). He states that this hunting/eating of flesh is but a variant of human sacrifice/cannibalism and has been programmed into the brain during the evolutionary process. However, he diverges from Eisler in saying, "It was at the time when Australopithecine primates were killing and eating baboons, and sometimes even one of their own, that spiritual and social structures began to evolve which made killing the foundation of cultural order'' (74–75). Accordingly, in archaic societies, ritual and myth dealing with sacrifice provided a mass outlet for these imprints in the brain. In more developed societies, which offer no such outlets, they can become individual psychoses. One would suspect that in Reformation–Counter-Reformation Europe during the sixteenth and seventeenth centuries, the breakdown of the existing order of things could lead to such mass counter-Christian psychoses as witchcraft and lycanthropy.

In addition to werewolfism as a psychosis, Eisler and others have said that it can also be a symptom of a disease such as rabies. The drug hyoscyamine (henbane) or stramonium also produces similar symptoms. Witches are said to have taken drugs to further a sensation of flying (Eisler 160).

It can thus be seen that the belief in the transformation of humans into predatory animals is a universal phenomenon, perhaps arising from hunting instincts but certainly being an aspect of cannibalism. Consequently, it is no surprise that in those regions of the world where the wolf ranges, lycanthropy is a characteristic phenomenon. Elsewhere, there are were-leopards (Africa), were-foxes (Japan), were-jaguars (South America), and so on.

Parallel to the Indo-European wolf bands are those of certain North American Indian tribes. For example, among the Nootkas there is an initiation ritual in which the werewolf band wearing lupine masks absconds with the supposedly dead initiate, whom they return the next day. He is then revived and also becomes a warrior werewolf (Eisler 150). A Chinese story quoted by Eisler is very much like parallel European folktales: ''A woodcutter [is] attacked in the evening in a wood by a big wolf . . . [he] mounts a tree and hits the wolf's forehead with a cut of his axe. The wolf remains lying on the ground until dawn, then disappears. His traces lead to the door of the hut of a peasant, who is found with a cut on his forehead. His sons kill the peasant, who while expiring transforms himself again into a wolf'' (Eisler 154).

A fairly recent case (in the 1940s) of lycanthropy among the Navajos indicates how tradition, folklore, and a psychotic condition combine. Alberta Hannum tells of a Navajo man who was thought to become a wolf at night by putting on a wolfskin, and was said to devour flocks of domestic animals as well as women. Another of his reputed activities was the digging up of corpses in order to get their jewels. He consequently became very wealthy. Hannum further indicates that lycanthropy had been a constant fear among the Navajos (76).

Before examining the lycanthrope in literature and in cinema, it would be illuminating to create a composite model of the life cycle of the werewolf, drawn from the traditions thus far discussed. To begin with, a werewolf can be the offspring of a normal mother if she has had intercourse with a possessed man. A variation of this is a woman who has had sex with a demonic spirit. Once the woman has been impregnated, a diabolical child is a foregone conclusion. This child can be a devil incarnate, as in the case of Ira Levin's *Rosemary's Baby*, or it can be a werewolf or some other type of monster.

Another and more common way in which a werewolf is created is by demonic possession or by external force. In both cases, as with birth from diabolical seed, the transformation is involuntary. In the matter of possession, the victim is sometimes described as weak-spirited (Villeneuve 43–44), but anybody can be taken over. Sometimes, a means of contagion is direct contact with a lycanthrope (Woodward 174). This is most commonly effected by a break in the skin, sometimes a scratch, but usually a bite by a werewolf. In folklore, wolf-people resulting from any of the above means spread the disease by biting. Of course, the voracious appetite of the werewolf leaves a relatively small number of victims alive. In some Eastern European traditions the power of the werewolf is difficult to resist. In some regions, the werewolf, as opposed to the vampire, cannot be warded off by religious items such as crucifixes; in other areas, crucifixes do the trick. In Romania, garlic rubbed around house apertures can repel the monster. Wolfsbane (aconite or monkshood), although very popular in films, is not an overly common lycanthrope repellent. This plant was, however, used to poison wolves. In Western Europe, particularly France, spells and pointed sticks can ward off werewolves.

A common way in which inner evil has been expressed in many periods of history has been through the external form of the body. Consequently, a totally bad person can supposedly become a monster, especially a werewolf or vampire. Another manifestation of inner evil is more indirect. In this case the individual engages in magic and witchcraft and consciously seeks to metamorphose into a werewolf. During a witches' sabbath, or analogous rite, often at a crossroads or at the entrance to a forest, the initiates leave bits of their own hair, and perhaps some skin or blood. These are dedicated to the Devil, who in turn gives the initiates an ointment by means of which they can become werewolves. One typical formula for such a salve contains such repellent items as parts of toad, snake, hedgehog, fox—of course wolf—and human blood or fat mixed with certain herbs (Villeneuve 55–56). Wolfsbane, although a repellent in some areas, also can play a role in transformation. "Wolfbane blooms under the autumn moon, and according to some legends, it is only at this time that the werewolf prowls the countryside" (Douglas 59). The full moon itself is generally a factor in metamorphosis. Sometimes it causes transformation at night; or, as in some French traditions, its appearance at noon on the day of the full moon causes the change.

Villeneuve quotes Jean Bodin's semi-rationalizing treatise *De la lycanthropie*, where, after applying the ointment, the sorcerer thinks that he is a wolf and acts accordingly. The Devil in turn surrounds the individual with a thick cloud of lupine shape, which makes others think he has really become a wolf (Villeneuve 56). This pseudo-transformation can also be achieved by means of certain magical formulas as opposed to the use of an ointment. Or as has been seen in some ancient sources, wearing a wolfskin garment, cap, or belt can also effect transformation.

Unlike ordinary mortals, the werewolf has two forms, one human and one lupine. In some traditions the human form of the werewolf is no different from that of anyone else. Other traditions diverge from this, and there is the belief that the lycanthrope as a person has certain telltale signs. Bristlelike hair grows from his palms. "Most humans who are werewolves will, of course, keep their palms shaven, but the roughness of the skin caused by such a procedure is almost impossible to disguise" (Douglas 57). Also, the index fingers on each hand are longer than the central digits. In addition to such signs, the werewolf can acquire a sign of a crescent or half moon on a thigh. In some traditions, the human form of the werewolf has scabby legs and sunken eyes that glow in the dark (Douglas 58).

As in the case of most human-to-animal transformations, the bestial shape is sometimes complete, sometimes partial. Consequently, the werewolf can appear as a biped or quadruped. If he stands on two feet, he sometimes retains other human remnants, but rarely traces of clothing. In totally bestial form, the werewolf has either shed his human clothes (as in the Roman tale of Niceros), or he has somehow absorbed them. Examples of both categories can be seen in two book illustrations. An etching by Maurice Sand for George Sand's 1858 book *Légendes rustiques* (Summers, frontispiece) shows a group of bipedal werewolves. On the other hand, a cut from a 1517 book by Johann Geiler von Kaiserberg shows a four-legged werewolf attacking a man (Summers 48). As a complete wolf, the werewolf is larger and more ferocious than the ordinary wolf. He can also have longer hair. This Eastern European tradition is reflected in the Slavic name for werewolf, *vlokodlak, vukodolak*, and other forms, the meaning of which is "wolf-haired" (Senn 19). This hair is sometimes silvery.

If a werewolf has been transformed into a beast by the full moon, he takes on his human form again when the moon sets and the sun rises. In those traditions where he becomes an animal by means of wolfskin garment or belt, he returns to human form after taking it off. If a salve has been used, it is washed off. If he has taken off or absorbed his clothing, he returns naked to human form. In most traditions, wounds suffered in the lupine state are carried over to the human form.

Traditions vary on how to eliminate a lycanthrope. In some, a stick with a metallic point piercing a vital area does the trick. In France such weapons often are of no avail unless they have been blessed in a chapel of St. Hubert. A silver object used as a club can also kill a werewolf, or, in more modern lycanthropy, a silver bullet (Douglas 66). Finally, since a werewolf is often a kind of witch or sorcerer, he can be killed by burning at the stake. Decapitation can be fatal to lycanthropes in certain traditions, as in Homer's Dolon story.

Although the werewolf makes an early appearance in literature, he has not often been the focal point of major literary works. This is especially true of the nineteenth century, when one would expect at least one outstanding lycanthropic classic. Instead, sensational popular literature was most often the vehicle for this theme. Even when such important writers as Alexandre Dumas (père) and Prosper Mérimée dealt with werewolves, those works fell below their usual standard. Certainly no single lycanthropic work can compare to Bram Stoker's classic

Dracula (1897). Perhaps the werewolf is not horrible enough; perhaps he is too human. He certainly lacks the vampire's cryptic and latently sexual nature.

In the twelfth-century poem, *William of Palerne, or the Romance of William and the Werwolf*, translated into English about 1350, lycanthropy plays an important role: the hero has become Roman emperor with the help of a werewolf (Skeat, passim). A helpful and benevolent werewolf also appears in the twelfth-century *Lay of the Bisclavaret* by Marie de France. In general, however, the werewolf was seldom used in literature before the nineteenth century. The lycanthrope does not appear in the first Gothic novels, such as Horace Walpole's *Castle of Otranto* (1765). In the Gothic tradition, but stressing a human monster, not a werewolf, is Mary Wollstonecraft Shelley's *Frankenstein* (1818). In keeping with both the Gothic horror story and the Romantic penchant for folklore was the penny magazine, or on a more refined level, the monthly literary magazine. They serialized tales of terror, including those about werewolves.

The first definitive werewolf story published in English was "Hugues, the Wer-Wolf" by Sutherland Menzies, which appeared in the *Court Magazine and Monthly Critic* in 1838 (Menzies 259–74), a British publication. The story begins innocently enough when the hero, Hugues, opens a chest which contains a wolf outfit, but takes a turn for the worse when he puts it on and becomes a werewolf. More famous is Captain Frederick Marryat's "White Wolf of the Harz Mountains," published in *The Phantom Ship* in England in 1839 after having been serialized in the *New Monthly Magazine* in 1837. Included in this tale are some of the essentials of the lycanthropic tale, such as a Central European locale and a marriage which takes an unexpected turn when a man discovers he has married a female werewolf. In this story within a story, Krantz, the narrator, tells of his marriage to a Transylvanian woman. Krantz's children are eaten one by one by a white wolf. The surviving children follow their stepmother and find she is a werewolf, whom Krantz shoots. He is cursed and is later devoured by a tiger (Bleiler 344).

The French werewolf hysteria of the sixteenth century is the subject of Catherine Crowe's "A Story of a Weir-Wolf," first published in *Hogg's Weekly Instructor* in 1846. Crowe's tale, although dealing with lycanthropy, is basically a romance. In it Manon Thierry out of jealousy accuses another woman and her father of witchcraft and werewolfism. Condemned to be burnt at the stake, they are saved and pardoned, and the accused woman even marries her true love (Crowe 184–89).

Many other stories dealing with lycanthropy were serialized in Britain and the United States during this period. Meanwhile in France, Alexandre Dumas (père) wrote *Le Meneur de loups* (The Wolf Leader), which was first published in 1857. This novel has an extremely complex plot and all the essential elements of the werewolf story. The evil Thibault has made a pact with the Devil, and after many twists of the plot becomes able to change himself into a wolf. He has only one thing to fear, however; and that is that one day a year he is vulnerable. At just such a time Thibault is wounded, and he finds himself in the cemetery where his late beloved is being buried. He dies and only a wolfskin remains; the rest of the body is missing. It appears that this is so because he gave himself so that his beloved would come back to life again. Villeneuve comments that the Dumas tale is not frightening, but says that *Monstre immortel* (Immortal Monster) of Prosper Mérimée, a contemporary of Dumas, is indeed chilling (207). This story, which deals with werewolves and cannibalism, has its roots in folklore. Also in the realm of folklore is George Sand's *Légendes rustiques*. Included in this 1858 book are three chapters on lycanthropes.

One of the classics of the horror genre, Robert Louis Stevenson's *The Strange Case of Dr. Jekyll and Mr. Hyde* (1886), has certain elements of lycanthropy. Dr. Jekyll discovers a liquid which can change him into the bestial Mr. Hyde, and another which permits him to regain his original form. As Mr. Hyde he is a murderer; as Dr. Jekyll he is a most virtuous man. The physical and mental metamorphosis of Dr. Jekyll is rather lupine, and the liquid with which this is done resembles the diabolical salve of the werewolf. Indeed, the eventual loss of control over the transformation process greatly resembles the inability of the werewolf to prevent his own metamorphosis. In both cases, something resembling sympathy is evoked from the reader. In fact, Stephen King considers *Dr. Jekyll and Mr. Hyde* to be a werewolf story (78–83).

The werewolf genre continued to be popular at the turn of the century and into the twentieth century. An example of this is Eden Phillpotts' 1899 collection of stories, *Loup-garou!* In this book Phillpotts describes the loups-garous as "horrid monsters akin to the vampire and the were-wolf" (qtd. in Summers 270). They are attracted by death although repelled by singing. The only things that can kill them are bullets which have been blessed.

In the twentieth century, werewolf tales have continued to appear in magazines and short story collections. Fred Whishaw's "The Were-Wolf," which was published in *Temple Bar* (November 1902), has Russia as its locale. In the story a cowherd takes the opportunity of the presence in the district of a huge marauding wolf to pretend he is a werewolf in order to steal. He is found out by the estate owner. Close to our conception of what a cinematic werewolf story should be like is Peter Fleming's 1931 story "The Kill." In a story within a story, Lord Fleer is about to adopt a Belgian orphan girl. He consequently does not acknowledge the illegitimate son whom his housekeeper is going to bear for him. The child, Vom, is born and put under a spell by the housekeeper. After her death Vom is reared by farmers, but unlike them he has an extra-long third finger, a sign of the werewolf. Ten years later, after a period of disappearance, Vom reappears and kills the orphan, now an attractive woman and Lord Fleer's heir. This tale is told by a young man to another man in a remote, deserted, fog-bound English railroad station. As it turns out, the teller is the new heir to the Fleer fortune and his listener is Vom, who kills him (Douglas 67–68).

Guy Endore's 1933 novel *The Werewolf of Paris* is considered by many to be a classic. It was the basis of the 1961 film, *Curse of the Werewolf*, although the setting was switched from nineteenth-century France to eighteenth-century Spain. In the tale, Bertrand Caillet, inheriting a familial curse, has "the stigmata of the werewolf . . . hairy palms, peculiar eyebrows, interlocking teeth" (Bleiler 178). As a teenager he begins to effect changing into a wolf. When he reaches maturity, his sex acts are followed by his eating up of his partner. After all kinds of atrocities, love calms him down, but eventually he ends up in an insane asylum and commits suicide.

Another vividly dramatic werewolf story is James Blish's 1950 "There Shall Be No Darkness." The setting is a Scottish castle where a party is in progress. The guest of honor is a Polish pianist whose eyebrows meet, whose index and middle fingers are the same size, and who has remarkably sharp teeth. When confronted by another guest, he metamorphoses into a wolf. Silver candlesticks ward him off. All the silver in the house is converted into silver bullets. As it turns out, the hostess, who is also a werewolf, is killed. Eventually, the pianist-werewolf is also killed (Douglas 68–69).

Two authors of the 1970s wrote werewolf novels which were adapted to films. The first, Gary Brandner, in *The Howling* (1977), wrote of a very peculiar California town where strangers disappear. Of course, they are devoured by the local folk, who are lycanthropes. Brandner wrote a sequel, *The Howling Two*, in 1979. Of a much higher caliber is Whitley Strieber's *The Wolfen* (1979), which deals with American Indian ancestral totems who have a lupine nature and appear in New York City.

Because the early lycanthropic tales were most often written for magazines, they are mainly short stories. "White Wolf of the Harz Mountains" is a story within a novel, and even *Dr. Jekyll and Mr. Hyde* is a novella. A notable exception is *Wagner, the Wehr-Wolf*, a "penny dreadful" novel published around 1857. Some of the more recent lycanthropic tales such as *The Werewolf of Paris, The Howling*, and *The Wolfen* are full novels. Plays dealing with werewolves have been rare. Films, on the other hand, have been a successful medium for lupine stories.

From its inception the cinema has been connected with magic and the fantastic. The very name of the predecessor of movies, the magic lantern, indicates this connection. Seeing moving pictures on a screen involved a radical departure from ordinary entertainment media and was a surreal experience by itself. In addition, at the beginning movies had few pretenses of literary excellence; they were more on the level of penny weekly magazines that featured sensational stories. Since performances were not live, fantastic effects both in filming and editing were not only possible but desirable. Consequently, horror, a type of fantasy, appears early in cinematic history. Film is a medium that is especially suited to the creation of horror. "There is its ability to conjure up the fantastic with conviction, the power of the camera to penetrate beneath the surface of the apparently normal and secure, its capacity for approaching each individual spectator, or drawing that spectator into itself, by the use of close-up—and finally its hypnotic effect, a film being viewed in the dark and consisting of moving shapes against a light-reflecting background, the effect being stronger when viewed slightly from below'' (Butler 9–10).

Although the rationalizing effects of the scientific and industrial revolutions devalued traditional mythical beliefs, science in the form of psychoanalysis opened a vast new mythical world, the unconscious. Movements in the arts of the first decades of the twentieth century, such as Expressionism and Surrealism, attempted to manifest on canvas or in literature elements of the unconscious mind. On a more popular level, cinema followed similar trends. Indeed, the loss of common religious and mythical beliefs was somewhat compensated for by films. Horror movies depicted countless fears and apprehensions of the unconscious, and, using monster figures from a variety of sources, created a new mythical genre. More than in literature, the success of a horror film was, and is, a fragile thing. Because of the patently unreal nature of the subject matter, any false move can reduce an audience to paroxysms of laughter.

The first major school of horror movies was in Germany. Here a combination of stresses of the period between World War I and the end of the Weimar Republic with the addition of strong Expressionist tendencies created a series of unique seminal films. Among the most renowned horror films produced during this era were the *Golem* (1914 and 1920 versions) and *The Cabinet of Dr. Caligari* (1919). The first important vampire picture was *Nosferatu* (1922).

Surprisingly, none of the German silent classics featured the werewolf theme. The earliest documented werewolf film is American, the 1913 Bison production of *The Werewolf*. Unlike more sophisticated German movies, this film has the basic approach of the penny supplements. ''Indian woman's husband is killed, but she thinks she was deserted; becomes witch and raises daughter to hate all white men; daughter becomes a werewolf; years later reincarnation of villain has his bride killed by reincarnation of the werewolf'' (Lee 3:533). The next werewolf movie to make an impact was the 1923 French production of *Le Loup-garou*, whose story deals with a murderer who after having been cursed by a priest becomes a werewolf (Willis 521). Finally, the Lee-Bradford production of *Wolf Blood* (1925) rounds out the repertory of silent werewolf movies. In this picture a ''man fears he is becoming a 'half beast' after receiving a transfusion of wolf's blood'' (Willis 533).

In film as in the realm of literature, *Dr. Jekyll and Mr. Hyde* far exceeds in quality its contemporary werewolf tales. The first successful film of the Robert Louis Stevenson classic (after a failed early attempt) was produced in the United States in 1920. Directed by John S. Robertson and starring John Barrymore, this film has been considered one of the best of the Jekyll-Hyde versions. Remarkable is the fact that Barrymore achieves transformation not by makeup but by facial contortions (Butler 28).

The advent of sound increased the possibilities of horror films. Universal Studios dominated the genre for nearly twenty years, beginning with its 1931 *Dracula*, starring Bela Lugosi. The same year saw a remake of *Dr. Jekyll and*

Mr. Hyde starring Fredric March, considered the best of the Dr. Jekyll films. The first lycanthropic film produced at Universal was the 1935 *Werewolf of London*. The basic key to this story is a mystical flower called mariphasa. It is, one would think, in the same magical category as the Homeric herb *moly* which prevents Odysseus from being turned into a pig by Circe. Apparently mariphasa grows only in Tibet, so that is where an English botanist goes to find it. He succeeds, but is bitten by a werewolf in the process. After the botanist returns to England, a Japanese scientist (actually the werewolf in human form) comes to him and asks for the flower; the scientist says that juice from the blossom of the flower will keep a person from becoming a werewolf. The botanist refuses to give the flower away. But he has been bitten; and, accordingly, at the time of the next full moon he becomes a murderous werewolf. The film says that a werewolf will be driven to destroy the person he loves most of all. The botanist attacks his wife, but he is slain by a silver bullet before he kills her (Douglas 73).

The werewolf film parallel in importance to the 1931 *Dracula* is *The Wolf-Man* (1941). This Universal movie, directed by George Waggner and starring Lon Chaney, Jr., and Claude Rains, which has often been severely criticized (Willis 534), praised with reservation (Butler 159), or totally lauded (Douglas 70–71), is nonetheless the archetype of werewolf films. The hero, Lawrence Talbot (Chaney), is reared in the sinister atmosphere of Transylvania, but he rejects peasant lore because he considers it superstition. He becomes a werewolf in the typical cinematic manner: while passing through a forest he wards off a lycanthrope who is attacking a woman, but he gets bitten in the process. He then becomes a lupine killer during the nights of the full moon. Puzzled by all this, Talbot is illuminated by an all-knowing gypsy woman played by Maria Ouspenskaya. Nothing helps, however, as was the case in *The Werewolf of London*. Another parallel with that film is that Talbot attacks a person close to him, this time his father (Claude Rains), and meets his demise by means of a silver object, this time a cane with a silver wolfhead tip.

Ever alert to box office success, Universal Studios extended the life of Lawrence Talbot in sequels as it had that of Dracula and the Frankenstein monster (the original *Frankenstein* had been produced in 1931). Indeed, if these horrendous beasts could reappear, why not have them meet each other? In the 1943 film, *Frankenstein Meets the Wolf Man*, Lawrence Talbot, ever desirous for a cure, is advised by a gypsy (Ouspenskaya again) to find Dr. Frankenstein, whose deep knowledge created the great monster out of human parts. Talbot finds the monster in a frozen state, but he discovers Dr. Frankenstein is dead. During the full moon the revitalized monster and the wolfman fight each other in the rebuilt laboratory. An end to the film, but as the audience knows, only a temporary demise of the monsters, is achieved when local Transylvanian villagers destroy a dam which drowns laboratory, Frankenstein monster, and wolfman.

After the wolfman's encounter with the Frankenstein monster, Dracula was added to the duo in the 1944 production *House of Frankenstein* and the 1945

House of Dracula. Not content to leave well enough alone, Universal had all three creatures do a reprise in the 1948 film *Abbott and Costello Meet Frankenstein*. Although ostensibly a horror-comedy, this movie is the end of the line for Universal Studio's wolfman.

Far from being dead, however, lycanthropy as well as other horror genres was revitalized during the 1950s and 1960s by Hammer Studios in England. These productions, although they were designed for the mass market, created a more folkloric, less absurd werewolf genre than the later Universal lycanthropic films. In the 1961 *Curse of the Werewolf*, loosely based on the Guy Endore novel, *The Werewolf of Paris*, Oliver Reed plays the lycanthrope. As in the book, lycanthropy is arrested by love, but love is foiled. Drake Douglas has high praise for the film: "All in all, *Curse of the Werewolf* is probably the most satisfying and intelligent of werewolf films" (75). On the other hand, Donald Willis, who unlike most critics has a negative attitude toward the film, calls it a "leisurely, rather dull horror film" (105).

Inevitably, the horror genre and the teenage exploitation movie were combined. Three self-explanatory examples are *I Was a Teenage Werewolf* (1957), *Werewolf in a Girls' Dormitory* (1961), and *Werewolf on Wheels* (1971).

In the 1980s werewolf films have again witnessed a renaissance, this time stimulated by phenomenal makeup techniques. The 1980 film, *Altered States*, directed by Ken Russell, although not technically a werewolf movie, deals with the lupine nature of man. A scientist trying to discover the primal state of humans reaches a lupine archetype, affirming Konrad Lorenz' theory of the Killer Ape or Burkert's Man the Killer (1–22). The 1981 film *An American Werewolf in London*, directed by John Landis, is a classic. Bitten by a monster on the Yorkshire moors, the hero (David Naughton) becomes a werewolf. Rick Baker's Oscar-winning makeup creates lupine snout, hair, and teeth on the werewolf as the audience watches. One of the most chilling scenes of the film occurs when a staid businessman encounters the lycanthrope in a deserted London Underground station. *The Howling* (1981), directed by Joe Dante, uses similar makeup techniques but is a less successful film. Here there are too many werewolves and too many cinematic inside jokes. A third 1981 film, *Wolfen*, directed by Michael Wadleigh, is a detective story with murderous American Indian ancestral spirits in lupine form as the object of the search. It is a fascinating film. Not so well done is *Ladyhawke*, a 1985 pseudo-medieval romance directed by Richard Donner. In it two cursed lovers are transformed into animals: she into a hawk during the day, and he into a wolf at night.

Werewolves have appeared on television in made-for-TV movies and in reruns of commercial films. An unexpected occasion for the appearance of a werewolf on television was in the Gothic soap opera *Dark Shadows*, which dealt with the supernatural. In 1968 a werewolf was added to the script. Headwriter Ron Sproat tells me that due to the exigencies of daytime television, a naked werewolf was impossible. Consequently, a mutant werewolf in a business suit was seen stalking the forest.

To sum up, films and television confirm the basic archetypal nature of the werewolf in the human psyche. The presence of werewolves on the screen might be a safe way of reifying them. As has been seen, such a safety valve was present in such pagan cultures as those of the proto–Indo-Europeans and the American Indians. With the advent of medieval Christianity, however, lycanthropy was suppressed; and this suppression led to periodic eruptions of lycanthropy in the form of sociopathic behavior. In recent times, psychoanalysis has seemingly directed many of the drives connected with lycanthropy into more constructive channels.

There are numerous studies of the werewolf, ranging from the general to the specific. The classic in the field remains Montague Summers' *The Werewolf* (1933). Unfortunately, Summers uses a nineteenth-century ecclesiastical approach, and he is obsessed with witchcraft. Consequently, he omits many folkloric elements that do not deal with that matter. Also important is Roland Villeneuve's *Loups-garous et vampires* (1963). Villeneuve gives a good survey of lycanthropy, but he does not go into much detail about werewolf literature. He omits films entirely. A general study of the werewolf is Basil Copper's *The Werewolf in Legend, Fact and Art* (1977). Also covering the entire field is Ian Woodward's *The Werewolf Delusion* (1979). Of interest to the general reader are Nancy Garden's *Werewolves* (1973), Bill Pronzini's *Werewolf!* (1979), and Jim Hoskins' *Werewolves* (1981).

Robert Eisler's *Man into Wolf* (1951) is essential for an understanding of lycanthropy from a psychological-anthropological point of view. Eisler's use of clinical case studies adds a broad dimension to his book. There is no single book on the werewolf in the ancient world. For this it is necessary to consult numerous articles as well as texts. Summers, Villeneuve, and others deal with the medieval and early modern periods in some detail. More specialized is Harry A. Senn's *Were-Wolf and Vampire in Romania* (1982), which in addition to describing Romanian lycanthropic lore compares it to werewolf traditions of medieval and early modern Europe.

General, but thorough, analyses of the werewolf in literature can be found in Everett Bleiler's *The Guide to Supernatural Fiction* (1983) and Marshall B. Tymn's *Horror Literature: A Core Collection and Reference Guide to the Best of Horror* (1981). The following works furnish useful information about werewolf films: Walt Lee's *Reference Guide to Fantastic Films* (1972–74); Donald C. Willis' *Horror and Science Fiction Films: A Checklist* (1972); Michael Weldon's *The Psychotronic Encyclopedia of Film* (1983); and John Stanley's *The Creature Features Movie Guide* (1984). All provide summaries and analyses of werewolf movies, but the Lee and Willis books are the most complete for the early films.

BIBLIOGRAPHY

Abbott, George Frederick. *Macedonian Folklore*. Cambridge: Cambridge University Press, 1903.

Abbott and Costello Meet Frankenstein. Dir. Charles Barton. With Lon Chaney, Jr., and Bela Lugosi. Universal, 1948.

Altered States. Dir. Ken Russell. With William Hurt and Blair Brown. Warner Bros., 1980.

An American Werewolf in London. Dir. John Landis. With David Naughton and Jenny Agutter. Polygram/Universal, 1981.

Baring-Gould, Sabine. *The Book of Were-Wolves: Being an Account of a Terrible Superstition*. London, 1865.

Beauvoys de Chauvincourt, Le Sieur de. *Discours de la lycanthropie ou la transformation des hommes en loups*. Paris, 1599.

Bleiler, Everett F. *The Guide to Supernatural Fiction: A Full Description of 1,175 Books from 1750 to 1960*. Kent, Ohio: Kent State University Press, 1983.

Bodin, Jean. *De la démonomanie des sorciers*: 2:6, *De la lycanthropie et si les esprits peuvent changer les hommes en bêtes*. Paris, 1580.

Bouget, Henry. *Discours des sorciers*. Lyon, 1590.

Brandner, Gary. *The Howling*. Greenwich, Conn.: Fawcett, 1977.

————. *The Howling Two*. Greenwich, Conn.: Fawcett, 1979.

Burkert, Walter. *Homo Necans: The Anthropology of Ancient Greek Sacrificial Ritual and Myth*. Trans. Peter Bing. Berkeley and Los Angeles: University of California Press, 1983.

Butler, Ivan. *Horror in the Cinema*. New York: A. S. Barnes; London: Zwemmer, 1970.

Cabaton, Antoine. "Le Loup-garou en Indochine et en Indonésie." *L'Ethnographie* n.s. 6 (1922): 55–58.

Clarens, Carlos. *Horror Movies*. London: Secker and Warburg, 1968.

Copper, Basil. *The Werewolf in Legend, Fact and Art*. New York, St. Martin's, 1977.

Crowe, Catherine. "A Story of a Weir-Wolf." *Hogg's Weekly Instructor* 3.64 (Edinburgh, May 16, 1846): 184–89.

Curse of the Werewolf. Dir. Terence Fisher. With Oliver Reed. Hammer, 1961.

Davidson, H. R. Ellis. *Gods and Myths of Northern Europe*. Baltimore: Penguin, 1964.

Dr. Jekyll and Mr. Hyde. Dir. John S. Robertson. With John Barrymore and Martha Mansfield. Paramount, 1920.

Dr. Jekyll and Mr. Hyde. Dir. Rouben Mamoulian. With Fredric March and Miriam Hopkins. Paramount, 1931.

Douglas, Drake. *Horror!* New York: Collier, 1969.

Dumas, Alexandre (père). *Le Meneur de loups*. Paris, 1857.

Eisler, Robert. *Man into Wolf: An Anthropological Interpretation of Sadism, Masochism and Lycanthropy*. London, 1951; rpt. New York: Greenwood Press, 1969.

Eliade, Mircea. *Zalmoxis: The Vanishing God*. Trans. Willard Trask. Chicago: University of Chicago Press, 1972.

Endore, [Samuel] Guy. *The Werewolf of Paris*, New York: Farrar and Rinehart, 1933.

Euripides. *Fabulae*. Ed. Gilbert Murray. 3 vols. 1902–9; rpt. Oxford: Clarendon, 1966–69.

Frank, Alan. *The Horror Film Handbook*. Totowa, N.J.: Barnes and Noble, 1982.

Frankenstein Meets the Wolf Man. Dir. William Neill. With Lon Chaney, Jr., and Bela Lugosi. Universal, 1943.

Garden, Nancy. *Werewolves*. Philadelphia: Lippincott, 1973.

Gernet, Louis. "Dolon le loup." In *Mélanges Franz Cumont*. Bruxelles: Secrétariat de l'Institut de Philologie et d'Histoire Orientales et Slaves, 1936. 1:189–208.

Gershevitch, Ilya, trans. *Yašt: The Avaestan Hymn to Mithra*. Cambridge: Cambridge University Press, 1959.

Gerstein, Mary R. "Germanic Warg: The Outlaw as Werewolf." In *Myth in Indo-European Antiquity*. Ed. Gerald Larson. Berkeley and Los Angeles: University of California Press, 1974. 131–56.

Gervase of Tilbury. *Otia Imperialia*. Ed. Felix Liebrecht. 3 vols. Hanover, 1856.

Gow, Gordon. *Suspense in the Cinema*. London: Zwemmer, 1968.

Hamel, Frank. *Human Animals*. London: William Rider, 1915.

Hannum, Alberta. *Spin a Silver Coin*. London: Michael Joseph, 1947.

Herodotus. *Historiae*. Ed. Karl Hude. 3rd ed. 2 vols. 1927; rpt. Oxford: Clarendon, 1967.

Hertz, Wilhelm. *Der Werwolf*. Stuttgart, 1862.

Homer. *Iliad*. Ed. David B. Monro and Thomas W. Allen. 3rd ed. 2 vols. 1920; rpt. Oxford: Clarendon, 1956.

Hoskins, Jim. *Werewolves*. New York: Franklin Watts, 1981.

House of Dracula. Dir. Erle C. Kenton. With John Carradine and Lon Chaney, Jr. Universal, 1945.

House of Frankenstein. Dir. Erle C. Kenton. With Boris Karloff and Lon Chaney, Jr. Universal, 1944.

The Howling. Dir. Joe Dante. With Patrick Macnee and Dee Wallace. Embassy, 1981.

Hurwood, Bernhardt J. *Vampires, Werewolves and Ghouls*. New York: Ace Books, 1968.

Jones, Louis C. "Italian Werewolves." *New York Folklore Quarterly* 6 (1950): 133–38.

Kienle, Richard von. "Tier und Völkernamen bei indogermanischen Stämmen." *Wörter und Sachen* 14 (1932): 32–39.

King, Stephen. *Danse Macabre*. New York: Berkley Books, 1982.

Kracauer, Siegfried. *From Caligari to Hitler*. Princeton: Princeton University Press, 1947.

Kroll, Walter. "Etwas vom Werwolf." *Wiener Studien* 55 (1937): 168–72.

Kyrou, Adonis. *Le Surréalisme au cinéma*. Paris: Editions Arcanes, 1953.

Laclos, Michel. *Le Fantastique cinéma*. Paris: Jean-Jacques Pauvert, 1958.

Ladyhawke. Dir. Richard Donner. With Matthew Broderick, Rutger Hauer, and Michelle Pfeiffer. Warner Bros., 1985.

Lee, Walt. *Reference Guide to Fantastic Films*. 3 vols. Los Angeles: Chelsea-Lee, 1972–74.

Leubuscher, Rudolph. *Über die Werwölfe und Tierverwandlungen im Mittelalter: Ein Beitrag zur Geschichte und Psychologie*. Berlin, 1850.

Lincoln, Bruce. *Priests, Warriors and Cattle: A Study in the Ecology of Religions*. Berkeley and Los Angeles: University of California Press, 1981.

———. "Homeric *lyssa*:'Wolfish Rage.' " *Indo-Germanische Forschungen* 80 (1975): 98–105.

Littleton, C. Scott. *The New Comparative Mythology*. 3rd ed. Berkeley and Los Angeles: University of California Press, 1982.

Marryat, Captain Frederick. "White Wolf of the Harz Mountains." In *The Phantom Ship*. London, 1839. Vol. 1, chap. 39.

Menzies, Sutherland. "Hugues, the Wer-Wolf." *Court Magazine and Monthly Critic* 13 (1838): 259–74.

Morgan, William. *Human Wolves among the Navaho*. Yale University Publications in Anthropology 11. New Haven: Yale University Press, 1936.

Müller, Konrad. *Die Werwolfssage: Studien zum Begriff der Volkssage*. Karlsruhe: Mack-lotsche Druckerei, 1937.

O'Donnell, Elliott. *Werewolves*. London: Methuen, 1912.

Ovid. *Metamorphoses*. Trans. Frank Justus Miller. 2nd ed. 2 vols. Cambridge: Harvard University Press, 1960.

Petronius Arbiter. *Satyricon*. Trans. W. Heseltine. In *Petronius . . . Seneca*. 1913; rpt. London: Heinemann, 1956.

Phillpotts, Eden. *Loup-garou!* London, 1899.

Pic, Xavier. *La Bête qui mangeait le monde en pays de Gévaudan et Auvergne*. Paris: Albin Michel, 1971.

Pronzini, Bill. *Werewolf!* New York: Arbor House, 1979.

Przyluski, Jean. "Les Confréries de loups-garous dans les sociétés indo-européennes." *Revue de l'Histoire des Religions* 121 (1940): 128–45.

Regino of Prüm. *Libri duo de synodalibus causis et disciplinis ecclesiasticis*. Ed. Was-serschleben. N.p., 1840.

Reynolds, George William MacArthur. *Wagner, the Wehr-Wolf*. London, [1857?].

Ridley, Richard A. "Wolf and Werewolf in Baltic and Salvic Tradition." *Journal of Indo-European Studies* 4 (1976): 321–31.

Sand, George. *Légendes rustiques*. Paris, 1858.

Schuster, Mauriz. "Der Werwolf und die Hexen." *Wiener Studien* 48 (1930): 149–78.

Senn. Harry A. *Were-Wolf and Vampire in Romania*. East European Monographs 99, Boulder. New York: Columbia University Press, 1982.

Skeat, W. W., ed. *The Romance of William of Palerne or William and the Werwolf*. London, 1867.

Sprenger, James, and Henry Kramer. *Malleus Maleficarum*. Cologne, 1486. Trans. Montague Summers. London: John Rodker, 1928.

Stanley, John. *The Creature Features Movie Guide*. New York: Warner Books, 1984.

Stevenson, Robert Louis. *The Strange Case of Dr. Jekyll and Mr. Hyde*. London, 1886.

Stewart, Caroline Taylor. *The Origin of the Werewolf Superstition*. University of Missouri Studies. Social Science Series 2.3. Columbia: University of Missouri, 1909.

Stoker, Bram. *Dracula*. London, 1897.

Strieber, Whitley. *The Wolfen*. New York: Bantam, 1979.

Summers, Montague. *The Werewolf*. London, 1933; rpt. New Hyde Park, N.Y.: University Books, 1966.

Taylor, Al. *Making a Monster: The Creation of Screen Characters by the Great Makeup Artists*. New York: Crown, 1979.

Tymn, Marshall B., ed. *Horror Literature: A Core Collection and Reference Guide to the Best of Horror*. New York: Bowker, 1981.

Ucko, Peter J., and Andrée Rosenfeld. *Palaeolithic Cave Art*. New York: McGraw-Hill, 1967.

Villeneuve, Roland. *Loups-garous et vampires*. Paris and Genève: La Palatine, 1963.

Weldon, Michael. *The Psychotronic Encyclopedia of Film*. New York: Ballantine, 1983.

The Werewolf. Dir. Henry McRae. Bison, 1913.

Werewolf of London. Dir. Stuart Walker. With Henry Hull, Warner Oland, and Valerie Hobson. Universal, 1935.

Whishaw, Fred. "The Were-Wolf." *Temple Bar* 76 (1902): 568–79.

Wikander, Stig. *Der arische Männerbund*. Lund: Ohlsson, 1938.

Willis, Donald C. *Horror and Science Fiction Films: A Checklist*. Metuchen, N.J.: Scarecrow Press, 1972.

Wolf Blood. Dir. George Chesebro and George Mitchell. With Marguerite Clayton, George Chesebro, and Ray Hanford. Lee-Bradford, 1925.

Wolfen. Dir. Michael Wadleigh. With Albert Finney and Diane Venora. Orion/Warner Bros. 1981.

The Wolf-Man. Dir. George Waggner. With Lon Chaney, Jr., and Claude Rains. Universal, 1941.

Woodward, Ian. *The Werewolf Delusion*. New York and London: Paddington Press, 1979.

_____ Giants and Fairies

19

Giants

Janis L. Pallister

Giants, whether appearing in folktales or in more sophisticated art forms, have the antinomic quality of being either wholly malevolent or wholly benevolent. While the origin of the concept of giants is too remote even to theorize intelligently over, tales regarding them may be "derived in part from dim traditions of primitive races living alongside more advanced peoples who had conquered the land but had not succeeded in extirpating the aborigines" ("Giant," *Encyclopaedia Britannica*), or these tales may be based on early encounters with such a people as the Watusi (Friedman 24).

Indeed, these stories may hinge upon poorly observed and badly reported instances of tribes or families of persons suffering from gigantism, or from an excess or defect of the materials of fetation. If this were the case, we would be dealing with gigantism the disease, which is always pituitary in origin, exhibiting extreme height—seven feet and over. More specifically, in humans it is caused by an oversecretion of growth hormone by the acidophilic cells in the anterior lobe of the pituitary. This ailment is genetically transmitted. Persons suffering from this disease have historically been displayed in freak shows and elsewhere as "monsters." Often they have been recruited by kings and potentates to serve as soldiers, bodyguards, and other types of wardens (C. J. S. Thompson 141–83). Magellan claimed he saw the "Giants of Patagonia" among the Tehuelche Indians of the New World. But there is no scientific evidence that such a race ever existed (Cohen 246–48). Yet people's belief in giants once allowed them to accept the "discovery" of the petrified Cardiff giant—a hoax perpetrated on the American public—as "proof positive of the biblical statement about giants in the earth" (Cohen 250–51).

Recent medical investigation sheds light on the story of David and Goliath, whose height was "six cubits and a span" (1 Samuel 17:21–58; 21:9; 22:10;

and 2 Samuel 21:19). It theorizes that if Goliath had indeed been suffering from this disease, he would have been quite weak, and therefore unable to win in combat. Such "giants" are always ill, and usually short-lived. Such a rational explanation, applied to the story of David and Goliath, as to the giants vanquished by heroes of the Arthurian cycle, or to the giant overcome by Jack the Giant Killer, sheds light on the giants' clumsiness and slow-wittedness; for mental retardation also frequently accompanies this illness. Indeed, more than one scholar has proposed that the legends of giants descend from the existence of some prehistoric race, hot-headed and not amenable to reason. The explanation would, however, have the unfortunate consequence of seriously undermining the major metaphors of these stories, and of attenuating the moral associations that accrue to these legendary "creatures"; for in the long run they are mythical monsters falling largely into the category of an evil force ultimately suppressed by an almost superhuman strength or great astuteness on the part of some virtuous "hero." In this case there is an important ethical sign here to be decoded. Sometimes, however, the giants themselves show superhuman charity and benevolence. In that case a different but equally valuable lesson is to be learned. Approaching the question more or less chronologically and certainly selectively, in this entry we will focus largely upon these two spiritual polarities.

In both the Greek and Norse mythologies, giants were primordial beings whom the gods overcame in battle, and who were then buried in the abyss of eternal darkness. In Norse mythology the rime-cold giant Ymir and his progeny are overcome by Bor, Odin, Vili, and Ve. From the various parts of the slain Ymir they fashioned the earth (Gayley 373; Bulfinch 241). The mountain giants Hrimthursar and Berg-riser are also beset by the hammer of Thor (Gayley 376). The Norse legends are woven into *The Ring of the Nibelung*, where the goddess Freia is the wage the giants claim for reconstruction of Wotan's (or Odin's) castle. This *Ring* was made famous by the operas of Wagner which revolve around these stories. But also well known are the paintings of Schnorr von Carolsfeld in the royal palace at Munich and the illustrations of the four operas by J. Hoffmann and by Th. Pixis (Gayley 536).

In Greek mythology earthbound giants were said to be the offspring of the blood spilt by the wounded Uranus; for clothes they wore the skins of beasts and for weapons they used rocks and tree trunks (Gayley 7). They included the mighty Alcyoneus, Pallas, Enceladus, and Porphyrion, who renewed the battle against the Olympian gods begun by the Titans, Cyclopes, and hundred-handed monsters (metaphysical giant-offspring of Uranus, or Heaven, and Gaea, or Earth). These early battles of the gods and giants of Greek mythology were sculpturally represented in marble on the north frieze of the Treasury of the Siphnians, now found in the Delphi museum (H. Gardner 133).

Yet, despite the supposed conquest of giant races, many attributes of the giant, and even legends regarding subsequent giants or giant races, occur in ancient mythology. Gigantic, for example, are two or three of the most remarkable divinities of Greece, notably Atlas and Chronos, the latter representing time, and conveyed as truly an ogre, since he is generally shown in classical and in neoclassical times as eating his children. One of the most memorable depictions of the giant Chronos, or Saturn—the god of sterile winter—is found in a masterpiece by Francisco de Goya, the great Spanish painter. Atlas, of course, would be diametrically opposed to Chronos: the fact that Atlas supported the earth upon his shoulders is beneficial to man, while Chronos, or time, is characteristically man's enemy. In any case, both are intimately associated with natural order, unlike the self-serving, anarchic giants of the creation myths of classical antiquity and of some other mythologies. Moreover, the classical creation mythology in which giants are involved has its sequels; for after Jupiter imprisoned the giants under Mount Etna, his brother, Pluto, god of Hades, ruler of the underworld, undertook—for fear of the light the giants' fall might expose—an inspection voyage in which he encountered Venus, who, with the arrows of her son Cupid, instilled in him a love for Proserpine (Persephone), whom he then abducted. Thus, giants are intimately connected with one of the chief allegorical stories of Greek and Roman mythology, endlessly retold from Ovid forward, and depicted in countless paintings from earliest classical times.

But there are other stories of giants coming from Greek and Roman antiquity. For instance, Pluto, or Hades, by virtue of a helmet given him by the giant Cyclopes, had the magical power to move about unseen but loathed by mortals. The Cyclopes also manufactured Neptune's trident and thunder for Jupiter. Here, then, the giant Cyclopes interact with other gods.

Yet, in Hesiod, the three Cyclopes themselves (Arges, Brontes, and Steropes) as well as the Titans and the Hecatonchires (or hundred-handed monsters) are, as we have said, the issue of the union of Uranus (the personified Heaven) and Gaea (or Earth). The Hecatonchires are represented in particular by Aegaeon, who could clasp whales in his arms (Hesiod, *Theogony* 147; Ovid, *Metamorphoses* 2.9–10; and Milton, "That nature is not subject to old age," line 59), as well as by Briareos (Hesiod, *Theogony* 713–16; Milton, *Paradise Lost* 1.229). Gyes, or Gyges, the hundred-armed son of Heaven and Earth, is described by Herodotus, and is the subject of a drama by Hebbel. As for the Cyclopes, they were often considered by the poets of classical antiquity to be man-eating inhabitants of Sicily, and at times were placed on a level with the gods. There was even an alter in the temple in Corinth devoted to them, and on that altar people offered sacrifices to them (Commelin 150).

While the Cyclopes and Titans are monstrous personifications of the physical world, and while they are said in the early myths to be not giants but rather the cause for the birth of giants from the blood of Uranus, they are, even so, often depicted as giants. These are the Cyclopes referred to, for example, in chapter 12 of Sannazaro's *Arcadia*. They appear also in R. Buchanan's "Cloudland," Pope's *Rape of the Lock*, Stephen Phillips' "Ulysses," and Robert Bridges' "The Return of Ulysses."

Cyclopes are interwoven into the myth of Neptune (or Poseidon), as well; and here we see the lord of the sea fathering several giants through mortals. Among these we should note Antaeus (whom Ovid describes), Orion, who, as the son of Neptune, was a giant; and, of particular importance here, the Cyclops Polyphemus. The latter is famous for his pursuit of the sea-nymph Galatea.

Polyphemus proclaims his passion in a lyric poem by Mnasalkes of Sikyon (ca. 250 .B.C.), and his love is also described by Theocritus in *Idyls* 6 and 11. Polyphemus' brutishness and power are fully demonstrated in Ovid's *Metamorphoses* (13.738 ff.). In Theocritus, we can only gather that Polyphemus is at least of gigantic proportions, if not indeed a giant; but in the *Odyssey* of Homer the monster and the giant are clearly fused.

In the *Odyssey*, Ulysses sojourns in the country of the Cyclopes, who, like some of the giants of the Arthurian cycle, and like the Fomoire—the enemies of the Tuatha De Danann in Irish "history" (Dillon 52)—inhabit an island of which they are the sole possessors. A cannibalistic and brutish Polyphemus is the master of the cave that Ulysses and his companions enter to explore. The adventures of Ulysses with this Cyclops, as, for example, the boring out of Polyphemus' eye, are depicted in Attic statuettes, as well as vase-paintings and reliefs.

Notable among the allusions to the Cyclops Polyphemus is a satyric drama, *The Cyclops* by Euripides, the only extant example of this ancient genre. Certainly one must also mention R. C. Rogers' "Blind Polyphemus," cited by Gayley (531). The Cyclops is spoken of in the Renaissance play of Jodelle, *Didon se sacrifiant* (act 1, lines 263–64, in Stone), whose plot is drawn from Virgil's *Aeneid*. In this great epic, the hero Aeneas is given armor made by Vulcan, god of fire, who has giants (including the rebellious Enceladus) and all the might of Etna to serve him. With this armor Aeneas does battle in Italy; and in his wanderings before reaching Italy, he too drifts to the coast of the Cyclopes (*Aeneid* 3.551–83), where he and his party meet Achaemenides, a Greek left behind in the Cyclopes' cave by Ulysses. Indeed, Aeneas himself sees the ogre Polyphemus, "massive and monstrous," and the whole tribe of Cyclopes (*Aeneid* 3.653–58). As Polyphemus appears in the freakish pursuit of the shepherdess Galatea, whose lover (Acis) he kills, and also as he emerges in the *Odyssey*, he is, like Caliban, symbolic of a deviant eroticism and the raw natural forces that oppose reason. He is also a sign of metaphysical evils that may beset humankind. So compelling has the story of the grotesque shepherd Polyphemus and of his love for Galatea been that a whole body of pastoral literature, beginning with Theocritus' idyl, has been based upon it. An early Greek fragment by Bion of Smyrna appears to be a lament of Polyphemus (Lang 183). In continental literature, Polyphemus' story was told by Poliziano in his poem "La giostra" and by Luis de Góngora y Argote in his "Fábula de Polifemo y Galatea" (1613); Lope de Vega also dealt with the subject. Such great sixteenth- and seventeenth-century painters as Raphael, Carracci, and Poussin executed frescoes and ceiling-paintings dealing with the story. The musician Handel set the tragedy of Acis and Galatea in a masque (ca. 1720), while John Gay created an opera on the subject in 1732. A formidable and most memorable painting of the Cyclops spying on a nude and sleeping Galatea was done in recent times (1898–1900) by the Symbolist artist Odilon Redon (Gerhardus, fig. 48; p. 79). The painting captures all the psychopathy implicit in the voyeurism of a monster deranged by unrequited love. Gustave Moreau's 1880 *Galatea* (Gerhardus, ill. 38; p. 69), which inexplicably shows a giant Polyphemus with two normal eyes and another in his forehead, is less moving, though such notables as J.-K. Huysmans and Marcel Proust proclaimed Moreau's genius. To the Pre-Raphaelites and the Symbolists the Cyclops Polyphemus represented poetic contemplation or imagination, so that the Moreau painting has its own historic importance, whatever we may think of its artistic merits.

In addition to those on the Cyclopes and other "true giants," many of the legends of classical antiquity have come to be associated with giants, even though in the beginning the figures in question may have been merely large and formidable, such as the race of Titans from the underworld, or the Great Mother Cybele, whom Baudelaire refers to as a "géante" (*Spleen et Idéal*, 5 and 19, in *Les Fleurs du mal*). Cybele, or Rhea, was the pretext for orgiastic rituals that would fit well into Baudelaire's view. She appears in Virgil's *Aeneid* (6.789; 10.252–53) and in Milton's "Arcades" (line 21). Ronsard mentions her frequently in *La Franciade* and elsewhere; Du Bellay also recalls her.

Along the same line, certain heroes may have come metaphorically to exert a "gigantic" effort against "gigantic" odds. This would have the effect of extending the Greek etymon *gigas* (*gigantos*), meaning mighty one; productive one; one giving birth. Such a person as the Green Knight from English medieval literature, or the legendary Little John of *Robin Hood*, or, in classical times, Heracles (or Hercules), is a *vir major* and not a *gigas*, an earthbound giant of myth, connected with birth or the creation of the earth. Yet the word "giant" is readily applied to the "large man," or the "great hero."

The confusion is heightened by the fact that such a *vir major* often must struggle with a true *gigas*. From Greek legend we have, for example, the often represented story of Heracles' struggle with the giant Antaeus, who, as we have said, was descended, like Orion, from Earth, and who, like Orion and the Cyclops Polyphemus, must, technically speaking, be supposed not to be altogether disproportionate to those human beings with whom they commingled, though poets and artists often tend to forget this. (Heracles himself was an earthly son of Jupiter.)

There is a magnificent Greek krater in the red-figure style done by Euphronios, ca. 510–500 B.C., and now in the Louvre, where Heracles is shown strangling Antaeus (H. Gardner 119; also see Gayley 221). A small-scale group by Pollaiuolo, done in 1475 and now in the National Museum of Florence (H. Gardner 483), also depicts this struggle. Heracles counts among those exploits excluded from the twelve labors not only the strangling of Antaeus, but also an encounter with Cacus, a giant who inhabited a cave on Mount Aventine, and who plundered the surrounding area, stealing the oxen of Geryon from the hero while he slept. Incidentally, in the *Divine Comedy*, Dante encounters Cacus in the form of a centaur in canto 25 of the *Inferno*, while in canto 31 he spies not only the biblical giant Nimrod (a stupid braggart) but also the classical giants Ephialtes (who represents senseless rage) and Briareus, as well as Antaeus (who symbolizes brainless vanity). All of them are placed in the ninth circle, or nether hell, for their rebellious pride, their violence, and their frivolity; and Dante concludes that Nature did well when she left off creating such vast animals as these.

In poetry, Pindar frequently celebrates Heracles' role in the clash between the giants (τίγαυτες) and the gods. As Pindar tells it, Heracles helped Zeus to slay Porphyrion, the king of giants; he also helped to put down Antaeus; and with Telamon, he defeated the giant herdsman Alcyoneus. Heracles quelled others of the giant races as well. (Pindar, *First, Fourth*, and *Seventh Nemean Odes*; *Eighth Pythian Ode*; *Sixth Isthmian Ode*.) For those who would view Heracles as a "giant," his confrontations with Antaeus, Alcyoneus, and others are examples of "gigantomachia," a combat between or among giants.

Tangentially, when we think of "giant" we may also think of such a heroic sculpture as the Laocoön group in the Vatican, an immortal representation of the struggle of Laocoön with the huge serpents (*Aeneid* 2.184–222). (The work was executed between 42 and 21 B.C. by the Rhodian sculptors Hagesandros, Polydoros, and Athenodoros.) We might point out at this juncture that the colossal statues of antiquity (such as the lost Colossus of Rhodes), or Rodin's monumental statues of Balzac, or the Christ of the Andes, are in some sense related to a consideration of giants and the gigantic; but they are not, strictly speaking, pertinent to a discussion of the fabulous, which is presently at hand. Besides, the huge snakes that seek to devour Laocoön and his son, both in Virgil and in the sculpture mentioned above, are an excellent example of the creation by the human imagination not only of races of giants having human characteristics, but also of a whole bestiary of giant, often totemic, animals. Thus we have giant ants of India, giant snakes, giant whales, giant cows (as Audhumbla, with Ymir), giant oxen (as Babe, with Paul Bunyan), giant mares (as in *Gargantua*), giant rabbits (as in *Alice*), giant apes (as King Kong), giant octopuses, the giant Leviathan, giant bees, giant birds, giant flies, imaginary giant birds (such as the griffon or the roc), and so forth. A consideration of giant-hearted heroes (including certain conceptualizations of Samson, or of Christ) and a discussion of giant animals, are, however, also largely outside the parameters of this study, although we will at times be forced to speak of the *vir major*, who is like a giant; and we will also be returning to "giant statues" in the context of popular culture concerning giants.

But giants are not restricted to Graeco-Roman and Norse antiquity. As we have already noted, there are biblical references to them, not only in the story of David and Goliath, but also in Genesis (6:4) and in Numbers (13:32–33), though the best interpretation of these passages reinforces the notion that some giants of antiquity may have been "mighty" or "Herculean" human types, and not mythic or poetic beings. Philo tends toward this conclusion: "When you hear that Moses spoke of the existence of giants, . . . what he writes is infinitely removed from fable. . . . He is depicting for you . . . men attached to their own will, to their own interests; slaves to their pleasures'' (qtd. in Darré 11).

Nonetheless, the spurious book of Enoch reminds one of the Greek creation myth, as it describes the birth, resulting from the union of heaven and earth, of cannibalistic giants whom God vanquished through his Archangels (Darré 12–13), though not before the giants had taught mankind the arts and the sciences. Jung sees these giants as proving themselves to be progressive elements who, like Cain, broadened and developed man's consciousness far more than the stay-at-home Abel. Jung writes, ''In this way they enlarged the significance of man to 'gigantic proportions,' which points to an inflation of the cultural consciousness at that period.'' The Deluge, however, represented the ''stroke from the unconsciousness'' that always threatens such an inflation (Jung, *Psychology* 421–22).

In general, whether fabled or real, biblical giants, are, like those of Greek and Norse legends, ultimately associated with brute force, and come finally to afford an evil presence. And, as suggested at the onset of this entry, giants are more often than not a malevolent force, to be challenged and overcome by the superior wit and the faith of their opponents. Thus Satan and his henchmen assume gigantic proportions in some contexts. Milton, like Dante before him (canto 34 of the *Inferno*), portrays Satan the Archfiend's parts ''in bulk as huge / As whom the fables name of monstrous size'' (*Paradise Lost* 1.196–97). Indeed, this fallen angel, of ''mighty stature,'' lies on the fiery sea of Hell ''Titanian,'' or like the Leviathan (lines 196–208); and, when he sets forth, his spear is larger than a Norway pine (lines 292–94). Milton's humanism permits a free flow between the ancient and the biblical lore concerning giants and the underworld. Of note, too, is Milton's introduction of the giant Harapha of Gath into the story of Samson (*Samson Agonistes*, lines 1065 ff.). Hughes (Milton 535–36) discusses the various personal and political interpretations of this invention by Milton and (577) proposes a Hebrew etymology for Harapha (the giant). That the scene with Harapha represents ''the final step in Samson's recovery of the chastened faith in himself and his divine guidance that makes his impending death a victory'' seems a quite plausible assertion on the part of Hughes (536). Milton creates this giant from 2 Samuel 21; but this episode of Samson and Harapha interrelates, of course, with the story of David and Goliath.

In the Judeo-Christian tradition, especially rich and complex are the works of literature and of art that deal with the battle in which the young David, armed only with a slingshot, defeats, is about to defeat, or has just defeated the Philistine Goliath. Because of David's role in this story as a salvation figure, and in Christian terms, as a type of Christ, artists throughout the centuries have been interested in showing his confrontations with Goliath, often in iconographic terms. The story is depicted in countless medieval cloister and cathedral carvings, in stained glass windows, and even in books of hours in miniature—a seeming contradiction, though this is explained by the role of David's psalms in the prayer life of the Church. Réau (vol. 2, pt. 1, pp. 260–63) gives many examples of the iconographic depiction of this particular instance of the *nanus contra gigantem* topoi, from the third century forward. The story of David and Goliath is shown, for example, in the Visconti Hours (Italian, fifteenth century). It illustrates, as is often the case, Psalm 143, "Blessed be the Lord my God, who teacheth my hands to fight, and my fingers to war." Here the swarthy, dark-eyed giant lies fallen, with an enormous club beside him. The presence of the club is important, for it is illustrative of Friedman's contention (33) that a lesser degree of civilization is associated with the giant; thus, his instruments of battle are crude. In reality, Goliath, who was only "large," and not a giant as we understand the term today, doubtless used a sword in his battle with David. The Visconti Goliath is, then, similar to the giants of the Arthurian legends, which we will discuss shortly; and the conceptualization of him contradicts the biblical account, in which Goliath bears a sword. On the other hand, in the biblical account the weapons of Goliath (a sword) and of David (a slingshot) show an interesting reversal of the usual concept of a giant as being crudely armed with a club, and naked, or else wearing animal furs, or being covered only with a great deal of his own hair. The conclusion must be that the biblical story represents the triumph of the virtuous cause, no matter what the tools. David, as the reader will recall, had refused arms that Saul offered him, preferring to confront the giant with only a slingshot and "the assistance of God." Thus it is a question of right over might here.

Readers will, of course, remember the great Renaissance renditions of the story: here the artistic portrayals of the battle of David and Goliath present equally interesting variations on the details of the story.

In sculpture, both Donatello's bronze *David* (1430), of a neoclassical thrust, and Verrocchio's bronze *David* (1465) show David holding a sword, and depict the severed head of Goliath. These two sculptures invite commentary. For if David is sometimes shown with a sword rather than with a slingshot, this is because after killing the giant with the slingshot he then cut off his head as a trophy for presentation to the authorities. Michelangelo has preferred to show David armed with his slingshot, while Bernini's Baroque sculpture of 1632 captures David's initial motion in which he launches the stone from his sling. Also of extreme power and beauty is the 1440 bronze relief panel on the Ghiberti doors in Florence, which shows David slicing off the giant's head; and he is most unquestionably a giant.

Notable among paintings of the story of David and Goliath are those of Michelangelo and Raphael in the Vatican, though the episodic intarsia after Lorenzo Lotto (ca. 1527) is also very arresting. In it Goliath is unequivocally a giant, as he is again in the two paintings in which David bears his enormous decapitated head, one by Caravaggio (ca. 1605) and the other, particularly startling, by Girolamo Forabosco (ca. 1665). (See *The Bible in Art*, ills. 158, 160, 164, 165, 166, and 167.). Noteworthy, too, is Hendrick Terbrugghen's *David and the Singers* (1623). Rembrandt chose to depict the young David presenting Goliath's head to Saul (1628), while Poussin showed David, preceded by musicians, carrying the head of Goliath impaled on the end of a stake (1627; now in the Prado).

Scenes of the story of David and Goliath can, as stated earlier, be viewed in medieval stained glass windows in many places of worship, such as those in the Sainte-Chapelle de Vic-le-Comte in Puy-de-Dôme, in the cloister of Saint-Aubin d'Angers, and in the *voussure*, or arch, of the rose window on the façade of the Cathedral of Reims. Outstanding in the Romantic vein is Burne-Jones' stained glass representation of David slaying Goliath in the lower frame of the King David panel of the Vyner Memorial Window in Christ Church Cathedral, Oxford, England. Here again the youthful David holds an enormous sword with which he is about to behead Goliath, who is this time shown as a large blond man, two to three times the size of David. Goliath's great frame fills more than half the available surface of the glass (Lee 153). In the twentieth century, Chagall, combining his mystic sense of Russian iconography and his interest, derived from his Judaism, in Old Testament stories, has executed a splendid lithograph of a princely young David. The frontal view shows David, with his sword in his right hand and the head of Goliath (of rather normal size) in his left. In another lithograph, Chagall shows David appearing before Saul with Goliath's head, scarcely bigger than his own, in his left hand (Chagall, pls. 63–64). These, like all of Chagall's illustrations of the Bible, are fresh in their approach.

Perhaps nowhere in literature has a more riveting description of the battle between these two great forces been given than in Du Bartas' *Divine Weeks* (*Second Week, Fourth Day*, lines 45–414). Though Du Bartas draws on the Bible and on Josephus for his narrative, the poet altogether overlooks the sophisticated society from which Goliath emerged: this "colossus," as he is called, is a giant of fable, extremely hairy, bristly like a hedgehog; he is as tall as a steeple and carries a sort of pointed, iron-tipped club as his lance. Linked to Cain by the ornament on his shield, he is a "monster" of ominous mien and bearing. David, in contrast, is like Orion, the great hunter of Boeotia. Thus, Du Bartas suggests a gigantomachia.

But "giants" occur in other legends and stories of the ancient world, beyond those of the Greek, Norse, and Judaic peoples. We find them mentioned in astonishing numbers in the ancient Hindu books; they figure in the legends of the Siamese, the Indians, and the Mongols. They are humanoid, and of monstrous size; their blood is red; their bodies are thin and tapered like a leaf, their sides are vertically disposed (Darré 13–14); and their origins recall those of the book of Enoch in the Judeo-Christian legend. Moreover, in the ancient Vedic books we find reference to "Kura, Kori, Kader, and Eriligarou," dogs, cocks, and wolves who, having become the sons of God, mixed their black blood with the white blood of European women and thus gave rise to a race of "giants" called the sons of the earth (Darré 14). In these instances, as is often the case for Greek and Hebrew "giants," the word has not yet taken on the meaning it has for us today, a being enormous beyond all human dimensions. "Giant" is, rather, a term designating a hero, or a demigod of considerable power and mortal grandeur, who is nonetheless not invincible. It is thus appropriate to reiterate that the Graeco-Latin word *gigans*, from which modern Western languages take their signifier for giant, derives from the Sanskrit *gô-jan*, meaning earth and giant. Thus, there is a relation of these figures to creation myths, to Gaea, Mother Earth, or, in the Hindu religion, to Gaya (Darré 14), who, in turn, is recalled in the collective psyche of the Northern peoples through the legendary Gayant (Darré 14–15).

The ancient Chinese, too, based their religious beliefs in part on the concept of giants, for they believed in the primordial colossal divine man called P'an Ku, who gave heaven and earth their names. His tears formed the rivers, his breath the wind, his speech the thunder. He was mortal, and at his death the parts of his body shaped the five holy mountains of China, as well as the sun and the moon. Likewise, in ancient Persia, Gayomart, the first man, was depicted as a huge figure that cast forth light. From the semen of his body, emitted at death, the primordial couple was said to have sprung. And even the American Indians of the Great Plains believed, with the Greeks and the Scandinavians, that giants were the first race of people to inhabit the earth. (See Teale 40–41).

It is ironic to observe, with Darré (16–18), that these ancient creation myths and stories of early man's struggles with contrary natural forces should almost invariably involve giants, often having mysterious origins and usually living apart from more civilized societies (as medieval giants do also), since modern anthropological discoveries dictate an opposite mythology. For, despite what Teale has to say on the subject (52–56), digs have, to date, turned up no skeletal remains of "giants" and, indeed, indicate that the oldest specimens of homo sapiens were often small, though sturdy. Cohen (250) asserts that the human being is, in fact, becoming taller, but the latest discovery of Leakey shows a three-million-year-old man to be quite similar to his twentieth-century descendents. It is because of this scientific evidence that we may insist upon the symbolic nature of legendary "giants," and thus may explain their persistence in medieval and modern times as psychologically generated.

Medieval literature and art present a plethora of giants—something of a new breed, usually not related to the giants of antiquity which we have been examining up to this point. (*Les Granz Geanz* of the twelfth century does, however, show knowledge of ancient and biblical giant lore.) The giant of medieval literature was not always evil. There was, after all, Rübezahl, a kindly giant living in the Bohemian forest; and in *Aucassin et Nicolete*, a French *chantefable* of the twelfth or thirteenth century, a giant herdsman, quite similar to the one in Chrétien de Troyes' *Yvain* (line 289 ff.), provides comic relief as he tells his sob-story to Aucassin and manages to get from him 20 *sous* to pay for a lost ox. Both he and the giant in *Yvain* are club-bearers, but Chrétien's monstrous creature is anything but comic (Hatzfeld 36–37).

Nor should we overlook, in this context, a "giant" so good, so holy, that he seems to have lost his attributes of giant and ogre over the ages. This is Saint Christopher, who is—leaving aside Saint Francis of Assisi—doubtless the most famous saint of Christendom. Jacques de Voragine in *The Golden Legend* says of him, "He was of gigantic stature, had a terrifying mien, was 12 *coudées* [twelve to eighteen feet] tall" (2:7). Saint Christopher belonged, before his conversion, to the class of dog-headed, cannibalistic ogre-monsters and giants we will be looking at shortly. Of course, his name, "Christ-bearer," like that of Atlas, a world-bearer, suggests that he would have to be a giant. The concept of the legendary "Saint Christopher" as a giant, to whom the Child Jesus revealed himself by transforming Christopher's staff into a palm tree loaded with dates, is, in fact, essential to the understanding of the saint's iconography. He is portrayed as a cynocephalic giant, perhaps through a fusion with Anubis, in Eastern icons (see Réau, vol. 3, pt. 1, p. 310). In Western art, the dog-head is usually lost (except in a twelfth-century miniature in the Abbey of Zwiefalten), but his gigantic size is usually retained. He is seen as a giant in many medieval books of hours, such as that of Catherine of Clèves; he is so represented by Memling in a wood engraving of 1423, and in one by Lucas Cranach of 1506. He has been painted by many great artists, such as Titian, Rubens, and Massys. And in 1933 the cycles of his life were portrayed in the frescoes of the church of Saint-Christsophe de Javel in Paris by Jacques Martin-Ferrières. (See further iconography in Réau, vol. 3, pt. 1, pp. 304–12.)

Yet, for the most part, giants in medieval literature and art do not represent saints, but, rather, brute nature or an evil force to be overcome by the superior wit and moral fiber of a warrior knight. Surely the most notable of medieval giant-ogres is Grendel, in the eighth-century anonymous Anglo-Saxon poem, *Beowulf*. The Danish Grendel and his mother are man-eating creatures conceived by a pair of those monsters born of Cain and banished by God, as punishment for Abel's murder (lines 104–8). To tie the evil giant to Cain is, in fact, a convention (cf. Du Bartas). Thus, the extra-biblical allegory relates the evil giant to the creation myth. It is interesting to note in this context that Beowulf, in presenting his credentials to Hrothgar, speaks of chasing the race of giants "from the earth" (lines 419–21). From this passage and from other aspects of the poem, there can be no doubt that Grendel is a formidable giant: Grendel and his dam are, in fact, said by the poet to be "giant monsters" (line 1347), and Grendel is called a "giant" (line 1614). He carries the bodies of thirty men he has killed at Herot back to his lair in the bogs (lines 121–25), and he can eat fifteen men or more on the spot (lines 1581–82). It is befitting, then, that the great Swedish warrior prince Beowulf, a Christian, should overcome the consummately evil Grendel, as well as his mother, for they are pagan. And Beowulf exterminates Grendel's mother with a sword "hammered by giants." Beowulf is, of course, an *exemplum* to be emulated. His is the good and the true path. In his words, thoughts, and deeds he is the embodiment of the Christian way of life. What makes his feat all the more awesome and Grendel all the more frightening is the fact that Grendel partakes of humanity. He and his dam use tools, and the dam's dagger (lines 1545–46) is in contrast to the fact that giants usually bear clubs as a mark of their uncivilized nature (Friedman 33).

Another poem in which the hero's courage is tested in the person of a giant is the fourteenth-century *Sir Gawain and the Green Knight*. The Green Knight is, as Goliath probably was, within human scale, although his energies are those of raw nature. Gawain, like Beowulf, is the ideal knightly hero, a Christian and a type of Christ in his temptation, and also a flower of chivalry. In this derivative of the Arthurian cycle we have the celebrated beheading-of-the-giant theme descending from the early Irish saga of *Fled Bricrennd*, or *Bricriu's Feast*, belonging to the Cuchulain cycle. In both stories, as in other romances (for example, *Le Livre de Caradoc*), the giant picks up his head after decapitation and is thus to be again overcome. (See Bruce 1:88–89). This motif recurs with variations in other Arthurian stories, as, for example, in the Old French works *La Mule sanz frain* and *Hunbaut*. Decapitation of the giant should, of course, be his ultimate undoing: David must decapitate Goliath; Beowulf, Grendel; and so on. To have the giant force reinstate itself is thus the epitome of magic and mystery. It is also the supreme challenge.

Other, even earlier, Arthurian romances in which giants appear are extremely numerous, and an account of all the versions of them as well as of their influences over subsequent literature and art is far beyond the scope of this entry. Yet, even though giants are among the "stock themes" of these romances (Bruce 1:312), one must take a careful look at this genre, which used what is called the *matière de Bretagne*, or Celtic material, and which reached its pinnacle in the late twelfth or early thirteenth century (Bruce 1:16), because the dynamics of good against evil inherent in situations where normal-sized human beings engage in conflict with giant creatures are here present.

The Giant Knight Mabonagrain in Chrétien de Troyes' *Erec* reminds us of the Green Knight, in that he is perhaps not truly a "giant." In any event, he holds a maiden captive in an enchanted garden near the palace of King Eurain, and Erec, of course, rescues this "damsel in distress." Indeed, rescue missions of this sort are common to Arthurian romance, and what foe could present a more formidable challenge to these heroic knights-errant than a giant? Thus, the protagonist of *Li Biaus Descouneus*, like Erec, rescues a girl (Clarie) from two giants, whom he slays, and in whose cave the party finds plentiful provisions (Bruce 2:194). Similarly, Fergus delivers two girls held captive by a giant at Mont Dolerous (Bruce 2:240). Many variations on this motif of men and maidens being delivered by valiant heroes from "giant" warriors, often designated as "Saxons," are cited by Bruce in his exhaustive study (2:191–92, 271, 319, 320, 322, 329, and 333–34). Throughout medieval literature there is a tendency to represent Saracens and Saxons as "giants"—doubtless designating the *vir major*, and not the *gigas*. For example, Baligant, in *La Chanson de Roland*, selects as one of his best squadrons the "Jaianz de Malpreis," and/or "Malprose" (lines 3253, 3285, 3518).

In many respects, the most famous and appealing of these Arthurian romances is the one dealing with Tristan and Isolde. Bédier's *Tristan*, woven from medieval French versions by Thomas, Béroul, and others, includes the episode that interests us here; it is one that is found in Gottfried von Strassburg's version of Tristan and in the Italian *Tavola Ritonda* (E. Gardner 165). In this adventure (Bédier, ch. 14), Tristan overcomes Urgan the Hairy, a clumsy giant who, armed with a crude club, is plaguing the land of Tristan's host. (We should note here the bestial hairiness and the club demarking the giant's uncivilized nature [Friedman 15, 31, 33, 161, 163].) Tristan wins this battle through his superior wit, prowess, and valor, all of which are served by his fine sword, which marks his greater degree of civilization. As an anticipated prize for ridding his host's land of this marauding giant, Tristan wins the famous dog Petit Crû (Petitto Araviuto), who is subsequently given as a gift to Isolde, and becomes inexorably interwoven with the adventures of Tristan and Isolde. (In other versions, however, Isolde already owns Petit Crû from the outset, and the dog drinks the magic potion at the same time as the star-crossed lovers.)

The story of Tristan and Isolde has been endlessly retold in art and literature, sometimes with the giant, sometimes without. Matthew Arnold has treated the subject somewhat autobiographically, and with great feeling, in his *Tristram and Iseult* (1852), where, however, the dog and the giant seem to be absent. Swinburne has also retold the story in his *Tristram of Lyonesse* (1882), where the struggle with the giant Urgan is told with considerable power. Urgan is called a "son of earth"; he is armed with mace and sword and is most ominous ("his eyes were night and flame"). In Swinburne's version, Tristan cuts off Urgan's huge right hand, as in the original story. The opera of Wagner and the beautiful film of Cocteau, *L'Eternel Retour*, have made the story known to the whole Western world, though Wagner's sublime opera is so ethereal as to be beyond the pale of little dogs and clumsy giants.

One must particularly single out, in addition to Tristan, a later Arthurian romance entitled *Le Chevalier du Papegau* (fourteenth century?), because in this otherwise lackluster work we have the rather original addition of a dwarf's son who becomes a giant, due to the fact that "he is suckled in the forest by a kindly unicorn" (Bruce 2:31). Here, then, is a coming together of several of the major topics of investigation in the present work.

The tales of Tristan, Lancelot, and other knights of Arthur's court are retold by Malory in the *Morte Darthur* (1469–70), and in the nineteenth century notably by Tennyson in his *Idylls of the King*. In this work we find Geraint in danger from a lance-bearing giant whom Enid spies; but the hero slays him without difficulty (*Geraint and Enid*, lines 121–66). Yet Tennyson's sense of myth led him to include the giant Arac in part 5 of *The Princess*; and the dying Merlin recounts how the Gleam flitted over a wilderness, glancing at Elf, Gnome, Griffin, and Giant ("Merlin and the Gleam," st. 4).

Despite the appearance of an occasionally benevolent or at least harmless giant in this vast body of literature involving Arthurian romance, most are ominous;

and the genuine purpose of their inclusion by all these known and anonymous authors is twofold. First, they are a part of the mythic and miraculous material that threw an aura of Celtic mist and even of "authenticity"—akin to local color—over the works; for giants were a part of early Irish "history." And second, on a deeper plane, the giants serve as one of the many devices (which also include serpents, dragons, and the like) for testing and ultimately displaying the extent of the hero's valor, prowess, and chivalry, and his passionate love for his lady, as well as his Christian devotion. (Such testing is reminiscent of the labors of Hercules.)

Particularly in literature, the influence of these medieval romances—coming both from the metrical and from the prose versions—was enormous. The tales of Arthur, and also of Charlemagne, continued to reappear and to multiply well into the sixteenth century and even later. Bruce (2:40–41) sees their traces in a wide variety of works, including Ariosto's *Orlando furioso* (which, first published in 1516, became a model for Spenser's *Faerie Queene*) and Torquato Tasso's *Gerusalemme liberata* (1581). In Spain and Portugal they had a major influence on *Amadís de Gaula*, a late thirteenth-century work in which several giants are, in one passage at least, mixed with ladies and knights at Constantinople, in a dance. On this work of the Spanish Middle Ages is based Montalvo's chivalric novel of 1508 concerning Amadís. Arthurian romance influenced Cervantes' *Don Quixote* (1605), as well as his *Galatea*, and also Montemayor's *Diana* (ca. 1558).

Probably one of the most giant-minded among these works is *Don Quixote*, a satire of the literature of knights-errant, bringing together themes from Arthurian and Carolingian medieval literature and the massive pastoral tradition mentioned earlier in this entry. Don Quixote, in emulation of the knights about whom he has read to the point that his mind is turned by their adventures, claims to have fallen from his horse Rozinante while fighting ten giants (*Quixote* 30), and, above all, combats windmills, thinking them to be giants. He is persuaded that the cursed necromancer Freston has transformed the giants into windmills, thus depriving him of the "Honor of the Victory" by which he may claim his lady-love Dulcinea (*Quixote* 44). Don Quixote also wants his fame to spread, so that anyone seeing him will say, "That's he who vanquished in single combat the huge giant Brocabruno . . . of the Invincible Strength" (*Quixote* 145–46); and he claims to have cut off the head of a giant as a *fait accompli*, though he has not (yet) done so (*Quixote* 251). In his "depraved Fancy," and in his sleep, he locks imaginary horns, too, with the giant enemy of the princess Micomicona; but in reality, Quixote has assaulted the inn-keeper's finest wineskins and set his chamber afloat with the best wine of the house (*Quixote* 303–5). Don Quixote and his windmills have been frequently represented in art and literature; we will cite here only Gustave Doré's great illustrations, which are among the finest he ever executed, and in which Don Quixote's fantasies about giants appear.

Giants figure in other genres of medieval literature, too, even though their presence in Arthurian romance is of primary importance. As we pointed out before, the Saracen knights (that is, the enemy) in such works as the anonymous *Chanson de Roland*, of the Carolingian cycle, or Bodel's *Le Jeu de Saint Nicholas* take on the proportions of giants, much as the Green Knight does. They also figure heavily in non-Arthurian medieval art; as Friedman shows (154–57), many efforts were made by artists of the time to depict the "monstrous races" (the Troglodytes, Epiphagi, Blemmyae, Amyctyrae, Cyclopes, Sciapods, and others). An especially frightening Cyclops, often reproduced, is found in Thomas of Cantimpré's *De naturis rerum* (Friedman, ill. 7; also in Baltrušaitis.) This Cyclops is naked, because the monstrous races, being uncivilized, wear no clothes, and are covered with hair; or else they wear animal skins (Friedman 31).

These "monstrous races" bear tangentially upon our investigation, and they are a dimension of giant lore as yet unexplored in this entry. The sciapod, for example, is a staple in the treatment of these races, and he is constantly depicted with his enormously enlarged foot shading him like an umbrella. So widespread is the lore of the sciapod that he even figures in a work as late as Flaubert's *Tentation de Saint Antoine*. Thus, both in literature and in art, a normal man may be thought to have a giant's foot or head (for example, *Chanson de Roland*, line 3221). These are obviously inaccurately observed and poorly depicted teratological phenomena; they are medical disorders. Attributes of the monstrous races are an extremely prevalent subject in medieval literature (as, for example, in *Le Jeu de Saint Nicholas*, or in the novels of the cycle of Alexandre le Grand.) Saint Augustine, in *The City of God*, is one of the many sources used for such material. Pliny is another. The monstrous races are also shown in the carvings on cathedrals and cloisters throughout Europe. Friedman's collection of illustrations is especially useful for sampling these frightening human types in medieval art, but it is understandably not comprehensive. And Montaigne, who in the late sixteenth century writes in several essays about human deformity (as do Paré and several other of his contemporaries), does not pass over giants. In particular, he considers the possible varieties of human life already mentioned by Pliny and Herodotus when he asserts that there are androgynes, headless men, quadrupeds, cyclopes, and sirens (bk. 2, ch. 12). He also recalls in this same essay the cynocephali and the apple-sniffers studied at length by Friedman. (See also Baltrušaitis, Céard, and Paré.)

Though it is obvious that the depiction of giants was very difficult for medieval and later artists, since the very effort to draw them attenuates their imaginary largeness, nonetheless the effort has been repeatedly made; as Friedman shows, medieval depictions of members of giant races often fill or dominate the frame, and sometimes the giants step outside the frame. In fact, Friedman writes, "This uneasy relationship of creature to frame suggests that the monstrous men are leaving the borders confining them to the static page and beginning to occupy landscapes; they cannot be contained in isolation" (154). The difficulties of drawing the giant and the symbolic meanings of how it is done and that it is done must give us pause. In my opinion, Gustave Doré, the great French engraver of the nineteenth century, best solved these problems in his illustrations of giants for numerous books, such as *Don Quixote, Gargantua*, and *Pantagruel*. We will presently return to the question of Doré's illustrations.

A discussion of giants and monsters of the Middle Ages and the Renaissance would also include coincidental mention of portrayals of the Mouth of Hell. Several especially notable examples can be found in the *Hours of Catherine of Clèves* (Flemish, fifteenth century). Here we find a monstrous head with seven human beings in its gigantic, toothy mouth; it has bulging, bloodshot eyes and sheds rays, like Lucifer. From later times, one might cite Bosch's *Garden of Delights*, which, on the left wing of the triptich, presents a huge humanoid monster, representative of punishment. Satan as a giant satyr-ogre is torturing and devouring lost souls in Pol de Limbourg's "Enfer," a miniature found in the *Très Riches Heures du Duc de Berry*. As a monstrous two-headed ogre he is also vividly portrayed in the sixteenth-century Last Judgment window in Fairford Church, Gloucestershire, England (Lee 31). He is most frightening.

Such enormous monsters and monster heads—which are, in fact, a permanent theatrical set for Hell in the medieval mystery plays—demonstrate the principle that that which is large is frightening or impressive; and for that reason they are often used in allegorical contexts. Sometimes a positive value may be attached to such enlargements, as in the 1559 drawing by Bruegel wherein the large allegorical figure of Hope stands on a huge anchor, which floats upon a raging sea of trouble (Klein 223–25).

On the other hand, in Spenser's *Faerie Queene* (1590–96), an allegorical work of great complexity, one of the vices, Pride (Orgoglio), is a most impressive giant. It is he who holds the Redcrosse Knight captive (bk. 1, cantos 7 and 8). This hideous giant, "horrible and hye," causes the ground to groan beneath him; and his stature exceeds "the hight of three the tallest sonnes of mortall seed" (1.7.8.4, 9). Spenser, echoing Hesiod and Natalis Comes, conceives this giant to be the offspring of Earth and Aeolus, the wind. He bears a great club, a snaggy Oak he had torn from his mother's bowels (the Earth's), and this club is "all arm'd with ragged snubbes and knottie graine." When beheaded by Prince Arthur, Orgoglio deflates, and his monstrous vanquished body is like an empty bladder (1.8.24). The spiritual symbolism of the entire episode, in which good triumphs over evil, is readily apparent, though some scholars view this episode from the *Faerie Queene* as an allegory of the Reformation, with the giant Pride representing the Roman Catholic Church, and, more specifically, its embodiment in King Philip of Spain.

As a late but important example of the influence of Arthurian romance one should also mention in passing another dream allegory in which monsters and giants (for example, Apollyon) play a role. This is John Bunyan's *Pilgrim's Progress* (1678–84), a work of the English Restoration.

The "triumph" of the Arthurian giant of medieval lore is, then, possibly unrivaled. Yet, fashioned perhaps in a very remote past, even tens of thousands of years ago, and coming down to us through the Middle Ages, there are also many "children's stories," or folkloric tales, revolving around giants. These stories have sometimes made their way into standard literature, where they are shared by children and adults; sometimes, however, they remain in the domain of the "fairy tale." Jessie Weston, for example, mentions a Celtic folktale in which the mysterious hand of a giant steals a child and a foal on the night of their birth. She compares this bogeyman's hand with the Black Hand in the Arthurian romances, but fails to link it to its counterpart, the Giant Hand of God appearing in early Christian iconography (for example, *The Bible in Art*, ill. 18). Here again, as with the foot, or the head, is an instance of focus upon some particular part of the giant's body.

Children's literature has, then, its own rich giant lore. In the seventeenth century, Charles Perrault recounted many of the Mother Goose fairy tales, though these stories were already known to most children of the Western world, as they are today. Among Perrault's Mother Goose stories, translated into English in 1729, are many ogres and giants. Bluebeard, for example, is to be classified as an ogre, while in "Le Petit Poucet" or "Tom Thumb" there is an ogre who has gigantic appetites (Perrault 175), and who, because of his seven-league "fairy" boots, can go from mountain to mountain and can step across rivers (177–78). In this literary retelling of the folk tale, Tom Thumb, though as small as a thumb and mute in the bargain, overcomes the evil ogre-giant by his superior wit and by his fundamental goodness.

The story of "Tom Thumb" is widely known in various versions, and, in fact, is a Mother Goose tale that existed long before Perrault. Deulin (325–77) studies the story's history and evolution. He finds far-flung variations on this archetypal story, even including a Zulu story about two small "Poucets" named Outhlakanyana and Umbadhlanyana who triumph over several gigantic cannibals. Deulin also cites a Flemish tale hitherto unnoted by scholars, entitled "Le Ptiat Pousset," as well as a Catalan story, "Lo Noy Petit." I might add that Antonine Maillet, in her *Rabelais et les traditions* (20 et passim), shows that Petit Poucet exists in Acadian folklore, too, probably coming from Brittany, and she alludes to him in her own novels, *Pélagie-la-Charrette* and *Cordes-de-Bois*.

Ogresses, who are seldom giantesses, would include the wicked witches in "Hansel and Gretel" and Chodzko's "Imperishable"; but they are present as a wicked stepmother or as the ogre's wife in many fairy tales collected by Perrault (1697), by the Brothers Grimm (1812–15), and by others. Snow White's stepmother is, for example, a rather famous would-be ogress, while there is a wicked mother of the "race ogresse" in "Sleeping Beauty."

Though ogres such as the Cyclops Polyphemus and the *Beowulf* Grendel and even Satan—in certain representations—belong to the adult world, and no doubt represent essential fears and paranoias, they also, as in children's stories, provide punishment motifs. But the ending to "Hansel and Gretel" (as well as to "Sleeping Beauty") points out an additional, perhaps more important, lesson. Wicked fairies, cruel godmothers, vile stepmothers—whether giantesses or not—rarely win. Additionally, we might suggest that they represent Jungian archetypes of the terrible mother figure, an unkind force to be undone. Yet, if such persons are so prevalent in these fairy tales, it should also be remembered that in the days of their invention women often died in childbirth, and mother substitutes, not always too kindly disposed, were common.

Ogres, as in "Tom Thumb" and in "Puss-in-Boots," do not fare better than their female counterparts, or their noncannibalistic brother giants. These ogres also frequently appear in children's literature, and, like the ogresses, can be viewed as symbolizing paternal and other authority figures. Indeed, the child-eating giant cyclops in "Jack and the Beanstalk," an old English tale collected by Andrew Lang, has usurped the very castle of Jack's father, or "taken his father's place." It is then up to Jack to act "like a brave knight's son," to show "an inquiring mind and great courage and enterprise," in gaining his fiefdom back from the horrid fee-fi-fo-fummer and his somewhat ambivalent wife (*World's Best* 144, 146).

Although the cannibalistic and the noncannibalistic giants of fairy tales parallel those of adult literature, in that they are sometimes "good" and sometimes "bad," they are more often bad than good. They therefore usually meet with an appropriate demise. Not only are they clumsy, but they have fatal powers. In "Puss-in-Boots," for instance, the ogre can make himself into various animals, big and small. He changes himself into a mouse at the bidding of Puss-in-Boots, whereupon he is devoured (Perrault, "Le Maître chat, ou le chat botté," pp. 134–35).

The stories of the threatening giant ogres in "Jack the Giant Killer" (of Cornish origins; collected by Andrew Lang) and of the giants in "The Brave Little Tailor" (of German origins) are extremely important, for these tales exhibit the redemption motifs central to Western civilization, here expressed through the theme of the small person overcoming the giant by wit and virtue. It is fascinating to note, moreover, the classic situation regarding weapons observable in "The Brave Little Tailor": the giants that the tailor has set against one another fight with their bare hands and with uprooted trees (that is, with clubs); they are finally killed by the little tailor with his sword. In "Jack the Giant Killer" the giant ogre has a bludgeoning club, while Jack uses a knife. Elsewhere, against giants armed only with clubs he uses a sharp sword, a cap of knowledge, and swift shoes or an invisible coat. This story contains, moreover, the beheading motif and other Arthurian paraphernalia we have previously discussed.

The illustrations of giants and ogres of the fairy tale are of varying quality and endless quantity. Doré, to whom I have referred several times in this entry, was the unsurpassed master at the depiction of the giant, in these as in more literary contexts. As I have said, the imaginary giant of *Don Quixote* seems most real (Doré 1:465), and Doré's rendition of Goliath is indeed stunning (1:15). The giants that serve to illustrate *Les Aventures du Chevalier Jaufre et de la belle Brunissende*, by Jean-Bernard Lafon, and to embellish Th. Gautier's translation of *Les Aventures du Baron de Munchhausen* (1:541, 543) are also very impressive—especially the latter, in which we have a picture of gigantomachia, or a battle between two giants (1:556), here holding their heads, and thus evoking the beheading motifs we have previously observed. Doré's illustrations of the giants of Rhenish mythology are numerous and most beautiful (1:597–632). But he is, above all, cited by critics for his illustrations of Rabelais and of Perrault, and for that reason it is appropriate to speak of him in the context of the fairy tale. Most memorable are the fearsome ogre giants of "Tom Thumb" and "Bluebeard." With their bulging eyes and fierce aspect, they seem virtually to leap off the pages in endless attack (1:397, 398, 407).

Lest one believe that giants have disappeared from modern children's literature, let us point out that in a very recent book by Jean Fritz, entitled *The Good Giants and the Bad Pukwudgies*, ancient creation myths and old Indian legends concerning giants are revived. In this story, the good giant Maushop, along with his wife Quant and their five sons, while opposing the mean small pukwudgies who are bent on much deviltry, creates Buzzards Bay and the islands of Martha's Vineyard and Nantucket, as well as the Elizabeth Islands.

In addition, Sara Teale's *Giants* (1979) will tell the older child and the casual reader all he/she wants to know about the lore and lifestyle of giants from many ages and cultures. It is narrated with great whimsy and is cleverly illustrated by a team of three artists directed by David Larkin. In this volume (163–67) can be found an adaptation of one of the best known original fairy tales of recent vintage, Oscar Wilde's *The Selfish Giant*. Here the giant pays a short seven-year visit to his friend the Cornish ogre. Upon returning, he does not like to find the local children playing in his beautiful garden. Mother Nature forthwith punishes him for his selfishness by making his garden barren. The end of this story, emanating from the depths of a very ancient fertility myth, finds the fierce and unloving giant grown gentle toward the children; and one day when the children come to play in his garden they find him lying dead, covered with a blanket of flowers.

As with children's literature, which is hard sometimes to separate from adult literature, folk customs and folklore are often intertwined with sophisticated literature. For example, Stith Thompson cites extensive references to giants and giant ogres in folk literature, including giants with one arm, with long teeth, with long hair, with no hair, with a stone heart; giant ogresses who throw their long breasts over their arms (an irregularity commonly ascribed by Europeans to aborigines, as can be seen in illustrations of early travel books); and so on. As it is not within the scope of this essay to study these many, many references, the reader who has that particular interest should use Thompson as a point of departure for a total exploration of the giant in folklore and popular culture.

However, we will consider those medieval folk customs in which the giant plays a principal role, because they are closely related to the drama. They exist yet today in village festivals, and are described at length by Darré, but Teale also mentions them (52); and C. J. S. Thompson discusses the traditions and the history of these wicker statues in England and elsewhere (135–37). Echoing Jessie Watson, Darré views the huge, burlesque mannequins displayed during popular festival parades as vestiges of very ancient fertility rites and of other pre-Christian celebrations (Darré 22–23). In Christian times, these festivities are associated with carnival before Lent, or feast before famine.

In these processions following fairs, as well as in the religious processions, citizens would display colossal statues of royal figures, of the Virgin, and of saints. So huge were these statues that they had to be drawn on carts by horses and oxen. The custom was widespread, but the Spanish parade for the feast of Corpus Christi is especially noteworthy. In France, at the Fête-Dieu of Angers, burlesque giants represented heretics in parades that were condoned and even initiated by the Church.

The European Middle Ages saw also the rise of the *ducasses* and the *kermesses* involving masquerades in which there were gigantic images. Among the figures in the Viennese parade of 1613, for example, were a rustic bride and groom, a huge statue of Bacchus, surrounded by artisans distributing wine to anyone with a goblet, and a gigantic wicker ox, drawn by an ox-powered sled of sorts and escorted by butchers (whose trademark the ox represented) mounted on horseback (Darré 33–34).

We are obviously here reminded of the folkloric giant Paul Bunyan and his companion Babe the Great Blue Ox. Paul Bunyan is a mythical hero of the American lumbercamps for whom there is "no known prototype" ("Bunyan," *Encyclopaedia Britannica*). He is reported to have created Puget Sound and the Grand Canyon. For hot-cakes, he is said to have used a griddle so large that men greased it by skating on it with sides of bacon for skates. Paul Bunyan appears in many children's books, but he has also been the subject of poems by Robert Frost, Carl Sandburg, and Richard Wilbur, an operetta by W. H. Auden and Benjamin Britten, and a ballet suite by William Bergsma.

It is correct to say that even normal-sized figures may, little by little, become larger, until they reach gigantic proportions. As Darré says (40), this would be done solely in order to impress the public more and more. Such may be the case with giant puppets, which have enjoyed a revival on American PBS stations. Should we not also mention here the colossal statues of Liberty and Uncle Sam, and the faces of four American presidents carved out of a mountain in South Dakota? The principle at work here is that the saint or culture hero, when not originally a "giant," gradually takes on the proportions of a giant, being the embodiment of power, and possessing a protecting or liberating force equal to that which a giant is supposed to have. Indeed it has been theorized that the very idea of giant came from early colossal statues, and not the reverse (especially by C. J. S. Thompson 130), though the presence of a giant mythology among Amerindians, where colossal statues did not exist, tends to militate against this opinion. One would rather contend that the concept had its origin in the presence of very tall and powerful men among ancient peoples—giants of the sort put on display or taken as guardsmen in historically documented cases dealt with at length by Thompson himself. In either case, a powerful visual impact is involved.

Though these folk parades flourished during the European Renaissance, it was nonetheless a period for the rebirth of learning; and during this era the intellectuals came to insist adamantly upon man's intrinsic worth. Questions about man as a physical part of the universe, and about his place in that universe, began to be raised. Issues of religion, aesthetics, and politics began to be treated in a far more aggressive and "objective" way than could be said of the medieval approach. Yet giants continued to thrive. "Bad giants" of the Arthurian romance and of folklore continued, as we have seen, through the sixteenth and seventeenth centuries, and the malevolent giants of antiquity even enjoyed a neoclassical revival with such poets as Ronsard, Du Bellay, Du Bartas, Milton, and others. Indeed, the Renaissance saw the birth of great mythographies, the first of which was Boccaccio's *Genealogia deorum*. (See, in the French translation of Boccaccio, book 5, ch. 67, "Des geans qui furent engendrez du sang des tytanes et de la terre," which includes a discussion of Goliath, and of Josephus' views on him.) This work of Boccaccio is complemented by Natalis Comes' *Mythologiae*, which, with other works of its kind, nourished Renaissance and neoclassical writers of several generations. (See especially Comes' "De Gigantibus," 194–96, where the giant is characterized as irrational, impetuous, libidinous, and lacking in discipline; also "De Cyclopibus," 275–78, where we learn that the Cyclopes lived in Lipara, and that "Polyphemus Galateam amavit.") These two great works quote critically and abundantly from ancient writers, and they are still useful reference works, particularly in reconstructing sources for Renaissance and neoclassical authors.

Two poets of the French Renaissance who, as members of the Pléiade, were engaged in this revival of antiquity were Ronsard and Du Bellay. Doubtless one of the most peculiar and arresting accounts of the struggle between giant and hero is found in Ronsard's "Hymne de Pollux et Castor"(1556), in which Pollux (Polydeuces), a member of Jason's Argonautic fleet and a "son of Jupiter," kills and beheads the gruesome, wrinkled Amycus, "son of Neptune," or Poseidon (Ronsard 2:213–16). The story of Castor and Pollux comes from Ovid and Theocritus (*Idyl* 22). Horace's *Second Epistle*, of which Du Bellay published a translation in 1552, deals with this famous pair of twins. They were a favorite Renaissance theme, and an opera was even written about them by J.-P. Rameau. But what makes the Ronsard poem so remarkable is that Amycus, a hairy ogre, in whose foul lair are found human remains and pools of blood, is a giant of medieval convention: he is extremely hairy and carries a club, evoking the giants of Chrétien de Troyes' *Erec* and *Yvain*, and retaining little of Theocritus' Amycus, a statuelike giant made of brass, who melts away at death. Although Ronsard spoke of giants elsewhere in his works ("Hercule chrétien," "Hymne des Astres," *La Franciade*), nowhere did he show more fully the violent clash of giant force and awkwardness with youthful virtue and dexterity than in this poem.

Du Bellay, too, recalls the giants of antiquity, the sons of the Sun and the Earth, in his "Prosphonématique" (1:159), an occasional poem written for the solemn entry of Henri II into Paris on June 16, 1549. He again refers to them in his *Musagnoemachie*, in the last strophe of his "De l'Innocence," and his

"Complainte du Désespéré" (line 427). But, regretting his "songes antiques," he turned to biblical subjects—considered by some to be equally of antiquity— and, toward 1552, gave us an unfortunate poem, in tedious dizains, entitled "La Monomachie de David et Goliath" (2:20–27). Here Goliath is scaly—a variation of the hairy giant—and is armed with a *grand'hache*. Nemrod (not Cain) is portrayed on his shield. David, who, like Du Bartas' David, calls Goliath a "mastin" (dog, or cur), is, of course, much more dextrous than the giant Philistine, the "Colosse." The moral of the story, perhaps derived from Horace, is clumsily spelled out and "universalized": brute force and pride (hubris), blinded by ire, and not guided by reason, can be outdone by weakness and humility, especially when that humility is shored up by faith.

As a consequence of this Renaissance revival of ancient myth, even into the age of Romanticism, poets such as Victor Hugo throughout part 4 of his *Légende des siècles* depict the struggle between giants and gods. In "Le Titan" (*Légende* 4), Hugo calls the giants "big sons" of Mother Earth, while human beings are said to be her "little sons." Somehow, the epic grandeur of the legend seems diminished in the image.

Yet, although these rebellious and grotesque giants of antiquity come back on the scene at the time of the Renaissance, good giants and philosophical giants nonetheless also appear now, almost for the first time; and they even enjoy great popularity and prominence. Sometimes these new giants are calculated on ancient, sometimes on medieval models; upon occasion they appear almost to be cut out of whole cloth.

Continuing the medieval tradition, the rather influential French tale of Valentine and Orson was published in Lyons in 1489. It was translated into Icelandic, Italian, German, and Dutch. In English it appeared in a 1550 version by Henry Watson, under the title *Historye of the Two Valyante Bretheren: Valentyne and Orson*. In one of the episodes of this romance Valentine and Orson must rescue their mother from a giant. Did Bruegel depict this giant in his "Masquerade of Orson and Valentine"? H. Arthur Klein cogently argues (119–21) that the central figure in this 1566 woodcut is indeed the giant of our story. He is dressed in skins and wears furs (Friedman 33–34), although his size is not shown here to be disproportionate to that of the other figures in the woodcut. He is thus a "giant" who has been neutralized.

To take another example, in a sixteenth-century Italian version of the Arthurian legend of Guiron (*Girone il cortese*), the daughter of the king of Northumberland bids Febus, former king of France, to slay the giants who make their home in a deep cave. This story is told by the son of Febus and the grandfather of Guiron, an old knight, himself of superhuman stature. Guiron, too, delivers his sometime friend Danian from a giant (E. Gardner 56–57).

Emerging from the medieval tradition, too, is Luigi Pulci's *Morgante*, or *Morgante Maggiore* (1483). This chivalrous epic in twenty-eight cantos is an unsynthesized series of comic incidents, scientific digressions, and lofty passages, all recounting the adventures of Orlando, the hero. He is a knight driven from the court of Charlemagne. Going to Pagania, Orlando meets three giants, two of whom he kills. The third is Big Morgante, with whom Orlando and his friend Rinaldo travel to infidel Africa. In the end, the two knights return to France to help the French in the famed Battle of Roncevaux, the subject of the *Chanson de Roland*. Orlando (Roland) is killed in this battle.

Shortly following *Morgante*, another comic giant, Le Fracasse, appeared on the scene, again in a comic spoof of chivalric romance. His antics are shown, along with those of Baldo—a descendant of Roland's cousin Rinaldo—in a work called *Le maccheronee* (or *Baldus*), first published in 1517, and written by Teofilo Folengo, under the pen name Merlinus Cocaius or Merlino Cocajo. The comic verve of this work sets it above parody, though some critics brand it as such. Of course, Folengo cannot be said to have invented the burlesque of chivalric romance, if Chaucer's Sir Thopas (1383?) and his encounter with the "greet geaunt" named sire Olifaunt be a burlesque, as I feel it is. Olifaunt is of the guardsman/herdsman type, apparently a Saracen—but he also has three heads!

All in all, then, and leaving aside works that continue the ancient and the medieval traditions that we have examined, the giants of Renaissance literature temporarily drop their fierce mien to become symbols of largesse and of humanism. Among the most famous of these "good guys" of the giant world are Rabelais' Gargantua and Pantagruel. *Pantagruel*, published in 1532, takes as its point of departure *Les Grandes et Inestimables Cronicques du grant et enorme géant Gargantua*, a book about three giants, Grant-Gosier, Galemelle, and their son Gargantua, and about the feats that the latter performed "pour le Roy Artus." Something of a parody of Arthurian romance, this book was also based upon French folklore; and, incidentally, the folkloric base for the legend of Gargantua (or Grand' Guele) is reconfirmed by Antonine Maillet in her *Rabelais et les traditions* (20, 27, 41), where we learn of the giant's existence, even today, in Acadian folktales. Still, Rabelais took inspiration for his giants not only from French folklore, but also from Italian forebears, and especially from Pulci, whose *Morgante* we have just spoken of. *Gargantua*, published in 1534, actually deals with the life of Pantagruel's father, and of his grandfather Grandgousier, and therefore precedes *Pantagruel* in most editions of Rabelais' *Oeuvres complètes*.

These two giants—who slip in and out of their gianthood with amusing results—surely epitomize Renaissance verve and exuberance in an altogether unique way. They are kings, of course; and while their enormous size gives rise to many hilarious episodes, the capacity of their minds, the extent of their virtue, and the degree of their civility are in sharp contrast to the evil monsters of the Middle Ages, half-beast and often ogre. In Rabelais' work the medieval *chanson de geste* is under satire, just as Arthurian romance is in *Don Quixote*, but, nevertheless, Gargantua and Pantagruel are creatures of the Renaissance, *bons buveurs, bons viveurs*. They are also studious and inquisitive. Moreover, they are archetypal models of the good and clement king. Antonine Maillet sees Rabelais' stories as universal in their thrust, and as pertaining to the quest for lost paradises (20).

Like Cervantes in *Don Quixote*, Rabelais' tone and comic spirit have had incalculable influence over subsequent literature, though his giants per se do not seem to have been easy to copy. However, Gargantua, at least, inspired the great giant "float," Gargantua Galaffre, first created in 1853 for the carnival of Bailleul. Because of its contemporaneity, one should also mention Antonine Maillet's charming play *Panurge, ami de Pantagruel* (1983); in it the giant has a literary revival of consequence. Here he voyages to the New World, and lands with his côterie on the shores of Acadia in Canada. Much of the conversation of the characters in this play reconstructs well-known passages from Rabelais.

The illustrations for the many editions of Rabelais' *Gargantua* and *Pantagruel* have shown us the limitations and the difficulties of rendering a visual interpretation of a giant. Some have succeeded better than others, but among the happiest, one should mention J. Le Clerc and J. Janot of the sixteenth century; Du Bourg of the eighteenth century; and Derain, in the Skira edition of *Pantagruel* (twentieth century). But the greatest, as I have already stated, was Gustave Doré of the nineteenth century. His realizations of Pantagruel and Gargantua as children who outmeasure everything around them are truly unforgettable. Samples from all of these artists can be readily viewed in the P. Jourda edition of Rabelais' *Oeuvres complètes*.

Can the giants of the *contes philosophiques*—that is, the giants of a Cyrano de Bergerac and of a Voltaire—be said to descend from the Renaissance tradition? It is hard to say. Strange and fantastic voyages bring the earth-born narrator of Cyrano's *Voyage dans la lune* to a moon inhabited by giant humanoid quadrupeds. And Voltaire's Micromégas, a giant from Sirius, is accompanied by a "dwarf" from Saturn in a "philosophical voyage" to the tiny earth, where humans seem to them to be but fleas, and whales from the Baltic Sea must be viewed under a microscope. Voltaire, of course, leaned upon Cyrano de Bergerac's *Histoires comiques*, his *Etats et empires de la lune*, and his *Etats et empires du soleil*, as well as Swift's *Gulliver's Travels*, for the creation of his *Micromégas*. Voltaire also borrowed from the traditional literature concerned with the "pluralité des mondes" (Lucretius, Fontenelle). But unlike these others, Voltaire's purpose is not only to "attack man's sense of importance as expressed in the anthropocentric theory of the Universe" (Voltaire 201), but also to show the law of relativity with respect to size, time, and space. More specifically, the imaginary or dream voyage of the giant to earth or of the earthman to another planet is for Voltaire, as for Cyrano and Swift, a pretext to satirize religion, politics, and customs of a particular state, or even of human beings in general.

Most likely these works of "speculative astronomy" and imaginary voyages pave the way for twentieth-century literature of science fiction and fantasy, in which "giants" still play a part. For giants are not an "endangered species" as Teale suggests (185–89). Not only are ancient legends regarding giants still being retold, both in adult and children's literature, but they are constantly appearing in books of science fiction and fantasy, under new "skins" and with new attributes. It would be difficult to trace the origins of these new giants. As stated, some may come from the early *conte philosophique* of Voltaire, or from a reading of Swift's *Gulliver's Travels*; they may be modified by the Gothic horror stories that involved ghoulish experiments and the creation of new species, such as Frankenstein's monster; and they may be fed, too, by more modern works featuring giant robots, as in the 1980 film *Saturn 3* with Kirk Douglas and Farrah Fawcett. Certainly the old relationship between the giant and the vegetation myth is also still alive, if not in American literature, at least in television commercials, which frequently show us the Jolly Green Giant, straddling the valleys around Le Sueur, Minnesota, accompanied by his small companion Sprout. But whatever the multiple sources, contemporary fiction can claim its own share of large, fabulous anthropoids.

Of great interest to writers of science fiction are the gravity problems revolving around giants. In this entry, we have seen how their supposed physiology might cause them to be rather easily outwitted. But, further, science fiction mythology holds that giants died out from their inability to support their weight (from fallen arches, bone erosion, and the like). Mud, and quicksand too, bring certain death to the giant. Therefore, the giant, like the dinosaur, had to become extinct and— if indeed he did precede man—to be replaced by a being with a more viable anatomy. (See also Teale 22.)

Be this as it may, in the domain of science fiction, we should mention the primordial earthbound giants (titanthrops) in *To Your Scattered Bodies Go*, from the Riverworld series by Philip José Farmer. They are, by the way, "good giants." Also of interest in the "monster" domain are the large creatures with six arms in Burroughs' *John Carter of Mars*. Very tall creatures figure memorably in C. S. Lewis' *Out of the Silent Planet*. Types of giants also figure in Arthur C. Clarke's *Rendezvous with Rama* and in Stephen Donaldson's novel *The Wounded Land*. At least a dozen more such examples can be found in Peter Nicholls' *Science Fiction Encyclopedia*. As a synecdoche (cf. the giant hand, the giant foot, the giant head, and other acromegalic members), we might cite the giant computer mind in the film *Colossus: The Forbin Project*. In the film *Star Wars* we had the large and hairy Wookie that growls and grunts. And so on.

Contemporary fantasy literature, too, is not without its share of "giants." Here we might mention J. R. R. Tolkien's Balrogs (giant devils) and his Ents (tree creatures who are large, old, powerful, and dangerous). Tolkien's link with ancient mythologies is sensed when we read the Old Norse myth concerning the formation of Midgard, or Middle Earth—the world of man—from the body of Ymir. This myth traces the birth of the first man (Aske) from an ash tree, and of the first woman (Embla) from an alder. In this Old Norse cosmology, the World Tree, a mighty ash called Yggdrasil, stood at the center of the universe. His three giant roots extended to the abodes of gods and giants (Teale 26, 38). There is doubtless some connection here with the prophetic trees of the forest of Dodona, which could reveal the secrets of Destiny in the name of Jupiter;

nor should we forget that Cyrano de Bergerac encountered talking oaks in his dream trip to the sun. And Piers Anthony's *Ogre, Ogre* gives us Smash, a huge half-breed ogre who, aided by the half-breed nymph Tandy, struggles to assert his essential humanity.

But even if one leaves aside twentieth-century science fiction and fantasy, one will still find giants in modern literature. For example, in 1936 Pirandello left unfinished a play, *I giganti della montagna*. This work, in three acts, whose intended denouement has been supplied by Pirandello's son, concerns a troupe of traveling actors. The play has its debt to the mythology of giants, being not only an allegory about mimesis or "fictitious reality" versus other "realities," but also about the slaves of the Mountain Giants and the slaves of Art.

Giants are not absent, either, from Miguel Ángel Asturias' *Hombres de maíz* (1949), a work of "magical realism," in which Indian peasants, with totemic identities that cause them to regard the grain as sacred, clash with their masters, avid for profit. The name of one of these peasants, Machotón (large, macho man), is of special significance to the present investigation.

In the world of art a powerful modern sculpture *Giovi e i Giganti* (Jove and the Giants) by Anne and Patrick Poirier was exhibited recently in Milan (*Art in America*, April 1984, s.p.).

In the course of this study, we have seen that evil giants and ogres invariably fall. Thus, they have become an important part of man's moral didacticism. Menestrier shows us their emblematic potential (21, 25, 91, 174–75, 368–69). With picture and motto, artists may use the legends concerning giants to demonstrate the results of impiety, of pride, of wars. Shakespeare, too, sees a valuable lesson to be drawn from giants, when he writes in *Measure for Measure*: "O! It is excellent / To have a giant's strength, but it is tyrannous / To use it like a giant" (II.ii.107–9).

When we consider the giant from the structural point of view, several reigning principles assert themselves. First of all, we may not even be talking about real giants most of the time when we say "giants" or "gigantic." To designate greatness, for instance, we speak figuratively of "giants," such as "giants of music" or "giants of literature." A sports team may call itself "The Giants." There are also the *Giants in the Earth*, that is, human conquerors of cruel Mother Nature, like the characters of Rölvaag, who took his title from the biblical passage regarding giants. Then, too, "giant" refers to relative size, as when the Spanish call a sunflower a "giganta," or when Leo Africanus says of the women of Tunis that they put on so many "fardels of linnen" around their heads that "they seem comparable to the heads of Giants" (249).

One might also use "gigantic" to designate a part, while the whole may not constitute a giant. Thus, in "Evadné" René Char suggests great sorrow by speaking of "a giant's tears." A normal-size human may have a giant's head (as a hydrocephalic), or a giant's foot (as a sciapod), or a giant's phallus (as Priapus or Silenus), or a giant's mind (as a computer). Such synecdoche is common to our thinking; and in any illustration or animation of "Jack and the

Beanstalk," nothing is more impressive than the giant's enormous foot slipping on the loose stone and falling, as a mark of his clumsiness and a presage that Jack will prevail. Nothing is more impressive, that is, except the many giants' heads that have to be delivered over to kings as proof that evil has lost to valor and as a prime trophy. (David, Beowulf, Jack the Giant Killer, and others make such presentations.) Parts of the giant's anatomy are often evoked, too, in geographical names—as in the Col du Géant, in the French Alps, or La Dent du Géant, the summit of Mont Blanc.

Voltaire's giants in *Micromégas* teach us an important lesson in relativity of size, as well as of time and space. A giant from one planet is a dwarf to a giant from a different planet, while to both giants human beings appear to be fleas or talking atoms. Yet, a normal man (Gulliver) can seem to be a giant to dwarfs (Lilliputians), but a dwarf to giants (inhabitants of Brobdingnag). Relatively is implicit, too, in the Spanish idiom that labels a little man who is taller than those around him, or a thing only important due to the inferiority of what surrounds it, a "gigante en tierra de enanos." All such comparisons have venerable precedents in reports brought back to Moses: "And there we saw giants, the sons of Anak, which come of the giants: and we were in our own sight as grasshoppers, and so we were in their sight" (Numbers 13:33).

It would seem, too, that a giant is larger than a giantess, judging from the Darré illustrations, and other indications found elsewhere. Yet the very word "giantess" has a bizarre ring to it, with the feminine diminutive attached to such an imposing noun as "giant." Amazons, the reader will recall, are commonly associated with large women; yet actually they are not giantesses, but women warriors who cut off their left breast in order to use their weapons better. Nonetheless, excepting Grendel's dam, a female giant must not be very ominous, especially if she is said to be beautiful. Still, the giantess, like the giant, has superhuman strength and anatomical capabilities commensurate with her size and otherworldliness. Thus, Rabelais tells us that Gargamelle delivered Gargantua through her left ear (*Gargantua*, ch. 6).

Giants, having, as it were, Gargantuan appetites, are capable of eating larger dinners than humans, and, indeed, of making their dinner of humans. Micromégas differs here: for lunch he eats a whole mountain, for he is not a man-eater. The giant in "Jack and the Beanstalk" eats elephant steaks and a whole roasted ox, and, when he can, whole children.

These anatomical differences make of the giant a space-conqueror, too. Gargantua and Pantagruel can travel from Chinon to Paris in a few steps. Micromégas can cover 30,000 feet in one step; and time to this inhabitant of the planet Sirius (as to Cyrano's lunar beings) is not the same as it is to us. At the age of 450 he enters adolescence. In a somewhat different context, Tennyson sensed the relativity of human time and giant time when he wrote in *The Princess*: "Would, indeed, we had been, / In lieu of many mortal flies, a race / Of giants living each a thousand years, / That we might see our own work out, and watch / The sandy footprint harden into stone" (3.250–54). But, no matter whether we live to be 20, 50, or 1,000, we never live long enough—or so Micromégas observes. And others with whom he comes in contact all agree with him.

The relativity of size to power is also an important factor in considering how giants interact with humans. The stories of David and Goliath, and of the knights-errant, prove that smallness can overcome bigness, when right, or wit, or some inherent disposition is on the side of the smaller force. Science demonstrates what our giant-slaying legends already suggested; for microscopic bacteria can lay low the gigantic human, and the even larger whale, "gentle giant" though he or she be.

The existence of giants in the human imagination shows, moreover, how much human beings like to consider enlarging and miniaturizing, sometimes out of pure whimsy. We find both traits at work in *Alice in Wonderland*, where Alice is at times large and at others small, relative to her surroundings. The characters in two recent films, *The Incredible Shrinking Woman* and *The Incredible Shrinking Man*, also have something to say about this. From their Lilliputian perspectives, all the rest of us become giants. Our fantasy, in which we can conceive of beings larger (or smaller) than life and then set up a situation in which we overcome them, seems to be the ultimate in wish fulfillment, with respect to metaphysical control.

Besides this, largeness in giants and in other things can be amusing (just as smallness is). Huge giants in a parade, large statues of Uncle Sam and of Mickey Mouse, the perspectives of Pantagruel and of Gargantua are comical. If, moreover, one should burn these hemp and papier-mâché statues after the merriment is over—as is often done—one again triumphs symbolically over the gigantic (cf. Teale 52).

But, conversely, that which is huge can be most frightening. Thus, the stories in which the small overcome the big, as "Jack the Giant Killer," or "Jack and the Beanstalk," teach the children who hear them hope and courage in the face of that which at first blush seems ominous, terrifying, and overpowering.

As Friedman points out (154), color and size polarities can be easily interchanged with moral polarities. The large in size can be regarded as morally and culturally defective, and as symbolic of brute force, or raw nature. Such is the case with the Cyclopes, or with the giants of the Arthurian legends, or the monsters and ogres we have mentioned here. On the other hand, the large in size can represent the large in heart; it can be a sign of liberality and of an expansive disposition, as is the case with Rabelais' giants. Significantly, Jung perceives the good giant to be an archetype of the "cosmic man" (*Man and His Symbols* 201).

Thus, we should not forget that the giant herdsman or the giant guard can sometimes represent a form of protection, rather than an obstacle to be overcome. Among such, we would have to number the many gigantic guards used in ancient times by Augustus Caesar, as custodians of the Sallustian Gardens, and in more recent history by François I, James I, and Charles I. Especially noteworthy is the formation in the eighteenth century of a famous regiment of gigantic guards—

all at least nine feet tall—by Frederick William of Prussia (C. J. S. Thompson 141–84). In addition, there are the many legendary giant guardsmen, such as Gog and Magog, protectors of the Tower of London, as well as those giants who guarded various cities of Belgium and Northern France; and there are certain "good" giant guardsmen of fiction. These latter might be regarded as an anima creation; but, of course, it depends on one's perspective as to whether such a giant is a guardian or a threat.

From the psychological and the moral point of view, the myths regarding bad giants represent the need for good to win out over evil—the need to undo it, to "decapitate it," the need to rescue our fellow men from it. Evil giants represent, also, the desire we have to believe that the small and seemingly helpless can overcome the large and powerful. This is an ever-present motif in our stories, in our films, in our comics. Though in some other contexts might overpowers right (for example, in La Fontaine's fables), in giant lore right can usually win out against might. In most tests presented in those stories where giants figure, brute force (raw nature) can be conquered through superior wit and tools, as well as through valor. Such dynamics are obviously political as well as moral. Besides, the evil deeds of monsters and giants transfer guilt from man to something extra-human or metaphysical. Perhaps these are some of the reasons why there are more evil than good giants in our literature.

Giants are the symbol for the expression of certain recurring beliefs in the mythologies of all races. Though they usually lack the stature of gods as well as the civilization and the cunning of man—therefore often becoming a symbol of a conquerable brute nature—they nevertheless symbolize other, even more intimate, aspects of the life experience. In Jungian terms, many of the stories of giants might be viewed as symbols of the Judeo-Christian ego's emergence from its pagan past. Similarly, the battles of gods against giants symbolize the struggle of right conscience against evil, or the freeing of the anima from parental domination, as also from the parent's "devouring" aspects that are personified in the ogre. Since the parent also represents something very large to the child, the common infantile dream of growing larger is intertwined in the stories of giants and mighty heroes. Jung himself studies this "dream" (*Man and His Symbols* 53–54); as an example of it he cites in particular Lewis Carroll's *Alice in Wonderland*.

The floating nature of the giant as symbol makes, then, for a dual archetype. The "bad" giant, whether earthbound or from another world, is a being of nature, a terrible parent figure to be feared and to be overcome. The "good" giant is a being to emulate—not only is he a "cosmic man," but a "superman." He does not have a magic suit, like Clark Kent; but he is large and may, in fact, have magic boots. The "good" giant (Gargantua, Pantagruel, Paul Bunyan) is a sign of our wish for expansiveness; he may also be an archetypal culture hero, as is Pecos Bill, "the first of the cowboys" (Teale 138–40).

Above all, giants appeal to our thirst for otherworldliness, for the miraculous, for the fabulous, for the extraordinary and the bizarre. And so we invent them;

never mind the epistemological problems these inventions invoke. *Star Wars* and *E.T.* speak to this need in us, but so do giants. Their function in our mythos is of sufficient importance for us to believe in them, if only in a sceptical and tentative manner.

BIBLIOGRAPHY

Baltrušaitis, Jurgis. *Réveils et prodiges*. Paris: Colin, 1960.

Baudelaire. *Les Fleurs du mal*. Paris: Hachette, 1951.

Bédier, Joseph. *Le Roman de Tristan et Iseut*. Paris: Piazza, 1929.

Beowulf. Trans. Burton Raffel. New York: New American Library, 1963.

The Bible in Art: Miniatures, Paintings, Drawings and Sculptures Inspired by the Old Testament. New York: Phaidon, 1956.

Boccaccio, Giovanni. *Généalogie*. New York: Garland, 1976.

Bruce, James Douglas. *The Evolution of Arthurian Romance*. 2 vols. Gloucester, Mass.: Peter Smith, 1958.

Bulfinch, Thomas. *Mythology*. New York: Dell, 1959.

"Bunyan, Paul." *Encyclopaedia Britannica*. 1965 ed.

Céard, Jean. *La Nature et les prodiges*. Genève: Droz, 1977.

Cervantes, Miguel de. *Don Quixote*. Trans. Peter Motteux, New York: Random House, 1930.

Chagall, Marc. *Illustrations for the Bible. Verve*. Issues 33–34. Paris, 1956.

Chaucer, Geoffrey. *Complete Works*. Ed. F. N. Robinson. New York: Houghton Mifflin, 1933.

Chrestien de Troyes. *Yvain*. Ed. T. B. W. Reid. Manchester, England: Manchester University Press, 1948.

Cohen, Daniel. *The Encyclopedia of Monsters*. New York: Dodd, Mead and Co., 1982.

Comes, Natalis. *Mythologiae*. New York: Garland, 1976.

Commelin, P. *Nouvelle Mythologie grecque et romaine*. Paris: Garnier, [1926?].

Costello, Peter. *The Magic Zoo: The Natural History of Fabulous Animals*. New York: St. Martin's, 1979.

Cyrano de Bergerac, Savinien de. *Voyage dans la lune et Histoire comique des etats et empires du soleil*. Ed. Willy de Spens. Paris: Union Générale d'Editions, 1963.

Darré, René. *Géants d'hier et d'aujourd'hui*. Arras: Imprimerie de la Nouvelle Société Anonyme du Pas-de-Calais, 1944.

Deulin, Charles, ed. *Les Contes de ma mère l'oye*. Paris, 1879; rpt. Genève: Slatkine, 1969.

Dillon, Myles. *Early Irish Literature*. Chicago: University of Chicago Press, 1948.

Doré, Gustave. *Das graphische Werk in zwei Bänden*. Ed. Günter Metken. 2 vols. München: Rogner and Bernhard, 1975.

Du Bartas, Guillaume de Salluste, Sieur. *Works*. Ed. Urban T. Holmes et al. 3 vols. Chapel Hill: University of North Carolina Press, 1935–40.

Du Bellay, Joachim. *Poésies françaises et latines*. 2 vols. Paris: Garnier, 1918.

Friedman, John B. *The Monstrous Races in Medieval Art and Thought*. Cambridge: Harvard University Press, 1981.

Gardner, Edmund G. *The Arthurian Legend in Italian Literature*. London: J. M. Dent and Sons, 1930.

Gardner, Helen. *Art through the Ages*. 5th ed. New York: Harcourt, Brace and World, 1970.

Gayley, Charles Mills. *The Classic Myths in English Literature and Art*. New York: Ginn, 1939.

Gerhardus, Maly, and Dietfried Gerhardus. *Symbolism and Art Nouveau*. Trans. Alan Bailey, Oxford: Phaidon, 1979.

"Giant." *Encyclopaedia Britannica*. 1965 ed.

Hatzfeld, Helmut A. *Literature through Art*. Chapel Hill: University of North Carolina Press, 1969.

Jung, Carl G. *Man and His Symbols*. Garden City, N.Y.: Doubleday, 1964.

———. *Psychology and Religion: West and East*. Vol. 11 of *The Collected Works of C. G. Jung*. Trans. R. F. C. Hull. Bollingen Series 20. Princeton: Princeton University Press, 1969.

Klein, H. Arthur. *Graphic Worlds of Peter Bruegel the Elder*. New York: Dover, 1963.

Lang. See Theocritus.

Lee, Lawrence, et al. *Stained Glass*. New York: Crown, 1976.

Leo Africanus, Johannes. *A Geographical Historie of Africa*. Trans. John Pory. London, 1600. Facsimile reproduction, New York: Da Capo; Amsterdam: Theatrum Orbis Terrarum, 1969.

Maillet, Antonine. *Rabelais et les traditions populaires en Acadie*. Québec: Les Presses de l'Université Laval, 1971.

Menestrier, Claude. *L'Art des emblèmes*. Paris, 1684. Facsimile reproduction, New York: Garland, 1979.

Milton, John. *Complete Poems and Major Prose*. Ed. Merritt Y. Hughes. New York: Odyssey Press, 1957.

Ovid. *Metamorphoses*. Trans. Rolfe Humphries. Bloomington: Indiana University Press, 1958.

Paré, Ambroise. *Des Monstres et prodiges*. Ed. Jean Céard. Genève: Droz, 1971.

———. *On Monsters and Marvels*. Trans. and ed. Janis L. Pallister. Chicago: University of Chicago Press, 1982.

Perrault, (Charles). *Contes en vers et en prose*. Genève: Skira, n.d.

Pindar. *Odes*. Trans. John Sandys. Cambridge: Harvard University Press, 1957.

Rabelais, François. *Oeuvres complètes*. Ed. P. Jourda. 2 vols. Paris: Garnier, 1962.

Réau, Louis. *Iconographie de l'art chrétien*. 3 vols. Paris: Presses Universitaires de France, 1955–59.

Ronsard, Pierre de. *Oeuvres complètes*. Ed. Gustave Cohen. 2 vols. Paris: Gallimard (Bibliothèque de la Pléiade), 1950.

Spenser, Edmund. *The Works of Edmund Spenser: A Variorum Edition*. Ed. E. Greenlaw et al. 11 vols. Baltimore: Johns Hopkins Press, 1932–57.

Stone, Donald, Jr., ed. *Four Renaissance Tragedies*. Cambridge: Harvard University Press, 1966.

Teale, Sarah. *Giants*. New York: Abrams, 1979.

Theocritus, Bion and Moschus. Trans. A. Lang. London: Macmillan, 1906.

Thompson, C. J. S. *The Mystery and Lore of Monsters*. New Hyde Park, N.Y.: University Books, 1968.

Thompson, Stith. *Motif-Index of Folk-Literature*. Rev. and enl. ed. 6 vols. Bloomington: Indiana University Press, 1955–58.

Virgil. *The Aeneid*. Trans. W. F. Jackson Knight. Baltimore: Penguin, 1956.

Voltaire. *Selections from Voltaire*. Ed. George R. Havens. New York: Appleton-Century, 1930.

Voragine, Jacques de. *La Légende dorée*. 2 vols. Paris: Garnier, 1967.

Weston, Jessie L. *From Ritual to Romance*. Garden City, N.Y.: Doubleday, 1957.

The World's Best Fairy Tales. Ed. Belle Becker Sideman. Pleasantville, N.Y.: The Reader's Digest Association, 1967; 1978.

20

Fairies

John Marshall Carter

Although fairies have been primarily associated with northwestern Europe (especially with the British Isles), fairylike beings such as the nymphs and dryads of classical mythology, the djinn (genies) of Arabic lore, and the peri of Persian lore appear in many cultures throughout the world. Fairies have certain features in common, but there are many different types of fairies, and the types vary greatly. Economic, scientific, and technological developments and the modifications of traditional fairy lore by writers and artists have helped change the perspectives on fairy beings. This entry will be an attempt to address fairies and their changing perceptions through history, literature, and art.

Because of the diversity of sources concerning fairies and because of the wide variety of fairy types, this entry will focus upon the fairy lore of the British Isles (England, Ireland, Scotland, and Wales), France, Germany, and Scandinavia—in essence, northwestern Europe. The organization of the entry will be as follows: fairy etymology; the grouping of fairies according to types; characteristics and activities of fairies; the relationship between human beings and fairies; concepts about fairyland; theories about the origin of the concept of fairies; a historical survey of fairy lore; the use of fairies in literature; their use in art; and the Fate of Faery.

An investigation of the origins of the words "fairy" and "elf" is essential to an understanding of fairies and fairy lore. Although there have been various theories about the origin of the word "fairy," the general consensus of opinion is with Latin and French origins. (For some theories current in the nineteenth century, see Keightley 4–13). Lewis Spence, among others, has expressed the widespread and accepted belief that "fairy" has a connection with the Fates of classical mythology (*Fairy Tradition* 114–15). It is clear that the word "fairy" is linked to the Latin *fata* (singular, *fatum*). Spence states that *fata* in late Latin and early Italian referred to a species of beings that involved the "mingling or confusion of ideas associated with *both* the classical Fates and the nymphic *Fatuae*," and that the term *fata* "came to be accepted in the Roman world under the form *hada* in Spain, *fada* in Provence, *fa'ae* in Gaul, and later *fee* in France, reaching Britain at last by Norman introduction as 'fay' " (*Fairy Tradition* 115). The noun "fairye" in English originally meant a state of enchantment, and it was not until later that the word was used to describe specific supernatural beings (Briggs, *Encyclopedia* 131).

The Old French forms "faerie," "faierie," and "fae" and the Middle French "feerie" and "fee" are also derived from the Latin *fata* ("Fairy," *Compact Edition of the Oxford English Dictionary* 1:952). Other forms of the word are: "feir," "feirie," "fai," "fayerie," "fayere," "pharie," "farie," "pherie," and "faerie."

The word "fairy" has a number of meanings and associations. It can signify an individual fairy being, and it can refer to the land or home of the fairies (fairyland). The words "faere" and "fairy" also have the medieval connotation of enchantment, magic, illusion, or dream (*OED*). In contemporary usage, one meaning of "fairy" is a male homosexual.

The word "elf" has a "Teutonic origin, and is the Middle English form of an older Anglo-Saxon *aelf*, having cognate forms in Icelandic *alfr*, Scandinavian *alf* and German *elf*' (Spence, *Fairy Tradition* 120). Although "elf" has been used as a synonym for "fairy," distinctions between elves and fairies have often been made in traditional lore.

Classifying fairies into types and groupings is difficult because of the variety of fairies and because of the overlapping of types. Classification is also complicated by distinctions made in separate areas and countries. In addition, the traditional lore concerning some fairy types has undergone a change over a period of time, and the same term may have had different meanings at different times. Another important point to keep in mind is that writers have often changed or modified traditional lore.

In this entry, four major groupings are used to classify different types of fairies or fairylike beings: (1) the fays; (2) certain monsters and demons having a connection with fairies and/or having some of the characteristics of fairies; (3) the nature fairies; and (4) the fairy people. (This classification is a modification of a classification of British fairies made by Katharine Briggs in her book *The Personnel of Fairyland*.) The four groupings are broad ones that have been adopted as a convenient means of classifying a body of material that is difficult to separate into distinct categories. As will be seen, some types of fairies can be placed in more than one of the groupings.

Although the term "fay" has been used at various periods to refer to several different types of fairy beings, it is mainly used in this entry to signify enchanters and enchantresses with supernatural powers. Whereas some fays are mortals, others are supernatural beings or are part human and part supernatural. Fays figure prominently in the Arthurian romances, two of the best known of the fays being the Lady of the Lake and Morgan le Fay.

The second grouping involves certain monsters, demons, or beings that have been associated with fairies and/or have some of the characteristics of fairies. An example of a monster that can be placed in this grouping is Tom Tit Tot, who is "a black thing with a long tail" and is an English version of Rumpel-stiltskin (Briggs, *Anatomy of Puck* 194–95). The djinn (genies) of Arabic lore may also be put in the second category (see the final entry of this book). They share a number of characteristics with traditional fairies, such as shape-shifting and stealing human beings from the human world and taking them to their world. Briggs places dragons and giants in this grouping (*Personnel of Fairyland* 16).

The third grouping (the nature fairies) is made up of a broad range of beings associated with natural objects or with the natural world. Some of the beings found here are: mermaids and many water-spirits (see the entry on mermaids); certain tree-spirits; and supernatural hags such as the Cailleach Bheur, a personification of winter. Sometimes, there is a thin line between creatures in the second grouping (monsters and demons) and those in the third grouping (nature fairies). For example, in Scottish lore, the nuckelavee is a frightening monster (half-man and half-horse) associated with water; and Jenny Greenteeth, an evil water-spirit of Lancashire streams that pulls people into the water and devours them, is a demon as well as a nature-spirit.

The final grouping (the fairy people) is the most important one and contains the beings that might be considered the "true" fairies. Two main subdivisions of the fairy people have often been made: (1) communal fairies, who belong to a group, tribe, or nation and live together, and (2) individual or solitary fairies, who are usually "associated with a place, or occupation, or household" (Leach 363). According to Lewis Spence, the solitary fairies were originally communal fairies, and "their alleged solitary status is to a great extent a result of their segregation as types in the popular mind" (*Fairy Tradition* 27). Although the division of the fairy people into communal fairies and solitary fairies has limitations and weaknesses, it is a useful one that helps suggest some major distinctions among traditional types of the fairy people.

Some of the fairies that live in groups have a loosely organized social structure, but others have a distinct social hierarchy, with a king or a queen (or both). Those with a monarchical society hold court and conduct affairs of state; and they spend much of their time dancing, singing, and feasting. For the most part, the communal fairies live in a fairyland, a land or place of their own distinct from the human world.

There are so many different types of communal fairies that only some of the more significant types can be singled out here. The Tuatha De Danann of Ireland and dwarfs and elves will be given special attention, and several other types of communal fairies will be discussed briefly.

The Tuatha De Danann (see Lady Gregory, *Gods and Fighting Men*) are perhaps the most important of the fairies with a monarchical society. According to tradition, the Tuatha De Danann conquered the Firbolgs, the original inhabitants of Ireland. When the Milesians later conquered the Tuatha De Danann, the Tuatha De Danann went to live in palaces found in an underground world, "in the depths of the earth, in hills, or under ridges more or less elevated" (Wentz 291–92). The Tuatha De Danann hold court and enjoy feasts and revelry. At times they go forth on a "faerie rade," riding in procession on magnificent horses. It is often said that the fairy people of Ireland (the Daoine Sidhe) are descendants of the Tuatha De Danann. (For an excellent discussion of Irish fairy kings and queens and the nature of Irish fairy society, see Logan, *The Old Gods*.)

Dwarfs live in underground kingdoms, each having its own king. They have long beards and wrinkled skin, and despite their short stature, their bodies are powerful. Many dwarfs are misshapen and hideous, with humpbacks, huge heads, flattened noses, and deformed arms, legs, and feet (sometimes the feet are like those of a goat or some other animal), but there are also handsome dwarfs, with "beauty or handsomeness of countenance, excellent proportion of body and limbs, and . . . fair hair" (Harward 29). In nearly all legends, dwarfs are renowned for their skill as smiths and craftsmen. They mine precious metals, and from them they shape swords, spears, and other objects with magical qualities. The dwarfs of Scandinavian mythology were maggots bred in the flesh of the slain rime-giant Ymir. By the decree of the gods, they were given human shape and intelligence (Brodeur 26).

In Scandinavian mythology, the Alfar or elves have a divine nature. The *Prose Edda* speaks of two types of elves: the dark elves, who "are blacker than pitch" and live in the earth, and the light elves, who "are fairer to look upon than the sun" and live in Alfheim or Elf-home (Brodeur 31, 43). In later tradition, various conceptions of elves developed. Some elves were conceived of as small, delicate beings that "dwell in the air, dance on the grass, or sit in the leaves of trees," but other elves were said to be "an underground people, who frequently inflict sickness or injury on mankind" (Keightley 78). According to Briggs, "elf" was "the Anglo-Saxon word for spirits of any kind, which later became specialized into creatures very like the Scandinavian light elves" (*Anatomy of Puck* 188). There was a widespread belief that the evil elves could cause a wound or illness by elf-shot, an arrow or a dart tipped with a flint arrowhead.

Several other types of fairies who live in groups or tribes are of interest. The pixies, who are found in Somerset, Devon, and Cornwall, enjoy playing tricks on people, especially leading travelers astray. The knockers, Cornish fairies who live in mines and make a knocking sound to warn miners of impending danger, are one of a number of fairylike beings associated with mines. Also found in Cornish lore are the spriggans, evil fairies who harm crops, steal human children, and commit other evil acts. They are of a small size, but can become very large by inflating their bodies. The Tylwyth Teg of Wales, who "live on an invisible island," are said to "dance in fairy rings," and human beings who join in the dancing "are made invisible and carried off for ever, unless they are rescued before cockcrow" (Briggs, *Anatomy of Puck* 195).

The solitary fairies are of two general types. Some of them have a connection with a human family, but others shun any connection with human beings. The hobgoblins, friendly spirits who live in houses and do domestic chores such as helping bread to rise and caring for unattended babies, belong to the first type. The brownie, a small fairy who wears ragged clothes of a brown color, is the best known of the household fairies. He will perform many tasks if he is well treated, but any mistreatment of him may cause him to do some damage. If he leaves a house, the good luck attached to it goes with him. Similar to the brownie is the lutin, a household spirit of Brittany (Wentz 190–91). Also of the brownie type is Puck, who was called Robin Goodfellow in Elizabethan times. Another solitary fairy is the banshee, a spirit who wails to foretell the death of a family member. The leprechaun, the fairy shoemaker, is the best known of the solitary fairies who shun contact with human beings. A leprechaun is a small, grotesque-looking man who wears a leathern apron and shoes with silver buckles and has "spectacles tilted on his sharp nose" (Spence, *Fairy Tradition* 106). If a person can catch a leprechaun, then the leprechaun is obligated to show where he keeps his buried treasure. But the person must never remove his eyes from the leprechaun for even a second, or he will slip away. And he has a store of tricks in reserve to keep his captor from getting the treasure.

Gnomes and trolls have often been grouped with fairies, but they seem to be distinct from them. A gnome is an elemental: one of four types of beings that Paracelsus (1493–1541) associated with each of the four elements (air, with sylphs; fire, with salamanders; water, with nereids; and earth, with gnomes). Gnomes are dwarflike beings who live beneath the earth and guard buried treasures. The word "gnome" is often used as a synonym for an elf or fairy. In Scandinavian mythology, trolls were originally gigantic beings associated with the subterranean world. They lived in mountain caverns, coming out only at night (sunlight turned them to stone). They craved human flesh and blood; but because they were dim-witted, human beings were often able to outwit them. In later tradition, trolls were represented as dwarflike beings that lived in caverns or subterranean dwellings. The dwarf trolls were not bloodthirsty monsters like the giant trolls and lacked their great strength, but they posed a threat to human beings because they had a fondness for stealing women and children and because they were more intelligent than the giant trolls. The dwarf trolls loved dancing, and often they possessed beautiful wives and great riches (Maple 2889).

The word "goblin" is a general term used to describe wicked or malevolent spirits (Briggs, *Encyclopedia* 194). In this general sense, the term can refer to a wide range of malevolent beings and spirits (for example, redcaps, kelpies, spriggans, and bugbears). Goblins are usually conceived of as misshapen, grotesque-looking beings that live in dark places, such as the goblins in George MacDonald's *The Princess and the Goblin*, who are "dwarfed and misshapen" creatures possessing great strength and cunning and living "away from the sun, in cold and wet and dark places" (4). The goblins in Christina Rossetti's well-known poem "Goblin Market" are "goblin men" with the features and attributes of various beasts such as cats, rats, wombats, and ratels. They tempt Lizzie to taste their deadly fruits, which are "like honey to the throat / But poison in the blood" (lines 554–55). In French folklore, goblins are household spirits of the brownie type that perform various tasks but have a mischievous nature.

Having looked at a number of fairy types, we will next investigate some of the ideas concerning the characteristics and activities of fairies. There will be a discussion of their physical appearance, dress, food, occupations, and pastimes, and of the nature of fairyland. In addition, the relationships that exist between fairies and human beings will be explored.

Most fairies have been envisaged as having a human or humanlike form. Writers often speak of fairies as "men." In *The Itinerary through Wales* by Giraldus Cambrensis (1146?–1220?), Elidorus gives the following description of fairies: "These men were of the smallest stature, but very well proportioned in their make; they were all of a fair complexion, with luxuriant hair falling over their shoulders like that of women" (390; qtd. in Briggs, *Anatomy of Puck* 18). Some fairies have an animal form or can assume one, and others have a form combining human and animal features. For example, Jimmy Squarefoot, a figure in Manx stories, has the shape of a pig or of a man with a pig's head; the kelpie, a Scottish water-fairy, usually appears in the form of a horse; and the urisk of the Scottish Highlands is part human and part goat (Briggs, *Encyclopedia* 242, 246, 420). When the form of the fairy is human, some kind of deformity or deficiency in its makeup is present in many cases. Thus the Elle-Women (Wood Wives) in Scandinavian folklore have the appearance of young, attractive women, but their backs are "hollow like a dough-trough" (Keightley 81). In the thirteenth-century French romance, *The Boke of Duke Huon of Burdeux*, the Fairy King Oberon is "crokyd shulderyd, but yet he hathe an aungelyke vysage, so that there is no mortall man that seeth hym but that taketh grete pleasure to beholde his fase" (no. 40, p. 63).

Although fairies may have one form that is their characteristic one, they were supposed to be capable of changing their shape. Moreover, fairies were said to have the power of making themselves invisible.

Size varies from fairy type to fairy type (Briggs, *Encyclopedia* 368–69). Some fairies are taller than human beings; at the other extreme are fairies only a few inches tall or even smaller. Many fairies are described as being somewhere between these two extremes—the height of approximately three feet is mentioned with some frequency. Extremely small fairies are rare in traditional lore, but they often appear in literary works. In Michael Drayton's *Nimphidia*, for instance, the Faery Queen and her retinue are so small that they can house themselves in a hazel nut (Latham 204–5).

Although many people today envisage fairies as winged creatures, the winged fairy seems to have little foundation in traditional fairy lore. It is unclear when wings were first associated with fairies, but the association may have been made "about the time when angels become predominantly feminine, and were popularly supposed to be departed spirits rather than beings of another order" (Briggs, *Anatomy of Puck* 9–10). The fairy with diaphanous wings became a commonplace in art in the nineteenth century, and this image has greatly influenced the way that people visualize fairies in our time.

Fairies are associated with green clothing, sometimes having green hair and skin as well. In Elizabethan fairy lore, green and white became the predominant fairy colors (Latham 86–87), as references in Shakespeare's *A Midsummer Night's Dream* and *The Merry Wives of Windsor* indicate. Yet, certain fairy types also like other colors of clothing and sometimes are found wearing exotic outfits, such as coats made from the wings of bats (*A Midsummer Night's Dream* II.ii.4–5). In *Pandaemonium*, Richard Bovet said that the fairies wore clothing of red, blue, or green according to the habits of the rural folk (Hazlitt 335).

Dancing has come to be associated with fairy beings. Thus Milton in *Comus* says that "the pert fairies and the dapper elves dance on the tawny sands and shelves" (lines 117–18), and in *Paradise Lost* he speaks of the "fairy elves" who dance by "a forest side / or fountain" (1.781–87). Fairies are said to use dancing as a means of locomotion as well as a pastime or entertainment. Some sources suggest that the fairies clasp hands when they dance, sometimes so feverishly that they leave fairy rings on the ground—barren spots on otherwise grassy ground.

Music always accompanies fairy appearances and dances. Oftentimes the fairies sing in high-pitched tones as they dance. This phenomenon always startles passersby. Although certain fairy beings attach themselves to human houses, the majority of their dances, songfests, and other revels occur in forests and fields.

Fairies enjoy many kinds of recreation and entertainment. Feasts and festivals are held that include a great variety of folk games. Hurling is a favorite sport of the fairies in Ireland; and in Wales the Tylwyth Teg play games with golden balls, in the same type of rings used for song and dance. Some fairies take great pleasure in hunting; and as mentioned earlier, the Tuatha De Danann ride in procession. Lady Wilde in her *Ancient Legends, Mystic Charms and Superstitions of Ireland* (1887) gives a vivid picture of the Tuatha De Danann riding on their magnificent fairy steeds: "A splendid sight was the cavalcade of the Tuatha-de-Danann knights. Seven-score steeds, each with a jewel on his forehead like a star, and seven-score horsemen, all the sons of kings, in their green mantles fringed with gold, and golden helmets on their head, and . . . each knight having in his hand a golden spear" (93).

Some of the fairy folk engage in different kinds of work and are known for their skill in certain occupations. In *The Secret Commonwealth*, Robert Kirk (1644–92) says that the fairies of the Scottish Highlands bake bread, spin, dye, and embroider (67, 73). The brownies and other household fairies are well known for their industrious nature, and the dwarfs are skilled as smiths. Throughout much of Europe, the fairies are famous for their ability as builders (Spence, *Fairy Tradition* 191–94).

Although fairies sometimes grow their own food, they often get their food from human beings by either stealing it or accepting it as a gift. In England in the sixteenth century, people usually put out bread for the fairies. According to some writers, fairies can extract the inherent vigor or the essence of food, leaving behind only a worthless residue (Kirk 67; Spence, *Fairy Tradition* 186). Fairies have a special fondness for dairy products—milk, cream, and butter.

Some fairies are friendly to mankind, but others are openly hostile. In Scotland, for instance, the Seelie Court may be beneficent, doing such good deeds as giving food to the poor; but the Unseelie Court inflict harm upon mankind (Spence, *Fairy Tradition* 128–29). The Host of the Unseelie Court (the unbaptized dead) fly through the air at night; they descend upon any human beings they find, lift them up, and carry them through the air, tormenting them and making them shoot arrows or darts at animals and other human beings (Wentz 108–9). Other evil fairies include the nuckelavee, the spriggans, and the korrigans (the korrigans are small fairies in Britanny who often steal human babies). In general, however, fairies are not actively friendly or hostile to mankind. All the same, fairies are sensitive to slights, and they usually punish or harm a person who violates their rules or breaks their taboos. Thus one must never call fairies by their true names but instead must use a substitute name that is complimentary or at least gives no offense (for example, the Good People, the Gentle Folk, the Gentry, the Wee Folk, or the People). It is always dangerous to enter an area or place that the fairies regard as belonging to them, and they may pinch a trespasser black and blue or inflict much more serious harm. At certain times, especially at Midsummer's Eve, the fairies are especially active, and a person intruding upon them runs the risk of being seriously harmed. People can protect themselves against fairies by such means as making the sign of the cross or uttering certain incantations. Fairies have a special fear of iron (Kirk 72–73).

Most fairies do not see anything wrong with stealing from human beings (Briggs, *Encyclopedia* 154, 158), and this includes the abduction of human beings themselves. Fairies steal women to serve as midwives when fairy children are born. And many types of fairies abduct men and women (especially those of great physical beauty) to be their lovers. In some cases human beings are not abducted by the fairies but go willingly with them, and have no desire to return to the human world once they have lived in fairyland. Most fairies have a reputation for stealing human children, and they usually leave a changeling (a fairy baby or an old fairy) in place of the human baby they steal. As a rule, changelings are deformed and ugly, and they usually display a spiteful, malicious nature. (For a good discussion of changelings, see Spence, *Fairy Tradition* 228–54).

Concepts concerning fairyland have varied as much as concepts concerning fairies. Fairyland is a place or a land distinct from the human world. Fairyland may be beneath the earth, on an island, in a forest, in a castle, in a country adjoining the human world, or in some other place. In *The King of Elfland's Daughter* by Lord Dunsany, fairyland or elfland is an enchanted land that adjoins the human world; one passes from "the fields we know" (the human world) through the frontier of twilight to an enchanted land where the colors are deeper than in "the fields we know" and where the air "glows with so deep a lucency that all things seen there have something of the look of our trees and flowers in June reflected in water" (17). Keats also conveys the mysterious nature of fairyland when he writes in "Ode to a Nightingale" of "magic casements, opening on the foam / Of perilous seas, in faery lands forlorn" (lines 69–70).

Fairyland has different symbolic meanings. Sometimes it is a utopia, a paradise that is full of joy and delights. Ossian, the Irish hero, falls in love with the beautiful fairy princess Niamh of the Golden Hair and goes with her across the Western Sea to Tir Nan Og (the Country of the Young), the most delightful of all the countries "that are under the sun." Honey and wine are abundant there, and days are passed feasting, playing, and drinking. Sweet music plays continuously. The mortal warrior can get his fill of the material things he cherished in life: swords, horses, hounds, armor, beautiful women, and a hundred strong retainers skilled in battle (Lady Gregory, *Gods and Fighting Men* 333–34). The Isle of Avalon is also a fairyland. The mortally wounded Arthur is taken there "so that his wounds might be attended to" (Geoffrey of Monmouth, *History of the Kings of Britain* 261). In Avalon even death might be defeated. But fairyland often has an association with sinister or evil things. The knight in Keats's poem "La Belle Dame sans Merci" falls asleep in the "elfin grot" of the beautiful fairy lady he met on the meads and dreams of "pale" kings, princes, and warriors, who tell him that "La Belle Dame sans Merci" has him "in thrall." The picture is one of horror and destruction: "I saw their starved lips in the gloam, / With horrid warning gaped wide" (lines 42–43). In the poem "The Changeling" by Charlotte Mew (1869–1928), the changeling does not want to leave his human family to live with the fairies in "their wet, wild wood." He says that "Black and chill are Their nights on the wold" (line 69), and that he will always be cold when he is with them.

Visits to fairyland by mortals involve danger. If they eat anything while they are there, they might never be able to return to their own world. Some of those who do return may lose their reason or may be half-witted the rest of their days. And some who come back from fairyland live for only a short time. In fairyland time passes much more slowly than in the human world. A few hours in fairyland may be many years in the human world. There is a widespread belief that fairies themselves are immortal—or at least they age very gradually. Human beings who enter fairyland do not usually grow older as long as they stay there, but if they return to their own world they began aging again or may become old very quickly. When Ossian desired to return to Ireland, Niamh of the Golden Hair told him that he must ride on a white horse and never set his foot upon the ground. If he touched the earth once, then he could never come back to the

Country of the Young. Ossian returned to Ireland, finding that things had greatly changed and that his people were no more. When he saw a stone trough in which his people had once washed their hands, he forgot Niamh's warning and got down from his horse. All at once, his years came upon him and he found himself lying on the ground, "an old man, weak and spent" (Lady Gregory, *Gods and Fighting Men* 337–41).

There has been much speculation about how the concept of fairies originated. One of the most plausible theories is that the concept grew out of the legends concerning races of people who were conquered by other races. The conquered people might conceal themselves from their conquerors in isolated and out-of-the-way places; at times they might spy on their conquerors and steal from them, perhaps taking some of their children and women. If some of the conquering people were able to return to their own people after visiting the places where the subdued race lived, they might describe the places they saw as strange and mysterious. Illustrations of this theory can be found in the Anglo-Saxon/Celtic world after the Anglo-Saxon infiltration of the British Isles and in the Anglo-Norman world after the Norman Conquest. As Pict and Scot were driven to the North and West by the Anglo-Saxons, they strove to preserve ancient traditions that had been at the very core of their religion and social organization. By the death of William the Conqueror in 1087, French-speaking Normans had driven Celtic and Anglo-Saxon people into the hinterlands of the British Isles. The century following the conquest witnessed a tremendous number of folktales centering around the conquered inhabitants of Britain.

Another important theory is that fairies are gods and heroes who have been displaced by another set of gods and heroes (Leach 363). Such a pattern is evident in Ireland, where the old gods were not eliminated after the triumph of Christianity but were given a new status, "and in different disguises they have lived on in the Irish countryside until the present day" (Logan 7).

Several other theories are of interest. Fairies may be the personification of the old animistic spirits. According to this theory, a spirit of the trees would be anthropomorphized into a dryad; and a water spirit, into an undine. Another theory is that fairies are a part of man's attempt to rationalize natural phenomena. For instance, the "Good People" of Ireland reflect the beauty and gentleness of their surroundings, but in the Scottish Highlands with their "dark-rising mountains" and their "mysterious cloud-shadowed lakes" the types of fairies are much fiercer (Wentz xxi). Fairies have often been associated with spirits of the dead, especially with those that live underground. There is a good probability that the concept of fairies originated in a cult of the dead (see Spence, *British Fairy Origins*). Christian belief explained fairies as fallen angels or as the spirits of persons who went to neither Heaven nor Hell.

A survey of fairies and fairylike beings through various periods will be useful in showing how ideas about such beings have developed and changed and how people in different times have viewed these beings. The following survey places changing concepts of fairies within an historical context.

Before the nymphs and the Fates of classical antiquity, fairylike beings appeared in the mythology of the ancient Near East. For instance, *Gilgamesh*, the Sumero-Babylonian epic of creation and life, contains a number of fairylike creatures among its pantheon of deities and beings, with some of these creatures inhabiting a middle position between the gods and men—a typical fairy feature, the habitation of a middle-earth.

In classical mythology, the nymphs, dryads, and some other beings associated with the natural world have attributes of nature fairies. The Fates, who preside over the destinies of men and sometimes appear at the birth of a child, are fairylike in the sense that they have a connection with destiny, prophecy, and birth. (In later literature, the fairy godmothers found in the fairy tales of Charles Perrault [1628–1703] and some other writers appear at christenings.) As mentioned earlier, fairies have often been associated with the dead, especially with spirits that live underground. Between the time of Homer and Alexander the Great, Greeks and Italians worshiped dead ancestors who, they believed, lived beneath the soil, "manesque sepulti," according to Virgil (*Aeneid* 4.34; see also Fustel De Coulanges, *The Ancient City* 15). The dead became demons or heroes to the Greeks, and "Lares," "Manes," and "Genii" to the Romans. The souls that had no resting place wandered the earth, becoming malevolent spirits that damaged crops, tormented the living, and brought diseases and plagues. Such spirits have obvious similarities to evil fairies such as the Unseelie Court of Scotland, the unbaptized dead who fly through the air at night and bring harm to animals and human beings.

The Hellenistic period (ca. 323 B.C.–ca. 146 B.C.) and the transitional era between the downfall of Rome and the Middle Ages were two historical periods that intensified a syncretic process of fairy beliefs. Alexander's conquests took Greek ideas into the non-Western world; the Roman conquests brought together Roman and non-Roman ideas. The Roman conquest of Gaul, for example, brought the Romans into contact with the Celtic peoples. The Celts have been associated with fairy beliefs since the ancient world (see Pliny the Elder, *Natural History* 30.4). Pliny is evidence of the link between Celtic Druidic practices and the fairy faith. G. Dottin remarked that the Druid priests of Ireland were thought to be able to understand the language of the gods and to predict the future (see *The Civilization of the Celts* 132). The Roman-Celtic assimilation was followed by other syncretisms during the late Republic and throughout the imperial period (ca. 27 B.C.–A.D. 476).

The chaotic conditions that resulted from the fall of the Roman Empire lend support to the theory that fairy beliefs could have grown out of the conquest of one people by another. After the disappearance of Roman legions, administration, and bureaucracy, Germanic tribes such as the Ostrogoths, Visigoths, and Vandals conquered various areas and became local sources of power across a fragmented Europe. Of particular interest to the student of fairy lore is the fate of the Celts. In France, they were pushed into the northwestern corner of the country by the Franks; in the British Isles, they were overrun by the Angles, Saxons, and Jutes.

The struggle of the Celtic people to cling to their own beliefs and traditions may have contributed to the development of the concept of fairies.

The Middle Ages was a fertile period for fairy lore. The pre-industrial and tribal character of the medieval period was conducive to fairy stories. Indeed, the troubadour and trouvère traditions, the rise and dominance of courtly love literature, and a populace tied intimately to the soil and tradition were catalysts for the wide dissemination of fairy lore, much of it based directly or indirectly on classical themes. For example, in the fifteenth-century verse romance *Sir Orfeo*, Sir Orfeo, who visits fairyland to regain his wife after the King of Fairy has abducted her, has obvious resemblances to Orpheus of classical myth, who goes to Hades to find his beloved Eurydice after she has died.

During the Middle Ages, most people believed in a host of supernatural beings such as devils, angels, sprites, and fairies. Although some accounts of fairies by medieval writers (for example, that by Giraldus Cambrensis of the fairy people seen by Elidorus) portrayed fairies in a favorable light, many medieval people feared them, linking them with devils and evil spirits. This attitude was reflected in the trial of Joan of Arc, where her accusers attempted to show that she had had dealings with fairies and asked her whether she did not believe that they "were evil spirits" (Scott 75–76, 123).

The waning of the Middle Ages carried in its wake a distinct reduction of spirituality. An old world was expiring, and a new one involving a scientific interpretation of nature was being born. Nicolaus Copernicus' *On the Revolutions of the Heavenly Orbs* (1543), which rejected the Ptolemaic conception of the solar system, was a landmark in the development of the new outlook. Although the new approach undermined many of the traditional beliefs, many people continued to accept the existence of fairies, and in the sixteenth and seventeenth centuries writers like William Shakespeare and Michael Drayton gave fairy lore a fresh impetus in literature.

The witchcraft mania in the sixteenth and seventeenth centuries intensified the negative image of fairies as devils or agents of Satan. The Puritans in particular condemned fairies and many other spirits as evil beings that sought to corrupt and destroy people. However, some serious scholarly works such as Robert Kirk's *The Secret Commonwealth* helped give a more balanced picture of fairies.

The Age of Reason, the period from the late seventeenth century to the late eighteenth century, was not in general a productive period for fairy lore. To the learned, fairies were a product of ignorance and superstition. To believe in fairies went against the dictates of reason.

There was a renewal of interest in fairy lore during the late eighteenth century and in the nineteenth century. In part, the interest was generated by a rejection of the Age of Reason with its faith in modernity, industry, and reason. Fairy lore provided a release from the pressures of modern society. German literature of the nineteenth century, for example, is nearly dominated by the theme of rebellion against the artificiality of modern society, a preference for forest and field over city and factories.

The twentieth century has witnessed a growing emphasis on specialization, and Fairy lore has not escaped this trend. Whereas once there were generalists like Robert Kirk and Thomas Keightley, now there are specialists devoted to the study of fairy lore. Even though scholars such as Katharine Briggs and Reidar Thorwald Christiansen have contributed greatly to our understanding of fairies and folklore, the general public today probably knows considerably less about fairy lore than it did in the seventeenth century.

The literature pertaining to fairies is extensive and varies greatly in quality. Some writers have a special insight into fairy lore and successfully capture the spirit of the fairy world, as does Shakespeare in *A Midsummer Night's Dream* when the Fairy Queen Titania says that the fairies have met in "forest, or mead, / By paved fountain or by rushy brook, / Or in the beached margent of the sea, / To dance our ringlets to the whistling wind" (II.i.83–86). William Butler Yeats, who believed in the existence of fairies, revealed his special insight into the fairy world in poems such as "The Stolen Child," "The Man Who Dreamed of Faeryland," and "The Host of the Air." In the latter poem, he conveys a feeling of danger, mystery, and fear when he writes of the Host of the Air, a malevolent branch of the fairy people. Another Irish writer, James Stephens, captures the beauty and magic of the fairy world in his novel *The Crock of Gold* when he describes the gathering of the hosts of the Sluaige Shee. On the other hand, some writers have prettified the fairies, with the result that they seem artificial and insipid. Many of the fairies in stories written during the late nineteenth century and the early twentieth century lack any real substance. They are often depicted as dainty beings with gauzy wings who sleep in cowslips and ride on moths and butterflies.

Although there are many types of fairy stories and a large number of motifs connected with them, several types and motifs are predominant. (For fairy motifs in folk literature, see Thompson, *Motif-Index of Folk-Literature*.) Most fairy stories deal with relationships between fairies and human beings. Stories of changelings are frequent, with most of these stories focusing on the malicious nature and actions of the fairy changeling and the efforts of the parents of the stolen child to get it back. In a few works, events are seen from the point of view of the fairy changeling, as in Charlotte Mew's poem "The Changeling." The story "The One and the Other" in Sylvia Townsend Warner's book *Kingdoms of Elfin* traces what happens to both the stolen human child (Tiffany) and the fairy changeling (Adam) during their lives; their paths finally cross in the human world when Tiffany, who has been cast out of the elfin kingdom because he is growing old, lies ill in an inn; Adam, who is trying to determine why fairies do not die, believes that Tiffany may be a fairy and draws blood from him to test it; and Tiffany bleeds to death. Many stories deal with the love between fairies and human beings, as that of Ossian for Niamh of the Golden Hair. These love stories are some of the most moving in fairy literature, with a deeply tragic note sometimes being struck. Visits to fairyland comprise an important motif. Sir Orfeo goes to fairyland to win back his wife; True Thomas in the medieval romance *Thomas and the Fairy Queen* visits Fairyland after he has made love to the Fairy Queen and has therefore put himself in her power; and Ossian cannot stay in the human world after he has looked upon Niamh, "a beautiful young woman" with "her cheeks redder than the rose, and her skin whiter than the swan upon the wave, and her lips as sweet as honey that is mixed through red wine" (Lady Gregory, *Gods and Fighting Men* 333). Rip Van Winkle in Washington Irving's well-known story visits a fairy realm, although it should be emphasized that the supernatural beings that Rip sees are "not fairies but the dead" (Briggs, *Vanishing People* 24). Many stories focus on punishments that fairies mete out to mortals because they have mistreated the fairies. But there are also numerous stories in which the fairies reward mortals for kind treatment or take pity on a person who has suffered unfairly in life. A comical tone characterizes a large number of stories that deal with certain fairy types such as brownies, leprechauns, and cluricauns (Irish fairies of the leprechaun type who enjoy guzzling liquor.)

A survey of fairy literature reveals that the literary treatment of fairies has changed through the ages and that certain fashions and trends have prevailed at different times. There is a large body of folk literature dealing with fairies, and this literature must be kept in mind when examining the work of specific authors. Some writers have presented the fairy world in terms of traditional lore, but others have modified this lore and invented new ideas about the fairy world.

As pointed out previously, fairylike beings appear in the mythology of the ancient Near East; and in classical mythology, the Fates and certain beings associated with the natural world (for example, the nymphs and dryads) have fairylike attributes. Homer and Hesiod are two of numerous Greek writers who describe fairylike beings. In Homer's *Odyssey*, for instance, the sirens seem to have some of the characteristics of the dangerous fairy ladies who lure mortals to destruction. Some of the Roman writers who mention fairy beliefs and/or fairylike beings are Virgil, Ovid, Pliny the Elder, and Apuleius. In the transitional period between ancient and medieval history, authors like the Neoplatonist Plotinus (d. 270) and Isidore of Seville (d. 636) describe beings of a fairy nature.

Several general types of fairies stand out in medieval literature. Of primary importance are the "aristocratic" fairies of a human shape that appear in Celtic stories and medieval romances. Early Irish stories contain references to fairy people and their kings and queens. In the Middle Ages these fairies were conceived of as living in an aristocratic society that resembled that in contemporary Ireland. Logan writes: "The spirit folk lived as the contemporary aristocracy lived, spending their days fighting, feasting, hunting and making love with beautiful maidens, of whom there seems to have been an endless supply" (13). Also of human form and of "aristocratic" mold are the fays of medieval romance such as the Lady of the Lake and Morgan le Fay—mortals, half-mortals, or supernatural beings who possess magical powers of enchantment (see Paton). An example of a fay who is a supernatural being is the Lady of the Lake in the German *Lanzelet* by Ulrich von Zatzikhoven, a water-fay who lives in a castle of gold on a beautiful island surrounded by an impassable wall (27–28). Morgan le Fay in Malory's *Morte Darthur* is a mortal with supernatural powers, but it appears that she is derived from a supernatural figure, the Celtic war goddess Morrigan (Paton 11–12). In many of the romances in which the female fays appear, the fay casts a spell of enchantment over a knight on whom she has bestowed her love; and through some magical agency connected with her he is drawn from the human world to her world, where "he dwells in utter forgetfulness of all things mortal, conscious only of the delights that the fay offers him" (Paton 5). The pattern here, of course, is the familiar one of a mortal's entry into fairyland and its bewitching effect on the person. Besides enchantresses like the Lady of the Lake and Morgan le Fay in the Arthurian romances, there are also male figures that have supernatural powers (for example, the Green Knight [in *Sir Gawain and the Green Knight*] and Merlin). Later, in the sixteenth century, Edmund Spenser in *The Faerie Queene* was to create a fairy world similar to that in the medieval romances.

A number of the medieval chroniclers of the eleventh, twelfth, and thirteenth centuries include a fairy story or motif here and there in their works, and the types of fairies they describe differ from the fays. In *De Nugis Curialium* (Of Courtiers' Trifles), Walter Map tells two noteworthy stories about fairies: in the story of Wild Edric, Edric takes a beautiful fairy woman as his bride (94–96); in the story of King Herla, the Fairy King (a red-bearded dwarf with a huge head) and many of his people attend Herla's wedding; later Herla and a large number of his men attend the Fairy King's wedding; after leaving the fairy kingdom, Herla and his companions must not dismount from their horses until a dog that the Fairy King gave Herla leaps from his arms, but because the dog never leaps down, Herla and his men are doomed to ride endlessly (15–18). Gervase of Tilbury in his *Otia Imperialia* writes of the Portunes, fairylike creatures that are not "quite half-an-inch high" and come into the homes of farmers at night, "warm themselves at the fire, and take little frogs out of their bosom, roast them on the coals, and eat them" (see the translation in Keightley 285–86). Gervase also describes the grant, a demon or goblin that is "like a yearling foal, erect on its hind legs, with sparkling eyes" and "often appears in the streets in the heat of the day, or about sunset" (see the translation in Keightley 286). In *The Itinerary through Wales*, Giraldus Cambrensis describes a subterranean race of fairy folk who are "of the smallest stature, but very well porportioned in their make" and who have "horses and greyhounds adapted to their size" (390). Another chronicler, Ralph of Coggeshall, describes Malekin, a human changeling who has fairylike attributes (120–21). He also tells the story of the Green Children, a boy and a girl who were found in Suffolk (120–21). They were human in form but had greenish skin; they spoke a language that nobody could understand, but in time the girl learned to speak English; and when asked what her country was like, she said that she and her companion had come from an underground country where all "the inhabitants, and all they had in that country, were of a greenish colour" and where "they saw no sun, but enjoyed a degree of light like what is after sunset'' (see the translation in Keightley 281–83).

The fairy and elfin lore found in the literature of Northern Europe during the Middle Ages deserves special attention because of its richness. Dwarfs, elves, water-spirits, household spirits, and other elfin beings appear frequently in Scandinavian and German literature. Of central importance to Norse mythology are the *Eddas*. The *Poetic Edda*, which was probably composed between the ninth and twelfth centuries, recounts the adventures of the Old Norse gods and heroes and speaks of dwarfs, elves, and giants. The *Prose Edda*, which was written by Snorri Sturluson during the early part of the thirteenth century, contains a description of the light and the dark elves and includes much information about dwarfs (their skill as craftsmen and smiths is emphasized). German tales mention dwarf-kings like Goldemar, Gibich, and Alberich. In the saga *Ortnit*, the dwarf Elberich plays a central role. The German epic *Nibelungenlied* contains elfin beings such as the dwarf-king Alberich (guardian of the Nibelung treasure-hoard that Sigfrid wins) and nixes (the water-spirits that the Burgundians see while they are traveling to the land of the Huns).

In Chaucer's *The Wife of Bath's Tale*, the Wife of Bath says that in the days of King Arthur the land was filled with ''fairye'' (supernatural beings), but that no elf can be seen now because the friars have driven them all away through their ''grete charitee and prayeres.'' However, the fairies were not to stay away, for the late Elizabethan age witnessed the greatest age of fairy poetry in England. Shakespeare, Drayton, and other writers drew upon native fairy traditions, enriched them with literary inventions, and created fairy poetry that appealed to different social groups. Briggs writes: ''The fairy poetry of Shakespeare, Drayton and Herrick was obviously meant to be taken lightly, but there was more reality behind it than there would be about such poetry written in the present day. The poets may not themselves have believed in fairies, but they knew that thousands of their fellow-countrymen believed in them'' (*Anatomy of Puck* 6–7). It was Shakespeare, of course, who was primarily responsible for bringing about the new attitude toward the fairies. Among the plays in which he includes fairy beings or refers to them are *Romeo and Juliet*, *A Midsummer Night's Dream*, *The Merry Wives of Windsor*, *Cymbeline*, *The Winter's Tale*, and *The Tempest* (Briggs, *Anatomy of Puck* 44–55). *A Midsummer Night's Dream*, which reveals his fullest picture of the fairy world, portrays the fairies as small beings with great supernatural powers. Oberon (the Fairy King) and Titania (the Fairy Queen) each have their own court with their retinue of attendants. Like most fairies in traditional lore, the fairies in this play involve themselves in human affairs and have relationships with human beings. Oberon says that Titania loves Theseus, Duke of Athens; and she accuses Oberon of loving Hippolyta, Queen of the Amazons. An argument concerning a changeling boy that Titania has in her care is the source of a quarrel between her and Oberon. The fairies in *A Midsummer Night's Dream* are not malicious or evil. Indeed, the play makes clear that they ''are spirits of another sort'' than the ''damned spirits'' that must return to ''their wormy beds'' before the coming of daylight (III.ii.378–95). Oberon seeks to help the young lovers, and at the end of the play he and Titania (after settling their quarrel) come to the palace of Theseus to bestow blessings upon the married couples. In this play as well as in the Queen Mab speech in *Romeo and Juliet*, the fairies are portrayed as very small beings. Puck speaks of the fairy elves as being small enough to hide in ''acorn cups'' (II.i.29–30). The diminutive fairy did not originate with Shakespeare, for very small fairies such as the Portunes were known in traditional lore prior to Shakespeare, and John Lyly had used diminutive fairies in his play *Endimion* before Shakespeare wrote his plays. However, Shakespeare helped establish a fashion for diminutive fairies (on diminutive fairies, see Briggs, *Encyclopedia* 98–102). *A Midsummer Night's Dream* also describes Puck or Robin Goodfellow, who is an example of a hobgoblin, a mischievous but friendly spirit of the brownie type. Puck describes himself as ''that merry wanderer of the night,'' and says that he makes jests to Oberon and makes him smile (II.i.43–44). He enjoys misleading travelers and plays tricks on people by changing his shape. Shakespeare popularized fairy lore and influenced the portrayal of fairies by English poets in the seventeenth century and afterwards. Following Shakespeare's lead, Drayton, William Browne of Tavistock, Robert Herrick, and some other poets described fairies as tiny beings of a beneficent nature. Drayton's poem *Nimphidia* uses a mock epic style (Briggs, *Anatomy of Puck* 56–61); and a playful tone is often present, as in the description of the Fairy Queen's chariot, which is made up of ''a Snayles fine shell,'' has wheels composed ''of Crickets bones,'' and is drawn by ''Four nimble gnats'' (Drayton, *Works* 3:129).

In the seventeenth and eighteenth centuries, a new type of fairy story appeared in the fairy tales of French writers such as Charles Perrault (1628–1703) and Madam D'Aulnoy (ca. 1650–1705). The principal type of ''fairy'' in these tales is the fairy godmother, a fairy being who influences the fate of human beings. As mentioned earlier, the fairy godmother is related to the classical Fates, who were associated with birth, destiny, and prophecy. The best known of the fairy godmothers is the one in ''Cinderella'' from Perrault's *Contes de ma Mère l'Oye* (Tales of Mother Goose), a beneficent being who uses magic to help Cinderella. However, the fairies in such tales can be malicious if they are wronged (a characteristic associated with the fairies of traditional lore). In ''Sleeping Beauty'' from the same collection, an old fairy who has not been invited to the christening of a princess puts a curse on her; and in ''The Fairy,'' also from Perrault, a fairy rewards a young woman for showing her kindness but punishes the woman's sister for mistreating her. These tales by Perrault and others had great appeal because they offered moral instruction.

The landmark work in the history of folktales is *Kinder- und Hausmärchen* (1812–15) of Jacob and Wilhelm Grimm. This collection of tales provided an impetus to collecting folktales throughout Europe. Although a few of the Grimm tales such as ''Rumpelstiltskin'' and ''The Cobbler and the Elves'' do deal with elfin or fairylike beings, most of the tales have little or nothing to do with actual fairies. Indeed, this statement is true in the case of most tales that are labeled "fairy tales."

Many writers in the nineteenth and twentieth centuries have collected fairy lore and have written studies of fairies. Sir Walter Scott made significant contributions to fairy lore in his *Minstrelsy of the Scottish Border* (1802–3) and his *Letters on Demonology and Witchcraft* (1830). In 1825, Thomas Crofton Croker published a work entitled *Fairy Legends and Traditions of the South of Ireland*, the first collection of oral tales assembled in the British Isles. Patrick Kennedy, in his *Legendary Fictions of the Irish Celts* (1866) and other works, did much to preserve the Irish folk and fairy traditions. Other writers who have contributed significantly to the preservation of Irish folklore and fairy lore include: Lady Wilde, *Ancient Legends, Mystic Charms and Superstitions of Ireland* (1887); Lady Gregory, *Gods and Fighting Men* (1904) and *Visions and Beliefs in the West of Ireland* (1920); and William Butler Yeats, *The Celtic Twilight* (1893) and *Fairy and Folk Tales of the Irish Peasantry* (1888). John F. Campbell's *Popular Tales of the Western Highlands* (new ed., 1890–93) comprises a great body of Scottish fairy lore. *The Fairy-Faith in Celtic Countries* (1911) by W. Y. Evans Wentz makes important contributions to an understanding of Celtic fairy lore. In *The Fairy Mythology* (1850), Thomas Keightley collected fairy lore from Europe and the Middle East and pointed out connections among various beliefs. The first book of Norwegian folktales was issued by Andreas Faye in 1833 (*Norske Sagn*). His work was followed by collections of tales by Peter Christen Asbjornsen (1812–85) and by Jorgen Moe (1813–82). Reidar Christiansen (b. 1886) made very important contributions to the study of Norwegian traditional narrative. (For an excellent collection of Norwegian folktales, see Christiansen, *Folktales of Norway*.) Katharine Briggs, author of a number of books on British fairy lore, has added greatly to the understanding of fairy lore. Two of her books, *The Anatomy of Puck* and *The Fairies in English Tradition and Literature*, provide an excellent survey of the uses of fairy lore in English literature.

The Romantic Revival that began in the latter part of the eighteenth century led to a renewal of interest in fairy lore. The fairy poetry of William Blake should be singled out as having special merit (Briggs, *Fairies in English Tradition* 161–64). By the middle of the nineteenth century, the work of the folklorists provided some writers of fairy stories new insights and approaches. George MacDonald in particular was able to capture the spirit of fairyland in *Phantastes*, *At the Back of the North Wind*, *The Princess and the Goblin*, and *The Princess and Curdie*. During the latter part of the nineteenth century and the early part of the twentieth century, much of the fairy literature lacked substance, with the fairies often being artificial and prettified creatures. Some modern writers such as James Stephens and J. R. R. Tolkien have succeeded in portraying fairy beings with imagination and power. In *The Hobbit* and *The Lord of the Rings*, fairy literature has "reached its highwater mark" (Briggs, *Fairies in English Tradition* 210).

Representations of fairies and fairylike beings can be found in book illustrations and other sources during the Middle Ages and the European Renaissance. In the eighteenth and nineteenth centuries, certain painters made fairies the subject of some of their works; and fairies have an appeal to twentieth-century artists, especially to illustrators of children's books.

Ancient art and architecture bear traces of the fairy tradition. In ancient Egypt, for example, sculptured reliefs and other works of art portray spirits that dwell in trees ("Monstrous and Imaginary Subjects" 252); and Bes, the Egyptian god of childbirth, was portrayed in statues as a deformed dwarf with a snub nose, although the portrayal may be based on that of human dwarfs. Greek and Roman art contains numerous representations of hamadryads and other nature-spirits. The Penates and the Lares, tutelary deities of the Romans, were represented in the form of images. (It appears that the brownie and certain other fairies of the hobgoblin type may have originated from the domestic Lar, the deity associated with the welfare and protection of a household [Briggs, *Vanishing People* 54]).

Fairies and fairylike beings were pictured in various ways during the Middle Ages and the European Renaissance. Because fairies were associated with devils and evil spirits, people often visualized fairies as having an animal form or a form combining animal and human elements. Thus an illustration from *Historia de gentibus septentrionalibus* by Olaus Magnus (1490–1557) shows satyrlike beings with tails dancing in a fairy ring (see the illustration in Briggs, *Anatomy of Puck*, opposite p. 16); and an illustration from the seventeenth-century ballad *Robin Goodfellow: His Mad Prankes and Merry Jests* depicts Robin Goodfellow as human to the waist and as goatlike below the waist (see Merivale, ill. 4). However, fairies were also pictured as having a human form (see, for instance, the illustration in Briggs, *Anatomy of Puck*, opposite p. 17). Representations of dwarfs and dwarflike beings can be found in illuminated manuscripts and other sources. For example, the Bayeux Tapestry contains the depiction of a dwarf; and although this figure appears to be that of a dwarfed human, the representation bears a resemblance to the dwarfs of fairy lore (see Parisse, pl. XL).

A number of painters in the eighteenth and nineteenth centuries made fairies the subject of one or more of their works. Henry Fuseli (1741–1825) in *Titania and Bottom* (an illustration to Shakespeare's *A Midsummer Night's Dream*) depicts a fairyworld that is "presided over by Titania, the Queen of the Fairies, who has just conjured up an ectoplasmic whirlwind of her elves, sprites, and gnomes to attend to Bottom" (Rosenblum and Jansen 56; see fig. 29). In Fuseli's *Titania's Awakening*, another illustration to *A Midsummer Night's Dream*, Oberon stands over the sleeping Titania as he prepares to awaken her. Oberon and Titania are depicted as majestic figures of human shape, but the painting also includes demons and other nightmarish figures.

The fairy world had a special appeal to a number of Victorian painters (see Maas 147–62). One of the most original of all fairy paintings is *The Fairy Feller's Masterstroke* (see color plate 42 in Rosenblum and Jansen) by Richard Dadd (1817–86), who was confined during much of his life to Bethlehem Hospital, an insane asylum. In this small painting (21" × 15"), a fairy woodchopper, who is going to try to split a hazelnut with one blow of his ax, stands with his ax poised in midair above his head as he readies to strike. Surrounding him is "a bewildering cast of fairy-tale characters, from Titania and Oberon and assorted winged elves and sprites to a grasshopper-like insect at the upper left which ceremonially trumpets this event" (Rosenblum and Jansen 273). Joseph Noël Paton (1821–1901) depicted Oberon and Titania and other fairy beings in paintings of a very detailed nature. John Anster Fitzgerald (1832–1906) portrayed fairies as they might appear in the dreams of mortals. In his works, the fairies are sometimes seen performing some erotic act, as in *The Captive Dreamer*, in which the female dreamer is being fondled by a number of devils and fairylike creatures. Richard Doyle (1824–83), an artist for *Punch*, was one of the most famous of the Victorian artists who portrayed fairies. In Doyle's illustrations to *Fairyland: A Series of Pictures from the Elf-World* (the illustrations accompanied a poem by William Allingham), diminutive fairies engage in a variety of activities and pastimes that include dancing with each other, riding in the air on the backs of moths and birds, and tilting with each other in tourneys. In Doyle's *The Fairy Tree*, a spellbound mortal looks at the limbs of a tree on which over two hundred individual fairies are depicted. The King of Fairyland is perched on a central branch, his heroic mustaches being attended by fairy maidens. A knight and court musicians resting on the same branch complete one of the Fairy Court scenes. On other branches, fairies are dancing, walking and running about, performing acts of tumbling, playing music, and doing other things. Whereas fairies in Victorian paintings are often winged, none of the fairies in *The Fairy Tree* has wings (Maas 157).

An artist who deserves special attention is the British illustrator Arthur Rackham (1867–1939). Although Rackham sometimes depicted winged fairies of the dainty or ethereal type, he was most successful in capturing the spirit of the fairy world when he portrayed elfin beings of a grotesque nature. These beings often have sharp facial features, pointed ears, and a wizened appearance. Most of Rackham's fairies are imbued with active life: they jump about, they point, they peer, they perform various tasks.

An impressive assortment of fairy illustrations in color and in black-and-white is contained in a recent book entitled *Faeries* (1978) by Brian Froud and Alan Lee. Here are found spriggans, the Tuatha De Danann, goblins, dwarfs, leprechauns, redcaps, and many other kinds of fairies, with a brief description of each type accompanying the illustrations.

Fairies have been part of mankind's spiritual beliefs for centuries. They have survived the various changes that have occurred in human thought over the ages and most likely will survive other changes that are to come. However, modern science and technology present a threat to their existence. What has been the effect of twentieth-century life and society on fairies? What will be the Fate of Faery?

Modern communications media have been both a blessing for and a blight on fairies. Fairy lore has reached a large audience through films. *A Midsummer*

Night's Dream was captured in all its magical splendor in 1935; and in 1939 Hollywood gave moviegoers a colorful, dazzling Fairyland in *The Wizard of Oz*. The Good Witch is a true fairy queen, resplendent with gauzy wings. Other films that deal with fairylike beings or have a fairylike atmosphere include *Snow White and the Seven Dwarfs* (1937), *The Dark Crystal* (1982), and *Gremlins* (1984). In *Gremlins*, the gremlins are depicted as thoroughly evil beings that wreck a town and kill human beings. (Gremlins are gnomelike creatures that airmen blamed for causing mishaps to aircraft. The first reference to gremlins can be traced to World War I [see Barber and Riches 72–74]). The world of advertising has not overlooked the fairy magic. General Mills has had great success with its fairy-inspired Lucky Charms cereal—"they're magically delicious," so the ad goes. Keebler Cookies are prepared by elves, according to television advertisements. The late 1970s and the early 1980s witnessed a gnome craze. The book *Gnomes* by Wil Huygen was a best-seller, and companies such as Gorham Textron had great success with their gnomes. More recently, Dr. Tom Clark, of Charlotte, North Carolina, began national distribution of his very intricately carved gnomes.

Although modern communications media have focused considerable attention on fairies, their association with tradition, with fields and forest, and the spiritual realm seems to be less strong today. Even in Ireland, where people have long accepted the existence of fairies, the belief in them is weakening. Logan writes: "Bulldozers now level fairy raths and sweep away fairy trees, and the Good People appear to be unable to defend and preserve their homes. No farmer nowadays would allow some of the milk from his milking machine to run off on the ground as tribute for the fairies. . . . Nobody ever applies to the fairies for permission and approval when he wishes to build a house. Fairy places and fairy passes are no longer treated with respect. All this is obvious to anyone who looks around at the Ireland of to-day" (133).

The scientific age, then, has had a demythologizing effect on people. However, despite all the adverse circumstances, fairy beliefs continue to survive. Writers like Tolkien and Briggs have breathed new life into fairy lore. In addition, many people today have found enduring values in the old beliefs. The continuing interest in fairy beliefs simply says that people today want to understand how they became what they are. As an antidote to the ills of a technological society, mankind will continue to turn to the fairies and fairy lore because they refresh the spirit and trigger the imagination.

BIBLIOGRAPHY

Allingham, William. *Fairyland: A Series of Pictures from the Elf-World*. Illustrated by Richard Doyle. London, 1870.

Arrowsmith, Nancy. *A Field Guide to the Little People*. New York: Hill and Wang, 1977.

Barber, Richard W., and Anne Riches. *A Dictionary of Fabulous Beasts*. London: Macmillan, 1971.

Bellows, Henry Adams, trans. *The Poetic Edda*. New York: The American-Scandinavian Foundation, 1923.

The Boke of Duke Huon of Burdeux. Trans. Sir John Bourchier. Ed. S. L. Lee. Early English Text Society, e.s. 40, 41, 43, 50. London, 1882–87.

Briggs, Katharine. *The Anatomy of Puck*. London: Routledge and Kegan Paul, 1959.

———. *An Encyclopedia of Fairies: Hobgoblins, Brownies, Bogies, and Other Supernatural Creatures*. New York: Pantheon, 1976.

———. *The Fairies in English Tradition and Literature*. Chicago: University of Chicago Press, 1967.

———. *The Personnel of Fairyland*. Cambridge, Mass.: Bentley, 1954.

———. *The Vanishing People: Fairy Lore and Legends*. New York: Pantheon, 1978.

Brodeur, Arthur Gilchrist, trans. *The Prose Edda*. By Snorri Sturluson. London: Oxford University Press, 1929.

Campbell, John F., ed. and trans. *Popular Tales of the West Highlands*. New ed. 4 vols. London, 1890–93.

Christiansen, Reidar, ed. *Folktales of Norway*. Trans. Pat Shaw Iversen. Chicago: University of Chicago Press, 1964.

Coulanges, Fustel De. *The Ancient City*. 1864. Garden City, N.Y.: Doubleday-Anchor, 1956.

Croker, Thomas Crofton. *Fairy Legends and Traditions of the South of Ireland*. 2nd ed. 3 vols. London, 1826–28.

Delattre, Floris. *English Fairy Poetry from the Origins to the Seventeenth Century*. London: Froude, 1912.

Dottin, G. *The Civilization of the Celts*. Trans. David MacRae. New York: Crescent Books, n.d.

Drayton, Michael. *The Works of Michael Drayton*. Ed. J. William Hebel. 5 vols. Oxford: Blackwell, 1931–41.

Duffy, Maureen. *The Erotic World of Faery*. London: Hodder and Stoughton, 1972.

Dunsany, Lord. *The King of Elfland's Daughter*. New York: Putnam's, 1924.

Eastman, Mary Huse, ed. *Index to Fairy Tales, Myths and Legends*. 2nd ed., rev. and enl. Boston: F. W. Faxon, 1926. Supplement, 1937; 2nd Supplement, 1952.

"Fairy." In *The Compact Edition of the Oxford English Dictionary*. Oxford: Oxford University Press, 1971. 1:952.

Froud, Brian, and Alan Lee. *Faeries*. New York. Abrams, 1978.

Geoffrey of Monmouth. *The History of the Kings of Britain*. Trans. Lewis Thorpe. Baltimore: Penguin, 1966.

Gervase of Tilbury. *Otia Imperialia*. Ed. Felix Liebrecht. 3 vols. Hanover, 1856.

Giraldus Cambrensis. *The Historical Works*. Ed. Thomas Wright. 1863. New York: AMS Press, 1968.

Gregory, Lady Augusta. *Gods and Fighting Men*. 2nd ed. New York: Oxford University Press, 1970.

———. *Visions and Beliefs in the West of Ireland*. 1920. New York: Oxford University Press, 1970.

Grimm, Jacob, and Wilhelm Grimm. *Grimm's Fairy Tales*. Trans. Margaret Hunt. London: Routledge and Kegan Paul, 1948.

Hartland, Edwin Sidney. *The Science of Fairy Tales: An Inquiry into Fairy Mythology*. London, 1891.

Harward, V. *The Dwarfs of Arthurian Romance and Celtic Tradition*. Leiden: Brill, 1958.

Hazlitt, W. C., ed. *Fairy Tales, Legends, and Romances Illustrating Shakespeare and Other Early English Writers*. 1875. New York: Georg Olms, 1977.

Hunt, Robert. *Popular Romances of the West of England*. 2 vols. London, 1865.

Ions, Veronica. *Egyptian Mythology*. New rev. ed. 1968. New York: Peter Bedrick Books, 1983.

Keightley, Thomas. *The Fairy Mythology*. 1850. New York: AMS Press, 1968.

Kennedy, Patrick, comp. *Legendary Fictions of the Irish Celts*. London, 1866.

Kirk, Robert. *The Secret Commonwealth of Elves, Fauns, and Fairies*. 1893. Stirling, Scotland: Eneas Mackay, 1933.

Latham, Minor White. *The Elizabethan Fairies: The Fairies of Folklore and the Fairies of Shakespeare*. 1930. New York: Octagon Books, 1972.

Leach, MacEdward. "Fairy." In *Funk and Wagnalls Standard Dictionary of Folklore, Mythology and Legend*. New York: Funk and Wagnalls, 1949. 1:363–65.

Logan, Patrick. *The Old Gods: The Facts about Irish Fairies*. Belfast: Appletree Press, 1981.

Maas, Jeremy. "Fairy Painters." In *Victorian Painters*. New York: Putnam's, 1969. 147–62.

MacDonald, George. *The Princess and the Goblin*. 1872. New York: Macmillan, 1930.

MacManus, D. A. *The Middle Kingdom: The Faerie World of Ireland*. London: Parrish, 1959.

Map, Walter. *De Nugis Curialium*. Trans. Frederick Tupper and M. B. Ogle. New York: Macmillan, 1924.

Maple, Eric. "Troll." In *Man, Myth and Magic*. Ed. Richard Cavendish. New York: Marshall Cavendish, 1985. 11:2889.

Merivale, Patricia. *Pan the Goat-God: His Myth in Modern Times*. Cambridge: Harvard University Press, 1969.

"Monstrous and Imaginary Subjects." In *Encyclopedia of World Art*. New York: McGraw-Hill, 1965. 10:250–72.

Owen, Dora, ed. *The Book of Fairy Poetry*. London: Longmans, Green, 1920.

Parisse, Michel. *The Bayeux Tapestry*. Trans. William Courtney. N.p.: Denoël, 1983.

Paton, Lucy Allen. *Studies in the Fairy Mythology of Arthurian Romance*. 2nd ed. New York: Burt Franklin, 1970.

Perrault, Charles. *Popular Tales*. Ed. Andrew Lang. Oxford, 1888.

Pliny the Elder. *Natural History*. Trans. H. Rackham et al. 10 vols. Cambridge: Harvard University Press, 1938–62.

Ralph of Coggeshall. *Chronicon Anglicanum*. Ed. Joseph Stevenson. Rolls Series 66. London, 1875.

Rhys, John. *Celtic Folk-Lore, Welsh and Manx*. 2 vols. Oxford: Clarendon, 1901.

Rosenblum, Robert, and H. W. Jansen. *19th-Century Art*. New York: Abrams, 1984.

Scott, Sir Walter. *Letters on Demonology and Witchcraft*. London, 1830.

———. *Minstrelsy of the Scottish Border*. 3 vols. London, 1802–3.

Scott, W. S., trans. *The Trial of Joan of Arc*. London: The Folio Society, 1956.

Sikes, Wirt. *British Goblins: Welsh Folk-Lore, Fairy Mythology, Legends and Traditions*. 1880. Yorkshire, England: EP Publishing Limited, 1973.

Spence, Lewis. *British Fairy Origins*. London: Watts and Company, 1946.

———. *The Fairy Tradition in Britain*. London: Rider and Company, 1948.

Stephens, James. *The Crock of Gold*. New York: Macmillan, 1937.

Thompson, Stith. *Motif-Index of Folk-Literature*. Rev. and enl. ed. 6 vols. Bloomington: Indiana University Press, 1955–58.

Tolkien, J. R. R. *The Hobbit*. Rev. ed. 1966. New York: Ballantine, 1981.

——. *The Lord of the Rings: A Trilogy*. London: Allen and Unwin, 1954–55.

Ulrich von Zatzikhoven. *Lanzelet*. Trans. Kenneth Webster. Rev. Roger Sherman Loomis. New York: Columbia University Press, 1951.

Warner, Sylvia Townsend. *Kingdoms of Elfin*. New York: Viking, 1977.

Wentz, W. Y. Evans. *The Fairy-Faith in Celtic Countries*. London: Oxford University Press, 1911.

Wilde, Lady. *Ancient Legends, Mystic Charms and Superstitions of Ireland*. 1887. London: Chatto and Windus, 1925.

Wood-Martin, W. G. *Traces of the Elder Faiths of Ireland*. 2 vols. London: Kennikat Press, 1970.

Yeats, W. B. *The Celtic Twilight*. London, 1893.

——, ed. *Fairy and Folk Tales of the Irish Peasantry*. London, 1888.

A MISCELLANY AND TAXONOMY

A Miscellany

Malcolm South

This entry uses five major groupings to classify most of the twenty main creatures, some of their variations, and many other creatures. For the most part, the entry deals with creatures that have received little or no attention in the Introduction and the previous entries. Many creatures (some are probably the favorites of certain readers) have been omitted here because of the limitations of space. However, an attempt has been made to make the coverage as varied and representative as possible.

Some idea of what a wide range of creatures can be included in a book on fabulous beings can be gained from examining Richard Huber's *Treasury of Fantastic and Mythological Creatures* and Heinz Mode's *Fabulous Beasts and Demons*. Huber's book, which contains illustrations but no discussion of the creatures included, has over 1,000 illustrations depicting dragons, unicorns, mermaids, satyrs, centaurs, griffins, sirens, harpies, basilisks, chimeras, Medusa, the Minotaur, the manticora, the phoenix, and hundreds of other creatures. Huber portrays traditional types of creatures as well as creatures invented by individual artists, and his book covers many periods and cultures. In addition to the creatures that we have covered in the previous entries, some of the other creatures included by Huber are the following. From ancient Egypt, there are soul-birds, gods, and hybrid animals; from the ancient Middle East, winged lions, a scorpion-archer, an eagle-headed creature, a humanized scorpion, Tiamat, Dagon, the demon Pazuzu, and other figures; and from ancient Greece, a winged lion, a panther-bird, a winged youth, Cerberus, Pegasus, and the Hydra. Numerous illustrations based on European sources portray devils, demons, Satan, Death, gargoyles, heraldic figures, sea monsters, figures from the zodiac, and many composite animals. From Islam come creatures such as demons, a goat-man, a bird with a human head, a bird-demon with a double head, and a lion with a stag's horns and a flaming tail. India is represented by demons, composite animals, and deities like Kali and Ganesha. There are Chinese demons, monsters, and fabulous animals, and there are figures from Tibet, Indonesia, the Philippines, Africa, pre-Columbian America, and other places. Mode's book has a "Glossary of Monsters" consisting of over 350 entries, with more than 300 of these pertaining to creatures besides the ones that we have discussed. Mode describes and traces the origins of most of these creatures and includes illustrations of many of them.

In order to give a focus to a complex body of material, I will group the fabulous creatures in this entry according to their physical makeup and/or their form (cf. Mode 18, 29–31). There will be five general sections. The first deals with man-animal combinations; the second, with fabulous animals; the third, with fabulous peoples and with imaginary beings that have a human or humanlike makeup; the fourth, with imaginary beings whose makeup differs somehow from that of the beings found in the previous groupings (of primary importance here are beings made up of plants, trees, or inanimate things); and the fifth, with imaginary creatures that have a variety of forms. These groupings are loose ones that have been adopted as a convenient means of organizing material that is difficult to classify. Much overlapping occurs, with some creatures falling into at least two of the groupings. The groupings, then, should not be regarded as making rigorous distinctions among different types of imaginary beings.

Creatures consisting of a man-animal combination have been represented in a variety of ways. The upper half of the body may be human and the lower half animal; the body may be human, with an animal head, or there may be a human head on an animal body. Numerous other variations are possible, especially if wings, horns, and an animal tail are added. The animal element in the combination may come from only one animal or may be from two or more. The posture of the creature helps determine whether we tend to think about it as having an animal or a human role (Mode 18). If the creature stands upright, its posture tends to be human; but if it sits on its haunches or is lying down, its posture usually seems to be that of an animal. Included in the man-animal grouping are creatures such as mermaids, sirens, harpies, the Gorgon Medusa, the sphinx, the Minotaur, the satyr, and the centaur.

The three major types of man-animal creatures are those half-human and half-animal, those with a human head and an animal body, and those with an animal head and a human body. The half-human, half-animal combination may suggest a binary or a dualistic nature, but the significance can vary widely. The symbolism of the second type—the human-headed animal—also varies. Often the human head suggests wisdom, intelligence, or the mind. Such symbolism seems to be the case with the lamassu—the winged, human-headed lions and bulls that guarded entrances to Assyrian temples and palaces. The form of the bodies—that of bull and of lion—embodies immense physical strength, and the addition of wings invests the creatures with supernatural power. But the head, the seat of intelligence, is human; and the faces have "a mien at once dignified and kindly'' (Gadd 14). The symbolism of the third type—the creature with an animal head and a human body—can have a broad range of meanings. Sometimes the animal head characterizes the nature of the creature. For instance, the head of an ass on a human body usually makes clear that the creature is stupid or foolish. Or the head may represent one major symbolic concept: thus a lion's head on a human body may symbolize the destructive power of time or death. However, the symbolism connected with the animal head may be much more complex than either of these two examples. This is especially true in the case of the animal-headed, human-bodied gods and goddesses that had great prominence in ancient Egypt. The heads given these deities might suggest the nature of the animals involved, but other symbolic meanings were also attached to the heads. Moreover, the animal-headed form was usually only one of the forms that the deity could have. For instance, the goddess Hathor, a sky-goddess who protected women and was a guardian of the dead, was sometimes represented as a cow-headed woman, but she also appeared in the form of a cow, ''a lioness, a snake (uraeus), a hippopotamus, and a tree nymph'' (Hornung 113). The animal and human forms of Egyptian deities symbolized supernatural powers whose real forms remained hidden and mysterious (Hornung 117). Some of the animal heads that appear on Egyptian deities are: crocodile, on Sebek, the crocodile-god; falcon, on Horus, a sun-god associated with the living pharaoh; ibis, on Thoth, patron of learning and scribe of the gods; jackal, on Anubis, god of the dead; ram, on Amon, a Theban god who was elevated to the position of ''king of the gods''; and scarab, on Khepri, the scarab-god associated with birth and renewal (Viaud 9–48).

The animal component in man-animal combinations has been drawn from numerous animals ranging from insects, scorpions, and spiders to horses, bulls, and lions; but only a relatively small number of animals have been the basis for combinations that have had lasting significance.

The lion has long held a place of special importance in animal symbolism because of his position as the king of beasts and because of his power and strength, fierceness, and majesty. It is easy to understand why various cultures have linked gods, demons, and heroes with the lion and why he has often been combined with the human form to create imaginary beings. The Great Sphinx at Gizeh, a recumbent lion with a human head, is one of the oldest of all figures combining human and animal features. Sphinxes were guardians of entrances to palaces and tombs in ancient Egypt, and, as already mentioned, the human-headed lions with wings had a similar function in ancient Mesopotamia. The Egyptian goddesses Sekhmet and Tefnut were each depicted as a woman having the head of a lioness, and the Assyrian god Utukku was also lion-headed and human-bodied (Mode 278). Tiamat, a deity symbolizing salt water in the Babylonian *Epic of Creation*, created a lion-man and other terrifying monsters to wage war against her enemies. In Hindu mythology the god Vishnu took the form of a lion-man (Narasimha) in his fourth reincarnation when he killed the evil king Hiranyakasipu. This king had been persecuting his son Prahlada because of Prahlada's devotion to Vishnu; when Prahlada declared one day that Vishnu was present everywhere, Hiranyakasipu impiously asked Prahlada whether he really thought that Vishnu could be in the pillars of his palace. All of a sudden, the god sprang out of a pillar as a lion-man and tore the king apart. Hiranyakasipu had thought that he could not die because Brahma had granted him a boon to the effect that he could not be killed by man, beast, or god; in his form as a lion-man Vishnu was not actually any of these, and Brahma's boon was consequently not violated (Stutley and Stutley 113). Another Hindu myth involving a lion-man concerns the god Siva, from whose forehead emerged a lion-headed, human-bodied demon in the form of a burst of energy. When this monster demanded food, Siva told it to eat its own hands and feet; it did so, but was so ravenous that it went on eating itself until it left only its face (Stutley and Stutley 148).

Like the lion, the bull has often been used as a symbol of power and potency. Bull-gods appear in a number of civilizations, especially in the ancient Middle East. The Sumerian god El and the Canaanite god Enlil, for instance, were associated with the bull; the sacred bull Apis was worshiped as a divine animal in ancient Egypt; and the killing of a sacred bull was part of Mithraism. The Minotaur, which may have had its origins in a Cretan bull-cult, is the most famous of a number of man-bull combinations. Enkidu, Gilgamesh's friend in the *Epic of Gilgamesh*, is a beast-man—half-man and half-bull; Sumerian legends speak of Hea-Bani, who has a human body and face and a bull's legs, tail, and horns (Barber and Riches 82); and the bucentaur is a type of centaur that is part human and part bull (or ox). In Greek mythology one of the forms assumed by the river-god Achelous, who could change his shape at will, is that of a bull-headed man.

The goat is a symbol of "the reproductive powers of the sun, and is given to various solar and atmospheric gods" (Elisabeth Goldsmith 125). The goat has long been associated with fertility and lechery. There are several types of man-goat creatures, with the satyr being the best known. Having affinities with the satyr are the Greek god Pan, who has the horns, legs, and ears of a goat; and the fauns, Roman deities of the forest, who are half-human and half-goat. Also similar in form to the satyr is the callitrice, an Ethiopian creature having a beard and a broad tail (Barber and Riches 34). Two other creatures half-goat and half-human are the urisk and the glaistig of the Scottish Highlands. The first usually frequents lonely places in the hills (especially near waterfalls) but at times may assist farmers with their work. Although the urisk is not evil, he may terrify travelers by following them in lonely places at night (Barber and Riches 110–11). The glaistig can assume a number of shapes but often has a form that is half-woman and half-goat. Like the urisk, she can be helpful to farmers, but when she appears as a water-spirit, she is evil and dangerous (Briggs 191). Devils have often been portrayed as being part human and part goat. At witches' sabbats, the Devil was usually said to have the form of a goat or a goat-man.

Mermaids and mermen are the most familiar of a number of imaginary creatures with a human-fish form. The oldest man-fish god was apparently the Sumerian god Oannes, who was credited with teaching men the arts of civilization. According to one account, Oannes had a fishlike body, a man's head beneath a fish's head, and humanlike feet attached to a fish's tail (Carrington 6; Shepard 6). The Syrian goddess Derceto or Atargatis has sometimes been called the first mermaid. Her story is a tragic one: because she offended Aphrodite, the goddess made her fall in love with a youth contrary to her will, and her sense of shame was so great after she bore him a child that she jumped into a lake. She was then transformed into a fish. Fishtailed beings appear in Greek mythology and art (for uses in Greek art, see Shepard). Glaucus, a fisherman of Boeotia, was transformed into a sea-god with a half-human, half-fish shape after he had eaten a herb that bestowed immortality on him. Triton, son of Poseidon and Amphitrite, ''is human from the waist up, fish-shaped from the waist down, a type which probably is to be traced to twy-form Oriental gods like the familiar Dagon of the Old Testament'' (Rose 64). Sometimes the word ''triton'' was used in the plural sense. Tritons usually have thick hair on their heads, gills beneath their ears, and a dolphinlike tail at the tip of the lower half of their bodies (Barber and Riches 144). They blow conch shells, and the sound calms the raging waves of the sea. A sea creature represented in Greek and Roman sculpture is the ichthyocentaur or the sea-centaur, which ''has the torso of a human being, the chest and forelegs of a horse and the tail of a fish'' (Shepard 70). People once thought that the sea and the land had creatures that were counterparts of each other (for example, dogfish and dog), and this concept helped foster the belief that sea creatures with a humanlike appearance must exist. The belief in such correspondences led to the acceptance of some very unusual fish-men—two of the most notable being the bishop-fish and the monk-fish. The former ''had a mitred head, a scaly body, with two claw-like fins in the place of arms, and a fin-like cloak,'' and the latter ''had a closely shaven head, with a variation of a monk's hood on its shoulder, two pinnate fins for arms, while the lower half of its body ended in a long curving fish-tail'' (Barber and Riches 26, 107).

Many fabulous creatures consist of a human-bird combination. Legends throughout the world tell of winged people, and many cultures have stories of the transformation of human beings into birds (especially swans). Birds can symbolize very opposite ideas—freedom, liberty, and beneficent ideas on the one hand and rapacity and destructive, evil forces on the other. The sirens and the harpies are the best known of the human-bird creatures having a destructive nature. The claws and the wings of birds often appear on human-bodied demons. Thus the Assyrian demon Pazuzu, who symbolized the southeastern storm wind and brought diseases, had largely a human form, but he was winged and had horns, bird-claws for feet, and lion-paws for hands (Mode 34). One of the most frightening bird-men is the Chemosit, a demon found in the mythology of the Nandi people in East Africa. He is half-man, half-bird, a one-legged creature with nine buttocks. ''His mouth shines red in the dark like a lantern, and he manages to walk with the help of a stick like a crutch'' (McHargue 75). He is fond of human flesh, with a preference for eating children instead of adults. In Japanese mythology the tengu, winged creatures that are part man and part bird and have long noses or beaks, have more of a mischievous nature than an evil one. Although they enjoy playing tricks upon people, they become angry if the tables are turned and tricks are played on them (Piggott 61). Garuda in Hindu mythology, the mount of Vishnu, has a bird's beak and wings and a man's body, arms, and legs. He instinctively hates evil and seeks to destroy the wicked (Ions 102–4). There has been a worldwide belief that the human soul can assume the form of a bird. An example of this belief is the ba: the ancient Egyptians thought that the soul lived on after death and could take the form of a ba, a bird-bodied creature with a human head.

Another frequent man-animal combination involves serpents. Greek mythology has several beings that are part serpent and part human: Echidna, the mother of the Hydra, Cerberus, and some other monsters, is human to the waist and a serpent in the rest of her body; Cecrops, the legendary founder of Athens, is part man and part serpent; the gorgons have snakes for hair; the legs of the gigantes consist of serpents; and Typhon, the son of Gaea and Tartarus, has a hundred dragon heads sprouting from his neck, and his body ends in a snake's tail or he has serpents from his thighs downward. In the ancient world, lamiae were believed to be monsters that drank the blood of children and preyed on young men. They were thought to have the power to change their shape, and they were represented in a variety of ways. Sometimes they were described as having a woman's face and breasts and a snake's body. In Keats's poem "Lamia," the woman with whom Lycius falls in love is a serpent-woman; at first she appears as a serpent, "a gordian shape of dazzling hue, / Vermillion-spotted, golden, green and blue"; then she changes into "a lady bright, / A full-born beauty new and exquisite." The nagas of Hindu mythology are semi-divine creatures that have a human form to the waist and a serpent's body below it; they have hooded heads with a human face, or sometimes they are depicted with one or more heads of snakes. They dwell in Patala, in the nether regions of the earth, living in splendid palaces and enjoying many kinds of pleasures. Jewels on their hoods dispel the darkness of the netherworld (Dimmitt and Buitenen 348–50). Although most nagas are regarded as demons, they are not innately evil, and some of them have gained a virtuous nature by means of a relationship with the gods (Ions 109). Garuda is the mortal enemy of the nagas and destroys them whenever he has an opportunity to do so.

A frightening man-animal creature is the scorpion-man, who apparently originated in the ancient Middle East. A scorpion-archer depicted on a boundary stone from Babylon shows what the form of this type of creature is like: he is human to the waist, and his lower half consists of a scorpion's body (Huber, pl. 4). In the Babylonian *Epic of Gilgamesh*, Gilgamesh finds the gate to Mount Khumbaba guarded by scorpion-men. A creature related to the scorpion-man is found in Revelation 9, where the fifth angel opens the bottomless pit and out of the smoke issuing from the pit come winged, human-faced locusts that have shapes "like unto horses prepared unto battle," hair like that of women, teeth like those of lions, and "tails like unto scorpions." Their stings do not kill but cause torment for five months like "the torment of a scorpion, when he striketh a man."

In contrast to the terrifying scorpion-man is the affable and amusing Hindu god Ganesha, a potbellied, four-armed man who has an elephant's head with one tusk (Ions 101). In some works of art he is shown seated in a relaxed manner, with beautiful maidens caressing him, fanning him, and offering him food (his ample potbelly makes clear that he is not sparing in his diet). According to one account about how he came to have an elephant's head (and several accounts give a different explanation of its origin), the goddess Parvati, having become annoyed with the god Shiva because he kept surprising her while she was bathing, made a man (Ganesha) and placed him as a guard outside her bath. When Ganesha kept Shiva from entering, he chopped off Ganesha's head. Parvati showed such grief about Ganesha that Shiva dispatched messengers to find him another head, and they returned with an elephant's head, which was then fixed on Ganesha's shoulder (Ions 101). Given the significance of the elephant in India, it is hardly surprising that the Indians have a god like Ganesha and that he remains one of their most beloved deities.

The second major grouping being used in this entry—fabulous animals— includes creatures ranging from those having the form of an actual animal to those having an imaginary form. Fabulous creatures made up of the parts of two or more animals appear frequently, and there are creatures that are not fully animal in form but have the animal element as the predominant one. A considerable number of fabulous animals are traditional types (for example, the unicorn, the chimera, and the griffin), but individual artists and writers are also always creating what might be considered "new" forms. As is true of man-animal combinations, only a small number of animals have been used to create most of the traditional types of fabulous beasts.

The lion has been used to form many imaginary animals. The griffin, with the body of a lion and the head, forepart, and wings of an eagle, is a creature associated with rapacity and guardianship—two concepts that the lion has symbolized in many cultures. The combination of eagle and lion in the makeup of the griffin unites the power of two creatures that have been traditionally regarded as primatial animals. In addition to the androsphinx (human-headed lion), Egyptian art also has the criosphinx (ram-headed lion) and the hieracosphinx (hawk-headed lion). One of the most terrifying figures in Egyptian mythology is Amun, who has the head of a crocodile, the body of a lion, and the hindquarters of a hippopotamus; he is called the "devourer of the dead" because he eats the hearts of those who are judged unfit after their souls are weighed during the final judgment in the hall of Osiris. Other composite animals involving the lion include the lion-centaur, the lion-headed bird, the chimera, and the ant-lion. The latter is one of the most unlikely of all animal composites (his front part is that of a lion and his rear part is that of a large ant), and he has been dealt one of the unfairest of all possible fates. He can find no nourishment of any kind, and the reason is his parentage: because he is the offspring of a flesh-eater (a lion) and of a "plant-eater" (an ant), "he cannot eat flesh, for that is contrary to the nature of his mother; and he cannot get nourishment from plants, for that is against the nature of his father: so he perishes because there is no food for him" (Carlill 189). A famous lion in mythology is the Nemean Lion, the killing of which was the first labor of Hercules. This beast was particularly dangerous because no weapon could harm it, and only through brute force—by strangling it—was Hercules able to kill it. In Revelation 4 one of the four beasts round the throne of God is "like a lion," and Revelation 9 speaks of horses that have heads "as the heads of lions." The symbol of St. Mark is the lion (usually a winged one). Some important lions in literature are the lion that befriends Una in Spenser's *The Faerie Queene*, the Lion in Lewis Carroll's *Through the Looking-Glass* (he and the Unicorn fight each other), the Cowardly Lion in L. Frank Baum's *The Wonderful Wizard of Oz*, and the lion Aslan (a Christ-figure) in C. S. Lewis' *The Chronicles of Narnia*.

Winged horses and other fabulous horses are found in many myths and legends. The Norse god Odin rides upon Sleipnir, a horse with eight legs. In Greek mythology Poseidon, the god of the sea, is credited with creating the horse; he keeps gold-maned horses with brazen hoofs in his palace in the sea; and as he rides over the waves of the sea in a chariot drawn by these horses, the waves grow smooth upon his approach. Horses are often associated with sky-gods. Thus in Greek mythology the sun-god Helios rides across the sky in a chariot that is pulled by swift horses, and in Norse mythology a horse named Alsvidur (the All Swift) draws the chariot of the moon-goddess Mani. An important mythical horse is Pegasus, the winged horse on which Bellerophon rides when he kills the chimera. (For an excellent study of Pegasus in art, see Yalouris.) After many triumphs Bellerophon becomes so proud that he tries to ride to heaven on Pegasus, but Zeus grows angry at his presumption and sends a gadfly to sting the horse, which throws off its rider. Hippocrene, the fountain sacred to the Muses, is said to have been made when Pegasus struck the earth with his hoof. Composite animals involving the horse include the hydrippus (part horse and part fish), the dragon-horse (with the forepart of a horse and with its body terminating in a dragon's tail), and the hippocamp (half-horse and half-fish, with a serpent's tail at the end of its body).

Mythical birds make up one of the largest categories of fabulous animals. (See Nigg, *A Guide to the Imaginary Birds of the World*.) The most important of all mythical birds, of course, is the phoenix, whose resurrection from its own ashes is a symbol of rebirth. A bird related to the phoenix is the Persian simurgh: according to some accounts, the simurgh lives for 1,700 years and dies on a pyre after the hatching of its young. The simurgh is one of a number of fabulous birds of immense size. Others include the Arabian roc, the Indian garuda, and the ziz (in Hebrew myth). The ziz is described as the biggest of all birds, and when he flies, he darkens the light of the sun (Costello 82). A widespread belief connects birds with thunder, lightning, and rain. Legends of the American Indians speak of the thunderbird, the thunder being produced by the sound of its wings. Mountain Indians conceived of the thunderbird as "a small red bird, which shot lightning arrows from its wing, the thunder being its wing rebounding" (Barber and Riches 143). On the other hand, the Pacific Indians conceived of the thunderbird as so immense that it has a lake on its back that is the source of rain. According to Chinese legends, the shang yang, a bird with only one leg, takes water into its beak from rivers and expels it in the form of rain (Borges 189). Birds have been regarded as having powers of divination and prophecy. The caladrius or charadrius, a completely white bird, will turn its head away from a sick person who will die; but if a sick person is destined to live, the bird looks at the person and draws the illness to itself; then it flies upward toward the sun, which destroys the illness (Curley 7–9). Whereas the caladrius can have healing powers, the Stymphalian birds of Greek mythology are destructive and death-dealing. They have brass claws and beaks and are able to shoot their feathers as if they were arrows. Some accounts describe them as man-eaters. One of Hercules' labors was to rid the lake at Stymphalus of these birds, and he was able to do this by scaring them with a brass rattle and shooting them when they flew away.

A number of creatures based on several other actual animals should be singled out. Mythical dogs usually have sinister associations. Cerberus, the dog that guards the entrance to Hades, is usually said to be three-headed (Hesiod gives the number of heads as fifty), and most of the time he is described as having the tail of a snake or a dragon and having snakes around his throat. In canto 6 of the *Inferno*, Cerberus is a three-headed, potbellied monster who flays and rips apart the sinners (the Gluttonous) in the Third Circle; his mouths gape wide; his body bristles and quivers; and he barks loudly. For his twelfth labor, Hercules carried Cerberus from Hades to the upper world, and then took him back to Hades. Another dog that is a guardian in the underworld is the dog Garm in Scandinavian mythology. There are many legends of supernatural dogs, especially in the British Isles, where the so-called black dogs are said to appear (see Brown). These creatures are of the size of a calf or larger, and their eyes shine in the dark. A person must not speak to or come into contact with one of these dogs, or he will die (Barber and Riches 46). Likewise, wolves usually embody evil. An example of this can be seen in the wolf Fenrir in Scandinavian mythology. The gods came to fear this creature so much that they sought to bind him, but because he always broke free of any chain put on him, a special chain was fashioned with which to imprison him. It was fashioned of invisible things such as "the roots of a mountain, the noise of a moving cat, and the breath of a fish" (H. R. Ellis Davidson 31). The chain did not look powerful, but it was unbelievably strong. Although Fenrir believed the chain to be incapable of holding him, he would not let it be put on him until one of the gods agreed to place one of his hands in his mouth as surety. Tyr did this; the wolf could not free himself, and he snapped his jaws together, biting off Tyr's hand. At the time of Ragnarok, when the destruction of the gods will occur, Fenrir will break loose. His jaws will stretch from the earth to the heavens; Odin and Fenrir will meet in battle; the monster will kill Odin, but Odin's son Vidar will avenge his father's death by killing the wolf (H. R. Ellis Davidson 31–32, 37–38, 59). Also appearing at this time of final destruction will be the Midgard Serpent, which encircled the earth and held its tail in its mouth. It will rise up out of the sea, spewing poison. The god Thor will kill it, but will die from its poison (H. R. Ellis Davidson 32, 37–38). The Midgard Serpent is an example of the Uroboros (Ouroboros), a serpent or a dragon that bites its own tail and usually appears in art in the form of a circle. The Uroboros is a symbol of eternity and cosmic unity. The multi-headed serpent or dragon is another type of monster found in many cultures, the most famous example being the Lernean Hydra, the killing of which was the second labor of Hercules. The Hydra was a water-serpent or a serpentlike water-creature with nine heads (the traditional number is nine, but some writers list as many as a hundred). When Hercules struck off a head of the creature, two new heads grew back in its place. The monster was eventually overcome by burning away the heads (thereby keeping them from growing back). Two other multi-headed serpents are Ananta and Kaliya in Hindu mythology; Ananta is the divine serpent on which the recumbent Vishnu rests in the cosmic ocean; Kaliya is the serpent-king in the river Yamuna who is overcome by Krishna while he is a boy. A mythical snake described by classical authors and included in the bestiaries is the amphisbaena, which has a head at each end; if one head falls asleep, the other one always stays awake (White 176–78). One of the most intriguing figures in any mythology is the Hindu monkey-god Hanuman. An offspring of the monkey-queen Anjana and the wind-god Vayu, Hanuman has marvelous powers. He can fly; he can become invisible; he can change his size, growing from a very small size to the size of a mountain. "In battle he was a terrifying figure, as vast as a mountain and as tall as a tower, with a yellow skin gleaming like molten gold; his face was as red as a ruby and his tail was of enormous length" (Ions 105). He also has the playful, fun-loving nature of a monkey, and his antics often get him into trouble. Because Hauman served Rama loyally, Rama bestowed immortality upon him (Ions 104–5).

Many sea-monsters are completely imaginary, but some are evidently the direct result of distorted accounts of actual animals. (For a brief discussion of types of sea-monsters and a bibliography concerning them, see Eberhart 265–305). Moreover, there is a possibility that in some cases an unusual sea- or lake-monster is a real animal that has not been identified. The celebrated Loch Ness monster (if indeed such a creature exists at all) could be some type of prehistoric animal that did not die out. Two water-monsters, leviathan and the kraken, deserve special attention. In a general sense, the word "leviathan" means a huge sea-animal, but more specifically the word is used to describe a monster mentioned in several places in the Old Testament. In fact, it is probably more appropriate to speak of monsters rather than a monster, for not the same creature seems to be described in all of the passages. In Psalm 74:14, leviathan seems to be a sea-dragon, and God is said to have broken "the heads of leviathan in pieces." In Psalm 104:26, leviathan is described as playing in the sea—seemingly a different kind of creature than that in Psalm 74. Another reference, in Isaiah 27:1, speaks of leviathan as "the piercing serpent" and "that crooked serpent." The fullest description of leviathan appears in Job 41, where the creature is said to be a fierce monster that "maketh the deep to boil like a pot." His teeth are "terrible round about," and he has scales that weapons cannot penetrate. The crocodile could be the basis of the monster described in Job 41 and Psalm 74, and the whale may be intended in Psalm 104. The Bible created an image of leviathan as a fierce, mysterious monster that is the adversary of God. Like leviathan, the kraken was regarded as a huge sea-monster. The creature was supposed to rest on the floor of the ocean for a long time; then it would rise to the surface. "The back of a fully grown monster was estimated to be 1 miles in circumference, and at first sight the creature looked like a number of small bumpy islands . . . with fish leaping about the shallows" (*Encyclopaedia of World Mythology* 217). Stories were told of mariners who had mistaken the back of the kraken for an island, gone onto the "island," built a fire for cooking a meal, and then had been drowned when the creature had submerged. The kraken was supposed to have large tentacles, and this fact has led to the assumption that the giant squid may lie behind the legend of the kraken. In his poem "The Kraken," Tennyson describes the kraken as sleeping "Far, far beneath in the abysmal sea"; he has lain there "for ages"; when the final doom of the world comes, the fires consuming the world "shall heat the deep," and the kraken will rise "roaring" to the surface and die there.

Several imaginary animals included in older works on natural history are of interest. The catoblepas, which may have been based on an actual animal, the gnu (Costello 111–14), is said to be an African animal that holds its head downward, close to the ground; if anyone sees its eyes, the person will die immediately. Another strange beast is the yale, which Pliny the Elder in book 8 of his *Natural History* describes as a black or tawny animal that is the size of a hippopotamus and has long, movable horns. It can adjust its horns in different directions depending on how it wishes to use them. Also described in book 8 of the *Natural History* are the leucrocotta and the crocotta. The former is supposed to be swifter than any other beast; it has the haunches of a stag, the head of a badger, and the neck, breast, and tail of a lion; its mouth extends to each ear, and there are "ridges of bone in place of rows of teeth" (8.30). The crocotta is said to be an Ethiopian beast that is the offspring of a dog and a wolf. It might be one of the hyenas, for Pliny says that its teeth are capable of breaking apart any food and that it eats something at a gulp and masticates it in its stomach. A creature that people in earlier times regarded with much wonder was the salamander, a lizardlike animal that could reputedly survive in fire without being burned because it was supposed to be so cold that it could put out fire by contact. It was considered very poisonous. According to an account in one bestiary, a person would die from eating the fruit from a tree around which a salamander had entwined itself (White 182–83). There is an actual animal called the salamander, but it does not have any particular resistance to fire.

A category of fabulous animals that deserves attention is that of the so-called "fearsome critters." These are fabulous creatures that grew out of humorous stories and tall tales of the American frontier and backwoods. For the most part, fearsome critters are ludicrous rather than fearsome. Nearly always, some element of great comic exaggeration is present in fearsome critters, either in their makeup or in their actions. Some of them consist of a union of the parts of two or more animals (for example, the jackalope, a creature with a jackrabbit's body and legs and a deer's head and horns). In some cases there is an adaptation of the body of a fearsome critter to its environment. Thus the legs of the sidehill dodger are shorter on one side than on the other—an adaptation that enables "it to keep its balance while feeding on the side of a steep mountain" (Botkin 374). Fearsome critters have some of the most original and amusing names that have ever been given to any imaginary creatures (for example, the dismal sauger, the fibbertigibbet, the Funeral Mountain terrashot, the goofang, the hymapom hog bear, and the philamaloo [see Botkin 374]). The truly wonderful thing about fearsome critters is that anyone can invent his or her own fearsome critter and make up the lore to go with it. (For an excellent study of comical creatures invented by American "storytellers," see Dorson, *Man and Beast in American Comic Legend*.)

The third main grouping in this entry—fabulous peoples and fabulous creatures with a human or humanlike appearance—covers a broad range of beings. Included here are the fabulous races of men, the Little People, and monsters such as the zombi and the Frankenstein monster. Most giants and many types of fairies fall into this grouping, but giants and fairies will not be discussed here because they are covered in separate entries.

When Othello gives an account of the story of his life to Desdemona's father, he mentions "The Anthropophagi, and men whose heads / Do grow beneath their shoulders" (I.iii.144–45). These are two of a number of monstrous races of people that were familiar to Europeans during Shakespeare's time. In *The Monstrous Races in Medieval Art and Thought*, John Block Friedman lists forty of these races (see ch. 1). Some of the fabulous ones (a number of races are real ones or distortions of real ones) are the following: the Astomi—the mouthless people, who cannot eat or drink but live by smelling flowers and fruits; the Blemmyae—people whose faces are on their chests; the Cynocephali—people who have the head of a dog and bark like dogs when they communicate; the Hippopodes—people who have the hoofs of horses in place of feet; the Panotii—the all-ears, people with ears long enough to reach their feet; the Sciapods—one-legged people, who use their single foot (a very large one) to shade their bodies from the sun; and the Straw-drinkers, noseless and mouthless people who have an orifice in their heads through which they take in food and drink by the use of straws. As Friedman points out, Europeans always associated the monstrous races with faraway places such as "India, Ethiopia, Albania, or Cathay, places whose outlines were vague to the medieval mind but whose names evoked mystery. As geographical knowledge grew, and the existence of many of the races began to appear unlikely, they were shifted to regions less well known— the Far North and ultimately the New World'' (1). A book that describes a large number of fabulous races and types of peoples is *Mandeville's Travels*.

Legends about the Little People are found in many cultures. Dwarfs, elves, and brownies (see the entry on fairies for information) are among the best known of these small people. Gnomes, which belong to a group of creatures identified with the four elements, are compounded of the element earth; they live beneath the earth and guard hidden treasures. They are usually depicted as grotesque- looking dwarfs who have beards and dress in gray or brown (Briggs 192–93; Borges 111). Some of the other beings that are Little People or are connected with them are the Domovoi (a Slavic household spirit that is covered with hair), the Leshy (a Slavic woodland spirit), and the Vodyany (also a Slavic woodland spirit). Hobbits, the creation of the English writer J. R. R. Tolkien, are also small people. They have good-natured faces, curly brown hair, and clever brown fingers. They like peace and order and enjoy their creature comforts, especially good food (*The Hobbit* 15–16).

Many people in our own time have claimed that they have seen huge, hairy creatures that have both apelike and humanlike features and walk upright. In Canada such a creature is called sasquatch; in the United States, bigfoot; in the Himalayas, the yeti; and similar creatures with other names have been described in other parts of the world. (For a detailed study of such creatures, see Halpin and Ames, *Manlike Monsters on Trial*.) Some persons who believe that these creatures might exist think that all of them might belong to the same species, but other persons have disagreed with such a conclusion. Photographs and plaster casts of footprints of humanlike creatures have been produced. And a film by Roger Patterson in California in 1967 (the authenticity of this film is in question) shows a gorillalike creature walking through a clearing. However, until there is more credible evidence, the existence of such creatures will remain only a tantalizing possibility.

An imaginary creature having some general resemblances to the sasquatch and the yeti is the "wild man," who is often found in medieval literature and art. Richard Bernheimer, in his excellent study *Wild Men in the Middle Ages*, describes the wild man as "a hairy man curiously compounded of human and animal traits, without, however, sinking to the level of an ape. It exhibits upon its naked human anatomy a growth of fur, leaving bare only its face, feet, and hands, at times its knees and elbows, or the breasts of the female of the species" (1). Wild men and women were said to live in remote areas of the forest and to avoid contact with human beings. Creatures of instinct and passion, they were unable to control their emotions; and like satyrs, with whom they share much in common, they were very lustful. There were not necessarily evil, but because of their lecherousness and their inability to control their emotions, they could be vicious and cruel.

A being that is associated with evil is the zombi, a dead person whose body has been reanimated by a sorcerer. Totally lacking in will, the zombi mindlessly obeys his master, who can use it for slave labor or can use it to carry out some evil plan. In Haiti, where the belief in zombis is widespread, a sorcerer is said to create a zombi in the following way. Having ridden backward to the victim's house, the sorcerer draws out the victim's soul through a crack in a door and imprisons the soul in a bottle. Before long the victim becomes sick and dies; after the victim has been buried, the sorcerer removes the corpse from the grave after performing certain rites of propitiation, and reanimates the body by placing under its nose the bottle holding the soul. In some accounts reanimation cannot occur unless the dead person answers to his name (Hill and Williams 294). A possible scientific explanation for zombis is that some kind of drug may be responsible for producing the trancelike state that characterizes them.

The monster in Mary Shelley's *Frankenstein* is also a creature that a person brings to life, but the Frankenstein monster is a "created" monster—created from dead bodies and produced by experimentation. *Frankenstein* does set forth a chilling picture of the horror that science can produce when it overreaches itself, and this explains in part why the book has a great hold on the modern imagination. But the book's real power is the empathy that it evokes for the monster—a being so misshapen and ugly that his own creator turns away from him with repugnance and horror. Along with his creator, the monster is condemned to pain, anguish, and remorse. He is victim and sufferer. Near the end of the novel, after Victor Frankenstein's death, the monster says: "I shall die. I shall no longer feel the agonies which now consume me, or be the prey of feelings unsatisfied, yet unquenched. . . . Some years ago, when the images which this world affords first opened upon me . . . I should have wept to die; now it is my only consolation" (Wolf, *Annotated Frankenstein* 330–31). Soon afterward the creature springs upon an ice-craft, and he is taken "away by the waves, and lost in darkness and distance." The most familiar image of the Frankenstein monster is that from the 1931 film starring Boris Karloff, where the monster is "tall, lurching, mute, shabbily clad, a humanlike thing with a square head and electronic pegs sticking out of his neck and a look of baffled innocence on his face" (Wolf, *Annotated Frankenstein* ix).

Another artificially created being, the golem of Jewish legend, is a clay figure of a man that has been brought to life. According to tradition, the creature can be animated by placing under his tongue a tablet inscribed with the *Shem ha-Meforash*, the most holy name of God, or by marking magical words ("God is Truth") on his forehead; removal of the tablet or a letter from the word "Truth" on the forehead (this changes "Truth" to the word "dead") results in the golem's destruction. In all legends the golem is huge and powerful, but whereas he is not usually dangerous in early legends, he poses a threat to someone in most modern stories. Sometimes he kills his creator. Although the golem has been traditionally portrayed as a mute, automatonlike creature that unthinkingly performs his master's orders, he appears in some modern stories as an articulate and intelligent being (Arnold Goldsmith 16–19). The most famous golem is the one that Rabbi Judah Loew of Prague is said to have created to protect the Jewish people against persecution. H. Leivick in his play *The Golem: A Dramatic Poem in Eight Scenes* and Abraham Rothberg in his novel *The Sword of the Golem* are among a number of twentieth-century authors who have written about the Golem of Prague (see Arnold Goldsmith).

Numerous legends tell of the transformation of animals into human beings, or vice versa. The werewolf is the best-known example of shape-shifting where a human being assumes the form of an animal. Some other examples are were-lions and were-leopards in Africa, were-tigers in Southeast Asia, were-jaguars in South America, and were-foxes in China. Stories of animals that are capable of changing into human form also abound in various cultures. In Japan, for instance, the fox, the badger, and the serpent in particular are said to have such an ability (Piggott 72–73).

The fourth grouping involves creatures whose physical makeup differs somehow from that of the beings in the previous groupings. To a large extent, the beings here are made up of plants, trees, or inanimate things. In some cases human or animal elements are combined with those from plants or inanimate things (for example, tree-men, plant- or tree-animals, and metal men). Often the external form is animal or human, and a creature may be regarded as a humanlike being (for example, Talos, the bronze giant that is guardian of the island of Crete) or as an animal (for example, the hound of the hedges in Charles G. Finney's novel *The Circus of Dr. Lao*, a creature that looks like a dog but is made up of the parts of plants). A being composed of inanimate things (either man-made ones or ones found in nature) can have almost any shape—that of a human being, an animal, a plant, or any inanimate object. It should be emphasized that the fourth grouping is very fluid and that it overlaps extensively with the second and the third groupings.

Plants and trees have been the basis for a variety of imaginary beings. (For information about "bizarre" plants, see Emboden.) Tree-people and human figures with branches growing from their bodies can be found in the art of ancient Mesopotamia and Egypt (Mode 187–88, 197). The Greeks believed that each tree had its own tree-nymph, a dryad or hamadryad, who was supposed to die at the death of the tree. Many children's stories and books have an episode in a forest where the trees have a humanlike intelligence and where their branches reach out to seize passersby (for example, chapter 19, "Attacked by the Fighting Trees," in L. Frank Baum's *The Wonderful Wizard of Oz*). Some stories and films deal with an invasion of the earth by plant-monsters from outer space. Thus the monster from outer space in the film *The Thing* (1951) is a form of vegetable life that preys on the men at an army station in the Antarctic, and in John Wyndam's novel *The Day of the Triffids* (film version in 1963), huge plants that have an extraterrestrial origin come close to destroying the human race. Now and then tree-men appear in literature, as in J. R. R. Tolkien's *The Lord of the Rings*, which describes the Ents, a race of beings that have a manlike form but resemble various trees. The Ents, who are shepherds of trees, are powerful beings who assist the forces of good to defeat the evil magician Saruman. The vegetable lamb or Barometz (the little lamb) was supposed to be a small lamb that grew from a fruit on a plant. The creature was attached to a stem, and when the creature had eaten all of the grass and herbage within its reach, it died (Costello 148–58). Another plant-animal is the barnacle goose, a goose that was said to originate from a barnacle formed on wood soaked in the sea, or from a tree that grew beside the seashore. There was a widespread belief in the existence of the barnacle goose during the Middle Ages, and the legend continued to have popularity to the end of the eighteenth century (Costello 135–47). A thorough study of the legend can be found in *Barnacles in Nature and in Myth* by Edward Heron-Allen.

Conceivably, any inanimate form or object can be represented in such a way that it can seem to be alive. Fairy tales, fables, and children's stories are full of inanimate objects that have life: the gingerbread boy that runs away in "The Gingerbread Boy"; the tin soldier that falls in love with the little dancer made of paper in Hans Christian Andersen's "The Steadfast Tin Soldier"; and the people made of china in chapter 20 of *The Wonderful Wizard of Oz*. Imaginary beings that are made of metal can be found with some frequency in literature. Talos, the bronze giant that is guardian of the island of Crete, is probably the best known of such figures. In the *Arabian Nights*, a brass boatman saves the third Kalandar from drowning (Borges 219–20). Then, of course, there are all those metal men and monsters that appear in science fiction stories. Houses are living beings in some stories: sometimes a house keeps people as prisoners, or renews itself by draining away the lives of people.

The fifth grouping pertains to creatures that have a variety of forms. Although there may be one prevailing shape, the being has other shapes as well. In general, the creatures in this grouping are supernatural beings that have the power to change their form. Among the beings that can be included here are devils, angels, the jinn (genies), and the ghilan.

Devils and demons have been depicted as having a human form, an animal form, a human-animal form, or some other shape. Often they have been represented as composite beings. Since a widespread belief has existed that devils can change their form, people have not tended to conceive of only one fixed form for a devil. However, in Christianity, the general conception of a devil is that of a humanlike creature with horns, tail, claws, and cloven feet. Often batlike wings are present. As mentioned earlier, devils have frequently been portrayed as part human and part goat. Artists and writers have given their imagination free rein in making Satan ugly and repulsive. For instance, he has been shown with "the horns of an ox, the ears of an ass, a tail ending in serpent's jaws, a body covered with ugly, grinning miniature faces, goat's legs, feet like vultures' talons, and a coiled, twisted and razor-sharp phallus" (Parker and Parker 141). But Satan is supposed to be capable of assuming a pleasing form, and he may appear in a guise such as that of a good-looking young man or an old man of kindly aspect. He may take the shape of someone's father, brother, or trusted friend. If he does have a human shape, something is often present that indicates his preternatural character—perhaps sharp, pointed teeth and/or clawlike fingernails. Yet more and more in modern literature it seems that the Devil looks pretty much like an ordinary mortal. Any detailed discussion of the Devil and demonology is beyond the scope of this entry, and only a few of the numerous studies pertaining to these subjects can be singled out here. Three excellent books by Jeffrey Burton Russell trace the concept of the Devil from the beginning through the Middle Ages: *The Devil: Perceptions of Evil from Antiquity to Primitive Christianity* (1977), *Satan: The Early Christian Tradition* (1981), and *Lucifer: The Devil in the Middle Ages* (1984). Some other studies that provide much useful information about the Devil are: *Satan, a Portrait: A Study of the Character of Satan through All the Ages* (1945) by Edward Langton; *The Encyclopedia of Witchcraft and Demonology* (1959) by Rossell Hope Robbins; *The Devil, Demonology, and Witchcraft* (2nd ed., 1974) by Henry Ansgar Kelly; and *A History of the Devil* (1974) by William Woods.

Many people tend to associate angels only with Christianity and Judaism, but they are also found in Islamism, Buddhism, Taoism, and Zoroastrianism (Wilson 23). Angels are servants of God or the gods (the word "angel" means "messenger") and act as intermediaries between human beings and God (Wilson 37). Angels are supposed to be bodiless and invisible because they are pure spirits (Gustav Davidson xxii), and writers have often described them as invisible beings or effulgent beings with no certain form. However, in art, they are usually portrayed as having a human form. Although some angels are said to be wingless, most angels are shown with wings. The models for the winged angel in Christian art were apparently certain winged figures like Eros (Cupid) and Nike (Victory) in classical art. Christian thinkers developed a large body of lore concerning the nature and the duties of angels. Above all, their duty is to serve God, in whatever way this is necessary. Some are engaged in the ceaseless adoration of God; some act as guardians in Heaven; some oversee the planets; and some carry out the will of God in the world. Authorities on angelology stated that different orders of angels exist, but no universal agreement could be reached about the exact number. One division that gained wide acceptance was that by the so-called Pseudo-Dionysius. According to this division, there are nine orders made up of three hierarchies: Seraphim, Cherubim, and Thrones, composing the first hierarchy; Dominions, Principalities, and Powers, composing the second; the Virtues, Archangels, and Angels, composing the third. An excellent guide to various angels is *A Dictionary of Angels* (1967) by Gustav Davidson. *Angels* (1980) by Peter Lamborn Wilson contains a large number of illustrations, some of them in color.

The jinn or djinn (genies) are good and evil spirits found in Arabic lore. They have transparent bodies made up of flame or vapor and can assume different forms such as those of human beings (often in the form of giants) and animals such as cats, black dogs, goats, and foxes. The way in which jinn treat a human being often depends on the behavior of the person. With the exception of those jinn of an evil nature, jinn in general do not usually harm people unless people mistreat them. Jinn are inclined to do good deeds for persons who have treated them kindly, but because jinn enjoy playing tricks on people, their behavior toward human beings usually has an unpredictable element. Jinn frequently abduct people and take them to their own world. There are many resemblances between jinn and fairies, and jinn may be regarded as a type of fairy beings. (See the entry on fairies.) Jinn often appear in the *Arabian Nights*, and many of them have a spiteful or malicious nature. Probably the best known of the tales involving jinn is "Alaeddin, or The Wonderful Lamp." When the jinni of the lamp first appears, he has the form of a hideous giant; and although the form he has in subsequent appearances is vague or is not described, it seems clear enough that he can alter his shape at will. He does not seem to be one of the evil jinn, but he has great powers and uses them in a terrifying way at times. He appears when the lamp is rubbed, and he and the other jinn of the lamp carry out all the commands that are given with the exception of Alaeddin's command that the egg of a rukh (roc) be brought to Alaeddin. This command could cause the jinni to destroy the person who gives it, but because the jinni knows that an evil magician is responsible for suggesting the command, he spares Alaeddin's life. (For an excellent discussion of jinn, see 'Djinn'' in *The Encyclopaedia of Islam*.)

The ghilan (singular, ghul), also found in Arabic lore, are fabulous beings that are said to live in lonely places and to lure travelers away from their companions and to devour them. The ghilan are believed to be capable of changing their shapes, and they are sometimes described as having very pleasing forms. A ghul can be killed by a single blow; but if a second blow is delivered, the creature comes back to life. (For more information about ghilan, see "Ghul" in *The Encyclopaedia of Islam*.)

As pointed out earlier, the groupings used in this entry are broad ones that have been adopted to give a focus to a complex body of material. Much overlapping takes place, and some beings (for example, those consisting of geometric shapes or of a part of the anatomy of a human being or an animal, such as a disembodied brain) do not seem to fit into any of the groupings clearly. We should not use these groupings (or probably any others) as rigorous classifications. The study of fabulous beings should involve a flexible approach that gives us freedom to explore new possibilities. In Peter Beagle's novel *The Last Unicorn*, the unicorn is troubled because most of the people in the "real" world think that they are seeing a mare when they see her. They cannot see the truth. "Seeing" unicorns, dragons, and other fabulous creatures requires an openness of mind and spirit. If we are to "see" them, we must have a willingness to make discoveries and hearts capable of sustaining wonder.

BIBLIOGRAPHY

Barber, Richard W., and Anne Riches. *A Dictionary of Fabulous Beasts*. London: Macmillan, 1971.

Bernheimer, Richard. *Wild Men in the Middle Ages: A Study in Art, Sentiment, and Demonology*. Cambridge: Harvard University Press, 1952.

Borges, Jorge Luis, with Margarita Guerrero. *The Book of Imaginary Beings*. Trans. Norman Thomas di Giovanni. New York: Discus-Avon, 1970.

Botkin, B. A. "Fearsome Critters." In *Funk and Wagnalls Standard Dictionary of Folklore, Mythology and Legend*. New York: Funk and Wagnalls, 1949. 1:373–74.

Briggs, Katharine. *An Encyclopedia of Fairies: Hobgoblins, Brownies, Bogies, and Other Supernatural Creatures*. New York: Pantheon, 1976.

Brown, T. "The Black Dog." *Folklore* 69 (1958): 175–92.

Burton, Richard F., trans. *The Book of the Thousand Nights and a Night: A Plain and Literal Translation of the Arabian Nights Entertainments*. 6 vols in 3. 1934; rpt. New York: Heritage, 1962.

Carlill, James, trans. *Physiologus*. In *The Epic of the Beast*. Ed. William Rose. London: George Routledge; New York: Dutton, 1924.

Carrington, Richard. *Mermaids and Mastodons: A Book of Natural and Unnatural History*. New York: Rinehart, 1957.

Costello, Peter. *The Magic Zoo: The Natural History of Fabulous Animals*. New York: St. Martin's, 1979.

Curley, Michael J., trans. *Physiologus*. Austin: University of Texas Press, 1979.

Davidson, Gustav. *A Dictionary of Angels, Including the Fallen Angels*. New York: Free Press, 1967.

Davidson, H. R. Ellis. *Gods and Myths of Northern Europe*. Baltimore: Penguin, 1964.

Davis, Wade. *The Serpent and the Rainbow*. New York: Simon and Schuster, 1985.

Dimmitt, Cornelia, and J. A. B. van Buitenen, eds. *Classical Hindu Mythology: A Reader in the Sanskrit Puranas*. Philadelphia: Temple University Press, 1978.

"Djinn." In *The Encyclopaedia of Islam*. New ed. Leiden: Brill, 1965. 2:546–50.

Dorson, Richard M. *Man and Beast in American Comic Legend*. Bloomington: Indiana University Press, 1982.

Eberhart, George M. *Monsters: A Guide to Information on Unaccounted for Creatures, Including Bigfoot, Many Water Monsters, and Other Irregular Animals*. New York: Garland, 1983.

Emboden, William A. *Bizarre Plants: Magical, Monstrous, Mythical*. New York: Macmillan, 1974.

Encyclopaedia of World Mythology. New York: Galahad Books, 1975.

Friedman, John Block. *The Monstrous Races in Medieval Art and Thought*. Cambridge: Harvard University Press, 1981.

Gadd, C. J. *The Assyrian Sculptures in the British Museum*. London: British Museum, 1934.

"Ghul." In *The Encyclopaedia of Islam*. New ed. Leiden: Brill, 1965. 2:1078–79.

Goldsmith, Arnold. *The Golem Remembered, 1909–1980: Variations of a Jewish Legend*. Detroit: Wayne State University Press, 1981.

Goldsmith, Elisabeth. *Ancient Pagan Symbols*. New York: Putnam's, 1929.

Halpin, Marjorie, and Michael M. Ames, eds. *Manlike Monsters on Trial. Early Records and Modern Evidence*. Vancouver and London: University of British Columbia Press, 1980.

Hill, Douglas, and Pat Williams. *The Supernatural*. New York: Hawthorn Books, 1965.

Hornung, Erik. *Conceptions of God in Ancient Eygpt: The One and the Many*. Trans. John Baines. Ithaca, N.Y.: Cornell University Press, 1982.

Huber, Richard. *Treasury of Fantastic and Mythological Creatures: 1,087 Renderings from Historic Sources.* New York: Dover, 1981.

Ions, Veronica. *Indian Mythology.* New rev. ed. 1982. New York: Peter Bedrick Books, 1984.

Kelly, Henry Ansgar. *The Devil, Demonology, and Witchcraft: The Development of Christian Beliefs in Evil Spirits.* Garden City, N.Y.: Doubleday, 1968.

Langton, Edward. *Satan, a Portrait: A Study of the Character of Satan through All the Ages.* London: Skeffington, 1945.

McHargue, Georgess. *The Impossible People: A History Natural and Unnatural of Beings Terrible and Wonderful.* New York: Holt, Rinehart and Winston, 1972.

Mandeville, John. *Travels of Sir John Mandeville.* Ed. A. W. Pollard. London: Macmillan, 1923.

Mode, Heinz. *Fabulous Beasts and Demons.* London: Phaidon, 1975.

Nigg, Joe. *A Guide to the Imaginary Birds of the World.* Cambridge, Mass.: Apple-Wood Books, 1984.

Parker, Derek, and Julia Parker. *The Immortals.* New York: McGraw-Hill, 1976.

Piggott, Julie. *Japanese Mythology.* New. rev. ed. 1982. New York: Peter Bedrick Books, 1983.

Pliny the Elder. *Natural History.* Trans. H. Rackham et al. 10 vols. Cambridge: Harvard University Press, 1938–62.

Robbins, Rossell Hope. *The Encyclopedia of Witchcraft and Demonology.* New York: Crown, 1959.

Rose, H. J. *A Handbook of Greek Mythology, Including Its Extension to Rome.* 5th ed. London: Methuen, 1953.

Russell, Jeffrey Burton. *The Devil: Perceptions of Evil from Antiquity to Primitive Christianity.* Ithaca, N.Y.: Cornell University Press, 1977.

———. *Lucifer: The Devil in the Middle Ages.* Ithaca, N.Y.: Cornell University Press, 1984.

———. *Satan: The Early Christian Tradition.* Ithaca, N.Y.: Cornell University Press, 1981.

Shepard, Katharine. *The Fish-Tailed Monster in Greek and Etruscan Art.* New York: George Bantal, 1940.

Stutley, Margaret, and James Stutley. *Harper's Dictionary of Hinduism: Its Mythology, Folklore, Philosophy, Literature, and History.* New York: Harper and Row, 1977.

Tolkien, J. R. R. *The Hobbit.* Rev. ed. 1966. New York: Ballantine, 1981.

Viaud, J. "Egyptian Mythology." In *New Larousse Encyclopedia of Mythology.* Ed. Felix Guirand. New ed. London: Hamlyn, 1968. 9–48.

White, T. H., ed. and trans. *The Bestiary: A Book of Beasts, Being a Translation from a Latin Bestiary of the Twelfth Century.* New York: Putnam's, 1954.

Wilson, Peter Lamborn. *Angels.* New York: Pantheon, 1980.

Wolf, Leonard, ed. *The Annotated Frankenstein.* New York: Clarkson N. Potter, 1977.

Woods, William. *A History of the Devil.* New York: Putnam's, 1974.

Yalouris, Nikolas. *Pegasus: The Art of the Legend.* Trans. Helen Zigada. N.p.: Mobil Oil Corporation, 1975.

A Taxonomy

The twenty main creatures and certain other creatures described in this book are classified according to the five major groupings listed in the "Miscellany." The creatures are arranged in alphabetical order under each grouping. As pointed out in the "Miscellany," the groupings are loose ones that have been adopted as a convenient means of organizing material that is difficult to classify. The werewolf is especially difficult to classify because its form changes. For the sake of convenience, the werewolf has been placed here under "Fabulous Animals."

1. HUMAN-ANIMAL COMBINATIONS

Ba
Bishop-fish
Bucentaur
Callitrice
Cecrops
Centaurs
Cheiron
Chemosit
Echidna
Fauns
Ganesha
Garuda
Gigantes
Glaistig
Glaucus
Gorgon Medusa
Harpies
Hea-Bani
Ichthyocentaur (sea-centaur)
Lamassu
Lion-men
Manticora
Melusine
Mermaids
Minotaur
Monk-fish
Nagas
Narasimha
Neck
Nuckelavee
Oannes

Onocentaur
Pan
Pazuzu
Pholos
Satyrs
Scorpion-men
Sileni
Sirens
Sphinx
Tengu
Triton
Typhon
Urisk

2. FABULOUS ANIMALS

Alsvidur
Amphisbaena
Amun
Ananta
Anka
Ant-lion
Basilisk
Black dogs
Caladrius (charadrius)
Catoblepas
Cerberus
Chimera
Criosphinx (ram-headed lion)
Crocotta
Dragon
Dragon-horse
Fearsome critters
Fêng-huang
Fenrir
Garm
Griffin (gryphon)
Hanuman
Hieracosphinx
Hippocamp (hippocampus)
Hippogryph
Hō-ō
Hydra
Hydrippus

Kaliya
Karkadann
Ki-lin
Kirin
Kraken
Leucrocotta
Leviathan
Loch Ness Monster
Midgard Serpent
Nemean Lion
Orthus
Pegasus
Phoenix
Roc
Salamander
Shang yang
Simurgh
Sin-you
Sleipnir
Stymphalian birds
Thunderbird
Unicorn
Uroboros (Ouroboros)
Werewolf
Yale
Ziz

3. FABULOUS PEOPLES AND FABULOUS CREATURES WITH A HUMAN OR HUMANLIKE APPEARANCE

Anthropophagi
Astomi
Banshee
Bigfoot
Blemmyae
Brownie
Cynocephali
Domovoi
Dwarfs
Elves
Frankenstein monster
Giants

Gnomes
Goblins
Golem
Gremlins
Hippopodes
Hobbits
Hobgoblins
Leprechaun
Leshy
Ogre
Panotii
Puck (Robin Goodfellow)
Sasquatch
Sciapods
Straw-drinkers
Trolls
Vampire
Vodyany
Wild people
Windigo (wendingo)
Yeti
Zombi (zombie)

4. CREATURES WITH A MAKEUP DIFFERENT FROM THAT IN THE PREVIOUS GROUPINGS

Barnacle goose
Ents
Plant-animals
Talos
Tree-animals
Tree-men
Vegetable lamb (Barometz)

5. FABULOUS CREATURES WITH A VARIETY OF FORMS

Angels
Devils
Fairies
Ghilan
Jinn (genies)
Lamiae

A Bibliography of Works Useful for the Study of Fabulous Creatures

This selective bibliography consists mainly of secondary sources. Most of the sources deal solely or largely with fabulous creatures, but some sources that do not give them major attention have been listed because they provide valuable information. Useful bibliographies can be found in Robinson, Mode, Costello, and Izzi.

Ashton, John. *Curious Creatures in Zoology*. London, 1890.

Baltrušaitis, Jurgis. *Réveils et prodiges*. Paris: Colin, 1960.

Barber, Richard W., and Anne Riches. *A Dictionary of Fabulous Beasts*. London: Macmillan, 1971.

Bernheimer, Richard. *Wild Men in the Middle Ages: A Study in Art, Sentiment, and Demonology*. Cambridge: Harvard University Press, 1952.

Blount, Margaret. *Animal Land: The Creatures of Children's Fiction*. New York: William Morrow, 1975.

Borges, Jorge Luis, with Margarita Guerrero. *The Book of Imaginary Beings*. Trans. Norman Thomas di Giovanni. New York: Discus-Avon, 1970.

Briggs, Katharine. *An Encyclopedia of Fairies: Hobgoblins, Brownies, Bogies, and Other Supernatural Creatures*. New York: Pantheon, 1976.

Carrington, Richard. *Mermaids and Mastodons: A Book of Natural and Unnatural History*. New York: Rinehart, 1957.

Clair, Colin. *Unnatural History: An Illustrated Bestiary*. New York: Abelard-Schuman, 1967.

Clébert, Jean-Paul. *Bestiaire fabuleux*. Paris: Albin Michel, 1971.

Costello, Peter. *The Magic Zoo: The Natural History of Fabulous Animals*. New York: St. Martin's, 1979.

Daniel, Howard. *Devils, Monsters, and Nightmares: An Introduction to the Grotesque and Fantastic in Art*. New York: Abelard-Schuman, 1964.

Dann, Jack, and Gardner Dozois, eds. *Bestiary!* New York: Ace, 1985.

Davidson, Gustav. *A Dictionary of Angels, Including the Fallen Angels*. New York: Free Press, 1967.

Debidour, Victor Henry. *Le Bestiaire sculpté du moyen âge en France*. Paris: Arthaud, 1961.

Dorson, Richard M. *Man and Beast in American Comic Legend*. Bloomington: Indiana University Press, 1982.

Eberhart, George M. *Monsters: A Guide to Information on Unaccounted For Creatures, Including Bigfoot, Many Water Monsters, and Other Irregular Animals*. New York: Garland, 1983.

Emboden, William A. *Bizarre Plants: Magical, Monstrous, Mythical*. New York: Macmillan, 1974.

Friedman, John Block. *The Monstrous Races in Medieval Art and Thought*. Cambridge: Harvard University Press, 1981.

Garner, Alan, ed. *A Cavalcade of Goblins*. New York: Walck, 1969.

Gould, Charles. *Mythical Monsters*. London, 1886.

Gubernatis, Angelo de. *Zoological Mythology or The Legends of Animals*. 2 vols. London, 1872; rpt. Detroit: Singing Tree Press, 1968.

Hall, Angus. *Monsters and Mythic Beasts*. Garden City, N.Y.: Doubleday, 1976.

Heron-Allen, Edward. *Barnacles in Nature and in Myth*. London: Oxford University Press, 1928.

Huber, Richard. *Treasury of Fantastic and Mythological Creatures: 1,087 Renderings from Historic Sources*. New York: Dover, 1981.

Izzi, Massimo. *I mostri e l'immaginario*. Rome: Edizioni del Graal, 1982.

Kappler, Claude. *Monstres, démons et merveilles à la fin du moyen âge*. Paris: Payot, 1980.

Klingender, Francis. *Animals in Art and Thought to the End of the Middle Ages*. Cambridge, Mass.: MIT Press, 1971.

Lehner, Ernst, and Johanna Lehner. *A Fantastic Bestiary: Beasts and Monsters in Myth and Folklore*. New York: Tudor Publishing Company, 1969.

Ley, Willy. *The Lungfish and the Unicorn: An Excursion into Romantic Zoology*. New York: Modern Age Books, 1941.

Livingston, Myra Cohn, ed. *Why Am I Grown So Cold?* New York: Atheneum, 1982.

Lloyd-Jones, Hugh. *Mythical Beasts*. London: Duckworth, 1980.

Lum, Peter. *Fabulous Beasts*. New York: Pantheon, 1951.

McCulloch, Florence. *Mediaeval Latin and French Bestiaries*. Rev. ed. Chapel Hill: University of North Carolinia Press, 1962.

McHargue, Georgess. *The Impossible People: A History Natural and Unnatural of Beings Terrible and Wonderful*. New York: Holt, Rinehart and Winston, 1972.

Mercatante, Anthony S. *Zoo of the Gods: Animals in Myth, Legend and Fable*. New York: Harper and Row, 1974.

Mobley, Jane, ed. *Phantasmagoria: Tales of Fantasy and the Supernatural*. Garden City, N.Y.: Anchor-Doubleday, 1977.

Mode, Heinz. *Fabulous Beasts and Demons*. London: Phaidon, 1975.

Nigg, Joe. *A Guide to the Imaginary Birds of the World*. Cambridge, Mass.: Apple-Wood Books, 1984.

Parker, Derek, and Julia Parker. *The Immortals*. New York: McGraw-Hill, 1976.

Randall, Lilian M. C. *Images in the Margins of Gothic Manuscripts*. Berkeley and Los Angeles: University of California Press, 1966.

Réau, Louis. *Iconographie de l'art chrétien*. 3 vols. Paris: Presses Universitaires de France, 1955–59.

Robbins, Rossell Hope. *The Encyclopedia of Witchcraft and Demonology*. New York: Crown, 1959.

Robin, P. Ansell. *Animal Lore in English Literature*. London: John Murray, 1932.

Robinson, Margaret W. *Fictitious Beasts: A Bibliography*. London: The Library Association, 1961.

Rowland, Beryl. *Animals with Human Faces: A Guide to Animal Symbolism*. Knoxville: University of Tennessee Press, 1973.

———. *Birds with Human Souls: A Guide to Bird Symbolism*. Knoxville: University of Tennessee Press, 1978.

Silverberg, Barbara, ed. *Phoenix Feathers: A Collection of Mythical Monsters*. New York: Dutton, 1973.

Slomann, Vilhelm. *Bicorporates: Studies in Revivals and Migrations of Art Motifs*. Trans. Eve M. Wendt. 2 vols. Copenhagen: Munksgaard, 1967.

Thompson, Stith. *Motif-Index of Folk-Literature*. Rev. and enl. ed. 6 vols. Bloomington: Indiana University Press, 1955–58.

Twitchell, James B. *Dreadful Pleasures: An Anatomy of Modern Horror*. New York: Oxford University Press, 1985.

Vinycomb, John. *Fictitious and Symbolic Creatures in Art, with Special Reference to Their Use in British Heraldry*. London, 1906; rpt. Detroit: Gale, 1969.

Wendt, Herbert. *Out of Noah's Ark: The Story of Man's Discovery of the Animal Kingdom*. Trans. Michael Bullock. Boston: Houghton Mifflin, 1959.

White, T. H., ed. and trans. *The Bestiary: A Book of Beasts, Being a Translation from a Latin Bestiary of the Twelfth Century*. New York: Putnam's, 1954.

Williamson, John. *The Oak King, the Holly King, and the Unicorn: The Myths and Symbolism of the Unicorn Tapestries*. New York: Harper and Row, 1986.

Wittkower, Rudolf. *Allegory and the Migration of Symbols*. London: Thames and Hudson, 1977.

Index

This index includes most of the fabulous beings described in the present work as well as a selection of authors and artists. In general, an author or artist is not indexed separately unless several references to him or her are given in at least two of the essays. However, limitations of space have not made it possible to include every artist and writer to whom there are several references. Gods and goddesses like Zeus and Athena and mythological heroes like Theseus and Bellerophon are not usually indexed separately. The entry on "Fabulous beings" pertains to only the Introduction and "A Miscellany," and the entry on "Angels" and the one on "Devils" pertain to only "A Miscellany."

About the Editor

MALCOLM SOUTH is Professor of English at East Carolina University. He is editor of *Topsell's Histories of Beasts* (1981) and has contributed articles to *The Modern Language Review*, *Studies in English Literature*, and *Tennessee Studies in Literature*. He has recently completed a work entitled *Soldiers of the Cross*, a study of the first Jesuit mission to England in 1580.

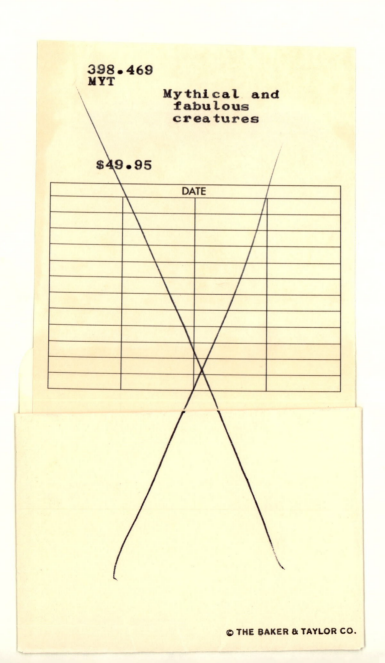

398.469
MYT

Mythical and
fabulous
creatures

$49.95

		DATE	